Democracy and Participation:

Popular protest and new social movements

Edited by **Malcolm J. Todd and Gary Taylor**
with a foreword by **Frank Furedi**

Merlin Press

First published in 2004
by The Merlin Press Ltd.
PO Box 30705
London
WC2E 8QD
www.merlinpress.co. uk

ISBN. 0850365384

British Library Cataloguing in Publication Data is available from the
British Library

Typography and layout by Design Studio, Sheffield Hallam University
Printed in the UK by Antony Rowe Ltd., Chippenham

Contents

Acknowledgements

The editors and publisher would like to thank the following for permission to reproduce copyright material in the volume:

Blackwell publishing for *'Alienation and Youth in Britain'* first published as *'A Generation Apart? Youth and Political Participation in Britain'*. Routledge for *'Women and Politics in Europe'* first published as *'Women and Political Power: Europe Since 1945'*, Chapter 3 of *'Making of the Contemporary World'*, by Ruth Henig and Simon Henig, Routledge (2000).

Colleagues and friends in the School of Social Science and Law at Sheffield Hallam University have engaged with many helpful discussions around some of the themes covered in this book. The Design Studio at Sheffield Hallam University has worked with us on the production of the manuscript. Merlin Press has been supportive of the project from the start. The contributors to this volume have been very patient as the compilation took place. Our thanks go to them all.

Malcolm J.Todd
Gary Taylor

October 2003

About the Authors

Paul Bagguley is Senior Lecturer in Sociology in the Department of Sociology and Social Policy at the University of Leeds. He has written widely on a range of social movements and social movement theory. He is currently carrying out research into the Bradford 'riots' of July 2001.

Peter Beresford is Professor of Social Policy and Director of the Centre for Citizen Participation at Brunel University. He is Chair of *Shaping Our Lives*, the national independent user controlled organisation core funded by the Department of Health to increase effective user involvement and improve the quality of support and services received by health and social care service user. He has experience as a long-term user/survivor of statutory mental health services and has been actively involved over a long period as writer, researcher and campaigner in issues of participation and empowerment.

Peter Campbell is a mental health system survivor. He was a founder member of *Survivors Speak Out* and *Survivors' Poetry*. Peter worked for fifteen years with pre-school and special needs children and has been a freelance trainer and writer in the mental health field since 1990. He has contributed chapters to numerous books on mental health. He is co-author of *Changing Practice: Mental Health Nursing and User Empowerment* and co-editor of From the Ashes of Experience: Reflections on Madness, Survival and Growth

John Carter teaches social policy and sociology at the University of Teesside. He has research interests in social theory and radical politics.

Nickie Charles is Professor of Sociology in the School of Social Sciences and International Development at the University of Wales Swansea. She is currently working on an ESRC-funded project, 'Social change, family formation and kin relations' which is a restudy of the classic study of the family and social change carried out in Swansea 40 years ago (Rosser, C and Harris, C *The family and social change*, RKP, 1965) and has recently published a book, *Gender in Modern Britain* (Oxford University Press, 2002). She is also researching the impact of feminist social movements in the context of devolution.

Kevin Farnsworth is a Senior Lecturer in social policy at South Bank University. He has previously published on the CBI and social policy, corporate structural power, and the role of business partnerships in combating social exclusion. Policy Press will publish his book *Corporate Power and Social Policy in Global Context* in the autumn.

Max Farrar teaches and researches in sociology at the School of Cultural Studies, Leeds Metropolitan University, UK. Previously he worked in adult education, at the Harehills and Chapeltown Law Centre, at the Runnymede Trust and as a freelance writer/photographer. His CV and short publications can be accessed through **www.maxfarrar.org.uk**. He is the author of *The Struggle for "Community" in a British Multi-Ethnic Inner City Area – Paradise in the Making* (New York and Lampeter: Edwin Mellen Press, 2002)

Frank Furedi is Professor of Sociology at the University of Kent at Canterbury. His books include *Culture of Fear: Risk-Taking and the Morality of Low Expectation* (Continuum, 2002) and *Paranoid Parenting: Why Ignoring the Experts May Be Best for Your Child* (Chicago Review Press, 2002).

Matt Henn is Principal Lecturer in Research Methods at Nottingham Trent University. Recently, he has been working on an ESRC-funded project that focuses on young people's engagement with the political process, and considers such wider issues as political participation, and citizenship. His other research examines elections in Central and East Europe, funded by the Nuffield Foundation.

Simon Henig is a Lecturer in British Politics at the University of Sunderland. His previous publications include *The Political Map of Britain* (Politicos Publishing, 2002), *Politicos Guide to the General Election* (Politicos Publishing, 2000) and *Women and Political Power: Europe Since 1945* (Routledge, 2000).

Elizabeth Lawrence is Principal Lecturer in Sociology and Sociology Subject Leader at Sheffield Hallam University. She is the author of *Gender and Trade Unions* (Taylor & Francis 1994). She is an active member of NATFHE, the University and College Lecturers' Union, and is currently an NEC member, National Negotiator and Regional Secretary.

Greg Martin completed his PhD at the University of Exeter in 1997 and since then has held posts in the Department of Sociology & Social Anthropology at Keele University and the Department of Sociology & Social Policy at the University of Leeds. He has written widely on social movements and is currently out of paid employment and travelling the world.

Dave Morland teaches Sociology and Philosophy at the University of Teesside. He has research interests in anarchism, technology and society, and the sociology of football.

Tessa Parkes is Senior Lecturer in Health and Social Care at the University of Brighton and has previously worked in the statutory and voluntary sector as a health worker. Her interests include lay participation in health and welfare services, mental health, social inequalities, and abuse in health/social care services.

Sally Ruane teaches health policy at De Montfort University, Leicester. Her research includes public-private boundaries in health, the private finance initiative and the General Agreement on Trade in Services.

Carlo Ruzza is Associate Professor of Sociology at the University of Trento (Italy) and has previously taught Sociology at the University of Surrey and at Essex University. He teaches courses on Ethnicity. In addition to focusing on peace movements, his research interests include other movements such those relating to anti-racism, and environmentalism, and broader advocacy coalitions that encompass movements in these areas together with other civil society actors.

John Steel teaches in the Department of Politics at the University of Sheffield and in the School of Social Science and Law at Sheffield Hallam University. His main research interests focus on the interaction of political thought and political action, particularly in relation to the development of radical ideas during the nineteenth century. In addition to his work in political theory, he has published widely in the field of educational research, where he has been keen to critically explore various 'meta-narratives' that affect theoretical debates and policy practice within the Higher Educational Sector.

Gary Taylor is Senior Lecturer in Social Policy at Sheffield Hallam University. He has written books on social and political theory, the media and social policy. He is currently writing a text on health policy.

Marilyn Taylor is Professor of Urban Governance and Regeneration at the University of the West of England. She has been involved in researching voluntary and community sector issues for many years and has written widely for academic, policy and practice audiences.

Malcolm J. Todd is Senior Lecturer in Sociology at Sheffield Hallam University. He is also presently (2003-2004) a Teaching Fellow, seconded part-time to the Learning and Teaching Institute at Sheffield Hallam University. He is the editor and author of a number of publications in the field of social and economic policy and also on teaching and learning in Higher Education. His most recent book is *Markets and the Welfare State: Public Sector Reform in Britain* (Sheffield Hallam University Press 2002).

Mark Weinstein is Senior Lecturer in Research Methods at Nottingham Trent University. His main area of research is in relation to youth activism in political parties and new social movements, and he also works on an ESRC-funded project, which focuses on young people's engagement with the political process.

Mick Wilkinson works as a Research Fellow at the University of Hull. His doctorate was in politics and his current research interests include: NGOs and the political process, the voluntary sector, policies for empowering grassroots communities, local governance, partnership working, political and economic migration, asylum seekers, youth homelessness and anti-poverty strategies.

Dominic Wring is Lecturer in Communication and Media Studies at the Department of Social Sciences, Loughborough University. He is particular interest in the historical role of marketing techniques and personnel in political campaigning. He is Associate Editor of Europe with the *Journal of Political Marketing*.

List of Abbreviations

The following abbreviations are used in the text:

ACM	Anti-Capitalist Movement
BMA	British Medical Association
CCT	Compulsory Competitive Tendering
CF	Conservative Future
CND	Campaign for Nuclear Disarmament
COSATU	Congress of South African Trade Unions
CRE	Commission for Racial Equality
DDA	Disability Discrimination Act (1995)
EF	Earth First!
ESF	European Social Forum
EU	European Union
FOE	Friends of the Earth
GATS	General Agreement on Trade in Services
GM	Genetically Modified
HRM	Human Resources Management
IMF	International Monetary Fund
LDYS	Liberal Democrats Youth Section
MSC	Manpower Service Commission
NGOs	Non Government Organisations
NIRC	National Industrial Relations Court
NSMs	New Social Movements
NSMT	New Social Movement Theory
NUT	National Union of Teachers
NUWM	National Unemployed Workers' Movement
PACs	Public Assistance Committees
PGA	People's Global Action
PFI	Private Finance Initiative
RTS	Reclaim The Streets
RMT	Resource Mobilisation Theory
SMEs	Small to Medium Size Enterprises
TGWU	Transport and General Workers' Union
TNCs	Transnational Corporations
UAB	Unemployment Assistance Board
UNESCO	United Nations Educational, Scientific and Cultural Organisation
VCOs	Voluntary and Community Organisations
VCS	Voluntary and Community Sector
WTO	World Trade Organisation
WSF	World Social Forum m.j.todd@shu.ac.uk
YL	Young Labour

List of Figures and Tables

Figures

Tables

FOREWORD – Reflections on some uncomfortable realities

What are the defining characteristics of political protest and of social movements today? Every generation seems to come up with its own answers and often counterposes its 'new' politics to the 'old' politics of a previous era. These days we write about 'new social movements' in order to distinguish them from the old. Terms like new politics and new social movements suggest at least a degree of continuity with the past and also point to some fundamental differences. As someone who has studied and participated in the 'old politics of protest', and finds it difficult to make sense of the term new social movement, I welcome the attempt to grapple with the issue addressed in the essays in this volume.

The issues of democratic participation and popular protest pose some of the most fundamental problems of our time. Now and again there are feeble attempts to counter the impression that we are going through a period of civic withdrawal and political disengagement. Occasionally we are told that the public is not really apathetic and that the youth is not so much apolitical as turned off by formal politics. Periodically surveys are published which attempt to show that everything is fine, young people are keen to volunteer or get stuck into local issues (For a review of this perspective, see Furedi, 2005). It is understandable that so many commentators are in a state of denial about the exhaustion of contemporary politics. Public disengagement does not only influence the sphere of politics, it represents a fundamental statement about society. It suggests that participation appears to have little purpose since nothing worthwhile can be achieved through it.

Disengagement

Increasingly, every election threatens to become an embarrassing reminder of the political wasteland that we inhabit. Apathy is no longer an adequate term of description for the steady erosion of the public's involvement in the political life of the United States. Since 1960, voter participation has steadily declined in almost every presidential election. Overall, the percentage of the electorate voting in presidential elections declined from 62.5 per cent in 1960 to 50.1 per cent in 1988. During the election in 1996, only 49 per cent of the voting age population bothered to cast their ballots – the lowest turn out since 1924. The election in 2000 continued this pattern, with only about 50 per cent of registered voters participating. The alienation of the public from the political process is particularly striking in relation to the election of 2000. Unlike the election of 1996, where the outcome was seen to be a foregone conclusion, the contest in 2000 was the most open for decades. Yet the number of Americans who voted was roughly the same as in 1996. According to the Committee for the Study of the American Electorate, 'the cumulative effect of voter disengagement during the past 30 years is that today, 25 million Americans who used to vote no longer do so' (BBC, 11.01.2000) Yet, voter participation in presidential elections appears positively high compared to the ballots cast for candidates running for a seat in the House of Representatives. These have averaged around 35 per cent in the nineties.

In the aftermath of 9/11, media pundits speculated that this tragic event and the growth of a sense of patriotism that it gave rise to might increase political participation. However, it soon became evident that not even such a major event could disrupt the pre-existing pattern of disengagement. The first 18 primaries prior to 5 July 2002 saw 'not just low turnout, but record low turnout – with only eight per cent of Democrats and seven per cent of Republicans going to the polls'. (Gitell, 2002).

Nor can European commentators feel smug about the political illiteracy of the American electorate. A leader in The Guardian titled 'Don't yawn for Europe. Apathy must not win the elections', written prior to the June 1999 elections, indicated that public disenchantment with political life is no longer confined to the other side of the Atlantic. In Britain, the facts speak for themselves. It is worth recalling that back in 1997, New Labour was backed by only 31 per cent of those qualified to vote. Voter turnout at this election was the lowest since 1945. 'The 1997 general election excited less interest than any other in living memory' concluded the authors of a Nuffield College Study of this event. Even the highly hyped public relations campaign surrounding devolution in Scotland and Wales failed to engage the public's interest. Voter participation in these 'history making' elections in 1999 indicated that the public regarded it as yet another stage-managed event. The majority of Welsh electorate chose the less than history making option of staying at home. Only 46 per cent of them bothered to vote. In Scotland a high profile media campaign designed to promote voter participation led to a 59 per cent turnout. And on the same day, polling booths in England were literally empty. Only 29 per cent of registered voters turned out for the 6 May local elections. The June 1999 UK elections to the European parliament represented an all time record low. Only 23 per cent turned out to vote. In one polling station in Sunderland, only 15 people turned up out of the 1,000 entitled to vote. In comparison to the General Election of 2001, that of 1997 looked positively exciting. Throughout the 2001 election campaign, apathy emerged as the dominant issue under debate. The turnout was an all-time low of 59 per cent at the 7 June, 2001 General Elections.

The steady decline of voter participation is directly linked to a much wider process at work. Lack of participation provides a clear index of disillusionment and public mistrust in the existing political system. Surveys of American public attitudes indicate that approval of the Government has steadily declined in recent decades. Whereas in 1958, over 75 per cent of the American people trusted their government to do the right thing, only 28.2 per cent could express a similar sentiment in 1990. Since the beginning of this decade trust in politicians has continued to decline. The 1996 'In a State of Disunion' survey conducted by the Gallup Organisation found that 64 per cent of the respondents had little or no confidence that government officials tell the truth.

A major study carried out by the Brookings Institution in May 2002 found that not even the wave of patriotism that followed in the aftermath of 9/11 translated into a durable growth of trust in the US Government. This survey showed that whereas in July 2001 only 29 per cent of Americans expressed a positive regard for their Government, in the aftermath of the events of September 11th, this figure almost doubled to 57 per cent. However, by May 2002, the public trust in federal government had fallen back to almost pre-9/11 figures. Although it stood at 40 per cent, experts felt the opportunity for the reforging of a relationship of trust had probably passed (Mackenzie and Labiner, 2001: 2–3).

Surveys in Europe point to a similar pattern. Studies carried out in the European Union indicate that around 45 per cent of the population is dissatisfied with the 'way that democracy works'. In Britain, surveys reveal a high level of public cynicism towards politicians. A Gallup poll conducted in April 1995 concluded that the opinion of most towards Members of Parliament was 'low' or 'very low'. A decade previously only a third had adopted this view. According to another survey, carried out in 1994, only 24 per cent of the population believed that the British government places the national interest above their party interests (Curtice and Jowell, 1995: 141, 148). Politicians consistently come at the bottom of the list of professions that the public trusts. A survey published by the ICM in June 1999 found that only ten per cent of the respondents stated that they trust politicians a lot, sixty-five per cent a little, and twenty five per cent indicated, not at all (*The Guardian*, 8:5:1999). A study carried out by the BBC in February 2002, indicated that many people under the age of 45 were disillusioned with politics and regarded politicians as 'crooks', 'liars' and a 'waste of time' (BBC, 28:02:2002).

During the nineties, the erosion of public trust was reflected in a national mood of suspicion towards the political system itself. What emerged was a brand of anti-politics, a cyclical dismissal of the elected politician and an obsession with sleaze and corruption in Westminster and Washington. The Clinton era was one of permanent scandal. Controversy surrounded the manner of Bush's election only to be followed by a series of corporate scandals that culminated with the collapse of Enron. The success of New Labour in portraying the Conservatives as a party of sleaze was crucial to its electoral success of 1997. In turn, the New Labour Government soon discovered that it too was not immune to the politics of the scandal. Within months of being elected, the New Labour Government was hit by a spate of minor scandals involving Labour MPs and Ministers. The issue of sleaze continued to haunt the Government as successive ministers were forced to hand in their resignation in 1998. The furore that surrounded Cheriegate in December 2002 – despite the absence of any allegation that the Prime Minister's wife had done anything illegal – indicates that cynicism towards Government is permanent feature of life.

The exhaustion of political life has little to do with political corruption, inept political leaders or insensitive bureaucracies. What has changed during the past two decades is the very meaning of politics itself. At the beginning of this century, political life was dominated by radically different alternatives. Competing political philosophies offered contrasting visions of the good society. Conflict between these ideologies was often fierce and sometimes provoked violent clashes and even revolutions. 'Left' and 'Right' were no mere labels. In a fundamental sense, they endowed individuals with an identity that said something very important about how they regarded their lives. Ardent advocates of revolutionary change clashed with fervent defenders of the capitalist system. Their competing views about society dominated the conduct of every day politics.

The end of the century offers a radically different political landscape. Politics today has little in common with the passions and conflicts that have shaped people's commitments and hatreds over the past century. There is no longer room for either the ardent defender of the free market faith, or the robust advocate of revolutionary transformation. It would be wrong to conclude that politics has become simply more moderate. Politics has gone into early retirement. The end–of–century ethos continually emphasises problems, which are not susceptible to human intervention. Theories of globalisation continually stress the inability of people and of their nation states to deal with forces that are beyond their control. The big issues of our time – the impending environmental catastrophe, threats to our health, killer bugs like SARS, weapons of mass destruction – are presented as perils that stand above politics. It is widely believed that the world is out of control and that there is little that human beings can do to master these developments or influence their destiny. Deprived of choice and options, humanity is forced to acquiesce to a worldview which Margaret Thatcher aptly described as TINA – There is No Alternative.

And if indeed there is no alternative, politics can have little meaning. Without alternatives, debate becomes empty posturing about trivial matters. Politicians are forced to inflate relatively banal proposals to the level of a major policy innovation. This is the age of 'micro–politics'. Politics has adopted the language of technocracy and presents itself through a depoliticised language of managerialism. Politicians now promise to 'deliver'. They carefully 'cost' proposals and offer 'value for money'. Policies are no longer good – they are 'evidence based'. Policies are rarely generated by a worldview – they are derived from 'best practice'.

The growth of a managerial political style has gone hand in hand with a shift from politics to the personal. Personalities and individual behaviour dominates the presentation of contemporary politics. As public life has become emptied of its content, private and personal preoccupations have been projected into the public sphere. Consequently, passions that were once stirred by ideological differences are far more likely to be engaged by individual misbehaviour, private troubles and personality conflicts. The private lives of politicians excite greater interest than the way they handle their public office. In Britain it is widely noted that the reality TV show Big Brother 'arouses passions that politics can no longer stir' (Thomson, 2002). In the US, plans are afoot to launch a television programme, titled the American Candidate. The aim of this programme is to use the reality TV format to pick a 'people's candidate' from its contestants. With so many people tuned of managerial politics is it any surprise that politicians are turning to reality television producers to learn how to engage with an otherwise disinterested public.

Disengaged Protest

Some critics of the prevailing social order believe that the public's disenchantment with contemporary politics provides an opportunity for the flourishing of radical dissent. However, confusion and distrust of the political system or suspicion towards authority are not inherently progressive responses. In such circumstances, cynicism, passivity and a sense of fatalism can influence public attitudes. Such attitudes do not preclude acts of protest. However, forms of protest that are influenced by such attitudes still express the politics of disengagement. To take one example, that of public protest against the military invasion of Iraq. One of the most prominent slogans of this movement 'Not in my name' clearly symbolises the mood of disengaged protest.

'Not in my name' is self-consciously framed as a personal proclamation. 'Not in my name' is not a political statement designed to involve others and does not seek to offer an alternative. It does not call on anyone to choose sides or even insist on a particular course of action. Insofar as it represents an attitude it is a prepolitical gesture. It is a statement of individual preference and represents an opt-out clause rather an attempt alter the course of events. As a metaphor for a shrug-of-the-shoulder, it represents a demand for personal disengagement rather for a fundamentally different approach to the war. It as much reflects a mood of anti-engagement as weariness towards war. That is why despite the mobilisation of millions on streets of Western capitals, this protest has had such little impact on society. Despite the fact that so many opposed the war, the absence of passion or the belief that protest could make a difference meant that the large numbers never amounted to a movement, at least in the old sense of the term. This is not surprising since the personal presentation of anti-war sentiment contains an implicit renunciation of social activism and protest.

Of course, disengagement is a troublesome concept. Certainly, people out on the streets of London or Seattle, protesting against capitalism or the invasion of Iraq do not think of themselves as disengaged. Today's activists continually point out the large size of many of the recent demonstrations. However, understanding the dynamic of mobilisations and protests cannot be gained through just counting numbers. Since the Cold War, we have seen on numerous occasions the phenomenon of self-consciously apolitical public mobilisations. The public outburst of emotionalism around the death of Diana, the so-called White Movement in Belgium, and the protests against paedophiles in the UK have been driven by people who are committed to make their own personal statement.

There are many activists who feel that their activism represents a valid form of engagement. No doubt it does. But engagement in a wider social sense is not reducible to individual activism. Political engagement involves action directed at influencing aspects of life of the wider public. It is not simply a personal statement but also part of a wider communal project. Engagement expresses an attitude and an orientation towards interaction with others. It is undertaken as part of a wider public dialogue that seeks to establish or alter the prevailing consensus on an issue or issues.

The clearest expression of disengagement can be seen in what is often depicted as the most attractive feature of contemporary social movements; its sheer numbers and diversity. The great variety of organisations that are called movements is truly breathtaking. It is claimed that the large variety of social movements are necessitated by the plurality of experiences and meanings in contemporary society (Melucci, 1988). However, it can also be argued that the pluralisation of experience is not so much a natural fact of life, but a self-conscious rejection of engaged dialogue. The attitude of live and let live can be seen as either a form of enlightened tolerance or as the renunciation of engagement through dialogue. I fear that it may represent the latter.

In the past the self-conscious cultivation of sectional interests was frequently characterised as sectarian. These days we don't use the word sectarian too often because movements are generally not inclined (or could not be bothered) to wrangle with one another. Yet such attitudes bear an uncanny resemblance to old-fashioned sect-like attitudes, in particular in their lack of interest in influencing the wider public. Such attitudes are bound up with the orientation of contemporary movements to issues associated with identity and life style. One of the most significant manifestations of political disengagement is the reconfiguration of activism as a form of lifestyle choice. Murray Bookchin's critique of 'lifestyle anarchism' provides an astute analysis of the way that the motif of self-expression comes to define the parameters of a particular form of activism (Bookchin, 1995). A similar critique could be made about a variety of other life style, identity or consumer focused organisations.

The politics of self-expression are extremely influential because it is continually affirmed through the signals transmitted by contemporary culture. Indeed self-expression is validated as a genuine and authentic act and is often favourably contrasted to what is perceived as the estranged artificial world of politics. The Italian sociologist Alberto Melucci claims that one of the distinct features of contemporary social movements is that people's participation within movements is no longer a means to an end. 'Participation in collective action is seen to have no value for the individual unless it provides a direct response to personal needs' (Melucci, 1989: 49). When movements become an in and of themselves, the link between protest and the politics of change becomes ruptured. There is nothing objectionable about individuals participating in organisations in order to become members of an emotional community. However, when the pursuit of self-discovery becomes an end in it self it represents merely another form of disengagement.

Some of the largest mobilisations in Europe during the nineties have been influenced by this trend of expressing 'personal needs'. The mass demonstrations in Spain, in July 1997, to mourn the murder of Miguel Angel Blanco by ETA, manifested a strange emotional dynamic. At times the crowd exuded a sense of intensity as if something tragic was just about to happen. At other times, a sense of anticipation – not unlike at pop festivals – helped create a feeling of exhilaration. Demonstrators told interviewers that they were not sure why they were there and some suggested that they too felt like victims. This reaction was self consciously cultivated by the crowd with the gesture of placing their hands at the back of their heads in the posture of surrendering prisoners.

Professionalising Protest

Some commentators have drawn attention to the fact that protest has become a normal feature of society (See, for example, Meyer and Tarrow, 1998). Whilst it is doubtful that all forms of protest can be absorbed as normal, the assimilation and professionalisation of protest is a striking feature of the contemporary political scene. Even some of the most spirited protest movements (anti capitalist, anti war) tend to be treated in Europe as normal protest. As someone who was a regular participant in demonstrations in the sixties and seventies, I am still shocked and surprised when I see protestors interviewed on television or hear the route of the march helpfully announced by broadcasters. That clearly was not the way that the media handled protestors involved in the Poll Tax protest, the miners' strike or the Vietnam demos. The normalisation of protest may well represent a stage in its institutionalisation.

The professionalisation of protest is strikingly evident in relation to consumer activism. Consumer and environmentalist activism also enjoys an unprecedented degree of adulation in the media and public life. Campaigns against road building, live animal exports, the fast food chain Macdonald's and trials of GM foods are characteristically portrayed as heroic acts of responsible citizenship. Often, the media depicted environmentalists who wrecked GM crop test sites as peoples' champions tackling giant American Goliaths. According to John Vidal, the environmental editor of *The Guardian*, 'the ecological-inspired critique of democracy is now exploding and the crop pullers should be seen as part of an international movement that, thanks to email and the web, watchdog groups and increasing networking, is throwing up new issues, philosophies, ethics, and legal arguments' (*The Guardian*, 17:08:1999). This representation of environmental activists as intellectual innovators, who are providing a morally exhausted society with a priceless philosophical contribution, is rarely interrogated. At every turn, environmental activists are praised for their altruism, social responsibility and moral outlook.

The adoption of the cause of consumer activism by the contemporary British and European political establishment raises interesting questions about its status as a movement. Consumer and environmental activists routinely attempt to portray themselves as disadvantaged radical outsiders who are continually battling against powerful vested interests. Environmental activists in particular claim that they represent a disenfranchised public who lack any significant access to the political system. However, judging by the highly positive representation of these 'outsiders' by the mainstream media, one could be forgiven for drawing the conclusion that this is very much a movement led by insiders.

The activism of consumer protestors should not confused with the activism sought by traditional social movements in the past. Unlike traditional social movements, lobbying groups are not interested in mobilising popular support per se. Campaigns organised by consumer activists are primarily media events designed to gain the maximum publicity. These campaigns are essentially public relations exercises oriented towards stimulating the interest of the media. The significance which advocacy groups, NGOs and campaigning groups attach to publicity is motivated by the realisation that their influence is intimately linked to their public profile. Indeed, it is their ability to gain profile which determines the degree of influence they can exercise over officialdom. Consequently, the machinery of consumer activism is single mindedly oriented towards gaining publicity through the media. A large active membership is quite unnecessary for an organisation devoted towards oiling the network of Britain's political oligarchy. Contacts in the media and friends in influential places are far more important than thousands of active supporters. Even when consumer activists take direct action, what counts is the presence of the television cameras. There is little point in protesting or demonstrating if it does not gain publicity for the group concerned. From this perspective an act is deemed to be effective if it makes the news. It does not matter whether anything has been achieved on the ground, publicity is all that counts. The typical Greenpeace stunt involving a small core of professional protestors, whose appearance is carefully crafted for the maximum dramatic effect, is emblematic of the political theatre of consumer activism.

For its part, the media uncritically embraces the consumer activist. They are the good guys. Unlike politicians they are not tainted by corruption or self-interest. They are typically portrayed as altruistic idealists, whose motives are beyond reproach. The media's celebration of consumer activism reflects a wider Establishment consensus about the semi-official status of this movement. In all but name the leadership of this informal network of non-governmental organisations has become integrated into the new Establishment. As Kevin Dunion, the Scottish director of Friends of the Earth boasted, after becoming the first eco-warrior to receive an OBE, 'There is now an alternative establishment that is being listened to'. He added that he was 'very pleased that Prince Charles made the presentation as he is a fellow environmentalist' (BBC Online Network, 7:07:1999). This 'alternative establishment' extends from the British aristocracy to representatives of Cool Britannia in the media.

The professionalisation of protest suggests that a significant section of social movements have been absorbed into the institutions a new political oligarchy. This development is most strikingly evident during the high profile international summits that provide the focus for so much of international protests these days. At these summits there is a place for everyone. The traditional politicians and their officials meet to decide the 'future of the world'. In the meantime they are lobbied by the legions of NGOs, who hold their slightly less conventional meetings in 'alternative' sites. And on the streets are the angry protestors, who have flown in from all over the world to air the views of people whose voices would not otherwise be heard.

The professionalisation of protest has important implications for democracy. Traditionally, public protest played a crucial role in the winning of democratic rights and in extending them. Participation through protest often appeared to have the potential for involving the public in a way that parliamentary democracy could not. Maybe that's the 'old' politics. With the professionalisation of protest it is far from evident whether its oligarchical activism is more democratic than the system of representative democracy. At least professional politicians need to get elected, whereas professional protestors have a warrant to speak on behalf of anyone without having to win a single vote.

Reengaging the protestor to a future oriented relationship with the public would be a positive development for democratic politics. Debating the relationship between democracy and protest may well help clarify the issues at stake.

©Frank Furedi
June 2003

References

BBC News, 'The United States of Apathy?', 11 January 2000.

BBC News, 'Politics is a "turn-off" for under 45s', 28 February 2002.

BBC ONLINE NETWORK, 1 July 1999.

Bookchin, M. (1995) *Social Anarchism or Lifestyle Anarchism: an unbridgeable chasm*, (San Francisco: AK Press).

Curtice, J. and Jowell, R. (1995) 'The sceptical electorate' in Jowell, R., Curtice, J., Park and Ahrendt, A. *British Social Attitudes: The 12th Report*, (Dartmouth) pp. 141 and 148.

Furedi, F. (2005) *Towards the self: the politics of disengagement* (forthcoming).

Gitell, S. (2002) *'Apathy at the Polls'*, *The Boston Phoenix*, 4 December 2002.

The Guardian, 8 June 1999.

Melucci, A. (1988) 'Social Movements and the Democratisation of Everyday Life', in Keane, J. (ed) *Civil Society and the State*, (London: Verso).

Meyer, D. and Tarrow, S. (1988) (eds) *The Social Movement Society: Contentious Politics For A New Century*, (Lanham: Rowman and Littlefield).

Thomson, A. (2002) ''Politics doesn't have to be like the Big Brother House', *The Daily Telegraph*, 4 December 2002.

Vidal, J. (1999) 'Seeds of dissent', *The Guardian*, 7 July 1999.

1. Introduction

Malcolm J. Todd and Gary Taylor

The purpose of this book is to provide a perspective on the current state of representative democracy in Britain. Specifically, it aims to investigate the importance of political protest and contemporary social movements not only as a means of holding elected political representatives accountable, but also as ways for diverse sections of the community to express their views. The essays contained within this edited volume are from a broad range of theoretical and disciplinary origins and they approach democracy and protest in a variety of ways. A number of the authors focus on the foundations, character and future of democratic participation in Britain, whilst others look specifically at the activities of 'old' and 'new' social movements and the various characteristics of political protest. Although the bulk of the essays are principally concerned with developments in Britain, many of the authors make comparisons with trends in the USA and in the rest of Europe. These comparisons provide us with some useful insights into the problems faced by a range of modern liberal democracies and, more generally, also steer us away from attributing these problems to the mistakes committed by any particular government or party. However, a common theme that recurs in these chapters is the belief that representative democracy is fundamentally limited in its ability to reflect the needs and desires of citizens in a contemporary western society like the UK. A number of our contributors claim that democracy today is far more than a set of institutions and political procedures and that democracy is, in fact, being continually forged and re-designed through our own activities.

It must be made clear at the outset that this edited volume makes no claim to be a comprehensive examination of all aspects of the debates surrounding the limits of modern western democracy. Further, the book is not an account of the emergence and growth of new social movements in the UK. It is, instead, primarily a collection that aims to introduce the reader to a series of issues, themes and perspectives that help us to frame these developments. We hope that this text will be able to make a modest contribution to discussions surrounding political protest and social movements in contemporary western liberal democracies.

In this introductory chapter, we start by taking a wide-ranging look at various aspects of the debates surrounding the so-called 'crisis of democracy'. This is followed by an examination of some the political ideologies that have framed our understanding of representative and direct democracy in the UK. Finally, we discuss some of the dynamics that may be involved with these developments and the implications this may be having for our current understanding of the nature of democracy and political protest in Britain.

The Exhaustion of the Old Politics?

Many people, including political scientists, politicians, journalists and new social movements activists have claimed that, at the start of the 21st-century, representative democracy is in nothing less than a state of crisis. And of particular concern to commentators in the UK are the difficulties that traditional political parties have encountered. The accounts they offer for this development are varied: There is very little difference today between the mainstream political doctrines and party programmes; the honesty and reputation of our elected politicians and of the mainstream political parties is in decline; a gap has opened up between the voter and the politicians, with parliamentary politics being unresponsive to the demands of the public; the electorate are depoliticised, disillusioned and unwilling to turn out in national and local elections; the electoral process itself is irrelevant to people's lives; Politics has become boring, technocratic and trivialised; the cut-and-thrust of politics has given way to the slick art of spin, leaving many people disinterested and disheartened.

Noreena Hertz is typical of a number of social commentators in recent years that claim people are no longer convinced that politicians can deliver on important issues. Real issues are being brushed aside and the electorate are being offered nothing more than a homogenous product. Hertz claims that traditional politicians no longer seem to capture the contemporary imagination and that politics has become:

> ... a product not really worth buying, another offer battling for the consumer's attention via ever more slick advertising campaigns rather than substance (and that) parties have become so similar that any one who disagrees with their fundamental tenets is necessarily left out, anyone who refuses to buy their message cannot find an alternative outlet to sell them another kind of product. (Hertz, 2001)

For some, this process of political disengagement and alienation has been a long time in the making. It is not the result of a temporary loss of faith by a distrustful public in our political leaders, but of a fundamental shift in attitude in western societies. This decline in confidence in representative democracy can be traced back to at least the 1960s. The growth of protest movements and social activism in Europe and America during the 1960s made many feel that national parliamentary politics could no longer deliver what was necessary to gain the consent and/or compliance of politically active youth involved in the peace movement, civil rights, the women's movement and in student politics (Putnam, 1995).

By the 1970s, this crisis in confidence in parliamentary institutions was undermined further by the inability of national political systems to deliver all they promised in the wake of significant socio-economic changes. Of particular importance were the oil price shock in the early 1970s and the ensuing intractable problem of economic decline. Leading western governments found that they were '... trapped between rising demands from citizens and declining resources to meet those demands' (Pharr, Putnam and Dalton, 2000:6). During this period, researchers found that young people had generally negative views about Britain's role in the international community and a general lack of trust in the workings of the British political system (see Chapter 10). Indeed, a number of observers have claimed that contemporary western societies are increasingly becoming characterised by a widespread and deep lack of trust in established forms of democracy (see Chapter 6).

This disenchantment with politics and politicians has not improved, despite attempts by governments to reduce the expectations of the electorate. During the 1980s, many western governments turned against excessive government intervention in social and economic policies and attempted to reduce the functions and responsibilities of the state and enhance and respect individual freedom. There was a political philosophy, which wanted to 'free' business, the public sector and the individual from the restrictions of 'big government'. It was argued that the era of the intrusive state was over and the fall of the Stalinist states of Eastern Europe economies reaffirmed the belief (espoused by Margaret Thatcher) that 'there is no alternative' to capitalism (see Foreword by Frank Furedi).

What is seen to be excessive state action has done little to stabilise society in the long run. But this sleight of hand, which in part attempted to restore the legitimacy of government by denying responsibility for such economic ills as unemployment, failed to recapture the trust of the public.

Although the free-market capitalism of the Reagan administration in America was popular during its early stages, confidence fell again by the close of the republican reign. In Britain, too, Margaret Thatcher drew upon the radical political economy of the New Right and appealed to many during the early 1980s – with far-reaching plans for domestic policy including the privatisation of nationalised industries and national utilities and the marketisation of public services like health, education and community care services (see Chapter 8). However, popular enthusiasm for such policies declined drastically in the latter half of the decade when, following the world capitalist recession in the 1980s, the Thatcherite 'project' was thought to be exhausted.

As noted, this lack of enthusiasm for parliamentary politics has been reflected in people's general lack of trust of government. In 1987, for example, less that half of the people in Britain believed that governments could be trusted to act in accordance with the public good (Pharr, Putnam and Dalton, 2000: 8-11). Similar trends continued throughout the 1990s. In America, in 1997, only 12 per cent of American people claimed that they had 'a great deal of confidence' in the executive and only 11 per cent had this level of confidence in the Senate. By 1998, only 3 per cent claimed that they trusted the government. This sense of apathy to formal politics also manifested itself in the number of people involved in political parties, which declined steadily over the post war period. In the USA, the number of people who took part in some political party fell in the period 1973-1993 by over 50 per cent. This has been attributed to the widely held belief that political parties are unresponsive to the interests of the public (Pharr, Putnam and Dalton, 2000: 11-16).

Indeed, it is often argued that voter apathy, declining membership of political parties and increased cynicism towards political leaders has pushed the modern democratic system towards a crisis of legitimacy. The existing system can only operate effectively if people agree to be governed and comply with the decisions made by government. This system is, however, crumbling under the weight of diverse pressures placed upon it. During the early 1990s it was argued that the popularity of politicians was in long-term decline, 'the erosion of public trust was reflected in a national mood of suspicion towards the political system itself. What emerged was a brand of anti-politics, a cynical dismissal of the elected politician and an obsession with sleaze and corruption in Westminster' (Furedi, Foreword).

Politicians are sometimes thought to live in a world of illusion. They are separated from the society they govern and from the lives of the people they are meant to represent. This apparent growing disconnection between elected representatives and the electorate is acknowledged by politicians from right, left and centre parties. In a BBC documentary in the early 1990s, a number of prominent politicians spoke of this problem. Chris Patten, the former Conservative minister and governor of Hong Kong, claimed that politicians have failed to make the necessary changes to the way they work, and that unless politicians change they may well 'go out of business'. Paddy Ashdown, the former leader of the Liberal Democrats, believed that politicians are dangerously out of touch with modern times and need to reassess their position in society and accommodate changes in British culture. Labour MPs have likewise argued that politicians must pay more attention to the views and activities of the citizen body. Calum MacDonald warned that politicians must take into account the range of single-issue groups in society and he claimed that the age of the old mass party is over (BBC2, 25.10.1993).

Although Tony Blair's New Labour government enjoyed a long honeymoon period when it came to power with a landslide victory in May 1997, it has done little to maintain the long-term interest of the electorate. For some observers, a weak conservative opposition has created few challenges for the government and has thus fuelled arrogance and complacency. The national political system makes extensive use of the print and broadcast media to cleanse its product for popular consumption and the government has taken a cautious approach on the majority of domestic issues in the hope no doubt of reducing potential opposition. According to Nick Cohen, modern British politics is dominated by opinion polls because the parties need to have the information necessary to predict the movements of floating voters. This has led to the increasing importance of knowing how to deal with the media and to the rise of the so-called spin doctors who pride themselves in being able to fine-tune the political system so as to make it responsive to what people want. All parties seek to attract the floating voters by appealing to what they call 'basic decent values' (Channel 4, 3.6.2001).

The British people, however, show disdain for the politics of spin. The working class, in particular, have become more contemptuous of the political system and this has manifested itself, in part, in declining turnout at elections of the inhabitants of the poorer constituencies in the UK. For example, at the European parliament elections in 1999, only 1.5 per cent of the voters of Sunderland turned out to vote (Channel 4, 3.6.2001). On the eve of the 2001 British general election, the polls showed that a low turnout was likely. This trend is true of many countries in Western Europe and in the USA. During the American presidential elections in 2000, over 90 million people (almost half of the electorate) did not vote (King, 2001; Hertz, 2001). We have also seen how the overall rate of voting is much lower at the majority of by-elections and at local elections in the UK and the USA (around 40 per cent in Britain, or closer to 30 per cent in the big cities). Anthony King attributed this to a range of factors. Firstly, it was said to stem from the decline in traditional religious and class loyalties that had formerly played an important role in motivating people. Secondly, the great ideological debates of the past have been replaced by arguments over the best ways to manage market capitalism – in this respect, there seems to be very little that separates the programmes of the main political parties. Finally, he claimed that young people are turning away from politics because they find politicians to be 'ill-mannered, irrelevant and often unintelligible' (King, 2001).

In fact, the turnout in the general election of 2001 was the lowest since 1918. It is said that this was because of the belief that the election was a foregone conclusion, that the campaign was too boring, that there is a general lack of interest in politics and the belief that there was an insufficient gap between the parties (Riddell, 2001). Although the Blair government sought to attribute the low turnout to the 'politics of contentment', commentators like Noreena Hertz claimed that it is the poorer sections of the community (rather than those who are served well by the government) that are less likely to vote. Groups who have traditionally been defended by the political left have become increasingly sidelined (Hertz, 2001).

In addition to the political disengagement of the poorer sections of the community, politicians have found it increasingly difficult to attract the interest of youth. A research study in the mid 1990s, conducted by the British left-leaning think-tank Demos, found that the portion of the voting population that has shown the most indifference to politics is the young (Mulgan and Wilkinson, 1995). This sense of growing alienation of young people from the political process and the democratic system was evident in the general election of 2001, where only 39 per cent of people aged 18-24 turned out to vote. Young people have withdrawn increasingly from formal parliamentary politics and are less inclined to be members of traditional political organisations. According to recent research, reported in this volume, this stems in part from the belief that young people feel powerless to exert effective influence on the national political system; that politics is based on an adversarial style of debate; that there is very little choice between the main political parties; that politics seems to be defined by scandals, sleaze, corruption and cronyism and that parliamentary politics is far too 'remote' to be of any interest or relevance (see Chapters 9 and 10).

Yet, although low voter turnout can be explained in part in terms of apathy and a mistrust of parliamentary politics, there is evidence to suggest that many people who abstained did so as a positive choice because they had a particularly low opinion of politicians and of the political system. A study conducted by MORI found that approximately 25 per cent of nonvoters were active citizens in that they took part in other political activities. These electors may, for example, be members of voluntary groups or attend public demonstrations (Riddell, 2001). According to some commentators, it could be, indeed, that significant sections of the population are unwilling to cast their votes because they are in fact better informed about the performance of government. This can have a detrimental effect if governments are unable to meet the standards expected of them. Governments have found it increasingly difficult to perform well in economic management and this can lead the citizens to turn away from politics and to regard politics as superfluous and incapable of providing feasible and long term solutions to economic problems (Pharr, Putnam and Dalton, 2000:20).

It would therefore be wrong to attribute the crisis of representative democracy solely to a lack of interest in political matters. Active citizens are also turning against traditional political institutions and are finding new ways to express themselves. This can be traced, in part, to mistrust in the existing system, to the lack of choice between the main parties and to the changing needs of the citizen body. According to a number of contributors to this volume, such developments reflect nothing less than a reconfiguration of British politics.

Democracy and Political Ideologies

The problems faced by modern politicians in gaining the trust of the electorate are by no means the only factors impinging upon the relevance, value and vitality of modern democracy. We should remember that democracy means rule by the many and that politicians have to accept that their will or should always be limits to what they can do. It is futile for politicians to complain about the apathy of the masses as if their profession is entitled to support. This support, it could be argued, must be earned by responding to and adapting to the needs of the electorate. Failure to do so will inevitably attract a heavy penalty.

There are clearly many forms of democracy. The right to vote would seem to be a necessary prerequisite for any form of democracy but the range of choice we have will differ between systems and the power held by the citizen will obviously be contingent upon the institutions and processes of each particular system. The national political systems of Britain, America and Western Europe operate according to the principles of representative, or indirect, democracy in which people transfer power to governments by means of direct elections. Rather than participate directly in governmental decision-making, we choose and elect representatives into parliamentary government to act on our behalf. Under this arrangement, an elected politician is provided with an authorisation to represent the electorate whilst the electorate, themselves, have relatively little power over their representatives once elected. Members of parliament in Britain, and of congress in the USA, are representatives and they are therefore free to prioritise their own views and interests above those of the electorate. Representative democracy, by definition, imposes a set of restrictions on political participation by the voting public. Of course, those people entitled to vote could ultimately exercise their power over how the government of the day performs by replacing their MP from a choice of groups of representation at the next general election. However, at that point, their success will often be determined by the fortunes of their own party rather than by their constituents having detailed knowledge of how their representatives used their power (Taylor, 1999: 34-36).

Modern liberal democracies rely not only upon the right for all to vote in a regular and secret ballot, but also upon there being a set of procedures in place that separate the powers of the state and ensure that political power is not abused (Dearlove and Saunders, 2000). Alongside these checks and balances of power on the government, there are also procedures that guarantee freedom of expression, debate and the liberty to form and join political groups or associations and express views through (lawful) public protests and campaigning (Dearlove and Saunders, 2000; Giddens, 2002; Heywood, 2002).

However, for those who argue for a system of direct democracy, these procedural aspects of the democratic system do little to create a politically informed and motivated body of voters. Indeed, voting in the general and local elections to express our views could in fact fuel political ignorance rather than liberate our political wills for, unless we take into account other views, we are unlikely to ever understand the composition of the common good. The 18th century French moral and political philosopher Jean-

Jacques Rousseau understood this point when he argued that in an ideal society it was the responsibility of all citizens to participate in the political affairs of the community and that this obligation was similar to that of paying taxes. In Rousseau's view, people should not be so preoccupied with their own affairs that they have no time for the affairs of state. Moreover, if we rely upon representatives we can relinquish our power to political elites and lose sight of our true freedom (Rousseau, 1968: 138-143). This line of thought, and the arguments associated with the classical Greek democratic theory, recognises the importance for democracy of active participation, where different interest groups should and could be much more immediately engaged in the institutions in which they live and work or which govern them (see, for example, Taylor, 1999; Cockburn, 1978).

It could be argued that for democracy to be real, citizens must be able to participate directly at some level in the decision making process. This was, indeed, the essence of 'direct democracy' in classical Greece. Under the Athenian system, during the fifth and fourth centuries BC, citizens were trusted to govern themselves. Rather than rely upon representatives, all those who were citizens were entitled and encouraged to speak in public assemblies and play an active part in making public policy. Through participation in mass meetings and debates, it was expected that citizens would also develop civic virtues and a broader political education (Taylor, 1999: 34).

It should be acknowledged that there is, of course, a vast difference in scale between the large contemporary nation state and the small city-states (*polis*) of classical Greece. It was also the case that the ancient Athenians excluded the vast majority of people from the rights and obligations of citizenship (immigrants, women and slaves, for example, were not citizens and had no vote). In fact, in Western Europe at least, it was not until the 20th century that people have benefited from full political participation with the franchise being secured by all social classes and women (Edye and Lintner, 1996: 66).

However, the practical relevance of this form of direct democracy is of limited value in modern society. Direct democracy of this kind is only workable in small communities – like that of the *polis* – where the members of the group can easily come together in a single physical place (Giddens, 1971: 181). Whilst acknowledging that the Athenian *polis* may have little application to the 21st century, one of its main contributions to western political thought relating to democracy lays in its insistence that democracy is dependent upon participation rather than upon the mere existence of a set of procedures that facilitate a properly monitored open electoral system. Advocates of participatory democracy, therefore, recognise that a democratic system depends upon people having the opportunity to engage in social and political activity, in an ongoing way, not just at election time. These advocates wish to see an improvement of the democratic spirit of people and tend to be drawn from left-of-centre of the political spectrum and advance the idea of a more active democracy as part of a package of proposed social reforms. They argue that if we were happy with the current distribution of power and resources, it would make little sense to campaign in favour of radical changes in the political system.

The way we view the modern democratic system will be influenced by a range of factors including our own particular ideological pedigree. It is, of course, not necessary for us to subscribe to any one particular ideology. Indeed, many people appear to draw their ideas from a variety of political streams. This cross fertilisation of ideas adds to diversity in society and assists us in communicating with fellow citizens. It would be a drab world, indeed, if we could only sign up for one philosophy and in doing so renounce the principles and supporters of other systems of thought. When looking at democracy, those searching for new ways to engage with the political system may well draw at least part of their inspiration from the intense ideological debates that have developed since the French revolution of 1789. This revolution promised to free the people from the bonds and tyranny of the *Ancient Regime* but ultimately failed to live up to the expectations of many. If we take a brief look at these modern ideologies, we will see that democracy is viewed in a variety of ways and that representative democracy in particular is often viewed with suspicion.

Liberal Fears

From a liberal perspective, democracy is one of the hallmarks of civilisation. Democratic principles often rest upon liberal assumptions about our abilities for rational thought, tolerance and sound judgement. Liberal theorists, however, have been concerned about those who are unable to live up to these standards. Many of the classical liberals of the eighteenth and nineteenth centuries (see, for example, Alexis de Tocqueville and J.S. Mill) felt that the French revolution had gone too far by tampering with property rights, and were generally fearful of the largely uneducated masses. It was argued that people are too often willing to sacrifice liberty for the promise of greater material security and that democrat's push the notion of equality too far. This line of reasoning states that people are not equal in their possession of talents and that they often experience frustration when they do not secure what they believe they are due. Under such conditions, the disaffected will grant the state increasing powers to improve their lot, which adds to the centralisation of power and the crushing of individual liberty. Such processes result in what is known as the 'tyranny of the majority' (Perry, 1993: 218).

This fear of the tyranny of the majority became an important feature of liberal social and political theory and found prominence in the work of the philosopher and political economist John Stuart Mill. Mill believed that the democratic aims of the French revolution, which had attempted to encourage self-government, had failed to materialise in practice. The will of the people was never more than the will of the majority and this majority maintained its position by attempting to suppress the minority. This tyranny of the majority was thought to be a social tyranny perpetrated by members of society rather than a political tyranny engineered by the government. In Mill's view, we need protection against '... prevailing opinion and feeling; against the tendency of society to impose, by other means than civil penalties, its own ideas and practices as rules of conduct on those who dissent from them' (Mill, 1859: 8). Limits must therefore be placed upon the jurisdiction of collective opinion.

Mill realised that the tyranny of the majority rested upon little more than the desire of people to impose their own preferences. He claimed that custom prescribed where to draw the line between the individual and social interference, and that it was often assumed that this line was clear and fixed. This line, however, differed significantly between nations and cultures. It depended upon such things as individual preferences, self-interest, and the values of the dominant or ascendant class. This social tyranny was already in existence, but Mill was convinced that it was about to be compounded by political tyranny. He believed that once the majority understand the power that they have, then individual liberty will ' ... probably be as much exposed to invasion from the government, as it already is from public opinion' (Mill, 1859: 12). His concern was that the government might increase its powers at the expense of individual liberty.

For Mill, democracy posed at least a potential threat to individual liberty. The more the state does, the more it can interfere in the life of the individual. Many liberals fear that the majority can be misguided and intolerant. The modern tabloid media, for example, are often thought to play upon the prejudices and envy of the so-called masses. They serve us a diet of sex scandals, celebrity lifestyles and political coverage that concentrates upon incidences of hypocrisy rather than the more serious and less newsworthy detail of policy and diplomacy (Taylor, 2000). This diet could turn many people away from politics, push them further towards their own personal interests and do little to equip the citizen with the information, insight and interest necessary to engage meaningfully with the democratic process. History shows, moreover, that 'popular opinion' can be manipulated to scapegoat minorities for problems existing at a systemic level. Liberals will sometimes point out that the 'cultured classes' in particular need to be vigilant in defending their own civil rights and values against the encroachment of mass democracy.

The Political Right

Theorists drawn from the political right are likewise sceptical about the value of representative democracy and have argued that democracy can have harmful effects upon the moral, social and institutional frameworks of society. The British statesman and political theorist Edmund Burke famously told his Bristol constituents in 1774 that parliament exists to represent the national interest, rather than the particular interests of local constituents, and that he was not willing to sacrifice his judgement for the opinions of his constituents (Burke, 1774). Many conservatives have cast doubt upon the capabilities of the general public, and of the working class in particular, to deliberate with sufficient care on political matters. British conservatives were critical of the democratic aspirations of the French revolution and warned that such abrupt political changes would end in tyranny. They supported minority rule and argued against parliamentary reform on the grounds that only a few had sufficient education, mature judgement and wisdom to rise above their own self interest and to prioritise the interests of the nation (Burke, 1791). Conservatives fiercely opposed the extension of the franchise (those entitled to vote) in the early 1830s on the grounds that this would disrupt the cherished features of the British constitution and undermine the social and political fabric of the nation. The Conservative Party was forced to reassess its position following the 1832 Reform Act, but this mistrust of extending democratic rights remained an important feature of conservative thinking for the bulk of the nineteenth century (Wright, 1970; Arnold, 1935).

The political right have often argued that there is a 'natural order' where politics is and should remain an elite activity. During the late nineteenth and early twentieth centuries, conservative theorists in Europe argued that the ideal of democratic government was an illusion and that society will always be divided between a small creative minority and a relatively passive majority. Roberto Michels' iron law of oligarchy, for example, shows how political groups can be captured by so-called ruling oligarchies (rule by the few) that have the necessary intellectual aptitude for political leadership and in turn expect little more than obedience from those they lead. Gaetano Mosca and Vilfredo Pareto argued similarly that elites, in the form of party professionals and politicians, are necessary for the smooth running of society and that these elites have distinctive qualities that separate them from the general public. From an elitist theory point of view, representative democracy is a sham – it is a 'camouflage for the oligarchic tendencies of power' and the idea of participatory democracy is both undesirable and impossible to achieve (Miller, 1991: 118).

Although modern conservatives no longer argue against working class people having the vote, some nevertheless remain sceptical about the ability of the working class to contribute much of value to the policy making process. Whilst accepting the importance of universal suffrage, many modern conservatives remain critical of active democratic participation whether this be in the form of demonstrations and protests or through pressure group activity. The New Right of the 1970s and 1980s, for example, drew upon right wing reservations over democracy to justify increasing the power of governing elites over the policy making process. For example, Margaret Thatcher tried to free her government of 1979-1990 from the undue influence of pressure groups. She believed that pressure groups tend to demand too much from the state and that they generally obstruct the free market economy. She was particularly critical of the trade union movement and did all she could to undermine the corporatist heritage of the post-war years by refusing to negotiate with the unions or involve them in the making of economic policy (Taylor, 1999: 63-64; see Chapters 5 and 6). For many on the right, representative democracy exists as a means to provide a mandate to govern rather than as a way for the masses to gain access to policy making.

The Political Left

Whereas the political right see mass participation as a threat to elite rule and capitalism, the political left have argued that representative democracies are elitist by nature and that this elitism stands in the way of true democracy. Karl Marx and Friedrich Engels argued that the French revolution was fought in the interests of the minority (the bourgeoisie) and that it did little to liberate the masses (Marx and Engels, 1845:139-143). Crudely expressed, they claimed that the state is part of a superstructure which rests upon, and is conditioned by, the needs of the economic base structure and that the bourgeoisie use the modern state to protect their own interests and to marginalise the interests of the working class (Marx and Engels, 1848; Marx, 1859). Given that the capitalist system was formed by, and is run in, the interests of the bourgeoisie, little can be expected from the political system by way of radical social reform. Marx himself argued that the working class should not rely upon the state because the interests of the bourgeoisie contaminated it and because it had become an instrument of class oppression designed for 'social enslavement' (Marx, 1871).

For many Marxists, democracy under capitalism is nothing less than pretence, an illusion that conceals the true extent of the exploitation endured by the working class. Such *bourgeois* democracy, they would claim, gives the impression that the state serves the will of the people and that it is free from the dominance of minority interests. Marxists point out, however, that the state and the existing system of representative democracy protect the economic interests of the minority and attempt to secure the compliance and passivity of the majority (see Chapter 4). In Marx's view, workers need 'direct democracy' – that is they need to form their own system of devolved 'communes' (run by a small group of delegates) rather than representatives (Marx, 1871).

A similar line of reasoning is also to be found in some forms of anarchism, though anarchists tend to place more emphasis upon the harmful effects of political authority and power rather than upon the needs of the capitalist economic system. Although many anarchists see themselves as advocates of direct democracy, some argue that direct democracy would do little to remove the main flaw in democracy and that the problem lies in the coercion of individuals which is symptomatic of systems resting upon 'majority rule'. This pushes some anarchists in the direction of 'consensus building' in which unanimity is required for policy to be made or before action is taken. Anarchists have tended to rely upon the revolutionary fervour of the dispossessed and marginalised and they have played a particularly important role in the direct action approach used in the anti-poll tax movement and in the anti-capitalist movement (see Chapter 4).

The dilution of left wing sentiment in national politics in Britain since the 1980s has created a space that some new social movements seek to fill. As is discussed elsewhere in this volume, the 1980s was a time in which British politics went through an important period of transition, with the decline of collective solidarity following the collapse of Labour support and the deterioration of trade union power undermined 'credible opposition to free market capitalism' (Chapter 3). Indeed, the dominance of the New Right in European and American politics during the 1980s transformed national political programmes and forced social democratic groups to the right in the hope of finding the elusive floating voter. Social democratic parties became increasingly willing to accommodate the interests of global capital. Globalisation is thought to exert pressure on Tony Blair's New Labour Party to make sure that state policies are in no real way a threat to dominant economic players. The New Labour leadership have, over the past ten years or so, discarded many of the polices that traditionally made the party appear distinctive. Critics of the current government have made the claim that voting New Labour, therefore, provides no real alternative to the previous Conservative administration in Britain (Chapters 3 and 8).

A number of commentators have argued that Marxists have failed to reflect the real needs of a post-material society (Inglehart, 1987). Indeed, the traditional Marxist parties have seemed a little antiquated to a new generation of left wing activists who, dismayed with the weakness of social democracy and the apparent redundancy of Marxist ideas, have turned towards the anti-capitalist movements. Many in the anti-capitalist movement argue that global capitalism stands in the way of true democracy and that direct democracy is necessary to counter the insidious influence of global economic power (see Chapters 2 and 3). For many on the left, capitalism is protected by representative democracy but challenged to its very core by active democratic movements, free from party ties and largely unwilling to compromise with what they regard as fundamental economic, social and political injustices.

Feminist reservations

There are, as Nickie Charles and Simon Henig make clear in this volume, considerable differences between various strands of feminist ideology and politics. However, notwithstanding the clear complexity of conceptualising feminism, an important underlying characteristic of the feminist view of democracy is to be found in its rejection of the liberal distinction between the public and private spheres. Susan Okin, for example, points out that liberals want to protect the private sphere from social and governmental intervention and that this 'private sphere' is often equated with 'domestic' life. Women are thought to inhabit this private sphere, whilst men assume control of the public realms of economic and political affairs. Given this control, men grant to themselves political rights and the right to control their own household. The feminist response is to declare that the 'personal is political'. This means that personal relationships are political because they involve an element of power. Modern feminists have thus sought to challenge power relations within the family with the aim of transforming gender roles. This refusal to accept the liberal distinction between the public and the private has also led some feminists to argue that the domestic sphere should be open to state intervention (Okin, 1991: 68-77).

In addition to transforming family relations, it is clear that many feminists want greater access to the 'public' sphere. Under a system of liberal democracy, there is the assumption that we all have equal access to power. However, this ignores the causes of sexual inequalities between women and men and of male domination over women (Hartmann, 1981). This inequality exists all over the world both an elite level (noted by the absence of women in key positions such as politics, relative to men) and at the mass level where women have endured exclusion from the public realm and have tended to be passive as citizens. Liberal democracy thus promises autonomy and self-determination, but fails to deliver because women are often excluded from the exercise of power. It has been argued that women are less likely to participate in politics because they are often constrained by the demands of the private domestic sphere. Inequalities in the sexual division of labour (women are still considered to have the main responsibility for care of all dependents) militate against women entering the public sphere. The private sphere thus has a direct impact upon levels of political participation (Schwarzmantel, 1994: 114-116 and 123-126).

According to many in the contemporary women's movement, the political system is controlled by men and dominated by a male agenda. Women are, therefore, encouraged by some feminists to form their own groups to deal with their own issues rather than to compete with men for power within patriarchal institutions. The contemporary women's movement has argued that politics does not take place solely in the public sphere and that it should be recognised that the personal is political. Conventional politics tends to be preoccupied with such issues as economic growth and with the redistribution of resources. Many feminists, on the other hand, have attempted to broaden the way we view the political system and point out that democracy should not be tied to the impersonal political realm but should take into account the importance of empowering people in their personal lives (see Chapters 12 and 13).

Feminists have looked for new ways to engage with the political process and have been attracted in particular to those social movement activities that look beyond narrow economistic views of politics. Instead of being anchored in economic squabbles, new social movements tend to be concerned with post-material issues and with questions about cultural reproduction, lifestyle issues and social identity. These movements have relied to a large extent upon the energy and imagination of women. The contemporary women's movement has inherited much from the left liberation movements of the nineteenth and twentieth centuries. It has concerned itself with social (abortion on demand, for example) and economic issues (equal pay, for example). Furthermore, since the 1970s, the women's movement has been concerned with a range of post-material values explored by new social movements. In this sense, the women's movement is hybrid in its motivation and its dominant concerns. Surveys conducted during the 1990s showed that women out-numbered men in such organisations as the Campaign for Nuclear Disarmament, Friends of the Earth and in the Animal Rights movement. It is argued that women are attracted to the 'politics of survival', that they seem more willing to advance the interests of humankind rather than those of a particular class and that they are at the forefront of movements driven by the desire to promote the 'culture of life' (see Chapters 12 and 13). For many feminists, active involvement in new social movements is necessary to counter the patriarchal agenda set by current parliamentary politics.

New Politics or Anti-politics?

Political ideologies have had a dramatic impact upon the conduct of modern politics for over two hundred years. They helped to make sense of the world from a class or gender point of view. Advocates of these ideologies ask us to suspend or at least relegate in importance the other facets of our social identities. Many would argue, however, that the age of ideology is coming to an end. The appeal of great ideological causes seem increasingly unattractive to a more diverse and complex citizen body. It could be, indeed, that the grand narratives of the past are now redundant and that we have entered a more fragmented and post-modern world which we inhabit with a variety of identities (Taylor and Spencer, 2002). Traditional social categories are seen to be breaking down and are being replaced by new fluid ways of defining ourselves. In particular, class-based systems of political representation are no longer as relevant and there is less pressure on political parties to act on behalf of a particular social group (Offe, 1985; see, also, Chapter 9 of this volume).

Martin Jacques has pointed out that post war Britain was based upon an old class hierarchy, rigid gender divisions and stable political institutions and that this old system is giving way to an increasingly diversified society in which people are losing sight of their place in the hierarchy. As society has become more affluent and complicated, traditional political parties and politicians appear to have lost their relevance. In Britain, the voting public no longer necessarily identify themselves with either of the main political parties. The old class antagonisms appear to have become rather less important in dictating the character of national political debate, and many politicians have lost their sense of direction following the fall of the communist bloc and the absence of war. For Jacques, many conservatives have suffered from a 'relaxation of focus' because their old class enemies no longer posed such an obvious threat. For socialists, the apparent triumph of free market economics in the 1980s and the affect of globalisation in the 1990s have undermined their former commitments. The political system has become fragmented and politicians seem unwilling to develop political visions, tie themselves to ideological causes and are apparently incapable of listening intently to grass root opinion. In Jacques view, if the system fails to represent diverse interests, it will increasingly lose its legitimacy (BBC2, 25.10.1993).

The 1980s and 1990s in the UK has been said to have been a period where individualism was in the ascendancy and collectivism was in decline and that this had forced political parties to change direction. It is argued that this rise in individualism expressed itself in a decline of class identity and solidarity. Political parties had to adapt to a more complex and diverse social structure and meet the challenge mounted by new social movements. Political parties became less significant to substantial sections of the political public. They lost their ideological coherence and began borrowing ideas from each other in a desperate attempt to find the right ideological cocktail to maintain and build support amongst the electorate (Fielding, 2000).

Decca Aitkenhead argues that without great ideological causes (like the post-war ambitious schemes to tackle social and economic problems), politics is rendered technical, dull and irrelevant to many people. Politicians have been successful in convincing many that the historic conflicts between the right and the left are no longer important. This has cut at the roots of 'domestic tribalism' and pushed young people in particular to 'travel the world' in search of something to believe in and something to belong to (Aitkenhead, 2002). Indeed, rather than engage in economic battles that appear to underpin 'traditional' politics, many people are turning towards issue-based politics (such as racism, sexism, animal rights, environmental issues and so on) promoted by new social movements. These are the issues that appear to exercise the current political imagination.

As the contributions to this volume demonstrate, the struggle for democracy has taken on powerful new forms in contemporary society. Whereas so-called 'old' social movements attempted to gain access to the state through parliamentary politics and focused mainly on economic redistribution, 'new' social movements focus increasingly (although not exclusively) on issues like social identity, culture, life-style and human rights concerns. Such movements tend to be defined by their focus on post-material values, their detachment from an identifiable political ideology, and their use of novel and unconventional methods of political action, combined with a rejection of hierarchical and bureaucratic organisation. It is the march, public demonstration, petition and the act of civil disobedience that have become important tactics for social movements to seek to exercise their power and influence policy (see Chapters 2, 3, 9 and 11).

This focus on the politics of identity has helped to undermine the notion of representative democracy and the relevance and appeal of traditional political thinking. New social movements, in there different manifestations, call into question the structures of representative democracy that are thought to curb citizen contributions to and participation in governance (Pichardos, 1994). Further, traditional ideologies, such as liberalism, conservatism and socialism, developed with specific class interests in mind. Liberalism traditionally advanced the interests of the middle class, conservatism defended the aristocracy and socialism looked forward to the time when the working class would free itself from slavery to the needs of the capitalist system. These ideologies were anchored quite firmly on the assumption that our identities are determined primarily by our economic positions in society. Feminists, nationalists and ecologists have challenged this assumption on the grounds that we are also influenced by our genders, nationality and our place in the environment respectively.

More recently, post-modernists have argued that as belief in tradition and religions have declined in western societies, we now live in a less certain age where little can be taken for granted. Each person, it is argued, has been forced to make new sets of decisions about their lifestyle and may, in consequence, have a multitude of social identities and is not thus able to be reduced to any single category (Craig, 1995). An argument is made in a number of the contributions to this volume is that if we are indeed multifaceted, it makes sense for us to express different parts of ourselves in different social groups. Whereas traditional representative democracy seeks to represent us in all things, participatory democracy gives greater scope for us to participate and be active on specific issues that concern us and thus contribute in a variety of ways to the political culture. This search for identity:

> implies making a distinction between old-style or emancipation politics and the new life politics. The former, for example, the labor movement, was concerned with issues like justice and equality and sought the autonomy of the individual. In contrast, life politics takes that autonomy as a given or as its pre-condition; now autonomous actors, unlike earlier ones, have the ability to make choices and contemporary political struggles are over what those choices will be (Craig, 1996: 6).

Yet, fundamental questions have been asked by those involved in discussions concerning the role of NSMs and their democratic status: What mandate do NSMs have in a democratic society? Who do they speak for? Who provides legitimacy for the actions of such groups? Overall, there is a concern that whilst NSMs may appear to enhance participation in politics (especially a radicalised youth), they do so in an inequitable way by furthering particularistic interests and not the interests of the collective body that have traditionally been pursued by a representative democracy (see, for example, Best, 2002; Furedi, Foreword).

The Importance of Social Capital

An important theme that is often raised in today's discussion of modern democracy is that of 'social capital'. As Paul Bagguley makes clear in this volume, social capital can be defined in a variety of ways. In essence, it is thought to mean a measure or expression of the amount of trust necessary for economic and social life. It is strengthened by the existence of strong civic associations, solidarity and loyalty, and 'social citizenship'. Social capital is not owned or possessed by anybody and thus differs significantly from physical capital. Social capital is to be found in the relationships that exist between people. It consists in the expectations we have of each other and in the extent to which we trust one another. The existence of social capital allows us to cooperate with others on common ventures and participate in the political life of the community (Rodger, 2000: 53-54 and 199).

For some commentators, however, democracy is in decline because of our general decline in such civic engagement. This has been attributed to the rise of television and other isolated leisure pursuits. The use of the Internet and sophisticated tele-communications systems is also having an effect upon the character of modern democracy. These new technologies, it is argued, are making it less important to have face-to-face contact with other citizens and are thought to reduce 'social capital' and make us less willing to participate in community activities (Margetts, 2000: 201). According to Robert Putnam, it is electronic entertainment – above all, television – that is 'privatising our leisure time' (Putnam, 2000: 283).

Indeed, evidence suggests that increasingly only a small minority of the population (often the well educated, middle-aged and middle-class) participate in political organisations on a local and/or national level in the UK and that this participation is also of a sporadic nature (Parry and Moyser, 1994). Membership of both the Conservative and Labour parties in the UK has fallen significantly over the past fifty years. In 1953, the Conservative Party had over 2.8 million members. However, by 1975 this had reduced to less than 1.2 million and, in 1993, the party had less than a 500,000 membership. The Labour Party, too, witnessed a similarly sharp deterioration in its membership from a high of over 1 million in 1952 to just over 300,000 in 1990 (Coxall and Robins, 1998: 84). In the United States, studies have shown that only 8 per cent of people have belonged to a political club or organisation and less than one in five people have ever contact with an official of national, state, or local government about a political issue or problem (Orum, 2001). For a number of commentators, large-scale disengagement by people from the public sphere may be having considerable implications for the shape of representative democracy (Putnam, 1995).

However, this view has been criticised as an explanation for the 'crisis in democracy' because it is far too deterministic and because it fails to take into account the variety of ways in which social capital is nurtured (see Chapter 6). It has been argued that social capital is far from in decline in Britain. Anthony Giddens, for example, suggests that there is evidence that citizens in late modern societies are not apolitical or indifferent to politics, and that people participate in different forms of civic engagement and belong to a wide range of communities of interests:

There are signs that interest in politics is actually on the rise, but is simply being channelled into directions other than orthodox party politics. Membership in civic groups and associations is growing and activists are devoting their energies to new social movements focused around single issues such as the environment, trade policy and nuclear non-proliferation (Giddens, 2001: 440).

The involvement of men in the social and political life of the community increased by approximately 7 per cent in the period 1950-1990. The involvement of women almost doubled, thus approaching the level of male participation. Indeed '... social capital has been sustained in Britain by virtue of the increasing participation of women in the community' (Hall 1999 cited in Margetts, 2000: 199). An increasing number of people in Britain are involved in some form of political participation beyond that of voting, but this political activity appears to be of an 'anti-party' type (Mulgan, 2001). Increased participation in single-issue groups owes at least something to growing cynicism towards politicians and towards the mainstream political process. During the BSE (or 'mad cow disease') crisis of the 1990s, for example, the British public remained resistant towards attempts by the government to play down the severity of contamination (Margetts, 2000: 199-200). Young people are also typically attracted to this form of politics. When young people engage in political activity it is often the case that they choose to participate in groups that shun bureaucratic and hierarchical structures in favour of groups involved in new forms of political expression. Young people are more likely to participate in voluntary groups rather than in political parties and that they do not necessarily regard this participation as 'political' in itself (see Chapters 9 and 10). Indeed, as Giddens notes, people are now much more likely to be involved in groups and associations than they used to. He cites research that shows that in Britain, twenty times more people belong to a voluntary or self-help group than are members of political parties (Giddens, 2002: 77).

The Labour Party, under Tony Blair, has been especially keen to see a role for the voluntary and community sector not just in increased services provision but also in encouraging its role to develop greater 'social capital' (see initiatives such as the Millennium Volunteers that encouraged young people to volunteer). It could be argued that the growth of voluntary and community groups has done a great deal to enhance social capital in society and to provide alternatives to traditional political institutions. They benefit indeed from the cynicism towards central and local government and from the unwillingness of many to surrender themselves and their communities to global economic forces. Voluntary and community groups have been instrumental in promoting active participation in communities and thus contribute significantly to participatory democracy. Voluntary participation is said to provide opportunities to take part in decision-making, thereby democratising the way services are planned or delivered. Voluntary groups are said to place a high value on personal contact with local people, with mobilising people and with helping to shape and steer the policy process. In many ways, these groups educate people into the realities of democratic participation. They inspire people to take an active role in their communities and thereby help to raise awareness of and confidence in their own abilities. Marginalised and under-represented members of the community can find an outlet for their interests and concerns in the voluntary and community sectors. These groups tend to understand the importance of diversity and tolerance, partly because they have developed in reaction to the narrowness of traditional political institutions and partly because their work will bring them into contact with a vast array of groups all vying for influence. In short, the argument goes that voluntary and community groups can enrich the democratic system by providing platforms for diverse sections of the community and by showing us that politics does not have to be left in the hands of the professional. They provide an effective counterweight to the power of both state bureaucracies and private enterprise (Ware and Todd, 2002; see also Chapters 15 and 16).

However, it should be acknowledged that there are very real concerns about the potentially anti-democratic nature of such developments. There are fears about the accountability of voluntary organisations, the lack of transparency in structure to governmental agencies and to the general public. There are important questions about the implications of shifting power and responsibility for our public services away from our elected and accountable politicians to unelected and less accountable authorities, interest groups, voluntary groups and non-governmental organisations (Ware and Todd, 2002). These are vital questions that underpin any debate about the notions of representative and participatory democracy.

The Renewal of Democracy?

The cynicism shown towards the main political parties does not in itself mean that we are becoming less political. Indeed, it could be argued that defining politics according to the activities of national political parties is far too restrictive and that a broader definition of politics should be used. Martin Jacques, for example, has argued that people are becoming more political, but that their political interests are not being expressed through traditional political organisations. People have access to more political options and '... the institutions of politics have been pushed to the margins of society existing on the outskirts of prosperity' (BBC2, 25.10.1993). Disillusionment with traditional political parties has led people to campaign actively for causes about which they feel strongly. Jacques argues that we live in a more democratised world in which '... power has become dispersed, the individual discerning and empowered'. In his view, national politics has failed to change and remains under the control of a small and unrepresentative political class. Jacques argues that we need a new conception of democracy and that representative democracy needs to be stimulated by exposure to direct democracy (BBC2, 25.10.1993).

It is important to recognise that modern democracy is becoming more fragmented and that there are multiple centres of power and a multitude of social groups that exert influence. Rather than seeing the state as the bastion of ultimate power, the idea of post-industrial democracy sees the importance of 'transnational relationships' and the 'multiplicity of partial governments'. Rather than consisting in competing for state power, individuals and groups are finding new ways to affirm themselves and realise their potential. It is argued by a number of the contributors to this volume that new social movements have the potential to play a particularly important part here. They are primarily driven by ideas of direct democracy that take into account both the importance of participation in the political process and the need to organise themselves democratically. Although the party system is in a state of crisis, new social movements have solid foundations within civil society and provide an essential means through which citizens can – by way of freedom of association – participate in the decision-making process and have a direct influence upon the political process (see Chapters 2 and 14).

We should remember, however, that the existence of a multitude of groups does not necessarily contribute towards a vibrant democracy. It has been argued that being offered resources with restrictions attached have institutionalised many social and community groups. These groups are thus effectively 'colonised' and used to legitimise and support the existing balance of power (see Chapter two). New social movements can therefore both serve and provide an alternative to the agenda set by parliamentary parties.

Concluding Comment

The chapters in this book demonstrate that whilst we live in a democratic age, it is clear that the nature of this democracy is changing constantly. Representative democracy allows the electorate to choose a government through voting but it does not allow much room for popular involvement in the policy and decision making process. Under representative democracy, the citizen is expected to be relatively passive. Political parties are there to mobilise support and they provide some opportunities for the general population to work on their behalf. It is clear that this form of democracy sees decision making as an elite activity supported by a popular mandate. Those who advocate the merits of participatory democracy, on the other hand, expect the involvement of the electorate to be beyond that of voting. They argue that we learn through taking part in social and political life and that social capital and civic virtues are more likely to develop through community activity than through passive obedience to government policy.

From the chapters that follow, it is evident that many people have in recent years expressed a concern about the limits of parliamentary politics and are turning away from traditional political organisations. The rise of new social movements provides new opportunities for the individual to learn about democracy and to participate with others on a multitude of projects. In doing so, it may be that the individual feels that she or he is making a small contribution towards the development of a strong participatory democracy. Yet, it is also clear that new social movements also present a series of challenges to representative democracy if sectional groups undermine broader public interests.

References

Aitkenhead, D. (2002) 'Bring back our tribes: politicians fret that the young aren't interested. But without ideology, politics is for anoraks', *The Guardian*, 5 February 2002.

Arnold, M. (1935) *Culture and Anarchy* (Cambridge: Cambridge University Press).

Best, S. (2002) *Introduction to Politics and Society* (London: Sage).

Birch, A.H. (1993) *The Concepts and Theories of Modern Democracy* (London: Routledge).

Burke, E. (1774) 'Speech to the Electors of Bristol' in B.W. Hill (ed.) *Edmund Burke on Government, Politics and Society* (Glasgow: Fontana, 1975), 156-8.

Burke, E. (1791) 'An Appeal from the New to the Old Whigs' in B.W. Hill (ed.) *Edmund Burke on Government, Politics and Society* (Glasgow: Fontana, 1975), 360-74.

Craig, P. (1995) 'Political Mediation, Traditional Parties and New Social Movements: Lessons from the Spanish Socialist Worker's Party', paper presented to the *Centre for Advanced Study in the Social Sciences*, Juan March Institute, Madrid, Spain, March,1994.

Dearlove, J. and Saunders, P. (2000) *Introduction to British Politics*. 3rd edn (Cambridge: Polity Press).

Fielding, S. (2000) 'A New Politics' in P. Dunleavy, A. Gamble, I. Holliday and G. Peele (eds) *Developments in British Politics* 6 (Houndmills: Macmillan), 10-28.

Frazer, E. (2000) 'Citizenship and Culture' in P. Dunleavy, A. Gamble, I. Holliday and G. Peele (eds) *Developments in British Politics 6* (Houndmills: Macmillan), 203-18.

Furedi, F. (2003) *Consuming Democracy: Activism, Elitism and Political Apathy.* http://161.58.137.22/furedi.html (Accessed: 2 June 2003).

Giddens, A. (2001) *Sociology.* 4th edn (Cambridge: Polity Press).

Giddens, A. (2002) *Runaway World: How Globalisation is Reshaping our Lives* (London: Profile Books).

Hartmann, H. (1981) 'The Unhappy Marriage of Marxism and Feminism: Towards a More Progressive Union' in L. Saegent (ed.) *The Unhappy Marriage of Marxism and Feminism: A Debate on Class and Patriarchy* (London: Pluto Press), 1-41.

Held, D. (1983) 'Central perspectives in the modern state' in D. Held et al. (eds) *States and Societies* (Oxford: Martin Robertson).

Hertz, N. (2001) 'Democracy in crisis: why we stayed away', *The Observer*, 10 June 2001.

King, A. (2001) 'Why a poor turn-out points to a democracy in good health', *The Daily Telegraph*, 21 May 2001.

Margetts, H. (2000) 'Political Participation and Protest' in P. Dunleavy, A. Gamble, I. Holliday and G. Peele (eds) *Developments in British Politics 6* (Houndmills: Macmillan), 185-202.

Marx, K. (1859) 'Preface to A Contribution to the Critique of Political Economy' in K. Marx and F. Engels, *Selected Works* (London: Lawrence and Wishart, 1977), 180-84.

Marx, K. (1871) The Civil War in France in K. Marx and F. Engels, *Selected Works* (London: Lawrence and Wishart, 1977), 271-307.

Marx, K. and Engels, F. (1845) The Holy Family in D. Mclellan (ed.) *Karl Marx: Selected Writings* (Oxford: Oxford University Press, 1977), 131-55.

Marx, K. and Engels, F. (1848) 'Manifesto of the Communist Party' in K. Marx and F. Engels, *Selected Works* (London: Lawrence and Wishart, 1977), 31-63.

Mill, J.S. (1859) On Liberty in S. Collini (ed.) *On Liberty and Other Writings* (Cambridge: Cambridge University Press, 1989), 1-116.

Miller, D. (1991) (ed) *The Blackwell Encyclopaedia of Political Thought* (Oxford: Blackwell).

Mulgan, G. (2001) 'Joined-up Government: Past, Present and Future'. Paper presented at the British Academy Conference on Joined-up Government, 30 October 2001.

Mulgan, G. and Wilkinson, H. (1985) *Freedom's Children* (London: Demos).

Offe, C. (1985) 'New Social Movements: Challenging the Boundaries of Institutional Politics', *Social Research,* vol. 52:4; 817-68.

Okin, S.M. (1991) 'Gender, the Public and the Private' in D. Held (ed.) *Political Theory Today* (Cambridge: Polity), 67-90.

Orum, A. (2001) *Introduction to Political Sociology.* 4th edn (Upper Saddle River: Prentice Hall).

Parry, G. and Moyser, G. (1994) 'A Map of Political Participation in Britain', *Government and Opposition*, vol. 79; 340-62.

Perry, M. (1993) *An Intellectual History of Modern Europe* (Boston: Houghton Mifflin).

Pharr, S., Putnam, R. and Dalton, R. (2000) 'A Quarter-century of Declining Confidence', *Journal of Democracy*, vol. 11:April; 5-25.

Pichardo, M. (1997) 'New Social Movements: A Critical Review', *Annual Review Sociology*, vol. 23; 411-430.

Putnam, R.D. (1995) 'Bowling Alone: America's Declining Social Capital', *Journal of Democracy*, vol. 6; 65-78.

Riddell, P. (2001) 'Lasting effect will be on MP's sleep', *The Times*, 7 December 2001.

Rodger, J. (2000) *From a Welfare State to a Welfare Society* (Houndmills: Macmillan).

Rousseau, J.J. (1968) *The Social Contract* (Harmondsworth: Penguin).

Schwarzmantel, J. (1994) *The State in Contemporary Society* (Hemel Hempstead: Harvester).

Taylor, G. (1999) *The State and Social Policy: An Introduction* (Sheffield: Sheffield Hallam University Press).

Taylor, G. (2000) *Freedom, Responsibility and the Media* (Sheffield: Sheffield Hallam University Press).

Taylor, G. and Spencer, S. (2002) 'Introduction' to G. Taylor and S. Spencer (eds) *Perspectives on Social Identity* (Sheffield: Sheffield Hallam University Press).

Ware, P. and Todd, M. (2002) 'British Statutory Sector Partnerships with the Voluntary Sector: Exploring Rhetoric and Reality', *The Social Policy Journal,* vol 1:3; 5-20.

Wright, D.G. (ed.) (1970) *Democracy and Reform 1815-1885* (London: Longman).

Audio-visual material

BBC2, *The incredible shrinking politicians.* 25 October 1993.

BBC2, *The day that Britain died, part 3.* 2 February 2000.

BBC2, *Waiting their turn: Minorities in a democracy.* 25 October 2000.

Channel 4, *Politics isn't working: the dumbed down election.* 3 June 2001.

Channel 4, *Politics isn't working: more unequal than ever.* 4 June 2001.

2. NEW SOCIAL MOVEMENTS AND DEMOCRACY

Greg Martin

The term 'new social movement' is problematic and below I set out some of the controversy that surrounds it. New social movement theory, however, is just one perspective amongst others in social movement studies (della Porta and Diani, 1999) and, as such, it provides us with a particular way of looking at and discussing issues to do with democracy and democratisation. One feature of new social movements is their concern with democracy from below or 'direct democracy', which differs from 'representative democracy'. Whereas the 'old' labour movement made its demands and aired its grievances via the apparatus of the state, new social movements question this mode of political organisation and interest intermediation, aiming at 'the creation of a new conception of democracy' (della Porta and Diani, 1999: 242) or a new model of democracy (Held, 1987). Movement actors are thus critical of liberal democracy and the party system and propose alternatives to parliamentary democracy. This represents a bottom-up, grassroots version of democracy rather than a top-down approach whereby participants in collective action must themselves, 'assume direct responsibility for intervening in the political decision-making process' (della Porta and Diani, 1999: 242).

Thus, the 'new' movements that emerged in the 1960s and 1970s were not only guided by the renewal of democracy (Eyerman, 2002: 444) but also placed great stress on their own internal democracy (Crossley, 2002: 150). While a perennial problem for all movement activists is 'institutionalisation' or becoming incorporated into the mainstream, even before this becomes a concern movements are faced with the challenge of trying to ensure that their own internal organisation and structure is and remains democratic and does not develop the characteristics of organisations they seek to avoid, e.g. hierarchy and bureaucratic management.

However, it is not just members of social movements that question dominant notions of democracy. A recent special issue of the current affairs magazine, *The Spectator*, published on 18th May 2002, asks whether democracy is doomed while sociologists and political scientists scrutinise the concept of democracy. The work of Ricardo Blaug (2002) is important here as he contrasts 'incumbent democracy' with the 'critical democracy' of which new social movements are an example. He also tackles what he sees as the 'blind hierarchism' of political theory and its failure to take radical organisational forms seriously (Blaug, 1999; 2000). The issue, here, is one of organisation and, more specifically, political organisation and this is relevant to my analysis, later in this chapter, of the anti-capitalist movement which, some have observed, lacks internal democracy and has a tendency to create hierarchies among its members (Beckett, 2002: 22).

Before I look at the anti-capitalist movement, I explore the ideas of prominent social movement scholars and, in particular, the works of Alain Touraine and Alberto Melucci both of whom have made significant contributions to the new social movements literature. Touraine and Melucci have different ideas about the nature and role of social movements in contemporary society and, indeed, both have differing theories of society. On the one hand, Touraine argues that we are entering a post-industrial or 'programmed society' which will be dominated by a central social conflict between two distinct opponents while, on the other, Melucci believes we now live in a 'complex society' where social movements are concerned with democratisation of everyday life. In the final part of the chapter, I consider how theories of new social movements might apply to the activities and campaigns of the anti-capitalist movement in a globalising world. I examine aspects of the debate over globalisation and especially those surrounding the local-global relationship and the question of whether the nation-state any longer has a meaningful role to play in global politics. I also consider the implications that this has for democracy and the emergence of a global civil society.

There is a small but growing literature on the anti-capitalist movement as well as intense speculation and conjecture about the possibilities and alternatives it proposes. Arguably, the anti-capitalist movement is worthy of analysis simply because, as Susan George has said, it represents the biggest resurgence of activism since the Vietnam War (Callinicos, 2001: 387). It is also perhaps the most significant of the 'new' new social movements which, in the UK, include the direct action of Earth First! groups like Reclaim the Streets and campaigns against the genetic modification of animal and plant organisms (Welsh, 2000: 53). Indeed, an analysis of the anti-capitalist movement raises issues about the nature of new social movements and the demands they make. I show how it contradicts certain aspects of new social movement theory demonstrating, for example, the persistent role of material and economic issues in contemporary 'new' social movements.

I also examine the tactics used by anti-capitalist activists as well as the character and social composition of the movement whose protest culture has been defined 'in terms of its modernity: its use of the Internet, its flexible, freelance activists, its international mobility, its youthful participants with their backpacks and trainers' (Beckett, 2002: 21). Moreover, I look at the implications that anti-capitalist protest has for democracy and the formation of a global civil society. Naomi Klein's (2000) book, *No Logo*, has generated huge interest in the power of brands, multinational corporations and possibilities for global resistance. However, some commentators are not sure whether her work adds up to a coherent theory (Parker, 2002: 161). While some argue that the only way to resist global forces is through 'local disruptions' (Sklair, 1995), others contend that even though new social movements have had a universalistic appeal, they have been unable to tackle global issues and continue to confront local issues, thrown up by globalisation processes, where the state remains an important player (Lentin, 1999). However, Baker (2002) questions the legitimacy of the state and those transnational institutions (e.g. NGOs) that are incorporated into global civil society, arguing that new social movements, such as the anti-capitalist movement, must retain their autonomy and independence if they are to be part of the formation of a truly democratic global civil society. Now, then, there appear to be any number of possible global futures but there is little doubt that 'more work needs to be done to assess the permanence of these transnational organisations and coalitions, as well as the claims that we have entered the dawn of a global civil society' (Ayres, 2001: 66).

Social Movements in Post-industrial Society

In this opening section, I examine some of the ideas of Touraine, which are important, I argue, when looking at contemporary campaigns against capitalism. Touraine's work is also significant because it has influenced Italian sociologist Alberto Melucci whose research around social movements and the democratisation of daily life is discussed in detail later in the chapter.

Along with Manuel Castells, Touraine is a key figure in the French school of social movement studies, which is premised on a neo-Marxist analysis of contemporary society (Hannigan, 1985). Thus, Touraine argues that society is dominated by a central conflict between the ruling class and a subordinate class. This conflict represents a struggle for the control of what he terms 'historicity' which is defined as the work society performs on itself 'by inventing its norms, its institutions and practices, guided by the great cultural orientations – pattern of knowledge, type of investment, and cultural model' (Touraine, 1981: 29) or, more simply, 'the capacity to produce an historical experience through cultural patterns' (Touraine, 1985: 778). The ruling class control the main cultural patterns of society (i.e. knowledge, investment, and ethics) which they impose on the subordinate group who fight this domination in order to define their own cultural patterns:

> The ruling class is the group of innovator-dominators which becomes identified with this production of society by itself, with its historicity, which it in turn utilises in order to legitimate its domination over the remainder of society, i.e. over the popular class, which is subjected to the ruling class but also challenges its domination in order to win back historicity for itself. (Touraine, 1981: 311).

For Touraine, social movements are not peripheral phenomena that neither exist on society's margins nor are they exceptional events. Rather, they are a central force in society. A social movement is a specific type of social conflict whose stake is the control of the main cultural patterns or historicity. According to Touraine, both opponents in this struggle are identified as social movements. For example, in industrial society, management would be considered a social movement in exactly the same way as labour. Moreover, both adversaries – both powerful and powerless – are collective actors capable, to some degree or other, of social action. Thus, the ruling class are never entirely capable of being 'identified with the central cultural values and norms' (Touraine, 1985: 774-775). Social movements, therefore, are never hegemonic because the struggle for domination is inexorable, although the fight may come to the brink of hegemonic crisis[1].

As society undergoes change so new class relations and, hence, new struggles emerge. Comparing contemporary society with the development of industrial society, Touraine argues, like Marx, that in any historical epoch 'new economic challenges come first before new social actors and

---

1   It is interesting to compare Touraine's ideas about struggles for control of historicity to the work associated with the Centre for Contemporary Cultural Studies which utilised Gramsci's notion of hegemony to show how working-class youth subcultures in post-war Britain attempted to win cultural space despite their subordinate structural position (Martin, 2002: 75).

conflicts take shape' (Touraine, 1985: 872). Although the workers' movement is now in decline, Touraine recognises that industrial conflicts have not disappeared altogether. However, we are witnessing the emergence of new conflicts that he believes are associated with a new 'societal type'. Therefore, he argues, there are aspects of a 'post-industrial' society evolving within the womb of industrial society. Research and development, information processing, biomedical science and techniques, and the mass media are all distinct components of this post-industrial societal type or 'programmed society'. Because of these developments, 'more and more domains of social life are opened up to technocratic projects of control' (Cohen, 1985: 702).

> ... bureaucratic activities or production of electrical and electronic equipment are just growing sectors of an industrial society defined by production of goods more than by new channels of communications and the creation of artificial languages. (Touraine, 1985: 781)

Touraine's argument is that just as the new societal type has not fully formed, so the new social movements are nascent and not yet organised. Thus, while 'it took some time in the nineteenth century to discover the "political capacity of the labouring classes"; we are only approaching an analogous stage in the evolution of the new social movements' (Touraine, 1985: 783). Touraine believes that new class actors and new struggles are emerging which reflect this transformation in society as 'we are living through the transition from industrial society to programmed society and hence experiencing the decline of a certain type of class relations and the emergence of a new generation of social movements' (Touraine, 1981: 9).

For Touraine, however, the programmed society departs radically from industrial society. While industrial society is organised around work and the relations of production, class domination in a programmed society takes the form of technocratic management controlling and running data or information apparatus. As 'resistance to this domination cannot be limited to a particular sphere, any more than can the domination itself' (Touraine, 1981: 6), the new social movement 'sets up a self-managing determination against technocratic management, i.e. one project of society against another' (Touraine, 1981: 9). This new conflict is thus spawned of the growing hold technocratic control has over society and its historicity. The stakes of these new struggles are 'self-management', 'just as social justice was in the workers' struggles' (Touraine 1981:22). Thus, it is Touraine's aim:

... to discover the social movement which in programmed society will occupy the central position held by the workers' movement in industrial society and the civil liberties movement in the market society by which it was preceded. (Touraine, 1981: 24)

Over the years, Touraine has researched a variety of social conflicts including the anti-nuclear movement in France and Solidarity in Poland. Using the method of 'sociological intervention', he and his co-workers have attempted to act as catalysts in collective action, raising the consciousness of movement members who are brought together so that they can grasp the full scope of their struggle and establish a group identity (McDonald, 2002). However, he has only been able to locate elements of the cultural revolt he seeks (Hannigan, 1985: 439) which may be because he works at such a high level of abstraction and thus has a tendency to impose his own interpretations on activists instead of trying to understand how they themselves make and modify meaning in their own settings (Davis, 2002: 9).

Moreover, even though Touraine is careful to highlight the emergent and transitional nature of contemporary society and the new social struggles, Jean Cohen (1985: 702-4) is critical of his theory of societal types and the notion that contemporary movements are radically discontinuous with earlier movements. This is because it conceals the continuity between the past and present, which is a criticism not only applicable to Touraine but, as I shall show, to new social movement theory in general. However, Cohen argues that contemporary movements have a similar orientation to that of older movements as they continue the theme 'society against the state' (Cohen, 1985: 665) in struggling for the democratisation of civil society (Cohen, 1985: 702). Moreover, she says that given the heterogeneity of contemporary movements it seems futile to speak of *the* new identity of these movements, as Touraine does, in terms of a core class conflict (Cohen, 1985: 665). These are all issues that will become relevant when I discuss, in the conclusion, the applicability of Touraine's thesis to contemporary anti-capitalist struggles. They are also concerns that Melucci takes up.

Democratisation of Everyday Life in Complex Society

The foregoing discussion of Touraine's work is important because it allows us now to reflect upon the work of Melucci who talks explicitly about new social movements and democracy in post-industrial or 'complex society'. Unlike Touraine, Melucci (1989: 80) does not wish to discover *the* central movement of post-industrial society, mainly because he believes that it is no longer helpful for us to treat social movements as epic characters moving on the stage of history. There are two reasons for this.

Firstly, he argues that rather than seeing social movements as unified entities, collective action ought to be seen 'as a social product, as a set of social relationships, and not as a primary datum or given metaphysical entity' (Melucci, 1988: 247). In other words, social movements are heterogeneous and made up of a plurality of meanings and orientations. Secondly, Melucci concurs with Touraine in believing that class struggle and the fight for citizenship characterised the industrial period. Moreover, it was characterised by the extension of political rights or the integration of excluded and underprivileged groups into the nation-state (cf. Scott, 1990: 10). While the struggle for democracy and citizenship has not ceased, Melucci argues that it now takes on a different form. For instance, the collective action of women raises the problem of rights, inequality and exclusion but women have also 'created meanings and definitions of identity which contrast with the increasing determination of individual and collective life by impersonal technocratic power' (Melucci, 1988: 247). Thus, we witness the emergence of identity politics or 'life politics' that differ from the 'emancipatory politics' that defined the industrial capitalist era (Giddens, 1991a).

For Melucci, then, concepts like liberation or emancipation are 'too strictly connected to the conceptual and linguistic horizon of industrial society' (Melucci, 1992: 67). Moreover, contemporary movements are not concerned principally with citizenship and do not demand access to state power by means of political processes. Traditionally, however, there has been a tendency amongst social movement scholars to focus on the political efficacy of collective action by studying mass mobilisations. Concentration of this visible face of movements has led to 'political overload' (Melucci, 1984: 822) and caused analysts to ignore the cultural dimension of contemporary collective action, which 'assumes the form of networks submerged in everyday life,' (Melucci, 1988: 248). Indeed, these networks make mobilisation possible and, as such, constitute the latent or hidden efficacy of social movements (Melucci, 1989: 73).

Crucial to Melucci's theory of social movements is his conception of what he terms complex societies which, 'in contrast to their late nineteenth-century industrial capitalist predecessors, are systems in which the production of material goods depends increasingly upon the production of signs

and social relations' (Melucci, 1989: 4). Such societies contain a fundamental paradox. On the one hand, highly differentiated systems increasingly produce and distribute resources for individualisation, self-realisation
and the building of personal and collective identities while, on the other
hand, they require more and more integration and must extend control over
the same resources in order to survive (Melucci, 1984: 827). This structural tension in complex systems throws up a number of dilemmas for post-
industrial democracy. Take, for example, the dilemma of 'dependent
participation' (Melucci, 1988: 255):

> The extension of the sphere of individual and collective rights neces-
> sitates planning, in order to co-ordinate the plurality of interests and
> decisions and to protect the corresponding rights of representation
> and decision-making. But each planning intervention necessitates a
> technocratic decision-making power, which inevitably curtails par-
> ticipation and effective rights. (Melucci, 1992: 69)

Here, there are clearly echoes of Habermas's colonisation thesis whereby movements 'arise at the seam between system and life-world'
(Habermas, 1981: 36) in order to resist or stave off the encroaching ratio-
nalisation of the life-world. Moreover, comparisons can and indeed have
been made between Melucci's ideas and Foucault's notion of the dispersal
of power (Bartholomew and Mayer, 1992: 147). Thus, Melucci believes
that contemporary movements act as 'revealers', unmasking the apparent
neutrality of power and rationality of the system and 'exposing that which
is hidden or excluded by the decision-making process' (Melucci, 1992: 68).
In this sense, the collective action of contemporary movements casts light
on the dark side of the moon (Melucci, 1997: 60).

Whatever type of political organisation might be envisioned in
advanced society, the problem of politics now confronts all complex systems and, Melucci says, that any project of democratisation cannot ignore
this. Unlike the industrial period where parliamentary institutions annulled
the problem of how to represent a plurality of interests which reduced representation to its 'bourgeois' forms (Melucci, 1988: 252), the problem in
post-industrial democracy is that 'there is an increase in the number of
groups capable of organising themselves, representing their interests and
extracting advantages from processes of political exchange; there is also a
fragmentation of political decision-making structures, giving rise to numer-

ous partial governments that are difficult to co-ordinate' (Melucci, 1988: 255). Thus:

> The problem of representation is tied to complexity and therefore cannot be annulled, whatever model of political organisation is envisaged. Representation involves the inevitable difference between representatives and those whom they represent [...] Any process of democratic transformation must necessarily take into account the difference between structures of representation and the demands or interests of the represented. (Melucci, 1988: 252)

What Melucci is saying here is the actors who produce social change and those who manage (i.e. institutionalise) it are not identical (Melucci, 1988: 254). Thus, the essence of democracy no longer consists in securing the competition of interests and the structures that make their representation possible because this version of democracy corresponded to a capitalist system where state and civil society were separated and the state 'translated the "private" interests formed in civil society into the terms of "public" institutions' (Melucci, 1988: 257). Melucci argues that this distinction is now unclear since the state can no longer be seen as a unitary agent as it is 'replaced from above by a tightly interdependent system of transnational relationships and subdivided below into a multiplicity of partial governments' (Melucci, 1988: 257) while in civil society 'the former unity (and homogeneity) of social interests has exploded' (Melucci, 1988: 257).

Therefore, it would be a mistake to think that democracy continues to be about the competition for access to governmental resources. In complex societies, democracy consists in enabling individuals and groups to affirm themselves and to be recognised for what they are or what they wish to be. This requires 'conditions for enhancing the recognition and autonomy of individuals and collective signifying processes' (Melucci, 1988: 258). The sense of belonging that this engenders is quite unlike being represented. Thus, there is pressure from the contradiction between belonging and representation which we must seek to resolve by facilitating certain 'rights of everyday life' (Melucci, 1988: 258) or 'a democracy of meanings' (Melucci, 1992: 70-3). That is, 'the right to makes one's voice heard by means of representation or by modifying the conditions of listening, as well as the right to belong or to withdraw from belonging in order to produce new meanings' (Melucci 1988: 258). A necessary precondition for such a democracy is the emergence of public spaces that are independent of the institutions of government, the party system and state structures:

> A new political space is designed beyond the traditional distinction between state and 'civil society': an intermediate public space, whose function is not to institutionalise the movements nor to transform them into parties, but to make society hear their messages and translate these messages into political decision making, while the movements maintain their autonomy. (Melucci, 1985: 815)

Inasmuch as these public spaces 'are intermediate between the levels of political power and decision-making and networks of everyday life, they are structurally ambivalent: they express the double meaning of the terms representation and participation' (Melucci, 1992: 71). Thus, it would be a mistake to think that there is an end to politics. Indeed, for Melucci politics has never been so important. However, it is a 'new politics' (Habermas, 1981: 33) requiring redefinition, as the demands of contemporary movements 'exist beyond political mediation and independently of its results' (Melucci, 1996: 216). In other words, contemporary collective action is both 'pre-political' and 'meta-political' which correspond respectively to the level of everyday life and the level at which new movements 'publicise the existence of some basic dilemmas of complex societies which cannot be resolved by means of political decisions' (Melucci, 1989: 222).

Melucci's conception of public space is similar to Habermas' (Delanty, 1999: 142) as well as to Touraine's idea of the expansion of civil society whereby contemporary movements contest the control of an increasing range of social activities (Cohen and Arato, 1992: 515). However, it also relates to one of the shortcomings of the new social movement paradigm. It has been argued that there is a rigid separation between social movements and politics, civil society and the state (Canel, 1992: 36). For instance, Bartholomew and Mayer (1992) argue that in his effort to avoid the 'political reductionism' of earlier theories Melucci falls prey to 'cultural reductionism'. This causes him to miss what is 'old' or traditional in contemporary 'new' social movements such as struggles for citizenship rights and the continued existence and relevance of material issues (Martin, 1998)[2]. Alan Scott has argued against the culturalism of new social movement theory saying:

> If there is a telos of social movement activity then it is the normali-
> sation of previously exotic issues and groups. Success is thus quite
> compatible with, and indeed overlaps, the disappearance of the
> movement as a movement. This argument is diametrically opposed
> to Touraine's analysis of social movements as pure forms of activity
> outside the political system. (Scott, 1990: 10-11)

Scott contests not the novelty of contemporary movements but the fact that they are regarded as apolitical because of their concern with social and cultural issues such as lifestyle and identity (cf. Taylor and Van Willigen, 1996: 125). He argues that contemporary movements are political phe-nomena precisely because they have emerged out of the failure of the insti-tutions of interest intermediation (e.g. interest groups and parties) to meet popular demands and feed them into the political system. Therefore, new forms of protest arise to voice concerns that are excluded from mainstream politics; 'new political movements' (Nedelmann, 1984) which bypass organisations and groups traditionally associated with processes of inter-mediation, finding alternative routes to articulate their demands.

Thus, there is debate and scepticism about the autonomy of contempo-rary social movements and the public space they inhabit (Plotke, 1990) and a belief that every movement must connect its demands to 'institutionally immanent possibilities' (Giddens, 1991b: 155). Other critics have used his-torical analysis to try to prove that new social movements are not actually new at all. For instance, Tucker argues that although identity formation is seen as a central goal of new movements, it was also a key aim of French syndicalists during the nineteenth century who 'had shared experiences and traditions of autonomy at the work place related to their possession of skill' (Tucker, 1991: 85). Similarly, D'Anieri et al. (1990) provide examples of past movements that resemble 'new' movements and Calhoun, too, points to the 'false novelty' (Calhoun, 1994: 24) of new social movements argu-ing that they do not exhibit a *de facto* discontinuity with the past. Indeed, new social movement theory is 'historically myopic' (Calhoun, 1994: 22) since it disregards the fact that supposedly new phenomenon's, such as the

---

2 Mooers and Sears (1992: 64) are critical of Melucci's heavy emphasis on the symbolic aspects of social life in complex societies where material production is replaced increasing-ly by the production of signs and social relations saying, rather pointedly, 'one wonders what people might eat in such societies [...] Of course, they eat signs'.

women's movement, had a long and deep-rooted history. Moreover, he claims that the novel features of new movements are features of *all* movements in their nascent stage (Calhoun, 1995: 174). Thus, before they undergo institutionalisation, incorporation and so on all movements have radical grassroots organisation and eschew conventional politics. Calhoun (1995: 179) also shows how the nineteenth and early twentieth century working-class movement was more multidimensional than new social movement theorists such as Melucci are willing to acknowledge.

Anti-capitalist Campaigns in Global Civil Society

The criticisms levelled at new social movement theory are also relevant to one of the newest of the 'new' social movements, the anti-capitalist movement. Below, for instance, I show how the anti-capitalist movement highlights the continued importance of material issues for collective action in a globalsing world. However, debates also surround the novelty of globalisation and of movements against global capitalism. Barker and Dale (1998) challenge the new social movement paradigm arguing that it is premised on the fallacious view that there has been a shift in the underlying structures of modern (capitalist) society. Similarly, for Tarrow (1998: 234), many of the features of the present day world economy are not as new as people claim but stretch back more than a century (cf. Lynch, 1998: 150). Moreover, Tarrow argues that transnational movements have historical parallels. The antislavery movement, for example, began in Britain in the eighteenth century and spread over the global during the early nineteenth century (Tarrow, 1998: 234). Ayres (2001: 55), on the other hand, argues that 'what is distinct about today's global economy is it neo-liberal character, which structures contemporary transnational contention'.

Egan (2001: 559) raises similar issues and identifies three questions that are central to debates around globalisation and which are relevant to a discussion of anti-capitalist struggles and democracy. Firstly, does globalisation represent a new stage of economic development or just a deepening and widening of existing capitalist social relations? Secondly, has global capital and the expansion of multilateral economic and political institutions caused the nation-state to become irrelevant? Thirdly, are there any longer alternatives to the hegemony of the market given the collapse of state socialism?

Another classic issue surrounding the concept of globalisation concerns the local-global relationship; it is perhaps here where we might resolve some of the issues regarding the novelty of global capitalism, and the nature of movement actors now involved in global struggles. In their examination of urban movements in a globalising world, Hamel et al. (2000) contest the traditional the view that urban social movements are preoccupied with local issues. They argue that urban movements have always been 'extra local' (Hamel et al., 2000: 2) although this is more pronounced in the present global epoch. Moreover, in his contribution to the book, Roth (2000) argues that the distinction between new movements and old movements is too rigid and it is a mistake to associate the former exclusively with post-material issues as new social movements have also addressed 'old' social problems such as unemployment, homelessness and poverty. The argument, therefore, is that urban movements continue to raise material concerns that arise out of the global expansion of capitalism. Many of the issues about new social movements and democracy are now tied to these kinds of debates about the relationship between the local and the global and the part played by the nation-state which some believe is gradually being supplanted by a global civil society. Indeed, global social movements are increasingly seen 'as the principal hope for the democratisation of a newly forming global civil society' (Nash, 2002: 438).

This is no less the case for Melucci who believes 'how to *exist with the other* in a planetary world is the moral challenge of our time' (Melucci, 1992: 53, emphasis in original). In other words, we need an ethic of coexistence, that is, 'a situational ethic, capable of lending dignity to the individual decision and repairing the links between genders, cultures, the individual and the species, living beings, the cosmos' (Melucci, 1997: 66). In a sense, a globalised world is, for Melucci, just a bigger version of complex society and his ideas around coexistence are like those about the recognition and acceptance of difference and autonomy but on a larger scale. Thus, globalisation has not altered the prevailing logic of the system but has just added greater instability and uncertainty which has led to a crisis of the international or interstate system:

The nation-states are losing their authority as, towards the top of the system, planetary interdependence and the emergence of transnational political and economic forces shift the locus of real decision-making elsewhere, while, towards the bottom, the proliferation of autonomous decision-making centres endows the 'societal' level of present-day societies with a power they never knew during the development of the modern state. (Melucci, 1997: 68)

What then are the implications for democracy and what might be the role of social movements and national states in a planetary society? Melucci argues that 'the planetarisation of the world system has called into question a restricted view of democracy as based simply on a competition for governmental resources and it has revealed the inadequacy of political institutions when facing the dramatic challenges of our time' (Melucci, 1992: 67-8). For Melucci, 'humankind must make an enormous effort to give political shape to its co-living; a political arrangement able to govern the plurality, autonomy and richness of difference but one, however, which also expresses humanity's shared responsibility for the fate of the species and the planet, and of each individual' (Melucci, 1997: 69).

While Melucci intimates the emergence of something resembling a global civil society where movements operate independently of the nation-state and seems able to incorporate globalisation into his general thesis about collective identities in complex society, he still appears reluctant to take material issues seriously. Thus, he says, 'for developing societies the future is still open to development, but they are at the same time entirely involved in the planetary system based on information' (Melucci, 1992: 73). Moreover, while Melucci sees the world system as a network of relationships between sovereign states, others argue that it continues to be defined according to the imbalance between the rich countries of the North and the poor countries of the South (Smith, 2001: 16). Indeed, as this 'global financial apartheid' (Hari, 2002: 24) is one of the main grievances of anti-capitalist activists it would seem that material and economic concerns continue to be crucial in a globalising world (Martin, 2002: 82)[3].

Melucci's work around social movements in a planetary society tells us little about how these collective struggles are played out locally which is probably because here, like Touraine, he is operating at a high level of abstraction. However, an early attempt at theorising the relationship between globalisation and social movements, proposed by Sklair (1995), does precisely this. Sklair's central argument is that while capitalism is increasingly organised on a global scale opposition to capitalist practices tends to be most effective locally[4]. Thus, while the labour and other movements working against global capitalism have had some notable successes,

---

3   This also demonstrates the ethnocentricity of (European) new social movement theory.
4   One variant of this form of collective resistance has come to be known as 'globalization from below' (Etzioni-Halevy, 2001).

they have generally failed globally (cf. Ayers, 2001: 55). Indeed, the problem for the labour movement now is how to form allegiances with new social movements; although others believe that the anti-capitalist movement in particular has given hope and opened up possibilities for rebuilding the Left (Gindin, 2001). Sklair's point is captured in the following quotation:

> The dilemma is that the only chance that people in social movements have to succeed is by disrupting the local agencies with which they come into direct contact in their daily lives, rather than the more global institutions whose interests these agencies are serving directly, or, more often, indirectly, while workers are often confused about whom (which representation of capital) to oppose when their interests (conditions of labour, livelihoods) are threatened. Increasingly, as capitalism globalises, subordinate groups find difficulty in identifying their adversaries. (Sklair, 1995: 499)

Sklair concludes that movements' 'prospects of challenging global capitalism locally and making this count globally, globalising disruptions, seems more realistic' (Sklair, 1995: 501). The global organisation of transnational corporations (TNCs) is too powerful for the local organisation of labour to resist. However, where TNCs have been challenged 'it has usually been due to local campaigns of disruption and counter-information against TNC malpractices which have attracted world-wide publicity' (Sklair, 1995: 501). The campaign against Nestlé infant formula is an example of a local disruption of TNC activities that can bring about a wider global challenge. Indeed, TNCs, 'if we are to believe their own propaganda, are continuously beset by opposition, boycott, legal challenge and moral outrage from consumers of their products and by disruptions from their workers' (Sklair, 1995: 507).

Lentin (1999) also examines the relationship between the global and the local. In assessing the contemporary relevance of new social movement theory in relation to global developments, she argues that the transnationalisation of collective action has come full circle. Thus, while the original new social movements (e.g. environmental, peace and women's campaigns) did have 'universalistic' agendas their criticism of the state encouraged it to hand over the solution to social problems to international bodies. While today's movements do act transnationally they are equally concerned with local or 'particularistic' issues which have emerged with the failure of nation-states to address continuing social problems within their borders (e.g. AIDS, homelessness and racism) which have been brought about by the dismantling of the welfare state and the concomitant disaffection and exclusion of some of the most marginalised groups in society[5]. Thus, Lentin argues that the state remains important and that transnational activity is less realistic which is a conclusion supporting those who critique new social movement theory for ignoring the contemporary significance of traditional politics and conventional political actors.

Like Lentin, Lynch (1998) believes that contemporary globalisation has implications for new social movements, that is, the universalistic movements analysed since the 1970s[6]. However, she argues that the effects of globalisation on these types of movements beg certain questions regarding the relationship between theorising about social movements and civil society. Thus, as new social movement theories are about movements in civil society now, in light of heightened globalisation, we need to look at the possibilities for the development of a global civil society and discover what the role of social movements – both national and transnational – is in this. Indeed, Lynch argues that transnational social movements contributed to the emergence of a global civil society. The peace movement, for instance, in its critique of militarisation and arms races 'deligitimised rigid conceptualisations of state sovereignty, legitimised the demobilisation of the state's coercive capacities, and encouraged guarantees of controls placed on the state by mechanisms of oversight' (Lynch, 1998: 163). However, the challenge now exists in relation to 'new' new social movements and how we make sense of what Lynch (1998: 166) calls the 'anarchic diversity' that currently characterises global civil society. In order to do this we need to look at the most likely successor of the labour movement and the new movements of the 1970s, namely the anti-capitalist movement. An examination of this movement throws up a number of issues pertinent to new social movement theory, democracy and the possibilities for the emergence of a global civil society. It also raises issues that are relevant to social movement's studies in general.

---

5   Some authors put these developments down to the emergence of post-Fordism (see Martin, 1998; 2001).

6   Interestingly, Lynch (1998: 162) contrasts these universalistic 'new' movements (e.g. feminism, peace and environmentalism) with the particularistic, 'old' social movements primarily identified with labour and class.

One of the most memorable and significant episodes of collective action associated with the anti-capitalist movement was the Battle of Seattle that took place at the end of November 1999. This was a high profile event whose primary focus was capitalism as a set of economic and social relations, the immediate target of which was the World Trade Organisation (WTO), which protestors saw as the symbol of a neo-liberal global free market (Welsh, 2000: 44). However, this wave of protest emerged out of the collective action of a number of interconnected groups and organisations and as such, it demonstrated the 'emergent capacity of global new social movement networks' (Welsh, 2000: 54). Similarly, Smith believes that although this was a single event – an 'iconic event' (Lofland, 1995: 203) – it illustrates that 'increasing globalisation and transnational protests have enduring effects on the organisation and character of social movements' (Smith, 2001: 1).

The Battle of Seattle comprised a diversity of groups including environmental and social justice groups who identified a single collective opponent in 'the practice of neo-liberal economic globalisation embodied in the WTO' (Welsh: 2000: 55). Moreover, Welsh argues that it is a truly global movement since 'the new network has adopted social justice as an axial principle, recognising that, via the environment (and trade), this effectively unites significant majorities in both North and South' (Welsh, 2000: 56). Thus, 'by joining movements for social justice with the environment as a global site for all civil societies, neo-liberalism is identified as the common enemy' (Welsh, 2000: 56). Here, then, is ample demonstration of Melucci's argument, discussed above, that contemporary movements and mobilisations consist of a plurality of groups and perspectives. It also supports Offe's (1985: 835) claim that in order to be effective new social movements must form 'strategic social alliances' that bring together 'old' with 'new' elements as well as class and non-class actors. Significantly, the anti-capitalist campaigners are also able to be effective through their use of new technologies such as the Internet and other electronic media.

Indeed, 'social movements have found new opportunities for political communication and mobilisation through media and information technology (particularly the Internet)' (Scott and Street, 2000: 215). This relates to what Charles Tilly calls 'repertoires of contention', which is a concept that 'seeks to capture the historical peculiarity of the methods of protest that agents use' (Crossley, 2002: 127). Along with networking via the use of new technologies such as mobile phones and e-mail, another tactic employed by anti-capitalist protestors is direct action. The use of e-mail, though, allows transnational movement organisations to sustain virtual networks (Diani, 2000: 394-6). However, these networks must not be regarded as social movements in their own right as they are 'less sustained, less unified, and less integrated into grassroots social networks than are true social movements' (Tarrow, 1998: 236). Tarrow argues that what are sometimes regarded as transnational movements might best be thought of as 'issue networks' rather than bona fide transnational social movement organisations, examples of which include Greenpeace, the European and US peace movement of the 1980s and Islamic fundamentalism (Tarrow, 1998: 239-40). Tarrow's arguments, here, about social movement organisation and transnational networks are relevant to the point I raised in the introduction regarding the implications that a discussion of democracy has for political organisation, new social movements, anti-capitalism and questions about the establishment of an autonomous global civil society.

As I mentioned, the work of Blaug is important as he is critical of the 'blind hierarchism' of political science that seems to disregard anti-hierarchical political forms such as new social movements (Blaug, 2000). This is because hierarchism is how we have come to conceive of organisation; which is largely the result of a particular reading of Weber (Albrow, 1992; Parker, 2000). Unfortunately, this causes us to see only 'the ineffectiveness of non-hierarchical co-ordination and the unassailability of current structures of power' (Blaug, 1999: 42). Even debates about civil society retain a hierarchistic orientation that regards the actions of deliberative groups as unimportant to the concerns of 'high politics'. Moreover, even when liberal democrats are concerned to look below the state and call for a deeper democracy they concentrate on the elite layer of think tanks, NGOs and various local government planning offices and public service committees and ignore associations within civil society (Blaug, 2002: 110). The irony is that hierarchy is not necessarily efficient and we are just as suspicious of its oppressive potential as we are of the chaos and disorder of anti-institutional and disorganised political forms (Blaug, 1999: 44-5). The orthodoxy of hierarchism thus:

> ... results in our spoiling those few opportunities which do emerge for open deliberation about those concerns that affect us all, so that, even when we change elites, we nevertheless continue to alienate our autonomy to proxies, to replicate illegitimate structures in our deci-

sion-making and to institutionalise hierarchically every inch of our collective lives. (Blaug, 1999: 47)

Indeed, for Blaug the current climate, especially in British politics, is wholly undemocratic. It represents a move away from deliberative participation towards an 'engineered democracy' whereby grassroots and self-help groups are subject to a process of colonisation, being offered resources with strings attached and threatened constantly by co-option (Blaug, 2002: 112-3). In other words, despite their radical organisation they become institutionalised and instrumental forms subject to bureaucratic procedures. Indeed, as I have said above, this is one of the central dilemmas for social movements but Blaug seems sanguine about the possibilities for non-hierarchical, anti-institutional and 'disorganised' forms of political organisation and, like others, sees possibilities in forms of critical democracy which includes the anti-globalisation protests of J18, Seattle and Genoa (Blaug, 2002: 106):

> The conclusion reached is that certain kinds of apparently disorganised radical collective actions, though so hard to see as to be almost impossible to accurately evaluate, in fact pose the single most significant threat to the power of global, national and even local elites. Anti-institutional radical forms have, therefore, because of a kind of tyranny of the visible, been seriously underestimated. (Blaug, 1999: 35)

Of course, the rejection of rational bureaucratic structures is nothing new to social movements. While a feature of 'new' social movement theory is that the movements resist the encroachment of a rationalistic system and attempt to offer alternative modes of social and political organisation, Rothschild-Whitt (1979) long ago looked at a range of groups that reject rational bureaucratic forms of organisation and attempt to develop a collectivist democracy. However, what are the possibilities for the alternative organisation of an anti-capitalist movement? Like Blaug, Fournier (2002) sees hope in the anti-corporate protests which invent organisational alternatives. Moreover, like Sklair (1995), she argues that these utopian grassroots movements offer points of disruption to a system that threatens to swallow up alternatives into a Third Way. Therefore, the age-old accusation that utopianism cannot coordinate action cannot be sustained (Blaug, 1999:

51). But what about on a larger scale? What are the possibilities for the development of a viable global civil society?

One of the key questions is whether there is space for global civil society between global corporate interests and the nation-state. From an organisational perspective, one issue is how can iconic events, such as the Battle of Seattle, sustain a movement? Another relates to the possibility of forming alliances, no matter how uneasy these might be, between a diversity of groups ranging from trade unions to environmental organisations that might unite anti-corporate activists (see Parker, 2002: 166). A crucial idea, here, is that corporate interests now determine policy and restrict serious democratic debate. Thus, the nation-state is irrelevant because corporate chief executives now run global government. With this in mind, 'the anti-corporate movement is now throwing its accusations much wider, and in the name of "citizens" concerned with democracy' (Parker, 2002: 167). However:

> Not all of this protest is anti-capitalist, or environmentally focused, or whatever, but perhaps its single unifying factor is a hostility to the corporation, and the figure of the Machiavellian manager who is organising the new world order for their own ends. (Parker, 2002: 168)

As others mentioned above, Parker highlights a number of dilemmas, problems and paradoxes inherent in anti-capitalist or anti-corporate activism. Thus, in an era of 'market populism' where 'consumer choice is the ultimate form of democratic accountability' (Parker, 2002: 180), anti-corporate protest 'dramatises the attractions and politics of being against management, but it also exposes the difficulties of what this might actually involve' (Parker, 2002: 181). In other words, it is easy to offer a critique and to decide to be 'against' but far harder to offer practical alternatives and decide what one stands 'for'. For Parker, one way of beginning to think about this is 'to reimagine what organisation might be without corporate managerialism' (Parker, 2002: 181).

Conclusion

An examination of the anti-capitalist movement brings us back to the work of Touraine who argues that post-industrial society will be defined by an antagonism between two distinct opponents. Although there is dispute as to how effective global (as opposed to local) challenges will be as well as their being scepticism surrounding the endurance of relations between diverse allied groups, Touraine's theory does appear to be borne out to some degree as anti-capitalist activists protest and rail against the increasing global domination of multinationals and corporate interests represented in institutions such as the World Bank, the WTO and the IMF. Campaigns for sustainable development embodied, for example, in indigenous peoples' movements (Feldman, 2002), also seem to support Touraine's argument that new movements will be involved in struggles for self-management. However, the campaign of anti-capitalists seems not to depart radically from previous struggles as they continue to be concerned with social justice and the expansion of capitalism, which they now combine, with issues of self-management.

This quest for autonomy also supports Melucci's claims that contemporary (new) social movements do not operate along conventional political lines but are concerned instead with the democratisation of everyday life which requires them to be organised as networks inhabiting an intermediate public space between state and civil society. Indeed, while the anti-capitalist movement causes us to remember the continuing relevance of material and economic concerns in a global world, the issue of autonomy or self-management lies at the heart of debates about new social movements, democracy and global civil society.

Baker (2002) argues that there are problems relating to the representativeness, accountability and legitimacy of NGOs and highlights the importance in making provision for the self-organisation of new social movements at grassroots level and outside of the state. Baker distinguishes between the kinds of institutions and groups that Lynch (1998: 163), mentioned above, says have contributed to the emergence of a global civil society (e.g. NGOs and other formal bodies and organisations) and other collective actors participating on the world stage that are not yet incorporated into transnational organisations. The anti-capitalist movement, along with other new social movements, therefore has to seek to remain independent and autonomous in order to be part of a genuinely democratic global civil society. However, it must also strive to make sure that its own internal structures reflect the democratic ideal.

In the introduction, I said that a persistent problem for social movement's activists concerns the lack of internal democracy that may develop which can tend to create hierarchies amongst participants. Exhibiting the kind of blind hierarchism discussed by Blaug, John Lloyd (2001) argues that the main problem for the global anti-capitalist movement is that it lacks the organisational characteristics of democratic government and therefore cannot provide an alternative despite claiming that it can. However, while Lloyd regards modern social democratic administrations as well-intentioned and almost helpless in the face of anti-capitalists, Beckett questions the democratic nature of social democracy, in a manner that has implications for the policing of social movements (Ellison and Martin, 2000), since 'there is a long history of social democrats acting intolerantly, and at times brutally, towards those further to the Left' (Beckett, 2002: 22). Therefore, Beckett concludes that 'the anti-capitalists appear to be alone on the Left in their ability to raise obvious questions about how the world works' (Beckett, 2002: 21).

Speaking from the Left, Callinicos' analysis echoes many of the points raised in the above. He argues that the success of the anti-capitalist movement's fight to resist neo-liberalism will depend on it building allegiances with the trade unionists that need to 'widen their horizons and see themselves as the key agent in a process of universal emancipation' (Callinicos, 2001: 395). In terms of alternatives, Callinicos is adamant that we must:

> ... return to the question of whether existing international institutions can be reformed to serve more democratic and humane purposes. From a socialist perspective, this question must be answered in the negative. Capitalism is driven by the logic of competitive accumulation, for which both human needs and capacities and the structures and resources of the planet itself are mere raw materials to be used and consumed. Since capitalism is an evolving system, institutions come and go as its structure and requirements change, but the same anti-human logic drives it. The key question is then to develop a different social logic, where the aim is no longer to maximise profits but to meet human needs in an environmentally sustainable way and on the basis of democratic and collective control of the world's resources. (Callinicos, 2001: 398-9)

References

Albrow, M. (1992) 'Sine Ira et Studio – or Do Organisations Have Feelings?', *Organisation Studies*, vol. 13:3; 313–29.

Ayres, J.M. (2001) 'Transnational Political Processes and Contention Against the Global Economy', *Mobilisation*, vol. 6:1; 55–68.

Baker, G. (2002) 'Problems in the Theorisation of Global Civil Society', *Political Studies*, vol. 50:5; 928–43.

Barker, C. and Dale, G. (1998) 'Protest Waves in Western Europe: A Critique of "New Social Movement" Theory', *Critical Sociology*, vol. 24:1/2; 65–104.

Bartholomew, A. and Mayer, M. (1992) 'Nomads of the Present: Melucci's Contribution to "New Social Movement" Theory', *Theory, Culture and Society*, vol. 9:4; 141–59.

Beckett, A. (2002) 'When Capitalism Calls', *London Review of Books*, 4 April; 21–2.

Blaug, R. (1999) 'The Tyranny of the Visible: Problems in the Evaluation of Anti-institutional Radicalism', *Organisation*, vol. 6:1; 33–56.

Blaug, R. (2000) 'Blind Hierarchism and Radical Organisational Forms', *New Political Science,* vol. 22:3; 379–95.

Blaug, R. (2002) 'Engineering Democracy', *Political Studies*, vol. 50:1; 102–16.

Calhoun, C. (ed.) (1994) *Social Theory and the Politics of Identity* (Oxford: Blackwell).

Calhoun, C. (1995) '"New Social Movements" of the Early Nineteenth Century' in M. Traugott (ed.) *Repertoires and Cycles of Collective Action* (Durham: Duke University Press), 173–215.

Callinicos, A. (2001) 'Where Now?' in E. Bircham and J. Charlton (eds) *Anti-capitalism: A Guide to the Movement* (London: Bookmarks Publications), 387-390.

Canel, E. (1992) 'New Social Movement Theory and Resource Mobilisation: The Need for Integration' in W.K. Carroll (ed.) *Organising Dissent* (Toronto: Garamond Press). 22–51.

Cohen, J.L. (1985) 'Strategy or Identity: New Theoretical Paradigms and Contemporary Social Movements', *Social Research*, vol. 52:4; 663–716.

Cohen, J.L. and Arato, A. (1992) *Civil Society and Political Theory* (Cambridge, Mass.: MIT Press).

Crossley, N. (2002) *Making Sense of Social Movements* (Buckingham: Oxford University Press).

D'Anieri, P., Ernst, C. and Kier, E. (1990) 'New Social Movements in Historical Perspective', *Comparative Politics*, vol. 22:4; 445–58.

Davis, J.E. (ed.) (2002) *Stories of Change: Narrative and Social Movements* (Albany: State University of New York Press).

Delanty, G. (1999) *Social Theory in a Changing World: Conceptions of Modernity* (Cambridge: Polity).

della Porta, D. and Diani, M. (1999) *Social Movements: An Introduction* (Oxford: Blackwell).

Diani, M. (2000) 'Social Movement Networks Virtual and Real', *Information, Communication and Society*, vol. 3:3; 386–401.

Egan, D. (2001) 'Constructing Globalisation: Capital, State and Social Movements', *New Political Science,* vol. 23:4; 559–64.

Ellison, G. and Martin, G. (2000) 'Policing, Collective Action and Social Movement Theory: The Case of the Northern Ireland Civil Rights Campaign', *British Journal of Sociology*, vol. 51:4; 681–99.

Etzioni-Halevy, E. (2001) 'The Globalisation of Democracy? Social Movements and the Limits of Transnational Accountability', *International Journal of Contemporary Sociology*, vol. 38:2; 146–70.

Eyerman, R. (2002) 'Music in Movement: Cultural Politics and Old and New Social Movements', *Qualitative Sociology*, vol. 25:3; 443–58.

Feldman, A. (2002) 'Making Space at the Nations' Table: Mapping the Transformative Geographies of the International Indigenous Peoples' Movement', *Social Movement Studies,* vol. 1:1; 31–46.

Fournier, V. (2002) 'Utopianism and the Cultivation of Possibilities: Grassroots Movements of Hope' in M. Parker (ed.) *Utopia, Ideology and Organisation* (Oxford: Blackwell), 189–216.

Giddens, A. (1991a) *Modernity and Self-identity* (Cambridge: Polity).

Giddens, A. (1991b) *The Consequences of Modernity* (Cambridge: Polity).

Gindin, S. (2001) 'Rebuilding the Left: Towards a Structured Anti-capitalist Movement', *Studies in Political Economy*, vol. 64; 91–7.

Habermas, J. (1981) 'New Social Movements', Telos, vol. 49; 33–7.

Hamel, P., Lustiger-Thaler, H. and Mayer, M. (eds) (2000) *Urban Movements in a Globalising World* (London: Routledge).

Hannigan, J.A. (1985) 'Alain Touraine, Manuel Castells and Social Movement Theory: A Critical Appraisal', *The Sociological Quarterly*, vol. 26:4; 435–54.

Hari, J. (2002) 'Now the protestors box clever', *New Statesman*, 1 April 2002; 23–4.

Held, D. (1987) *Models of Democracy* (Cambridge: Polity).

Klein, N. (2000) *No Logo* (London: Flamingo).

Lentin, A. (1999) 'Structure, Strategy, Sustainability: What Future for New Social Movement Theory?', *Sociological Research Online*, vol. 4:3. http://www.socresonline.org.uk/socresonline/4/3/lentin.html

Lloyd, J. (2001) *The Protest Ethic: How the Anti-globalisation Movement Challenges Social Democracy* (London: Demos).

Lofland, J. (1995) 'Charting Degrees of Movement Culture: Tasks of the Cultural Cartographer' in H. Johnston and B. Klandermans (eds) *Social Movements and Culture* (London: UCL Press), 188–216.

Lynch, C. (1998) Social Movements and the Problem of Globalisation', *Alternatives*, vol. 23; 149–73.

Martin, G. (1998) 'Generational Differences Amongst New Age Travellers', *The Sociological Review*, vol. 46:4; 735–56.

Martin, G. (2001) 'Social Movements, Welfare and Social Policy: A Critical Analysis', *Critical Social Policy*, vol. 21:3; 361–83.

Martin, G. (2002) 'Conceptualising Cultural Politics in Subcultural and Social Movement Studies', *Social Movement Studies*, vol. 1:1; 73–88.

McDonald, K. (2002) 'L'Intervention Sociologique After Twenty-five Years: Can it Translate into English?', *Qualitative Sociology*, vol. 25:2; 247–60.

Melucci, A. (1984) 'An End to Social Movements?', *Social Science Information*, vol. 23:4/5; 819–35.

Melucci, A. (1985) 'The Symbolic Challenge of Contemporary Movements', *Social Research*, vol. 52:4; 789–816.

Melucci, A. (1988) 'Social Movements and the Democratisation of Everyday Life' in J. Keane (ed.) *Civil Society and the State* (London: Verso). 245-259.

Melucci, A. (1989) Nomads of the Present (London: Hutchinson Radius).

Melucci, A. (1992) 'Liberation of Meaning? Social Movements, Culture and Democracy', *Development and Change*, vol. 23:3; 43–77.

Melucci, A. (1996) *Challenging Codes* (Cambridge: Cambridge University Press).

Melucci, A. (1997) 'Identity and Difference in a Globalised World' in P. Werbner and T. Modood (eds) *Debating Cultural Hybridity* (London: Zed Books). 58-69.

Mooers, C. and Sears, A. (1992) 'The "New Social Movements" and the Withering Away of State Theory' in W.K. Carroll (ed.) *Organising Dissent* (Toronto: Garamond Press). 52-68.

Nash, K. (2002) 'Political Sociology Beyond the Social Democratic Nation-state', *Sociology*, vol. 36:2; 437–43.

Nedelmann, B. (1984) 'New Political Movements and Changes in Processes of Intermediation', *Social Science Information*, vol. 23:6: 1029–48.

Offe, K. (1985) 'New Social Movements: Challenging the Boundaries of Institutional Politics', *Social Research*, vol. 52:4; 817–67.

Parker, M. (2000) 'The Sociology of Organisations and the Organisation of Sociology: Some Reflections on the Making of a Division of Labour', *The Sociological Review*, vol. 48:1; 124–46.

Parker, M. (2002) *Against Management* (Cambridge: Polity).

Plotke, D. (1990) 'What's So New About the New Social Movements?', *Socialist Review*, vol. 90:1; 81–102.

Roth, R. (2000) 'New Social Movements, Poor People's Movements and the Struggle for Social Citizenship' in P. Hamel, H. Lustiger-Thaler and M. Mayer (eds) *Urban Movements in a Globalising World* (London: Routledge).

Rothschild-Whitt, J. (1979) 'The Collectivist Organisation: An Alternative to Rational-bureaucratic Models', *American Sociological Review*, vol. 44; 509–27.

Scott, A. (1990) *Ideology and the New Social Movements* (London: Unwin Hyman).

Scott, A. and Street, J. (2000) 'From Media Protest to E-protest: The Use of Popular Culture and New Media in Parties and Social Movements', *Information, Communication and Society*, vol. 3:2; 215–40.

Sklair, L. (1995) 'Social Movements and Global Capitalism', *Sociology*, vol. 29:3; 495–512.

Smith, J. (2001) 'Globalising Resistance: The Battle of Seattle and the Future of Social Movements', *Mobilisation*, vol. 6:1; 1–19.

Tarrow, S. (1988) 'Fishnets, Internets and Cadnets: Globalisation and Transnational Collective Action', *Social Movements, Protest and Contention*, vol. 7; 228–44.

Taylor, V. and van Willigen, M. (1996) 'Women's Self-help and the Reconstruction of Gender: The Postpartum Support and Breast Cancer Movements', *Mobilisation*, vol. 1:2; 123–42.

Touraine, A. (1981) *The Voice and the Eye* (Cambridge: Cambridge University Press).

Touraine, A. (1985) 'An Introduction to the Study of Social Movements', *Social Research*, vol. 52:4; 749–87.

Tucker, K.H. (1991) 'How New are the New Social Movements?', *Theory, Culture and Society*, vol. 8:2; 75–98.

Welsh, I. (2000) 'New Social Movements', *Developments in Sociology*, vol. 16; 43–60.

3. ANTI-GLOBALISATION, ANTI-CAPITALISM AND THE DEMOCRATIC STATE[7]

Kevin Farnsworth

The 1990s marked, according to Francis Fukuyama, the end of history, brought about by the collapse of Communism and the dawn of a new, more stable future, under capitalism. The radical Left was thought to have been buried with the fall of the Berlin Wall and the collapse of the Soviet Union. In Britain, the defeat of militancy within the Labour Party and the decline of trade unionism over the 1980s spelled the demise of any credible opposition to free market capitalism. Old Labour gave way to 'New Labour', social democracy gave way to the Third Way, and opposition to Rightist and Centrist politics all but disappeared.

However, the turn of the new century brought with it a new challenge to the political establishment, the likes of which had not been seen since the 1960s. Whilst various political struggles had taken place during the 1970s, 1980s and 1990s, including organised industrial unrest, the emergence of single-issue protest, most markedly around environmentalism, and the Poll Tax demonstrations in the UK, the new struggle is different. Most obviously, political unrest since the 1960s has been relatively narrow in political focus, centring on wage claims, conditions of work, tax equity or the protection of local environments. This new movement, on the other hand, draws together a range of interests to fight on all of these fronts simultaneously and over all continents. The most visible signs of the movement have been the mega-demonstrations in Seattle, Genoa, Quebec and, more recently, in Barcelona. Each of these attracted several hundred thousand demonstrators and much media attention. But what exactly is this new movement about, what are its demands, how does it fit in with democratic or parliamentary politics, and where is it heading? This chapter sets out to address each of these questions.

Is the Movement Anti-Globalist?

The new movement is most commonly described as an anti-globalisation or anti-capitalist movement, and the extent to which these are accurate

7 I am grateful to Meir Shabat for his insightful comments on an earlier draft.

descriptions are questions that have occupied activists, academics and journalists for the whole of its short history. Whether the movement is anti-capitalist or anti-globalisation is an important question since it helps those
within it, as well as those outside and those against it, to define its objectives and organising principles. There is certainly a strong resistance to the
present guise of economic and political globalisation that is accused of
undermining economic and social development. This has led some commentators, especially those who are critical of the movement, to accuse
those within it as being politically unrealistic, naïve and of standing in the
way of progress since global communications, global trade, global travel
and even global communities are viewed as irreversible signs of 'progress'.
In reality, those who oppose globalisation make up a very small part of the
movement. Whilst key thinkers in the movement, including Bello (2000)
and Hines (2000), do advocate trade restrictions, localised production and
direct local democracy, it would be inaccurate to suggest that the movement as a whole is anti-globalist. Indeed, many of the dominant groups
within the movement embrace globalisation; they view political and economic globalisation as offering the potential for greater economic development and equality as well as offering the opportunity for international
political solidarity. Most of the major organisations within the movement,
including two of the key players in the UK – *Globalise Resistance* and
People's Global Action (PGA), seek, in fact, to build a global political
movement. Indeed, many within the movement increasingly resist the label
of 'anti-globalisation'. As George Monbiot, a key thinker within the movement, points out, hardly anyone within the movement uses the term to refer
to him or herself anymore (cited in Hari, 2002: 20). Having said this, many
within the movement have focused a great deal on the problems that globalisation and the associated spread of neo-liberalism presents for workers
in the developed and developing world. It is this form of globalisation –
globalisation 'World Bank style', the spread of corporate monoculture, the
power and dominance of global corporations and corporate-led neo-liberalism – that the movement opposes most vigorously. The globalisation and
regionalisation of government, through the European Union, NAFTA,
World Bank, International Monetary Fund and World Trade Organisation
offers no protection since these institutions are viewed as further privileg-
ing the interests of international capital at the expense of human rights and
democratic institutions at all levels. Moreover, globalisation has spurred
the growth of global elite networks between corporate and governmental
interests (Sklair, 2001). Klein is probably right when she suggests that a

key objective of the movement is to 'embrace globalisation but ... wrest it from the grasp of the multinationals' (Klein, 2000: 31). In response, the movement seeks to *'globalise protest'*, through *'global solidarity'* for the establishment of *'global citizenship'*, *'global democracy'*, and *'global justice'*.

Is it Anti-Capitalist?

This suggests that anti-capitalism would be a more accurate description of the movement than anti-globalisation. According to McNally 'For the first time in decades, it is possible to realistically envision the emergence of a new radical left – an activist anti-capitalist left' (2001:76). This does not alter the fact, however, that the movement is a diverse one, made up of various groups, each with different aims and aspirations. If we consider any of the major demonstrations so far – in Seattle (1999), Quebec City (2001), Gothenberg (2001), Genoa (2001), Porte Allegre (2001) and Barcelona (2002) – anarchists, communists, socialists, trade unionists, social democrats, debt-relief groups, environmentalists, Catholics, pacifists and Christian democrats have all marched in unison. This diversity is one of the key features that distinguish this from other movements in recent memory. It is also, some would argue, one of its key strengths, though the coming together of these groups was probably borne more out of the general weakness of the left, a matter we will return to later. It is certainly true that the incorporation of mainstream religious organisations, the voluntary sector and, most importantly, the trade unions, has lent the movement legitimacy and strength in numbers, although politicians and the media who prefer to concentrate on the more radical elements of the movement often overlook this fact.

The fact that the movement is so diverse is, on the face of it, at odds with the suggestion that it can be anti-capitalist. Clearly, many who have participated in the various demonstrations would not refer to themselves or their organisations in such terms. Whilst the movement is made up of different groups, gathering in different places around different themes, including opposition to immigration controls, third world debt, war and imperialism and protests against capitalism, there is a unifying idea to which most groups subscribe, which suggests that large and powerful corporate interests are at the heart of many of these social and politico-economic problems, and it is this realisation that has come to define the movement. As Monbiot, in an interview with Bygrave (2002) puts it:

I think the great majority of people who have joined this movement started off with a vague sense that something was wrong and not necessarily being able to put their finger on what it was ... Having a sense that power was being removed from their hands, then gradually becoming more informed, often in very specific areas because what you find in our community of activism is some people who are very concerned about farming, those who are very interested in the environment, or labour standards, or privatisation of public services, or Third World debt. These interests tie together and the place they all meet is this issue of corporate power.

Klein agrees that the focus of activists and organisations tends to settle on corporate power and that activists are becoming much more sophisticated in their worldview of the operation of the global economy (Klein, 2000: 266). As the movement matures it also appears that it is becoming more anti-capitalist. Tony Juniper (2002), director-designate of Friends of the Earth UK, outlines the evolution of thinking for many environmentalists within the movement:

For the past 10 years, we've been locating ourselves more in the bigger economic debate and less in the "save the whales" type debate. Talking about rainforests led us into talking about Third World debt. Talking about climate change led us to talk about transnational corporations. The more you talk about these things, the more you realise the subject isn't the environment any more, it's the economy and the pressures on countries to do things that undercut any efforts they make to deal with environmental issues. By the time we got to Seattle, we were all campaigning on the same basic trend that was undermining everybody's efforts to achieve any progressive goals. That trend is the free market and privileges for big corporations and rich people at the expense of everything else.

Starr's research also supports this view. All the major groups that make up the movement, according to her, identify corporations, especially multinational corporations, as their common enemy. The introduction to the 'Guide to the Movement' in the UK (George et al., 2001), in fact, states that the enemy is the 'whole corporate system'.

Thus, even if differences exist in the methods employed by different groups to try to address various social, political and economic problems, the movement has been surprisingly successful at uniting these diverse interests beneath an anti-capitalist banner. This has been made easier by the emergence of neo-liberal hegemony, which dominates the policies of international governmental agencies and nation states and helps to unite those who oppose it.

Whilst many within the movement are opposed to large and transnational corporations, however, they are not necessarily opposed to *capitalism*. Many do advocate the revolutionary overthrow of the capitalist system and clearly locate the problem with global capitalism. As Guy Taylor (2002), spokesperson for Globalise Resistance puts it:

> I am keen to stick with the name of "anti-capitalism" as it points the finger at where the problem lies, in the system rather than with particularly nasty individuals or corporations (although these do very much exist).

Others, however, push for no more than stiffer regulations on big business and resistance to the domination of neo-liberalism within international governmental agencies and nation states. Even if it is possible to argue that anti-capitalism is the most obvious and consistent message, it is by no means the only one; the movement fights many different battles on many different fronts: against inequality; poverty; low pay and exploitation; environmental degradation; sexism and patriarchy; and imperialism and warfare. After reviewing the key texts of the movement, Dale (2001: 372) summarises its biggest concerns as being opposition to:

> the further commodification of human life; 'to the plunder of 'natural capital' and the imperilling of plant Earth as a future habitat; to exploiting and 'social exclusion'; and to the corporate takeover of public space and the political process.

The connections between this range of social and environmental ills and corporate power appear to be enough to override differences in the movement where much narrower differences have divided the left in the past. Individuals and organisations within the movement have been prepared to put aside differences on longer-term objectives, and have instead focused on immediate injustices, drawing strength from diversity as the World Social Forum (WSF, 2002) puts it:

We are diverse – women and men, adults and youth, indigenous peoples, rural and urban, workers and unemployed, homeless, the elderly, students, migrants, professionals, peoples of every creed, colour and sexual orientation ... diversity is our strength and the basis of our unity. We are a global solidarity movement, united in our determination to fight against the concentration of wealth, the proliferation of poverty and inequalities, and the destruction of our earth. We are living and constructing alternative systems, and using creative ways to promote them. We are building a large alliance from our struggles and resistance against a system based on sexism, racism and violence, which privileges the interests of capital and patriarchy over the needs and aspirations of people.

From this, the connections between the dangers of corporate power and other social ills are clear; but overall the movement is perhaps more accurately defined by its concerns for global citizenship or global justice than its anti-globalism or anti-capitalism. In fact, Monbiot suggests that today no one term accurately describes the movement, though he does feel that the 'global justice movement' is a more accurate one (cited in Hari, 2002: 20). But ultimately, each commentator on the movement and each activist within it will choose to identify the movement in ways that fit best with their own understanding or agenda. What is most surprising, and most important, is how, despite these differences, the movement retains some coherence and unity. This is undoubtedly borne of the fact that, in recent years, the left has been so weak that only cooperation and unity has offered any possibility of power and influence, a fact that has focused the minds of many organisations and activists on its most important goal: to build and expand the movement. There have been signs recently that this unity is being increasingly challenged, however, as subsequent sections will testify.

The Failure of Democracy and the Rise of the Movement

We have already noted that the growth and expansion of the movement since 1999 took many by surprise. Ironically, it also grew most quickly and powerfully within a Europe dominated by 'left-wing' governments. In 1998, 13 out of 15 EU governments were led by social democratic or socialist coalitions. Indeed, one explanation of the rise of the movement is massive disappointment in these regimes, most of which continued to defend and enthusiastically follow neo-liberal policies. As Klein (2000:

341) puts it, '[Voters] tried to reverse conservative trends by electing liberal, labour or democratic-socialist governments, only to find that economic policy remains unchanged or caters even more directly to the whims of global corporations'.

The shift to the right by politically institutionalised social democratic parties has left a gap that has been filled by the rise of non-institutionalised struggle. This new movement appears to have little or no faith in parliamentary democracy. Whilst the movement has gone from strength to strength, voter apathy has increased, and voter turnout has fallen to record lows. Activists and organisations within the movement are much less likely to be tied to political parties as those on the left have been in the past. The gap between activists on the left and social democratic parties has seldom been wider. As Gindin (2001: 93) notes, in the Canadian context:

Our vision and our project – building a movement that changes how we think about politics, extending the range of what's possible, and considering a fundamental challenge to capital – is simply on a different terrain ... when it comes to political practice and overall agenda, the movements and (social democratic parties) have come to speak different languages.

Generally speaking, the movement appears to have lost faith in democratic politics. This is not surprising given that social democratic governments themselves have often defended their abandonment of policies designed to control capital by effectively stating that the pressures of globalisation were shaping their choices. As Tony Blair explained in 1995 and 1999 respectively:

The determining context of economic policy is the new global market. That imposes huge limitations of a practical nature ... on macro-economic policies. (*Financial Times*, 22 May 1995)

If the markets don't like your policies, they will punish you. (Tony Blair, speech to the Economic Club, Chicago, 23 April 1999)

Statements such as these explain why globalisation has often been considered to be the enemy of greater equality and justice and why anti-globalisation has been a rallying force amongst some groups on the left (though, as discussed above, it is certain forms of globalisation that are opposed rather than globalisation per se). What has emerged from 'demo-cratic' parliamentary politics is a 'one-size-fits-all' neo-liberalism that has eroded the boundaries between national capitalist models (Budd, 2001: 174). In response, the movement seeks to reinvigorate democracy through non-institutionalised politics.

Concerns have been expressed about the increased role and power of international and regional governmental bodies in prioritising the interests of business and increasingly overriding the decisions of locally or nation-ally elected governments. The only way to control this shifting power, activists argue, is to internationalise regional and global protest. The best and most successful illustration of this was the defeat of the proposed Multilateral Agreement on Investment (MAI) in 1998. This proposal, spon-sored by the OECD, would have changed the balance between govern-ments and corporations by allowing the latter to prosecute the former in international courts for limiting investments or capital flows without good reason, even if states believed that doing so would protect local markets or their citizens. Any state preventing the expansion of GM foods on the basis of concerns about health or local environments, but not hard and fast evi-dence, for example, could have been prosecuted by international compa-nies and forced to open their markets. In the end, the MAI was defeated, partly because of the coordinated activities of the movement (Desai, 2001) a fact that has inspired and given hope to subsequent actions. It also forced international negotiators and politicians to publicly defend the proposal and, to some extent, subjected this area of international trade negotiation to a degree of democracy according to Desai (2001: 61).

By the end of the 1990s, the evolving movement had also drawn inspi-ration from the extraordinary story of the Zapatista uprising in Chiapas, Mexico, in 1994. The Zapatista movement was made up largely of indige-nous Indian peasants, who struggled for land rights, better social conditions generally and against cuts in workers rights as a result of globalisation (Chomsky, 1999: 124). Although the Mexican government initially brand-ed them as terrorists and tried to curb the rebellion with military force, they eventually agreed to withdraw from two key areas in Chiapas because of a massive guerrilla campaign and widespread public support. In March 2001, ordinary Mexicans and the President himself welcomed the Zapatistas to Mexico City. Bolivia provided another hopeful story for activists, where, following the insistence of the World Bank, the water supply of Cochabamba was privatised in 1998 with the result that the price of water increased by 200%. The fierce popular protest that followed forced the

Bolivian government to reverse the privatisation, though Bechtel, the company that initially took over the water supply, is now attempting to sue the Bolivian government for $250m in compensation (Shultz, 2002).

Successful campaigns have also been fought closer to home. By challenging corporate power, the movement has helped to revive important democratic rights within the workplace, such as the right to form trade unions; and workers appear to have found a new confidence in campaigning for better working conditions and pay. It seems that every part of the public sector has experienced some form of industrial action over the past two years.

There have also been successes by environmentalists and debt campaigners. In both areas, probably more has been achieved, and more quickly, through direct action, demonstrations and educational campaigns to oppose state and corporate activities than could have been achieved through parliamentary or traditional means alone. Today both governments and corporations are at pains to promote and display their environmentally friendly credentials, even if at times this does not translate into effective policies. Even when governments and corporations have tried to counter the arguments of environmentalists, such as on the safety of genetically modified farming, environmentalists have managed to convince consumers that these products and farming methods create more dangers than benefits. In many countries, including the UK, GM trials have had to be halted in the face of this widespread opposition.

Actions around environmental degradation have also met with some success. Despite the lamentable progress made by the international community on environmental protection, especially given the US's attempts during the recent Johannesburg Earth Summit to reverse its decision to sign up to the Kyoto protocol, environmentalists have at least managed to place the issue onto the political agenda in most countries. Even corporations have come to recognise the importance of environmental performance to future sales, and increasing numbers are actively seeking the backing of prominent environmentalists in an aim to win over increasingly demanding and well-informed consumers (Cahal, 2002).

On the issue of debt relief too, governments have been forced into action to try to alleviate the burden of debt on developing countries. The movement as a whole, and the specific actions of campaign groups such as Jubilee 2000, helped place this issue on the political agenda.

Companies have also been forced to counter the charges made by the movement that they undermine human rights and exploit workers in developing and developed countries. By bringing these issues to the attention of consumers, the movement threatens to undermine the sales and profits of the offending companies, by exposing the exploitation of labour by, in particular, clothing companies such as The Gap and Nike.

This disappointment in the democratic process, combined with a newly established faith in the merits of non-institutionalised struggle, has led to an expansion in the size of the movement in recent years. It has also led to a growth in direct action against Banks and giant corporations, particularly large American corporations such as McDonalds and Starbucks, symbols of wealth and privilege such as expensive sports cars, and the repressive arm of the state.

Demonstrations and the Response of the State

It is important to note that different parts of the movement play different roles within the demonstrations. The majority prefer to march peacefully. Some stress the importance of challenging directly the authority of the police. Others focus on attacking symbols of wealth and privilege. Whether one supports this action or not, it is important to view such action as a rarely used, but significant, form of protest. Very rarely is it *mindless* as politicians or the media often brand it; often it is rational, coordinated and targeted. When direct action does, in fact, degenerate into *mindless* untargeted violence against property (it hardly ever extends to violence against civilians), those within the demonstrations often redirect efforts towards what are viewed as legitimate targets. Nevertheless, whatever form protest takes, it often brings demonstrators into direct conflict with the police and army.

The reaction of governments towards the movement has steadily tightened in response to its growing size and its methods. Governments and the popular media charge the movement with lacking a justifiable and coherent political goal and as violent and thuggish. Tony Blair derided them as a 'travelling circus', interested only in mindless violence. Nevertheless, despite these charges, the movement as a whole has clearer political objections and objectives than many others that have preceded it. This movement perhaps presents a bigger threat to governments, however, since it challenges the present management of global capitalism and thus the authority of nation states themselves.

The response of those states has been to introduce and justify heavy and repressive police and military control. Even moderate leaders, sympathetic to leftist causes, have tried to dissuade people from taking part in demonstrations. Ken Livingstone, himself no stranger to leftist causes and demonstrations, warned those who were considering joining a rally in London on May 1st 2001 – international labour day – that they would face a tough zero-tolerance and well-armed police force. In the event, demonstrators and innocent bystanders were forcibly, and some civil liberties groups argue illegally, detained in Oxford Circus for up to 8 hours (Bright and Harris, 2001).

Demonstrators also face restricted movement, internationally coordinated surveillance, long arrests for minor incidents and the use of excessive and even illegal violence. Police in London have openly bore live arms against protesters since 2001, as did police in Gothenburg during the EU summit in June 2001 and in Genoa in July 2001. Three protesters were shot and injured by the Swedish police in Gothenburg, whilst Genoa witnessed the first fatality of the movement when the Italian paramilitary police shot a young protestor in the head. Protesters also witnessed new levels of state violence at the hands of the Italian police, culminating in one of the worst attacks on innocent civilians in recent years when almost one hundred demonstrators were brutally beaten by police during a nighttime raid of one of the official accommodation shelters. The attack happened late at night whilst most of the people inside were sleeping.

Demands and Strategies of the Movement

Since the interests of the movement are many and varied, so too are the demands made; though it is worth pointing out again that, since opposition to big business lies at the heart of the movement, the most important campaigns centre around countering corporate power. What divides the movement is agreement on how best to do this. As highlighted above, for thinkers such as Bello (2000) and Hines (2000) it is important to reverse the processes of globalisation and revert to localised production and localised democracy, though, as noted above, theirs is a minority view within the movement as a whole. For Klein (2000), the key problem is the power and influence of large corporations and mega-brands; hence, she advocates stronger scrutiny of the practices of transnationals so that the power and legitimacy of these and other companies is challenged. Focusing on individual corporations, however, risks individualising a problem that is far more widespread than the bad practices of the largest transnationals according to Harman (2000). For Pettifor (2001: 52) and George, (2001:

22), the focus should be on the regulation and control of international finance, so that capital is controlled by democratic institutions according to the principles of human rights rather than corporate rights. Others, such as Bourdieu maintain that neo-liberalism and the retreat of the state is the main issue to be confronted. In placing the emphasis on state activities and ideology, of course, such views shift the focus away from capitalism.

As far as the key organisations within the movement are concerned, it is the building of the movement and establishing a critical mass and a visible presence that are most important. To take a small but influential cross section of organisations – Socialist Alliance, Globalise resistance, ATTAC, the World Social Forum, People's Global Action, the Anarchist Federation, the World Development Organisation, the Wombles and Ya Basta! – all place the greatest emphasise on continuing efforts to build a world movement in opposition to corporate power and neo-liberal globalisation. Concerns about human rights and participatory democracy also lie at the heart of the movement. In fact, for Dale (2001: 373), participatory democracy, rather than anti-capitalism, is the 'common project'. Yet, for many within the movement, true democracy is not possible under contemporary global capitalism. To restore democracy, People's Global Action argues that we need to develop diverse 'forms of organisation at different levels, acknowledging that there is not a single way of solving the problems we are facing.' Beyond this, only direct and localised forms of democracy, independent of government and economic powers, would guarantee human rights. One of the key aims of the United Kingdoms Socialist Alliance is to expose the powers that corporations have over states. They see the state as increasingly unwilling and unable to effectively regulate, supervise and control large corporations. Its aim is to restore the power and authority of democratic states and 'galvanise mass opposition to the injustice, inequality and environmental damage which the market causes' (Socialist Alliance, 2000)

The World Social Forum, an organisation established to counter the neo-liberalism of the business-dominated World Economic Forum, similarly argues for the restoration of genuine, as opposed to corrupted, democracy that responds to the demands of the electorate rather than the demands of large corporations. It goes on to argue that activists within the movement should:

stand in opposition to a process of globalisation commanded by the large multinational corporations and by the governments and international institutions at the service of those corporations' interests, with the complicity of national governments. (WSF, 2002)

ATTAC offers one solution to both reduce the short-termism of capital and raise additional revenue for governments: the Tobin Tax. The so-called Tobin Tax, named after James Tobin, would impose of levy of around 0.05-0.25 per cent on foreign-exchange transactions, a policy that is designed to deter speculative financial flows, which can undermine national economies. ATTAC (1999) argues that:

Even at the particularly low rate of 0.1%, the Tobin Tax would bring in close to $100 billion every year. Collected for the most part by industrialised countries, where the principal financial markets are located, this money could be used to help struggle against inequalities, to promote education and public health in poor countries, and for food security and sustainable development. Such a measure fits with a clearly anti-speculative perspective. It would sustain a logic of resistance, restore maneuvering room to citizens and national governments, and, most of all, would mean that political, rather than financial considerations are returning to the fore.

The Anarchist Federation (2003), on the other hand, rejects any attempt to reform capitalism as flawed and fruitless:

as they fail to challenge capitalism itself. Unions also work as a part of the capitalist system, so although workers struggle within them, they will be unable to bring about capitalism's destruction unless they go beyond these limits.

The Socialist Alliance (2001) would agree, though unlike anarchists, who would oppose socialist statism, argue that it is necessary to replace corrupted forms of capitalism with:

a popular socialist republic, based on democratic common ownership and democratic control of the key sectors of the economy, a system based on social justice and ecological sustainability.

Despite these revolutionary aspirations, however, most groups, including socialists, embrace reformism whenever they unite behind the myriad causes of the movement. Whilst some groups believe that true reform, and true democratic accountability cannot be achieved without the revolutionary overthrow of capitalism, most organisations campaign around reformist issues either because they are reformists at heart or as a pragmatic solution in order to both mitigate against some of the worst excesses of global capitalism, and to help strengthen and build the movement. Focusing on a broad range of issues allows different groups to campaign around issues that concern current and potential members, thereby providing some scope for the further expansion of the movement. Globalise Resistance, for example, claims to unite:

> Christians campaigning for debt relief, environmentalists opposing GM food, trade unionists fighting privatisation in their workplaces and students demanding that education be free to all.

The ability to appeal to all these groups is facilitated by the tendency of organisations within the movement to emphasise campaign-focused reformism rather than ideology. By abandoning ideology, for example, Ya Basta! claims to have adopted a world view that is more encompassing, allowing it to focus on factors such as:

> the profound modification of the production system, the dominant role of information, the importance of the environment and other themes until now considered more 'social' than 'political'.

Although this shift in Ya Basta!'s thinking originally caused splits between it and other groups on the left, Ya Basta! claims that it is now able to form links with a whole range of sympathiser ideas:

> Recently ... we have seen a point of commonality in the struggles we are doing together, a sort of re-acquaintance with people who can appreciate the big results obtained by our struggles ... (Hobo, 2000, cited in Wright, 2000).

As already indicated above, the clearest division within the movement centres on the strategies employed during demonstrations. In order to achieve their aims, Globalise Resistance and the World Social Forum, for example, have tended to urge peaceful protest. Some within the moment have gone as far as condemning it outright. Others, such as the Wombles, have urged direct and sporadic action against the state and large corporations. Still others, especially the anarchist groups, have deliberately not advocated any one strategy but have stressed the importance of individual expressions of opposition, anger and resentment against the state and capitalists. The result has been a clear division between those who seek to demonstrate peacefully and those who see forms of direct action as being more important. This division around tactics has created deeper tensions as the movement has matured and as violence has arisen with increasing regularity. Those who advocate more peaceful demonstration, for example, have tried increasingly to distance themselves from those who cause damage to property. The key difficulty for those within the movement is that, on the one hand, such action creates media interest and publicity, but on the other, this publicity is often negative, doing little to further expand and win support for the movement, and allowing journalists and politicians to more easily condemn the movement as a whole.

Many within the movement distinguish between legitimate targeted forms of protest, which can be taken to be a demonstration of strength and unity within the movement, and illegitimate forms of violence, which are targeted towards innocent members of the public or merely result in bad publicity for the movement as a whole. Although episodes of random and untargeted violence are extremely rare, such acts risk undermining the movement and bringing condemnation from those who would otherwise be sympathetic to the movement and its objectives.

Others within the movement stress passive resistance as a key part of their own strategies during demonstrations. The so-called 'pink-bloc' dress as pink fairies or in drag costume and hurl such 'weapons' as teddy bears or flowers at the police as their chosen form of protest against machismo and violence, including that targeted at protesters by the police. Still others have more directly condemned the use of violence by some individuals and organisations within the movement. Monbiot (2000) has been scathing in his attacks on vandalism and violence:

> The violence on May Day was the direct and predictable result of both the absence of boundaries and the abdication of responsibility ... As the nutters in the crowd smashed up shops and defaced the Cenotaph, they must have believed they were precipitating the assault on the entire world order, which Reclaim the Streets, had promised but had wholly failed to deliver ... It achieved the otherwise impossible feat of making the government's anti-terrorism bill

appear sane. It made the police look like society's guardian angels, and it allowed every reactionary in Britain to feel that he or she had been justified in dismissing the direct action movement as an inarticulate threat to human life.

A year later, Monbiot further tried to distance the majority of activists from the 'nutters':

some of the key planning meetings for the big demonstrations have become dominated by a handful of aggressive and overbearing men. People questioning their plans are dismissed as "reformists" or "middle-class wankers" ... [N]on-violent direct action has gradually been displaced by anything-goes direct action. (*The Guardian*, Tuesday May 1, 2001)

This not only illustrates the line some activists such as Monbiot are willing to draw between legitimate and illegitimate forms of protest, it also represents an attempt by some within the movement to push forward with clearer and unifying strategies and greater coherence than has been managed before. Others, however, point to the risk that such a strategy could pose in turning a large and diverse movement that employs different strategies into a small, fragmented and more disciplined one (McNally, 2001).

Future for the Movement

Quite what will happen to the movement in the near and distant future remains to be seen. Whilst the organisers of the movement continue to make optimistic noises about the present state and future of the movement, others are already writing its obituary. The cause of the premature death of the movement, according to Alan Beattie writing in an article for the *Financial Times* during November 2001, was the attacks on the World Trade Centre during the previous September:

In the two large meetings since the attacks – the World Trade Organisation conference in Doha, Qatar, and the International Monetary Fund and World Bank meetings in Ottawa, Canada – the large crowds of demonstrators against the institutions, and economic liberalisation in general, have been sharply diminished. (*Financial Times*, Nov 28th, 2001)

More recently, Johann Hari (2002) argued in the New Statesman that the movement 'has dropped well below the public's radar, and talk of its death is in the air'. What in fact seems to have happened is that the media is increasingly ignoring the movement. Mike Bygrave (2002) found, when he investigated 'where all the protesters had gone' in an article for the Observer eight months after Beattie's that the movement showed few signs that it was in decline:

an estimated 250,000-plus protesters turned up in Barcelona in March for the EU summit. As many as rallied at Genoa last year, only this time the (peaceful) protest was almost totally ignored by the media.(Bygrave, 2002)

Even more recently, in October 2002, up to 500,000 protesters attended the European Social Forum (ESF, the younger sister-organisation of the WSF) in Florence. The movement has also helped to boost the numbers of those marching against the attacks on Afghanistan and Iraq. Whilst Hari (2002), writing before the Florence forum, sees anti-war demonstrations as the only thing presently keeping the movement alive, anti-war and anti-imperialism have in fact been key concerns of the movement since its inception. At the moment, it is not so much the continued existence of the movement that we must wonder about, but whether it can continue to expand.

In many ways, the current strength of the movement is borne out of the past weakness of the left. The last two decades have been particularly bad ones; the left has been disenfranchised and become disillusioned and fragmented. As a result, many on the left have been prepared to find common causes with others in recent years, and have done so successfully within the confines of the movement. The paradox is that, if the left had been stronger, it probably would have continued to fight too many battles within it to join together and have even the modest impact it has so far had. The problem is that, as the current movement gains confidence and tries to move forward, it may again begin to fragment.

Divisions have emerged recently, especially on the question of the objectives and future direction of the movement. The biggest problem confronting the movement, and threatening to weaken it, concerns its future focus: whether it should be short-termist and reformist, or whether it should be long-termist and ideological. As the movement begins to focus on the specifics it is much more likely to fragment; yet it is inevitable that, as it matures, it will aim to more clearly define itself.

The objectives of the World and European Social Forums have been to more clearly map out the principles and objectives of the movement and develop a more positive, and in some ways reformist, agenda (Williamson, 2002). Both were established in order to discuss and debate issues and formulate strategies rather than as forms of protest against, or as gatherings to disrupt, the key meetings of business or governments. Key voices within the movement are already calling for more coherent and forward looking messages around which to organise. Part of the rationale for this, according to Monbiot, is that without a clear and coherent objective, the movement risks degenerating into pointless and mindless acts of violence. This, according to Monbiot (2000), is what happened during the May Day demonstrations discussed above, where the futility of 'digging up Parliament Square' was 'so utterly frustrating and disempowering that the more hot-headed protesters could almost be excused for wanting to do something more spectacular'. Moreover, violent protesters are criticised for effectively bullying those who oppose direct action into silence:

Though the physically and psychologically powerful people who hector the doubters at some of the meetings impose their will on everyone else, they argue that it is undemocratic to decide how the group as a whole should behave. If some people want to be violent, that's up to them. While nearly all the protesters opposing globalisation, corporations and environmental destruction are peaceful, they – or perhaps I should say we – have become reluctant to demand that our movement abides by the principles of non-violence. We call upon the world to exercise collective responsibility for the state of the planet. Yet we seem unprepared to exercise collective responsibility for the state of our own movement ... If violence holds sway, it will deliver the movement into the hands of its enemies. Many protesters have argued that seeking to tackle it would be divisive. But if we can't divide ourselves from violence, then violence will divide us from society. (Monbiot, 2001)

For Monbiot, the need is for greater responsibility and coordination. He also suggests that the movement needs to turn against certain organisations in the movement, and in particular 'the proponents of "localisation"' and, rather, unite in order to seek to establish a global parliament (cited in Hari, 2002: 22).

Whilst others have been less prescriptive than Monbiot, they have also concluded that a more united and coherent approach is essential to the future of the movement. Gindin, for example, states that:

> we cannot build unity, coordinate activity, affect the political culture of the country, make democratic decisions and build the kind of social power that can challenge capitalist power without structures and resources. (Gindin, 2001)

Clearly, there is a battle of ideas, objectives and identity within the movement. Whilst some are extremely uncomfortable with imposing discipline and control over the movement, others view this as essential to its future. The risk is that such moves will alienate some groups, especially those who generally oppose formal structures and organisational discipline, especially the various anarchist groups. Whilst it is possible for groups to unite against capitalists, it is difficult to see how diverse groups could ever unite behind clear strategies for the future. As Anarchists will never support state solutions advocated by many socialists, and socialists are unlikely to settle for regulated capitalism, as favoured by some organisations within the movement.

For Klein, any attempt to centralise the movement will limit its ability to protest around many different issues. For McNally (2001), any attempt to control the behaviour and strategies of activists within the movement would risk alienating the 'engine' of the movement: disaffected youth. The young already feel little engagement with institutional politics, including the trade union movement, and appear to place more faith in direct action as a way of venting anger and pushing for radical, rather than piecemeal, changes. To try to impose controls on them risks shutting out an important element of the movement; one that helped to revive and give hope to the left in the 1990s. McNally (2001) also criticises Monbiot and others for their condemnation of those who engage in direct action. According to him, to vilify members of the movement is a high-risk strategy that may lead to divisions and prevent open and democratic debate (Mcnally, 2001). Whilst it may be true to argue that only a minority of protesters take part in direct violent action, many more within the movement may lend them tacit support or may be unwilling to condemn such behaviour. Hence, such a policy may well create much deeper splits and divisions than merely ostracising the obvious minority who engage in such activities. Instead, McNally urges the movement to capitalise on the energies of all its members:

> There is no simply either/or at issue here; it is not a question of direct action or mass action. What is required is the political vision to weave together direct action and mass action approaches in order to develop the energy and enthusiasm of direct action in concert with the larger mass mobilising and movement-building approaches of mass action tactics. (McNally, 2001: 855)

The key for McNally, and in this he is joined by Moody (2001: 293), is to unite activists with organised and unorganised labour. Together, both can unite in strength to oppose corporate power and neo-liberalism, but to do this the movement as a whole needs to make its message more appealing to trade unionists, that is, the movement needs to focus on shorter-term reformist goals as well as longer-term strategies.

Whether diverse interests continue to unite under shared objectives, or whether it will split remains to be seen. The likelihood is that broad coalitions on the left will continue to be formed, and that different groups will continue to march together on basic issues on which they agree, although there are likely to be more efforts made to control and coordinate activities (as happened in the ESF meetings in Florence).

However, whatever happens to the movement, it has at least had the effect of presenting a challenge to global capitalism where politicians appear to be unwilling to do the same. It has offered somewhere for people to go where they can feel that their voice matters and feel that their democratic right to protest may make a difference where their democratic right to vote has failed. It has helped, to 'kick-start a profound rethinking about globalisation among governments' according to George Soros. More generally, it has helped to revive important democratic rights within the workplace, such as the right to form trade unions, and workers appear to have found a new confidence to campaign on issues they feel strongly about, from better working conditions to improved pay settlements.

Even if it has had this impact on political institutions and on political parties, however, it has failed to impact decisively on electoral results. In western democracies at least, the political right has recovered, and in some countries, the far-right have gained strength. The neo-liberal hegemony, meanwhile, remains largely intact. Clearly, the movement will have to do more if it is to encourage wider opposition to neo-liberal globalisation. Whether or not it can do this will depend on the outcome of current debates concerning its future direction.

References

Anarchist Federation (2003). http://flag.blackened.net/af/ (Accessed: October 2002).

ATTAC (1999) *Platform of the international movement ATTAC: International movement for democratic control of financial markets and their institutions.* http://attac.org.uk/attac/document/plateformeintlen.pdf?documentID=2 (Accessed: November 2002).

Bello, W. (2000) 'UNCTAD: Time to Lead, Time to Challenge the WTO' in *Globalise This!: the Battle Against the World Trade Organisation and Corporate Rule* (Maine: Common Courage Press). 163-174.

Bright, M. and Harris, P. (2001) 'Police 'broke the law' in May Day stand-off', *Observer*, 6 May 2001.

Budd, A. (2001) 'Western Europe' in S. George, G. Monbiot, L. German, T. Hayter, A. Callinicos and K. Moody (2001) *Anti-capitalism: A Guide to the Movement* (London: Bookmarks Publications). 173-184.

Bygrave, M. (2002) 'Where did all the protesters go?' *The Observer,* 14 July 2002.

Cahil, M. (2002) 'Eco campaigners go corporate as global firms set out to prove they really are green-aware', *The Independent*, 14 January 2002.

Chomsky, N. (1999) *Profit Over People: Neo-liberalism and Global Order* (London: Seven Stories Press).

Dale, G. (2001) '"Merging Rivulets of Opposition": *Perspectives of the Anti-capitalist Movement*', Millennium, vol. 30:2.

Desai, M. and Said, Y. (2001) The New Anti-capitalist Movement: Money and Global Civil Society in *Global Civil Society Yearbook* (London: London School of Economics).

George, S. (2001) 'Corporate Globalisation' in S. George, et al. (2001) *Anti-capitalism: A Guide to the Movement* (London: Bookmarks Publications). 11-26.

George, S., Monbiot, G., German, L., Hayter, T., Callinicos, A. and Moody, K. (2001) *Anti-capitalism: A Guide to the Movement* (London: Bookmarks Publications).

Gindin, S. (2001) 'Comment: Rebuilding the Left: Towards a Structured Anti-capitalist Movement', *Studies in Political Economy*, vol. 64:Spring.

Hari, J. (2002) 'Whatever happened to No Logo?', *New Statesman*, 11 November 2002; 15(732).

Harman, C. (2000) 'Anti-capitalism: Theory and Practice', *International Socialist*, vol. Autumn.

Hines, C. (2000) *Localisation: A Global Manifesto* (London: Earthscan).

Juniper, T. (2002) 'Where did all the protesters go?', *The Observer*, 14 July 2002

Klein, N. (2000) *No Logo* (London: Flamingo).

McNally, D. (2001) 'Mass protest in Quebec City: From Anti-globalisation to Anti-capitalism', New Politics, vol. Summer.

Monbiot, G. (2000a) 'No way to run a revolution: one of Britain's most effective direct action movements has lost the llot', *The Guardian*, 10 May 2000.

Monbiot, G. (2000b) 'Streets of shame', *The Guardian*, 10 May 2000.

Monbiot, G. (2001) 'Violence is our enemy', *The Guardian*, 1 May 2001.

Moody, K. (2001) 'Unions' in S. George, et al. (2001) *Anti-capitalism: A Guide to the Movement* (London: Bookmarks Publications). 291-302.

People's Global Action (2002) *Manifesto.* http://www.nadir.org/nadir/initiativ/agp/en/PGAInfos/manifest.htm (Accessed: 10 February 2003)

Pettifor, A. (2001) 'Debt' in S. George et al. (2001) *Anti-capitalism: A Guide to the Movement* (London: Bookmarks Publications). 43-56.

Shultz, J. (2002) 'Bechtel Strikes Back at Bolivia' *Trasnationale.* http://forums.transnationale.org/viewtopic.php?t=118&highlight=bolivia+water (Accessed: 12 November 2002).

Sklair, L. (2000) *The Transnational Capitalist Class* (Oxford: Blackwell Publishers).

Socialist Alliance (2001) *Constitution of the Socialist Alliance*, December 1 2001. http://www.socialistalliance.net/about/constitution.html (Accessed: August 2002).

Socialist Alliance (2000) *Manifesto: For the Millions, Not the Millionaires.* http://www.socialistalliance.net/manifesto/intro.htm (Accessed: January 2001).

Starr, A. (2000) *Naming the Enemy: Anti-corporate Social Movements Confront Globalisation* (London: Zed Books Ltd).

Taylor, G. (2002) 'We haven't gone away', *The Observer*, 21 July 2002.

Williamson, L. (2002) 'Anti-globalisation's appetite for destruction wanes', *The Guardian*, 8 November 2002.

Wright, S. (2000) *Changing the World (One Bridge at a Time)? Ya Basta after Prague.* http://www.geocities.com/swervedc/yabasta.html (Accessed: August 2002).

WSF (2002) '*Call of Social Movements: Resistance to Neoliberalism, War and Militarism: for Peace and Social Justice*'.
http://www.forumsocialmundial.org.br/main.asp?id_menu=4_2&cd_language=2 (Accessed: December 2002).

4. ANARCHISM AND DEMOCRACY

Dave Morland and John Carter

Among contemporary political ideologies, anarchism is not alone in its repudiation of democracy. But in no other ideology is the rejection of democracy so central to its political narrative. Anarchy by definition is regarded as a society without rule or government. It is an ideology that campaigns for the abolition of the state and the elimination, as far as possible, of all other modes of hierarchy, power, oppression and subjugation. Kropotkin, the leading anarchist theoretician of the nineteenth century, contends that anarchists are committed to a society 'where the functions of government are reduced to a minimum, and the individual recovers his full liberty of initiative and action for satisfying, by means of free groups and federations – freely constituted – all the infinitely varied needs of the human being' (1970a: 46). In essence, anarchists are, as George Woodcock, the noted historian of the movement, observes, unswerving in their enmity towards authority. Similarly, they eschew any rigid organisation that suffocates liberty and spontaneity (Woodcock, 1975: 7, 15).

In contemporary vocabulary, anarchism has become synonymous with a commitment to abstention from democratic electoral processes and assemblies, favouring instead a strategy of spontaneous and autonomous direct action. In part, this popular perception is undoubtedly a legacy of individual acts of anarchist terror. During the nineteenth century, the popular image of anarchism was that of the armed insurgent. Joseph Conrad's novel, *The Secret Agent*, is arguably the most famous literary representation of this image. However, this understanding of anarchism is also indebted to its own highly visible denunciation of hierarchy and authoritarianism. Anarchism and democracy are seemingly incompatible; the former committed to the latter's demise. Refuting the value of electoral politics as a means to transform society, anarchists have long been associated with revolutionary campaigns that actively seek to bypass democratic channels of opposition and change. As Woodcock (1975) has commented 'Democracy advocates the sovereignty of the people. Anarchism advocates the sovereignty of the person' (p.30). In essence, this reflects the nature of the anarchist objection to democracy. Sharing sentiments with Rousseau, anarchists such as Kropotkin claim that engaging with representative democracy is tantamount to surrendering one's sovereignty (1992: 120).

Anarchism is, therefore, opposed to democratic structures and government, but is equally distrustful of all modes of hierarchical organisation and dictatorship that threaten to jeopardise individual freedom and autonomy. If there is one crucial difference between anarchism and other radical political ideologies, it is this: Anarchists demand no government as the outcome of revolution. All others demand a revolutionary government, whether elected or dictatorial (Kropotkin, 1970b: 237-8).

This chapter explores the reasons behind the anarchists' hostility towards democracy. It begins by focusing on the arguments employed by some of the leading classical anarchists of the eighteenth and nineteenth centuries. In highlighting their concerns, we intend to illustrate the strategic and philosophical objections the classical social anarchists aimed at democracy. More importantly, we shall be suggesting that the entire edifice of the anarchist argument against democracy hinges on the prefigurative nature of anarchism itself. In other words, anarchism's commitment to overturning capitalism by only employing a strategy that is an embryonic representation of an anarchist social future dictates its fundamental opposition to democratic government and practices. We continue our analysis by identifying how that prefigurative element of anarchism has become a vitally important component in the recent anti-capitalist movement's campaigns and strategy. Consequently, we represent anarchism not as some moribund or defunct sect long forgotten in the cobweb-ridden corridors of political history. Rather, we view it as a dynamic and increasingly relevant ideology that is breathing life into some of the most significant global protest movements we have witnessed over the last 40 years or more.

The Classical Heritage

Before commencing our exploration of the classical anarchists' views of democracy, there is a qualification to be made to the argument advanced thus far. As Robert Graham has argued, the 'relationship between anarchism and democratic theory has always been ambiguous' (1989: 71). The reason for this uncertainty is that whilst anarchists have given short shrift to representative democracy many of them (such as Bakunin, Kropotkin and, more recently, Bookchin) have pointed toward direct democracy (the Paris Commune being looked upon with particular favour) as the basis for a future anarchist society. But even anarchist support for direct democracy is deeply ambivalent. The basis of this equivocation is a firm belief that democracy as such embodies an element of authoritarianism that anarchists find difficult to live with. For classical anarchists, democracy is inextricably linked to majoritarianism. Furthermore, majoritarianism represents a real danger to individual liberty or autonomy (Vincent, 1992: 137; Miller, 1984: 38). For Godwin, national assemblies that operate based on majoritarianism not only deprive individuals of the right of private judgement, but in doing so 'contribute to the depravation of the human understanding and character' (Marshall, 1986: 116). These central tenets of anarchism still resonate in contemporary writings. Clark illustrates how the anarchist critique of present political organisations, which focuses on 'coercion and authoritarianism', inspires a much broader appraisal of authoritarian social relations grounded in economics, the family, class, race and education (1984: 128). In light of this, and in the context of anarchism's implacable hostility toward the state, elections, as Powell (1991) has noted, 'become a matter of inconsequence. Moreover, not only do they entail the withdrawal of personal autonomy in the determination of an individual's life, but by positive participation in them, they also imply a moral approval of the existing political system' (1991: 50).

As Marshall has observed, anarchists recognise that democracy is preferable to other modes of government, such as monarchy or aristocracy, but they 'still consider it to be essentially oppressive' (1992: 22). Cadogan has commented that 'it remains the case that representative government mandated by the vote, with all its property qualifications, is absolutely better than personal government by divine right' (1991: 109-110). This is a common sentiment, and one expressed somewhat earlier by Proudhon. The French anarchist deliberated that democracy was superior to monarchy if only because it enabled 'reason to substitute itself for the will' (1840), a view shared by Godwin (Marshall, 1986: 111). Nonetheless, the position of anarchism remains ambiguous here. Proudhon stood for and was successfully elected to the Constituent Assembly in June 1848. He soon became disillusioned with his experience and it is unclear why Proudhon adopted this strategy. The most plausible explanation appears to be that he thought engaging in electoral politics at this time could accelerate the political goals of the working classes. Similarly, the Spanish anarchists were known on at least one occasion to be somewhat less than dogmatic in their hostility toward 'participation in the Frente Popular elections in February 1936' (Guérin, 1989: 123). However, these are exceptions to a general rule under anarchism. Mostly anarchists have opined that the introduction of ballots and majority voting sweeps reason aside as democracy creates citizens that recoil from responsibility and freedom. Accordingly, anarchists decry the process of representation that is the hallmark of parliamentary democracy. Bakunin denounces representative democracy as 'based on the pseudo-sovereignty of a sham popular will, supposedly expressed by pseudo-representatives of the people in sham popular assemblies' (Bakunin, 1990: 13).

If anarchists have disagreed over many things, on this issue they stand shoulder to shoulder. Anarchists regard political parties with disdain. They are viewed as manipulative and intolerant, and symbolise, for Godwin, a straitjacket restraining intellectual development and freedom (Marshall, 1986: 118). Moreover, it is worth recalling that anarchists are in the business of eradicating the state, and to believe that parliamentary democracy can deliver this objective is rather naïve (Miller, 1984: 13). One problem here is that elected representatives are frequently, if not inevitably, ideologically incorporated into capitalism. To put it another way, even if representatives are elected on radical manifestos they are gradually co-opted by the ruling classes. However, a second and more fundamental problem precludes faith in the parliamentary road to anarchism. The most cogent argument marshalled by anarchists against representative democracy is that aligned to their account of human nature. Both Bakunin and Kropotkin, for instance, assume a lust for power within human nature (Morland, 1997: 92-93, 142-3). To place one's trust in elected representatives as a strategy for overturning the state is extremely misguided. As Bakunin warns, no 'one should be entrusted with power, inasmuch as anyone invested with authority must, through the force of an immutable social law, become an oppressor and exploiter of society' (Maximoff, 1964: 249). Kropotkin echoes these sentiments in his essay, *Must We Occupy Ourselves with an Examination of the Ideal of a Future System?* Here Kropotkin clearly identifies a will to power in human nature and issued a prophetic caveat that 'any group of people entrusted with deciding a certain set of activities often of an organisational quality always strives to broaden the range of these activities and its own power in these activities' (1993: 25). Interestingly, it was the former syndicalist, Michels, developing perhaps the most famous account of elite theory in his work, *Political Parties* (1911), that illustrated both how the socialist movement was itself susceptible to oligarchy, and actually furnished 'the most appropriate and fruitful ground for the observation of these tendencies' (Cited in Beetham, 1977: 5-19).

Identification of a will to power in human nature permeates anarchist praxis and revolutionary strategy. Insofar as representative democracy embodies the principles of an authoritarian, centralist, hierarchical state, then, anarchists can have no truck with parliamentary politics when con-

sidering their objectives of a decentralised, non-hierarchical, federal decision-making structure through spontaneous direct action. 'Like the rule of
despots, representative government ... 'Kropotkin argues, '... will always
seek to extend its legislation, to increase its power by meddling with everything, all the time killing the initiative of the individual and the group to
supplant them by law' (1992: 125). The prophetic nature of Kropotkin's
warning derives from the insistence on the commensurability of means and
ends in anarchist revolutionary methodology. This was most famously
expressed in Bakunin's dispute with Marx over the nature and future direction of the International Working Men's Association, occasionally referred
to as the First International. Marx was a member of the General Council of
the IWMA, which after internal disputes about strategy and direction,
decided to remove the autonomy of the federations of the First
International. In response to this, the anarchists of the Jura Federation distributed a document, the Sonvillier Circular, to other federations in the
IWMA. Supporting Bakunin against Marx, the Circular outlined the anarchists' concerns over the centralisation of the organisation. 'How can you
expect an egalitarian and free society to emerge from an authoritarian
organisation? It is impossible. The International, embryo of the future
human society, must be from this moment the faithful image of our principles of liberty and federation, and reject from its midst any principle leading to authority and dictatorship' (Joll, 1979: 87).

Herein lays the essence of the major quarrel between anarchists and
Marxists. The Marxist commitment to the centralisation of revolutionary
strategy is anathema to anarchism. Expressed in terms of a revolutionary
dictatorship of the proletariat, Bakunin sees no merit in Marx's tactic of
transferring political power from the state to the people. There is no real
difference, he argues, between a revolutionary dictatorship and the state.
They both 'represent the same government of the majority by a minority in
the name of the presumed stupidity of the other. Therefore they are equally reactionary, both having the direct and inevitable result of consolidating
the political and economic privileges of the governing minority and the
political and economic slavery of the masses' (Bakunin, 1990: 137).
Kropotkin made similar criticisms of Lenin's revolutionary strategy, arguing that the method by which the Bolsheviks were seeking 'to establish
communism ... makes success absolutely impossible' (Marshall, 1992:
333). More widely, anarchists believe that the revolution should arise from
the ground up. It should be a spontaneous movement of the people themselves. Calls from socialists for a workers' state or a revolutionary govern-

ment are terribly dangerous. For as Kropotkin has cautioned, an u..
ship leads 'to the death of all revolutionary movement' (1970b: 243).

The anarchist critique of many contemporary Marxist movements is that they are non-prefigurative and inextricably linked to highly structured and centralised forms of organisation, premised on Lenin's view of the Party and Marx's concept of the Dictatorship of the Proletariat (Marx, 1974: 355). The former of these was rooted in the example of the Bolshevik Party in a leadership role vis-à-vis the whole working class, underscored by democratic centralism. The latter saw the need for a disciplined and centralised force to fight the final battle with capitalism and extirpate the last remnants of the bourgeois mode of production. Only then, after the old order had been vanquished at some future date, could the 'withering away of the state' commence and the structures of the Party atrophy. As such, for Marxists, a more libertarian future can only be reached by authoritarian means. Engels makes this point perfectly clear, both in his letter to P. van Patten on 18 April 1883 (Engels, 1975) and in his better-known essay, *On Authority*. Here Engels reacts to anarchist concerns over the nature of the revolution. 'But the anti-authoritarians demand that the political state be abolished at one stroke, even before the social conditions that gave birth to it have been destroyed. They demand that the first act of the social revolution shall be the abolition of authority. Have these gentlemen ever seen a revolution? A revolution is certainly the most authoritarian thing there is; it is the act whereby one part of the population imposes its will upon the other part by means of rifles, bayonets and cannon – authoritarian means, if such there be at all; and if the victorious party does not want to have fought in vain, it must maintain this rule by means of the terror which its arms inspire in the reactionists' (Engels, 1874).

Concentration on the commensurability of means and ends reflects the prefigurative nature of anarchism. That anarchists consider it imperative that revolutionary change begins from the bottom up in spontaneous direct action is indicative of their thinking that revolutionary strategy should establish a mould from which the social future should emerge. It is for these reasons that anarchists have long been associated with campaigns of direct action, and have frequently been labelled as radical activists. That is, people taking control of the revolutionary process themselves, a revolution from the bottom up without direction from a hierarchical and centralised party. To this end, anarchism has been identified with syndicalism. For both anarchists and syndicalists are sceptical of the involvement of outsiders in their attempts to transform society, and both regard most if not all forms of action as legitimate within the revolutionary arsenal of direct action.

To be sure, there is significant overlap between anarchism and syndicalism, but there are also some crucial differences. Moreover, it is in these dissimilarities that further reinforcement of the anarchists' critique of democracy is to be found. To begin with there is suspicion in anarchist quarters that syndicalism's dependence on trade unions may lead to sectional disagreements. Further, trade unions are particularly susceptible to economic and ideological incorporation into capital. More significantly for anarchists such as Kropotkin there is an unwarranted emphasis on the industrial proletariat at the expense of other groups in society such as the peasants or, for Bakunin, the lumpenproletariat. This latter critique is also directed more widely at Marxism. Anarchists have always questioned the political significance attached to the industrial proletariat by Marxists and others. It is certainly not clear to anarchists that the industrial working class will be the leading revolutionary group in society. If anything, it is precisely this group that is likely to be deflected from revolutionary objectives towards satisfaction of class demands (Miller, 1984: 128-133). In other words, if any group is likely to be influenced and thereby succumb to the economic and political allure of democratic regimes it is, for anarchists, the working classes. Accordingly, universal suffrage entices those sectors of society with the promise of social mobility and other rewards, whether they are by nature economic, social or welfare. It is, then, the dispossessed and disenfranchised that represent the most revolutionary sector of society for anarchism. Indeed anarchists would point out that it was literally the disenfranchised, those that had deliberately avoided electoral registration, that played a key part in recent opposition to the poll tax (See for example, Karycinska (1991) and Burns (1992).)

In more recent times, anarchism has revisited its relationship with democracy. There have been notable attempts by philosophical anarchists to reconcile liberty with authority. Wolff's excellent short treatise, *In Defense of Anarchism*, is a spirited endeavour to illustrate how universal direct democracy maintains the autonomy of individuals that are still required to accede to the authority of law. From a different perspective, Robert Graham utilises Carole Pateman's concept of self-assumed obligation to argue that there is a form of direct democracy that anarchists could subscribe to without reservation (1989: 170-171). Reflecting classical anarchists' commitment to federalism, self-assuming obligations amount in a participatory democracy to political obligations to other citizens only.

Pateman's model, outlined in her text *The Problem of Political Obligation*, embodies horizontal relationships rather than the vertical relationships of authority that are the hallmarks of state institutions. Further, Pateman claims that direct democracy is not inextricably linked to majority rule. Those in a minority can either consent to a majority decision or refuse to recognise it as binding and dissent.

Unquestionably, anarchists reject the tyranny of the majority and strive to create a future society based on freedom and autonomy. Anarchists are reluctant to present blueprints for change, as they do not wish to foreclose debate over the shape or nature of future society. Once again, this reluctance to draw detailed plans for a future anarchy reflects the prefigurative nature of the movement and its ideology. However, anarchism does embody a number of important goals that suggest an outline for the future. It is more than coincidence that most of the classical anarchists envisage a future of freely federated communes that are organised in a decentralised community that incorporates some notion of direct democracy. To achieve those objectives anarchists insist that the means of change must be consistent with and mirror the principles that underscore those ultimate objectives. To that end, efforts to achieve these ends that rely on the ballot box, on representative democracy or any kind of political party, whether revolutionary or otherwise, are futile and doomed to failure. Anarchists may be painfully aware of a long hard struggle ahead before they can even begin to see sight of their goals. Nevertheless, they are steadfast in their determination not to attempt foolish shortcuts that by their very nature jeopardise their central objectives and principles. For the classical anarchists, any revolutionary strategy must comprise in embryonic form the aims and objectives of a future anarchist society.

Anarchism, Democracy and the Anti-Capitalist Movement

There are various reasons for diverting a discussion on anarchism and democracy into an analysis of the current anti-capitalist movement (ACM). In practical terms this is simply because the ACM is comprised of a large number of groups and individuals who would describe themselves as anarchists or who embody libertarian sentiments. As Graeber has argued, 'anarchism is the heart of the movement, its soul; the source of most of what's new and hopeful about it' (2002: 62). Conversely, it might be said that the coming together of a mass movement against capitalism over the last 5-10 years has given anarchism as an ideology a much-needed shot in the arm.

However, in the context of our discussion of anarchism and democracy there is a more pressing reason to study the ACM. This is that the ACM is itself highly prefigurative and seeks to pursue struggles in ways that combine means and ends. As such, abstract libertarian attitudes towards power and decision making come to life and are embedded in the nature of day-to-day organisation and action.

Before considering the way that anarchist principle is played out in the ACM, we need to briefly consider the scope of the movement itself. In this, we would follow the usual convention of describing the movement as a heterogeneous network of international, national and local campaigns. At a minimalist level, these hang together through their self-proclaimed or de facto opposition to the globalised free market and its institutions/effects. In this sense, it is a movement positioned around an often vague but nonetheless powerful sentiment, which has appeared in a particular historical context (the post Cold War victory of the market and the disappearance of the Stalinist left). Practically though this is a movement of movements – incorporating peace advocates; debt campaigners; street partyers and reclaimers; animal rights groups; sex workers, sweat shop activists and environmentalists (to name but a few).

This is not really the place to launch a grand typology of the ACM. Rather we need to pull out from the movement specific tendencies and notions that display its anarchist core. However the first step towards doing that is to note that the ACM contains within it ideas and organisations that are explicitly *not* anarchistic. These belong to the various Leninist and Trotskyist parties who have temporarily put their transitional programmes on hold in order to catch the coat tails of this new vital movement. In the UK, the predominant Marxist presence in the ACM would be the Socialist Workers Party and its high profile front, Globalise Resistance (for an account of the SWP's role in the ACM see Leeds Earth First! 1999). Explicitly, these Marxist groupings are non-prefigurative and cling on to highly structured and centralised forms of organisation (premised on the previously discussed Leninist view of the Party and Marxist concept of the Dictatorship of the Proletariat).

As noted above, the ACM as a whole displays strong anarchistic tendencies and is certainly 'more anarchist than Marxist'. That anarchism itself is of a non-monolithic, diverse nature with regard to its analysis, types of action and 'body language'. One way to bundle these diverse trajectories is provided by Murray Bookchin in his controversial tract, *Social Anarchism or Lifestyle Anarchism: an unbridgeable chasm*. In Bookchin's typology social anarchists are those adopting a class analysis of society and seeking to deploy it in a direct assault on capitalism as a socio-economic system. As such, their goal is explicitly revolutionary with a target of complete systemic transformation. Lifestyle anarchism is however, for Bookchin, a post-modern phenomena rooted in post-materialist values. Consequently lacking structural analysis, its focus is not and cannot be a systemic assault on capitalism per se. Instead, lifestyle anarchism is seen as a disparate set of campaigns seeking individual autonomy and self-expression, in a variety of realms from the cultural to the spiritual and mystical. It is worth noting here that Bookchin's categorisation has been denounced by contemporary anarchist writers like Bob Black. For Black, there is no such thing as lifestyle anarchism. Rather it is a pejorative marker that Bookchin employs to identify those he disapproves of (Black, 1997).

There is then a sense in which the ACM's anarchism can be seen as an admixture of the social and lifestyle, a diverse patchwork of revolts and intuitive rebellions. Within this, there probably is a distinction to be drawn between those anarchists who see the need for national federations and a relatively high degree of organisation and those preferring autonomy and localism. However, the general description of the movement as *prefigurative* still holds. As such, all contemporary anarchists would agree on the need for non-hierarchical organisations in which decisions are a work in progress and made by those affected (with rights for minorities to mount challenges, pursue alternatives or withdraw their consent at any time). Similarly, there is a do-it-yourself ethic in which activists seek to encourage the activism and participation of others, rather than to establish control over them (McKay, 1998). In stark contrast to the Marxist left, there is also what might be called a de-privileging of formal organisations and a disinterest in signing up members. Rather, to use the phrase favoured by *Reclaim the Streets*, contemporary libertarian groups should be regarded as 'organised coincidences' with an emphasis on the production of spontaneity and autonomous action.

This process of doing and encouraging – the propaganda of the deed – happens of course in distinctive places. As such, there are geographically based groups working in specific towns and cities (sometimes as parts of wider federations). For many anarchists this local work is of prime importance as it takes place within real communities. It also forms the ideal contexts in which prefigurative direct democracy can flourish. However, the link between the local and the national has become more complex and mediated in the electronic age through the media of e-mail, websites and discussion lists. These forms of communication can both connect remote places as well as enriching purely local interactions and activism (as, for example, with the *Bristol Activists* e-discussion list, 2002).

Decision making then in the contemporary ACM should perhaps be regarded as an organic and networked process, with a momentum towards action that works through different geographical locations and organisational settings. This is not to claim an equality of influence in the process or to ignore the fact that certain groups have sufficient kudos to often play a determining role in certain actions. However, through the medium of open meetings and organising committees, the ability to influence is largely determined by willingness to become involved. As such, decisions are ultimately contingent upon and played out in the unglamorous work of designing leaflets, web site posting and room booking. This is particularly so as most anti-capitalist groups lack the permanent administrative and secretarial structures so central to mainstream political life.

This absence of a supporting bureaucracy leads onto an important theoretical issue. For in conventional politics a distinction is usually drawn between the *decisional* and *executive* functions – a distinction that is present in both formal state structures and the political parties. In central and local government, this denotes a specific group of people who have the formal power to decide – councillors, MPs, Ministers – decisions that then acquire a legal status and formal authority. These subsequently are passed to another group for implementation purposes – officials and civil servants. They then have legal powers to enforce certain actions and exclude others and in doing so, override dissent and the will of minorities. A similar distinction between decision makers and implementing bureaucracy can be found in the political parties – between the Labour/Tory leadership and their Millbank/Central Office staff, for example.

It should be noted immediately that this is a somewhat formalistic presentation of the decision-making and implementation process in conventional politics. There are in fact many points at which policy can be influenced and created and formal decisions are really part of a wider policy cycle. However, it is important to note the 'separation of powers' that sits at the heart of traditional democratic theory and practical politics. This however is absent from (or at least only minimally present) in anarchist politics. For obvious reasons the idea of having powerful central committees is rejected because such structures offend principles of autonomy and spontaneity. In practice there is a near total overlap between those who decide what to do and those who actually do it – embodied in the concept of the *activist*. In passing, it should be noted that this integration of decision making and implementation is not unique to anarchist politics and has been a feature of feminist politics and many other new social movements for thirty years or more. With this integration, however, anarchist principles are given an organisational form. As Graeber has argued, the ACM's anarchist ideology is 'immanent in the anti-authoritarian principles that underlie [its] practice' (2002: 72).

There are, of course, times when decisions as to a particular course of action have to be made, in the context of specific meetings or conferences. With the anarchist rejection of representative democracy, this really leaves a choice between forms of direct democracy and *consensus building*. Many favour the former, as 'direct democratic voting on policy decisions within free associations is the political counterpoint of free agreement.' (Anarchist FAQs, 2002). In a libertarian future, free associations would be workplace or community gatherings comprised of all of the citizens involved, forming themselves into a horizontal political authority (as well as being a model for present day anarchist politics). Direct democracy in this context should not be seen as a form of *majority rule* and minorities would have full rights to continue arguing and propose alternatives, as well as the right to leave – rights of *voice* and *exit*.

Though most anarchist and anti-capitalist movements combine elements of direct democracy and consensus building, the latter should be regarded as a distinctive way of deciding. For rather than voting and creating winners/losers, consensus building seeks to create unanimity and solutions that are acceptable to all – and only proceeds when that agreement has been reached. This itself may simply be the product of ongoing discussion and debate or could involve techniques designed to articulate and resolve the different views. Perhaps more prevalent in North America, these mechanisms include the use of 'spokes councils' and affinity groups within specific meetings or conferences (see Graeber, 2002: 70-2). Anarchist opponents of consensus building as a basis for decision making, argue however that these processes can give too much blocking power to small minorities and operate as a barrier to progress. For this reason consensus building may also apply undue psychological pressure onto small groups of dissenters and individuals (Anarchist FAQs, 2002). Furthermore, Bookchin has argued consensus building may foster a lowest common denominator effect in which safe options are pursued. As such, it 'precludes ongoing dissensus – the all important process of continual dialogue, disagreement, challenge and counter challenge, without which social as well as individual creativity would be impossible' (1995: 17).

Principle in Practice: the Mayday Protests

In the post-war period, Mayday in the West has been sanitised and lost its connection to both a tradition of working-class militancy and its earlier incarnation as a neo-pagan festival of misrule and revelry. It might still see workers on the streets, but only in an orderly procession to an officially sanctioned meeting point, to hear Labourist politicians and union leaders. Since 1999, however Mayday has been reclaimed for both older traditions and has become a key fixture in the anti-capitalist calendar. The way in which this has happened says much about the centrality of anarchist ideas and forms of mobilisation – as do the nature of the protests themselves. For the recent Mayday mobilisations can be seen as prefiguration in action and as acts of organised spontaneity. They also illustrate the way the movement has had to refine its tactics in response to policing strategies.

The revival of more vibrant Mayday protests should of course be seen in the context of mass street protests against globalised capital that became a feature of the late 1990s (for example the anti-WTO protests at Davos of 1998 and the international Day of Action against Capitalism of June 18th 1999). In this new setting, groups of class war anarchists and ecologists met in Bradford in 1998 to plan direct actions for the following Mayday (for a more detailed history see Do or Die, 2000 and Urban 75, 2002). This saw successful events in London and elsewhere in 1999 and the start of what may now have become a tradition. Subsequent protests have seen a major organising role played by established anti-capitalist groups such as *Reclaim the Streets* and *Earth First!* However, larger general gatherings such as the annual Anarchist Bookfair have started to take more direct responsibility – along with open organising meetings and conferences.

Each Mayday from 2000 onwards has really operated at two interlinked levels. Firstly the day has seen a series of specific actions run by individual groups of campaigners, such as Critical Mass bike rides, anti-fur actions, debt campaigns and McProtests. Secondly, though, each year has had a particular theme or strategy, developed by the organising committee:

Guerilla Gardening – In 2000 an attempt was made to reclaim Parliament Square by ripping up the tarmac and planting flowers and shrubs in it. This was later followed by Winston Churchill's cele-

brated tonsorial transformation (as well as the less celebrated deface-
ment of the Cenotaph).

Mayday Monopoly – In 2001 the Mayday organising committee created a Monopoly Board (on its website) suggesting particular places
of interest in the centre of London – banks, the arms trade etc. –
which protestors might like to 'visit'. As the day unfolded, activists
became trapped within a police cordon in Oxford Street and were
illegally detained there for several hours.

Mayday in Mayfair – In 2002 there was a concerted effort to avoid
being penned and those attending were encouraged to remain on the
move to keep the Met guessing. As such, the emphasis was on promoting self-organised affinity groups to promote their own actions
rather than announcing a single event or assembly point (though the
general area of Mayfair with its wealth and Embassies was highlighted by organisers as the target zone).

The 2002 Mayday website made a clear attempt to rediscover older traditions of Mayday by suggesting participants mount a game of 'Carniball',
something akin to the mass village football games that ebbed and flowed
over great distances in the countryside. Organisers also encouraged a travelling circus of 'jesters, jugglers, minstrels, show girls, gypsies, pagan sor-
cerers, ring masters, ring mistresses and clowns.' (Mayday Collective,
2002). As such, capitalism was confronted by something that was at once
both 'fluffy' and determined, deploying humour and disobedience against
money. This saw a series of running (non-violent) skirmishes with police
throughout the day as well as a more sustained piece of partying in Soho in
the evening (around a Sex Workers Pride event). All this was in contrast to
a TUC/Globalise Resistance march and rally taking place on Mayday in
central London. This protest embodied a quite different politics and organisational strategy – turn up at the pre-determined muster point; march along
a marshalled, police agreed route; listen to speeches and go home. This
division between direct action and carnival on the one hand and sanctioned,
traditional protest on the other, continued in 2003. Around the theme of
Weapons of Mass Construction a number of actions took place against
firms who had benefited from the Iraq War, alongside a predictable TUC
march to Trafalgar Square.

TACT and the Anarchist Travelling Circus

Two planned UK developments provide further examples of the way that anarchist attitudes towards democracy and decision-making are central to questions of strategy:

(T)emporary (A)nti-(C)apitalist (T)eams – As in any form of politics the existence of a wide variety of groups has both its strengths and weaknesses. In particular, the vitality of difference and autonomy can often militate against the formation of effective alliances and campaigns. This is precisely so in a movement that values localism and is inherently suspicious of centralisation and hierarchy, even when these are pursued in the name of effectiveness. Such sentiments have led to social and lifestyle anarchist groups finding it difficult to join anything other than the most minimal federations. One solution recently proposed is the idea of *Temporary Anti-Capitalist Teams (TACT)*. These are intended to be short-term fluid coalitions that might take place within individual communities (for example, campaigning against a road development) or on a wider scale. Practically this would involve individuals and groups agreeing to work together for the duration the specific project, providing mutual support, sharing ideas and mounting joint actions. These would be leaderless alliances and would not require anyone to 'join' a new organisation (for more details see TACT, 2002).

The Anarchist Travelling Circus – In a parallel development plans have recently come together for a series of protests around the UK and beyond, adopting the name provided by Tony Blair when describing anti-capitalist protestors. This will see a number of events taking place from Mayday 2003 through to the G8 summit in France the following month. Planned actions are likely to include gigs and street parties, protests, film shows and food. Distinctively, the *Anarchist Travelling Circus* will seek to work with existing local campaigns, groups and social centres – adding an impetus and level of support to real struggles and movements rather than imposing a central template. Consequently, in as much as there is an organisational centre to the *Circus*, it is likely to generate ideas and operate as a network. This is reflected in the way that proposals for the Circus have come together. As with the rebirth of Mayday, this has seen open meetings at the *Earth First!* gathering and Anarchist Bookfair, as well as ongoing suggestions and debates on e-discussion lists.

Conclusion

Anarchists then reject that which is most cherished in modern political systems – the idea that the popular will is best expressed through the isolated action of voting and the selection of representatives. This rejection proceeds from libertarian first principles and the view that democratic processes ultimately validate systems of authority and repression. In this way, anarchists regard the democratic model as inevitably linked to the generation of hierarchy in general and the modern state in particular. As such, that which is supposed to represent the voice of the people is deeply implicated in power structures that serve to limit and oppress.

In place of democracy, anarchists promote participatory decision making in non-hierarchical settings. With this, they are using a decisional process embedded in everyday life and in the day-to-day operation of real communities. This organic and natural way of reaching conclusions – through discussion and involvement – is central to the emerging anti-capitalist movement that has flourished over the last five years. With this, anarchist ideas and ways of working have found their way to the heart of modern radical politics.

References

Anarchist FAQs (2002) *What Does Anarchism Stand For?* Available online. http://www.geocities.com/CapitolHill/1931/secA2.html#seca211 (Accessed: 1 September 2002).

Bakunin, M. (1990) *Statism and Anarchy* (Cambridge: Cambridge University Press).

Beetham, D. (1977) 'From Socialism to Fascism: The Relation between Theory and Practice in the Work of Robert Michels. I. From Marxist Revolutionary to Political Sociologist', *Political Studies*, vol. 25:1; 3-24.

Bookchin, M. (1995) *Social Anarchism or Lifestyle Anarchism: An Unbridgeable Chasm* (San Francisco: AK Press).

Bristol Activists (2002). Available online. http://groups.yahoo.com/group/bristolactivists (Accessed: 1 September 2002).

Burns, D. (1992) *Poll Tax Rebellion* (Stirling: AK Press).

Cadogan, P. (1991) 'Freedom to Vote? Freedom from Voting?', *The Raven*, vol. 4:2; 101-13.

Clark, J. (1984) *The Anarchist Moment: Reflections on Culture, Nature and Power* (Montréal: Black Rose Books).

Do or Die (2000) *May Day: Guerrilla? Gardening?* Available online. http://www.eco-action.org/dod/no9/may_day.htm (Accessed: 1 September 2002).

Engels, F. (1975) 'Letter to P. van Patten, 18 April 1883', in Marx Engels: *Selected Correspondence* (Moscow: Progress Publishers).

Engels, F. (1874) *On Authority.* Available online. http://csf.colorado.edu/psn/marx/Archive/1872-Auth/ (Accessed: 2 December 2002).

Graeber, D. (2002) 'The New Anarchists', *New Left Review*, vol. 13; 61-73.

Graham, R. (1989) 'The Role of Contract in Anarchist Ideology' in D. Goodway (ed.) *For Anarchism: History, Theory and Practice* (London: Routledge). 150-175.

Guérin, D. (1989) 'Marxism and Anarchism' in D. Goodway (ed.) *For Anarchism: History, Theory and Practice* (London: Routledge). 109-126.

Joll, J. (1979) *The Anarchists* (London: Methuen).

Karycinska, Z. (1991) 'The Exercise of Real Power', *The Raven*, vol. 4:2; 126-9.

Kropotkin, P. (1970a) 'Anarchist Communism: Its Basis and Principles' in R.N. Baldwin (ed.) *Kropotkin's Revolutionary Pamphlets* (New York: Dover Publications). 44-78.

Kropotkin, P. (1970b) 'Revolutionary Government' in R.N. Baldwin (ed.) *Kropotkin's Revolutionary Pamphlets* (New York: Dover Publications). 236-250.

Kropotkin, P. (1992) 'Representative Government' in *Words of a Rebel* (Montréal: Black Rose Books). 118-144.

Kropotkin, P. (1993) 'Must We Occupy Ourselves with an Examination of the Ideal of a Future System?' in *Fugitive Writings* (Montréal: Black Rose Books). 13-68.

Leeds Earth First! (1999) *Vampire Alert.* Available online. http://www.leedsef.org.uk/swp.htm (Accessed: 1 September 2002).

Marshall, P. (ed.) (1986) *The Anarchist Writings of William Godwin* (London: Freedom Press).

Marshall, P. (1992) *Demanding the Impossible: A History of Anarchism* (London: HarperCollins).

Marx, K. (1974) 'Critique of the Gotha Programme' in *The First International and After: Political Writings*, Volume 3 (Harmondsworth: Penguin). 339-359.

Maximoff, G.P. (ed.) (1964) *The Political Philosophy of Bakunin: Scientific Anarchism* (Glencoe: Free Press).

Mayday Collective (2002) *Mayday in Mayfair.* Available online. http://www.nadir.org/nadir/kampagen/ourmayday/may1st.htm (Accessed: 29 April 2002).

McKay, G. (ed.) (1998) *DiY Culture: Party and Protest in Nineties Britain* (London: Verso).

Miller, D. (1984) *Anarchism* (London: Dent and Sons).

Morland, D. (1997) *Demanding the Impossible: Human Nature and Politics in Nineteenth-Century Social Anarchism* (London: Cassell).

Powell, T. (1991) 'The "Purists", the "Realists" and the Straitjacket: Emma Goldman, the Spanish Anarchists, and the February Elections, 1936', *The Raven*, vol. 4:2; 148-64.

Proudhon, P-J. (1840) *What is Property?* Available online. http://sailor.gutenberg.org/etext95/pprty10.txt (Accessed: 4 December 2002).

TACT (2002) *Temporary Anti-capitalist Teams*. Available online. http://www.red-star-research.org.uk/tact/tact2.html (Accessed: 1 September 2002).

Urban 75 (2002) *History of Mayday*. Available online. http://www.urban75.org/mayday02/history.html (Accessed: 1 September 2002).

Vincent, A. (1992) *Modern Political Ideologies* (Oxford: Blackwell).

Wolff, R.P. (1976) *In Defense of Anarchism* (New York: Harper Torchbooks).

Woodcock, G. (1975) *Anarchism: A History of Libertarian Ideas and Movements* (Harmondsworth: Penguin).

Wright, S. (2000) *Changing the World (One Bridge at a Time)? Ya Basta after* Prague. http://www.geocities.com/swervedc/yabasta.html

5. IDEAS AND INTERESTS:
The Struggle for Democracy and Free Speech during the Nineteenth Century

John Steel

How does the concept of democracy relate to the idea and practice of freedom of speech? Why is freedom of speech so important to democratic systems? The relationship between freedom of speech, democracy and protest is both theoretically and historically intertwined. Struggles for democratic representation have often gone hand in hand with calls for freedom of speech, either as a component of democratic reform, or as a means to secure greater democracy. Though we could refer to and explore many examples of that struggle, this chapter will focus on just one – the struggle for democracy in England during the nineteenth century. I have chosen to focus on this period because of its raw and vibrant intellectual and political climate, a climate that was particularly colourful during the first part of the nineteenth century. New ideas from the enlightenment, ideas that asserted freedom, accountability and human progress sought to challenge the powerful yet stagnant regimes of church and state. Democracy was the political system that would ensure that privilege and corruption would cease, and freedom of speech, mainly through freedom of the press would buttress the democratic process.

This chapter then will provide an historical and theoretical insight into the relationship between freedom of speech (expressed as freedom of the press) and democracy during this turbulent period of English history. The chapter will firstly outline the social and political context of the period before moving on to highlight the importance of the press to this particular story. From here, we will explore the ideas of two of the most influential thinkers of the late eighteenth/early nineteenth centuries – Jeremy Bentham and Thomas Paine. We will then go on to look at how their ideas influenced the radical press with particular emphasis on the utilitarian Philosophic Radicals and the working class radicalism that was inspired by Paine. Before concluding, this chapter will attempt to show how, in the end the battle for freedom of speech and democracy was eventually won and in particular, in whose interests this victory was gained. This analysis will not only highlight what a turbulent period of English history this was, but also the connection between political ideas and political action.

Context

Britain at the beginning of the nineteenth century was a country of great power and wealth; it was also a place of enormous change and upheaval. Moreover, the defeat of Napoleon at the battle of Waterloo in 1815 seemed to confirm Britain as the global power, economically and militarily. London was increasingly recognised as the world centre of finance and the motor force of capitalist expansion. In addition to Britain's economic growth, its Empire was also expanding, more so than any other country at this time. Such a period of change and flux impacted greatly on life in Britain. The socio-economic changes that were well underway by the beginning of the nineteenth century, impacted significantly on the demographics of Britain. For example, the population grew massively from 12 million at the beginning of the century to 31 million in 1885 (Beales, 1969: 15). This growth in population was reflected in the growth of towns and cities, for example: Liverpool had grown from 82,000 in 1801 to 202,000 in 1831; Leeds from 53,000 to 123,000, with towns like Sheffield and Birmingham doubling in size during the same period (Woodward, 1992: 2). Such demographic changes also affected the nature of the population as a better-educated workforce was sought after to work in the factories of these growing towns and cities.

Intellectual life also mirrored the changes in Britain's economic and social sphere. New ideas, which were influenced in part by the revolutions in America (1776) and France (1789), found a new and receptive audience. The extent and ferocity of such changes acted as a catalyst to the upsurge in radicalism and political activism which sought dramatic changes in the social and political landscape of Britain. The focus of much of this radicalism was the British system of government which was widely seen as corrupt and unrepresentative of the majority of the people. Given this background, and the long tradition of dissent in Britain, the climate for protest and conflict was ripe.

The Press

Since the time of Elizabeth I, there had been strict controls over the press in England. Though these controls wavered from time to time, those in power had always sought to prohibit and censure 'dangerous' views expressed in print. It was most often during times of great anxiety for those in power, times when their power was threatened, that the control of the press was at its most austere. If we look at the turn of the nineteenth century in particular, we see that the increasing spread of democratic ideals made the authorities particularly nervous. This, and the continuing war with France, only added to the paranoia of the government. Such paranoia meant that those in power felt the need to curtail the spread of dangerous ideas. After the Peterloo Massacre[8] in 1819 concern about rising radicalism prompted the government to introduce the notorious Six Acts which sought to inhibit the rise of democratic reform by a number of means. Within these Acts there was to be a curtailment or licensing of public meetings; the prevention and punishment of literature that was deemed blasphemous or seditious, and an increase in the infamous 'stamp tax' to four pence for each copy. This tax was first introduced in 1712 in order to control the spread of 'dangerous' pamphlets and newspapers (see Wickwar, 1928). The idea was that the taxation would push up the price of publications and such a high price would inhibit the circulation of 'dangerous ideas' particularly amongst the working classes. During these times of revolt and unrest, there was a great increase in 'blasphemous' and 'seditious' literature, literature that were of course deemed illegal. By the beginning of the 1830's, the battle between radical publishers and government became what Joel Wiener (1969) terms the 'War of the Unstamped'.

The increasing complexity of a burgeoning industrial society, coupled with the associated problems brought about by massive social and economic change, presented the authorities with a wide range of critics and dissenters. Moreover, with a greater opportunity for the dissemination of critical and dissenting ideas through mass-produced printed material, political struggle and the mechanics of protest entered a new more vigorous phase of expression. Dissenting pamphlets and newspapers provided the prosecuting authorities with no shortage of targets. Such pamphlets were produced by small publishers and widely sold in industrial towns and cities. Given the political turmoil of the time, it is no surprise that most of the prosecutions for seditious libel during the early part of the nineteenth were centred on two key issues: the first concerned the war with France; the second, political reform.

As we can see then, this particular time of English history is one of great social and political turbulence and this is evident within the struggle for

---

8   At a rally at St. Peters field in Manchester, the yeomanry charged and killed eleven people. This later came to be known as the Peterloo Massacre.

free speech and democracy in the early part of the nineteenth century. However, thus far what is missing from this picture is any sense of the ideas that lie behind the popular protest movements for parliamentary reform. It would therefore be helpful if we looked at some of the intellectual influences of the day. For this we can now turn to Thomas Paine and Jeremy Bentham.

Paine and Bentham

Thomas Paine (1736-1809) is an important thinker in terms of struggles for free speech and democracy. Arguments that asserted freedom of speech often went hand in hand with arguments that sought to extend the franchise. The political establishment in Britain and America regarded Paine as a dangerous radical, yet in Paris he was viewed as a moderate (Hobsbawm, 1997: 54). His ideas resonate through much dissenting literature of the time. Paine distrusted the aristocracy, arguing that hereditary systems of government 'degenerate into ignorance'; and the people at large should run their own affairs through democratic representation. Indeed, 'Paine devoted his life to methods of scattering and subdividing power, to ensuring that it was not monopolised by any single pair of hands or particular "faction". (Keane, 1996: xiv)'

> The fact therefore must be that the individuals themselves, each in his own personal and sovereign right, entered into a compact with each other to produce a Government: and this is the only mode in which Governments had a right to arise, and the only principle in which they have a right to exist (Paine, 1995: 122).

Paine was attempting here to provide a theoretical account of what had happened in America in 1776 and what was happening in France in 1789. In defending the Revolutions against hereditary interests, in favour of notions of natural rights and common interests, Paine was providing a politicised formula for democracy that was both influenced by the democrats of ancient Greece, and by the Enlightenment belief in science and progress. Pamphleteers and agitators took to Paine's words and set about reprinting and disseminating his work, much to the concern and annoyance of those in power. Moreover, his arguments for liberty of the press, particularly in relation to democratic accountability were powerful ammunition for radicals and dissenters during the first forty years of the nineteenth century. It was clear that robust and open public debate 'had confirmed Paine's view that a "free press" was a fundamental ingredient of republican liberty (Keane, 1996: 463-4). Paine's vision of democracy was one that was open to all and as such accountable. Accountability was a necessary component of Paine's view of democracy and this sentiment was carried through by dissenters and radicals into the nineteenth century.

However, Paine's ideas were not the only ones to influence the radical spirit of the age. Jeremy Bentham (1748-1832) was a highly influential thinker and the founder of utilitarianism. The main focus of Bentham's intellectual energies was political and legal reform. His aim was to reorganise the structure of social institutions around purely rational principles. Such rational principles would provide the framework for ending corruption and self interest in government and ensuring the best political system. Bentham argued that the only criterion for evaluating legal and political institutions was the degree to which they increased or decreased the general happiness amongst the greater number of people in the country. For Bentham it was human nature that people seek happiness and avoid pain. From this starting point it is possible to view all human activity as either good in that it promotes happiness; or bad as it brings about pain or unhappiness. This is the principle of utility.

> Nature has placed mankind under the governance of two sovereign masters, pain and pleasure. It is for them alone to point out what we ought to do, as well as to determine what we shall do. [...] They govern us all in all we do, in all we say, in all we think: every effort we can make to throw off our subjection, will serve but to demonstrate and confirm it (Bentham, 1970: 11).

This assertion then is the primary statement Bentham makes in his seminal work, *An Introduction to the Principles of Morals and Legislation* published in 1789. In this text, Bentham briefly sets out the premise of the principle of utility and then in detail how it should be applied to society and the legal system. The principle of utility was the cornerstone of Bentham's political philosophy; all of his recommendations for good government and the appropriate legal and political systems stem from this principle. Bentham argued that the main business of government was to secure the interests, indeed the happiness of society at large. It was the task of good government to increase the stock of happiness for the majority of society. For Bentham democracy was the system of government which would pro-

mote the greatest happiness for the greatest number as the people themselves would be able to rid themselves of bad or corrupt representatives and
replace them with ones that shared the interests of the people.

Though writing at roughly the same time, Paine and Bentham offer justifications of democracy that rest on differing moral and epistemological
conceptions of man. Thomas Paine in his *Rights of Man* argues that all governments should be held accountable at all times; not to some divine entity, but to the people at large. For Paine, in order for a democratic society to
operate effectively, and according to certain inalienable 'natural rights',
those in government should be held accountable by a free and unrestricted
press.

Bentham, too, argued that democracy was the best political system.
However, this was not based on a conception of natural rights as it was for
Paine; for Bentham, notions of rights were nothing more than 'nonsense on
stilts'. Democratic institutions were viewed as the best form of government
because they were the systems most likely to promote the greatest happiness for the greatest number. It was in relation to Bentham's principle of
utility that all actions and all systems should be judged and not some
abstract notion of rights whether they be 'liberty', 'equality' or 'fraternity'.
In terms of freedom of speech, this was seen by both as essential for
democracy, as both Bentham and Paine thought that freedom of speech,
usually via freedom of the press, was necessary for holding those in power
accountable to the people. However, the basis on which such a system is
based differs both morally and epistemologically. For Bentham democracy
was not to be justified in terms of abstract notions of natural rights as it was
for Paine, but in terms of utility. As Arblaster notes:

> Since each person pursued his or her own well being, it followed that
> each person would vote in his or her own interest. The sum total of
> individual votes ought therefore to promote the utilitarian objective
> of the greatest happiness of the greatest number. The only people
> who could be trusted to pursue the good of the people were the peo-
> ple themselves, acting through their elected and accountable repre-
> sentatives. (1987: 44-45)

Accountability is one of the cornerstones of democracy and freedom of
speech has a major part to play in the effective working of a democracy.
Indeed, it is the notion of accountability that connects free speech and
democracy together. In short, freedom of speech, usually via a free and

unrestricted press, is necessary to ensure good government, primarily by holding those in power accountable in the public arena. In doing so, any perceived wrongdoing or error enacted by government, can be challenged in an open arena of public debate that is facilitated by freedom of speech.

In a democracy, it is important that the sovereign people have at their disposal all information regarding the dealings of government. Information regarding the practices, procedures and outcomes of political life needs to be made available to all within a democracy so that governments can be seen to be operating according to the wishes of the sovereign people. For example, at the end of the 18th century the MP John Wilkes was prosecuted for publishing works that were considered both blasphemous and obscene, more famously he was prosecuted for publishing the proceedings of Parliament. The controversy surrounding this affair was a very important development in the struggle for freedom of speech, and as Patricia Hollis (1970: 28) notes, during the 1770's Wilkes's struggle had eventually established the right of newspapers to report Parliamentary debates. Ultimately this means that the people at large were now in a position to receive information about the workings of government and ultimately be better informed about the political process. We can see then that for a democracy to operate according to its fundamental principles, accountability is a key component. In other words, the people must have information about decisions made in their name within democratic systems, as such their representative are fully accountable. However, related to the dissemination of information relating to the activities of the peoples' representatives is the important notion that the people also have the opportunity to publicly censure their representatives. Hence, freedom of speech is necessary to allow such censure to occur unhindered from government interference. It is this notion of accountability that makes freedom of speech essential to democratic government.

The ideas from radicals such as Paine and Bentham greatly impacted practices and institutions that dated back as far as the Reformation. These systems of governance were now starting to look out of place in this new and fast changing world of the industrial age. Cracks and contradictions were beginning to appear in the machinery of government and dissenters inspired by Bentham and Paine and other radical thinkers would seek to expose and exploit such fissures and weaknesses. What we will do now is look more closely at how the ideas of Bentham and Paine influenced, in different ways, the struggle for free speech and democracy.

Ideas in Action

Part of the struggle for free speech and democracy was fought through the radical press; criticisms of the corruption and self-interest of those in power were common in dissenting newspapers and pamphlets. As we have seen, the different ideas of Bentham and Paine were highly influential during the struggle for democracy during the nineteenth century. What we will do now is explore how these ideas informed the practice of radicals and agitators by looking at the ideas contained in the radical press. During the early part of the nineteenth century, the utilitarian press inspired much radical activity. True to Bentham's principles it sought to challenge corruption and greed in government. Much of the utilitarian press intended to inform and educate the masses in the virtues of utilitarianism, and make Bentham's ideas accessible to a wider range of readers. Collectively the followers of Bentham were known as the Philosophic Radicals; this group of middle class men sought to spread the word of utilitarianism and educate the working classes in the virtues of utilitarian thinking and practice. For the Philosophic Radicals, education in particular was seen as a possible saviour of the working classes as they thought that the poor conditions of the working classes were caused mainly by ignorance. The poor conditions of the working classes were a direct result of their lack of knowledge in matters of politics, economics and philosophy; such knowledge could, however, be provided through the press. The problem was that this was impossible as the taxes on the press raised the price of literature and placed such information out of the reach of many. Such taxes became known as the taxes on knowledge.

The argument was that if the working classes could have the means of attaining information, they would then be in a position to better themselves. This prompted John Arthur Roebuck MP, to publish a series of pamphlets collectively known as Pamphlets for the People. Contained within these pamphlets were utilitarian inspired articles on why and how the existing system of government should be changed and why there should be greater freedom of the press. The aim of the pamphlets was to enlighten the working people and demonstrate the virtues of utilitarianism. It was argued that not only would people become better educated and therefore able to escape their miserable plight, but also that they would become morally sound individuals. Within this remit, the object of the pamphlets was to 'instruct' people in their relative duties as citizens; 'to point out to them the rights that they ought to seek to attain.' It was argued that 'mere' possession of power was not sufficient to ensure good government, what was also necessary was greater knowledge and sound morality. As the *Westminster Review* (1930: 246-247) argued at every opportunity – '[m]orality, as applied to the conduct of individuals, is reducible to being the rule, the general observation of which would provide the greatest happiness amongst those who are to be affected by its consequences.' Such morality and knowledge in the mass of the people would ensure that society would improve, and it was towards this end the pamphlets were published.

In asserting freedom of the press, Roebuck is not only providing justification of a repeal of the stamp tax, he also provides an analysis of why such a system emerged in the first place. He argues that not only does the government make law unintelligible to those that have not studied it, but clarity relating to the law has become hidden, 'buried' within statute upon statute. Moreover, such laws are designed to protect the rich, as they are generally unintelligible to the common person. According to Roebuck, the working people are made ignorant of the information that would protect them from prosecution and hardship.

Ignorance and dependency are states to which working people were doomed because the means to end such ignorance were beyond them. Although highly critical of the laws and their application, utilitarians such as John Roebuck and his friend Francis Place did not just direct their energies towards a critique of the system but also outlined in great detail what the essential features of a good, that is, morally sound and just government are:

> A good government, I take to be that which – 1, insures to every man against oppression, whether foreign or domestic, his personal safety, his property, and his reputation; and – 2, which sagaciously employs the resources and powers of the whole people to perform such necessary labours as cannot so well be done by individual exertion. (Roebuck, 1835-35: 7)

Though the ideas of Bentham and his followers the Philosophic Radicals sought to challenge the corruption of the old regime through the application of utilitarian principles, it is also possible to see that these ideas in practice had another aim, that of socialising the so-called lower orders into the burgeoning system of laissez faire capitalism. Indeed inherent in much of the utilitarian writing of the time was a strong paternalist thrust particularly in the works of utilitarian James Mill, where the emphasis on virtue and political economy are clear[9].

One of the key features of the Philosophic Radicals is their unflinching paternalism as is evident in the works of Roebuck and indeed James Mill. However, early dissenters had a choice, they could indeed follow the works of Bentham and the Philosophic Radicals, or they could look to the work of Paine for inspiration and guidance. Many working class radical did just this. Thomas Paine's *Rights of Man* inspired many radicals towards the end of the eighteenth century and its impact was no less at the beginning of the nineteenth.

After the war with France, there was an expectation that the living conditions of the poor would improve. However this did not materialise, even the middle and upper classes were starting to suffer to some degree. Without any radical reform in the political structure of Britain, reform which gave men the right to have a say in the running of their country, there would be no rest for those who sought to challenge the patronage, corruption and privilege at the heart of the British political system. Those who did challenge the excesses of political privilege provided the so-called 'lower orders' with the ammunition to generate a critical consciousness that would eventually seek to replace the 'oafish' patronage of Parliament with a more democratic system of government. As Hollis (1970) argues in *The Pauper Press*, the working-class justification for freedom of the press, particularly during the early part of the nineteenth century, rested primarily on the extension of the franchise and the repeal of taxes on the poor. The 'Unstamped' press during this time was chiefly concerned with highlighting the injustices of privilege and the corruption inherent within such a non-representative system of government.

One such challenger of the *status quo* was Major John Cartwright (1740-1824) an ex-sailor and early pioneer of the cause of political reform (he was politically active even before the French Revolution); he was active in many of the radical movements of the time. Imprisoned in 1813 for his views, he published a number of reformist works including *Take Your Choice* which was his main work on radical reform and which forms the basis of much of his political philosophy.

---

9 There have been a number of excellent critiques of the middle class struggle for freedom of the press during the nineteenth century, critiques which emphasise paternalism and a level of social engineering. See J. Curran, 1983; J. Curran & J. Seaton, 1999; J. Wiener, 1969, and P. Hollis, 1970.

At the same trial at which Cartwright was being fined £100 for *Take Your Choice*, another political agitator and publisher was also under indictment at the same hearing. Thomas J. Wooler (1786-1853) was not as lucky as Cartwright was as he was imprisoned for fifteen months for similar charges to that of Cartwright. Thomas Wooler was a radical reformer who in 1815 started to publish the radical pamphlet *Black Dwarf,* which John Cartwright supported financially and to which he contributed regular articles and letters. *Black Dwarf* was a sharply satirical pamphlet aimed at making 'public men look ridiculous' (Wickwar, 1928: 57). In some contrast to other pamphlets, Wooler's *Dwarf* held nothing back in its calls for political reform and justice for the poor. Wooler advocated the notion of 'open constitutionalism' where debates about new forms of political organisation were out in the public sphere and open to scrutiny of government and people alike (Wickwar, 1928; Thomas, 1969). The *Black Dwarf* was particularly adept at presenting the *status quo* in stark terms and was often the target of censorship measures and prosecutions. Like other radical pamphlets, the *Black Dwarf* was vehement in its criticism of the 'establishment press' in which the interests of those in power were represented. Such 'corruption of the press' was perceived as a vehicle of exploitation as the 'so-called' middle-class radical press looked to protect the interests of the rich by appealing to working class sensibilities.

The *Black Dwarf* was particularly eloquent when it came to arguing that censorship of such pamphlets was useless, as they only reflected the existence that many working people were experiencing. Unlike the utilitarian radical press, which patronised and preached to the poor, the *Black Dwarf* sought to highlight the self interested nature of the middle class press and did not patronise its audience. As we have seen, the paternalism of the utilitarians saw that the poor needed to be educated as to the causes of their misery and *guided* accordingly. Wooler and Cartwright knew that working men and women were more than capable of realising and understanding the causes of their misery without such paternalistic and overtly moral guidance. Moreover, they were quite capable of coming up with their own solutions to their problems and need not be patronised by the middle-class press, radical or not.

E. P. Thompson in *The Making of the English Working-class* notes that the period of the radical press during the early 1820s was very important in that it paved the way for the emergence of a distinct class consciousness when 'there came a climactic contest between Old Corruption and Reform.' (1980: 781). This is evident in the writings of the working-class radicalism of the day, as the powers of the press were seen as a constituent part of the movement for reform within the context of the interests of the poor, which were not solely parliamentary. Such interests fermented within the context of such radicalism and laid the seeds of working-class movements that were to come much later.

This aspect is evidenced in the work of another pro-reform pamphleteer – William Cobbett (1763-1831). Cobbett was initially a Tory, but after travelling in France and America he became influenced by the work of Thomas Paine; as a result he became more radical and by 1806 was a strong advocate of Parliamentary reform. The first time that Cobbett felt the wrath of the libel laws was in 1810 when a year earlier he had, criticised the use of German troops by Britain to quell a mutiny in Ely. The result was a conviction for seditious libel and a resulting sentence of two years in Newgate prison. (Thomas, 1969). On his release, Cobbett continued to attack British policy in the pages of the *Political Register*; in particular he attacked censorial newspaper taxes. In his popular *Political Register,* Cobbett was vehemently outspoken, reacting against the privileges of the establishment and the liberties they took to the detriment of normal working people. In the hope of stirring up unrest and dissatisfaction amongst the working class Cobbett changed the *Political Register* from a newspaper to a pamphlet and reduced the price to two pence (later to be known as 'Twopenny Trash'). As a result, Cobbett's *Political Register* soon had a circulation of 40,000 and was now the main newspaper/pamphlet to be read by the working classes. As with many of the pro-reform pamphleteers, Cobbett was also a vehement advocate of a free press that he saw as necessary in order to contribute to widespread liberty in general. As Osbourne notes: 'Basic to Cobbett's ardent championing of a free press was his insistence upon the ability of people to choose correctly between truth and error if an argument was presented without favour' (1966: 59).

Cobbett was sure that if he could make people aware of the system upon which their misery was founded, they would understand how and in what way government could be reformed. Issue 'No. 18' of his *Political Register* was one of Cobbett's most celebrated attacks on the political system in Britain. In the pamphlet, Cobbett criticised the nature of its constitutional make up and lambasted those in power for exacting vast amounts of taxes from the working people of the country:

As to the cause of our present miseries, it is the enormous amount of taxes, which the government compels us to pay for the support of its armies, its placemen, its pensioners, and for the payment of the interest of its debt. That is the real cause has been a thousand times proved; and, it is now so acknowledged by the creatures of the government themselves. (*Political Register*, No. 18, November 2, 1816, col. 435.)

He continues:

The remedy is what we have now to look to, and that remedy consists wholly and solely of such a reform in the Commons, or People's House of Parliament [...]. We must have that first or we will have nothing good [...]. (*Political Register*, No. 18, November 2, 1816, col. 435 and 454.)

Twenty thousand copies of the famous 'No. 18' were sold within two weeks, forty-four thousand within a month, and two hundred thousand within the next year (Osbourne, 1966: 54). Wickwar notes that '[I]t was then for the first time that one who was conscious of being a writer with a social message tried to speak to (my emphasis) the people instead of speaking for them, to lead them instead of patronising them, and to educate them instead of lecturing their unheeding Government.' (1928: 54)

As the reform movement took hold, increasingly men were prepared to risk fines or imprisonment for the sake of advocating greater democracy. William Hone (1780-1843) was one such radical reformer. Hone was an auctioneer and bookseller who after his move into publishing in 1818 soon found himself at the mercy of the Attorney General for blasphemous libel. Much of Hone's publications involved parody particularly aimed at the Royal family and the ministers of Government. Hackwood describes Hone's writing at this time as 'always topical and full of invention, and by a happier combination of caricature and satire, they oftener than not accomplished the particular purpose they aimed at [...].' (1912: 219). In 1817, Hone published the pamphlet entitled *Hone's Weekly Commentary,* this short-lived periodical being replaced by the cheaper (two pence) *Reformer;* both publications lambasting the current political set up, and such diatribes were to result in getting Hone and his supporters in trouble.

Clearly, the arguments of the radicals and dissenters highlighted above provide arguments that are similar to those expressed by utilitarians and later by liberal commentators. Notably the fundamental stress on rationality, the search for truth and the assertion of public accountability in politics via a free press. However, though accountability in government and the search for truth are asserted in much the same way as the utilitarian and later liberal activists, a crucial difference is an emerging sense of class cohesion within working class discussions of freedom of the press. The notion of accountability and truth are increasingly being articulated in the interests of the working classes themselves rather than a middle-class elite who act as guides or leaders for the poor as we saw with the Philosophic Radicals. Moreover, working class arguments were generally couched in terms of notions of rights (echoing Paine), again this is something antithetical to utilitarians.

Cobbett, Cartwright and Hone saw themselves not as leaders of the working classes as such, but as facilitators to their incorporation into the machinery of politics and political practice. Though at this stage familiar arguments were employed, the emphasis of these arguments was increasingly focussed on the social whole, and particularly on working-class interests within this social whole. Thus within these early attempts at a broader more inclusive social analysis within the working class press, notions of class identity and class cohesion are starting to develop. This notion of class identity would be reinforced later in the nineteenth century in the works of Henry Hetherington, George Jacob Holyoake and the revolutionary Julian Harney.

Victory for Democracy and Freedom of Speech?

Cries for political reform that had so long fallen on deaf ears were heard and could no longer be ignored, and in 1832 the First Reform Act ensured that the franchise was widened, if only in a limited sense. However, the aristocracy and landed interests remained politically dominant. Moreover, middle-class interests had won the day as the movements for working-class enfranchisement dwindled. In 1832 'the vote was extended to more of the middle-class, with many of the working-class actually losing their votes. There was still only one in seven adult males who could vote' (Pearson and Williams, 1984: 29). Though relatively limited, the extension of the franchise seemed to dampen down disquiet amongst the middle classes. The extension of the franchise and the redistribution of seats in the House of Commons meant that the impetus for prosecutions against the press ultimately waned as the amount of dissent apparently decreased.

This point provides a good indication of the primary motivation behind middle-class radicalism, as the calls they made for increased political representation wavered as their political power increased. It would eventually become no longer expedient to advocate total freedom of the press, as this would only encourage the so-called lower orders to challenge the political system that was now bearing fruit for the middle classes. According to Erskine May, along with the franchise 'the freedom of the press had been assured, and the journalists had won the 'utmost latitude of criticism and invective' in their treatment of public figures and political affairs.' (Cited in A. Jones, 1996: 13).

Although Erskine May's applause was well founded, other more minor obstacles to a truly free press, namely the stamp duty, remained. The notion of a tax on the press continued to irritate smaller publications and even sections of the established press, such a system ran contrary to the laissez-faire ethos of the day. However, as Curran and Seaton (1999: 12-13) point out, from the government's viewpoint, the tax was perceived as useful in that it served a number of ends. Firstly, a tax on the press would ensure that readership would be restricted to the middle classes; also, the system of tax would ensure that the ownership of newspapers would be largely restricted to the propertied classes. Furthermore, the Chancellor saw it as a great source of revenue, and it would take vast amounts of pressure and persuasion to make him repeal the tax.

In 1836, with the passing of the Acts 6 & 7, William IV reduced the four pence tax to one penny. This seemed to appease many agitators, who then eventually went on to concentrate their energies on other political struggles[10]. However, the end of the post-publication taxation system also impacted on the ability of the working-class press to reach their intended readership, as increasing compliance with the law meant that the radical papers would now have to raise their prices, thus making them out of reach for a great number of their working-class readership. This of course also meant that by 1837, the clandestine radical press had disappeared (Curran, 1999:12-13).

In 1848 a group of working-class and middle-class repealers which included Collet, Hetherington, Holyoake and Watson formed 'The Association for the Repeal of Taxes on Knowledge' as they were still unhappy with the one pence duty. This group, following earlier years' examples, challenged the authorities to a courtroom battle over the so-called tax on knowledge when they produced in 1853 the *Potteries Free*

---

10 Most notably the Chartist movement and the Anti Corn Law movement.

Press, an unstamped penny weekly. When prosecutions from the stamp office followed, petitions were organised and enough support was generated to draw up a bill which sought to abolish the remaining duty, the bill was presented to Parliament in 1855. Eventually, after much debate, Lord Palmerston declared that he had confidence in the people not to allow a degradation in the press and that the so-called evils which were anticipated would not emerge. At last and after much argument, the free market was seen to be by far the most powerful force in the area of the press as it allowed for the best to succeed and the worst to fail. The stamp tax was repealed in 1855 (Jones, 1996: 21-24). Eric Glasgow commenting on the growth of publishing in Victorian England highlights the growing power of the market and its impact on the commercial publishing industry when he notes that publishing 'became a distinctive feature of the "free market" economy and the triumphant capitalism which had followed the development in England of the Industrial Revolution' (Glasgow, 1998: 395-400).

After the repeal of the last stamp tax, it was generally safe to assume that the liberty of the press was eventually won in legal terms at least. The notion that an outside body should interfere with the 'natural' processes of the market was held up as being socially irresponsible as the health and prosperity of society would suffer. The forces of capitalism, the motor of social progress, should not be interfered with if the health of the country was to remain good. As the tide of support became evident across the country it was no surprise when in his Budget of 1861, Gladstone finally repealed the stamp duty on paper. As Thomas (1969: 214) argues, finally after nearly four hundred years of struggle the war against formal censorship of the press was won.

We can see that the final battle against press control was won on generally economic and political grounds. Middle class interests and the force of capital won over the old orders of power and their restrictions on emerging notions of freedom and democracy. Moreover, the victorious middle-class fight for freedom of the press was fought ultimately in terms of winning the means to attaining, then maintaining its power base over the so called 'lower orders'. It could be argued that massive social movements alone and the threat of revolution were solely responsible for the gradual shift in the progress towards a free press, but this would negate the force of historical processes that were to culminate in the industrial revolution and its associated impact on structures of power and power relations. It is clear that the main influence in the movement of the free press was that of the development of the free market and the massive tide of social change that went with it.

The force of the free market in capital *and* ideas ensured that eventually press legislation had to be curbed and ultimately halted as contradictions within the system were highlighted and critiqued. The control of the press by the machinery of the state was seen as a contradiction within the emerging capitalist system itself, and was inconsistent with the very foundations of *laissez-faire* philosophy. Within this battle, the radical working-class press, and the interests which they represented were defeated. It is worth quoting James Curran when he notes:

> The decline of the radical press in the second half of the nineteenth century must be situated in its wider social context: the defeat of the militant working-class movement; the lack of developed consciousness that rendered the working-class vulnerable to ideological incorporation; and the development or extension of a number of agencies of social control mediating consensual values which became, to a lesser or greater extent, internalised by the majority of the population; A crucial factor, however in the eclipse of radical journalism was the industrialisation of the press. (Curran, 1983: 67)

Conclusion

This chapter has sought to combine an historical and theoretical study of freedom of speech and democracy, in doing this I have concentrated on the struggle for freedom of speech and democracy during the nineteenth century in England. We have seen how particular ideas, most notably those of Bentham and Paine influenced middle and working class struggles respectively, for greater democratic representation and inclusion in the political process. We can see here how the notion of interests surface in political struggles. In particular, class interests of those radicals and agitators who sought to change the system of government and influence the political process. It is clear that the notion of accountability is one that is crucial to the democratic process, but the philosophical basis upon which that accountability is sought differs considerably. Moreover, though freedom of speech is necessary to allow for accountable systems of government, we have also seen that freedom of speech can be used as a powerful political tool to challenging the status quo and establish new forms of power and authority. Though freedom of speech and democracy are connected and one cannot really have a working democracy without freedom of speech, justifications for freedom of speech can emanate from other sources such as the search for truth and the expression of individual liberty as detailed by John Stuart Mill in *On Liberty* in 1859. After the battle for a free press had been won, and the franchise was extended, it would be John Stuart Mill who would highlight the dangers of public opinion on individual development and liberty. Rather than accountability as such, Mill stressed individual liberty and the search for truth which would provide probably the strongest philosophical defence of freedom of thought and action of the nineteenth century, a defence that has influence even today. It has been the purpose of this chapter to highlight how freedom of speech relates to the concept of democracy by drawing upon the struggle for democracy during the early nineteenth century in Britain. Within this exploration we have seen how different political and philosophical ideas underpinned arguments for democratic representation and freedom of speech. In short we have seen how political ideas have informed political action within the context of particular struggles. We have also seen how particular interests were served during the struggle for democracy and more specifically how conceptions of freedom of speech were utilised for different political ends. It would be worth remembering that within all social movements, interests are asserted and power sought; the struggle for democracy during the nineteenth century provides just one example of the ways in which interests are articulated and power sought. Freedom of speech remains a powerful political tool, moreover, its significance emphasises the importance of debate and dialogue. We may also be aware of the way in which ideas permeate through different media within political discourse, but should always be prepared to critically engage with such ideas, and ask 'in who's interests are such ideas intended to serve, and for what ends?'

References

Arblaster, A. (1987) *Democracy* (Buckingham: Open University Press).

Beales, D. (1969) *From Castlereagh to Gladstone 1815–1885* (London: Nelson).

Bentham, J. (1970) *An Introduction to the Principles of Morals and Legislation* (London: Methuen).

Curran, J. (1983) 'The Press as an Agency of Social Control: An Historical Perspective' in G. Boyce, J. Curran and P. Wingate (eds) *Newspaper History:*

From the Seventeenth Century to the Present Day (California: Sage Publications Inc). 51-75.

Curran, J. and Seaton, J. (1999) *Power Without Responsibility, The Press and Broadcasting in Britain* (London: Routledge).

Glasgow, E. (1998) 'Publishers in Victorian England', *Library Review*, vol. 47:8; 395–400.

Hackwood, F.W. (1912) *William Hone His Life and Times* (London: T. Fisher Unwin).

Hobsbawm, E. (1997) *The Age of Revolution 1789–1848* (London: Weidenfeld and Nicholson).

Hollis, P. (1970) *The Pauper Press, A Study of Working Class Radicalism of the 1830's* (London: Oxford University Press).

Jones, A. (1996) *Powers of the Press* (Aldershot: Ashgate Publishing, Scholar Press).

Keane, J. (1996) *Tom Paine A Political Life* (London: Bloomsbury Publishing).

Osbourne, J.W. (1966) *William Cobbett* (New York: Rutgers).

Paine, T. (1995) *Rights of Man* (Oxford: Oxford University Press).

Pearson, R. and Williams, G. (1984) *Political Thought and Public Policy in the Nineteenth Century* (London: Longman).

Political Register, No. 18, 2 November 1816.

Roebuck, J.A. (1935–36) *Pamphlets for the People*, vols 1 and 2.

Thomas, D. (1969) *A Long Time Burning, The History of Literary Censorship in England* (London: Routledge and Kegan Paul).

Thompson, E.P. (1980) *The Making of the English Working Class* (London: Victor Gollancz).

Wiener, J. H. (1969) *The War of the Unstamped: The Movement to Repeal the British Newspaper Tax, 1830-36* (London: Cornell University Publications).

Westminster Review, vol. 13, January 1830.

Wickwar, W.H. (1928) *The Struggle for Freedom of the Press, 1819–1832* (London: George Allen and Unwin).

Woodward, L. (1992) *The Age of Reform, England 1815–1870* (Oxford: Oxford University Press).

6. UNEMPLOYMENT, PROTEST AND CRISES OF DEMOCRACY:
A comparison of some social capital, mass society and social movement society theses

Paul Bagguley

Social scientific common sense might suggest that high levels of unemployment in the archetypal 'Western democracies' would generate a crisis of the democratic functions of the state. Those economically deprived through unemployment might be reasonably expected to protest in ways that challenge the government, that threaten the outcomes of the democratic process. Government policies might be changed or whole governments might be expected to fall in the face of an uprising by the unemployed.

However, things are rarely that simple. There is no straightforward connection between the experience of unemployment and the political responses to it. There are many contextual factors that have shaped the political responses of the unemployed, and protest is only one. Similarly, protest by the unemployed is only one source of democratic crisis that could be generated by high unemployment. Unemployment could lead to political withdrawal, so that the democratic crisis that ensues is that more insidious type: a crisis of participation. If people do not exercise their democratic rights by voting, then the democratic system loses legitimacy in its own terms. This is indeed, what appears to be happening in Britain:

> More than five million fewer people voted in the 2001 election than did so in 1997, which itself had a lower turnout than its predecessor did in 1992. The word crisis is often abused in contemporary accounts of politics. But if this is not a crisis of democratic politics in Britain, then it is hard to know what would be. (Whiteley et. al., 2001: 786)

Barely 54 per cent of the adult population voted in the 2001 general election and in some constituencies only one third of the electorate bothered to turnout. Whilst unemployment is a factor that reduces the likelihood of an individual voting, and constituencies with higher levels of unemployment have lower turnouts, most of the decline in voting can be explained by general dissatisfaction among the population at large with party leaders, their policies and their 'boring' campaigns (Whiteley et. al., 2001: 776). I shall be arguing that the relationship between the unemployed and democracy is a more complex and interesting story than simple claims about withdrawal from politics suggest.

In this chapter, I want to explore the implications for democracy of unemployment and the protests it may generate. I shall not engage in detailed debates about how to define democracy, I shall take as given that societies in Western Europe and North America are 'democracies'. However, I will be using the term democracy in two distinct ways. Firstly, to refer to the democratic control over and accountability of state institutions. Secondly, to refer to democratic rights and participation in organisations that are part of the public sphere or civil society. I shall be discussing in later sections the changing relationships between the unemployed, protest and both of these senses of democracy.

The theoretical part of my argument starts from three broader approaches to analysing politics in democratic societies. Each of them has something general to say about the relationship between protest and democracy, and from each of them can be derived some specific claims about the unemployed, democracy and protest. It is some of these claims that I wish to question and challenge here. The first – mass society theory – is quite old, and I resurrect it only for the reason that I feel that its ghost haunts many contemporary discussions about the current state of politics and culture. Mass society theory claims that in modern societies individuals have become 'detached' from meaningful relationships and as a result turn away from normal democratic politicians towards volatile mass social movements to solve their problems. For my representative of mass society theory I have elected to use Kornhauser (1960).

Secondly, I will consider one of the most influential theories to have emerged since the early 1990s the idea of social capital. As we shall see theories of social capital, as they have been applied to politics and the state of democratic societies, share many themes from the older mass society theory. Indeed the similarities are so striking at certain points one is tempted to see social capital theory as merely mass society theory resurrected under a new name. For my discussion of social capital theory, I have elected Putnam (2000) as my principal representative.

Thirdly, I shall discuss the idea that contemporary democracies have become 'social movement societies'. This again shares some similarities with mass society theory and social capital theory in that it sees contemporary societies as characterised by a widespread lack of trust in established forms of democracy. However, it critically differs from them in not seeing this as necessarily a bad thing and in certain respects directly contradicts them. To represent this way of thinking Meyer and Tarrow (1998) have been elected.

The final theoretical argument that I shall consider is specific to protest by the unemployed. Piven and Cloward's work on what they refer to as poor peoples' movements also suggests that democracy is quite central to understanding the dynamics and impact of protest by the unemployed. Each of these theoretical arguments about protest and democracy is then considered in relation to protests by the unemployed in Britain in the 1930s and 1980s in order to examine empirically the relationship between the unemployed, protest and democracy.

Mass Society, the Unemployed and Democracy

Kornhauser's mass society theory is very much a product of its time. In many ways, it is an analysis of how and why fascism and communism emerged in Europe in the first decades of the twentieth century. Kornhauser understands mass society in contrast to traditional communal forms of society, pluralist societies and totalitarian (fascist and communist) societies. He sees all societies as divided between political elites who take decisions and the mass of the population who are not centrally involved in political processes. In a pluralist or democratic society the political elite is easily influenced by the mass of the population through elections, and in totalitarian societies, since there are no free elections, the elite cannot be easily influenced by the mass of the population. However, in a totalitarian regime the masses are constantly 'mobilised' by elites in support of the regime. In a mass society elites are accessible to and can be easily influenced by the masses, and at the same time the elites seek to keep the masses mobilised, in effect using them for their own political ends. A mass society lacks 'intermediate organisations' that mediate between individuals and government. These might be churches, trade unions and other kinds of permanent associations of people. As a result Kornhauser describes mass society as an 'atomised' society of individuals. People are isolated from each other with little meaningful organised social interaction between them (Kornhauser, 1960: 39-43; 76-93).

A characteristic of the mass society is the widespread existence of 'mass movements'. These have 'remote and extreme' objectives, where the individuals involved have a weak sense of responsibility. They do not think about the consequences of their actions. These mass movements favour an 'activist mode of response' to issues. They engage in various forms of direct action with little prior debate outside of routine politics. They often respond to remote and abstract symbols or slogans. Mass movements mobilise those social groups who are most marginal to society, those who are most 'atomised'. They are not members of intermediate organisations. These types of movements lack a clear internal organisational structure, so that there is no way in which 'members' can control the 'leaders'. Consequently, totalitarian groups such as communists and fascists may capture and manipulate mass movements (Kornhauser, 1960: 43-51).

Kornhauser sees involvement in mass movements as a search for self-identity on the part of atomised individuals. These atomised individuals mainly come from the unemployed, the marginal middle classes, intellectuals, and the lower sections of the working class, and others who are not part of intermediate organisations. What are the social conditions that produce mass movements and a mass society? Firstly, if democracy is weak with few rights to form public associations and few legal protections for individual liberty then people are likely to seek redress for their problems through mass movements. Secondly, rapid industrialisation and urbanisation may create the conditions for mass movements by creating new marginal groups and undermining established intermediate organisations such as churches. Finally, economic recession and social breakdown may reveal the underlying weaknesses of an urbanised democracy and suddenly increase the numbers in marginalised circumstances such as the unemployed, as well as undermining the economic basis of intermediate organisations (Kornhauser, 1960: 119-28; 177-82).

Kornhauser paid particular attention to the unemployed and mass movements. He argued that high unemployment lead to increased support for fascist and communist parties. This could be explained using his framework through the way in which unemployment is a socially isolating experience that undermines self-respect and leads to withdrawal from intermediate organisations. He sees unemployment leading to either mass action or mass apathy. Those who are very isolated from others become apathetic, whilst those who are only isolated from the wider society but retain some face-to-face contacts are attracted to mass movements (Kornhauser, 1960: 90-3; 96; 217-18). It is clear then that it is the absence of membership of intermediate organisations that integrate individuals into the wider society that is critical for Kornhauser's explanation of mass movement participation among the unemployed. Mass activism he saw as giving the unemployed something to do, in short it provided them with a sense of self-identity, as well as appealing to their needs for something to be done about their economic circumstances (Kornhauser, 1960: 160-7).

Kornhauser's arguments were subject to a certain amount of critical scrutiny during the 1960s (Gusfield, 1962; Pinard, 1968), and one is tempted to consign his ideas to the dustbin of intellectual history. However, the arguments that Kornhauser put forward have this habit of coming back to haunt us in different forms and under different labels, and this is especially the case when there are debates about the decline of democracy and the political consequences of unemployment.

The theory has been criticised for its normative assumptions. It assumes that pluralism is the norm for modern societies and that this implies that conflicts are disruptions of the normal harmony and threats to pluralism, rather than being authentic conflicts of interests and beliefs. It presents a rather utopian view of pluralist society, and therefore fails to see how mass society rather than encouraging extremism may actually function to promote social conformism, through mass communications, national systems of mass education, etc. (Gusfield, 1962). In contrast, pluralist societies may encourage extremism when some groups are excluded from normal political processes. Furthermore, attachment to intermediate organisations may promote conflict rather than secure social integration and social order (Gusfield, 1962: 27). Pinard (1968) developed these points further, arguing that intermediate organisations might help to mobilise people into social movements positively sanctioning the kinds of mass movement of which Kornhauser and others were so critical. They can act to diffuse and communicate the ideas and propositions of emergent social movements. To Gusfield's point about the real nature of conflicting interests in pluralist conditions, Pinard adds the claim that social strain is a crucial precondition of mass mobilisations. Whereas mass society theory sees strains as forces that threaten attachments to intermediate organisations, Pinard argues that strains may lead intermediate organisations into opposition to the established social order.

Both Gusfield and Pinard conclude with arguments that are the polar opposite of mass society theorists such as Kornhauser. In particular, they argue that a pluralist society with its intermediate organisations is more prone to the emergence of social movements than a mass society, because the intermediate organisations may act as mobilising structures and networks for emergent social movements. As I shall argue below this is precisely a theme taken up by more recent theories of the emergence of a 'social movement society', and is supported by the evidence about protest amongst the unemployed. A mass society of atomised individuals is less likely to have social movements because isolated individuals are more difficult to mobilise, and mass communications and mass education can help to ensure social conformity. Finally, they also reveal the normative and judgmental character of mass society theory, where it sees social movements and protest as somehow deviant and a threat to democracy. These kinds of issues are currently being rehearsed again in current debates about the role of social capital in contemporary democracies, and it is these that I turn to next.

The 'Social Capital' Debate

Debates around the 'state of democracy' in recent years have made extensive use of the concept of social capital (Putnam et. al., 2000; Putnam, 2000). Whilst there are other definitions of social capital in circulation (Bourdieu, 1997; Coleman, 1997) Putnam's has become the most widely used in relation to politics and democracy. He argues that 'social capital refers to connections among individuals – social networks and the norms of reciprocity and trustworthiness that arise from them' (Putnam, 2000: 19).

Putnam suggests that the social contacts provided by networks provide a 'value' that enables individuals or groups to be more productive. This might mean their businesses are more successful because they know the 'right people', or it might mean that their neighbourhoods are simply friendlier places to live in because they have many good acquaintances. These networks or social capital are formed because it suits individuals' own interests, but also because the group benefits as well. Group benefits from social capital arise from the 'norm of generalised reciprocity' which means that individuals participate in and contribute to social capital not in the expectation that they will immediately benefit, but they might expect something in return at some point in the future from other participants. Putnam distinguishes between inclusive 'bridging social capital', which connects different kinds of people, across classes, genders, ethnicities, etc., and exclusive 'bonding social capital', which connects similar types of persons for example within a class, gender or ethnic group. Whilst bonding social capital is strong in terms of loyalty, it can generate conflict with those not included. Hence, Putnam tends to prefer bridging social capital. In relation to the quality of democracy, it is specifically argued that:

> Low levels of overall social capital and social trust in any given soci-
> ety contribute to poor governmental performance, which in turn
> adversely affects all citizens to varying degrees; as a consequence
> they will give the government low marks. (Putnam et al., 2000: 26)

According to Putnam, social capital decline is the main reason why democracy is in decline in Western societies, but what explains the decline in social capital? Primarily it is the emergence of the 'TV generation'. Since the 1960s, he argues that younger people are spending more time involved in 'electronic entertainment' than in developing social capital and becoming involved in collective pursuits. Social capital decline is mostly explained by:

> ... the effect of electronic entertainment – above all, television – in
> privatising our leisure time has been substantial. My rough estimate
> is that this factor might account for perhaps 25 per cent of the decline
> ... and most important, generational change – the slow, steady, and
> ineluctable replacement of the long civic generation by their less
> involved children and grandchildren ... this factor might account for
> perhaps half of the overall decline. (Putnam, 2000: 283)

Putnam's argument might superficially be read as a sociological analysis. It is, however, clearly an instance of methodological individualism. Individuals choose to participate in social networks for what they may gain from them. Any social consequences such as norms, trust or good government follow on from this. Yet, social capital stops us from being selfish and promotes more effective and efficient government. The emphasis on efficient and effective outcomes of high levels of social capital also reveals its economistic biases.

Putnam's account of social capital both in general and in relation to the health of democracy has been criticised on a number of grounds. Firstly, he tends to neglect the role of the state in creating the conditions for flourishing social capital. Social capital depends on certain kinds of liberties or citizenship rights for instance, which can only be guaranteed by certain types of state. In this sense, his application of the concept can be seen as ahistorical. Secondly, he tends to see the decline of social capital as non-economic, that is, based on individuals choosing to do different things with their spare time. Yet, he also sees strong social capital as a prerequisite for economic success, but declining social capital might be an effect of economic decline. Thirdly, social capital can be negative, in that it can give rise to 'anti-democratic' movements. Fourthly, he gives a rather deterministic interpretation of how social capital influences democracy. Fifthly, Putnam's concept of social capital ignores social structure and related concepts. We have seen how he sees social capital, its networks, and norms as emerging from the rational choices of individuals. Hence, he tends to neglect issues of class, power and the substantive content of political actions (Fine, 2001).

The theory of social capital has become an instance of neo-classical economists' colonisation of other social sciences (Fine, 2001). It seeks to measure the sociability and civic mindedness of people in a quantitative manner, and to subsequently manage society according to middle class values (Walters, 2002).

Much of what is discussed under the category of 'social capital' is standard meat and drink for sociologists. The currently dominant understanding of social capital sees it as consisting of social networks, trust and the norms that help sustain those networks and trust relations (Putnam, 2000: 19). Declining social capital is used as a kind of meta-narrative of social ills. Indeed the highly problematic relationship that has been found between legitimacy and social capital reflects this.

In direct contrast to this social movement theorists have long argued that social networks can help us understand the dynamics of social movements precisely because their must be relations of trust among those participating. Consequently, strong social movements might be read as an outcome of strong 'social capital', or at least different kinds of 'social capital'. Diani's discussion is one of the few to explicitly try to apply the concept of social capital to social movement analysis (Diani, 1997). However, his account adds much more to the arguments of social capital theorists, seeing networks as extending not just among potential social movement participants, but also between movements and elite politicians. He also sees movements as creating social capital as well as drawing upon it. In Diani's account one feels that social capital as a concept becomes redundant as much of what he argues is better captured using conventional sociological accounts of social networks, power and collective identity.

As social movements generate criticism of government we might reverse Putnam et al.'s simple causal sequence and argue that high levels of social capital enable citizens to challenge and criticise governments thus emphasising their poor performance and encouraging widespread disaffection. Tarrow has argued something akin to this; using the 'mad cow' disease issue in Britain as one of his examples, he concluded that:

> ... new activism may be creating networks of working relations between citizens and their governments even as those same citizens express their dismay to survey researchers about the performance of the latter. (Tarrow, 2000: 288)

From the social capital perspective, the unemployed might be thought to constitute a 'threat' to democracy because they lack social capital. However, this brief discussion of the most influential accounts of social capital theory shows that it has some serious limitations. Furthermore, these limitations are shared to some degree with mass society theory, and are counterbalanced by the claims of those who argue that contemporary societies are becoming 'social movement societies'.

Towards a Social Movement Society?

The idea of a 'social movement society' has developed from two sources. The first (Tarrow, 1994) and developed in more detail by Meyer and Tarrow (1998) has emerged largely from American analyses of social movements. The other originates in German sociology (Neidhardt and Rucht, 1991; Rucht and Neidhardt, 2002). Here I shall be considering both versions of the theory.

The Meyer and Tarrow version involves three central claims. Firstly, protest is now a normal, routine feature of contemporary societies. It is no longer exceptional or abnormal and occurring at times of crisis. Of course the pace and level of protest may still increase at particular points over particular issues, but the mere occurrence of protest may no longer be taken as a sign of social and political crisis. This is in direct contrast to mass society theory which would see a social movement society as a society in 'crisis', and it would be seen as a sign of a failing democracy.

Secondly, protest is used more often by a wider range of types of people and over a wider range of issues than before. Consequently, protest cannot be simply explained as the political resort of the poor or socially marginalised. This claim is also in contradiction with the arguments of Kornhauser, who suggested that it was precisely those who were poor or socially marginalised who were attracted to social movements.

Finally, it is claimed that the institutionalisation and professionalisation of social movements may be turning them into a tool of mainstream politics. All of these arguments suggest that social movements can no longer be seen as the province of those social groups and issues of contention that are on the margins of conventional politics. Rather than being outside of democracy or a challenge to it, social movements have changed the ways in which democracy is done, performed or carried out (Meyer and Tarrow, 1998: 4). This was also a feature that Kornhauser failed to appreciate fully. He failed to see that social movements could be 'normalised' in this way by contemporary democratic states.

A rather different approach to explaining the emergence of the social movement society is taken by Rucht and Neidhardt (2002). They emphasise the combination of three structural features of contemporary societies in generating and sustaining social movements. These are structural strains, mobilising structures and societal opportunity structures. Structural strains arise from processes of modernisation of societies. Initially this gave rise to strains such as class inequalities. However, over time as societies have become more complex there are a wide variety of strains, such as environmental problems, ethnic conflicts and gender-based conflicts. Furthermore, the proliferation of strains and associated demands for governments to do something about them has increased demands for citizen participation in governmental decision-making. In short a demand for more democracy. These circumstances are most likely to give rise to many smaller situationally specific social movements rather than a single over-arching class based movement (Rucht and Neidhardt, 2002: 16-17).

Mobilising structures consist most basically of social networks among potential participants. Increasingly it is suggested that these networks are to be found among specific social groups, such as the young. These provide alternative sources of collective identity, and if social movements can stabilise them into more enduring social milieus then they can form the basis of more sustained social movements. Societal opportunity structures refer to opportunities for social movements to act. These opportunities may be the failure of political parties or interest groups to respond to certain strains in society, increased media coverage of political decisions and strains so that people are more likely to find out about strains. The media are also a means for social movements to gain the attention of both the public and politicians. It summary it is being suggested that strains have become more or less permanent, whilst mobilising structures are more available and the failure of political parties and the attention of mass media provide greater opportunities for the development of movements (Rucht and Neidhardt, 2002: 18-23).

Straight away we can see that both versions of the social movement society theory overlap with mass society theory in seeing more protest around, but radically depart from it in not seeing protest as something done by marginalised and isolated social groups in society. It does not see social movements as evidence of the failure or dysfunction of democratic pluralist society. Rather it is seen as evidence of the vitality of democracy, with social movements becoming 'institutionalised' alongside established political parties and pressure groups and in competition with them for peoples' attention. Similarly, it shares some concerns with social capital theory. However, whilst social capital theory tends to be too dismissive of social movements in comparison to its normative preference for 'conventional' politics, SMS theory blurs the distinction between the two.

In some ways, the relative strengths and weaknesses of these two ways of theorising about the social movement society are mirror images of each other. Rucht and Neidhardt emphasise structural strains, common experiences of deprivation, collective identities, mobilising structures and political opportunity structures. Meyer and Tarrow emphasise the role of the state and its agencies such as the police, forms of social movement organisation and repertoires of contention.

We shall see below that some of these specific claims are strongly supported by evidence about protest by the unemployed. However, what social movement society theorists do not seem to be able to explain very well is what kinds of movements occur in which circumstances. During the 1930s, there was extensive protest by the unemployed in Britain, but during the high unemployment of the 1980s, it was largely absent. To begin to answer that question we have to turn to those who have specifically examined protest by the unemployed.

Piven and Cloward

Piven and Cloward's analysis of Poor Peoples' movements still stands as one of the most important contributions to understanding protest by the unemployed. Their analysis is built around two sets of arguments. The first is concerned with the role of economic, social and political crises as the background factors giving rise to protest, and the second is concerned with how protest is shaped by social institutions such as the state.

The 'crisis' factors include the breakdown of economic routines, which mean that people no longer have regular employment. Dominant ideologies and beliefs lose their grip on the population. They no longer offer people convincing explanations of the events around them, for example, when there is an economic recession. Finally, there is a crisis of support for established political parties. As those parties are no longer able to offer people convincing policies for their problems then they lose support from those sections of the population that traditionally supported them.

The factors shaping protest concern those institutions that people come into contact with on an everyday basis. These institutions are experienced as the most immediate and visible origins of deprivation and oppression and provide immediate targets for protest. For the unemployed this often means the immediate administrators of state benefits for the unemployed rather than the government directly. These institutions also shape the collective base of protest by bringing people together in particular places and at particular times. Finally, institutions shape the strategies and tactics of protest (Piven and Cloward, 1977: 18-22).

According to Piven and Cloward, protest is the way in which the unemployed gain concessions from elite groups in society, but they do this indirectly through highly disruptive protest such as rioting or other forms of violent disruption. Yet, this disruptive protest is only effective when it affects the electoral prospects of political parties.

Democracy appears in Piven and Cloward's argument at two points. The first and most evident is where a 'crisis of democracy' is a prerequisite for successful protest by the unemployed. Where their protests only gain concessions in the context of a crisis of electoral support for established parties. The second is less evident from their general argument. There must be some kind of direct electoral influence over the welfare institutions that the unemployed are protesting against. In order to pursue and develop these arguments further I shall make a comparison between two periods of mass unemployment in Britain: the 1930s and the 1980s.

The Unemployed, Democracy and Protest in the 1930s and the 1980s

In the first part of this section, I want to examine the relationships between unemployment, democracy and protest during the 1920s and 1930s. This is a critical period to consider since there was widespread protest by the unemployed at various points during this period. However, the 1930s in particular contrast with the 1980s. During the 1920s and 1930s there was widespread if spasmodic protest by the unemployed organised by the National Unemployed Workers' Movement (NUWM). In the 1980s, there were attempts to organise the unemployed, but there was no widespread protest certainly not on the scale of the 1930s.

Using this contrast between the 1930s and the 1980s, I want to make two principal arguments about the relationship between the unemployed, democracy and their protests. Firstly, that the scope of democratic control over state welfare is critical in providing the opportunity for protest. In the 1920s and 1930s this was called 'public assistance'. This picks up certain themes from Piven and Cloward's discussion of how institutions shape protest and develops some issues from the social movement society theorists' claims about political opportunity structures. Secondly, I shall show that mass society theory and social capital theory are wrong to suggest that the lack of organisational membership can be used as an explanation of protest as an alternative to more conventional forms of politics. On the contrary, high levels of membership of 'intermediate organisations' such as trade unions or working men's clubs were closely related to the mobilisation of protest among the unemployed in the 1930s. This also picks up the themes of mobilising structures from the debate about the emergence of a social movement society.

Unemployment in the 1920s and 30s was exceptionally high being over 10 per cent for much of the period and reaching 22 per cent of the working population in 1932 (Beveridge, 1960: 47). However, the most widespread protests took place in 1935, showing that it was not the level of unemployment that mattered. What triggered the protests in 1935 was the reform of the administration of unemployment benefits that meant that not only were the levels of benefit cut, but that the administration was centralised. Many of these protests were organised by the National Unemployed Workers' Movement. In the early 1930s many of the longer term unemployed received benefits from locally administered 'Public Assistance Committees' (PACs) that were run by county councils. Locally elected councillors ran these 146 PACs. Although limited by central government regulations local PACs had some autonomy over the conditions and levels of benefit for the unemployed. This meant that persuading local PACs to treat the unemployed more leniently was a realistic goal for the NUWM. These activities were monitored by the government as in the following case of Lewis Jones who was an NUWM activist who was elected to the County Council:

... the tendency of the Relief Sub-Committees in the area was to grant the maxima of the scale... This tendency was accounted for in part by the Communistic activity in the Area and particularly by the activity of Mr. Lewis Jones a Communist who has recently been elected a member of the County Council for the Tonypandy division. Mr. Jones has set himself out to educate his constituents as to their rights to Public Assistance. This he does in various ways. He has for example a motor van with a loudspeaker by means of which he broadcasts to all in doubt as to their rights and invites all with a grievance to report their cases to local communist agents whose names and addresses are given; the agents pass on the particulars to Mr. Jones who then gives advice. He also holds crowded meetings every Sunday night in the Judges Hall, Tonypandy at which he makes such statements as that there are hundreds of people in the Area not receiving the assistance to which they are entitled and advises them how this may be rectified. (Asserted Laxity in the Operation of Public Assistance and a Description of the Activities of Mr. Lewis Jones. PRO. MH. 79/312. Quoted in Webster, 1985: 229-30)

This shows how the administration of unemployment relief functioned as a political opportunity for the NUWM. The PACs' local democratic autonomy enabled the NUWM to act collectively on behalf of individuals and the unemployed in general, but only within those places where they were able to influence the PACs. In some places, the PACs remained unsympathetic towards the unemployed; hence, it provided an opportunity for protest and not a certainty of protest. What this illustrates then is that the unemployed used democracy as an opportunity for collective action, rather than turning away from democracy or being a threat to it.

In 1935 when the locally accountable PACs were abolished and a national Unemployment Assistance Board (UAB) created, there was widespread opposition from the unemployed. The creation of the UAB meant two things. Firstly, it was a board appointed by central government and elected representatives could not influence its decisions in any way. It was a straightforward bureaucracy and not directly accountable. Secondly, it created national levels of public assistance for the unemployed, and for those living in areas where the local PACs had been most generous this meant significant cuts in the levels of assistance that they were receiving. When this was announced in January 1935 there were widespread protests in South Wales and the North of England organised by the NUWM. Over the weekend of 2-3 February, over 300,000 people demonstrated in South Wales, and on 6 February a demonstration of 30,000 people in front of Sheffield town hall ended in a 'riot' (Miller, 1979; Moore, 1985). The immediate response of the government was to restore the cuts, but they gradually moved towards national scales over the next few years.

These protests by the unemployed did not just depend on the opportunities afforded by some degree of democratic control over public assistance. The protests had to be organised and central to their organisation was the NUWM. However, the NUWM was stronger in some parts of the country than others. The Rhondda in South Wales was one such area. One reason why this area was a significant location of protest amongst the unemployed was not no just that there were high levels of unemployment, but that there were high levels of organisational membership amongst the unemployed. This point is demonstrated in table 6.1 below.

Table 6.1

Organisational Membership Amongst the Unemployed in Selected Localities, 1936

Locality	Long-term Unemployed	None	Trade Union	Working Mens Clubs	Organisations per person
Rhondda	63%	19.7%	38.5%	18.7%	1.46
Liverpool	23%	48.2%	5.3%	2.7%	0.51
Blackburn	38%	32.5%	25.8%	4.5%	0.89
Leicester	11%	47.6%	11.9%	5.9%	0.57

Source: Calculated from Pilgrim Trust (1968), table II p. 13 and table LIX p. 274

Table 6.1 presents evidence that clearly contradicts the claims of both mass society theory and social capital theory. It shows that in those places with the highest levels of long-term unemployment, the unemployed also had the highest levels of membership of organisations. At one extreme was the Rhondda coal-mining district where 63 per cent of the unemployed were 'long-term' unemployed. At the other extreme is Leicester where 11 per cent of the unemployed were classified as long-term and there were much lower levels of organisational membership. Add to this the evidence of where protests by the unemployed during this period were the strongest, and there is a strong correlation between social capital or attachment to formally organised public associations and protest by the unemployed. In short, a vibrant 'grass-roots' democracy is necessary for protest by the unemployed.

One way of thinking about these places with high levels of organisational membership is as local 'social movement societies'. Unlike the predictions of social capital theory, membership of local organisations does not just encourage 'normal' democratic politics, it also enables protest. In contrast, certain of the arguments of social movements society theorists about the importance of organisations to the mobilisation of protest are vindicated.

The 1980s also saw high levels of unemployment, with over three million unemployed by the middle of the decade (Bagguley, 1991: 6). Whereas we have seen that in the 1930s there were at times large-scale protests by the unemployed, the 1980s saw a quite different response. During the 1980s, the political responses of the unemployed to their situation were much more tightly controlled by the trade union movement than during the 1930s. Furthermore, as the unemployment benefits system was by now a centralised national bureaucracy, there was now democratic accountability to provide a political opportunity for collective action by the unemployed.

During the 1980s, the national labour movement directed protest against unemployment, whilst during the 1930s the NUWM was an organisation of the unemployed, although controlled by the Communist Party. There are two kinds of labour movement action against unemployment during the 1980s that I want to discuss. The first concerns the 'Peoples' Marches for Jobs' in 1981 and 1983, and the other concerns the creation of TUC centres for the unemployed. Both illustrate the ways in which protest can be regulated and normalised under the conditions of a 'social movement society'. In the 1980s protest by the unemployed became an example of an expanded democratic politics, rather than a challenge to democracy.

The 'Peoples' Marches for Jobs' were organised by local and regional labour movements, and involved long distance marches from different parts of the country meeting up in London. Although they involved the unemployed as marchers, the unemployed did not do the organising, this was done by a range of labour movement organisations that wanted express some kind of broad concern with the level of unemployment and its consequences. Unlike the NUWM during the 1930s which also organised similar long distance marches of the unemployed that were known as 'hunger marches' (Kingsford, 1982), the Peoples' Marches for Jobs lacked clearly defined goals or demands. In the 1930s, the NUWM's hunger marches usually had some clearly defined demand of the government to create jobs or raise the level of financial support for the unemployed. In contrast, the Peoples' Marches for Jobs aimed merely to mobilise as broad a range of people as possible against the Conservative government:

> There are a lot of people in this world outside the trade unions, outside the Labour Party, who have got ideas and solutions. The idea of the March was to try to tie this together so that the March itself would bring forward some alternative based on a people's alternative. (Benn, Carter and Dromey, 1981: 7)

Little of consequence happened because of the People's March for Jobs. There were no identifiable changes to government policy. The TUC's centres for the unemployed were more sustained attempts to organise the unemployed in some way during the 1980s. The first of these started in the late 1970s, however, their activities were the subject of intense debate within the labour movement. Some saw the centres for the unemployed as political bases to create 'unions' of the unemployed modelled in part on the NUWM. However, unions wanted to retain the unemployed as a special category of members and they saw the centres for the unemployed as places run by the unions for the unemployed. They would provide the unemployed with advice about welfare rights and other services, education and leisure activities.

The labour movement attempted to generate funding to support the unemployed centres, but largely failed; only raising £52,000 in 1983 for example (Bagguley, 1991: 121). The alternative was to seek some kind of government funding through what was called the Manpower Service Commission (MSC), which supported various projects to attempt to 'manage' the problem of unemployment for the government. The consequence of the MSC funding the centres was that they were not allowed to engage in any political activity, and even providing advice about welfare rights could prove to be seen as 'political'. The vast majority of unemployed centres were funded by the MSC, so that by 1982, the centres had over 200 employees funded by the MSC, and by 1985, there were over 200 centres around the country (Bagguley, 1989: 258).

Compared to the 1930s the 1980s saw relatively little protest by the unemployed, and we can now see that there were two main reasons for this. The first concerns the bureaucratic and undemocratic way in which benefits for the unemployed are now run compared to the early 1930s when they were run by the Public Assistance Committees of the locally elected

County Councils. This supports one of Piven and Cloward's key arguments that the unemployed can only protest against those institutions that they have some kind of role within. Without their democratic role in electing those who ran the local PACs, by the 1980s there was little that they could directly influence to their own benefit. The second concerns the ways in which the labour movement controlled the centres for the unemployed by insisting that their role be largely non-political. This was reinforced by the centres becoming funded by the MSC, which prevented them from encouraging political activity. This second aspect illustrates how the institutionalisation and professionalisation of a movement, a feature emphasised by some social movement society theorists (Meyer and Tarrow, 1998: 4), can actually block rather than encourage protest. As Meyer and Tarrow suggested the labour movement became through the centres for the unemployed a 'tool' that the government used to control political responses to unemployment.

Conclusions

In this chapter, I have examined the relationship between democracy, unemployment and protest. I began by reviewing three influential discussions about the relationships between democracy and protest. In the first, mass society theory, democracy and protest are counterposed to one another. Widespread protest is seen as evidence of a democracy in crisis, and the unemployed among other marginalised social groups were seen as susceptible to protest and therefore a threat to democracy. Social capital theory is the second approach that I have considered. This shares some common characteristics with mass society theory, in that it emphasises membership of organisations as being central to a healthy democracy. From this approach one could surmise that the unemployed withdraw from democratic participation as they lack social capital or membership of organisations. This again tends to suggest that they are a threat to democracy. Thirdly, I examined some recent ideas about the role of social movements in contemporary societies. The social movement society idea suggests that social movements and their forms of protest have become a normal part of contemporary democratic activities. For this to be sustained they argued that there must be social networks and membership of organisations for people to be mobilised into movements.

Piven and Cloward suggested that the unemployed are only able to protest at times of crisis and in particular against those institutions that they are able to influence through democratic activities. When we examined in more detail the relationship between the unemployed democracy and protest in Britain, we find that in the 1930s there was extensive protest, but limited protest in the 1980s. Aspects of the social movement society argument and Piven and Cloward's ideas can help to explain this contrast. In the 1930s, there were organisations of the unemployed that were willing to mobilise them in protest actions, and there were readily available targets for protest, the locally elected Public Assistance Committees, who could give the unemployed concessions. In the 1980s, the organisations attempting to mobilise the unemployed either had vague or non-political goals. Furthermore, the labour movement's centres for the unemployed had to avoid protest activities to retain their funding. Finally there was a lack of realistic targets for the unemployed to protest against that could offer them concessions. We can see that democracy in both senses, in the sense of electoral politics, and in the sense of membership of organisations and has shaped the protests of the unemployed.

References

Bagguley, P. (1989) *Organising the Unemployed: Politics, Ideology and the Experience of Unemployment.* DPhil thesis (University of Sussex: Brighton).

Bagguley, P. (1991) F*rom Protest to Acquiescence? Political Movements of the Unemployed* (London: Macmillan).

Benn, T., Carter, P. and Dromey, J. (1981) 'Coming in from the Cold', *Marxism Today*, vol. 25:12; 6-13.

Beveridge, W. (1960) *Full Employment in a Free Society* (London: George Allen and Unwin).

Bourdieu, P. (1997) 'The Forms of Capital' in A.H. Halsey et al. (eds) *Education: Culture, Economy, Society* (Oxford: Oxford University Press). 46-58.

Coleman, J.S. (1997) 'Social Capital in the Creation of Human Capital' in A.H. Halsey et al. (eds) *Education: Culture, Economy, Society* (Oxford: Oxford University Press). 80-95.

Diani, M. (1997) 'Social Movements and Social Capital: A Network Perspective on Social Movement Outcomes', *Mobilisation*, vol. 2:2; 129-47.

Fine, B. (2001) *Social Capital versus Social Theory: Political Economy and Social Science at the Turn of the Millennium* (London: Routledge).

Gusfield, J.R. (1962) 'Mass Society and Extremist Politics', *American Sociological Review*, vol. 27:1; 19-3.

Kornhauser, W. (1960) *The Politics of Mass Society* (London: Routledge).

Meyer, D.S. and Tarrow, S. (1998) 'A Movement Society: Contentious Politics for a New Century' in D.S. Meyer and S. Tarrow (eds) *The Social Movement Society: Contentious Politics for a New Century* (Lanham: Rowman and Littlefield). 1-28.

Miller, F.M. (1979) 'The British Unemployment Assistance Crisis of 1935', *Journal of Contemporary History*, vol. 14; 329-52.

Moore, B. (1985) *All Out!* (Sheffield: Sheffield City Libraries).

Neidhardt, F. and Rucht, D. (1991) 'The Analysis of Social Movements' in D. Rucht (ed.) *Research on Social Movements: The State of the Art in Western Europe and the USA* (Boulder: Westview Press). 421-464.

Pilgrim Trust (1968) *Men Without Work* (New York: Greenwood Press).

Pinard, M. (1968) 'Mass Society and Political Movements', *American Journal of Sociology*, vol. 73:6; 682-90.

Piven, F.F. and Cloward, R.A. (1977) *Poor Peoples' Movements: Why they Succeed, How They Fail* (New York: Pantheon Books).

Putnam, R.D. (2000) *Bowling Alone: The Collapse and Revival of American Community* (New York: Simon and Schuster).

Rucht, D. and Neidhardt, F. (2002) 'Towards a "Movement Society"? On the Possibilities of Institutionalising Social Movements', *Social Movement Studies*, vol. 1:1; 7-30.

Tarrow, S. (1994) *Power in Movement: Social Movements, Collective Action and Politics* (Cambridge: Cambridge University Press).

Tarrow, S. (2000) 'Mad Cows and Social Activists: Contentious Politics in the Trilateral Democracies' in S.J. Pharr and R.D. Putnam (eds) *Disaffected Democracies: What's Troubling the Trilateral Countries?* (Princeton, NJ.: Princeton University Press). 270-290.

Walters, W. (2002) 'Social Capital and Political Sociology: Re-imagining Politics?', *Sociology*, vol. 36:2; 377-97.

Webster, C. (1985) 'Health, Welfare and Unemployment During the Depression', *Past and Present*, vol. 109; 204-30.

Whiteley, P. et al. (2001) 'Turnout', *Parliamentary Affairs*, vol. 54; 775-88.

7. Trade Unions

Elizabeth Lawrence

Trade unionism developed in industrial and industrialising countries as a response to employment conditions under capitalism. Trade unions have subsequently in Eastern Europe and in the former Soviet Union also played a role in defending workers' interests in command economies. Within 'Third World' countries trade unions have often been a major force for democratic change.

In various ways trade unions have been involved in movements for democracy in the societies in which they exist. This can be seen, for instance, in the support of British trade unions for Chartism and women's suffrage in the Nineteenth Century and in the role of COSATU (Congress of South African Trade Unions) in the Twentieth Century in the overthrow of apartheid and the struggle for a non-racial, democratic South Africa. This involvement of trade unions in movements for democracy arises partly because the essential function of a trade union, namely collective bargaining over pay and other terms of employment, cannot be conducted under political regimes that deny basic democratic rights of free organisation and assembly. It also equally arises from political perspectives that see trade unions as part of a wider labour movement, along with political parties, campaign groups and community organisations, with a responsibility to contribute to the achievement of social justice.

The role of trade unions as agents of democratic change has also led to an emphasis, among activists, political commentators and scholars, on the importance of democracy within trade unions. If trade unions are to exercise power in society, through representing people at work, then it is important that they are internally democratic. Internal democracy is vital to representativeness and to the moral authority of trade unions. This aspect of union organisation and government will be dealt with later in the chapter.

The Continuance of Industrial Relations

Trade unions had their origins in workers' response to the harsh working conditions of early industrialisation. The factory system, by bringing groups of workers together in conditions where they could perceive common interests, fostered the development of trade unionism. Writers such as Marx and Engels (1848), Engels (1845) and Thompson (1976) have shown how workers responded to factory conditions by forming collective organisations. Many early trade unions included in their remit arrangements for the payment of burial expenses and provisions for widows and orphans. In the absence of a welfare state, workers endeavoured to create their own forms of welfare, under their own control. The early trade unions often organised first on a local level and on a trade or craft basis (Pelling, 1969). These unions attempted to enforce a local rate of pay for the job, a form of unilateral regulation by workers. Later collective bargaining developed as a means of attempting to gain some control over pay and conditions of employment. Trade unions also campaigned for legal reforms to improve the situation of workers, such as limits on the length of the working day, e.g. the 1847 Ten Hours Act, and the introduction of factory inspectors. In this activity unions moved beyond the limits of the immediate workplace as the focus of their struggles. Some of this legislation, however, also produced divisions within the working class. For instance 'protective' legislation limited the employment of working women, or in the case of the 1844 Mines Act excluded women from some areas of employment. When this happened without alternative and better employment being provided, it was not a gain for women workers (Pinchbeck, 1969).

During the Twentieth Century social and political commentators at times proclaimed that trade unions were no longer necessary or relevant, as employment conditions and living standards for the working class improved. One example of this claim was the embourgeoisement thesis of the 1950s and 1960s (Zweig, 1961). Another example was the general anti-collectivism promoted by Margaret Thatcher, British Conservative Prime Minister 1979-1990. It should be noted that this argument was neither valid in the advanced capitalist economies, where workers still needed trade unions to protect them from redundancies, workplace hazards, low pay, long working hours, discrimination, harassment and bullying, nor in many 'Third World' countries, where workers experienced standards of exploitation at least as severe as those suffered by workers in Europe and North America during earlier stages of capitalism (Klein, 2000).

Many textbooks on Industrial Relations in the late 20th century began by explaining that Industrial Relations still exists as a field of academic study and of social life, despite the decline in levels of trade union membership and the growth of the non-unionised workplace (Edwards, 1995). The argument was that the process of rule-making in relation to workplace behaviour, pay and conditions of employment still exists, even if much of this no longer took place through collective bargaining between trade unions and employers. Industrial Relations as an academic discipline has been defined as 'a system of rules' (Dunlop, 1958) or as the 'struggle over the processes of job regulation' (Hyman, 1975). While functionalist writers such as Dunlop (1958) focus on the aspect of regulation and Marxist writers such as Hyman (1975) focus on the aspect of conflict and control, they both identify an area of activity between employers and their organisations and workers and their organisations, whose study constitutes the basis of an academic discipline, namely Industrial Relations.

During the 1990s the term 'Employment Relations' came into vogue. It was a term preferred by personnel managers, now often re-designated Human Resources managers, as a way of downplaying the importance of trade unions. Human Resources Management (HRM), with its emphasis on direct communication between managers and workers, on the use of appraisal and on devolution of personnel functions to line managers, was seen by some as an employers' strategy for de-collectivising workplace relations and reducing trade union power (Bacon, 1999).

Despite re-labelling under the influence of HRM, the fundamental features of employment in a capitalist society, including the basic inequality of bargaining power, concealed under the contract of employment, persist in Britain in the Twenty First Century. Hence the need still for forms of collective organisation of workers, especially trade unions. The different political and social experiences of different generations need to be addressed next, since they have a bearing on the future of trade unions as collective organisations and the meanings trade union membership has for people at work.

The Political and Social Experience of Different Generations

One of the notable features of British society, more so than of many countries on the continent of Europe, has been the different political and social experience of different generations. This is particularly the case in respect of knowledge of, and involvement with, trade unions.

In Britain the generations born in the 1950s and 1960s lived through a period of expanding trade union power. In the 1970s union membership grew to the point where slightly over half of the total working population belonged to a trade union. In 1979 union density in the UK stood at 56.9 per cent (McIlroy, 1995: 25). The political struggles of the 1970s over trade union law and pay restraint showed the power of sections of organised labour. It is useful to recount briefly the key events of that period.

In 1969 the Labour Government planned to 'reform' industrial relations by bringing in legislation to reduce the power of the trade unions. This was presented in a White Paper, titled *'In Place of Strife'*. The approach to reform was different from that advocated by the Donovan Commission of 1968, which had advocated reform through the strengthening of collective bargaining machinery and the integration of formal and informal systems of industrial relations. The proposals in 'In Place of Strife' included legislation for compulsory ballots before workers took strike action. They were dropped because of opposition from both trade unions and back-bench Labour MPs.

The Conservative Government of Edward Heath (Prime Minister 1970-74) then produced legislation in the form of the Industrial Relations Act (1971). This Act included provision for compulsory pre-strike ballots, banning of closed shop agreements, registration of trade unions, the formation of a National Industrial Relations Court (NIRC), and rights for individual workers to take legal action against trade unions. The majority of trade unions refused to co-operate with the Act. The Liaison Committee for the Defence of Trade Unions was formed to co-ordinate rank and file resistance to the Industrial Relations Act.

In 1971 there was a May Day demonstration of half a million workers against the Industrial Relations Act. Branches of the LCDTU and councils of action (often based on local trades union councils) were formed in many parts of the country. A head-on confrontation between the Government and the trade unions occurred in 1971 arising from a dispute in the London docks. Five dock workers were jailed under the Industrial Relations Act for unofficial picketing. There was widespread sympathy in the trade union movement for the jailed dockers and the likelihood of growing industrial action in solidarity with them. The Official Solicitor then intervened to arrange for the freeing of the five dockers before the political crisis escalated. The credibility of the Industrial Relations Act was seriously undermined.

Struggles over labour law marked British industrial relations for the remainder of the Twentieth Century. The Labour Governments of 1997-present, however, unlike the Labour Government of 1974-79, did not repeal most of the legislation of the preceding Conservative Governments of Margaret Thatcher and John Major.

During the early 1970s trade union opposition to the 1971 Industrial Relations Act, eventually led to the downfall of the Conservative Government of Edward Heath. In 1972 and in 1974 the National Union of Mineworkers successfully took strike action against government-imposed statutory pay limits. In 1972 the opposition was to a 7 per cent pay limit, in 1994 to a pay norm of £1 plus 4 per cent. Many trade unionists supported the mineworkers. The dominant trade union view of the time was opposition to government-imposed pay limits and support for a return to free collective bargaining.

During the 1974 Miners' Strike the Conservative Prime Minister, Edward Heath, put the country on a three-day week. Factories were only permitted to operate for three days per week to save energy. Offices could operate for five days per week, but could only use electricity on three days per week. This was in the days when many office workers still used manual typewriters and paper filing systems. Many people experienced the three-day week as a government-imposed lockout on the working class. Heath then called a General Election and went to the country on the theme of 'Who governs Britain?' He lost the election. The Labour Government, which succeeded him, repealed the 1971 Industrial Relations Act.

During the period of the 1974-79 Labour Government there were various positive advances in employment rights. These included a right to claim unfair dismissal, rights to maternity leave and maternity pay, and legislation against sex and race discrimination. Jack Jones, then leader of the TGWU (Transport and General Workers' Union) advocated a policy called the Social Contract. This was a deal between unions and the government in which the unions would support pay restraint in return for improvements in the 'social wage' including welfare benefits and legislation supporting workers' rights. There were forms of what would later be identified as 'partnership', such as the National Economic Development Council, in which trade union leaders were consulted on economic policy. The Social Contract encountered growing opposition among the ranks of trade union members who objected to pay restraint.

The events of the 1970s led to positive appreciation among workers of what trade unions could achieve in respect of employment rights. There were, however, also political and media attacks on trade unions, playing on a theme of the dangers caused by excessive trade union power to the economic health of the country. These attacks reached their peak in 1979, the so-called 'winter of discontent' when various strikes by low-paid public sector workers led to some disruption of hospital and local government services.

Generations who grew up in the 1979-1997 period knew only a Conservative government and a series of defeats for organised labour. During this period changes in labour law substantially weakened the power of unions. McIlroy (1991) summarised these changes as: (a) reducing individual employment rights, especially through lengthening qualifying periods to take cases to industrial tribunals (now called employment tribunals) and qualifying periods for maternity rights, (b) reducing trade union immunities, thus criminalising secondary action, (c) reducing support for collective bargaining, by removing legislation which supported it, and (d) disorganising the unions, through abolition of the closed shop and legislation on union governance, elections and political funds. These changes were introduced piecemeal in a series of acts.

Worker solidarity was redefined as secondary industrial action and made unlawful. Margaret Thatcher, Conservative Prime Minister 1979-1990 proclaimed that there was no such thing as society, only the family and individuals. There was an ideological onslaught on collectivist values. In 1984-5 the Conservative Government engaged in a major political battle with the National Union of Mineworkers, then the strongest and most militant trade union in Britain. The dispute occurred over pit closures. The miners were eventually defeated. This was partly because they were divided. Pit closures were not a unifying issue in the way a struggle for a pay rise in 1972 and 1974 was. Heavy policing of pit communities marked the miners' strike. Press coverage focused largely on the issue of picket line violence. Eventually economic hardship forced many miners back to work and the strike ended with a return to work without a settlement. The defeat of the miners' strike was a major setback for organised labour.

For the generation of young people in Britain coming to adulthood at the beginning of the Twenty First Century, their experiences of labour history are very different from their parents' generation. They may have had no personal experience or knowledge of trade unionism and their world view has been partly shaped by the anti-collectivist discourse of the Thatcher period. Some young people nowadays approach the labour market with a sense of fatalism, and hold a perspective in which employers have all the power and workers have to take the jobs on the terms on offer or not at all. If people are convinced that trade unions can do nothing to improve their pay and conditions, they will be less likely to join a trade union, let alone become active in one. Many university students, working part-time to finance their studies, experience employment in non-unionised sectors of the economy, especially shops, restaurants and bars. This is not a starting point in working life that is likely to give a positive view of the benefits of union membership, although it may show the need for union organisation.

The second half of the Twentieth Century showed marked swings in the status and respectability of trade unions. During the Second World War unions were (junior) partners in production for the war effort, in a struggle against fascism. Since fascist governments on the continent of Europe had smashed the organised trade union movement, the struggle against fascism was seen as the cause of the labour movement. In this period trade union leaders made headway for their members in a number of bargaining areas, in return for contributing to wartime production. Following World War II, for a number of years in the UK trade union leaders enjoyed a period of respectability, becoming in some ways part of the establishment, with consultation by governments on matters of economic policy and life peerages for retired union leaders. This continued for much of the 1960s and during the Labour Government of 1974-79. It was only with the election of a Conservative Government under Margaret Thatcher in 1979, that the pattern changed significantly. Trade union representatives were no longer routinely included in a variety of government bodies and quangos. Regular consultations with unions over economic and employment policy ceased. Trade unions were 'out in the cold'. So for the generation born around or soon after World War II trade unions were in some ways part of the establishment, indeed were criticised by 'New Left' radicals in the late 1960s and early 1970s for being too much part of the establishment. For young people born since 1979, trade unions were organisations subjected to marginalisation by government and exclusion from the corridors of power. This attitude to the unions has largely continued under the Labour Governments led by Tony Blair since 1997. Under the leadership of John Monks, TUC General Secretary since 1993, the TUC and individual trade unions in the UK have, in varying degrees, espoused the notion of social partnership, as a strategy for bringing unions back into the centre of the political stage (Taylor, 2000). The impact of the 1979-1997 period, however, meant that trade unions faced a long journey back.

The Decline in Trade Union Membership

Many trade unions in Britain in the 1990s had to face up to the implications of a declining number of members. Membership decline arose partly from changing patterns of employment. Loss of jobs in industries such as coal mining, engineering, manufacturing, and steel led to loss of union members for unions recruiting in these industries. Within the private sector there has been a growth in the number of SMEs (small to medium size enterprises). Cully et al. (1999) report that only 7 per cent of small businesses with a working owner present had a recognised trade union. This would suggest that employer opposition might be an important factor in blocking the growth of unionism in this sector. Public sector unionism was relatively less affected by loss of membership.

Another aspect of the picture, however, until fairly recently has been the failure of unions to invest resources in recruitment work (Kelly and Heery, 1989). At one time unions did not need to do much actively to recruit members. Many people assumed it was 'natural' to join the union when starting work. Moreover greater employment stability meant that once an employee had joined a trade union, the union often had a member for several decades. The growth of temporary contract working and employment instability hit union membership in a number of ways. Workers on a temporary contract may perceive less benefit in joining a trade union, because they see their position with their employer as only temporary. It is also harder for employees on a temporary contract to assert employment rights, if they fear the consequence of doing so will be the non-renewal of their contract. While this may not necessarily be a deterrent to union membership, it is likely to discourage union activism. Moreover higher rates of labour turnover meant unions had to keep recruiting new employees to the union. This particularly affects unions organising in highly casualised industries such as hotel and catering.

During the 1990s the TUC and its affiliated organisations became concerned about the increasing average age of trade union members, which was in the late forties. This meant that unions were faced with the prospect of many of their members, including their lay activists, reaching retirement age within the next ten to fifteen years. Unless younger generations of workers could be recruited, trade unions faced possible extinction as collective organisations. This led unions to question whether younger workers see trade unions as no longer relevant. One quotation used to address this problem was the view that unions are a good thing for blue-collar workers with problems, but not relevant for white-collar workers with opportunities. This is not a viewpoint, which is hostile to trade unionism, but is one that sees it as personally irrelevant.

Trade union renewal and growth among younger workers also relates to the extent to which the young people of the early Twenty First Century are a politicised and socially aware generation. Many young people are interested in issues regarding the environment and animal rights. Others have also become involved with anti-globalisation campaigns. These issues do not automatically connect with traditional labour movement concerns, regarding jobs, pay and conditions, although there is potential overlap with environmental and globalisation issues, if the political connections are made. To do this requires a trade union perspective, which goes beyond immediate workplace concerns, and a political analysis, which relates issues of environment, globalisation, capitalism and imperialism. Mann (1973) proposed that class consciousness consists of four elements: class identity (defining oneself as a member of the working class and identifying with others in the same position), class opposition (identifying the capitalist class as a distinct class with opposing interests), class totality (seeing class relationships as affecting the whole of society) and alternative consciousness (the ability to imagine a different society. Anti-globalisation protesters, advancing slogans such as 'Another World is Possible' clearly have what Mann referred to as alternative consciousness, although they may not possess a strong class identity.

There is some indication that unions are now more popular as far as their public image is concerned. There are no longer the kinds of press debates about problems of excessive trade union power, which took place at the end of the 1970s. A July 2002 *Guardian/ICM* opinion poll showed 59 per cent of voters thinking strikes planned by public sector workers, in local government, rail and underground, were justified, while only 29 per cent considered them unjustified (*Guardian*, 30th July, 2002). The willingness of the public to support strike action, which could cause them personal inconvenience, is a good test of trade union popularity.

The TUC is tackling the issue of recruitment and organisational renewal with the New Unionism project and the Organising Academy. The Organising Academy has focused on recruiting young people as union organisers. Its work is discussed in a later section of this chapter.

Hyman (2002) identifies five possible union responses to declining membership. These are: (1) providing more services to attract members, (2) mergers, (3) a renewal of unionism based on an organising approach, (4) seeking partnership with employers, and (5) campaigning on human rights. He notes that some of these approaches are in conflict with others. For instance seeking partnership with employers, and hence greater respectability, does not sit easily with a focus on grassroots organising or linking up with other groups concerned with human rights issues. Nonetheless the response of the trade union movement in Britain in the 1990s showed all these possible responses.

Kelly (2002) identifies four methods used by unions internationally to revive their power. These are international solidarity action, coalition building, accessing political power and corporate campaigns. Again these approaches are not always complementary. The examples he quotes, however, do provide some evidence of a revitalisation of the trade union movement.

What are Trade Unions for?

The attempt to make trade unions more relevant to younger people raises the issue of the purposes of trade unions. The question of 'what are trade unions for?' has been debated many times both within the labour movement and among academics. It is useful therefore to summarise briefly these debates and discuss their implications for the future of trade unionism.

The academic literature on Industrial Relations has traditionally distinguished between a welfare unionism and a business unionism philosophy (Jackson, 1982). The welfare unionism philosophy is associated with the social-democratic values of many European trade union unions. It focuses on achieving social benefits for all working people and sees the trade union as part of a wider labour movement. The business unionism philosophy is associated with the approach of many North American trade unions. In this view the union is a business, which is there to deliver services and agreements on pay and conditions for its members, but does not have a wider social or political role. In practice, however, most unions spend most of their time and resources on matters concerned with jobs, pay and conditions. Therefore, while the distinction between welfare and business unionism is useful, for instance in studying relationships with political parties, it does not imply that in all respects unions with different philosophies act differently. Nonetheless the welfare unionism philosophy sits more comfortably with trade unions playing a wider social and political role.

The purpose of trade unions has also been debated within social-democratic and socialist political theory. For instance Flanders (1970) argues that unions should be organisations that represent workers' interests in the workplace. He rejects both the Marxist view that unions should be involved in a struggle for socialism and a bourgeois view that unions should control workers' demands in the wider interests of 'society'. Others such as Anderson (1977) present the Leninist view that trade union consciousness is insufficient for the socialist transformation of society and that a political party is necessary. Within this perspective socialists should be active in unions, but need to struggle against bureaucracy in the unions and against accommodation with the capitalist system.

Trade union responses in Britain to membership decline in the 1980s and 1990s have as Hyman (2002) indicated been varied. At times there has been an emphasis on promoting unions as providers of services to members. This approach was advocated by Bassett and Cave (1993), when they argued unions should be an emergency service for people at work, with union membership sold on a similar basis to AA membership. This is an approach similar to a business unionism philosophy, in that union membership is viewed only in terms of the benefits it delivers to individuals. Within this perspective members are seen as recipients of services, not as union activists, and internal union democracy is either treated as relatively unimportant or is evaluated principally in consumer satisfaction terms, with the assumption that if members are not satisfied they can leave the union and join another one. This view does not encourage unions to take on a wider social and political role, since the criterion of effectiveness is the level of service delivered to individual members. One of the limits of this approach is the question of when individual members' problems should be perceived as social issues. For instance if a union is representing individual members, who are experiencing violent assaults in the workplace, when does it define the problem in wider social terms, related perhaps to poor levels of service provision, or unacceptable behaviour on the part of 'customers', or indeed the promotion of customer care policies, in ways which neglect the rights of employees.

Unions have also, however, as in the TUC's New Unionism project, focused on organising and campaigning in a more dynamic way, which seeks the active involvement of the membership. This also lays the basis for potential links with local community struggles, campaigns with human rights and anti-globalisation organisations. Thus these different perspectives on the role of trade unionism have implications for the internal organ-

isation of the union, the view of the membership, as either active participants or recipients of a service, and whether it is important for unions to be
democratic. They also have implications for the extent to which trade
unions reach outwards and seek to build alliances with other groups in society, who are also seeking social change.

Trade Union Democracy

If union democracy is important, there are still debates as to how democracy within unions should be defined. The academic literature on union
democracy and government has taken two main approaches to the definition of union democracy. One approach has been to measure democracy in
terms of levels of membership participation (Ramaswamy, 1977). On this
test, most unions, like many other voluntary organisations and political parties, can be judged undemocratic. For instance in many union elections,
only a minority of members votes, even though they have the opportunity
to do so in a postal ballot. Union constitutions, however, are formally democratic, in that members have the opportunity to participate, vote in elections and stand for office.

The other major approach to the definition of union democracy has been
to examine the right of opposition groups within unions to exist and organise, circulate material and contest elections (Lipset, Trow and Coleman,
1956). The presence of organised oppositions is seen as beneficial in
encouraging membership participation, since it presents members with a
choice of policies and leaders. If an opposition group has a genuine chance
of winning union elections and/or changing policies, then this can be seen
as a good indicator of union democracy. Within British trade unions at the
start of the Twenty First Century there were a number of victories by the
left in union general secretary elections (e.g. Bob Crow RMT, Billy Hayes
CWU, Mick Rix ASLEF, Mark Serwotka PCS and Derek Simpson, AMI-
CUS). In many cases these election results indicated a degree of political
shift among the union members.

The impact of feminism and other equality movements on trade unionism has added another dimension to the definition of union democracy.
There is now more concern over how far unions are representative of their
members in terms of gender, race, disability and sexuality. In some cases
unions have addressed this issue through the establishment of advisory
committees and conferences for oppressed groups and through the creation
of reserved seats on their national executives. One of the most thorough-

going attempts to address equality issues occurred with the formation in 1993 of UNISON from three unions (COHSE, NALGO and NUPE). The UNISON constitution includes principles of proportionality, fair representation and self-organisation (McBride, 2001).

Trade Unions, Equality Movements and 'New Social' Movements

One of the major changes in the British trade union movement in the last quarter of the Twentieth Century was the impact of equality movements. These movements challenged and redefined areas of trade union policy; they added new issues to the bargaining agenda; and they led to some reexamination and revisions of trade union structures.

Trade unions had held a limited women's rights agenda for a long time, at least since the 1888 TUC resolution in favour of equal pay. For much of this time, however, the trade union agenda on women's rights was largely confined to equal pay and related equality issues in the workplace. Many trade unions also supported the principle of the family wage, the belief that male workers had the right to earn enough to support a family, even though this principle in some ways undermined women's claims for equal pay. The impact of Second Wave Feminism was to achieve a considerable widening of the union agenda on women's rights. The Working Women's Charter Campaign in the 1970s and 1980s linked demands for equality in the workplace with equality in society, working on the principle that women cannot be equal at work without equality in the wider society. In the 1970s too several trade unions affiliated to the National Abortion Campaign, taking up a position of opposing restrictive legislation on abortion and supporting the demand for a woman's right to choose. In 1979 the TUC called a national demonstration in opposition to the Corrie Anti-abortion Bill. This was the first time that a national trade union federation had called a demonstration in support of women's abortion rights. The winning of unions to a pro-choice position was a major achievement by women's rights activists in the unions, since it involved not only winning support for a pro-choice case, but also winning the argument that women's abortion rights are a trade union issue (Lawrence, 1994).

In terms of race policy again there was a major change in the trade union position in the last quarter of the Twentieth Century. For much of the Twentieth Century official trade union policy was to support immigration controls as the basis for good race relations (Miles and Phizacklea, 1977;

Phizacklea and Miles, 1980). The approach, like Labour Party policy of the time, focused on integration and assimilation. This policy defined problems of race relations in terms of a rapid entry of immigrants with a different culture, not in terms of white racism. Thus for a long time trade unions adopted a colour-blind approach to race relations. Two strikes in the 1970s were important in shattering this complacency. In both of these strikes, Mansfield Hosiery Mills and Imperial Typewriters in Leicester, black workers went out on strike over discriminatory practices, while white workers continued to work (Sivanandan, 1990). This racial divide in the workplace made some trade union leaders realise that unions needed to be more active in challenging racism, including among their members. Subsequently the TUC and affiliated trades unions have taken a more active stance against racism and have promoted various initiatives to tackle racial inequality.

In the case of disability for a long time this had been seen by trade unions as more of a welfare issue than an equal rights issue. Unions had supported employment in sheltered workshops and services for disabled ex-servicemen and women. The National League of the Blind and Disabled had been in existence since 1890 as a TUC-affiliated union. The campaigns by disability rights activists in the 1980s onwards for full civil rights challenged trade unions, like the rest of society, to re-examine assumptions about the abilities of disabled workers. The TUC did support campaigns for anti-discrimination legislation. While the 1995 Disability Discrimination Act (DDA) was not the comprehensive piece of equality legislation disability rights activists had sought, it provided scope for further educational and campaigning work by trade unions. Trade union officers were also involved in representing members in disability discrimination cases; often where employers did not understand the concept of a 'reasonable adjustment' as required by the DDA.

Winning union support for lesbian and gay rights involved challenging accepted boundaries of the public and the private. Like women's abortion rights, issues of sexuality were at first difficult to raise at trade union meetings. Many union members were reluctant to see these matters as trade union issues. Many unions, however, now do have comprehensive anti-discrimination policies, which include lesbians and gay men. Unions have been involved in campaigning against workplace discrimination and for reform of pension schemes, so that they include provision for same sex partners.

The equality movements not only challenged the policy positions and bargaining agenda of trade unions. They also persuaded unions to change some of their ways of operating to make unions more inclusive. For instance women's rights activists campaigned for the provision of crèche facilities at union meetings and for the payment of childcare expenses. Engaging with disability rights required unions to address issues of access to union meetings, and production of union material in an accessible format. The choice of safe and culturally acceptable venues for union meetings is also a matter which unions have had to address.

In 2001 the TUC conference adopted an equality clause as a condition of affiliation to the TUC (see Appendix 1). All unions are required to have an equality clause in their constitution. This was a clear statement that equality is mainstream trade union business (*Labour Research* Vol. 91, No 3, March 2002). Unions will also be required to engage in more effective equality monitoring of their own structures. This includes counting the number of women and minorities on executive committees and in leadership positions at all levels of the union. Equality auditing of union structures can contribute to the renewal of the trade union movement.

Other social movements as well as equality movements have also affected unions. Anti-globalisation protests have linked protestors concerned with environmental issues, world trade, and Third World debt cancellation with trade unions. At the protests at the World Trade Summits in Genoa in 2001 and Barcelona in 2002, trade union contingents played a major role in the demonstrations. The development of social forums at a city level, in which these various affinity groups can meet with trade unions and exchange viewpoints, may encourage trade union renewal and radicalism. It may also help unions connect with radicalising young people who do not automatically see trade unions as an obvious channel for their political activity.

New Unionism and the TUC Organising Academy

'New Unionism' is a label given by the TUC to a number of projects to revitalise the labour movement. Two essential elements of 'New Unionism' are the organising approach and the work of the TUC's Organising Academy. The TUC's 'New Unionism' project aimed to propagate a model of unionism based on the principle of organising rather than servicing members. The argument put forward was that trade unions had slipped into a mode of activity in which full-time officials and lay officers provide services, principally representation and collective bargaining, for a largely inactive membership. For trade unions to grow and be effective they needed to shift resources from servicing existing members to recruiting and organising new ones. Thus the organising model emphasises the principle that the members are the union. In practice it is sometimes easier for unions to espouse this model than to translate it into day-to-day ways of working, since members expect a service in return for their subscription and may leave, if not provided with representation when they need it.

In 1998 the TUC set up the Organising Academy. The Organising Academy has now trained over 150 new union organisers. Affiliated unions employ Academy trainees, usually for a period of a year. They are given training by the TUC but are allocated projects by the individual unions they work for. . Many of these trainees have gone on to permanent employment with trade unions. The TUC Organising Academy brings young people into union activism. Some Academy trainees have previous union experience; others have been active in the National Union of Students or various campaign groups. Prior trade union experience was not a condition of recruitment, unlike in the case of many other full-time trade union posts. Academy trainees have engaged in focused recruitment projects. Some projects have focussed on in-fill recruitment, namely raising the level of union density in a workplace where the union already has members and recognition. Much of this work is based on the recognition that the single biggest reason why many workers have never joined a trade union is that no one has ever asked them to join. Other projects have focused on greenfield recruitment, endeavouring to build up membership as a basis for a claim for union recognition. In these contexts Academy organisers are more likely to face employer hostility and resistance. They may for instance be unable to meet workers, distribute literature or hold meetings on workplace premises.

The Organising Academy had often adopted the 'like recruits like' principle in terms of union recruitment. Thus, there has been a conscious effort to recruit organisers who are young, female and black in an attempt to appeal to un-unionised groups of workers, by employing union organisers from the same background. The work of the Organising Academy is not only about recruitment, but also about building up workplace organisation. Thus the aim is to create a self-sufficient organising group of lay union activists within a workplace, who can continue organising and recruitment work, once the full-time union organiser has moved on to another project. The Organising Academy is also becoming an apprenticeship route into full-time union office holding. This could create a tension if it blocks opportunities for other lay activists to obtain posts as union employees.

Partnership at Work or Conflict?

As Hyman (2002) notes one trade union response to declining membership levels has been partnership projects. The TUC under John Monks' leadership embraced the concept of partnership as a way of regaining respectability and support for trade unions. Within the European Union there is a definition of social partners, namely employers and trade unions, who are engaged jointly in matters of economic regulation and social welfare. Given the way unions in Britain were out in the cold during the period of Conservative Government (1979-1997) it is understandable that partnership seemed an attractive alternative to exclusion. The partnership approach at the level of society, however, is based on a concept of a social market, support for state welfare provision and regulation of the economy. These are not the economic policies pursued by the Labour Government in Britain. On the contrary Labour economic policies under Tony Blair's leadership involved a continuation of many aspects of Thatcherism, including maintenance of restrictive labour laws and support for economic deregulation. Thus the economic basis at the state level for social partnership is lacking.

One of the major tensions between the British trade union leadership and the Labour Government arose from the failure of the Government to repeal the Conservative anti-union laws. Indeed the organisation of lawful industrial action became more difficult when the courts ruled that while unions no longer needed to give employers the names of those members being balloted for industrial action, they needed instead to supply detailed profiles, which would allow employers to minimise the effect of industrial action. The task of supplying a detailed profile by site, grade, part-time or full-time status and similar features was an even more difficult one than supplying an accurate list of names.

Individual employment rights have also not been improved to the extent trade union leaders wished. The trade unions wished to see employment rights start from day one of employment, so that employers could not use temporary contracts to remove employment rights. While a national minimum wage has been established, the level is considerably lower than the trade unions would like. In 2002 the national minimum wage was £4.20 per hour for workers over 22.

The partnership agenda poses the question of how far are employers committed to partnership. At local level many trade unionists see little evidence of commitment to partnership on the part of employers. Within the public sector partnership projects can come into conflict with decisions by the Labour Government to privatise public services. An area where partnership between trade union leaders and the Labour Government has come near to breaking point is privatisation. Unions have been actively involved in campaigns against privatisation in the health service, railways, education and the post office. In 2002 SERTUC (South East Region of the TUC) held a conference against privatisation. Union opposition to privatisation has been based both on a belief that it will lead to deteriorating services for the public and on concern regarding the impact on workers' pay and conditions.

The privatisation issue is also leading to splits between the Labour Party and those unions affiliated to the LP. On 16th March 2002 a Socialist Alliance conference on trade union political funds attracted around 1000 participants. In 2002 the CWU (Communication Workers' Union) decided to cut by 50 per cent its donations to the Labour Party. Motions on disaffiliation from the Labour Party had been debated at a number of trade union conferences. For instance at the UNISON Conference in 2001, one delegate posed the question 'why feed the hand that bites you?'

Conclusion: the Future of Trade Unions

Will trade unions be relevant to future generations? First, in answer to this question it can be argued that people at work need representation, both individual and collective. An individual worker who is involved in disciplinary or grievance proceedings will usually benefit from being represented. Individual workers who experience bullying, harassment or discrimination are more likely to receive justice if they have trade union representation. At this basic level it can be argued that trade unions are always potentially relevant to people at work, so long as trade union representatives are permitted to carry out this representative function. Collective representation is also relevant while employees experience improvements in their pay and conditions arising from collective bargaining. Neither of these forms of representation requires active engagement from most members with the work of the trade union for most of the time, unless called upon to take industrial action in support of collective bargaining.

Much of the academic literature on union participation has identified it with commitment to occupational roles and with work being a central life interest (e.g. Lipset, Trow and Coleman, 1954). There may have been a decline in both professional-bureaucratic and traditional-proletarian orientations to work. In this sense the question of the future of trade unions is part of a wider question of whether there is a future for occupational associations of any kind, as part of civil society. Younger workers may have a more instrumental orientation to work, partly because of labour market experience, partly because of more consumerist values. Nonetheless attachment to work and to work-based organisations can grow over working life. The instrumental orientation can also co-exist with forms of militant industrial protest. It would be wrong to conclude therefore that because many younger workers may be more leisure-oriented than work-oriented that this necessarily leads to non-membership or non-involvement with trade unions.

Is there a union renaissance or revival going on? Many trade unions would like to give this impression. Clearly in the UK there has been some stabilisation in union membership figures and some modest increase. Trade union federations in several countries have adopted a more dynamic approach to union organisation and recruitment. There has not been a massive rebirth of unionism, at the time of writing (2002), but there has been some increase in industrial militancy and in pay expectations. Kelly (1998) has argued that patterns of union activity can be related to long waves of economic development. According to this model strike waves are more likely to occur during transition periods between upswings and downswings in the economy, suggesting a possible revival of union activity early in the Twenty First century.

One of the key questions to trade union revival at the beginning of the Twenty First Century is the question of how far can organised labour link up with anti-globalisation struggles and other social movements for peace, justice and human rights. For instance there are possible dynamic alliances of workers and consumers, using selective consumer boycotts of products, around issues of labour conditions in the Third World and environmental issues. Labour unions in the Third World are facing many of the same challenges that faced workers in Europe and North America in the 19th and early 20th centuries, including battles over the right to organise. They are facing the same struggles over pay, unsanitary working conditions, long working hours and lack of freedom for workers living in premises owned or controlled by employers. For instance the situation of women textile workers in free trade zones, as reported by Pilger in 2002, has many similarities with the situation of women textile workers in New England early in the Twentieth Century, prior to the famous Bread and Roses strike of 1912, in which over 20,000 mainly female textile workers won a major dispute over pay and working hours. There is a material basis for coalitions concerned with justice for workers, fair trade and protection of the environment.

Trade unions participated in protests against globalisation, e.g. Genoa 2001, Barcelona 2002, and took part in the European Social Forum in Florence, Italy, in November 2002. Many individual union activists and sections of the leadership of trade union are demonstrating their willingness to make the political connections between issues of workers' rights and other social and political questions. They do subscribe to the belief that 'Another World is Possible'.

Appendix 1 – TUC Model Equality Clause

The objects of the union shall include:

a)   the promotion of equality for all including through:
      i) collective bargaining, publicity material and campaigning, representation, union organisation and structures, education and training, organising and recruitment, the provision of all other services and benefits and all other activities;
      ii) the union's own employment practices.

b)   to oppose actively all forms of harassment, prejudice and unfair discrimination whether on the grounds of sex, race, ethnic or national origin, religion, colour, class, caring responsibilities, marital status, sexuality, disability, age or other status or personal characteristics.

References

Ackers, P., Smith, C. and Smith, P. (eds) (1996) *The New Workplace and Trade Unionism* (London: Routledge).

Anderson, P. (1977) 'The Limits and Possibilities of Trade Union Action' in T. Clarke and L. Clements (eds) *Trade Unions under Capitalism* (London: Fontana).

Bacon, N. (1999) 'Union Derecognition and the New Human Relations: A Steel Industry Case Study', *Work, Employment & Society*, vol. 13:1; 1-17.

Bassett, P. and Cave, A. (1993) *All for One: The Future of the Unions* (London: Fabian Society).

Beardwell, I.J. (ed.) (1996) *Contemporary Industrial Relations: A Critical Analysis* (Oxford: Oxford University Press).

Briskin, L. and McDermott, P. (eds) (1993) *Women Challenging Unions: Feminism, Democracy and Militancy* (Toronto: University of Toronto Press).

Clarke, T. and Clements, L. (eds) (1977) *Trade Unions under Capitalism* (London: Fontana).

Cully, M., Woodland, S., O'Reilly, A. and Dix, G. (1999) *Britain at Work, as Depicted by the 1998 Workplace Employee Relations Survey* (London: Routledge).

Davis, M. (1993) *Comrade or Brother: The History of the British Labour Movement 1789-1951* (London: Pluto).

Dubin, R. (1973) 'Attachment to Work and Union Militancy', *Industrial Relations,* vol. 12:1; 51-64.

Dunlop, J.T. (1958) Industrial Relations Systems (New York: Holt).

Edwards, P.K. (ed.) (1995) *Industrial Relations: Theory and Practice in Britain (Oxford: Blackwell).*

Engels, F. (1845) 'The Condition of the Working Class in England' in K. Marx and F. Engels (1975) *Collected Works Vol. 4 1844-1845* (London: Lawrence and Wishart), 477-519.

Fairbrother, P. (1994) *Politics and the State as Employer* (London: Mansell).

Flanders, A. (1970) *Management and Unions* (London: Faber and Faber).

Gallie, D., Penn, R. and Rose, M. (eds) (1996) *Trade Unionism in Recession* (Oxford: Oxford University Press).

Goodman, G. (1985) *The Miners' Strike* (London: Pluto Press).

Hyman, R. (1975) *Industrial Relations: A Marxist Approach* (London: Macmillan).

Hyman, R. (2002) 'The Future of Unions', *Just Labour: A Canadian Journal of Work and Society*. www.justlabour@yorku.ca

Jackson, M.P. (1982) *Trade Unions* (London: Longman).

Kelly, J. (1988) *Trade Unions and Socialist Politics* (London: Verso).

Kelly, J. (1998) *Rethinking Industrial Relations, Mobilisation, Collectivism and Long Waves* (London: Routledge).

Kelly, J. (2002) *Union Revival: Organising Around the World*, TUC, November 2002.

Kelly, J. and Heery, E. (1989) 'Full-time Officers and Trade Union Recruitment', B*ritish Journal of Industrial Relations*, vol. 27:2; 196-213.

Kelly, J. and Heery, E. (1990) 'British Trade Unionism 1979-1989: *Change, Continuity and Contradictions, Work, Employment & Society* (special issue); 29-65.

Klein, N. (2000) *No Logo* (London: Flamingo).

Labour Research Department (2002) 'Women in Unions Face Glass Ceiling', *Labour Research*, vol. 91:3; 10-12.

Lawrence, E. (1994) *Gender and Trade Unions* (Basingstoke: Taylor and Francis).

Lipset, S.M., Trow, M.A. and Coleman, J.S. (1956) *Union Democracy* (Glencoe: Free Press).

McBride, A. (2001) *Gender Democracy in Trade Unions* (Aldershot: Ashgate).

McCarthy, W.E.J. (ed.) (1985) *Trade Unions* (Harmondsworth: Penguin).

McIlroy, J. (1991) *The Permanent Revolution: Conservative Law and the Trade Unions* (London: Spokesman).

McIlroy, J. (1995) *Trade Unions in Britain Today. 2nd edn* (Manchester: Manchester University Press).

Mann, M. (1973) *Consciousness and Action among the Western Working Class* (London: Macmillan).

Marx, K. and Engels, F. (1848) 'Manifesto of the Communist Party' in K. Marx and F. Engels (1976) *Collected Works, Vol. 6* (London: Lawrence and Wishart), 477-519.

Miles, R. and Phizacklea, A. (1977) *The TUC, Black Workers and New Commonwealth Immigration*, 1954-1973 (University of Bristol SSRC Research Unit on Ethnic Relations).

Moody, K. (1988) *An Injury to All: the Decline of American Unionism* (London: Verso).

Mort, J-A. (ed.) (1998) *Not your Father's Union Movement: Inside the AFL-CIO* (London: Verso).

Pelling, H. (1969) *A History of British Trade Unionism* (Harmondsworth: Penguin).

Phizacklea, A. and Miles, R. (1980) *Labour and Racism* (London: Routledge and Kegan Paul).

Pilger, J. (2002) *The New Rulers of the World* (London: Verso).

Pinchbeck, I. (1969) *Women Workers and the Industrial Revolution, 1750-1850* (London: Frank Cass and Co. Ltd).

Ramaswamy, E.A. (1977) 'The Participatory Dimension of Trade Union Democracy: A Comparative Sociological View', *Sociology*, vol. 11:3; 465-80.

Ramdin, R. (1987) *The Making of the Black Working Class in Britain* (London: Wildwood).

Saunders, J. (1989) *Across Frontiers: International Support for the Miners' Strike 1984/85* (London: Canary Press).

Sivanandan, A. (1990) *Communities of Resistance: Writings on Black Struggles for Socialism* (London: Verso).

Taylor, R. (1994) *The Future of the Trade Unions* (London: Andre Deutsch).

Taylor, R. (2000) *The TUC, From the General Strike to New Unionism* (Basingstoke: Palgrave).

Thompson, E.P. (1976) *The Making of the English Working Class* (Harmondsworth: Penguin).

Virdee, S. and Grint, K. (1994) 'Black Self Organisation in Trade Unions', *Sociological Review*, vol. 42:2; 202-26.

Wrench, J. (1989) 'Unequal Comrades: Trade Unions, Equal Opportunities and Race' in R. Jenkins and J. Solomos (eds) *Racism and Equal Opportunities in the 1980s* (Cambridge: Cambridge University Press).

Zweig, F. (1961) *The Worker in an Affluent Society* (London: Heinemann).

8. UK Anti-Privatisation Politics

Sally Ruane

This chapter seeks to explore the character and limitations of anti-privatisation political activity in Britain, particularly in relation to the welfare state. It conceptualises privatisation as a refashioning of the relationship between capital and the decommodified sectors of the state and it explores the potential for resistance amongst those arguably most affected by it: service producers and service users.

Among others, Carter and Fairbrother (1995) and Kerr (1998) have signalled how restructuring within the state has brought about a rearticulation in class relations in the workplace: changes in both the labour process and class relations of authority, control and sometimes ownership. Changes in the dominant mode of control of labour and the creation of a higher service class enjoying greater managerial control and relatively high levels of remuneration have implications for the ways in which people experience their work, the potential for conflict and the ability of the workforce to take collective action. In this chapter, I shall consider how the experience of a radical public policy, which has refashioned the relationship of state to capital, might or might not have the potential to mobilise to resistance. At the same time, part of this restructuring has modified the relationship of users and recipients to welfare services and benefits, through fees as well as changes in the quality and quantity of services. Some of these developments threaten the 'social wage' enjoyed by the citizen: the collective benefits transferred to individuals and families in cash and kind via the state (Bryson, 1992). This raises the possibility of user engagement and resistance.

The chapter first identifies some of the main types of policy initiative that have deepened capitalist penetration of the state; following this, it considers the principal actors in anti-privatisation politics and how anti-privatisation activity fares on Byrne's (1997) protest campaign – social movement continuum. It then explores in more detail how experiences in services work and consumption promote or constrain resistance among producers and users. It finishes with a discussion of the constraints and opportunities faced by anti-privatisation activists.

A Restructuring of the State

Nelson (1995) observes that capital is seeking to pursue new avenues of profitability, not so much through a geographical expansion into new markets but through the penetration of those spheres of activity that, for decades at least, had been conducted in the non-commodified zones of the state. Many of these activities entail the production of services not goods. At the supranational level, the General Agreement on Trade in Services (GATS) has been negotiated under the auspices of the World Trade Organisation, to establish a legal framework within which cross-border trade and investment in services can flourish. It seeks to remove 'barriers to trade' in services, extend market access by overseas companies to service sectors and constrain state service regulation. It is against this backdrop that in this chapter we focus upon policy developments at the national and local level, which have furthered the penetration by capital of decommodified services, specifically welfare services, and at the possibilities and constraints facing a politics of anti-privatisation.

Margaret Thatcher, drawing upon the radical political economy of the New Right, advocated the superiority of the market and contract mechanisms in the allocation of goods and services. This was seen first among nationalised industries and later among utilities. Public sector monopolies were criticised for 'crowding out' alternative and competing goods and services suppliers, thereby constraining the scope for the accumulation of capital (Bacon and Eltis, 1978) and a challenge was issued to professionals, bureaucrats and other groups in the public sector who were construed under public choice theory as self-interested empire-builders. In the welfare sector, government policies gave significant fillips to commercial provision in some ancillary services such as cleaning and catering but also in caring sectors such as residential care for older people. Cox (1986) has observed how little political opposition to these moves there was, apart from trade union campaigns and half-hearted gestures from an enfeebled shadow cabinet.

Privatisation policies have since been introduced by successive governments regardless of political colour and the terrain judged ripe for 'enclosure' now encompasses the institutions and services which form the core of the welfare state. There are distinct types of these so-called 'public-private partnerships' (PPPs). One brings commercial activity directly into the state sector. Compulsory Competitive Tendering (CCT) (and latterly Best Value) established a competitive market in the provision of *ancillary* services within local government, health and education. This constituted a recommodification of previously devalorised activities. The contracting-out of *professional* services has not been applied on a general basis but has been used in a more limited way. For instance, where Local Education Authorities (LEAs) fail OFSTED inspections, other authorities and suppliers from the independent sector may be invited to tender for those services. Alongside this, we have the prospect of private 'senior management teams' running some NHS services through 'franchising' (Cox, 1996).

Another approach has been to establish organisational structures and procedures that make much more likely the fostering of commercial activity in the provision of services. The principle of the 'enabler state' contracting for services from a range of competing suppliers in the commercial, voluntary and statutory sectors accompanied the organisational separation of purchaser and provider roles. For instance, whilst 2 per cent of home help and home care contact hours were supplied by the independent sector in 1992, by 1998, the figure was 45 per cent (Johnson, 2001). A variant of this model can be seen in the use of planning procedures to supplement NHS hospital capacity with capacity within the independent health care sector (DoH, 2000). This means that some NHS patients will now receive NHS-funded health care which is supplied by a for profit provider, which now engages in the planning process of health care. The highly controversial private finance initiative (PFI) which combines commercial involvement in the planning and design of services and infrastructure as well as in the long-term running and maintenance of those services and infrastructure (Kerr, 1998; Ruane, 2002) entails a degree of privatisation which is broad in scope (planning, design, service provision) and lengthy in duration.

There has been widespread restructuring of the public bodies responsible for delivering welfare services – often away from centralised, hierarchical structures in which all are employees of the state, towards a decentralised, fragmented proliferation of agencies in which the management function has changed from one embracing control, co-ordination and unifying functions to one which emphasises the first of those. For example, in the 1980s, the Civil Service was restructured through the Next Step programme, establishing multiple agencies with chief executives and semi-autonomous managerial structures with discretion to provide services according to proxy market criteria and indicators (Carter and Fairbrother, 1995). Such restructurings are relevant not only because they have resulted in changes in the labour process and in relations of authority and control, thereby shaping the way state employees experience and make sense of their work but also because they may establish the structures, roles and procedures which serve as a stepping stone for subsequent privatisation. Private sector managerial practices such as individual performance review and budget management are also important since these techniques help shape the values and ethos of the service as well as preparing it (through the greater exercise of control over staff and the intensification of work) for survival in the market.

Other reforms have transferred part of the burden of paying for services away from the state (through redistributive taxation) and onto the user. In higher education, it is no longer grants but loans which are means-tested and although these can be obtained at advantageous rates within a regulated framework, the principle that the individual is responsible for covering his or her own maintenance costs during the university years is established (Kendall and Holloway, 2001). Moreover, tuition fees are also now covered in part by the individual.

Taken as a whole, these developments mark a significant encroachment by business upon the welfare sector, conceptualised by Whitfield (2001a) as an emerging 'corporate welfare complex'.

Anti-privatisation politics now occur in a different climate. The Labour leadership is itself an energetic and enthusiastic prosecutor of privatisation policies. There is no serious front bench resistance to privatisation, with both Conservatives and Liberal Democrats accepting a role for the private sector. A 'new consensus' appears to have emerged. The Greens alone of significant national parties oppose privatisation.

Extra-Parliamentary political action opposing privatisation has accelerated over the past few years. Much of this has been trade union activity with high profile campaigns, including actual and threatened strike action. These are often related either to the prospect or the consequences of transfer of groups of workers into private sector employment, which has accompanied PFI schemes and other public-private partnerships. Trade unions at the national level have adopted a range of tactics. Both Unison and the GMB, which have substantial public sector memberships, have established pro-public sector campaigns: 'Positively Public' and 'Keeping Public Services Public', respectively. Both have commissioned research, for instance in relation to the companies engaged in privatised services and the anticipated consequences of privatisation models, particularly PFI.

Much anti-privatisation political activity has a strong trade union character – unsurprising since most left activists are likely to be strong trade unionists – but there are other social groups involved as well. Perhaps the most politically engaged user group is the council house tenant or resident. Tenants' and residents' associations have been organised into federations. These user groups, which, because of the spatial character of their organisation, take on some of the flavour of community groups, are actively engaged alongside trade unions (e.g. UCATT, TGWU) in a national campaign called Defend Council Housing. This maintains a sophisticated website which carries information about proposed stock transfers and the voting results of areas where stock transfer has already been tested at the ballot box. Defend Council Housing has recorded some stunning victories in its campaigns for 'No' votes in stock transfer ballots (for example, in Birmingham in 2002).

There also exist locally based radical political groupings composed of diverse activists who work together around a range of political issues, including privatisation. These groups bring together radicals from different occupational groups and employment settings (and none) although there is a strong public sector bias. The Tyneside Socialist Forum, for instance, is comprised of greens, environmentalists, community activists (including clergy), radical lay Christians, non-aligned radicals, as well as socialists from various political parties (and none). Many, though by no means all of these are middle class professionals working in the public sector. All of these are users – and often critics – of at least some public services even if they do not principally identify as such.

Many of these organisations have sought to develop alliances. Both nationally and regionally, trade unionists have forged links with and made use of radical academics whose technical and theoretical expertise can be used to critique specific policy applications and help educate members. The numerous anti-privatisation conferences, seminars and workshops that have been held over the past few years fulfil their literal function, bringing different people together and serving as a springboard for action and further networking. Many organisations make creative use of the internet: websites are used for the dissemination of factual information, analysis and the advertising of conferences, demonstrations, lobbies and other events; they are used for the presentation of statements or declarations or petitions which the visitor to the website is invited to sign; they are used for the exposition of principles, values and aims and for specific policy proposals. Some websites even contain discussion forums via which site visitors are encouraged to debate.

Anti-Privatisation Politics: a Protest Movement?

Given a range of anti-privatisation activists and organisations, it is worth considering how best to conceptualise this activity. It is possible to discern features characteristic of a range of positions on Byrne's (1997) 'protest campaign-social movement' continuum. At one end the anti-privatisation continuum, collective action may take on a 'protest campaign' character (e.g. attempts to obstruct the implementation of a specific scheme) but at the other, values are promoted which pose a radical challenge to the status quo (for instance in an anti-capitalist demonstration). Byrne suggests that social movements are comprised of those whose values and principles are non-negotiable; these are the source of cohesion for social movements and their incorporation into policy requires a 'thorough-going revision of some of the basic ideas which underpin the whole functioning of [the] system' (Byrne, 1997: 17).

What we find in anti-privatisation politics is rather different. Despite the much-argued case for a campaign which is *offensive* and positive rather than merely *defensive*, anti-privatisation politics have emerged as a direct result of government policies which have undone previous pro-public measures, arrangements and institutions (Whitfield, 2001b). They focus principally upon defending *even if* the goals of extending the socialisation of the means of production are present. In the main, these broader, more far-reaching goals are not much in evidence. The main focus is upon trying to prevent threatened or potential privatisation moves or to reverse those that have already been taken.

Rather, then, than attempting to bring about a popular conversion to values which are so radical they 'break the limits of compatibility of a system' (Byrne, 1997: 17), anti-privatisation protest seeks the *restoration* of values, principles and policies which increasingly appear to belong to a previous. Perhaps, though, the notion of incompatibility is not entirely without application. Regulation theorists (see, for example, Jessop, 1994; Cerny, 1990) have emphasised the distinctive phases of capitalism that 'require' different institutional and regulatory infrastructure. A reasonably generous welfare state and a corporatist framework for economic and employment policy obtained in many Western European countries under Fordism. Under the emergent, post-Fordist, globalised phase of capitalism, the values of socialisation and public service ethos do increasingly come to appear as 'outdated' or incompatible.

It is still possible to argue, then, that anti-privatisation politics can propose a revision of basic ideas, which is not merely restorative, and reformist but a fundamental challenge to the emergent order. It is possible to see, as a result, that trade union attempts to operate within the fold of the Labour Party and 'tug' a Labour government which has embraced the notion of globalised capitalism back to traditional labour values, face limitations, as Labour leadership disregard for the anti-PFI vote at the Labour Party Conference in 2002 illustrates. Here we might see that party and pressure group politics, seeking concessions, compromise and damage limitation, face a crisis which has the potential to 'expel' such politics out into the sphere of the extra-parliamentary, tactically non-conventional world of the protest movement. It is possible to see an anti-privatisation movement as embryonic or emergent.

Re-Articulating Class Relations in the Workplace

There are two groups we might consider to be most affected by radical restructuring and who might offer resistance to it. One comprises those who produce welfare services, in a professional or 'support' capacity, and the other consists of those who use these services. The first could be expected to resist because of the reshaping of class relations (of ownership and/or control) in the workplace, which have almost everywhere entailed an intensification of work and an intensification of the extraction of surplus labour. Users could be expected to resist because of encroachments on the social wage. We begin with a consideration of welfare service workers.

The professional employee-employer relationship, through the exchange of commitment to meeting client needs for generous wages and control over the service, entails trust. Whilst some have argued that this 'pact' leaves the professional class intrinsically conservative, others have claimed that the service class, because of both its function and its possession of cultural capital, is able to produce a social critique of the status quo giving rise to the alternative politics of the new social movements (Webb, 1999).

Historically, under the welfare state, professionals offered their services to all on a citizenship basis rather than a market or ability-to-pay basis. Hanlon (2000) argues that their own material interests were served by this *and* by the expansion of public services and increasing state involvement in sectors such as health, education and employment. There is some evidence that individuals sympathetic to the ideals of the welfare state and citizenship-based access to public services self-selected for these career opportunities. Byrne (2002) argues that professional work in the public sector offered the prospect of rising not from but *with* the working class (since these were institutions largely brought about by the political actions of this class earlier in the century) and appealed disproportionately to those brought up in politicised working class families. All of this contributes to the possibility of a progressive service sector. However, the restructuring of the public sector under first the Conservatives and now New Labour has set in motion a new dynamic.

The introduction of centralised financial control, auditing, rationing and cost cutting has degraded and proletarianised service work and undermined the trust basis of service class employment with political and ideological consequences (Webb, 1999). With trust-based employment relations disrupted, morale low and insecurity high, Webb predicts that professionals will become increasingly self-protective or indifferent, threatening their potential for radicalism. Moreover, a divide has emerged between professional management strategists who adopt 'entrepreneurial values' and devalued welfare professionals who cling to their 'caring values'.

It is the uneven and fragmenting impact of the reforms that Hanlon emphasises. Restructuring the public sector presents not merely threats in the form of auditing, cost-accountability and rationing but also *opportunities* of career advancement, enhanced status and pecuniary reward for those willing to endorse either practically or ideologically the commercial and entrepreneurial turn. The struggle is fought in terms of individual careers, daily practices and professional identities and ideologies. Professionals are social actors who give meaning to and make judgements and choices about the options facing them. Hanlon (2000) argues that, 'The changing nature of people's work is reshaping them politically; the outcomes of this reshaping will be key determinant in the future of the welfare state'

Some will endorse entrepreneurial approaches and will actively position themselves within managerial elite enjoying enhanced control and high levels of remuneration. Others will merely want to keep their jobs but may be forced to practice in ways which are inimical to their values and which may have a corrosive effect on those values. Professionals may come to believe that they can no longer provide good quality services on a citizenship basis.

In making decisions about how to respond to the degradation of work, service professionals' options are shaped by, among other things, the meanings they confer upon the changes they experience at work, meanings informed in part by wider social discourses. These contain several elements or themes which recur: the welfare state is too expensive and cannot be sustained; taxes cannot be raised to fund better public services because of the threat to international competitiveness; the public sector is very wasteful; the public sector needs to learn from the private sector which is less costly, better managed and more efficient; the public sector needs to modernise and to find new models of service delivery.

Thus, degradation and standardisation may not be experienced as exploitation and the professional might consider cuts justifiable in order to reduce waste or stronger management essential given the size and complexity of the institution; or s/he might consider a reduction in the quality of service offered inevitable in the context of a government policy of increased access. In these circumstances, professionals will not feel they can justifiably – legitimately – resist, either individually or collectively and professional associations and trade unions will face corresponding legitimacy difficulties with their own members and the wider public.

The NUT has been pursuing anti-privatisation initiatives and the BMA has researched, reported on and provided a forum for discussion on issues relating to privatisation for some time. However, a perusal of the websites would indicate that, with one or two exceptions, professional associations have devoted limited activity to resisting privatisation, but rather have focussed on pay and conditions, professionalism, workload and casualisation.

Moreover, despite the challenge posed to public professionals through changes in the material conditions of work and authority relations at work, there has been comparatively little political collaboration with non-professional workers in the welfare state. There are several reasons for this, including the fact that professional and non-professional workers have traditionally been organised in different unions and associations. In particular, the selective pursuit of CCT has served over the past twenty years to sustain a critical difference in the employment positions and work experiences of professionals and ancillary workers in such sectors as health and education. The latter have been subjected to the threat of regular competition for their own jobs. By the early 1990s, most affected services were provided by 'in house' teams but on terms, conditions and pay relatively worse than they had previously enjoyed (Kerr and Radford, 1994). Professionals in these services did not face this threat. It is true that the position in local government and the civil service was somewhat different since some white collar, technical and professional roles were included in the legislation in the early 1990s. Market testing has resulted in a reduction in the number of civil service jobs and both in-house and transferred staff have complained of increased workloads, resource shortages, stress and insecurity. However, in other respects contracting has had a less serious impact on white-collar workers in that the pressure to contract out is less severe and protection of quality is more central (Colling, 1999). Nonetheless, the Public and Commercial Services Union remains one of the few major professional groups that have launched a national campaign against privatisation (www.pcs.org.uk/02natprivatisation.htm).

Colling (1999) points out that outsourcing of these working class jobs has not resulted in any straightforward way in a heightening of class awareness. Distinctive patterns of tendering and service configuration have fragmented workforces, exposing them to varying degrees of competitive pressures and developing divisions. The consequences for trade unions of these tendering and outsourcing policies have been significant, although they have varied across and within sectors (Corby, 2000). Pay and conditions have been retarded, with any earnings growth accompanied by job cuts and increased productivity: that is, the pay-effort bargain to attain these earnings changed (Colling, 1999). Indeed, attempts to increase productivity have made use of increased monitoring or supervision of effort levels, job role expansion and work intensification.

The introduction of PFI as a mode of financing, developing and running public sector infrastructure has threatened whole sectors of an institution's workforce with long-term en bloc transfer to private providers. The exclusion of professional spheres of activity from the early waves of PFI served to drive a divisive wedge between the 'threatened' ancillary and the 'safe' professional groups. In the health sector, The RCN's belief in the late 1990s that 'PFI doesn't affect our members' helped prevent the possibility of a joint front to resist the advance of PFI in the hospital sector (Ruane, 2000) and some professionals welcomed new facilities and equipment, even if purchased through private money. Thus, at both the national and the local level, resistance to individual schemes was diluted. The prospect of franchising and privately managed stand alone diagnostic and treatment centres, along with a potential expansion in the role of private acute care, however, may lead to a reappraisal on the part of professional groups, particularly as the potential implications of GATS sink in. It comes as no surprise that it is the trade unions representing 'support' workers which have until now taken the lead in anti-privatisation activity.

The Users of Public Services as a Potential Source of Political Opposition

Users are potential participants in a politics of anti-privatisation, partly because of the introduction or extension of fees and partly because of the reduction in quantity or quality of services available. Some hospital PFI schemes have reportedly brought about a reduction in beds, resulting in unwanted service reconfiguration (Houldcroft, 2002). Access to good quality services is thereby threatened on several fronts. If producers of services can be expected to struggle in the workplace over relations of authority and ownership and the wage-effort bargain, users of services could be expected to resist a reduction in the 'social wage' in the form of state services and cash benefits. We might expect user resistance either where services are universal or a broad swathe of the population, commanding a range of resources, is affected or where users are able to organise effectively.

It is possible for individuals or households of different income levels to establish distinct patterns of consumption and standards of living. However, in relation to public services, especially 'universal' services, experiences may be more shared. Although outside welfare, the rail service brings the point home. Rail passengers of all incomes must use the same train services. Although these can be income differentiated in terms of travelling comfort, quality of food and service, the reliability, punctuality and safety of train services affect and inconvenience all who use them, regardless of income. Moreover, the impact is profound: this inconvenience disrupts the individual's ability to organise the rest of his or her daily routine effectively. The high profile tragedies of recent years, for instance at Hatfield and Potters Bar, have threatened literally millions of passengers with the prospect that the trains and the tracks they are travelling on may be fatally dangerous. Media reports have explicitly linked this to privatisation (Clark, 2002).

Social housing is accessed predominantly by the elderly, low paid and workless. It is, therefore, not conducive to a commonality of experience across classes. However, social housing is enormously significant for hundreds of thousands of low paid workers since it affords them security of tenure across changes in employment status. Occupants of social housing are more likely to share with each other experience of the service: they live in often spatially segregated areas and are organised into tenants' groups or associations. Therefore, as well as sharing common experience of the conditions of the lived-in environment, they already have institutional struc-

tures and definite processes for the discussion of problems and the organisation of action for redress. Moreover, many tenants' associations are long-
standing with a membership that includes older people from the politicised
working class of the post-war decades.

Consumption of health and education services can be contrasted. Access
to and consumption of education services is to a considerable extent determined by income level. Schools have well defined catchment areas; this
means that schools are likely to vary in relation to the profile of the children they cater for and in relation to the additional resources parents provide for the school and the sorts of difficulties teachers have to deal with in
the lives of the children. The exercise of the right to 'parental choice' has
exacerbated differences among schools. However, differences in access to
quality education do not end there. For the well off, it is possible to buy an
entire childhood of education in the private sector, although purchase of
private secondary education only is more common. This is superior to state
education in a number of ways: classes tend to be smaller, resources more
generous, opportunities for extra-curriculum activities more numerous and
diverse and outputs in terms of exam results better. This approach to education also tends to reduce dramatically children's contact with their less
advantaged peers. Higher education is shared but paying the fees and for
the maintenance of the student is easier for the better off family.

The situation is somewhat different in health. Certainly, better off
households may be able to take out private medical insurance or can access
private health care on a fee-for-service basis where less well off households
may not. However, it is not possible to purchase a childhood's or adulthood's access to private health care in the way in which a childhood of education can be purchased privately. Private health care is not
comprehensive: some interventions cannot be purchased (e.g. organ trans-
plants), fees can quickly become unaffordable and insurance policies are
limited in scope. There are no emergency and accident provisions comparable with those of the public sector. Access or the possibility of access to
the National Health Service is always necessary. There is, therefore, a partial commonality in the experience of the service among different sections
of the population.

However, the comparative cohesion and political engagement of the
tenants' organisations around council housing are not to be found in equal
measure in user groups associated with other services within the welfare
state, including health. User action in relation to health services illustrates
this where hundreds of health service user groups have been formed 'rep-

resenting' patients, carers and relatives and varying in size, structure, access to financial resources and the range of issues campaigned around (Allsop, Baggott and Jones, 2002). There are significant limitations to the reformism of these organisations and these limitations do not lie solely in the financial costs of or short timescale for consultation. The largest and most highly organised groups have been unmistakably incorporated into the policy process. An illustration can be found in the Patients Association, which lobbies the government for policy change, raises the salience of issues through the media and undertakes research. It is often invited to represent patients' views on committees, think tanks and working parties that shape future policy. For instance, the PA attends meetings of the Partners' Council, a consultative body established by the National Institute of Clinical Excellence (www.patients-association.com). Suspicions of corporatism are strengthened by the views of civil servants who suggest involving such groups in the policy process is a pragmatic means of helping 'create a consensus about what was possible' and 'minimis[ing] overt criticism' (Allsop, Baggott and Jones, 2002). These are not initiatives that involve an opposition of patient to the political parameters of the service: its mode of funding, structure, relationship to private interest and so forth.

Discussion

By far the most coherent anti-privatisation activity is undertaken by a handful of trade unions. This is because their public sector members are in direct line of fire and because they have the financial and organisational resources to run campaigns, fund research, access information about specific local developments and make use of media contacts. They are also national organisations with a national profile and some of their leaders are recognisable to the non-membership public. They are in a good position to articulate the concerns and anxieties of all who oppose privatisation. Their role in helping frame or define the meaning, implications and anticipated consequences of current pro-private reform cannot be overestimated. The public – all users of public services and some workers within them – are aware of the broad thrust for privatisation. It does not matter so much that they know the specifics of a given scheme or sector but how their ideological framing of that thrust is shaped. The meaning attributed to a particular policy is shaped by a range of competing discourses: those of ministers, 'experts', newspapers, friends and workmates and those of individuals or organisations with which the individual identifies. The pro-privatisation agenda in welfare has not been driven from below: there is no push for it from the Labour Party rank and file or the general public. It is a policy that has developed on the 'inside' and is being imposed from the top. Because of this, Tony Blair and ministers of state have had, on numerous occasions, to explain and justify the policy on public platforms. This suggests that the definition of the policy, its meaning in terms of consequences and interests served and interests threatened, is at the least open to debate. This creates a political opportunity for those who would resist the policy.

Other groups opposed to privatisation tend to be smaller and to command fewer material resources although they can often mobilise non-material resources such as expertise, skills and specialist knowledge. Local groupings of wider networks of left political activists tend not to sustain a permanent infrastructure of office and researcher. Although the Internet has speeded up, intensified and widened communications, these groups are often lacking in time and money. Like trade unions, they are often not exclusively preoccupied with anti-privatisation. Because of their limited time and material resources, they are particularly vulnerable to 'events' (as Macmillan put it), as the derailing by September 11th of the growing anti-privatisation campaign of the summer of 2001 demonstrates. Although some insisted 'politics as usual' was the best way to defy terrorism, at least one trade union dropped any attempt to raise privatisation issues through the mass media because media attention had turned elsewhere. At the same time, many left activists prioritised anti-war activities. These illustrate how command over resources and political opportunity interact to shape outcome.

War or the threat of war served in 2001 to halt a growing momentum and momentum is what is required in developing a successful protest against privatisation. But surely relevant also was the decision at the same time by Unison to step down their public campaign and enter a series of negotiations with government. The internal union wrangling (www.unison.co.uk) over the resultant PFI-related 'Retention of Employment' proposal illustrates the dilemma trade unions face: they can negotiate concessions for members within the framework of government policy or they can engage in battle over the policy itself, utilising industrial, including strike, action. They can do both of course, but the consequences of one approach might fatally affect the outcome of the other and only the latter leaves open the possibility of sustained approaches, which engage, convince and galvanise the public.

There are many reasons for the low level of political activism in the UK but, after a decade or two of 'There is No Alternative', a belief (and even experience) that effort achieves comparatively little must rank high above them. Mobilisation theory (Kelly, 1998) suggests that individuals are more likely to participate in collective action if they believe that action will be efficacious. Interaction with others is essential for individuals to ascertain how others define the situation and whether enough of them are prepared to take action to make a difference. But even this assumes a 'public interest'. In the context of employment, the interests of workers are contested: they are not reducible, as are employers', to profit and employers and trade unions compete to define workers' 'real interests'. How much more the 'contingent products of social construction' (Kelly, 1998) are the 'real interests' of the public: the battle at the 2002 Labour Party Conference over PFI centred precisely on this struggle to define the public interest. The challenge of left activists and unions alike is to convert the manifest public unease about (at least aspects of) privatisation into a politically meaningful force (Travis and Maguire, 2002).

This is all the more important given the wedge driven by Blair and Labour ministers between the public and 'producer interests' (White, 2002) and Blair's conviction that there is genuine public backing for new PFI schools and hospitals regardless of longer-term costs. Engaging with community groups is strategically essential. There have been few political successes enjoyed by anti-privatisation activists and the most notable – ballot defeats for the transfer of council housing stock – are the outcome of painstakingly developed alliances.

One of the difficulties facing campaigners against privatisation is that pro-private policy is pursued by Labour, which has traditionally defended and extended the scope of the public. Those attached to Labour face a difficult cognitive task in resolving the meaning of a pro-privatisation leader in a social democratic party. This difficulty is aggravated by the absence of a persistently and publicly communicated *internal* source of an alternative definition of party policy: that it is *not* a third way or essential modernisation but that it is a rolling back of the hard-won gains of social democracy. A recent history of 18 years in opposition adds further to the difficulty of those unsure how to make sense of the policy and philosophy shifts within the Labour Party. The partial political paralysis brought about by this cognitive dissonance has led some to wonder whether only the Labour Party can privatise the welfare state (Ruane, 2000).

Social movements have been conceptualised by some (Byrne, 1997) as an alternative to class-based action, and as emerging in the wake of the failure of collective action by the industrialised working class to bring about radical social transformation. This has established social movements and class-based action as in some way oppositional or contradictory theories of social change. However, in relation to anti-privatisation politics, at least, combining social movement and class perspectives seems a more fruitful way forward. Anti-privatisation politics cannot yet be conceptualised as constitutive of a political or social movement. They do, however, form the basis of a potential or emergent protest movement. Moreover, they do so with a foundation in the organised working class and with, despite all of the limitations and obstacles identified above, the *potential* of alliances with radicalised middle classes because of a refashioning of class relations in the workplace and with service users because of the concomitant threat posed to the social wage. Resource Mobilisation theorists suggest that movements emerge out of networks, groups and movements which already exist among those who are dissatisfied and aggrieved. At present, there are examples of organised groups and examples of alliances but as yet, organisation and activity have not yet developed sufficient momentum for a 'take-off'.

References

Allsop, J., Baggott, R. and Jones, K. (2002) 'Health Consumer Groups and the National Policy Process' in S. Henderson and A. Petersen (eds) *Consuming Health: the Commodification of Health Care* (London: Routledge). pp. 48-65.

Bacon, R. and Eltis, W. (1978) *Britain's Economic Problem: Too Few Producers* (London: Macmillan).

Baggott, R., Allsop, J. and Jones, K. (2001) *Participation and Representation in Health Policy: the Role of Health Consumer Groups, Final Report to the ESRC.*

Bryson, L. (1992) *Welfare and the State* (London: Macmillan).

Butler, P. (2002) 'Hospitals one step closer to private management', *The Guardian*, 11 February 2002.

Byrne, D. (2002) *A Middle Class Created by Social Democracy: Public Sector Service Class People in Post-industrial Britain and Northern Ireland.* Unpublished paper presented at the conference, 'How Class Works', State University of New York, June 2002.

Byrne, P. (1997) *Social Movements in Britain* (London: Routledge).

Carter, B. and Fairbrother, P. (1995) 'The Remaking of the State Middle Class' in T. Butler and M. Savage (eds) *Social Change and the Middle Classes* (London: UCL Press). pp. 133-147.

Cerny, P. (1990) *The Changing Architecture of Politics* (London: Sage).

Clark, A. (2002) 'Not-for-profit successor welcomed despite doubts about who is in the governance driving seat', *The Guardian*, 4 October 2002.

Colling, T. (1999) 'Tendering and Outsourcing: Working in the Contract State?' in S. Corby and G. White (eds) *Employee Relations in the Public Services* (London: Routledge/Cardiff University). pp. 136-155.

Corby, S. (2000) 'Employee Relations in the Public Services: A Paradigm Shift?', *Public Policy and Administration*, vol. 15:3; 60-74.

Cox, A. (1986) 'Privatisation and Public Enterprises in Britain 1979-1985', *Teaching Politics*, vol. 15:1; 30-59.

Department of Health (2000) *The NHS Plan: A Plan for Investment, A Plan for Reform* (Cm4848-1 London: HMSO).

Hanlon, G. (2000) 'Sacking the New Jerusalem? The New Right, Social Democracy and Professional Identities', *Sociological Research Online* 5:1. www.socresonline.org.uk/5/1/hanlon.html

Houldcroft, L.. (2002) 'Shock for hospital as Trust chief quits', *The Journal*, 27 September 2002, Newcastle.

Jessop, B. (1994) 'The Schumpeterian Welfare State' in R. Burrows and B. Loader (eds) *Towards a Post-Fordist Welfare State* (London: Routledge). pp. 13-37.

Johnson, N. (2001) 'The Personal Social Services' in S. Savage and R. Atkinson (eds) *Public Policy under Blair* (London: Palgrave). pp. 174-191.

Kelly, J. (1998) *Rethinking Industrial Relations* (London: LSE/Routledge).

Kendall, I. and Holloway, D. (2001) 'Education Policy' in S. Savage and R. Atkinson (eds) *Public Policy under Blair* (Basingstoke: Palgrave). pp. 154-173.

Kerr, D. (1998) 'The PFI miracle', *Capital and Class*, vol. 64:Spring; 17-27.

Kerr, A. and Radford, M. (1994) 'TUPE or not TUPE: Competitive Tendering and the Transfer Laws', *Public Money and Management*, vol. 14:4; 37-46.

Nelson, J. (1995) *Post-industrial Capitalism* (Thousand Oaks, CA: Sage).

Ruane, S. (2000) 'Acquiescence and Opposition: The Private Finance Initiative in the NHS', *Policy and Politics*, vol. 28:3; 411-24.

Ruane, S. (2002) 'PPPs – The Case of PFI' in C. Glendinning, M. Powell and K. Rummery (eds) *Partnerships, New Labour and the Governance of Welfare* (Bristol: Policy Press). pp. 199-212.

Travis, A. and Maguire, K. (2002) 'Majority backs fire strike and wants PFI halted', *The Guardian*, 26 September 2002.

Webb, J. (1999) 'Work and the New Public Service Class', *Sociology,* vol. 33:4; 747-66.

White, M. (2002) 'Blair beaten but defiant on public services', *The Guardian*, 1 October 2002.

Whitfield, D. (2001a) *Public Services or Corporate Welfare* (London: Pluto Press).

Whitfield, D. (2001b) *Keeping the Private out of the Public.* Unpublished presentation given at a national conference, Leicester, November 2001.

9. POLITICAL ACTIVITY AND YOUTH IN BRITAIN

Mark Weinstein

Recently there has been a rise in interest in young people's political behaviour. The past few years have seen the publication of a number of important studies that explore young people's perception of formal political institutions, their trust in the system, their understanding of what politics means to them, as well as their attitudes towards political parties and elections (Wring et al., 1999; White et al., 2000; Henn et al., 2002). However, this relatively healthy interest in youth has not always been the case.

In the years succeeding the Second World War, British political science was deeply absorbed with the explanatory power of social class to the almost total exclusion of other socio-demographic characteristics. Butler and Stokes' *Political Change in Britain* (1969) provided the keystone study. Heavily influenced by the discipline in America (Lazarsfeld et al., 1944; Campbell et al., 1960), they argued that allegiance to a political party was inherited through childhood socialisation, developing into a deep psychological attachment between the individual elector and their party that would endure over time. This partisan alignment worked in tandem with a strong class alignment as voters expressed their identification with their chosen parties at the polls, with working class electors voting for the Labour Party and middle class voters casting their ballots for the Conservative Party (see Crewe, 1983; Robertson, 1984; Franklin, 1985).

Given the strength of the relationship between class and voting behaviour at the time, maybe it is not that surprising in retrospect that British political science of the period talked with a single voice about 'the elector', 'the citizen' and 'the voter'. The oft-cited quote of Pultzer (1967: 98) that 'class is the basis of British party politics; all else is embellishment and detail', could easily be adapted as a critique of the narrow focus of conventional British political science throughout this period. Within this homogenised view of society the focus rarely shifted away from the explanatory power of social class. Whilst the family unit was regarded as the key transmission mechanism through which people were socialised into the political system (Jennings and Niemi, 1974), young people did not feature on the political agenda in any meaningful way. Rather, there was the implicit assumption that the experiences of youth were not worthy of differentiation from those of the population as a whole. The lack of interest in youth was not exclusive; historical religious differences between Catholics and Protestants were no longer seen to be politically salient, and regional, ethnic and gender differences were regarded to be of only of minimal importance. In 1964, Rose (1964: 18) was able to state that 'today politics in the United Kingdom is greatly simplified by the absence of major cleavages along the lines of ethnic groups, language or religion'. However, the invisibility of youth was something that would change at the turn of the 1970s.

From 'Old' to 'New' Politics

The period from the late 1960s marked a fundamental change in the character of British political life as the hitherto stable relationship between class and political behaviour entered a period of dealignment (Crewe, 1984; Harrop and Miller, 1987). Faced with the phenomena of dealignment, British political science developed a variety of theories that sought to explain electoral behaviour, many of which demonstrated a growing appreciation of the sophistication and complexity of political attitudes and electoral behaviour (Dunleavy, 1980; Himmelweit et al., 1981; Rose and McAllister, 1986). Others, however, claimed that the entire basis of politics in advanced Western societies was in the process of transformation with the rise of new social movements based on social, rather than class cleavages (Barnes et al., 1979; Dalton, 1988).

Underpinning the rise of these new movements was the argument that society had experienced an intergenerational shift towards a post materialist perspective (Inglehart, 1977). Inglehart argued that young people, in particular, were increasingly rejecting the growth agenda of the main political parties, and questioning the values, priorities and consensual goals at the heart of the system. He argued that these new political cleavages were mobilising specific *generational* segments of society with support for political change coming from a new social base with youth at the forefront of a new political agenda centred on environmentalism, opposition to the development of nuclear power and armaments, and anti-growth politics (Inglehart, 1984; Offe, 1985; Crook et al., 1992).

1968 and All That

Inglehart's contention that there was a new generation of post materialists maturing in the late 1960s offered a theoretical explanation for the 'waves of dissatisfaction and protest' (Barnes and Kasse, 1979: 9) that appeared to sweep across advanced Western societies at this time. A core of protestors emerged who appeared to be dissatisfied with the society in which they lived and who were looking for fundamental social change. The rise in youth-led political protest was closely related to the emergence of a rebellious youth culture in the 1960s (Osgerby, 2000; Marwick, 1988).

During 1967 and 1968 a series of mobilisations drew in a new generation of young radicals protesting against the war in Vietnam (Lent, 2001) and students revolted at the London School of Economics as part of a wave of militant student protests in European and American cities inspired by the role of students in the general strike in France in 1968 (Birchall, 1987). In 1970 the first national women's liberation conference was held, the Gay Liberation Front held its first meeting and Friends of the Earth (FOE) – a new, radicalised, environmental movement – was formed in 1971 in response to the first major road building programme of the post-war period (McNeish, 1999). Greenpeace soon joined FOE on the environmental scene.

Noticeably, these mobilisations appeared to be youth led and, as was noted by Kasse and Marsh (1979), the protestors had very little interest in what is usually called 'politics'. Cotgrave's (1982) 1979 study of environmental groups found that 30 per cent per cent of those involved in these mobilisations were under 30 years old and Van Liere and Dunlap's (1980: 191) study of environmentalism was able to conclude that 'age is negatively correlated with environmental concern'[11]. Towards the end of the 1970s a reinvigorated Campaign for Nuclear Disarmament (CND) resurfaced, refreshed by what was perceived to be an upping of the anté in the nuclear arms race by NATO's decision to base Cruise and Pershing missiles in Europe. Coxall (2001: 35) estimates that at its height in the mid-1980s, CND had 45,000 members whilst another 100,000 belonged to local peace groups. During this time a series of national mobilisations regularly attracted in excess of 100,000 demonstrators to the streets of London. Once again many of these mobilisations had a high concentration of youth. Parkin's (1968) study of CND uncovered a membership in which 55 per cent per cent of people were in the 15-25 age group, and Byrne's (1988) research, carried out at the height of the 1980s mobilisations, found that 71 per cent

---

11 This finding was not limited to any individual country. See, for example, Kriesi's (1989) study of Dutch social movements that reached similar conclusions about age and the potential for Mobilisation.

per cent of CND members were under the age of 40, 24 per cent per cent of them being under the age of 25.

A New Style of 'Youth' Politics?

From their previous invisibility, young people suddenly became central to an understanding of political behaviour. For the first time a number of clearly discernable 'youth issues' were identified, as was a distinctive, new, style of politics that appeared to be particularly attractive to the young. In particular, it was suggested that the anti-bureaucratic and non-hierarchical structures of such organisations, combined with the use of unconventional methods of political action to appeal specifically to young people (Melucci, 1989; Della Porta and Diani, 1999; Byrne, 1997). Anti-bureaucratic in their own right, they rejected the conventional structures and traditional political leadership patterns that characterised most of the old political movements, whether they are political parties, trade unions, or civil rights-based groups. Whilst the old politics was built on established, centralised and hierarchical organisations, the new politics called for forms of political expression that were symbolic, providing a sign for society that reached far beyond the particular message that they sought to communicate (Melucci, 1989).

The new political organisations exhibited qualities and behavioural patterns that went sharply against the established political grain, not just in the issues around which they coalesced and the anti-growth ideology they espoused (Dalton et al., 1990). They were also differentiated from past political incarnations by their preference for direct political action, often remaining intentionally outside of the framework of conventional politics. Such an approach contrasted markedly with the functioning of older left-wing political organisations and campaigns that sought to buy interest and influence at the negotiating table. New social movement organisations, in contrast, remained deliberately outside of the system, exerting pressure on policy directly by their actions and the influence that they had on public opinion.

From New Social Movement to Radical Direct Action

Coxall (2001: 36) estimates by the mid-1980s the environmental movement had a membership approaching two million people. However, as the eighties progressed well-established groups such as FOE and Greenpeace tended to adopt an increasingly conventional pressure group strategy, with the result that by the end of the decade British environmental groups had grown into relatively formal and bureaucratised organisations. Whilst FOE introduced a number of central co-ordinators in the mid-1980s, Greenpeace UK (which had started with just six members of staff in 1980) had evolved into an organisation of eight separate sections by 1993 (Diani and Donati, 1999: 19). Groups such as FOE and Greenpeace also began to sponsor their own scientific evidence to challenge that of the government and multinational corporations. This development is best seen in the debate around climate change and global warming, where it became more and more common for environmental experts to engage in debate with their opponents (Connelly and Smith, 1999: 83), downgrading the importance of rank and file mobilisations in the eyes of many activists. Indeed, the professionalisation of environmental politics and the greater emphasis placed on technical knowledge has, more recently, extended into an engagement with national governments and multinational corporations that many grassroots activists in the movement would regard as unacceptable. For example, in 2001 representatives of FOE joined with the World Wildlife Fund and Transport 2000 to meet their opposite numbers from Monsanto, Du Pont, Balfour Beatty and Cargill's at a 'Getting Engaged' seminar (Rowell, 2001).

This turn from participatory campaigning organisations towards centralised media-oriented lobbying strategies paved the way for the rise of the direct action movement that we know today (Wall, 1999). New groups emerged to carry the mantel of the radical environmental movement in the late 1980s and early 1990s. The myriad of groups and individuals who participated in these actions soon coalesced into a living community of activists, forming a partnership that was to be broadly sustained over a number of years at a series of high profile protests. The issue that rejuvenated and revitalised the environmental movement was the building of new roads. In 1988 the Department of Transport published its *London Road Assessment Studies,* detailing plans to spend £12-20 billion on road widening, bypasses and the construction of an inner-M25. In response to this, Alarm was formed as a London-wide alliance against road building, which by the end of 1989 boasted over 150 local groups (McNeish, 1999: 69-70). Alarm adopted a decentralised structure enabling each local group to retain autonomy in action under the banner that 'each group had to oppose all roads in the Assessment not just those in their own backyard' (Stewart,

1997: 9). The following year the government's White Paper *Roads to Prosperity* was the catalyst for a new wave of protest action.

When Twyford Down in Hampshire came to prominence in late 1992 there was a well-established network of groups throughout the country ready to act and the fight against the extension of the M3 motorway (McNeish, 1999). Alarm UK worked in tandem with other groups such as the Dongas Tribe, and Earth First! (EF). Drawing inspiration from the organisation of the same name in America, when EF emerged in 1991 it was the antithesis of the established environmental lobby (Lent, 2001) devoid of formal membership lists, lacking officers to talk to the media, or of any apparent chain of command that could be identified by an outsider, EF was extremely hard to pin down as an 'organisation' (Byrne, 1997: 146). It was the actions of EF, amongst others, at Twyford Down that inspired the protest at the M11 extension in East London and then again at the site of the proposed Newbury Bypass between 1995-7 (Lent, 2001). Other notable milestones in the 1990s included the fight against the extension of the M77 near Glasgow between 1994-5, and the campaign against the new runway at Manchester Airport between 1995-7 (Griggs et al., 1998).

Many of the groups that were involved in these actions have since broadened their focus to campaign against other forms of development such as opencast mining, the building of shopping centres on greenbelt land and the planting of genetically modified crops. Once again, new groups emerged. Reclaim The Streets (RTS), an organisation that proudly describes itself as a 'disorganisation', emerged from EF and was instrumental in a series of 'street parties' against car culture (McNeish, 1999: 71). The party spirit that was present in the radical environmental movement in the 1990s grew out of the rave dance scene that spread across Britain in 1988, heralded as the 'second summer of love' (Lent, 2001: 216). A new layer of young people were effectively politicised by their resistance to the government's attempt to close down their illegal parties. Going to an illegal rave quickly became a political act of defiance: a statement about the state's interference in their choice of lifestyle. The rebellious 'do-it-yourself' festival spirit of illegal raving and the grassroots democratic politics and direct action of the anti-roads movement led to the formation of a myriad of groups and networks in the campaign against the Criminal Justice Act in 1994 (McNeish, 1999: 74). The spirit of radical direct action was brought to Britain's cities. Tactics that had been employed in the protest camps – tunnelling, tree-dwelling, and 'locking-on' by using a series of chains encased in concrete tubes – were enlivened by the arrival of the urban street party. RTS street parties became common in the mid to late 1990s with activists blocking off a street, setting up a sound system and stopping the traffic to have a party in the middle of the road.

In the minds of the protestors these parties were a great success, bringing the negative effects of car culture onto the political agenda. Indeed, the direct action movement won a number of victories during the 1990s. By 1996 it appeared as though the government's road building programme was to be scaled down significantly and the campaign against genetically modified food appeared to be similarly successful. The summer of 1998 saw the destruction of 25 of the 325 test fields of genetically modified crops by supporters of GenetiX Snowball, and the Genetic Environmental Network (Coxall, 2001), with significant victories being scored against some of the most powerful agro-industrial corporations in the world (Borger, 1999). These perceived successes brought new recruits to the radical direct action community, won over to the idea that they could change the world without needing a membership card for any organisation or needing to sign up to a manifesto. In the past few years RTS has been instrumental in many of the more explicitly anti-capitalist actions of the late 1990s and early 2000s such as the 'guerrilla gardening' action and graffiti spraying of the Cenotaph in May 2000. Many RTS activists have also participated in the anti-capitalist/anti-globalisation protests against organisations such as the International Monetary Fund and the World Trade Organisation at Seattle, Genoa, and Gothenburg (Rikowski, 2001).

Somewhat surprisingly, it was the Countryside Alliance, a group that was formed from a variety of country sports campaigns to oppose the government's plans to ban hunting with hounds, that organised the largest mobilisation of the 1990s, drawing 250,000 people onto the streets of London in March 1998 (Grant, 2002: 141). Protest action from the centre-right of the political spectrum has been a rare commodity in post-war British politics with Parry et al's (1992: 227) statement that 'direct action is primarily a matter for the left' being largely unchallenged. However, there are indications that such activities may become more commonplace. As hunting with hounds has now been banned in Scotland, and a ban looks more likely to become law south of the border, a split has occurred within the Countryside Alliance, with the newly formed Countryside Action Network and the Real Countryside Alliance promising a shift in their activities towards the techniques used by the radical environmental movement (Beckett, 2002).

Youth and Direct Action Participation

The task of estimating the age distribution of social movement participation in Britain with any degree of accuracy is an extremely difficult one. As far back as the late 1970s the argument has been made that young people are more likely to be drawn to unconventional protest activity (Marsh, 1977; Barnes et al., 1979). Such a conclusion was endorsed by Parry et al (1992) in their landmark study of political participation in Britain, the fieldwork for which was carried out in 1985. Parry et al. (1992: 234) found that 40 per cent per cent of those with a propensity to direct action were under 29 years-old – the only participant type in their study in which the youth cohort was over represented[12].

There are few formal social movement organisations that maintain detailed membership, let alone those broken down by socio-demographic characteristics. For example, FOE and Greenpeace, the two largest organisations in the environmental movement with the most resources at their disposal do not keep membership information broken down by age distribution (Grey, 2002; Croft, 2002)[13] . Furthermore, membership of such organisations is inherently unstable and subject to short-term fluctuations. Jordan and Maloney analysed official records to uncover that only 35 per cent of those who joined FOE in 1991 re-joined in 1992 while Amnesty International lost 24.5 per cent of its existing membership that year. Furthermore, they estimate that the general turnover rates for environmental groups may be somewhere in the region of 30 to 40 per cent a year (1997: 166).

There are also very many people involved in the direct action community who are not members of *any* organisation. Support for movement causes does not necessary imply membership of an organisation, and only a limited number of activists who are involved in the more radical mobilisations that have been witnessed in recent years are card-carrying members of any group. Rather, people take part in actions that one or a combinationof groups may have proposed, but they do so as unaffiliated individu-

---

12 It should be borne in mind, however, that many of these studies are attitudinal studies that measure protest potential rather than protest activity itself: there is a significant difference in an individual telling a researcher that they are sympathetic to unconventional political protest and actually engaging in such activity themselves.

13 This is not just the case for age: 'Information on the number of women involved with movements other than the women's movement is virtually non-existent' (Byrne, 1997: 76).

als who are sympathetic to the broad goals of a particular campaign or action. The real contribution is measured in doing things rather than being a number on a membership list that can be used to impress potential bargaining partners that their particular organisation is deserving of a seat at the negotiating table. Numbers only become important in key mobilisations and even then many such actions do not depend on large turnouts. Whilst lamenting the 'dearth' of empirical evidence for whom social movement activists are, Byrne (1997: 62-3) does say that that empirical material that is available is broadly consistent:

> The picture that emerges is one of social movements apparently holding a particular appeal for one segment of society, those who are well educated (and thus middle class) and who are not employed in the private sector. If there were such as thing as a 'typical' supporter of a social movement, he or she would be a graduate working in the public sector with an income that was above average but below that of similarly qualified people in the private sector... the more active a supporter someone is, the closer he or she conforms to this stereotype.

McNeish (1999) found the same thing in his 1996 study of Alarm UK, EF and RTS activists. He found that activists sympathetic to the campaigns of these groups tended to come from all social class backgrounds, and that generally the younger the respondents the less interest they had in traditional political processes. Moreover, 'for the eco-activist wing of the movement the political system is simply anathema' (1999: 76).

However, this view is a contested one, and there are those who say that the simple equation of youth with radical environmentalism should be resisted. Bennie and Rudig (1993), for example, used the 1989 and 1992 Eurobarometre studies and a survey of Green Party members at their highpoint in 1989 to portray a somewhat contradictory picture of young people's relationship to environmental activism[14]. It is significant that when asked about the most important issues of the day, the young are clearly thE most willing to place the environment high on their political agenda. Yet whilst, young people do demonstrate higher levels of environmental concern, this concern does not necessarily manifest itself into environmental

---

14 The Greens polled 14.5 per cent in the UK in the European elections, including 30 per cent of those 18-21 year-olds who did vote (Bennie and Rudig 1993: 7).

action. In their everyday actions young people do not stand out as particularly environmentally aware, and whilst they are slightly more likely to be members of mainstream environmental organisations, Bennie and Rudig claim that they are *less* likely to be active members. Most recently, Lent (2001: 224) has argued that the image of radical environmental movements being composed overwhelmingly of 'angry young people' is 'absurd'.

The Decline of Party Membership

The rise in new social movements and direct action politics is often contrasted with the decline in political parties. It is clearly the case that the rise in new social movement activities has allowed for a different possibility of 'doing' politics – one that was widely regarded as being far more attractive to young people. Thus it has been argued that the environmental movement may attract members for the very reasons that political parties are struggling (Dalton et al., 2000): they typify a non-partisan style of politics that offer a more fluid and varied organisational life for their members. Indeed, the argument that the rise of protest politics can be directly related to the decline of mainstream political parties in advanced western democracies is one that is commonly heard (Berry, 1984; Grant, 1995; Lawson and Merkl, 1998). Although few would challenge Seyd and Whiteley's (1992: 204) contention that new social movement organisations 'provide a more rewarding type of political participation for many people than a political party', convincing evidence that young people have turned away from the parties towards such organisations is very hard to come by.

What is certain is that the main political parties have experienced a steady decline in their memberships since the hey-day of the 1950s[15]. In 1964, 9.4 per cent of all registered voters were members of one of the three main political parties. By the time of the 1997 General Election this figure had fallen to just 2 per cent (Webb and Farrell, 1999: 47). Table 9.1 paints a sorry picture of the decline of mass membership parties.

---

15 Scarrow (1996) raises an interesting point in posing the question whether mass party recruitment in the third quarter of the twentieth century was in itself the aberration, rather than party decline in the fourth quarter.

Table 9.1
Individual Membership of the Labour, Conservative and Liberal Democrat parties in Britain 1950-1998

Year	Conservative	Labour	Liberal Democrat
1945		487,000	
1947	1,200,000	608,000	
1948	2,249,000	629,000	
1953	2,806,000	1,005,000	
1960	2,800,000	790,000	
1964		830,000	278,690*
1966		776,000	234,345*
1970	1,500,000	690,000	234,345*
1974	1,500,000	692,000	190,000*
1979	1,350,000*	666,000	145,000*
1983	1,200,000*	295,000	145,258*
1987	1,000,000*	289,000	137,500*
1988	1,000,000*	265,000	
1989	750,000**	294,000	82,000**
1990		311,000	
1991		261,000	
1992	500,000	280,000	100,000*
1993		266,000	
1994		280,000	
1995		365,110**	
1996		400,465**	
1997	400,000**	405,238**	100,000**
1998	204,000**	387,776**	
2000	318,000^	311,000^	71,641^
2002	330,000^	280,000^	76,023^

*† Scarrow (1996: 75), * Webb and Farrell (1999: 48), ** Seyd and Whiteley (2000: 3), and ^ Wintour (2002: 5). Note that the Liberal Party became the Liberal Democrats in 1988. The 1988 figure for the Liberal Democrats is estimated on the basis of the numbers voting to elect a new leader, and 1998 figure for the Conservatives is based on the numbers participating in the ballot on the party's European strategy.*

In looking at the figures for the post-war period it is apparent that the decline in party membership is far from a recent phenomenon. Labour's membership has fallen from a high of 1,005,000 in 1953, following a downward path through the 1960s and 1970s to a low point of 261,000 in 1991. The party's fortunes have revived somewhat with the launch of the New Labour modernisation project, but having set themselves a target of

450,000 for 2000 (Maguire, 2001), membership has dropped once again in the wake of the party's election triumph in 1997. The Conservative Party has experienced an even more precipitous decline. From a highpoint of 2,806,000 in 1953, the party has experienced a continual erosion of its membership through to a figure of 204,000 in 1994. That membership had increased to 330,000 by 2002 may provide some encouragement for the party, even if these current figures do represent a shadow of former glories[16].

Youth Participation in British Political Parties

Whilst there are numerous histories of Conservative and Labour govern-ments and biographies of great party leaders, the quality of information on the nature of political party memberships is limited to a few recent studies (Rudig et al., 1991; Seyd and Whiteley, 1992; Whiteley et al., 1994; Scarrow, 1996). Whiteley et al's study was the first to research the Conservative Party using a national random sample[17]. They uncovered an average age of 62, with only 1 per cent of members being under 25 (1994: 42-3). Whilst the Conservative Party's membership is the least youthful, the age profile of the other mainstream political parties in Britain is far from healthy as a barometer of their future prosperity; the average age of Labour Party members was 48 in 1992 (Seyd and Whiteley, 1992: 32) and the Liberal Democrat's had a similar profile with their average age being estimated at 49 in 1995 (Rudig et al., 1995: 392).

Not surprisingly, there has been even less research into youth member-ships of mainstream political parties. Consequently, it is very difficult to obtain accurate information on memberships of youth organisations or to make meaningful historical comparisons about activity levels. In the 1950s the Young Conservatives was a buoyant organisation with a membership of around 100,000 (Layton-Henry, 1973). In the early 1990s Whiteley et al (1994: 106) found that younger Conservative members were significantly

---

16 Of course, these membership figures do need to be treated with a healthy degree of scepticism. Scarrow (1996: 78-9) cautions that when interpreting official membership fig-ures we have to bear in mind that not only do they come from internal party sources but they have also been subjected to significant changes both in counting mechanisms and party membership criteria over the years.

17 Prior to Whiteley et al's 1992 study of the Conservative Party, the research that had been undertaken on the party had tended to concentrate either on particular constituency associations (Bealey et al. 1965) or party officers (Butler and Pinto-Duschinsky, 1980).

more active than the older members, with 18-25 year-olds twice as likely to be highly active when compared to members overall. Estimates for the Conservative Party's current day youth organisation, Conservative Future(CF), are far from reliable. The party does not have a national membership database and is not able to put a reliable figure on the total membership of the party or its profile, although CF's national organiser estimates that around 10,000 would be a 'realistic figure' for their organisation (Pugh, 2001). Research by Leonard and Katwala (1998) suggested a figure in the region of 30,000 for membership of the Labour Party's youth organisation. This corresponds to an estimate of between 28,000 and 30,000 for Young Labour (YL) and a further 5,000 in Labour Students (Angus and Higgs, 2001). The Liberal Democrats youth section, Liberal Democrats Youth and Students (LDYS) are unable to identify their full membership, as the application form to join the Liberal Democrat Party does not contain an age identifier. However, they estimate that their potential membership might be as high as 5,000, whilst being confident that they know of 1,800 active members (Davies, 2001).

These low levels of activism within the mainstream political parties are part of an apparent decline in young people's participation in conventional political activity as measured by a variety of commonly used indicators. In terms of voting at recent elections for instance, young people continue to turnout in lower numbers than do their older contemporaries. Certainly, the rate of voting turnout amongst young people in recent elections has followed a steady downward trend. In the 1992 national election, only 61 per cent of 18-24 year olds voted (Butler and Kavanagh, 1997: 295), and in 1997 the estimated turnout rate for 18-24 year olds was only 68 per cent (Jowell and Park, 1998). In 2001, turnout in the general election sunk to a post-war low of just 59 per cent (Kimberlee, 2002), with only 39 per cent of young people casting a vote (MORI, 2001)[18]. As well as being less likely to vote in elections when compared with older age cohorts, young people have consistently fewer memberships of formal groups of various kinds (Parry et al., 1992: 158), express less interest in politics (Park, 1999), and are much less likely to offer a party political identification (Heath and Park, 1997; Jowell and Park, 1998; Wring et al., 1999).

---

18 It should be noted that whilst young people are less likely to vote in elections, data from the 1989 European Assembly election does confirm that the main socio-demographic correlates of green voting across Europe are youth and education, of which youth is the marginally more important (Rudig et al., 1993).

Young People's Voluntary and Campaigning Activity

However, a number of studies have suggested that whilst young people may be less interested in formal 'politics' than other (older) age groups they may be concerned about matters that are essentially 'political' in nature, but that these concerns lie beyond the boundaries of how politics is conventionally understood. As White et al. (2000) demonstrate, once young people are invited to discuss politics in their own terms (thus widening the definition of politics), then there is evidence of much higher levels of interest and activity by young people. Bhavnani's (1994) ethnographic study raises the possibility that the young people she talked with could have provided instances of activity that they themselves may not have defined as 'political' but which could be placed within the domain of politics. In a series of enlightening passages it is quite clear that, for Bhavnani's subjects, 'politics' as represented by parties and politicians simply does not connect with their everyday lives in any meaningful way. Of the views expressed in her interviews, three keep reappearing: 'that politics is boring, that politics is difficult to understand, and that there was no point in voting' (Bhavnani, 1994: 139). In another study of young people, Gaskin et al. (1996: 3) also found that whilst their subjects tended to 'show a distinct alienation from mainstream politics' these people also saw work with voluntary organisations 'as a route to social and political action'.

Indeed, there are a number of studies which indicate that young people do have a high rate of participation in various forms of voluntary and campaigning activity – the end results of which were intended to achieve some political and social change – without regarding this action as necessarily 'political' (Gaskin et al., 1996; Industrial Society, 1997). Roker et al. (1999) question the preoccupation with participation in conventional 'politics' and turnout at elections. Their data, gathered from a multi-area school survey of 14-16 year-olds, challenges the prevailing negative images of young people as inactive, showing a much greater level of involvement in voluntary and campaigning activities across a range of social, environmental and political issues than common stereotypes would suggest.

Conclusion

So, how many young people actually take part in some form of political activity in Britain today? The short and simple answer is, probably not many, whilst the more honest answer must be that we don't know. Byrne

(1997: 3) points out that 'we must remember that political activism of all kinds is a minority sport in Britain. The great majority of the 5 million people who are officially members of one of the organisations that make up the environmental movement, for example, are fairly passive, rarely extending beyond possession of their membership card (Coxall, 2001: 115). High profile cases of political protest have actually been based on very small numbers of people taking part (Coxall, 2001: 36) and it is often the tactical ingenuity of those involved that has brought their activities to the attention of the media, and success for their cause. This corresponds with the situation in Britain's political parties, with only a minority of members participating in the lives of their party by doing things such as attending branch meetings (Scarrow, 2000: 95). The limited evidence that is available would tend to suggest that younger members are significantly more active than older members, with 18-25 year-olds being twice as likely to be highly active when compared to members overall (Whitely et al., 1994: 106), but this research is limited to the Conservative Party and is now somewhat out of date.

Using a variety of well established indicators it is clear that young people are far less likely to participate in conventional political activity than their older counterparts. The evidence for their participation in unconventional protest activity is far less compelling. Whilst the visible impression represented in the media may suggest a high level of activism amongst youth, harder evidence is unconvincing. It is clear that more research is needed to provide an accurate and reliable answer to this important question.

References

Angus, M. and Higgs, L. (2001) *Personal Interview*, 19 October (unpublished interview: London).

Barnes, S. and Kasse, M. (1979) 'Introduction' in S. Barnes, M. Kasse, K. Allerbeck, B. Farah, F. Heunks, R. Inglehart, K. Jennings, H. Klingermann, A. Marsh and L. Rosenmayr (eds) *Political Action: Mass Participation in Five Western Democracies* (London: Sage), 13-26.

Barnes, S., Kasse, M., Allerbeck, K., Farah, B., Heunks, F., Inglehart, R., Jennings, K., Klingermann, H., Marsh, A. and Rosenmayr, L. (1979) *Political Action: Mass Participation in Five Western Democracies* (London: Sage).

Bealey, F., Blondel, J. and McCann, W. (1965) *Constituency Politics* (London: Faber).

Bentley, T., Oakley, K., Gibson, S. and Kilgour, K. (1999) *The Real Deal: What Young People Really Think About Government, Politics and Social Exclusion* (London: Demos).

Bennie, L. and Rudig, W. (1993) 'Youth and the Environment: Attitudes and Actions in the 1990's', *Youth and Policy*, vol. 42; 6-21.

Berry, J. (1984) *The Interest Group Society* (Glenview, Ill.: Little Brown).

Bhavnani, K.K. (1994) *Talking Politics: A Psychological Framing of Views from Youth in Britain* (Cambridge: Cambridge University Press).

Birchall, I. (1987) 'France 1968: All Power to the Imagination' in C. Barker (ed.) *Revolutionary Rehearsals* (London: Bookmarks).

Butler, D. and Kavanagh, D. (1997) *The British General Election of 1997* (Hampshire: Macmillan Press).

Butler, D. and Pinto-Duschinsky, M. (1980) 'The Conservative Elite 1918-78: Does Unrepresentativeness Matter?' in Z. Layton-Henry (ed.) *Conservative Party Politics* (London: Macmillan), 186-209.

Borger, J. (1999) 'How the mighty fall', *The Guardian* 2, 22 November 1999.

Byrne, P. (1988) *The Campaign for Nuclear Disarmament* (London: Routledge).

Byrne, P. (1997) *Social Movements in Britain* (London: Routledge).

Campbell, A., Converse, P., Miller, A. and Stokes, G. (1960) *The American Voter* (New York: Wiley).

Connelly, J. and Smith, G. (1999) *Politics and the Environment: From Theory to Practice* (London: Routledge).

Cotgrave, S. (1982) *Catastrophe or Cornucopia* (London: Wiley).

Coxall, B. (2001) *Pressure Groups in British Politics* (Harlow: Pearson).

Crewe, I. (1983) 'The Electorate: Partisan Dealignment Ten Years On', *West European Politics*, vol. 6; 183-215.

Crewe, I. (1984) 'The Electorate: Partisan Dealignment Ten Years On' in H. Berrington (ed.) *Change in British Politics* (London: Frank Cass), 183-215.

Crook, S., Pakulski, J. and Waters, M. (1992) *Postmodernisation: Change in Advanced Society* (London: Sage).

Croft, S. (info@foe.co.uk) (2002), *FOE Membership*, 5 August, Email to Mark Weinstein (mark.weinstein@ntu.ac.uk).

Dalton, R. (1988) *Citizen Politics in Western Democracies* (Chatham, NJ.: Chatham Publishers).

Dalton, R., Keuchler, M. and Burklin, W. (1990) 'The Challenge of New Movements' in R. Dalton and M. Keuchler (eds) *Challenging the Political*

Order: New Movements in Western Democracies (Cambridge: Polity Press), 3-20.

Dalton, R., McAllister, I. and Wattenberg, M. (2000) 'The Consequences of Partisan Dealignment' in R. Dalton and M. Wattenberg (eds) *Parties Without Partisans: Political Change in Advanced Industrial Democracies* (Oxford: Oxford University Press), 37-63.

Davies, L. (2001) *Personal Interview*, 18 October (unpublished interview: London).

della Porta, D. and Diani, M. (1999) *Social Movements: An Introduction* (Oxford: Blackwell).

Diani, M. and Donati, D. (1999) 'Organisational Change in Western European Environmental Groups: A Framework for Analysis' in C. Rootes (ed.) *Environmental Movements: Local, National, Global* (London: Frank Cass), 13-35.

Dunleavy, P. (1980) *Urban Political Analysis* (London: Macmillan).

Evans, G. (ed.) (1999) *The End of Class Politics?* (Oxford: Oxford University Press).

Franklin, M. (1985) *The Decline of Class Voting in Britain: Changes in the Basis of Electoral Choice 1964–1983* (Oxford: Clarendon Press).

Gaskin, K., Vlaeminke, M. and Fenton, N. (1996) *Young People's Attitudes Towards the Voluntary Sector: A Report for the Commission on the Future of the Voluntary Sector* (Loughborough: Loughborough University).

Grant, W. (1995) *Pressure Groups, Politics and Democracy in Britain*. 2nd edn (Hemel Hempstead: Harvester Wheatsheaf).

Grant, W. (2002) *Pressure Groups and British Politics* (Hampshire: Macmillan).

Griggs, Howarth and Jacobs (1998) 'Second Runway at Manchester', *Parliamentary Affairs*, vol. 51; 358-69.

Grey, J. (julia.chase-grey@uk.greenpeace.org) (2002) *Membership of Greenpeace UK*, 5 August, Email to Mark Weinstein (mark.weinstein@ntu.ac.uk).

Harrop, M. and Miller, W. (1987) *Elections and Voters: A Comparative Introduction* (London: Macmillan).

Heath, A., Jowell, R. and Curtice, J. (1985) *How Britain Votes* (Oxford: Pergamon Press).

Heath, A. and Park, A. (1997) 'Thatcher's Children?' in: R. Jowell, et al. (eds) *British Social Attitudes: the 14th Report. The End of Conservative Values?* (Aldershot: Ashgate), 19-32.

Henn, M., Weinstein, M. and Wring, D. (2002)' A Generation Apart? Youth and Political Participation in Britain', *British Journal of Politics and International Relations,* vol. 4:2; 167-92.

Himmelweit, H., Humphreys, P. and Jaeger, M. (1981) *How Voters Decide* (London: Academic Press).

Industrial Society (1997) *Speaking Up, Speaking Out!* (London: Industrial Society).

Inglehart, R. (1977) *The Silent Revolution: Changing Values and Political Styles among Western Publics* (Princeton, NJ.: Princeton University Press).

Jennings, M. and Niemi, R. (1974) *The Political Character of Adolescence* (Princeton, NJ.: Princeton University Press).

Jordan, G. and Maloney, W. (1997) *The Protest Business* (Manchester: Manchester University Press).

Jowell, R. and Park, A. (1998) *Young People, Politics and Citizenship: A Disengaged Generation?* (London: Citizenship Foundation).

Kasse, M. and Marsh, A. (1979) 'In Conclusion: The Future of Political Participation in Western Democracies' in S. Barnes, and M. Kasse, et al. (eds) *Political Action: Mass Participation in Five Western Democracies* (London: Sage), 523-36.

Kimberlee, R. (1998) 'Young People and the 1997 General Election', *Renewal,* vol. 6:2; 87-90.

Kriesi, H. (1989), 'New Social Movements and the New Class in the Netherlands', *American Journal of Sociology*, vol. 95, 1078-116.

Lawson, K. and Merkl, P. (eds) (1998) *When Parties Fail: Emerging Alternative Organisations* (Princeton, NJ.: Princeton University Press).

Layton-Henry, Z. (1973) 'The Young Conservatives: 1945-70', *Contemporary History,* vol. 8:2; 143-56.

Lazarsfeld, P., Berelson, B. and Gaudet, H. (1944) *The People's Choice: How the Voter Makes up his Mind in a Presidential Campaign.* 1st edn (New York: Columbia University Press).

Leonard, M. and Katwala, S. (1997) 'It Was the Young Wot Won It!', *Renewal,* vol. 5:3/4; 108-16.

Lent, A. (2001) *British Social Movements Since 1945: Sex, Colour, Peace and Power* (Hampshire: Palgrave).

Maguire, K. (2001) Big fall in Labour Membership, *The Guardian*, 6 June 2001

Marwick, A. (1988) 'The 1960s – was there a Cultural Revolution?', *Contemporary Record,* vol. 2:3; 18-20.

Marsh, A. (1977) *Protest and Political Consciousness* (London: Sage).

McNeish, W. (1999) 'Resisting Colonisation: The Politics of Anti-roads Protesting' in: P. Bagguley and J. Hearn (eds) *Transforming Politics: Power and Resistance* (London: Macmillan, 67-84).

Melucci, A. (1989) *Nomads of the Present: Social Movements and Individual Needs in a Contemporary Society* (London: Century Hutchinson).

MORI (2001) 'How Britain Voted in 2001', *British Public Opinion*, vol. 24:3/4; 3.

Offe, C. (1985) 'New Social Movements: Challenging the Boundaries of Institutional Politics', *Social Research*, vol. 52:4; 817-68.

Osgerby, B. (1998), *Youth in Britain Since 1945* (London: MacMillan).

Park, A. (1995) 'Teenagers and their Politics' in R. Jowell, J. Curtice, L. Brook and S. Witherspoon (eds) *British Social Attitudes: The 12th Report* (Aldershot: Dartmouth). 43-60.

Parkin, F. (1968) *Middle Class Radicalism: The Social Bases of the British Campaign for Nuclear Disarmament* (Manchester: Manchester University Press).

Parry, G., Moyser, G. and Day, N. (1992) *Political Participation and Democracy in Britain* (Cambridge: Cambridge University Press).

Pugh, D. (2001) *Personal Interview*, 23 October (unpublished interview: London).

Pultzer, P. (1967) *Political Representation and Elections in Britain* (London: Allen and Unwin).

Rikowski, G. (2001) *The Battle in Seattle: Its Significance for Education* (London: Tufnell Press).

Robertson, D. (1984) *Class and the Britain Electorate* (Oxford: Basil Blackwell).

Roker, D., Player, K. and Coleman, J. (1999) *Challenging the Image: Young People as Volunteers and Campaigners* (London: Youth Work Press).

Rose, R. (1964) *Politics in England: An Interpretation* (Boston, Mass.: Little Brown).

Rose, R. and McAllister, J. (1986) *Voters Begin to Chose: From Closed Class to Open Elections in Britain* (London: Sage).

Rowell, A. (2001) 'Green Activists and Multinationals "Get Engaged" at Controversial Rendezvous', *The Big Issue*, 8 July 2001.

Rudig, W., Bennie, L. and Franklin, M. (1991) *Green Party Members: A Profile* (Glasgow: Delta Publications).

Rudig, W., Franklin, M. and Bennie, L. (1993) *Green Blues: the Rise and Decline of the British Green Party*, No. 95, Strathclyde Papers on Government and Politics (Strathclyde: Strathclyde University; Department of Government).

Rudig, W. et al. (1995) 'The Membership Dynamics of British Centre Parties: From Liberals and Social Democrats to Liberal Democrats' in J. Stanyer, and J. Lovenduski (eds) *Contemporary Political Studies* Vol. 1 (Exeter: The Political Studies Association). 386-402.

Scarrow, S. (1996) *Parties and Their Members* (Oxford: Oxford University Press).

Scarrow, S. (2000) 'Parties Without Members?: Party Organisation in a Changing Electoral Environment' in: R. Dalton and M. Wattenberg (eds) *Parties Without Partisans: Political Change in Advanced Industrial Democracies* (Oxford: Oxford University Press), 79-101.

Seyd, P. and Whiteley, P. (1992) *Labour's Grassroots: The Politics of Party Membership* (Oxford: Clarendon Press).

Seyd, P. and Whiteley, P. (2000) *Towards a More Responsible Two Party System: The British Party System Reconsidered.* Paper presented at the panel on 'Responsible Parties in Comparative Perspective' at the Annual Meeting of the American Political Science Association, Washington DC., August 31 to September 3 2000.

Stewart, J. (ed.) (1997) *Alarm Bells* (London: Alarm UK).

Topf, R. (1995) 'Beyond Electoral Participation' in H-D. Klingerman and D. Fuchs (eds) *Citizens and the State* (Oxford: Oxford University Press).

Van Liere, K. and Dunlap, R. (1980) 'The Social Bases of Environmental Concern', *Public Opinion Quarterly*, Vol. 44; 181-97.

Wall, D. (1999) *Earth First! and the Anti-roads Movement: Radical Environmentalism and Comparative Social Movements* (London: Routledge).

Webb, P. and Farrell, D. (1999) 'Party Members and Ideological Change' in G. Evans and P. Norris (eds) *Critical Elections: British Parties and Voters in Long-term Perspective* (London: Sage), 44-63.

White, C., Bruce, S. and Ritchie, J. (2000) *Young People's Politics: Political Interest and Engagement Amongst 14-24 year-olds* (York: Joseph Rowntree Foundation).

Whiteley, P., Seyd, P. and Richardson, J. (1994) *True Blues: The Politics of Conservative Party Membership* (Oxford: Clarendon Press).

Wring, D., Henn, M. and Weinstein, M. (1999) 'Young People and Contemporary Politics: Committed Scepticism or Engaged Cynicism?' in J. Fisher, P. Cowley, D. Denver and A. Russell (eds) *British Elections and Parties Review* Vol. 9 (London: Frank Cass Publishers), 200-216.

10. Alienation and Youth in Britain

Matt Henn, Mark Weinstein and Dominic Wring

Conventional wisdom suggests that young people are becoming increasingly disengaged from politics and the democratic system (see Wring, Henn and Weinstein, 1999). Current thinking is that this development calls into question the legitimacy of the political system itself, and that this is leading to the rise of a disenchanted and irresponsible youth generation. This is characterised by their apparent 'unwillingness to obey the law, to play by the rules, or to pay for the needs of others' (Mulgan and Wilkinson, 1997: 218). A number of predominantly quantitative-based studies have measured this apparent youth disillusionment using such indicators as (declining) party membership, political attitudes, and voting behaviour. In particular, only 39 per cent of 18-24 year olds turned out to vote at the 2001 General Election, compared with 59 per cent of registered voters (MORI, 2001).

Like their older contemporaries, young people in Britain appear to be sceptical of the way the British political system is organised and led. This is not a new revelation. Public discontent with politics can be traced back to the 1940s. Data from early Gallup and Mass Observation studies demonstrate the concerns of the British electorate throughout the 1940s and 1950s (Mass Observation, 1948; Cantril, 1951). Discontent with the British political system became a visible phenomenon from the 1970s onwards with the publication of a series of key studies that uncovered a general sense of dissatisfaction with the functioning of democracy in Britain, one that was more pronounced amongst young people (Royal Commission, 1973a; Marsh, 1977). This picture of the general population was supplemented by two studies specifically addressing young people's attitudes towards politics and government. In comparing young Britons with their American, German and Italian counterparts, Dennis, Lindberg and McCrone (1971) paint a negative picture of young Britons' support for government and political institutions, demonstrating a generally unfavourable sense of national identity and a critical disposition towards Britain's role in the world. In a similar vein, Hart (1978: 46) uncovered a 'lack of basic trust or faith amongst British teenagers' in the functioning of British democracy.

The events of the succeeding years have done little to challenge Marsh's (1977: 115) contention that in general people regard politics as 'a remote and unresponsive system run by cynical and aloof politicians'. If anything, the growing sense of remoteness and disenchantment with politics has vindicated the authors of the minority report of *The Royal Commission of the Constitution* (Royal Commission, 1973b) who urged urgent action to address what they perceived to be deep-seated problems with the functioning of British political institutions.

Evidence from a number of recent studies suggest that at present there appears to be widespread disillusion with politics and political institutions, with a series of recent indicators suggesting that young people are less engaged than older age cohorts[19]. Drawing on conventional political science indicators, and relying on predominantly quantitative approaches, such studies tend toward a characterisation in which young people appear to be set apart from the rest of the population (Parry, Moyser and Day 1992; Park, 1995; Gaskin, Vlaeminke and Fenton, 1996; Heath and Park 1997; Jowell and Park 1998; Industrial Society, 1997; White, Bruce and Ritchie, 2000). This perceived gap might be explained by either a generational or life cycle effect[20]. Parry, Moyser and Day offer tentative support to the life cycle interpretation in relation to conventional (electoral) political participation (1992: 170), whilst also identifying signs of a 'generational imprint' (1992: 160) in relation to unconventional (protest) politics. Heath and Park (1997), whilst cautiously prefacing their comments with the caveat that generational and life cycle effects can never be definitively disentangled, lend guarded support to life cycle factors. Jowell and Park (1998: 14) are slightly less hesitant in concluding that the 'trend towards less engagement in politics among the young ... appears to signal a generational change rather than just an effect of the life cycle at work'.

---

19 See the chapter by Weinstein in this collection for an analysis of youth political participation rates.

20 For an explanation of the life cycle theory of political behaviour, see Verba and Nie (1972) and Nie, Verba and Kim (1974) who suggest that political participation is low in early years, rising at the onset of adulthood, reaching a peak in middle age, before falling off in latter years. For an explication of the generational thesis, see Inglehart (1971; 1977), Barnes and Kasse et al (1979) and Dalton (1988). This approach differs from the life cycle view of political behaviour in contesting that generations of people are socialised predominately through shared historical experiences in their formative years. Furthermore, it is proposed that the values held by distinct generations do not disperse with the passage of time but endure over their life span.

However, the evidence from the key studies of the 1990s fails to offer conclusive support for either of the two theoretical conceptualisations, and the only area in which there appears to be unanimous agreement is in relation to the difficulty of disentangling the complex mixture of life cycle and generation effects. Rather, research throughout the 1990s has tended to lend support to Parry, Moyser and Day's (1992: 155) contention that 'all in all ... it seems impossible to rule out either process'. Indeed, even major proponents of the generational argument agree that there is no definitive way of rejecting either life cycle or generational interpretation (Abramson and Inglehart, 1992: 201)[21].

Research Design

In this chapter, we aim to examine whether young people are alienated from politics in Britain – by exploring their attitudes to political processes, institutions and players. However, we are also interested in gaining insights into what informs their views on these matters. Inevitably, this involves us in a search for *meaning*, in which we propose not only to develop an understanding of their orientation to 'formal' politics, but also to reveal their subjective experiences of politics, as well as their perspectives on what politics actually means to them. In addition, we will examine whether they are concerned about matters that are essentially 'political' in nature, but that lie beyond the boundaries of how politics is conventionally understood (and studied).

In order to explore these issues, we have adopted a longitudinal research design, combining quantitative (panel survey) and qualitative (focus groups) methods. The first stage of this research was conducted in June 1998. This was a regional panel survey of 1,597 'attainers'[22] drawn randomly from across Nottinghamshire using the electoral register as our sam-

---

21 For a fuller discussion of the difficulties of distinguishing between life cycle, generational and period effects see Franklin (1985: 22-23) and Jowell and Park (1998: 5-8).

22 Attainers are first-time entrants onto the electoral register, who therefore have only limited experience of 'formal' politics. We recognise that not every young person of attainer age was captured by this method – indeed, approximately 14 per cent of 18-19 year olds are not registered to vote, which compares with only 2 per cent of those aged 50 or above (Arber, 1993: 81). Nonetheless, the vast majority of our target group was eligible for inclusion through this method.

pling frame[23]. The second wave of this panel survey (carried out in June 1999) is assessed in this chapter. Participants included all those from the original 1998 sample who had indicated that they were interested in taking part in further research for the project. Of this group of 867, returns were received from 425 young people – an overall response rate of 49.6 per cent[24]. Based in Nottinghamshire, and using the electoral register as our sampling frame, our survey cannot therefore be representative of all young people of this age group in Britain. However, our intention is to present an indicative picture of youth orientation to, and understanding of, politics. Our combined methods approach would seem to provide a reasonable basis upon which to achieve this objective.

Given their relative inexperience politically, this age cohort is unlikely to have formed deep-seated views about politics, parties, politicians and political institutions (especially when compared with their older contemporaries). The panel survey method therefore enables us to monitor changes in the political views and outlook of young people as they accumulate experience of engaging with formal politics (through elections in this case)[25].

The panel survey data was augmented by a series of six focus groups[26] held in August 1999 that were designed to uncover some of the deeper perceptions and meanings that the young people in the survey attached to politics and political activity. Through this research, we were able to gain a

---

23 Full details about the design of the 1998 panel survey, including who the survey participants are, how they were originally included within the study, and why Nottinghamshire is such an interesting case for analysis of young people's political views and concerns, can be found in the first Nottinghamshire County Council report (Wring, Henn and Weinstein, 1998).
24 In this chapter, we compared the views of the 425 respondents who took part in the 1999 survey, with the views of the same people as they were expressed in 1998, and not with the full 1,597 members of the earlier study. This is so that we can compare like with like. Where the data have revealed differences over time between the two waves of our panel study, we can therefore conclude that this indicates actual differences in the views and attitudes of our respondents.
25 At the time of the 1999 second-wave survey, respondents had had at least one opportunity to vote (the 1999 European Parliamentary election), although the majority were also eligible to vote at the 1999 May local elections (excluding only those living in the Nottingham City local authority boundary).
26 The focus groups were constructed using the 1999 panel survey data. The membership of the groups was as follows: those who were generally enthusiastic (group 1) or broadly sceptical (5) about politics; those who had left (3) or remained in the education system (4); those who identified with a variety of contemporary youth concerns and post-materialist issues (environmentalism, animal rights, and so on) (2); and a general mix of young people (6).

deeper insight into their views and opinions than was possible through the panel survey alone. For example, where the survey respondents indicated that they strongly disagreed with the statement, *It is important to vote in local elections*, the focus group research afforded us the opportunity to delve into the reasons behind such a response. Survey research by itself does not aim to provide this depth of insight, and in this respect the focus groups provided an opportunity to contextualise the data gained from the survey, and supplement that data in very important ways. The focus groups also allowed the participants to express themselves in their own words using their own language – as we shall see in the *Results* section below, this is important, given that the young people in our focus groups were encouraged to communicate to us their meaning of 'politics', rather than respond to conventional definitions.

Results

The main findings from the survey and from the focus groups are integrated and reported in the following sections. Figures from the survey that are reported in brackets refer to 1998 data and are reviewed in order to give some indication of any shift in overall views and orientations amongst our survey members.

Political Engagement

The results indicate that, far from being apolitical and apathetic, young people do have an interest in political issues (see Table 10.1).

Table 10.1 Young people's political engagement (%)

	A great Deal	Quite a lot	Some	Not very much	None/ not at all
Generally speaking, how often would you say that you talk about politics with your friends or family?	4.7 (5.4)	14.4 (16.5)	31.8 (32.1)	37.4 (33.0)	11.8 (13.0)
How much interest do you normally have in national politics?	5.6 (9.4)	27.8 (25.2)	37.9 (37.0)	22.1 (21.2)	6.6 (7.1)
How much interest do you normally have in local politics?	1.9 (4.3)	10.7 (9.9)	32.2 (37.6)	44.1 (34.0)	11.1 (14.2)

(1998 results in brackets for this and all subsequent tables). Base: 425 respondents, 1999 panel survey wave 2 (1998 panel survey wave 1 data reported in brackets)

Firstly, we found from the survey that a majority of this age cohort does discuss politics with their friends and family at least 'some' of the time, if not more often (50.9 per cent). We then wanted to find out how much interest young people had in political affairs. When asked about national politics, over seven respondents in ten replied they had some or more interest, the same proportion that had reported so a year previously. Interestingly, there were significant levels of engagement with local affairs, which by definition are less high profile, and do not receive the same media attention as national issues. More than two-fifths (44.8 per cent) said they had at least 'some' interest, four times the number who had none (11.1 per cent), but marginally less than had indicated an engagement with local political affairs in the first wave of the survey a year previously (51.8 per cent).

These results seem to contradict the conventional view that young people take little interest in political affairs. We tested these ideas further through the focus groups. We found from these sessions that the research participants recognised that there was some apathy amongst certain layers of young people when it comes to voting and elections, but that they considered that professional politicians should shoulder some of the blame for this state of affairs. A consistent message expressed in all of the focus groups, was that politics is not aimed at young people. This reflects the findings of much previous qualitative research (Bhavnani, 1994; White, Bruce, and Ritchie, 2000) that suggests that if young people appear to exhibit a lack of engagement with politics, it is because they perceive the world of formal politics to be distant from their lives, and broadly irrelevant – that politics has little meaning for them. A common complaint was that 'there is no encouragement for us to take an interest'. An overwhelming majority of the participants agreed that if politics were targeted more at young people, then they would take a more active interest:

'All politicians complain that they are not getting through to the younger generation, but they don't give the younger generation any real reason to be interested in politics'.

'Young people choose to exclude themselves because they find no connection with themselves [and politicians]'.

There was a general consensus that political parties were at least partially responsible for any youth apathy that might exist, because they persistently failed to actively encourage young people to take an interest in politics: *'they don't give us any incentives to want to know about it [politics]'*. Therefore, the focus group participants were concerned that young people were generally *'encouraged to be passive'*. The point was frequently made that, instead of blaming young people for a lack of interest in politics, politicians and political parties should take the lead both in trying to connect with young people, and in finding ways to transform politics into a more engaging and meaningful process and activity. At present however, they were criticised for both failing to target their communication towards youth, and for consistently ignoring 'youth' issues. Ambivalence to 'formal' politics was therefore less an indication that young people were apathetic or naturally disinterested in politics, and more a product of their frustration that politicians and officials would not address their views and desires. Some adopted a fatalistic approach, symptomatic of a general mood of powerlessness:

'Why bother – we're never really going to change things'

'I'm not going to change their mind'

'We've got no interest because we don't think there's going to be any change. If we thought there was a chance to change [things] we'd probably be interested'.

Political Agendas

As a further indicator of young people's level of engagement with political affairs, we asked our respondents – through the questionnaires – what issues were of central political interest to them[27]. The results suggest that, contrary to the notion that young people today have no interest in political matters, they are relatively serious observers of political affairs: the majority (75 per cent) answered this question, and their responses were both serious and typically well thought through. Europe was the issue of most salience to our survey group[28] (see Figure 10.1 below), followed (in rank order) by education, war and militarism, and the environment.

---

27 An open question asked 'Which community, national or international issue are you most concerned about?'. This open question was coded into 16 different categories, with only the first answer volunteered actually recorded.
28 However, given the proximity of our survey to the 1999 European Parliamentary elections (questionnaires were sent out the day after the election), and the intense media coverage given to European matters at the time, this is perhaps not particularly surprising.

Figure 10.1 Agenda of youth concerns (%)

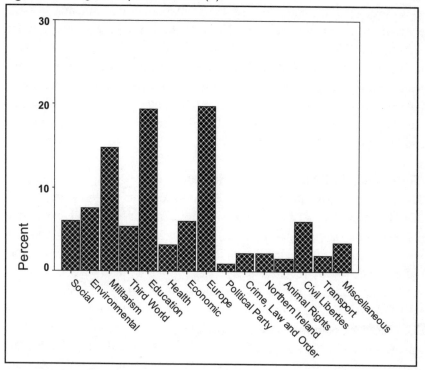

Base: 425 respondents, 1999 panel survey wave 2

The focus groups too, considered what contemporary matters were of importance to young people. In a discussion about local government, the young people involved were asked what sorts of issues they would like to raise with their local councillors, given the opportunity. The responses that were given were very detailed and showed a clear understanding and awareness of events and affairs happening in their local communities. Several young people focused on issues relating to the local built environment and the way in which planning decisions affect their communities – such as the development of the local economy, the state of the housing stock, modernisation of shopping areas, traffic systems and so on. A number of very localised environmental issues were also discussed, as were issues relating to the provision and funding of education.

Together, these findings indicate that young people *are* interested in politics, and they appear to have their own agenda. This agenda focuses on a particular youth perspective (for instance, nearly all of the responses to the survey question categorised under the heading 'education' as the main issue of concern, cited the abolition of the university maintenance grant system, and the introduction of university tuition fees). It also gives emphasis to broadly post-materialist issues. Militarism, environmental matters, civil liberties, solidarity with the Third World, animal rights, were ranked 3rd, 4th, 5th, 8th, 14th respectively out of the 16 categories used to summarise the data from this open question. The concern with environmental matters was also given special attention in the focus group discussions. Finally, the qualitative responses from the focus groups clearly indicate that young people are both aware of, and interested in topical, immediate and localised issues.

Confidence in Professional Politicians

The data from both the panel survey and the focus groups indicate that there is a crucial lack of confidence in politicians, at both local and national levels – this lends support to findings reported in other studies, and provides an insight into young people's apparent disconnection from formal politics. The survey revealed that this age group is highly sceptical of the notion that political parties and elected representatives genuinely seek to further young people's interests and act upon their concerns. A pattern of dislocation from formal politics is revealed when respondents were asked for their opinion of politicians (see Table 2). As was the case in the first wave of the panel survey a year previously, only a minority (19.9 per cent) agreed that politicians care about young people like myself, whilst majorities took the somewhat sceptical line that, once elected, politicians lose touch with people pretty quickly (54.4 per cent), and that parties are only interested in people's votes, not in their opinions (57.5 per cent). Similarly, respondents were more likely to agree (46.5 per cent) than disagree (36.3 per cent) with the contention that, it doesn't matter which party is in power, in the end things go on much the same.

However, the survey revealed that young people do not agree with the notion that *politicians are all the same*. Perhaps this reflects respondents' abilities to discriminate between individual MPs (some of whom may be recognised by our young panel to perform their duties well), and MPs as a collective body that may appear to be out of touch with voters generally. If this is the case, it suggests that, far from being politically lazy and disinterested, young people are relatively sophisticated (but sceptical) observers of the political scene.

Table 10.2 Youth perception of formal politics (%)

How much do you agree or disagree with each of the following statements?	Agree	Neither/Nor	Disagree
Politicians care about young people like myself	19.9 (16.9)	41.9 (42.5)	38.1 (40.5)
Politicians are all the same	25.7 (23.1)	25.0 (20.5)	49.3 (56.5)
Once elected, politicians lose touch with people pretty quickly	54.4 (49.6)	32.0 (32.6)	13.7 (17.7)
Parties are only interested in peoples votes, not in their opinions	57.5 (55.0)	26.4 (26.8)	16.0 (18.1)
It doesn't matter which party is in power, in the end things go on much the same	46.5 (50.4)	17.2 (17.6)	36.3 (32.0)

Base: 425 respondents, 1999 panel survey wave 2 (1998 panel survey wave 1 data reported in brackets)

The focus group data reinforce the suspicion that young people have of professional politicians, and shed further light on where this scepticism comes from. The general consensus was that the political parties only really bother to communicate with people prior to elections, or if there is something particularly wrong that needs to be addressed. This view is typified by the following comments:

'The way I see it, politicians only tend to claim an interest in people when it's time for elections. If it isn't an election then they don't bother'.

'That's the only time they want to speak to you – when they want your vote'.

'It's as if they don't care. Once they've got your vote, that's it, finished'

Typically, the young people in the focus groups had a negative image of party politics that consisted of politicians shouting at each other in the House of Commons. Such an adversarial style of politics is regarded as remote and boring, rather than inspiring – it had very little connection with young people's everyday lives. These findings reinforce the notion that politics is remote; politics is conducted by people who are *different*, and whose interests and concerns are disengaged from the lived experience of young people.

Confidence in the Democratic Process

Interestingly, the results from both the focus groups and the survey indicate that whilst young people place relatively little trust in the custodians of the political system, they do nonetheless display important signs that they are engaged with, and have a high degree of faith in, the democratic process itself.

Having reached the age of assent more than 12 months previously, all our respondents had now had the opportunity to vote in at least one election. In line with the record levels of abstention reported for both the 1999 local elections and the European election (Henn, Weinstein, Wring 2000:7), a majority of our respondents decided not to vote in these contests. Nonetheless, higher than expected numbers reported that they had exercised their voting prerogative in these elections (see Table 10.3 below).

Table 10.3 Reported voting (%)

	Yes	No
Did you vote in the recent local election on May 6th 1999?	42.7	57.3
Did you vote in the recent European parliamentary election?	38.9	61.1

Base: 425 respondents, 1999 panel survey wave 2

Somewhat paradoxically, although the level of intention to vote at the next national parliamentary election was high, the survey respondents were unsure which political party they would support in such a contest. In the previous wave of the survey, 77.6 per cent reported that they proposed to cast their vote at the election, and over eight in ten of the 1999 wave of the panel stated the same (83.7 per cent)[29]. However, they were still left unsure which political party they would support when the time arises, with only 44.1 per cent claiming to have already made this decision (this compares with 46.8 per cent in 1998 – see Table 10.4).

---

29 According to Heath and Taylor (1999: 168), the size of deviations between reported turnout (as measured in the British Election Studies series) and the official turnout since 1964 averages 9.9 per cent. We can assume therefore that the expected turnout as reported by the young people in our survey is likely to over-estimate the actual turnout at the next general election.

Table 10.4 Intention to vote, and party identification (%)

	Yes	No	Don't know[*]
Do you intend to vote in the next parliamentary general election?	83.7 (77.0)	16.3 (5.7)	0.0 (17.3)
If you do intend to vote (in the next parliamentary general election), do you know which party you will vote for?	44.1 (46.8)	55.9 (53.2)	

Base: 425 respondents, 1999 panel survey wave 2 (1998 panel survey wave 1 data reported in brackets)
* In the 1999 survey, the question was asked without a "Don't Know" option.

Their stated interest in the next national election is reflected somewhat in the strong commitment that they claim to have for the democratic process. Table 10.5 illustrates this, suggesting that by large majorities, the survey respondents considered that it is important to vote in both national elections (73.2 per cent) and in local contests (61.6 per cent), with only a fraction expressing support for the negative contention that *voting is a waste of time* (6.4 per cent). However, their support for the idea of voting had fallen somewhat over the twelve months since this same group was last surveyed, with corresponding figures of 81.6 per cent, 72.4 per cent, and 2.4 per cent respectively.

Table 10.5 Perception of importance of voting (%)

How much do you agree or disagree with each of the following statements?	Strongly Agree	Agree	Neither / nor	Disagree	Strongly Disagree
Important to vote in national elections	36.7 (44.1)	36.7 (37.5)	23.8 (16.7)	2.1 (0.9)	0.7 (0.7)
Important to vote in local elections	17.4 (26.4)	44.2 (46.0)	32.2 (25.7)	5.6 (1.7)	0.5 (0.2)
Voting is a waste of time	1.9 (0.5)	4.5 (1.9)	20.0 (16.3)	42.6 (42.9)	31.1 (38.4)

Base: 425 respondents, 1999 panel survey wave 2 (1998 panel survey wave 1 data reported in brackets)

The focus groups too revealed a high degree of support for the idea of elections, although respondents who had actually cast their votes at the ballot box were typically somewhat disappointed with the outcomes of the process. Several first-time voters complained of feeling a sense of anti-climax, frustration and disappointment. There was a strong feeling from some quarters that having had the opportunity to vote, they did not feel significantly empowered. This was even more demoralising given that many of the research participants had expected the act of voting to represent an important and symbolic landmark in their transition into full citizenship.

Nor did voting make them really feel like they were involved in the decision making process. A focus group member said: '*I feel no different to when I couldn't vote. I can't move political molehills never mind mountains*'. Even a participant from the 'enthusiast' group 1, commented: '*There was a lot of hype and it was a big let-down*'. Several people related this concern to the commonly endorsed view that the main parties were quite similar in outlook and thus offered them a limited electoral choice. Linked to this, many participants agreed that they didn't feel well informed, and complained that they lacked access to the type of material that could rectify this personal shortcoming. These findings from the focus groups perhaps help to account for the small decrease in levels of support for elections revealed in the survey, and mentioned above (Table 10.5).

To pursue this issue, we asked the focus group participants to take part in a qualitative sentence completion exercise. They were asked to set out their thoughts about voting and elections, as a reaction to the part-sentence, 'Now that I have had an opportunity to vote, I feel…'. The responses from each of the 45 young participants have been coded and reproduced in Table 6 below. Their written responses were unequivocal. Whilst nearly a fifth (18.7 per cent) of respondents were satisfied both with the general process of voting (category 7), and that their voices would be listened to in a serious way by politicians and decision-makers (category 5), over eight in ten (81.3 per cent) held negative views now that the elections were over (categories 1-4, 6, and 8-9). The largest group (28.8 per cent) of the young people in our study considered that casting their vote in an election had made, and would continue in the future to make, no difference to their lives or to the world around them. A noticeable minority stated that there was no party that shared their concerns (11.7 per cent), whilst one in six (16.6 per cent) claimed to be disappointed that there was insufficient political information available upon which to make an informed choice about how best to cast their vote. Again, this more qualitative data helps to reveal some of the subjective experiences of politics that the young people in our study have, and provides an insight into what lies behind their apparent disconnection from formal politics.

Table 10.6 'Now that I have had an opportunity to vote, I feel..' (focus group sentence completion exercise)

	Number	Percent
1. No different than from before I had voted	8	13.6
2. I will (continue to) abstain from voting in the future	2	3.4
3. Insufficiently informed about elections and politics to make my vote count	10	16.9
4. Disappointed that my vote had not made a positive change to my life/ that my views will not be listened to	17	28.8
5. Contented that my vote had made a positive change to my life / that my views will be listened to	3	5.1
6. Disappointed generally with the process of voting	3	5.1
7. Contented generally with the process of voting	8	13.6
8. That there was no party that generally reflected my interests and concerns	7	11.9
9. There are no issues that I feel strongly about	1	1.7

Figures in the 'Number' column total more than 45, because some focus group respondents wrote more than one answer

Increasing Young People's Political Participation

Whilst they may be generally frustrated that the outcomes appear to provide them with little opportunity to influence the world around them, young people are clearly predisposed to the idea of elections. So, how might this general support for the democratic process be translated into increased participation in elections?

In the Government's *Representation of the People Act 2000*, certain proposals were suggested that were designed to solve the problem of low election turnout in Britain. In the survey, we asked the young respondents whether they considered that these methods would increase or decrease their likelihood to vote in elections. The results indicate that in all but one case, the largest group of respondents claimed that such scenarios would make no difference to their likelihood to vote (see Table 10.7). The one exception to this rule was that a majority of young people (55.9 per cent) claimed that spreading voting over more than one day would increase their attendance at elections[30]. Nonetheless, the findings clearly indicate that for all cases, those who view the introduction of these procedural changes pos-

---

30 At present, voting in Britain for local, national and European election contests takes place on Thursdays only.

itively outweigh the numbers of those who view them negatively. This isperhaps not surprising, given that people are unlikely to report that making the voting system more flexible would reduce their propensity to vote. The net turnout differences between those who would be more likely to vote, against those who would actually be less likely to do so, is set out in Table 10.7.

Table 10.7 Proposals to increase voter turnout (%)

Would you be more or less likely to vote if:	More	Less	Make no difference	Net turnout increase (+/-)
Vote in a public place (such as a supermarket)	35.8	6.4	57.8	+29.4
Vote over more than one day	55.9	1.9	42.2	+54.0
Polling stations were open for 24 hours	38.6	2.1	59.2	+36.5
Vote by post	45.5	6.6	47.9	+38.9
Vote by phone	40.0	11.6	48.5	+28.4
Vote from home (via the Internet or by digital TV)	40.3	10.8	48.8	+29.5
Voting was compulsory	41.8	10.7	47.5	+31.1
Access to polling stations was improved	19.7	0.5	79.8	+19.2

Base: 425 respondents, 1999 panel survey wave 2

These ideas were further tested through the focus groups. Most groups welcomed the proposals to change the way in which voting was conducted. In particular, there was again popular support for the proposal to extend the voting time period beyond a single day. Participants thought voting in supermarkets, on the telephone or through the Internet would probably encourage turnout amongst young people. Where there had been a good deal of consensus in most of the discussion about the proposed electoral procedural changes, the subject of compulsory voting caused a marked divergence in opinion when it was raised in the focus groups. Some welcomed the proposal because they felt it to be an elementary democratic duty of citizens to go to the polls. One person cited the Australian system as an example of how this can work[31]: *'In Australia, I think there's a law*

---

31 Voting at federal elections has been compulsory in Australia since 1924. The penalty for failing to do so is a $20 administrative fine.

that makes it compulsory, I think that could be quite a good idea'. But other participants, noticeably in the 'sceptics' focus group, adopted a contrasting standpoint. One member of this group drew support when they stated:

'It's your right to vote for the party you want. If there's no party you shouldn't have to vote. You've got the right not to vote'.

Fellow group members continued with a sustained attack on a rule change they believed would be *'impractical', 'stupid', 'undemocratic', 'counter-productive'* and encouraging of uninformed participation.

However, before we asked about these ideas for increasing electoral turnout among young people, we again invited our young participants to take part in a qualitative written sentence completion exercise. We presented them with the part sentence, 'I would be more likely to vote in the future, if...', and asked them to respond. The findings of this open-ended exercise are reproduced in Table 10.8. Significantly, the data indicate that the young people in the focus groups were more responsive to issues of political substance than they were to the procedural, mobilising mechanisms examined above. The results suggest that young people would be more likely to cast their vote in electoral contests if: they had more information about the political parties (26.7 per cent); there were a party that they considered represented their views (11.7 per cent); there was evidence that their views would be seriously listened to by politicians and decision-makers (18.3 per cent); or there was a greater choice of political parties available (6.7 per cent). Combining these four categories, we can observe that issues of political substance have a higher priority amongst young people than do introducing initiatives designed to increase the accessibility of voting, by a margin of 3.5:1. This qualitative data provides an interesting insight into young people's response to the procedural initiatives that have been suggested (and in some cases piloted) that are designed to mobilise the electorate and increase voting turnout. While these reforms were generally received favourably, none of the participants appeared to believe that they were crucial for enhancing the democratic process – accessible information about the parties, the candidates, and the issues was seen to be the key to improving election turnout.

Table 10.8

'I would be more likely to vote in the future, f..' (focus group sentence completion exercise)

	Number	Percent
1. More information about the parties and candidates was available	16	26.7
2. There was a party that generally reflected my interests and concerns	7	11.7
3. The parties listened to my opinions/ my vote would make a difference to my life	11	18.3
4. The parties could be distinguished from each other/ greater choice of political parties	4	6.7
5. Voting was made more accessible (more polling stations, extended voting period), and the process was clearer	11	18.3
6. Greater feedback on the outcomes of elections	5	8.3
7. Will always vote regardless	3	5.0
8. Payment incentive	3	5.0

Figures in the 'Number' column total more than 45, because some focus group respondents wrote more than one answer

Conclusion

As a number of previous studies have concluded, in terms of their behaviour and attitudes, young people are certainly less positively disposed towards the political process than their older contemporaries. But are they a politically alienated generation?

There is evidence that young people in Britain are becoming increasingly critical of the political set-up, and withdrawing from formal politics. They vote less, they participate less in terms of memberships of ostensibly 'political' organisations, and they have less favourable views towards the political system than older age groups, or previous youth cohorts. Current research elsewhere suggests that there is a legitimacy crisis as far as the British political system is concerned that is deeper for young people than it is for older age groups, indicating a possible cohort effect.

But what accounts for their apparent withdrawal from formal politics? Our research was designed to contribute towards an emerging body of knowledge that seeks to use qualitative techniques to explore youth political behaviour and attitudes, to build up an understanding of why young people appear to be somewhat disengaged from formal politics, and to address such issues from their own perspectives. Our findings suggest that although uninspired by, or even sceptical of, political parties and professional politicians, young people are sufficiently interested in political affairs to dispel the myth that they are apathetic and politically lazy. But they are also interested in a new style of politics. While they may eschew much of what could be characterised as 'formal' or conventional politics, they are interested in a different type of politics that is more participative, and which focuses on localised, immediate (and some post-material) issues.

Somewhat paradoxically, they are also still committed to the idea of elections and the democratic process. There is a civic orientation amongst the young to the democratic process: representative democracy is generally seen to be a very good thing and the young people who have participated in this study clearly signify their desire to be able to play a more active (and even) role within it. This is a particularly important finding, given that having had the opportunity to vote for the first time, they are left somewhat frustrated by the process outcomes – the words and deeds of those who have ultimately been elected to positions of political power through the elections. What is even more surprising is that the young people who participated in our study indicated that they could be persuaded to turn out to vote in larger numbers in the future.

By all accounts, these findings would suggest that young people might, to some extent, be politically alienated, although that is not to say that they are apolitical or apathetic. More, it is that they feel as if they have no ability to influence the course of political events, because the political system is too remote and inaccessible for them to engage with it meaningfully and effectively. They therefore have a correspondingly low level of political efficacy – they feel relatively powerless and unable to influence the political process. This is particularly frustrating, given that they are interested in political affairs. They are therefore alienated, but engaged, sceptics – they are interested in political affairs, feel powerless to influence the political process, and distrustful of those who are elected to positions of power and charged with running the political system.

References

Abrams, M. (1959) *The Teenage Consumer* (London: Press Exchange).

Abramson, P. and Inglehart, R. (1992) 'Generational Replacement and Value Change in Eight West European Societies', *British Journal of Political Science*, vol. 22:2; 183–228.

Almond, G. and Verba, S. (1963) *The Civic Culture,* (Princeton, NJ.: Princeton University Press).

Arber, S. (1993) 'Designing Samples' in N. Gilbert (ed.) *Researching Social Life* (London: Sage).

Barnes, S. and Kasse, M. (1979) *Political Action: Mass Participation in Five Western Democracies* (London: Sage).

Beck, U. (1982) Risk Society (London: Sage).

Bennett, S., Flickinger, R. and Stacci, R. (2000) 'Political Talk Over Here, Over There, Over Time', *British Journal of Political Science*, vol. 30; 99–119.

Bennie, L. and Rudig, W. (1993) 'Youth and the Environment: Attitudes and Actions in the 1990s', *Youth and Policy*, vol. 42; 6–21.

Bhavnani, K.K. (1994) *Talking Politics: A Psychological Framing of Views from Youth in Britain* (Cambridge: Cambridge University Press).

Budge, I. (1971) 'Support for Nation Among English Children: A Comment, *British Journal of Political Science*, vol. 1:3; 389-92.

Butler, D. and Kavanagh, D. (1997) The British General Election of 1997 (Hampshire: Macmillan Press).

Bynner, J. and Ashford, S. (1994) 'Politics and Participation: Some Antecedents of Young People's Attitudes to the Political System and Political Activity', *European Journal of Social Psychology*, vol. 24:2; 223-36.

Bynner, J., Ferri, E. and Sheperd, P. (1997) 'Changing Lives in the 1990s' in J. Bynner, E. Ferri, and P. Sheperd (eds) *Twenty-something in the 1990s: Getting On, Getting By, Getting Nowhere* (Aldershot: Ashgate).

Cantril, H. (ed.) (1951) *Public Opinion*, 1935–46 (Princeton, NJ.: Princeton University Press).

Cloonan, M. and Street, J. (1998) 'Rock the Vote: Popular Culture and Politics', *Politics*, vol. 18:1; 33-8.

Crace, J. (2000) 'The new citizens', *The Guardian*, 15 February 2000.

Crick, B. (1998) *Education for Citizenship and the Teaching of Democracy in Schools: Final Report of the Advisory Group on Citizenship* (London: Qualifications and Curriculum Authority).

Dalton, R. (1988) *Citizen Politics in Western Democracies* (New Jersey: Chatham House).

Frankfort-Nachmias C. and Nachmias, D. (1996) *Research Methods in the Social Sciences* (London : Edward Arnold).

Franklin, B. (1994) *Packaging Politics: Political Communications in Britain's Media Democracy* (London: Edward Arnold).

Franklin, M. (1985) *The Decline of Class Voting in Britain: Changes in the Basis of Electoral Choice 1964-1983* (Oxford: Clarendon Press).

Gaskin, K., Vlaeminke, M. and Fenton, N. (1996) *Young People's Attitudes Towards the Voluntary Sector: A Report for the Commission on the Future of the Voluntary Sector* (Loughborough: Loughborough University).

Government of The United Kingdom (2000) *Representation of the People Act 2000* (London: The Stationary Office Limited).

Hart, V. (1978) *Distrust and Democracy* (Cambridge: Cambridge University Press).

Heath, A. and Park, A. (1997) 'Thatcher's Children?' in R. Jowell et al. (eds) *British Social Attitudes: The 14th Report. The End of Conservative Values?* (Aldershot: Ashgate).

Heath, A. and Taylor, B. (1999) 'New Sources of Abstention?' in G. Evans and P. Norris (eds) *Critical Elections: British Parties and Voters in Long-term Perspective* (London: Sage Publications Ltd).

Henn, M., Weinstein, M. and Wring, D. (2000) *Young People and Citizenship: A Study of Opinion in Nottinghamshire* (Nottingham: Nottinghamshire County Council).

Industrial Society (1997) *Speaking Up, Speaking Out!* (London: Industrial Society).

Inglehart, R. (1971) 'The Silent Revolution in Europe: Intergenerational Change in Post-industrial Societies', *American Political Science Review*, vol. 65(4):991–1017.

Inglehart, R. (1977) *The Silent Revolution: Changing Values and Political Styles Among Western Publics* (Princeton, NJ.: Princeton University Press).

Jowell, R. and Park, A. (1998) *Young People, Politics and Citizenship: A Disengaged Generation?* (London: Citizenship Foundation).

Kavanagh, D. (1972) 'Allegiance Among English Children: A Dissent', *British Journal of Political Science*, vol. 2:1; 127-31.

Kavanagh, D. (1980) 'Political Culture in Britain: The Decline of the Civic Culture' in G. Almond and S. Verba (eds) *Civic Culture Revisited* (Boston, Mass.: Little Brown and Company).

Kimberlee, R. (1998) 'Young People and the 1997 General Election', *Renewal*, vol. 6:2; 87–90.

Kimberlee, R. (2002) 'Why Don't Young People Vote at General Elections?', *Journal of Youth Studies*, vol. 5:1; 85–98.

Leonard, M. and Katwala, S. (1997) 'It Was The Young Wot Won It!', *Renewal*, vol. 5:3/4; 108–16.

Lewis, P. (1978) *The Fifties* (London: Heinemann).

London Youth Matters (1997) *The Kids Are Alright?: What It's Like to Be Young in London in the 1990s* (London: London Youth Matters).

Marsh, A. (1977) *Protest and Political Consciousness* (London: Sage).

Marsh, D. (1972) 'Beliefs About Democracy Among English Adolescents: What Significance Have They?', *British Journal of Political Science*, vol. 2:2; 255-9.

Mass Observation (1948) *Puzzled People: A Study in Popular Attitudes to Religion, Ethics, Progress, and Politics in a London Borough* (London: Gollancz).

Miles, S. (2000) *Youth Lifestyles in a Changing World* (Buckingham: Open University Press).

MORI (2001) 'How Britain Voted in 2001', *British Public Opinion*, vol. 24:3/4; 3.

Mulgan, G. and Wilkinson, H. (1997) 'Freedom's Children and the Rise of Generational Politics' in G. Mulgan (ed) *Life after Politics: New Thinking for the Twenty-first Century* (London: Fontana Press).

Nie, N., Verba, S. and Kim, J-O. (1974) 'Political Participation and the Life Cycle', *Comparative Politics*, vol. 6; 319-40.

Oppenheim, A.N. (1992) *Questionnaire Design, Interviewing and Attitude Measurement* (London: Continuum).

Osgerby, B. (1998) *Youth in Britain Since 1945* (London: MacMillan).

Panebianco, A. (1988) *Political Parties: Organisation and Power* (Cambridge: Cambridge University Press).

Park, A. (1995) 'Teenagers and their Politics' in R. Jowell, J. Curtice, L. Brook, and S. Witherspoon (eds) *British Social Attitudes: The 12th Report* (Aldershot: Dartmouth).

Parry, G., Moyser, G. and Day, N. (1992) *Political Participation and Democracy in Britain* (Cambridge: Cambridge University Press).

Roberts, K. (1995) *Youth and Unemployment in Modern Britain* (Oxford: Oxford University Press).

Roker, D. (1997) *Challenging the Image: Young People as Volunteers and Campaigners* (Brighton: Trust for the Study of Adolescence).

The Royal Commission on the Constitution (1973a) Vol. 1, *Report*, Cmnd. 5460 (London: HMSO).

The Royal Commission on the Constitution (1973b) Vol. 2, *Memorandum of Dissent,* Cmnd. 5460 (London: HMSO).

Swaddle, K. and Heath, A. (1992) 'Official and Reported Turnout in the British General Election of 1987' in D. Denver, and G. Hands (eds) *Issues and Controversies in British Electoral Behaviour* (London: Harvester Wheatsheaf).

Verba, S. and Nie, N. (1972) *Participation in America: Political Democracy and Social Equality* (New York: Harper and Row).

White, C., Bruce, S. and Ritchie, J. (2000) *Young People's Politics: Political Interest and Engagement Amongst 14–24 year-olds* (York: Joseph Rowntree Foundation).

Wilkinson, H. (1996) 'But will they Vote? The Political Attitudes of Young People', *Children and Society*, vol. 10:3; 242-4.

Williamson, H. (1997) 'Status Zero Youth and the Underclass: Some Considerations' in R. McDonald (ed.) *Youth, The 'Underclass' and Social Exclusion* (London: Routledge).

Wring, D., Henn, M. and Weinstein, M. (1999) 'Young People and Contemporary Politics: Committed Scepticism or Engaged Cynicism?' in J. Fisher, P. Cowley, D. Denver, and A. Russell (eds) *British Elections and Parties Review Vol. 9* (London: Frank Cass Publishers).

11. Social Movements and the Struggle Over 'Race'

Max Farrar

In this chapter, I will analyse some of the effects on the political culture in the UK of social movements, since the 1970s, which have taken 'race' as their problematic. 'Race' has been a burning issue in recent British history arguably ever since the anti-black 'riots' in Liverpool in 1919, and certainly since those in Notting Hill and Nottingham in 1958 (Fryer, 1984). However, this chapter focuses on the new social movements that were formed at the start of the 1970s, which engaged in political action in support of social and racial equality. This is not to minimise the importance of the activities of liberals working in opposition to racism, which resulted in Race Relations Acts passed from 1966 to 2000, but it is intended to move our attention away from reformist politics.

This chapter focuses the extra-parliamentary movements of black and white Britons in which the status of racial categories is at stake. This emphasis is chosen for two reasons. Firstly because their vigorous protests have had such widespread effects on political and social life in the UK, and secondly because they have been largely ignored in the sociological and political literature on 'race'. Despite Paul Gilroy's comment many years ago that the social movement around 'race' in the 1980s 'has passed largely unacknowledged by left writers' (Gilroy, 1987a: 134), much work remains to be done in this field. One chapter of Alistair Bonnett's *Anti-Racism* (2000) is devoted to 'practising anti-racism', but this contains only the barest mention of the Anti-Nazi League, and makes no other reference to British social movements on 'race'. Mairtin Mac an Ghaill's (1999) examination of 'anti-racism and ethnic minority community mobilisation' is based on categorical distinctions (derived from Bonnett, 1993), between 'racial rejectionists' (i.e. racists), 'multi-culturalists' and 'anti-racists'. These distinctions run against the line taken in this chapter. Further, Mac an Ghaill is concerned with the theoretical underpinnings of the analysis of anti-racism, rather than with providing the much-needed empirical material on actual mobilisations. The concept 'power' appears in the title of another useful book on racism by Bhattacharyya, Gabriel and Small (2002), but, again, the focus is conceptual and not on those movements in Britain which have campaigned for power. Fortunately, there are some exceptions. A. Sivanandan (1982, 2000) has consistently applied the theory of class struggle Marxism to black British social movements and trade union struggles over 'race'. Cathie Lloyd (1998; 2001; 2002) has offered valuable analytical and empirical material on social movements around 'race' in the UK and in Europe. But, surprisingly perhaps, books that take 'race' and British politics as their focus (Miles and Phizacklea (eds) (1979), Goulbourne (ed.) (1990), Saggar (1992), Solomos and Back (1995)) make almost no mention of the relevant social movements. This chapter begins to redress this.

Because 'race' is a contested concept and social movements are also the subject of theoretical dispute, the chapter starts with a brief discussion of the relevant theories. It sets the framework for the argument put forward here: that the most significant of these social movements have undermined the viability of the concept of 'race'; have fundamentally dislocated the assumption that British culture is coloured white; and thus that they have forced a reconfiguration of the notion of British identity. These changes are currently being worked out in the new literature on British citizenship (Parekh, 2000; *Parekh Report 2000*; Stevenson 2002); an important discussion, which, for reasons of space, is not entered into here.

One other introductory point needs to be made, concerning the method employed in researching this chapter. I was actively involved in several movements, which focused on 'race' issues in the 1970s and 1980s, and some of the material used here comes from my own documents, notes, and memories. Perhaps because of the lack of academic attention on these movements, there is very little accessible documentation, even in specialist libraries, despite the proliferation of leaflets, pamphlets and newspapers issued within these movements. Some material is available on the worldwide web. While I have started interviewing key figures in these movements, much more careful 'oral history' needs to be done (a start has been made; see Harris and White (eds) (1999)), and librarians should be encouraged to acquire materials held in personal collections by activists, so that they can be collated, stored and indexed[32]. One major gap in this chapter, for instance, is any analysis of the role played by the various branches and tendencies within the Indian Workers Association. De Witt John (1969) is the authoritative source for the origins of this important Association, and

---

32 When established, the National Museum and Archives of Black British History and Culture will be a major asset.

Ramdin (1987) provides extensive information on its activities in the 1970s and 1980s. Perhaps because of their commitments to either the Soviet or Chinese styles of Communist Party, these associations were not always organic to the movements described here. But their continual presence in the struggle to eradicate racial discrimination should be properly analysed in the future. This chapter should therefore be considered to be 'work in progress'.

'Race' and Social Movement Theory

'Race' is a bogus concept. Committees of experts assembled by the United Nations Educational, Scientific and Cultural Organisation (UNESCO) have, since their first statement in 1950, systematically undermined notion that it is a valid scientific concept (Montagu, 1972). In 1970, the sociologist John Rex inserted these expert statements into the broader academic culture in this form:

> Race is a taxonomic concept of limited usefulness as a means of classifying human beings ... human population groups constitute a continuum ... the genetic diversity within groups is probably as great as that between groups ... "All men [sic] living today belong to a single species and are derived from a common stock". (Rex, 1983: 4-5)

Building on his writings since the 1960s, Michael Banton (1998) explained the genealogy of the concept of 'race' in European social thought. He noted that 'race' was set out and widely circulated in popular and intellectual circles from the middle of the Nineteenth Century. Racial categorisation replaced an earlier Christian account that all humans (of whatever skin colour) are the children of God with a spurious 'science' of fundamental biological difference. Supposedly different types (such as Caucasian, Negroid, Mongoloid, Asiatic and so on) were identified and labelled by the leading social and scientific thinkers of the day. Robert Miles (1982; 1989) argued that the concept 'race' has no validity whatsoever, placing it in inverted commas to signify its utterly dubious status. His argument is that white societies, since their first colonies in South America and the Caribbean, engage in a process of racialisation of non-white 'others'. This process takes skin colour, hair type, shape of eye and such like as indicators of essential biological difference. Racist ideology claimed that the non-'Caucasian' types of eye, nose, skin colour etc. are also signifiers of cultural inferiority, and thus provided justification for the economic exploitation and social exclusion of non-whites. Stuart Hall (1992), in an essay written specifically written for students, enlarged this work with a synthesis of Foucauldian and Marxist theory applied to a reading of European colonialism. Writing about the historical experience of dark-skinned people of African origin, Paul Gilroy (1993; 1997; 2000) has made the case for a replacement of racial categories with a notion of diasporic social identities. Such identities are mobile, hybrid, and continually changing, constructed from the huge variety of cultural and economic positions in which non-whites are placed throughout the globe. A similar argument should be made for white-skinned people. Gilroy (1987b; 1992) has also argued that the concept of 'anti-racism' is now a hindrance to political progress in this field because it fetishises the concept of 'race' and colludes in the reduction of 'race' to culture. Yet, the concept of 'race' lives on in sections of popular and political culture, seemingly undamaged by this intellectual assault. One reason for this is the continued publications of academics that persist in arguing that 'races' are essentially different (Carlton Coon (1982) claims to have identified 68 of them). Another reason for this persistence will emerge later in this chapter: the continued activities of social movements of black people, and of whites, who reject the rejection of 'race'.

As a further preliminary to analysing actual social movements on 'race', we need to examine some of the literature on social movements. The published theoretical and empirical work has so far failed to turn its attention to movements of black people, or whites with an interest in 'race', in the UK. First, what are social movements? Paul Byrne argues that: 'social movements ... are amorphous entities ... hard to delineate in organisational, tactical or ideological terms'. There are some common features, however: social movements have an 'expressive' politics, non-negotiable basic values, and collective identities; they operate in networks outside the orthodox channels of representative democracy, and they make a fundamental challenge to the existing order' (Byrne, 1997: 11-23).

Analysts of social movements are somewhat split between the 'resource mobilisation' theories and the 'new social movement' theories. The former provide useful purchase on the methods used by, and the material achievements of social movements, while the latter focus more on the concepts of identity and networks. Della Porta and Diani (1999) attempt to reconcile the two camps, but Melucci has argued that, since the late 1990s, there has been a tendency to abandon new social movement theory in favour of the rational choice models adopted by the resource mobilisation theorists (Lentin, 1999). Because 'race', and its abolition, is inextricably linked to questions of identity, and the 'race' movements have been concerned with fundamental change, the discussion here draws mainly from the sociology of new social movements.

The theory advanced by Manuel Castells (1983) is the most nearly relevant to the 'race' social movements. His more recent work provides a rather limited set of conceptual tools than are required. This work suggests that social movements can be separated from other forms of political action by the primary importance they give to the creation and enactment of a distinctive social identity, by the type of adversary they choose to attack, and by their 'societal goals' – the 'vision of a new kind of social order, or social organisation' which they are trying to achieve (Castells, 1997: 71). These are familiar characteristic features of social movements. However, in the case studies that he offers in the 1997 book, Castells is too eager to reduce each to an identity held in common, a single enemy and an agreed goal. In his brief discussion of 'African American identity', he even appears to accept the validity of the concept of 'race' (1997: 53-9). In the 'race' movements, as we shall see, while some accept Castells' assumption about the concept of 'race', there is little agreement on identity, adversary or goals. Alberto Melucci (1996) also emphasises 'identity' as a focal concern for social movements, but stresses their organisational method as another distinctive feature. Movements form fluid non-hierarchical networks and reject the fixed structures established by political parties and pressure groups. Again, while this applies to some 'race' movements, it certainly does not apply to the field as a whole, which has witnessed the rise and fall of several groups which have claimed the status and form of political parties, as well as the operation of quite tightly organised core groups within the networked movement.

Castells' earlier theory of urban social movements directs our attention to each of these important issues, but to several others besides. Having reviewed a wide range of city-based campaigns in Europe and America, from gay movements to tenants associations, Castells distinguished three types of movement defined principally by what he later called their 'societal goals':

Those, which are organised around 'collective consumption demands' – those that seek to de-commodify the services, provided by the city, to transform them from exchange values into use values.

Those which are engaged in 'the search for cultural identity, for the maintenance or creation of autonomous local cultures, ethnically-based or historically originated'; these 'community' movements seek to defend people's face-to-face communication, their 'autonomously defined social meaning' against the invasion from above of media messages and its standardised culture. He called these 'community movements'.

Those that aim for neighbourhood self-management, local participation and autonomy, against centralised power structures; these are the characteristic goals of what Castells calls 'citizen movements'. (Castell, 1983: 319-21)

This approach enables us to capture important features of some black social movements – their search for cultural identity, their campaigns for adequate welfare and social provision (preferably de-commodified, or free), and, particularly in those that based themselves in specific inner-areas of the major UK cities, the demand for local control of neighbourhood facilities and a recognition of their rights as British citizens. Castells' category of 'citizen movements' might also stretch to the anti-deportation campaigns that have been a feature of British political life since the late 1970s, and those of the early twenty-first century that defend refugees and asylum-seekers. The question of whether these movements are revolutionary in intent was answered by Jean Cohen (1985), who argued that their emphasis was on structural reform; they adopted a type of 'self-limiting radicalism'. Again, this is hardly true of the militant black movement of the 1970s and early 1980s, which saw itself as spearheading revolutionary change.

However, there are several gaps in this approach. One is a consideration of the embodied and expressive elements of 'race' social movements, issues which are effectively addressed in Hetherington's (1998) study of 'new age' movements and which Gilroy (1987a) briefly attempted to include in his comments on black urban politics in the 1980s. I shall address this in my examination below of movements such as Rock Against Racism.

A second problem lies in Castells' thin approach to the issue of 'community'. In my own study of black and white social movements I have emphasised goals which Castells underplays, such as the search for emotional intimacy, social solidarity and social justice, captured in what I call the social imaginary of 'community', which is characteristic of the movements operating over the past thirty years in the multi-cultural inner city area of Chapeltown, Leeds (Farrar, 2002a). The utopianism, which underpins this imaginary, is observable in the anti-capitalist social movements of the late 1990s and early 2000s; sometimes they acknowledge the inspiration they gained from radical black movements and earlier carnivalesque movements. A less optimistic feature of my own study, which has been analysed rather differently by Gilroy (1987a), is the use of the tactics of violence and fire in the so-called 'riots', which punctuated the 1970s, the 1980s, and 2001.

Thirdly, Castells, in common with most of the social movement theorists, pays too little attention to the international dimensions of social movements. While this will be redressed by studies of the anti-capitalist movements that emerged in the late 1990s, the movements around 'race' in the UK had from the start a keen focus on the global dimensions of the issues they addressed.

In summary, then, this chapter will analyse 'race' social movements in terms which problematises the notion of 'race'; will suggest limitations, as well as applications of Castells' urban social movement theory; and will focus on the bodily and artistic aspects, as well as the violence, contained within an extremely diverse set of movements linked only by their common interest in the question of 'race'. The global aspects of these movements will be mentioned in passing.

Early 'Race' Movements

A defining moment for the black social movements in the 1970s was the trial of what became known as the Mangrove Nine. Nine black (British Caribbean) people were arrested during a demonstration in August 1971 against police harassment of Frank Critchlow, the owner of the Mangrove restaurant in Notting Hill, London. Demonstrations, occupations, sit-downs and so on are the stock-in-trade of social movements, and the intensity of the bodily experience in these activities is rarely commented upon. Yet, demonstrators are often turning their bodies into the targets of physical aggression by police officers and counter-demonstrators. Both on these occasions and on those where there is joyful, exuberant non-violent action, the rush of adrenaline is experienced physically by many of the participants. One of the leaders of the Mangrove demonstration, Darcus Howe, had already been campaigning against police malpractice, and when members of the British Black Panthers arrived to support the demonstration the police took the opportunity to arrest radicals who, according to a report in the Guardian newspaper, they had already had under surveillance for a year (Fryer, 1984: 394). Violence was exerted here and arrests were made. Charges included incitement to riot, attempted murder of police officers and assault. The fact that an all-white jury acquitted the nine proved, according to Darcus Howe, that 'This race thing, you have to be very careful how you deal with it because you can win people over' (Interview 6.8.2002).

Howe was already familiar with the theory advanced by his uncle, the Trinidadian Marxist CLR James. As he puts it, *'Facing Reality* (1958) was my text'; it is a refined mix of theory and studies of working class practice which stresses the need for autonomous organisation of the black working class, within an overall strategy of unity with militants in the white working class as revolutionary forces develop. Howe briefly joined the Black Panthers, which included Althea Jones and Barbara Beese, but from 1974 until the mid-1980s was the editor of the monthly journal Race Today. He subsequently became a leading figure in the Race Today Alliance, which included the Black Parents Movement and the Black Students Movement[33]. Although there were differences of emphasis within the Alliance, with John La Rose in particular having a greater regard for the legacy of George Padmore (Interview with John La Rose 13.9.2001, Alleyne, 2002), it was committed to the view that 'race' is inextricable from 'class'.

The Mangrove trial, and the many other campaigns against police harassment documented in the pages of *Race Today* throughout the 1970s, exemplified the confidence of this tendency within the black social movements that racism is not an inevitable and insurmountable feature of white society. White working class people were, in this analysis, capable of recognising what they had in common with black workers. In that sense, they were undermining the salience of the category 'race', while campaigning vigorously against racism. Private and public meetings, press releases and leaflets, the filling of the court-room galleries with family and supporters, pickets of court houses and demonstrations – all these tactics were frequently utilised in most cities throughout the 1970s. Black mili-

---

33 Leila Hassan, John La Rose, Gus John and Linton Kwesi Johnson were among the other key members.

tants formed a social movement with 'justice' as its immediate goal. This movement emphasised the central role of the arrested youth and their families, a legal defence team led by black lawyers and/or anti-racist whites who showed no deference to the police or the judges, and the mobilisation in demonstrations and court-room pickets of supporters of the accused. The Alliance was, however, as committed to workplace struggles as it was to neighbourhood-based actions, and as interested in political militancy within the Asian population as in the Caribbean groups. *Race Today* covered political events anywhere in the world with a significant black population, taking a Marxist-internationalist perspective[34]. The Alliance was a tightly organised and disciplined group which saw itself at the centre of a wider social movement of black people and those of their white supporters who adopted Jamesian politics. It had members in Bradford (publishing Bradford Black magazine between 1977 and 1980) and supporters in other cities. Nevertheless, the Alliance always adopted what was then called a 'mass politics' and is now more often seen as 'movement' politics.

Its rejection of the Leninist theory of a revolutionary party functioning as the leadership of the working class distinguished the Alliance from two other black organisations in the 1970s, the Black Unity and Freedom Party (BUFP) and Samaj-in'a Babylon. The BUFP published a newspaper, *Black Voice*[35]. Samaj was formed by a group of British Asians who left the Socialist Workers Party, issuing its first newspaper in September 1976. Soonu Engineer was a leading member, and most, but not all, of its correspondents were Asian. In March 1977, it added 'in'a Babylon' to its title, indicating its willingness to cover the struggles of British Caribbeans as well as Asians. It included articles on Rastafarianism, and it reported on arrested Caribbean youth known as the Islington 18 and the Lewisham 21 in its August-September 1977 issue. Just as *Black Voice* indicated its solidarity with the republican movement in the north of Ireland, the Samaj group was not ideologically hostile to white people as a whole. It described itself as 'a socialist paper for black people and those involved in the fight against racism', that is, whites who identified with black struggle. However, it was clear about its principal focus: 'the struggles of black workers here and internationally' (Samaj-in'a Babylon, March 1977).

---

34 Moore (1975) effectively utilises Race Today to summarise the struggles of the early 1970s.

35 My 1988 issue is Volume 19 so it was presumably founded in 1969.

There was much evidence available in this period to justify the argument that black workers, particularly British Asians, would engage in sharp confrontations with their employers. A social movement emerged with 'workers' rights' as its central theme. The three month strike by the predominantly Asian workforce at Imperial Typewriters in Leicester which began in May 1974, championed by *Race Today*, may have resulted in the closure of the factory, but it demonstrated not only the militancy of the Asian workers, but the willingness of Asian women to play a central role in the organisation of the strike (Ramdin, 1987: 271-280). The epic strike at the Grunwick photographic factory in north London, from August 1976 to July 1978, also ended in defeat for the workers, but witnessed an intensity of struggle rarely seen in British trade union history (Ramdin, 1987: 280-309). Mrs Jayaben Desai, a central figure throughout the strike paid tribute to the massive support offered to the Asian strikers, mainly women, by white trade unionists. She also understood the contradictions within white racism: 'Ordinary trade union members ... who come to our picket line ... support us because I think they understand how we suffer. Some may have racialist attitudes, but there is also genuine sympathy' (Samaj-in'a Babylon, April-May 1977).

It is clear that all three of these black organisations emphasised their ideological and organisational autonomy from the parties and campaigns of the predominantly white far left, but never excluded alliances with whites that supported their political position. Further, the division between people of African and Asian origin was seen as a product of colonialism and racism, and was expected to be eradicated over time. For them, 'race' was a significant, but not the only, source of oppression and alienation in white society. In this they were quite distinct from the other important formation within the black social movements of the 1970s, the group based in Notting Hill, London, which published a newspaper called *Grassroots*. Issues of this newspaper published in 1976 and 1978 cover similar issues to those included in the Marxist-oriented papers – racist attacks, police harassment, unjust deportations – but the paper indicates its commitment to what has been described as 'cultural nationalism' by its exclusive emphasis on issues relating to people of African origin. The significance it placed on education, family life, and 'black heroes' (where black is the code for African), and the stress it gave to Africa Liberation Day (celebrated in May 1978 with a march and a week-end of cultural and educational events) indicated its aspiration for a social and cultural life in the UK which is quite separate from that of white citizens. In this it has close links with those in the

Rastafarian movement, also prominent in this period, which, following Marcus Garvey, advocated a physical return to Africa by black Britons (Owens, 1979; Jones, 1987). While this formation rarely imposed its organisation on white society, since it had little or no interest in the demonstrations, conferences and so on organised by the wider movements around 'race', its influence among young black people was significant, because it expressed the deep alienation many felt within white society.

Brief reference has been made to the role of whites within the 'race' movements, and this must now be addressed. White racists have also organised in a form that fits within the parameters of social movements. The National Front (NF), the predominant organisation of British Nazis in the 1970s, adopted a populist approach to politics, campaigning vigorously against immigration and against British Caribbean youths' alleged proclivity to crime. A membership organisation, it continually sought to expand its influence by recruiting among white football supporters and by spectacular (and provocative) actions, such as demonstrating against the Imperial Typewriters' strikers, and marching through neighbourhoods where black British people lived (e.g. Bradford on 24th April 1976, deliberately provoking a violent confrontation with Asian youth and their white supporters (Webster, 1977: 173, 195). Like most social movements, it advocated symbolic action as a key tactic for increasing its influence in British politics: 'What is it that touches off a chord in the instincts of the people. . ? It can often be the most simple and primitive thing ... a flag ... a marching column ... the sound of a drum' (NF leader John Tyndall, quoted in Walker, 1977: 145). This symbolic, embodied, performative approach to politics is characteristic of social movements of both the left and the right. Unlike the left social movements, however, the NF sought Parliamentary representation. Eighty of its 176 candidates obtained more than 10 per cent of the vote in the local government elections of 1976 in the wake of hostile tabloid reaction the arrival in the UK of British Asians expelled from Malawi. In Leicester, it fielded 48 candidates, gaining 43,733 votes (averaging 18.5 per cent of the total votes cast) (Webster, 1977: 195-8). These indicators of entrenched racism alarmed the left.

The end of the 1970s was therefore a very difficult time for Britain's black population. Surveyed in 1982, 53 per cent of British Caribbean's and 51 per cent of British Asians, said 'things had got worse' for them over the previous five years. While the economic recession was the main reason for this for the majority of these, 41 per cent of Caribbeans and 49 per cent of Asians said racism was the reason (Brown, 1984: 277-8). The rise in support for the National Front, the catalogue of reported violence exerted against black Britons, and racist remarks by pop icons stimulated one of the major social movements of the 1970s and early 1980s, Rock Against Racism (RAR) and the Anti Nazi League (ANL). The former was established in 1976 by members and sympathisers of the Socialist Workers Party whose understanding of the importance of popular culture matched, perhaps overshadowed, their Party's focus of workplace struggle. Rooted in the iconoclastic underground newspapers, theatre groups and youth music cultures of the 1960s, the founders of RAR (including Red Saunders, Roger Huddle, Syd Shelton and David Widgery) were a world apart from the dead men on leave (Lenin's apt phrase) who populated the revolutionary left. They formed RAR in specific response to David Bowie's comment to Playboy magazine that he sympathised with fascism, and his dressing in Nazi regalia at Victoria station (Widgery, 1986: 41), and to Eric Clapton's shout to the crowd at a gig that they should "Vote for Enoch Powell ... Stop Britain becoming a black colony ... get the foreigners out" (Samaj-in' a Babylon, March 1977).

David Widgery's book Beating Time (1986), subtitled 'riot 'n' race 'n' 'n' rock and roll' provides marvellous commentary and photographs of this period and the movement he did so much to form. Ruth Gregory, who, unusually for a newspaper editor, was a painter and graphic designer, ran RAR's magazine *Temporary Hoarding*. It has never been matched in political journalism for its creative layout, its serious content (Widgery accurately describes it as 'dub Marxism'), accessible style, and for its sheer energy and commitment. Nazi iconography was creeping into the body-displays adopted by some early supporters of Punk rock bands like the Sex Pistols, Sham 69 and Angelic Upstarts, and around the second-wave Ska band, Madness. Temporary Hoarding gave prominence to Pistols' singer Johnny Rotten's condemnation of racism in general and Nazism in particular. The explosion all over the country of RAR reggae/punk gigs, where dreadlocked blacks and safety-pinned whites enthusiastically shared the same space for the first time effectively expelled both the nazi regalia and the actual Nazis from the movement. Pogo-ing[36] was perhaps the most dramatic example of the embodiment of this new culture for white youths. The cool, rhythmic, intimate dance style of early reggae was equally expressive among black youths, but it was beginning to be replaced by more energetic

---

36 A dance form that consisted of young people, mainly men, leaping up in the air and crashing into the people packed into the space nearby.

forms of black dance in which the body was bent and arms were out-stretched. Personal styles of clothing and hair at RAR gigs and carnivals eschewed all mainstream pop conventions, creating new modes with bewildering rapidity. All these performances involved the creation of a personal symbolic order by bricolage (Hall and Jefferson, 1976; Hebdige, 1979) to match the non-racial order they aimed for in society.

RAR's innovation – mass cultural politics – came at a time when small groups of whites in all the major cities had been organising anti-fascist and anti-racist campaigns since the early 1970s, often distributing the anti-fascist magazine *Searchlight*. Many, such as the Leeds Coalition Against Racism and Fascism, set up in 1974 by members of Big Flame, a mainly white far left group which supported political autonomy, had disputed *Searchlight's* one-sided emphasis on nazi groups, arguing that racism in the wider society was in many respects the more significant issue. Big Flame's pamphlet 'The Past Against Our Future' (1978) went further, arguing that the sexual and gender oppression that underlay Nazism was almost as important as its racism. Despite these sorts of commitments, local groups mainly agreed to join the single-focused Anti Nazi League when it was formed in late 1977, since, with the SWP's organisational flair and its wide backing from trade unions, left MPs and other worthies, and with RAR as its creative vanguard, the ANL was clearly able to mobilise a much larger movement than the could the small anti-racist, anti-fascist groups. A combination of RAR Carnivals and massive anti-nazi demonstrations successfully marginalised the National Front and considerably reduced its vote at the 1979 election[37]. Eighty thousand people attended the first RAR/ANL Carnival, rocking politically to The Clash, The Tom Robinson Band, Steel Pulse, X-Ray Specs and others (30th April 1978, Victoria Park, London). One hundred thousand attended the second (24th September 1978, Brockwell Park, London), while 35,000 carnivalled in Manchester in the autumn of 1978, 5,000 in Cardiff, 8,000 in Edinburgh, 2,000 in Harwich and 5,000 in Southampton (Renton, 2002). Widgery puts the total figure even higher, claiming that 400,000 people took part in the carnivals of 1978. At its height there were 52 RAR groups organising around the UK (Widgery, 1986: 91, 95). Between 1977 and 1979, nine million ANL

---

37 Its vote in Leicester dropped to 5 per cent in the 1978 local elections, it failed to retain its deposit in any seat at the 1979 general election, and the National Front then split into three factions (Widgery, 1986: 111).

leaflets were distributed and 750,000 badges were sold. Large numbers of Labour Party and Trade Union branches affiliated (Renton, 2002).

The predominantly white left, aided by RAR but as yet unsupported by the ANL, mobilised thousands, including many young blacks, to stop the National Front marching through Lewisham (an area of black settlement in London) in August 1977; 7,000 young Bengalis demonstrated after the racist murder of Altab Ali in East London, joined the following month by 4,000 ANL supporters (Renton, 2002). On 23rd April 1979, the police killed Blair Peach during a huge demonstration in Southall (an the area of London with a high proportion of British Punjabi residents), initiated by the Southall Asian Youth Movement and supported by the ANL, against the decision to allow the National Front to hold a meeting at Ealing Town Hall. Ten thousand people joined the mourning procession (CARF, 1981). One of the significant consequences of this upsurge of self-organisation amongst British Asians was the formation of Southall Black Sisters in November 1979, a group that has campaigned ever since both for women's rights in general and against all forms of religious fundamentalism in particular (SBS, 1990; Patel, 2002)[38].

Throughout this period, a social movement of unprecedented proportions was created. Although Gilroy (1987a) correctly criticises the ANL for its implicit reinforcement of British nationalism (with its argument that the Nazis were sham patriots) and its narrowing-down of the complex agenda of RAR, his is the only academic work, which provides a proper appreciation of this movement's achievements. Its last Carnival, in Leeds in 1983, show-cased the tendency in youth culture which most explicitly took up the challenge of the abolition of 'race': Two-Tone, the revival of Jamaica Ska played by bands such as The Specials, The Beat and The Selecter composed equally of black and white British musicians (listen to 'The Best of Two Tone' CD, Chrysalis (1993)).

The important part played by the Asian Youth Movements (AYMs), which formed in most towns and cities with a sizeable population of British Asians during the late 1970s, is even less well documented. Yet the AYMs initiated their own demonstrations, issued their own propaganda and functioned as a thorn in the flesh of the newly emerging Asian establishment in the towns in which they were based. Every anti-fascist demonstration had

---

38 Mirza (ed.) (1997) captures much of the relevant theory and some of the activism of black British women.

a large contingent of Asian youth; if anyone still held any doubts about the status of young British Asians as active and politically aware members of British society, the AYMs forcibly ejected those illusions and defeated the 'between two cultures' argument (Anwar, 1981) at the same time. CARF (1981: 54-7) discusses the Southall AYM and highlights one its other achievements: bridging the gap between young Asians and young Caribbeans in Southall. It made good links with the organisation that mobilised Caribbean youth in that area, the significantly named People's Unite Education and Creative Arts Centre. The police at the demonstration in 1979 at which Blair Peach was killed smashed this centre up.

The turning of a decade is an arbitrary point at which we take stock of the recent past, and in terms of the impact of these social movements on the political culture of the UK, it is reasonable to assert that the 1970s was the time in which a new social actor made its presence decisively felt in British society: black citizens found their militant voice, and the establishment was forced to make ad-hoc responses. Its main efforts were in Parliamentary legislation. The Race Relations Act of 1976 strengthened the provisions of the 1965 and 1968 Acts by outlawing both indirect and direct discrimination, and the Race Relations Board was replaced by the Commission for Racial Equality, charged with the duty to 'work towards eliminating racial discrimination; to promote equality of opportunity; to influence policy, and promote and encourage research in race relations; and to keep the functioning of the Act under constant review', as well as helping people with their complaints and acting against institutions found to have exerted indirect discrimination (Hiro, 1992: 226). With 86 branches throughout the UK, some were optimistic for the CRE. The radical movements held no illusions, and even Lionel Morrison argued that CRE offices did black organisations a disservice by claiming to represent black opinion in their neighbourhoods (Walker, 1977: 219). Nevertheless, the UK has legislation and enforcement mechanisms, which are the envy of anti-racists among our European partners (Forbes, 1995).

Aside from this legislative response, there were four important consequences for the shape of British politics as a whole. One was the ability to secure a principle that is as clear today as it became then: the right to autonomous self-organisation based on a particular source of oppression (in this case, racism). This principle is secure only in the sense that it is widely acknowledged to be the operative principle in all social movements; it remains bitterly disputed by the predominantly white parties of the far left and the Labour Party[39].

Secondly, these movements created a new form of politics: the cultural politics of everyday life. Although RAR deserves the credit for translating this into mass politics, Caribbean reggae musicians such as Bob Marley and Peter Tosh and the poet Linton Kwesi Johnson initially established the fusion of cultural activity and political commitment in the early 1970s. It was, and is, expressed most vigorously within the Caribbean neighbourhoods of the UK by the annual West Indian-style Carnivals held each year (Connor and Farrar, 2003). The theorist of this fusion was CLR James, and Creation for Liberation, an arm of the Race Today Alliance headed by Johnson, promoted political culture in black neighbourhoods for some time after RAR and dissolved. This understanding, which was so clearly manifested by Reclaim the Streets in the 1990s, owes as much to the cultural politics of the 1970s 'race' movements as it does to the Situationists to whom it most often referred (Jordan, 1998).

Thirdly, a generation of white youth was formed which admired black culture, hated racism and began to mix comfortably with British Asians and British Caribbeans. It was in this period that it began to be possible to use the term 'black' generically, in recognition of what people of Asian (South and East) and African (UK, Caribbean and US) descent had in common in predominantly white societies. Despite the impact of cultural nationalism behind the scenes, in the public sphere, especially among young people, the foundations were being laid for 'race' to be understood as phenotypical, not genotypical, as constructed, not essential. So long as racism existed, the concept of 'race' would not disappear, but for the major black radical movements at least, it was not to be taken as the essential feature of their social existence.

The fourth and perhaps most important consequence arose from these three developments. Both multi-culturalism and anti-racism were losing their relevance in the everyday lives of young people living in the ethnically diverse cities of the UK. 'Race' was becoming less personally divisive issue for them than it had been for their black and their white parents. This is not for a moment to suggest that racist atrocities ceased, but it is to

---

39 On the former, the exemplary story of the fateful clash between the leadership of Socialist Workers Party and its black members organised around its paper Flame remains to be told. In brief, Flame was extinguished. On the latter, see the demise of Labour Party Black Sections, which had been organised by Labour Party members influenced by black social movements but who remained, nevertheless committed to the reformist politics of Labour (Shukra, 1990).

suggest that, in the neighbourhoods, clubs, colleges and schools in which black and white young people grew up and worked together, an ease of association developed across the cultures. Although it took another few years for 'whiteness' studies to enter the academic domain, key thinkers in this field (e.g. Ware, 1992; Ware and Back, 2002) formed their politics and their ideas in the 1970s cultural politics mileux, alongside radical blacks. 'Being white' is now the focus of critical interrogation, but it is no longer taken as the automatic signifier of indissoluble difference, any more than 'being black' had been for the radical black movements of this period. As we shall see below, this development was uneven – contrary forces emerged during the 1980s. Nor were the deeper, socio-psychological layers of white racism eliminated. Nevertheless, from this period onwards, the claim that the UK was simply white or universally racist held diminishing credibility.

Later Movements

Events took place in the mid-1970s and the early 1980s, which the mass media called 'riots' and which radicals, black and white, called 'rebellions' or 'insurrections'. I seek to replace all these terms with 'violent urban protest' (Farrar, 2002b). The following briefly summarises the major protests:

- On 5th November 1975 British-Caribbean youth in Chapeltown, Leeds, stoned police cars, severely injuring two officers, and fought pitched battles with the police who arrived to rescue their colleagues (Race Today, December 1975).
- Over the August Bank Holiday weekend in 1976, much larger groups of British Caribbean youth fought with the police at the Notting Hill Carnival in London Race Today, September 1976).
- Five years later violent protest broke out in the St Paul's area of Bristol (2nd April 1981, 100 arrests), in Brixton, London (9th-13th April, 244 arrests), Finsbury Park, London (20th April, 91 arrests), Southall, London (3rd July, 23 arrests), Toxteth, Liverpool (3rd-8th July, 200 arrests)
- On the night of 10th July 1981, violence took place in Moss Side (Manchester, with 53 arrests), throughout London (385 arrests), Birmingham (42 arrests), Wolverhampton (22 arrests), Liverpool

(65 arrests), Preston (24 arrests), Hull (27 arrests) and Luton (one arrest).

- Over the week-end of 10th-11th July 1981 there was further disorder in Manchester, London and Birmingham, and in another 25 cities and towns, including Leeds, Bradford and Tunbridge Wells, with a further 1,065 arrests. Too little emphasis has been placed on the fact that thousands of white youths were involved in the July 1981 events. (For further details, see Benyon and Solomos, 1987: 3-15; Farrar, 1982: 7; Gilroy, 1987: 237-40; Hiro, 1992: 85; Kettle and Hodges, 1982.)[40]

Gilroy (1987a) argues that these activities exhibit many of the features associated with social movements, and he emphasises their normative, moral and purposeful aspects (particularly the demand for social justice), as well as the exuberance and joyfulness exhibited by many participants. All these are important observations; particularly in view of the unthinking condemnation, they receive from mainstream politicians and the mass media. But one other feature must also be stressed: the terrible fear they provoke among most inner city residents, the shame experienced by families afterwards, and the acute disruption they cause in the local political process. In Chapeltown, for instance, most of the key activists in the urban movements of the 1970s, which had campaigned so successfully over educational issues in the 1970s (Farrar, 1992), refused to participate in the defence committee set up for those arrested in 1981. Instead, they turned all their attention to an institution created by the city council, the Harehills and Chapeltown Liaison Committee, which tied them ever more closely to the local state as the 1980s progressed. While a new generation of activists did emerge in the mid-1980s, who, significantly, were willing to campaign successfully as mixed groups of whites, British Asians and British Caribbeans, the council was able to accelerate the process of ethnic segmentation, professionalisation and individualisation which was developing in the UK as a whole, stimulated by Mrs Thatcher's brand of Conservatism (Farrar, 1999).

---

40 Protest against the police by black British youth has been a persistent stimulus for political activity throughout the period considered in this chapter. Injustices are catalogued in Policing Against Black People (IRR, 1987) and this phenomenon is analysed sociologically in Cashmore and McLauhglin (eds.) (1991).

Employing Castells' terms, the movements of the 1970s were effective on all three dimensions – in their 'collective consumption' demands, over their 'identity' issues, and as 'citizens' movements', even including revolutionary elements within the movement. But, apart from the new radicals demonstrating over police and council racism, the movements of the 1970s largely collapsed in the subsequent decade into reformist pressure activity. In particular, they demanded (and largely obtained) equal opportunity policies in public sector bodies. Cain and Yuval-Davis (1990) describe the emergence of salaried, 'professional' spokespeople, the separation of Asians and Caribbeans, an increasing focus of welfare issues instead of political rights, and the dependence of local organisations on public funding (and thus the restraint of their radicalism). Those committed to the probably out-dated revolution/reform binary opposition critique these developments as 'mere reformism', but it is important to recall that these activities – of what we might call ethnically segmented local pressure groups – delivered significant improvement to the material fabric of the multi-cultural inner city area known as Chapeltown (Farrar, 2002a), and other similar areas also witnessed these developments in housing, local community centres, environmental improvement and the like. These reforms may have arrived anyway, but they were certainly kick-started by the violent urban protest of 1981. It is an irony that few of the youths who fought and flamed throughout the first seven months of that year benefited from the reforms they precipitated.

Only one major campaign arose out the violent urban protests in 1981: the defence of twelve members of the United Black Youth League (UBYL). These young British Asians living in Bradford had made petrol bombs in preparation for a rumoured attack by fascists in the wake of the 'riots' in July of that year. Two of the defendants, Tarlochan Gata-Aura and Tariq Mehmood Ali, had been members of the Bradford Asian Youth Movement. Gata-Aura had also had long experience of trying to work within the mainly white organisations of the far left, and of Samaj-in'a Babylon, finally forming the UBYL, a radical local organisation which aspired to black unity. The defence campaign fractured several times in the lead-up to their month-long trial in Leeds Crown Court in April 1982, but it finally succeeded in distributing thousands of leaflets and posters and mobilising huge numbers of British Asians and their white and British Caribbean supporters. Radical barristers, experienced in trials in which racism is the key issue, combined with massive public support succeeded in persuading a jury of seven white and five black people that the UBYL members were justified in making these preparations. The jury accepted the slogan raised by militants throughout the 1970s that 'self defence is no offence'[41].

One other event in the early 1980s provoked a mass demonstration, mainly of British Caribbeans. The fire at a party in New Cross, London, on 18th January 1981, at which thirteen black youths died, provoked outrage within the black community when it became clear to them that it had been started by a petrol bomb thrown by racists. 'Thirteen dead and nothing said' was shouted at meetings and at the New Cross Massacre Black People's Day of Action on 2nd March; no member of the white establishment had even bothered to send condolences to the bereaved families. One thousand people attended a meeting immediately after the fire and 20,000, mainly but not exclusively British Caribbeans, joined the Day of Action, marching for eight hours from New Cross to Hyde Park (in London). Another of the marchers' slogans, 'Blood ah go run is justice nah come' was particularly prescient, since the Day of Action took place just a month before violent urban protest in Brixton, London, in the wake of the mass arrests in the police's 'Swamp '81' campaign. Skilfully co-ordinated by members of the Race Today Alliance, this was the largest demonstration of black Britons ever seen in this country and showed every sign of turning itself into a mass social movement. It seems probable that the outbreak of urban protest over the following four months undermined that possibility, and while the legal challenges to the official response to the fire (that it was an accident) continued until July 1982, no conclusion was reached which satisfied the families or the campaigners[42].

It might be possible to fit mass campaigns such as those for the UBYL defendants or the New Cross victims within Castells' category of a citizen movement, since they are fiercely opposed to centralised power structures. Their equal emphasis, however, on 'autonomously defined social meaning' and self-identity places them within Castells' 'community movement'. What Castells' typology fails to capture is the intense concentration within these movements on justice and equal rights, regardless of ethnicity. While these movements are rooted in everyday life and utterly practical in their demands, a longing for a world in which skin colour is irrelevant and justice and solidarity will prevail is at the heart of these events. Thus the con-

---

41 See *Race Today* August/September 1982 for an analysis of the campaign and the trial.
42 For further details, see issues of Race Today for 1981 and 1982 and the document issued by the 20th Anniversary New Cross Massacre Action Committee (2001).

cept 'utopian', with positive connotations, should be attached to these movements.

Another social movement – against deportations – developed during the 1980s, which also hardly fits within the classic movements paradigm. As practical and rooted as the ones just described, but less utopian, protests and demonstrations took place throughout the 1980s against the operation of immigration laws. (Several of these have been documented by Steve Cohen (1981; 1986; 2001; 2002); see also Bhattacharyya and Gabriel (2002), Wilson and Lal (1983), Gordon (1984).) Cohen joined the revolutionary left in the late 1960s, became a barrister, worked as a play leader and then took a job in the South Manchester Law Centre (SMLC) in 1977 (Interview 16.9.02). Nasira Begum went to the SMLC in 1978 requesting help with threatened deportation. Her visit led to three years of legal actions linked to public campaigning before she was given leave to stay in the UK. It established principles which are replicated in all effective social movements around racial justice. Regular, open, democratic meetings – at which Nasira always played a key part – directed the campaign, which emphasised the importance of making links with all those facing a similar plight (Cohen, 2002). The most public of these, for Anwar Ditta's right to bring her children to join her in Rochdale, in which Tarlochan Gata-Aura played a leading part, lasted from 1977 to 1981. It had generated such momentum that a television company paid for blood tests to be done to refute the government's claim that the children were not Anwar's; it filmed the results being announced (*World in Action*, 16.3.1981). Three days after the programme was broadcast, entry clearance certificates were issued (Cohen, 2002). Of the many other campaigns of the 1980s, detailed in the radical publications of that decade and sometimes getting coverage in the mainstream media, that for Viraj Mendis produced the most publicity. Mendis was granted sanctuary in the Church of the Ascension in Hume, Manchester, for 671 days before it was smashed into by police and Mendis was arrested, on 18th January 1989. He was put on a plane to Sri Lanka two days later (Cohen, 2002).

As Cohen points out, the 1990s saw very few campaigns around immigration/deportation issues in Greater Manchester, and nor were there many elsewhere. At the start of the twenty first century, however, there are signs of renewed militancy over the related issue of asylum seekers and refugees. Formed in 1995, the National Coalition of Anti-Deportation Campaigns (NCADC, 20002) had issued 27 Newsletters by September 2002, detailing the dozens of cases and campaigns that have taken place in recent years.

None, however, have achieved the kind of support that was witnessed in the 1980s, and it would be hard to claim that a mass social movement was still in operation[43]. This is partly because successive Labour Home Secretaries' pronouncements on 'bogus asylum seekers' and 'clearly unfounded' anti-deportation campaigns (Dunstan, 2002) have narrowed the space in the dominant political discourse for a resurgence of anti-racist campaigning. 'Race', under Labour, seems to have been pushed into a strange new shape: if you are a citizen of the Commonwealth or the European Union (white or not) your rights are more or less respected; if you are not, you are irredeemably 'Other'. Despite the rhetoric of equal opportunity and the celebration of ethnic difference, some non-white British citizens argue that their status will never be fully respected, and another factor has come into play that has depleted political militancy around 'race'.

Ethnic particularism (Paul Gilroy's useful concept) was present in the cultural nationalism of the 1970s, but the movements described above dwarfed it. It gained ground in the 1980s as ethnically-specific jobs were created under the 'race equality' programmes promoted by Labour councils, assisted by those aspects of Conservative government policy which were seeking to ameliorate the effects in the inner cities of its economic policy. The mass demonstrations by British Muslims against Salman Rushdie's novel *The Satanic Verses* (1988) (Appignanesi and Maitland (1989)) announced not simply that this religious group could form itself into a social movement of remarkable size and force, but that Muslims felt compelled to assert the particularity of their identity and needs. Avtar Brah (1996: 168) has argued that during and after the *Verses* protests the UK witnessed the 'focus on cultural difference as the primary signifier of a supposedly immutable boundary: a view of the Asian as "alien" par excellence; the ultimate Other'. In response, a significant section of British Muslims became more strongly committed to Islam than they had before; the effect on young Muslims was particularly marked. Tariq Modood (1988) put the theoretical seal on what was already emerging in the social movements – Asians were not 'black', he argued. It was from this point onwards that 'the inclusive notion of blackness' emphasised by the 1970s and 1980s movements came under threat (Solomos and Back 1996: 134). The resurgence of religious divisions in India during the 1990s as the

---

43 Nevertheless, around 5,000 people demonstrated in support of asylum seekers and against deportations of migrant workers in London in the summer of 2002.

avowedly secular the Congress Party lost power, as Sikhs grew more militant in their demand for a separate state called Khalistan, as Indian Hindus became increasingly violent in their hostility to Indian Muslims, and the rise in tension between India and Pakistan (culminating in the threat of war in 2002) all contributed to an increased focus among significant sections of the British Asian population on the particular beliefs and practices of their various religions. All this was embodied in everyday life by the proliferation of types of clothing and headwear that symbolically announced the devotees' allegiances. The parallel move among some British Caribbeans was towards Afrocentrism (Asante, 1988; 1993). Afrocentricity is defined as 'a perspective which allows Africans to be subjects of historical experiences rather than objects on the fringes of Europe ... [it] is the Afrocentric study of African phenomena' (Asante, 1993: 2).

This academic aim translates for its adherents into the view that whites are incapable of overcoming their racism, a growing commitment to living, as far as possible, separate lives from whites, combined with an immersion into whatever aspects of African culture they can acquire. Symbolically manifested in the wearing of African clothing and artefacts, or in the uniforms of the Black Muslims, in UK academic circles it is expressed in studies such as Hylton (1999) and *The African Centred Review*. While it might be expected that these types of ethnic particularism would lead their followers into militant campaigns on behalf of putative members who are victims of injustice, this rarely takes place. There might be several reasons for this: their intensely cultural focus might distance them from 'politics'; joining social movements would draw them into unwelcome contact with other cultures; victims of injustice might be thought of as of lower status. For whatever reason, the ethnic particularists only promote the interests of their own group. While, as we have seen in the anti-Rushdie protests, they are capable of creating a social movement of their own, normally they restrict themselves to pressure group activity, on a limited range of issues specific to their ethnic group. In so doing, they reinsert the category of 'race' into political and popular discourse, staking the claim that there really is something essentially different and untranslatable about their biology and/or their culture.

Such groups rarely make the headlines, whereas at least one campaign, with deep roots in the radical black movements of the previous three decades, did so throughout the second half of the 1990s. The murder of Stephen Lawrence, a young British Caribbean Londoner, on 22nd April 1993, the dogged insistence of his parents that racism was its motive and that the police had failed properly to investigate, the eventual emergence of a co-ordinated alliance of lawyers and protesters, culminating in the MacPherson report in 1999, ruptured yet again the fabric of British 'race' relations. Cathcart (1999) provides full details of the case and its legal ram-ifications, but minimises the role of the campaign. Initially supported by the now-defunct Anti Racist Alliance, the public only became fully aware of the case when Imran Khan, a socialist solicitor who had worked in one of the radical police monitoring groups set up the Greater London Council in the 1980s, contacted Southall Rights in 1995 for support. Suresh Grover, one of the founders of Southall Rights, which had been doing case work and campaign work throughout the 1980s and 1990s, had long experience of building political movements in which racist and class oppression is the key focus, but 'race' is not understood in essentialist terms. He had learned inside these movements that a persistent legal challenge by radical lawyers had to be combined with public meetings and sophisticated use of the press if Doreen and Neville Lawrence's wishes were to be fulfilled[44]. The alleged perpetrators were acquitted when they were finally brought by private pros-ecution to the criminal court in April 1996. However, the agreement by the 1997 Labour government to set up a public enquiry was to provide some comfort when Lord MacPherson pronounced, after taking evidence from March to September 1998, that there was institutional racism in the Metropolitan police force. The explosion of discussion that greeted this finding baffled 'race' movement's activists, since this had been their expe-rience for so many years. The finding, however, was placed in the context of Lord Scarman's (1982) report into the Brixton protests of 1981, which had found that racist practices took place, but that racism was not institu-tionalised in the Metropolitan force. Officially sanctioning this condemna-tion of the structure of London's policing meant that not only police forces nationally, but public bodies in general were forced yet again to examine themselves. It led directly to the Race Relations (Amendment) Act of 2000, which placed a duty on public bodies to take active steps to ensure that dis-crimination was not taking place in their institutions. From a social move-ments point of view, Suresh Grover was then able to initiate the National Civil Rights Movement (NCRM) in 1999. At the time of writing (September 2002) this is publicising and assisting eighteen separate cam-

---

44 Television coverage of these events produced a spectacle that delighted anti-essentialists – a British Caribbean family represented and supported by British Asians, British Caribbeans, and their white friends.

paigns against police malpractice. The NCRM is another example of the tendency we might identify as the 'movement against "race"'. While the majority of these campaigns are for black people (Asian and Caribbean), and almost all of its Executive Committee members are black, the Movement supports the 96 victims of the Hillsborough football stadium disaster, most of whom were white, and a white Irish Catholic killed by a mob of Loyalists (NCRM, 2002).

Conclusion

This chapter has attempted to chart the major radical and revolutionary movements, which took 'race' as their focus during the three decades from 1970 onwards. It has risked over-simplifying a complex history by creating a narrative line around the idea that this period has witnessed a sharp divergence between movements which have fetishised and reified 'race', and those which have de-essentialised the concept, understanding it as socially constructed within capitalist societies, holding no greater significance than other sources of oppression such as class and gender. Again risking over-simplification, and without intending to under-estimate the weight of feeling of real distinction, it has suggested that those movements which seek to reinstate 'race' as a valid biological or cultural concept have been systematically undermined not only by the activities of their opponents in the other social movements but by profound changes in the culture of everyday life. Exemplified most clearly in popular music and fashion, 'racial anti-essentialism' seems to be the dominant force in the UK of the twenty-first century. This was summed up for me during an interview in research for this chapter with Pal Luthra. Mr Luthra, whose origins are Indian, had been active in the black socialist movements in the UK of the late 1970s and 1980s. When I asked him how he would define his identity today, he said: 'It has to be as a Londoner, rather than anything else ... I am more of a foreigner there [India] than here ... London residents have a multitude of family identities, relationships which don't make sense in a traditional way; trying to put labels on people is quite difficult' (Interview 22.7.02). Increasingly, as a cause and an effect of the movements against 'race', this comment applies to more and more UK citizens, whatever their skin colour.

References

Alleyne, B. (2002) *Radicals Against Race – Black Activism and Cultural Politics* (London: Berg).

Anthias, L. and Lloyd, C. (eds) (2002) *Rethinking Anti-racisms – From Theory to Practice* (London: Routledge).

Anwar, M. (1981) *Between Two Cultures – A Study of Relationships Between Generations in the Asian community in Britain* (London: Commission for Racial Equality).

Asante, M.K. (1988) *Afrocentricity* (Trenton: Africa World Press).

Asante, M.K. (1993) *Malcolm X as Cultural Hero and Other Essays* (Trenton: Africa World Press).

Banton, M. (1998) *Racial Theories.* 2nd edn (Cambridge: Cambridge University Press).

Benyon, J. and Solomos, J. (eds) (1987) *The Roots of Urban Unrest* (Oxford: Pergamon Press).

Bhattacharyya, G. and Gabriel, J. (2002) 'Anti-deportation Campaigning in the West Midlands' in L. Anthias and C. Lloyd (eds) *Rethinking Anti-racisms – From Theory to Practice* (London: Routledge).

Bhattacharyya, G., Gabriel, J. and Small, S. (2002) *Race and Power – Global Racism in the Twenty-first Century* (London: Routledge).

Bonnett, A. (1993) *Radicalism, Anti-racism and Representation* (London: Routledge).

Bonnett, A. (2000) *Anti-racism* (London: Routledge).

Brah, A. (1996) *Cartographies of Diaspora – Contesting Identities* (London: Routledge).

Brown, C. (1984) *Black and White Britain – The Third PSI Survey* (London: Policy Studies Institute).

Byrne, P. (1997) *Social Movements in Britain* (London: Routledge).

Cathcart, B. (1999) *The Case of Stephen Lawrence* (London: Viking/Penguin).

CARF [Campaign against Racism and Fascism] (1981) *Southall – The Birth of a Black Community* (London: Institute of Race Relations/Southall Rights).

Cashmore, E. and McLaughlin, E. (eds) (1991) *Out of Order? Policing Black People* (London: Routledge).

Castells, M. (1983) *The City and the Grassroots* (London: Edward Arnold).

Castells, M. (1997) *The Power of Identity* (Oxford: Blackwell).

Cohen, J. (1985) 'Strategy or Identity – New Theoretical Paradigms and Contemporary Social Movements', *Social Research*, vol. 52:4; 663-716.

Cohen, S. (1981) *The Thin End of the White Wedge* (Manchester: South Manchester Law Centre).

Cohen, S. (1986) *What Would You Do if Your Fiancée Lived on the Moon?* (Manchester: Manchester City Council).

Cohen, S. (2001) *Immigration Controls, the Family and the Welfare State* (London: Jessica Kingsley Publishers).

Cohen, S. (2002) 'Resistance From Below – Fighting Against Deportations and for Family Unity in Greater Manchester', Journal of North West Labour History, vol. 26.

Coon, C.S. (1982) *Racial Adaptations* (Chicago: Nelson-Hall).

Connor, G. and Farrar, M. (forthcoming) 'Carnival in Leeds and London, UK – Making New Black British Subjectivities' in M.C. Riggio (ed.) *Carnival in Action* (London and New York: Routledge).

Della Porta, D. and Diani, M. (1999) *Social Movements – An Introduction* (Oxford: Blackwell).

Dunstan, R. (2002) 'Growing Up Under New Labour', *National Campaign of Anti-Deportation Campaigns Newsletter*, Issue 27.

Farrar, M. [aka Paul Holt] (1982) 'Riot and Revolution: The Politics of an Inner City', Revolutionary Socialism [The journal of Big Flame] Issue 8:Winter 1981-1982.

Farrar, M. (1992) 'Racism, Education and Black Self Organisation', *Critical Social Policy*, Issue 35:Autumn 1992.

Farrar, M. (1999) 'Social Movements in a Multi-ethnic Inner City: Explaining their Rise and Fall over 25 years' in P. Bagguley and J. Hearn *Transforming Politics: Power and Resistance* (London: Macmillan). pp. 87-105.

Farrar, M. (2002a) *The Struggle for "Community" in a British Multi-ethnic Inner City Area – Paradise in the Making* (New York and Lampeter: Edwin Mellen Press).

Farrar, M. (2002b) 'The Northern "Race Riots" of the Summer of 2001 – Were they Riots, Were they Racial? A Case-study of the Events in Harehills, Leeds'. Paper presented to the BSA 'Race' and Ethnicity Study Group Seminar, City University, London, 18 May 2002.

Forbes, I. (1995) 'Institutionalising Anti-discrimination in Europe' in A. Hargreaves and J. Leaman (eds) *Racism, Ethnicity and Politics in Contemporary Europe* (Aldershot: Edward Elgar).

Fryer, P. (1984) *Staying Power – The History of Black People in Britain* (London: Pluto Press).

Gilroy, P. (1987a) *There Ain't No Black in the Union Jack* (London: Hutchinson).

Gilroy, P. (1987b) *Problems in Anti-racist Strategy* (London: Runnymede Trust).

Gilroy, P. (1992) 'The End of Anti-racism' in J. Donald and A. Rattansi (eds) *'Race', Culture and Difference* (London: Sage). pp. 49-61.

Gilroy, P. (1993) T*he Black Atlantic-Modernity and Double Consciousness* (London: Verso).

Gilroy, P. (1997) 'Diaspora and the Detours of Identity' in K. Woodward (ed.) *Identity and Difference* (London: Sage). pp. 299-346.

Gilroy, P. (2000) *Between Camps – Race, Identity and Nationalism at the End of the Colour Line* (London: Allen Lane, The Penguin Press).

Gordon, P. (1984) *Deportations and Removals* (London: Runnymede Trust).

Goulbourne, H. (ed.) (1990) *Black Politics in Britain* (Aldershot: Avebury).

Hall, S. and Jefferson, T. (eds) (1976) *Resistance Through Rituals* (London: Routledge).

Hall, S. (1992) 'The West and the Rest: Discourse and Power' in S. Hall and B. Gieben (eds) *Formations of Modernity* (London: Polity/Open University Press). pp. 275-332.

Harris, R. and White, S. (eds) (1999) *Changing Britannia – Life Experience with Britain* (London: New Beacon Books/George Padmore Institute).

Hebdige, D. (1976) *Subculture – The Meaning of Style* (London: Routledge).

Hetherington, K. (1998) *Expressions of Identity – Space, Performance, Politics* (London: Sage).

Hiro, D. (1992) *Black British – White British* (London: Paladin).

Hylton, C.A.H. (1999) *African-Caribbean Community Organisations: the Search for Individual and Group Identity* (Stoke-on-Trent: Trentham Books).

IRR (1987) *Policing Against Black People* (London: Institute of Race Relations).

Jones, S. (1988) *Black Culture, White Youth: the Reggae Tradition from JA to UK* (Basingstoke: Macmillan).

Jordan, J. (1998) 'The Art of Necessity: The Subversive Imagination of Anti-road Protest and Reclaim the Streets' in G. McKay (ed.) *DiY Culture – Party and Protest in Nineties Britain* (London: Verso). pp. 129-151.

Lentin, A. (1999) 'Structure, Strategy and Sustainability – What Future for New Social Movement Theory?', *Sociological Research Online*, vol. 4:3.

Lloyd, C. (1998) 'Anti-racist Mobilisations in France and Britain in the 1970s and 1980s' in D. Joly (ed.) *Scapegoats and Social Actors – the Exclusion and Integration of Minorities in Western and Eastern Europe* (London: Macmillan). pp. 155-172.

Lloyd, C. (2001) 'The Changing Face of Anti-racism – Social Movements and Global Civil Society'. Paper presented to the British Sociological Association 'Race' Forum conference on 'New European Identities', SOAS, University of London, 14 September 2001.

Lloyd, C. (2002) 'Anti-racism Social Movements and Civil Society' in L. Anthias and C. Lloyd (eds) *Rethinking Anti-racisms – From Theory to Practice* (London: Routledge). pp. 60-77.

Mac an Ghaill, M. (1999) *Contemporary Racisms and Ethnicities* (Buckingham: Open University Press).

MacPherson, W. (1999) *The Stephen Lawrence Inquiry* (London: HMSO Cm 4262-1).

Melucci, A. (1996) *Challenging Codes – Collective Action in the Information Age* (Cambridge: Cambridge University Press).

Miles, R. (1982) *Racism and Migrant Labour* (London: Routledge and Kegan Paul).

Miles, R. (1989) *Racism* (London: Routledge).

Miles, R. and Phizacklea, A. (eds) (1979) *Racism and Political Action in Britain* (London: Routledge and Kegan Paul).

Mirza, H.S. (ed.) (1997) *Black British Feminism – A Reader* (London: Routledge).

Modood, T. (1988) '"Black" Racial Equality and Asian Identity', *New Community*, vol. 14:3. 397-404.

Montagu, A. (1972) *Statement on Race* (New York: Oxford University Press).

Moore, R. (1975) *Racism and Black Resistance in Britain* (London: Pluto Press).

NCADC (2002) *National Coalition of Anti-Deportation Campaigns.* www.ncadc.org.uk [Accessed: 23 September 2002].

NCRM (2002) *National Civil Rights Movement web-site.* www.ncrm.org.uk [Accessed: 23 September 2002].

Owens, J. (1979) D*read – The Rastafarians of Jamaica (*London: Heineman).

Parekh, B. (2000) *Rethinking Multiculturalism – Cultural Diversity and Political Theory* (Basingstoke: Macmillan).

Parekh Report (2000) *The Report of the Commission on the Future of Multi-ethnic Britain* (London: Profile Books).

Patel, P. (2002) 'Back to the Future – Avoiding Déjà Vu in Resisting Racism' in L. Anthias and C. Lloyd (eds) *Rethinking Anti-racisms – From Theory to Practice* (London: Routledge). pp. 128-148.

Ramdin, R. (1987) *The Making of the Black Working Class in Britain* (Aldershot: Wildwood House).

Renton, D. (2002) *'The Anti-Nazi League 1977-1982'*. www.dkrenton.co.uk [Accessed: 11 July 2002].

Rex, J. (1983) *Race Relations in Sociological Theory.* 2nd edn (London: Routledge and Kegan Paul).

Saggar, S. (1992) *Race and Politics in Britain* (London: Harvester Wheatsheaf).

Scarman, L. (1982) *The Brixton Disorders, 10-12 April 1981 – the Scarman Report* (Harmondsworth: Penguin).

Shukra, K. (1990) 'Black Sections in the Labour Party' in H. Goulbourne (ed.) *Black Politics in Britain* (Aldershot: Avebury).

Solomos, J. and Back, L. (1995) *Race, Politics and Social Change* (London: Routledge).

Solomos, J. and Back, L. (1996) *Racism and Society* (Basingstoke: Macmillan).

Sivanandan, A. (1982) *A Different Hunger* (London: Verso).

Sivanandan, A. (1990) *Communities of Resistance* (London: Verso).

SBS, Southall Black Sisters (1990) *Against the Grain* (London: Southall Black Sisters).

Stevenson, N. (2002) 'Cosmopolitanism, Multiculturalism and Citizenship'. Paper presented to the British Sociological Association, Leicester, 27 March 2002.

Twentieth Anniversary New Cross Massacre Action Committee (2001) 'The New Cross Fire 18 January 1981 – 13 Dead. Nothing Said. We Will Not Forget', A4 document, four pages, obtainable from New Beacon Books, London N4 3EN.

Walker, M. (1977) *The National Front* (London: Fontana).

Ware, V. (1992) *Beyond the Pale – White Women, Racism and History* (London: Verso).

Ware, V. and Back, L. (2002) *Out of Whiteness – Color, Politics and Culture* (Chicago and London: Chicago University Press).

Widgery, D. (1986) *Beating Time* (London: Chatto and Windus).

Wilson, A. and Lal, S. (1983) *But My Cows Aren't Coming to England* (Manchester: South Manchester Law Centre).

12. FEMINISM, SOCIAL MOVEMENTS AND THE POLITICAL ORDER

Nickie Charles

Feminism, as political ideology and social movement, represents a profound challenge to conventional ways of doing and understanding politics. Rather than seeing politics as an activity that takes place exclusively in the public sphere and involving political parties, feminists argue that we 'do' politics in every sphere of our lives, even the private and personal. Furthermore, conventional definitions of politics are gendered; thus, what men do in the public sphere is defined as politics while women's activities are seen as extensions of their familial and domestic roles or as social and/or welfare rather than political activity. It is not only conventional politics which is gendered. 'Alternative' politics is also gendered with new social movements noted for their relatively high proportion of women activists. This has not, however, been taken into account by social movement theorists who claim that new social movements challenge the political order but, despite the emergence of feminist social movements, do not explore their effect on the gender order. Indeed, most social movement theory fails to recognise the salience of gender to understanding social movements both empirically and theoretically and leads to feminists claiming that gender has not yet been integrated into mainstream social movement theory (Taylor and Whittier, 1998; Taylor, 1999; Moghadam, 2001).

In this chapter I discuss the challenge posed by feminism to our understanding of 'politics as normal' and 'alternative politics', situating this challenge in the context of that posed by 'new social movements' to the political order (Dalton and Kuechler, 1990). I look first at the way the challenge of new social movements has been theorised and the problematic place of feminist social movements within such theorising. I then look at the challenge of feminism and feminist social movements to conventional politics, focussing on the feminist critique of the public-private divide which underpins liberal democracy. Following this, I discuss 'alternative' politics, showing how social movement theory has analysed contemporary social movements in apparently gender-neutral terms and arguing that both social movements and the categories of social movement theory are gendered. This discussion will highlight the gendering of social movement politics and draw out the implications of women's way of doing politics for a new practice of politics. Finally, I suggest that contemporary social movements are locked in a struggle over the gender order.

Challenging Politics as Normal

It has been argued that some contemporary social movements, among them the women's movement, the ecology movement, the peace movement and the youth movement, represent a new paradigm of politics that has the potential of transforming the political order (Offe, 1990; Kuechler and Dalton, 1990). The old political paradigm was based on issues of economic growth, distribution and security and resulted in the post-war consensus between labour and capital that heralded the establishment of welfare states. In exchange for this settlement, the labour movement abandoned its long-term project of a socialist transformation of capitalism. The accepted form of politics was representative democracy 'mediated through party competition' (Offe, 1985: 823). Politics was to be taken care of by political parties while citizens concentrated on their work and families that were, by definition, not political. Social and political conflict was resolved by 'collective bargaining, party competition, and representative party government' while the values on which civil society was based were 'social mobility, private life, consumption, instrumental rationality, authority, and order' (Offe, 1985: 824).

The 'new' social movements present a fundamental challenge to this settlement and to the 'established routines of "doing politics"' and attempt 'to redefine the accepted boundaries of the political' (Eyerman and Jamison, 1991: 149-50). Their central concerns are 'cultural reproduction, social integration, and socialisation' rather than material production and reproduction and issues of distribution (Habermas, 1981: 33). They are concerned with issues of territory, space of action, life-world, identity, and survival. They value autonomy and identity and are opposed to manipulation, control, dependence, bureaucratisation and regulation. They question the ideas of progress and economic growth, which underpin the previously dominant political paradigm and represent 'resistance to tendencies to colonise the life-world'; they are about creating social spaces and searching for 'personal and collective identity' (Habermas, 1981: 35-6).

According to Melucci, new social movements operate primarily on the symbolic level. The movement is the message; the form taken by the movement is itself a challenge to dominant cultural codes and embodies different ways of understanding and relating to the social world. Social movements 'perceive' and 'name' the world in new ways, ways which make visible power relations which were previously invisible (Melucci, 1989: 75). They create new knowledges (Eyerman and Jamison, 1991). Thus, new ways of understanding power and the state have emerged from the feminist movement and feminist standpoint theorists argue that knowledge is socially located, with specific knowledges being produced by different social groups and associated social movements (Cooper, 1995; Harding, 1991).

Social movements are also prefigurative in that social movement actors live their lives in different ways and according to different sets of values: change on an individual and personal level is seen as an intrinsic part of wider social change. They embody post-material values, their social base differs from that of 'old' social movements and their action is aimed not at the state but civil society. New social movements are seen as providing an alternative or oppositional culture, lifestyle and organisation; they are a form of cultural practice prefiguring a new type of society. Moreover, social movement culture is important in sustaining the networks and collective identities necessary for political action (Staggenborg, 2001; Taylor and Whittier, 1992; Carroll and Ratner, 2001). Their organisational form itself provides a critique of the hierarchical bureaucratic organisation on which conventional politics is based. They have no leaders, they practise direct democracy, groups constituting the movement are autonomous, there is no central organisation coordinating the movement, and there are lateral connections between the groups rather than relations between the base and the leadership (Gerlach and Hine, 1970; Roseneil, 1995). Thus, new social movements provide a new political paradigm in terms of their values, issues, organisation and modes of action. However, while some social movements are unequivocally regarded as new, such as the ecology movement and the peace movement, there is ambiguity about the newness or otherwise of the women's movement and the nature of the challenge it poses to the political order.

Feminist Social Movements

New social movements have been defined by some as cultural or social rather than political and as relating to civil society rather than the economy: their prime concern is therefore with issues of culture and meaning rather than distribution and this in part is what gives them their newness. The women's movement, however, engages in a politics of (re)distribution as well as a cultural politics of recognition (Fraser, 2000) and is said to straddle the modern/post-modern divide (Barrett, 1992). This has led some social movement theorists to argue that it is not a new social movement but that it exhibits some features of new social movements alongside others which are characteristic of old social movements. Habermas, for instance, argues that the women's movement has the character of 'bourgeois-socialist liberation movements', which concern themselves with rights and inclusion in the polity, but it is linked to the new social movements by its concern with lifestyles as well as with rights. Touraine's comments on the women's movement share the ambiguity expressed by Habermas. On the one hand, women's liberation movements are modernising movements because they aim to extend the social and political participation of women but, at the same time, they include 'a more radical tendency which rejects an equality which appears to be imitative of the dominant male model and asserts the specificity of women's culture, experience and action' (Touraine, 1985: 777). In Touraine's view, 'leftist-inspired ... feminist movements ... are not clearly social movements' (1992: 144). In similar vein Melucci argues that the women's movement has gone beyond demands for equality and inclusion in the masculine world to stress difference and people's right to be different. It 'has raised a fundamental question concerning everyone in complex systems: how communication is possible, how to communicate with "another" without denying the difference by power relations' (Melucci, 1985: 311). He makes an interesting and somewhat idiosyncratic distinction between feminism and the women's movement, arguing that feminism concerns those women who were active in the early years of second wave feminism and have subsequently created feminist institutions and contributed to the transformation of institutional life generally: an equal rights feminism. While the women's movement 'comprises a much more articulated variety of submerged phenomena, in which the cultural dimension predominates over direct confrontations with political institutions ... It is within these submerged networks that the female difference becomes the basis for the elaboration of alternative symbolic codes at odds with the dominant cultural and political codes' (Melucci, 1989: 95). Thus, he is arguing that visible public mobilisations of women no longer exist, but women's collective action persists in daily life, occasionally surfacing in single-issue campaigns. The women's movement has become mainly symbolic and exists in submerged networks, supporting an alternative 'women's culture' (Melucci, 1988: 95). By separating these two dimensions of the women's movement and naming them differently, he manages to fit the 1980s women's movement to his theoretical construction of new social movements as cultural and symbolic rather than political (see also Kuechler and Dalton, 1990: 282). This avoids his having to modify his theory, but it constructs the women's movement in a way that is not recognisable to feminists of either the 1970s or the 1980s (see, for example, Roseneil, 1995). It also marginalises the significance of oppositional cultures to the political activities of social movements, maintaining an arbitrary distinction between politics and culture and between 'old' and new social movements. The feminist movement challenges this separation, demonstrating that politics is about culture as well as struggles over distri-bution (Roseneil, 1995; Charles, 2000), and does not fit neatly into the categories developed by new social movement theorists.

The Feminist Challenge

The Personal is Political

The women's movement revealed that what was previously thought to be outside the realm of politics was fundamentally political and that cultural values support (or challenge) particular gendered relations of power. Thus, in connection with the private domain of the family, feminists have shown not only that state policies have hitherto supported male power and authority within the home but also that cultural values underpin this support. They argue that the balance of power needs to be shifted within the private sphere, through state intervention, such that women's and children's rights are recognised as well as those of men. Thus, what is defined as private has been shown to be structured by unequal gender relations, which are supported by the state (politics) as well as by a system of cultural values that enhances men's dominance. The women's movement defined domestic violence as a public rather than a private issue and in this sense the personal was most decidedly political. In contrast, they also argued that the decision to have an abortion rather than carry a pregnancy to term was something that was a woman's alone and should not be dictated by husbands, fathers, the church or the state. Thus, the feminist movement contested the very definitions and boundaries of the political, a challenge that was epitomised in the slogan 'the personal is political'. This constituted a challenge to the foundational categories of liberal democracy.

Underpinning conventional understandings of liberal democratic politics is an analytical separation between the public and the private with men belonging in the public and women in the private (Siltanen and Stanworth, 1984). The equation of politics with the public domain and the definition of men as public and women as private underpin 'malestream' explanations of gender differences in political behaviour and marginalise women in relation to the political. Indeed the boundaries of public and private are themselves politically constructed and, hence, contested (Siltanen and Stanworth, 1984); furthermore, they are gendered. Attempts to confine women to the private realm in the nineteenth and early twentieth century were challenged by women's successful struggles for inclusion in the polity by means of the vote, access to education, married women's property rights and so on. This has led to women's inclusion in the public realm and, as Walby has argued, can be conceptualised as a shift from private to public patriarchy (Walby, 1990). It does not, however, challenge the gendering of the public and private spheres. Women are included in the public domain but remain under the control of men and one of the ways in which this control is maintained is through the virtual male monopoly on political power and the continuing ability to treat politics as a male preserve. Second wave feminism poses a more fundamental challenge to the boundaries of the public and private, redefining politics to include women's activities as well as men's, showing that the public-private divide is gendered and redefining what is personal and what is political.

Feminist political practices also confound the public private divide. This happens when 'boundaries between the public and private spheres' are transgressed and the private sphere is made public, as in the Greenham Common women's peace camp (Roseneil, 1996: 101). It also happens when women's activities, particularly their organising activities within communities, take place within the neighbourhood, an 'expanded private sphere' which is, at the same time, a public sphere (Stall and Stoecker, 1998: 732). Thus, the boundaries between household and neighbourhood, the private and public, are not fixed and women's political practice challenges them. Indeed women's activities in the public sphere are often based on their roles within the private sphere (Schirmer, 1989), which, at the same time, can lead to a transformation in those roles. The women's movement has clearly challenged the boundaries between the public and the private, showing them to be gendered and subject to change. Indeed the slogan 'the personal is political' draws attention to the gendered power relations, which structure both the private and public domains.

There are however disagreements about where the boundaries of the public and private should be drawn. Dissolving any distinction between public and private and regarding 'all aspects of social existence as if they were an undifferentiated expression of male power' and defining 'power as the essence of politics' is resisted by those who want to maintain a distinction between public and private but to map the connections between the two spheres for men as well as women (Phillips, 1991: 94-5). Ann Phillips, for instance, argues that the public-private distinction is needed but that it should not be equated with a division between men and women.

Democracy at Home

As well as showing that the public-private divide is gendered, feminists challenge liberal definitions of democracy, arguing that, in its wider feminist definition, democracy should embrace what goes on within the household and within intimate relations as well as what goes on in the domain of formal politics (Phillips, 1991: 95). Thus the rights of women to live free of the fear of violence need to be respected by the men with whom they live, in the allegedly private domain, and in order to protect these rights there has to be political involvement (Siltanen and Stanworth, 1984).

However democracy within families and households 'is not really a matter of regulation, imposition, guarantee' but more about empowering women by giving them access to resources (whether in the form of equal pay or refuge provision) so that they are no longer dependent on men within the domestic sphere but are able to negotiate with them from a position of equality rather than subordination (Phillips, 1991; Charles, 1995). Additionally 'there is a distinction between spheres within which democracy can be imposed and spheres within which it should be enabled': in the domestic sphere it is the latter but feminists are concerned that women are empowered in this sphere partly through the operation of the realm of formal politics (Phillips, 1991: 119). And while recognising the significance of gendered power relations in daily life, Phillips argues that attempts to democratise 'every-day life should not become a substitute for a more lively and vital political life' (Phillips, 1991: 119). In a sense, defining the private so that it encompasses women's reproductive choices involves its democratisation. Reproductive decisions could hitherto be made by men on behalf of 'their' womenfolk and, in many parts of the world, still are. What feminists have demanded is that these rights be exercised by individual women rather than men (either individually or collectively), not that the right to exercise them be abolished.

The women's movement has redefined politics and democracy so that they are no longer confined to the public sphere; in so doing it has challenged the public-private divide. Such redefini-tions and challenges desta-bilise the settlement between labour and capital and the confinement of politics to political parties and the public sphere. Furthermore, they show that the categories underpinning liberal democracy are gendered and fuel debates about the changing basis of politics.

A New Basis for Politics?

One of the issues which has emerged in the wake of the challenge posed by new social movements is whether there is a realignment of politics taking place (see for e.g. Evans and Norris, 1999). Thus from the 1960s there has been debate as to whether the class basis of politics is changing. Political scientists have found evidence that gender and ethnicity affect voting patterns with ethnic minorities and younger cohorts of women being more likely to support the Labour Party (Norris, 1999; Saggar and Heath, 1999). In the US and Britain there is evidence of the emergence of a modern gender gap in voting patterns with younger women being more inclined to support the Democratic and Labour parties than their male peers. This reverses the traditional gender gap where women were inclined to vote more conservatively than men and which still characterises older generations (Norris, 1999). There is therefore evidence that social cleavages other than class are significant in affecting conventional political behaviour.

The emergence of new social movements with no clear link to the labour movement or the working class has also been taken as a sign that the class-basis of politics is weakening. They are taken to be both product and accelerator of a shift from a politics based on class to a politics based on other social cleavages such as gender, ethnicity, sexuality, religion or cultural identity. This has been conceptualised in terms of a societal transformation. Thus in capitalist industrial societies the main social cleavage and the basis of politics was class, with the labour movement as the central social movement, while in the information society (or post-industrial or post-modern society) the central social movement is likely to be the ecology movement (Touraine, 1985; Eder, 1993) or (as has recently been argued) the women's movement (Touraine, 2002). According to Touraine, the women's movement is 'everywhere, in all countries and parts of the world' (Touraine, 2002: 94). He suggests that political issues can be framed in terms of gender in ways that polarise societies throughout the world, thus recognising the profoundly gendered nature of contemporary politics. This may represent a paradigm shift insofar as it is a move away from class-based politics and from an understanding of politics in class terms. This view has similarities with those of feminists who argue that many contemporary social movements, not only the new social movements beloved by new social movement theorists, are locked in struggles over the gender order (Nelson and Chowdhury, 1994; Walby, 1996). Thus, the New Right and right-wing counter movements want to restore the family (with its 'traditional' gender division of labour), the market, private property and religion/science as the foundations of civil society and morality. New social movements, on the other hand, seek to reconstitute civil society, to politicise the institutions of civil society such as the family, production and work (Offe, 1985). This will take place in 'an intermediate sphere between "private" pursuits and concerns and institutional, state-sanctioned modes of politics' (Offe, 1985: 819-20) which is a sphere which can be defined as both private and public and where much of women's political activity takes place (Stall and Stoecker, 1998).

Part of this discussion focuses on the social basis of new social movements and the extent to which this is symptomatic of a move away from class politics (Maheu, 1995). Thus, it has been argued that new social movements are class based but that their base is middle class rather then working class. This has led some commentators to argue that what new social movements represent is a 'new politics of class' rather than a new form of politics, which is not related to class (Eder, 1993; Kriesi, 1989). Moreover, there is evidence that new social movements draw their membership largely from that sector of the middle class working in creative and welfare occupations (Bagguley, 1995; Byrne, 1997). These groups can be seen as the traditional intellectuals defined by Gramsci (Bagguley, 1992) whose distance from both the values and immediate imperatives of capitalist production and from the two main classes, capital and labour, allows them to take a critical stance towards it (Lovell, 1987). Thus new social movement politics, the politics of the green movement, the peace movement and the women's movement, is conceptualised as a new form of class politics, which differs radically from the politics of the working class as far as it is politics of a class but not on behalf of a class (Offe, 1985: 833). The demands of the new movements are not class specific but universalistic or particularistic and cannot be understood as representing class interests. This type of analysis, however, persists in foregrounding class whereas other bases of social division such as gender, ethnicity and sexuality may be just as pertinent.

In contrast with class, there is a dearth of information about the gender composition of 'new' social movements despite the significant presence of women within them. Studies of CND in Britain in 1982 and 1985 found that there were equal numbers of women and men supporters while in 1991 women constituted 62 per cent and men 38 per cent of supporters (Byrne, 1997: 76). Similarly, membership of Friends of the Earth, a social movement organisation, was 66 per cent women in the mid-1990s (Stephenson, 1998: 102). The relatively high participation of women in social movement politics marks it off from 'politics as normal', yet it is claimed that the evidence from Britain about the gender base of social movement support is inconclusive (Byrne, 1997). Evidence from the US and elsewhere, however, suggests that women's participation in social movements is much higher than in conventional politics (women hold up at least half the sky in new social movements) and in several women are in a majority. Thus, women form the backbone of the peace and environmental movements in the US and globally (West and Blumberg, 1990: 18), the animal rights movement is 'overwhelmingly female and middle class' (Einwohner, 1999: 56) and, by definition, the women's movement is exclusively female. The failure, particularly by those studying social movements in Britain, to analyse social movements in terms of gender, even though their gender composition is so different from that of conventional political organisations, is indicative of the conti-nuing strength of the class-based paradigm in social movement research.

Evidence also suggests that gender affects both the ways social actors engage with politics and the values underpinning their engagement. Thus, it has been argued that women engage in a 'politics of survival' and that it is not self-interest that motivates them but 'a politics of love and caring' (West and Blumberg, 1990: 15). New social movements are characterised by 'altruism' and post-material values and they aim for 'collective social gain' (Dalton et al., 1990: 8). This is what has led to the view that their politics is the politics of a class but not on behalf of a class. However, it could just as plausibly be argued that it is a politics of gender on behalf of humankind, reflecting the relatively high proportion of women active in new social movements and their different ways of doing politics. Thus, women's altruistic 'politics of love and caring' is, it has been argued, rooted in women's 'sense of connectedness and continuity with other persons and the natural world' (Diamond and Hartsock, 1981). These claims are not derived from essentialist notions of women's and men's difference but from a recognition of the fact that women's 'life experiences and social location give them an awareness of the importance of care' (Mackay, 2001: 191). Men who are engaged in 'the practice of caring work will [also] develop perspectives, skills and insights, and modes of thinking related to that practice' (Mackay, 2001: 137). This ties in with the membership of new social movements being drawn from middle-class, creative and welfare occupations where women are relatively well represented. In addition there is evidence that women view politics differently from men, they are more interested in solving problems and prefer consensus and consultation to engaging in the games that it is necessary to play to be successful in conventional politics (Mackay, 2001). These ways of working are not in evidence in conventional politics but are precisely how the politics engaged in by new social movements has been characterised.

As well as the politics of new social movements being gendered, the issues that they take up can also be understood in gendered terms. Women 'initiate, pursue, and support issues concerning bio-social production and reproduction, that is those questions having to do with control over, responsibility for, and care of people and other natural resources' (Jonasdottir, 1985: 42): issues such as peace, environmentalism, animal rights, welfare issues and so on. The gender composition of new social movements and the values that inform them suggest that they can be conceptualised as representing a politics of gender. This is given added weight when we consider that ecology, peace and animal rights have all been defined as feminist issues and framed in terms of gender (Adams, 1990; Mies and Shiva, 1993). Indeed, it has been suggested that feminist issues in politics can be defined as follows:

(1) women support the issue to a greater degree than men; (2) the issue stands outside of the traditional right/left scale; (3) the issue tends to be met with emotional reac-tions in the political arena; and (4) the issue lacks certi-fied cultural authority or at least has an ambiguous political status. (Peterson, 1981: 9 cited in Jonasdottir, 1985: 42)

Using this definition, peace and the environment are feminist issues, they represent a culture of life rather than the 'culture of death', which is the 'basis for capitalist accumulation' (Shiva, 1989: 13 cited in Miles, 2001: 145). Indeed, in opinion polls on the war in Afghanistan after September 11th 2001, women were consistently found to be less enthusiastic about the war than men (Bunting, 2001) as they were at the time of writing about the prospects of war with Iraq (*Guardian*, 17/9/02).

It can therefore be argued that gender is central to the politics of new social movements and that they cannot be fully understood without considering this. Indeed, many contemporary social and political movements are implicitly or explicitly engaged in conflict over gender and the organisation of 'reproductive, domestic, productive, communal and political activities' (Nelson and Chowdhury, 1994: 11). The women's movement has spawned counter movements such as the anti-abortion movement and there are many fundamentalist religious movements, which have as a central goal the strengthening of men's control over women (Moghadam, 1995). However, despite the obvious importance of gender to social movement politics, it has neither been recognised by, nor incorporated into, mainstream social movement theory.

Challenging Social Movement Theory

As well as downplaying the gender basis of social movement poli-tics, social movement theory ignores the gendered nature of the concepts it uses to analyse social movements. Resource mobilisation theory (RMT), for instance, relies on the notion of a rational actor and explores processes of mobilisation into social movements, utilising organisation theory and likening social movements to capitalist industrial enterprises. Social movements are organised based on instrumental rationality and have leaders who pursue strategies, provide mobilising frames for action and galvanise their members into action. In contrast, new social movement theory (NSMT) focusses on the structural conditions which give rise to social movements, arguing that capitalist industrial society is undergoing a fundamental transformation which is both hastened by and reflected in the emergence of new social movements. They conceptualise this transformation as a shift away from a society structured by class. These two schools have dominated social movement theory during the past two decades but latterly there has been some convergence between them (see for e.g. Johnston and Klandermans, 1995). This results from critiques of RMT for its neglect of culture and of NSMT for its neglect of politics. These critiques assert the political and cultural dimensions of all social move-ments, not only those that have emerged since the 1960s in Western Europe and North America, but do not address the gender bias of social movement theory's central concepts, an issue which is central to the feminist critique (Scott, 1990; Swidler, 1995; Taylor and Whittier, 1995; Tucker, 1991).

The feminist critique of existing social movement theory focuses on RMT's reliance on the concepts of rational actor, bureaucratic organisations and strategic action and NSMT's neglect of changes in gender relations and the gender order in explaining the emergence of social movements (Ferree, 1992; Rothschild-Whitt, 1979; Roseneil, 1995). Feminists are not alone in criticising rational choice theory and the notion of a rational actor underpinning RMT, but what is striking is that it is only feminist authors who have incorporated a consideration of gender into their accounts; others, by implication, regard rational action as a gender-neutral concept (Crossley, 2002; Dalton et al., 1990). RMT's reliance on the notion of a rational actor implies that potential participants in social movements are devoid of any analytically significant social characteristics such as gender, ethnicity, class or age. In effect, this means that the rational actor, unencumbered by ties of any sort and free of emotions, demonstrates 'universal attributes of human nature' (Ferree, 1992: 41). Countless feminist theorists have pointed out that these supposedly gender-neutral, universal attributes are actually those associated with white, middle-class males in Western societies (Hekman, 1990; Smith, 1988). As Ferree puts it, 'Feminist theory emphasises that the values that appear most "natural" and "objective " today are those derived from the experiences of nineteenth century, white, Western, middle-class men ... Rational choice theory itself embodies such values' (Ferree, 1992: 41). It rests on a separation of emotion and reason and a devaluing of the former and assumes self-interest, with its attendant problems of costs and benefits and selective incen-tives, to be the only motivation for action. It is impossible to understand social movements if it is assumed that the only basis for participation is self-interest (see also Dalton et al., 1990; Crossley, 2002). Ferree argues that human action is based on other types of rationality such as value-rationality and that the motivation for action is broader and more diverse than self-interest. Neglecting this by focussing on rational action impoverishes RMT and means that it cannot explain satisfactorily people's commitment to social movements.

This elevation of rational or instrumental action is also addressed by Rothschild-Whitt in her discussion of forms of organisation. She argues that collectivist organisation, which characterises new social movement organisations at least in their early stages, is based on substantive or value rationality. This contrasts with bureaucratic organisation, which is associated with instrumental rationality. She argues that most discussions of organisation focus on the latter, including those of resource mobilisation theorists (see also Cohen, 1985: 675), but many social movement organisations, such as cooperatives, women's refuges and so on, are organised as collectives and cannot be conceptualised as bureaucracies. Following Weber, she defines a value rational approach to social action as being 'marked by "a belief in the value for its own sake ... independent of its prospects of success"' (Weber, 1968: 24 in Rothschild Whitt, 1979: 509). Weber did not develop an ideal-typical organisation based on value rationality. However, Rothschild-Whitt argues that a collectivist organisation that is non-hierarchical arrives at decisions through a process of consensus building and practices direct democracy is the ideal type associated with value-rationality. There are no leaders and followers and no specialisation of tasks. Skills are shared and everyone knows how to do all the tasks associated with the organisation. Unlike bureaucratic organisations the incentives to participate are not only material but consist more importantly of value fulfilment and 'solidary incentive such as friendship' (Rothschild-Whitt, 1979: 515); emotions are therefore recognised as important to this type of organisation (Hercus, 1999). This form of organisation is common within contemporary social movements and is sometimes referred to as embodying feminist or woman-centred values (Taylor, 1999). It is contrasted to bureaucratic organisations and rational action both of which are associated with masculinity in western cultures.

Feminists argue that organisations, including social movement organisations, are not only gendered but also have associated gender cultures (Acker, 1990), and there is some evidence that the gender culture of organisations is influenced by their gender composition (Holt and Thaulow, 1996). Thus, bureaucratic organisations are constructed on assumptions of masculine characteristics and behaviour, stressing rationality and hierarchy, and the existence of a gendered division of labour that privileges men. They 'are governed by a masculine ethic of rationality and reason that necessitates setting emotions and personal considerations aside' (Taylor, 1999: 20). This is true of conventional politics which is 'tied to powerful male cultural symbols and is premised upon male norms and values. It is also premised upon the caring and daily maintenance of male politicians being carried out by women' (Mackay, 2001: 158). Bureaucracy as a concept is criticised for its gender blindness and its failure to notice that male careers in bureaucratic organisations have historically relied on women's performing routine non-career jobs within the organisation and providing domestic circumstances conducive to the furtherance of male careers (Witz and Savage, 1992). RMT's over-emphasis on one specific organisational form therefore lays it open to accusations of gender bias. It also renders it difficult for RMT to analyse the different forms of organisation and action that characterise the women's movement (Buechler, 1993).

RMT has also been criticised for focussing on strategic action and assuming that all social movements develop strategies. Strategy is associated with 'instrumental rationality, cost-benefit analysis and military-like planning' and is particularly inappropriate in analysing movements such as Greenham where there was no discernible strategy (although there were goals) and action was often based on 'affective and emotional impulses' (Roseneil, 1995: 98; c.f. Cooper, 1995). Furthermore, a focus on tactics and strategy obscures the 'gendered dynamics and tensions within movements' (Taylor, J, 1998). The concepts on which RMT is based are therefore gendered. This renders them problematic for analysing social movements, obscuring both the gendered social processes whereby social movements are constituted and their engagement in a politics of gender.

Neither NSM theory nor RMT – nor, indeed the recent amalgamations of the two – have responded to the feminist challenge by producing a gendered theory of social movements. It is almost as if social movement theory exists in a parallel, gender-neutral universe. The men who produce it, like the men in new social movements on whom West and Blumberg comment, tend to take on the leadership roles and, even though women may 'assume leadership roles, their contributions may go unrecognised and unrecorded' (West and Blumberg, 1990: 24). Indeed, the absence of women theorists from this domain of sociology, with the notable exception of Jean Cohen, is remarkable (Cohen, 1985). Feminists have researched women's movements in a theoretically informed way (e.g., Freeman, 1975; Staggenborg, 1991; Matthews, 1994; Roseneil, 1995; Taylor, 1999; Charles, 2000) but have neither entered the realms of abstract theory nor have their insights been incorporated by male theorists. However, from their research the outline of a gendered theory of social movements is emerging. Feminist social movement scholars attempt to integrate different levels of analysis. Thus structural issues and issues of identity, both collective and individual, are linked and action is conceptualised as gendered and as having dimensions other than rationality. Moreover, both the political and cultural dimensions of social movements are considered, one is not divorced from the other in order to make social reality fit better with social theory. The significance of experience and emotions to the formation and transformation of collective identities is also recognised (Hercus, 1999). As Jean Cohen puts it, 'we could attempt to correlate changes in organisational forms, targets, and tactics of collective action with changes in the locus and technology of power and resources, alterations in the relation between state, economy, and society, and transformations in the experiences and struc-tures of everyday life ... ' (Cohen, 1985: 690). Changes in gender relations are part of 'the experiences and structures of everyday life'.

Gendering Social Movement Theory

A theory, which takes gender fully into account, needs to make 'explicit the role of social movements both in affirming and challenging the gender order' (Taylor, 1999: 26). As well as being analysed as a response to changes in industrial capitalism and as bringing about societal transformation to a post-industrial or information society, social movements need to be understood as a response to changes in the gender order or patriarchy (Roseneil, 1995). Empirical research shows that the political environment or political opportunity structure in which a social movement emerges is gendered. This environment is created not only by governmental and state activity but also by other social movements. Thus, second wave feminism was the 'big sister' of the women's peace movements of Britain and the U.S in the 1980s, and constituted part of the political opportunity structure, which made the Greenham Common women's peace camp possible (Roseneil, 2000). Similarly the UN decade for women and interna-tional conferences such as the UN women's conference in Beijing (which was itself an outcome of feminist organising at national and international level as well as within the UN) together with 'transnational women's networks' (Moghadam, 2001) have had the effect of creating a sympathetic political climate for the sustenance of women's organisations around the world (Charles, 1993; Craske and Molyneux, 2002; Abdulhadi, 1998). Political parties, trade unions and the state (local and national) also form part of the political opportunity structure and their domination by men has been shown to affect the outcome of struggles that are waged by women (Ferree and Roth, 1998). Conversely, when the number of women in positions of power within such organisations reaches a critical mass, it is more likely that women's demands will be heard and taken seriously (Charles, 2000).

The response to social movements on the part of social and political actors such as the media and individuals or counter movements is also affected by gender. Thus, the opposition of a US animal rights group to

hunting was easily dismissed by male hunters as emotional and unscientif-
ic because of the overwhelmingly gendered image of the animal rights
group and the fact that most of the activists were women (Einwohner,
1999). This meant that their arguments were not taken seriously and their
protests were unsuccessful. The gender of the target group, in this case the
hunters, was also significant in affecting the outcome of protests as they
were all men and hunting is seen as a quintessentially masculine endeavour. This example illustrates how gender can delegitimate social movement
protest; there is a perception that, unlike men, women do not need to be
taken seriously.

Within social movement organisations, as in other organisa-tions, it is
often men who take on leadership roles. Thus organising at the level of the
community, on the margins between the public and the private, 'is the part
of social movement work that occurs closest to the grass roots and is most
often done by women' (Stall and Stoecker, 1998: 731). However, although
it is women who do this grassroots organising it is often men who take on
the leadership positions within social movements (West and Blumberg,
1990: 24). This is not necessarily in the face of oppo-sition from women
although sometimes this is the case. Thus in the abortion movement in
Ireland men tried to take control by 'moving to the front of marches in
order to lead them, controlling discussions, rejecting revolving leadership
positions, and insisting on parliamentary voting procedures and standardised meeting rules in the name of democracy' (Taylor, J, 1998: 688). This
was countered by women who engaged in gendered forms of action that
'drew on signifiers of domestic womanhood' thereby excluding men. In
other movements men take leadership roles because there is a recognition
by movement activists that gender affects the perceived legitimacy of the
movement and that it can be easy for women to be dismissed as 'a bunch
of hysterical housewives' (Neal and Phillips, 1990: 252) or as emotional
and irrational and therefore not to be taken seriously (Einwohner, 1999).
Similarly, there is an assumed gender division of labour within social
movements which means that men lead and women follow and support. In
a US steel strike, for instance, the male leadership discouraged women
from undertaking picket duty and assumed that they would be in charge of
the food and the kitchens (Fonow, 1998). Similar battles were fought during the 1984-5 miners' strike in Britain when women insisted on participating in picket lines and public meetings as well as fulfilling their
expected welfare and support role.

The micro-level of mobilisation and movement formation involving the formation and transformation of collective identity is also gendered (Gamson, 1997). Thus, the collective identity of the women's self-help movement is based on 'members' shared experiences as white, middle-class, heterosexual women, thereby drawing on conservative norms of femininity' (Taylor, 1999: 27). Similarly, many issues are framed in gendered terms. For instance, the women's peace movement defines peace as a women's or feminist issue. This can take the form of a maternalist politics which defines women's support for peace in terms of motherhood and protecting the planet for our children, with slogans such as 'You can't hug kids with nuclear arms' (Strange, 1990: 209) or a feminist politics which identifies militarism and war with the violence endemic to male-dominated, capitalist and racist societies. Supporting peace is linked to opposition to all forms of violence, which include sexism and violence against women. Collective identities are constructed on the basis of women's commonalities, their exper-iences as mothers, as givers and preservers of life and as in harmony with animals and nature. Indeed constructing collective identities involves defining and framing issues in gendered terms. Thus feminists argue that the violence, exploitation and dominance that are constituent parts of militarism are also essential to capitalism and patriarchy thereby analysing opposition to militarism in gendered and classed terms and defining peace as a feminist issue (Strange, 1990: 221).

The structure and organisation of movements are, as we have already seen, gendered and range from bureaucratic, hierarchical and specialist organisations, on the one hand, to collectivist, non-specialist and directly democratic organisations, on the other (Martin, 1990). The assumption that rational action provides the key to understanding social movements involves a gendered definition of social action and defines much of the activity taking place within social movements as irrelevant to understanding their nature. Emotional (affectual) and value-rational action (Rothschild-Whitt, 1979) are critical to the emergence and development of social movements and in the formation and transformation of identity and consciousness which takes place within them (see Charles and Hughes-Freeland, 1996, for feminist accounts of identity formation and transformation in social movements; Taylor, 1999; Hercus, 1999).

If social movements are analysed in terms of gender then it becomes clear that the issues they take up can be framed in gendered terms, that the political opportunity structure is shaped by gender, as is the response to social movements on the part of social actors. Collective identities are similarly gendered, as are the organisational forms that characterise social movements, their value base and their ways of doing politics. This is evident in the high proportion of women active in new social movements and, as we have seen, affects how they are perceived by wider society and how legitimate they are seen to be. This gendering of social movements is something that has not been widely researched, in contrast with their class basis, and has not been incorporated into social movement theory.

The Challenge of New Social Movements

Analysing social movements in terms of gender is taking seriously Eyerman and Jamison's claim that social movements bring about epistemological shifts and change the way we understand the world. If we look at social movements through the lens of gender, our picture of their challenge to the political order involves more than a dealignment from class and a redefinition of politics to include social and welfare issues, environmental issues, issues of representation and so on. What the evidence presented here suggests is that the challenge of new social movements to conventional politics may go deeper than this. It is possible that the new social movements are actually challenging the gender order in so far as they are asserting a different set of values and a different way of doing politics, which can be defined as gendered. Thus post-material values, which characterise new social movements, can be seen as gendered and as characteristic of women's (and some men's) way of doing politics. They are based on an ethic of care, which stresses the connectedness of all life on earth and emphasises cooperation rather than competition and control. This ethic underpins new social movements and marks them off from the old self-interested, rights-based movements. The value basis of new social movements and women's way of doing politics, together with the gendered nature of social movements and the way that the issues can be understood in terms of gender, suggests that new social movements, whether or not they are explicitly feminist and whether or not men take on leadership positions within them, represent a challenge to the gender order, a challenge which is resisted by all those move-ments which seek to reinforce men's control over women and nature.

References

Abulhadi, R. (1998) 'The Palestinian women's autonomous movement: emergence, dynamics, and challenges' in *Gender and Society*, 12(6): 649-673.

Acker, J. (1990) 'Hierarchies, jobs, bodies: a theory of gendered organisations' in *Gender and Society*, (2): 139-158.

Adams, C. (1990) *The sexual politics of meat* (Polity Press: Cambridge).

Bagguley, P. (1995) 'Middle-class radicalism revisited' in T, Butlers and M. Savage (eds) *Social change and the middle classes* (UCL Press: London, pp. 293-309).

Bagguley, P. (1992) 'Social change, the middle class and the emergence of "new social movements"' in *Sociological Review*, 40(1): 26-48.

Barrett, M. (1992) 'Words and things: materialism and method in contemporary feminist analysis' in M. Barrett and A. Phillips (eds) *Destablising theory: contemporary feminist debates* (Polity Press: Cambridge, pp. 201-19).

Buechler, S.M. (2000) *Social movements in advanced capitalism* (Oxford University Press: Oxford).

Buechler, S.M. (1993) 'Beyond resource mobilisation? Emerging trends in social movement theory' in *The sociological quarterly*, 34(2): 217-35.

Bunting, M. (2001) 'Women and war', *Guardian*, 20 September.

Byrne, P. (1997) *Social movements in Britain* (Routledge: London and New York).

Carroll, W.K. and Ratner, R.S. (2001) 'Sustaining oppositional cultures in 'post-socialist' times: a comparative study of three social movement organisations' in *Sociology*, 35(3): 605-629.

Charles, N. (2000) *Feminism, the state and social policy* (Macmillan and St Martin's Press: Basingstoke and New York).

Charles, N. (1995) 'Feminist politics, domestic violence and the state' in *Sociological Review*, 43(4): 617-40.

Charles, N. and Hughes-Freeland, F. (1996) (eds) *Practising feminism: identity, difference, power* (Routledge: London).

Cohen, J.L. (1985) 'Strategy or identity: new theoretical para-digms and contemporary social movements' in *Social Research* 52-4: 663-716.

Cooper, D. (1995) *Power in struggle: feminism, sexuality and the state* (Open University Press: Milton Keynes).

Craske, N. and Molyneux, M. (2002) (eds) *Gender and the politics of democracy in Latin America* (Palgrave: Basingstoke).

Crossley, N. (2002) *Making sense of social movements* (Open University Press: Milton Keynes).

Dalton, R.J. and Kuechler, M. (1990) (eds) *Challenging the political order: new social and political movements in western democracies* (Polity Press: Cambridge).

Dalton, R.J., Kuechler, M. and Burklin, W. (1990) 'The challenge of new movements' in Dalton, R.J. and Kuechler, M. (1990) (eds) *Challenging the political order: new social and political movements in western democracies* (Polity Press: Cambridge, pp. 3-20).

Diamond, I. and Hartsock, N. (1981) 'Beyond interests in politics: a comment on Virginia Sapiro's "When are interests interesting? The problem of political representation of women"' in *American Political Science Review*, 75(3): 717-23.

Eder, K. (1993) *The new politics of class: social movements and cultural dynamics in advanced societies* (Sage: London).

Einwohner, R.L. (1999) 'Gender, class, and social movement outcomes: identity and effectiveness in two animal rights campaigns' in *Gender and Society*, 13(1): 56-76.

Eyerman, R. and Jamison, A. (1991) *Social movements: a cognitive approach* (Polity Press: Cambridge).

Evans, G. and Norris, P. (1999) (eds) *Critical elections* (Sage: London).

Ferree, M.M. (1992) 'The political context of rationality: rational choice theory and resource mobilisation' in A.D. Morris and C.M. Mueller (eds) *Frontiers in social movement theory* (Yale University Press: New Haven, CT, pp. 29-52).

Fonow, M.M. (1998) 'Protest engendered: the participation of women steelworkers in the Wheeling-Pittsburgh steel strike of 1985' in *Gender and Society*, 12 (6): 710-728.

Fraser, N. (2000) 'Rethinking recognition' in *New Left Review*, 3 (May/June): 107-120.

Freeman, J. (1975) *The politics of women's liberation* (David Mckay: New York).

Gamson, J. (1997) 'Messages of exclusion: gender, movements, and symbolic boundaries' in *Gender and Society*, 11(2): 178-199.

Gerlach, L.P. and Hine, M.M. (1970) *People, power, change: movements of social transformation* (Bobbs-Merill: Indianapolis).

Travis, A. and White, M. 'War on Iraq: the mood shifts' *Guardian* (2002) 17 September.

Habermas, J. (1981) 'New social movements' in *Telos*, 49: 33-7.

Harding, S. (1991) *Whose science? Whose knowledge? Thinking from women's lives* (Open University Press: Milton Keynes).

Hekman, S.J. (1990) *Gender and knowledge: elements of a post-modern feminism* (Polity: Cambridge).

Hercus, C. (1999) 'Identity, emotion, and feminist collective action' in *Gender and Society*, 13(1): 34-55.

Holt, H. and Thaulow, I. (1996) 'Formal and informal flexibility in the workplace' in S. Lewis and J. Lewis (eds) *The work-family challenge* (Sage: London).

Johnston, H. and Klandermans, B. (1995) (eds) *Social movements and culture* (UCL Press: London).

Jonasdottir, K. (1985) 'On the concept of interest, women's interests, and the limitations of interest theory' in K.B. Jones and A.G. Jonasdottir (eds) *The political interests of gender* (Sage: London, pp. 33-65).

Kriesi, H. (1989) 'New social movements and the new class in the Netherlands' in *American Journal of Sociology*, 94(5): 1078-116.

Kuechler, M. and Dalton, R.J. (1990) 'New social movements and the political order: inducing change for long-term stability? in Dalton, R.J. and Kuechler, M (1990) (eds) *Challenging the political order: new social and political movements in western demo-cracies* (Polity Press: Cambridge, pp. 277-300).

Lovell, T. (1987) *Consuming fiction* (Verso: London).

Mackay, F. (2001) *Love and politics: women politicians and the ethics of care* (Continuum: London and New York).

Maheu, L. (1995) (ed.) *Social movements and social classes, Sage studies in international sociology 46* (Sage: London).

Martin, P.Y. (1990) 'Rethinking feminist organisations' in *Gender and Society*, 4: 182-206.

Matthews, N. (1995) *Confronting rape: the feminist anti-rape movement and the state* (Routledge: London and New York).

Melucci, A. (1989) *Nomads of the present: social movements and individual needs in contemporary society* (Hutchinson Radius: London).

Melucci, A. (1985) 'The symbolic challenge of contemporary move-ments' in *Social Research*, 52: 789-816.

Mies, M. and Shiva, V. (1992) *Ecofeminism* (Zed Books: London).

Moghadam, V.M. (2001) 'Transnational feminist networks: Collective action in an era of globalisation' in P. Hamel, H. Lustiger-Thaler, J.N. Pieterse, S. Roseneil (eds) *Globalisation and social movements* (Palgrave: Basingstoke and New York, pp.111-139).

Moghadam, V.M. (1996) 'Introduction and overview' in V.M. Moghadam (ed) *Patriarchy and economic development* (Clarendon Press: Oxford, pp. 1-15).

Moghadam, V.M. (1995) 'Gender dynamics of restructuring in the semiperiphery' in R.L. Blumberg, C.A. Rakowski, I. Tinker and M. Monteon (eds) *Engendering wealth and well-being* (Westview Press: Boulder, Col, pp. 17-37).

Miles, A (2001) 'Global feminist theorising and organising: life-centred and multi-centred alternatives to neoliberal globalisa-tion' in P. Hamel, H. Lustiger-Thaler, J.N. Pieterse, S. Roseneil (eds) *Globalisation and social movements* (Palgrave: Basingstoke and New York, pp.140-165).

Neal, D.M. and Phillips, B.D. (1990) 'Female-dominated local social movement organisations in disaster-threat situations' in G. West and R.L. Blumberg (eds) *Women and social protest* (Oxford University Press: Oxford, pp. 243-255).

Nelson, B.J. and Chowdhury, N. (eds..) *Women and politics world-wide* (Yale University Press: New Haven and London).

Norris, P. (1999) 'Gender: a gender-generation gap?' in G. Evans and P. Norris (eds..) *Critical elections: British parties and voters in long-term perspective* (Sage: London. pp. 148-80).

Offe, C. (1990) 'Reflection on the institutional self-transformation of movement politics: a tentative stage model' in R.J. Dalton and M. Kuechler (eds) *Challenging the political order* (Polity Press: Cambridge, pp. 232-50).

Offe, C. (1985) 'New social movements: challenging the boundaries of institutional politics' in *Social Research*, 52 (4): 817-68.

Taylor, V. (1999) 'Gender and social movements: gender processes in women's self-help movements' in *Gender and Society*, 13(1): 8-33.

Peterson, A. (1981) 'Kvinnofragor, kvinnomedvetande och klass' (Women's issues, women's consciousness, and class) in *Zenit*, 70: 5.

Phillips, A. (1991) *Engendering democracy* (Polity Press: Cambridge).

Roseneil, S. (2000) *Common women, uncommon practices: the queer feminisms of Greenham* (Cassell: London and New York).

Roseneil, S. (1996) 'Transgressions and transformations: exper-ience, consciousness and identity at Greenham' in N. Charles and F. Hughes-Freeland (eds) *Practising feminism: identity, differ-ence, power* (Routledge: London and New York, pp. 86-108).

Roseneil, S. (1995) *Disarming patriarchy: feminism and political action at Greenham* (Open University Press: Milton Keynes).

Rothschild-Whitt, J. (1979) 'The collectivist organisation: an alternative to rational-bureaucratic models' in *American Sociological Review*, 44: 509-27.

Saggar, S. and Heath, A. (1999) 'Race: towards a multicultural electorate?' in G. Evans and P. Norris (eds) *Critical elections: British parties and voters in long-term perspective* (Sage: London, pp. 102-23).

Schirmer, J. (1989) '"Those who die for life cannot be called dead": women and human rights protest in Latin America' in *Feminist Review*, 32: 3-29.

Scott, A. (1990) *Ideology and the new social movements* (Unwin Hyman: London).

Shiva, V. (1989) *Staying alive: women, ecology and development* (Zed Press: London).

Siltanen, J. and Stanworth, M. (1984) 'The politics of private woman and public man' in J. Siltanen and M. Stanworth (eds) *Women and the public sphere: a critique of sociology and politics* (Hutchinson: London, pp. 185-208).

Smith, D. (1988) *The everyday world as problematic: a feminist sociology* (Open University Press: Milton Keynes).

Staggenborg, S. (2001) 'Beyond culture versus politics: a case study of a local women's movement' in *Gender and Society,* 15(4): 507-530.

Staggenborg, S. (1991) *The pro-choice movement: organisation and activism in the abortion conflict* (Oxford University Press: New York, Oxford).

Stall, S. and Stoecker, R. (1998) 'Community organising or orga-nising community? Gender and the crafts of empowerment' in *Gender and Society*, 12(6): 729-756.

Stephenson, M. (1998) *The glass trapdoor: women, politics and the media during the 1997 general election* (Fawcett: London).

Strange, C. (1990) 'Mothers on the march: maternalism in women's protest for peace in North America and Western Europe, 1900-1985' in G. West and R.L. Blumberg (eds) *Women and social protest* (Oxford University Press: Oxford, pp. 209-224).

Swidler, A. (1995) 'Cultural power and social movements' in H. Johnston and B. Klandermans (eds) *Social movements and culture* (UCL Press: London, pp.25-40).

Taylor, J. (1998) 'Feminist tactics and friendly fire in the Irish women's movement' in *Gender and Society*, 12(6): 674-69.

Taylor, V. (1999) 'Gender and social movements: gender processes in women's self-help movements' in *Gender and Society*, 13(1): 8-33.

Taylor, V. and Whittier, N. (1998) 'Guest editors' introduction: special issue on gender and social movements part I' in *Gender and Society*, 12(6): 622-625.

Taylor, V. and Whittier, N. (1995) 'Analytic approaches to social movement culture: the culture of the women's movement' in H. Johnston and B. Klandermans (eds) *Social movements and culture* (UCL Press: London, pp.163-187).

Taylor, V. and Whittier, N. (1992) 'Collective identity in social movement communities: lesbian feminist organisation' in A.D. Morris and C.M. Mueller (eds) *Frontiers in social movement theory* (Yale University Press: New Haven, CT, pp. 104-29).

Touraine, A. (2002) 'The importance of social movements' in *Social Movement Studies,* 1 (1): 89-95.

Touraine, A. (1992) 'Beyond social movements?' in *Theory, culture and society,* 9 (1): 124-45.

Touraine, A. (1985) 'An introduction to the study of social movements' in *Social Research,* 52 (4): 749-87.

Tucker, K. H. (1991) 'How new are new social movements?' in *Theory, culture and society,* 8: 75-98.

Walby, S. (1996) 'The "declining significance" or the "changing forms" of patriarchy?' in V. Moghadam (ed) *Patriarchy and development* (Clarendon Press: Oxford, pp. 19-33).

Walby, S. (1990) *Theorising patriarchy* (Basil Blackwell: Oxford).

West, G. and Blumberg, R.L. (1990) 'Reconstructing social protest from a feminist perspective' in G. West and R.L. Blumberg (eds) *Women and social protest* (Oxford University Press: Oxford, pp. 3-35).

Witz, A. and Savage, M. (1992) 'The gender of organisations' in M. Savage and A. Witz (eds) *Gender and bureaucracy* (Blackwell/The Sociological Review: Oxford, pp. 3-62).

13. WOMEN AND POLITICS IN EUROPE

Simon Henig

There has been much discussion about the reasons why so many women became involved in the women's protest movements of the 1960s and 1970s. Clearly, the activism and feminist writings of American women in the early and mid 1960s inspired many women in Europe. Peace campaigns like the Campaign for Nuclear Disarmament (CND) movement in Britain and the student protests of the late 1960s in many west European countries also drew growing numbers of women into political activism. By the mid 1960s, women had increasing access to further and higher education. At the same time, the mass marketing of labour saving devices reduced the amount of time that needed to be spent on housework, and the growing availability of contraceptives enabled women to control their fertility and to limit family size. Furthermore, the 1960s were a time of economic growth in Western Europe, and increasing numbers of women, both married and single, were drawn into employment. As more opportunities opened up for women, they became more aware of the discrimination they faced in the work place and of the contradictions between the emancipated role outside the home that they were increasingly able to play and the traditional expectations which still defined a women's place in society.

As we shall see, second wave feminism contained many diverse strands, and took different forms from country to country. In its ambitious aim to transform society, it encompassed a range of agendas including economic issues, sexual concerns, family issues, and the use of language and interpretations of history. As a result of its campaigns, and their impact in reformulating the political agenda, it had a major impact throughout Western Europe, being described by the Danish feminist Drude Dahlerup as "one of the most important social movements of the post-war period" (Dahlerup, 1986: 1). By raising new issues and causing old ones to be redefined and by influencing public opinion, women's activities in the 1970s significantly broadened the political agenda. They were also successful in bringing into existence a growing feminist consciousness. This chapter will first discuss the various strands of second wave feminism and assess what the many different women's groups aimed to achieve and will then examine its specific impact in nine European countries. By the 1970s, women were becoming prominent in new forms of political campaigning linking environmental concerns with anti-nuclear protests, and were increasingly active in informal local networks. This chapter will assess these developments and the distinctive contribution they made in broadening political agendas by the end of the 1970s.

Categories of Feminist Groups

It has been argued that the women's movements of the late 1960s and 1970s "typically consist[ed] of two branches", an older branch of liberal or moderate groups aiming to achieve equal rights for women within the existing social system, and a younger, more radical and ideologically motivated branch wanting to transform society in accordance with feminist principles (Lovenduski and Hills, 1981: 6). 'Equal rights', 'liberal' or 'welfare' feminism was particularly strong in Sweden and Norway, and was influential in Denmark and in Holland. Very different in its aims and objectives was radical or socialist feminism, which argued that working through existing political structures would merely serve to perpetuate the oppression of women. Rooted in the 'New Left' protest movements of the late 1960s, radical and socialist feminists campaigned to break down the male domination of society and to work for the liberation of all oppressed people, particularly women. While socialist feminists placed the blame for the exploitation and oppression of women on class as well as gender, radical feminists emphasised sex as the fundamental division in society. Socialist and radical feminists were particularly effective in their campaigns in Italy and Spain, and were also prominent in France, Denmark and Britain, though acrimonious debates between the two groups and with liberal feminists increasingly undermined their effectiveness.

While 'women's rights' groups campaigned to secure equality for women by exerting pressure on existing political structures, feminists that are more radical argued that women had to create new political structures and a new political discourse. Arguing that domestic issues hitherto regarded as personal such as child-rearing, housework, marriage and love were in fact issues loaded with profound political significance, their claim "the personal is political" challenged and greatly expanded traditional definitions of what should be regarded as 'political'. Furthermore, they pointed out that broader conceptions of what could be regarded as legitimate political activity, which was not confined to conventional political frameworks, included the self-help projects, networking and co-operative ventures in which women had always been active at local level.

Thus, one aim of the more radical feminist groups in the 1970s was to draw public attention to the continuing oppression of women by men through high-profile activities. An example in August, 1970, was the attempt by nine French radical feminists to lay a wreath to the wife of the Unknown Soldier in the Arc de Triomphe in Paris, on which was inscribed "there is one about whom even less is known than the Unknown Soldier: his wife". Four months earlier in Copenhagen, a group of about fifteen Danish women marched down the main pedestrian area "audaciously and grotesquely dressed, caricaturing the commercialised image of women as stupid sex object. On their route, they shouted feminist slogans ... At the main square ... they took off all their artificial female attributes – bras, roll-ons, artificial eyelashes and wigs – and threw them into a wastebasket on which was written 'Keep Denmark tidy' (Dahlerup, 1986: 93, 217).

A second aim was to construct new political frameworks through which women could work to achieve their goals, free from male domination. Not only was it argued that women's approaches to political activity were very different to those of men, seeking to work through loose networks in a flexible way rather than to construct hierarchical structures, but that their concerns were also seen to be more practical and immediate, centring on health issues, the provision of day care centres and safe refuges and on environmental problems. Thus the 1970s saw the emergence of well-women centres, rape crisis centres and safe women's refuges all staffed and run by women.

However, the most significant aim was to challenge the traditional view that issues such as contraception, abortion and divorce were not legitimate political concerns. These issues were in fact highly political, argued feminists, and were a striking illustration of the continuing way in which men oppressed women and defined the political agenda to ensure their dominance. Only women should be given the responsibility and the right to control their own fertility and thus free abortion on demand became one of the central goals of feminist groups throughout Western Europe, and the principal battleground on which they waged their struggles against male-dominated political parties and governments.

As we shall see, significant changes in legislation relating to issues such as abortion and divorce took place in the 1970s across Western Europe, which resulted from the efforts of feminist activists, though the new laws were frequently more limited than women campaigners had demanded. In countries such as Norway and Sweden where such legislation was already more favourable to women than elsewhere, campaigns centred instead on equality issues. We shall consider the activities in these two countries first, then turn to Denmark and Holland, and then look at Italy, Spain and France, before turning to Britain and (West) Germany.

Sweden and Norway

In Sweden, women's sections had developed since the turn of the century "in virtually every party, union, professional, social and religious organisation in the nation" (Adams and Winston, 1980: 139). The result was that 'reformist' feminism had become a strong force influencing the political agenda, especially of the Social Democratic party, which had dominated Swedish government since the 1930s. Early in the 1960s, a woman journalist, Eva Moberg, wrote a pamphlet The Conditional Emancipation of Women which "sparked a national 'sex role' debate" by questioning why, just because women gave birth to children, they should also be allocated all the washing, cooking and domestic chores (Kelber, 1994: 101). The result was that by the end of the decade the Swedish government explicitly adopted the goal of a society based on independent individuals and began to formulate an official sex equality policy to recognise this. A number of measures followed, including provision for the separate taxation of married couples, the right of all to work, and the establishment in 1976 of a Parliamentary committee on Equality. The implementation of a 'parents' insurance' programme enabled fathers as well as mothers to stay home during the first year of a child's life, and working mothers were assisted by the provision of new day-care centres. In 1980, an Ombudsman for Equality was appointed.

Perhaps it was hardly surprising, therefore, that there was little radical feminist activity in Sweden in the 1970s. Legislation regarding reproductive rights was in advance of other European countries; laws prohibiting abortion were first reformed in 1938 and since the 1950s, contraceptive advice centres were available to all women over the age of 15. In 1975, an abortion act was passed which enabled women to have abortions on demand and provided a full range of supportive public services, and subsequently rape within marriage was recognised as a criminal offence (Lovenduski, 1986: 277). Thus, women's groups and organisations within Sweden achieved success in achieving their goals by working within existing political structures, which perhaps explains the relative weakness and ineffectiveness of the few radical feminist groups that were formed in the late 1960s.

In Norway, while new feminist groups emerged in the late 1960s and 1970s aiming to 'transform structures along feminist principles', they were willing to work alongside established women's organisations on a range of issues including demands for a more liberal abortion law, secured in 1978, and for equal pay (Lovenduski, 1986: 12). Quite soon, strong links formed between the different women's groups, as they all worked together across party, class and ideological lines to explain the workings of the electoral system to women voters and to campaign for the election of as many women as possible both at local and at national level. As in Sweden, the goal in the early 1970s was to secure equal opportunities for and equal treatment of women. Thus in 1972 the Equal Status Council was established, which replaced the Equal Pay Council, which had existed since 1959. However, radical feminist groups argued strongly that women needed additional help to enable them to compete on equal terms with men, otherwise the pursuit of equality would simply lead to the "assimilation of women into the male-created and dominated public realm on unequal terms" (Lovenduski, 1986: 17). They stressed the fact that women's approaches to politics were different to those of men, and that formal political structures needed to reflect female as well as male political cultures. The result in 1978 was the adoption by the Norwegian Parliament of the legally groundbreaking Equal Status Act, which, while it promoted equality between the sexes, aimed particularly to improve the position of women, by giving them special rights because of their sex. The Act recognised that, because only women experienced pregnancy and childbirth, their situation was different to that of a man and required positive discrimination to enable them to secure real equality. Thus strong campaigning and close collaboration between a range of different women's groups and organisations laid the foundations in the 1970s for a dramatic transformation of the Norwegian social and political system over the following 20 years.

Denmark and the Netherlands

In these two countries, radical feminist groups emerged in the 1970s to challenge existing social and political structures and to campaign for liberation for women. At the same time, long-established 'women's rights' groups were exerting pressure within the political system to secure greater equality for women, and the interaction of these different approaches resulted in the adoption of many important new measures in both countries.

A number of loosely-organised, diffuse feminists groups of mainly young and middle class women emerged in Denmark at the beginning of 1970, from the New Left and student movements. They were inspired by the example of female activists in the United States and Britain, and wanted to challenge both the existing Danish patriarchal social structure and the older women's groups who they alleged had not fought strongly enough to overturn it. They used direct action to get across their message, operating under the banner of the 'Redstockings', a name they borrowed from the New York Redstockings. Two examples of their tactics help to explain why they quickly attracted the attention of the Danish media:

> On Mother's Day (in May, 1970, in Copenhagen) a group of women entered a public bus and refused to pay more than 80 per cent of the fare because women get only 80 per cent of the salary of men. They were – peacefully- arrested and fined, but they refused to pay more than 80 per cent of the penalty...

> During a beauty contest (in summer 1971, in Aarhus) a group of Redstockings interrupted the event, conducted by a popular TV host, and protested against the exploitation of women as sex objects and women competing for the benefit of men only. (Dahlerup, 1986: 226)

The radical feminist movement spread from Copenhagen to other major Danish cities such as Aarhus and Odense, and set up Women's Houses to act as the meeting point for feminist activists. A Feminist Festival was held in Copenhagen in 1974, which attracted 30,000 visitors, to listen to the speeches and enjoy the music of all-women bands and became the first of many such events. At the same time, radical feminists campaigned with other groups to demand free abortion and equal pay. In 1973, a liberal abortion act, which had been passed in 1970, was replaced by a Termination of Pregnancy Act, which provided for free abortion on demand during the first 12 weeks of pregnancy. It was followed in 1974 by the Social Assistance Act, which established a wide network of day care and recreation centres for children and young people subsidised by public municipal funds. In addition, the 1976 Equal Pay Act provided for equal pay for equal work (Kelber, 1994: 141-2).

At the same time, the older-established women's groups and women in Parliament were continuing their efforts to secure greater social and workplace equality for women. The Commission on the Status of Women in Society, which had operated in the 1960s and early 1970s, was replaced in 1975 by an Equal Status Council whose task was to work to eliminate inequality "in the hiring, training, promotion and working conditions of women and men" and to "oversee affirmative action in the public sector and education". The Council became statutory three years later with the passing of the Equal Treatment Act, which specified equal treatment of men and women in employment, education and other areas (Kelber, 1994: 141). Subsequently, in each county an 'equality consultant' was appointed to enable women to improve their position in the labour market and to break down sex segregation. A symbolic but important change in the marriage law was passed in 1984, whereby a woman could keep her own family name on marriage unless she explicitly chose to take the name of her new husband, and the same provision was available to men. Radical feminist groups were scathing about the shortcomings of such moves towards 'equal status', yet there is no doubt that the combination of "the indirect impact of the new movement through its renewal of the feminist debate and the direct effect of actions by feminists working inside the political institutions" brought about considerable social and economic changes which greatly benefited women (Dahlerup, 1986: 241-2).

There were striking similarities between events in Denmark and in the Netherlands. In the latter country, radical feminist groups emerged in the late 1960s out of student protest campaigns and quickly attracted national attention. In particular, the 'Dolle Mina' group, arising out of student and left-wing politics, built up a wide following and organised many consciousness-raising events, which were fully covered by the Dutch media. By 1982, it was estimated that there were nearly 160 feminist groups, covering a quarter of all Dutch towns (Katzenstein and Mueller, 1987: 46). Radical feminists focused their activities strongly at grass-roots level, campaigning to establish rape crisis centres, women's health groups and adult education centres to encourage women returners. However, their greatest achievement was to redefine the abortion issue as a women's issue whereas hitherto it had been seen as a "medical or psychological problem" (Dahlerup, 1986: 64). Though the new abortion bill of 1981, which came into force in 1984, was paradoxically somewhat less liberal than the existing system in practice (because the previous law had become widely discredited), nevertheless women's groups had forced change on unwilling political parties and had mounted a successful challenge to the way in which issues like abortion were perceived by Dutch politicians.

At the same time, long-established women's groups, some operating in women's wings of political parties and in trades unions, worked to increase the numbers of female political representatives. The Dutch Association for Women's Interests sought to mobilise voters to vote for women candidates and put pressure on parties to nominate more women candidates. A major objective was to speed up the achievement of social equality between the sexes, and in 1974 an Emancipation Commission was set up as an independent advisory body to help the government to formulate a coherent policy for the emancipation of women. In 1977, a State Secretary was appointed to co-ordinate and to promote an emancipation policy, supervised by a special Emancipation Council, and a year later a state sub-department was established for the 'Co-ordination of Equality Policy' in addition to a special parliamentary committee on emancipation policy. Government subsidies were made available to help projects that promoted women's emancipation, and 'femocrats', activists from the women's movement, were recruited into government departments to give advice and assistance with the establishment of such projects at local level. Once again, as in Denmark, despite the misgivings of some radical activists, the parallel efforts of radical feminist groups and of older more traditional women's organisations had proved very successful, in helping to establish in the Netherlands "the most extensive and comprehensive [sex equality apparatus] in Europe" (Lovenduski, 1986: 276).

Italy, Spain and France

In the late 1960s, these three large Catholic countries were not as advanced as the four northern European countries we have just considered in terms of attitudes towards the social and economic emancipation of women. Outside the major urban areas, a strong Catholic Church worked closely with traditional local and regional networks to emphasise the family responsibilities and domestic roles of women. However, the 1960s was a decade of economic expansion and of widening educational opportunities that laid the foundations for change. In all three countries, new feminist groups became active in the 1970s and pressed strongly for divorce law and abortion reforms and for greater economic equality.

In France, feminist activity grew out of the student protests of May 1968. Over 100 feminist groups, some of them very small, ranging from revolutionary and radical groups to those advocating syndicalist, socialist or reformist approaches, emerged in the following two years (Jenson, 1996:

73-108). Though many of the groups have been described as rather intellectual and elitist in approach, sometimes aloof, largely Paris-dominated,
and often bitterly opposed to each other (Lovenduski, 1986: 95), they were
able to join forces effectively in a campaign to secure a more liberal abortion law. Contraception had been legalised in France in 1967 and this
opened the way for a campaign to repeal a law of 1920, which had banned
contraception and abortion. As in the Netherlands, French feminist groups
argued that control of fertility should be solely a woman's responsibility
and that she should have the right to decide whether or not to have an abortion. The forces of opposition – centred on the Catholic Church, the parties
of the Right and conservative doctors – were strong, and feminist activists
therefore sought national publicity to demonstrate that large numbers of
women who could afford to secure abortions elsewhere were flouting the
existing laws. They also tried to encourage more women to seek abortions.
Their aim was to force the government to take action against those who
were breaking the law and openly admitting it, thus forcing a confrontation
situation and demonstrating how ineffective and socially divisive the existing ban on abortion actually was (Dahlerup, 1986: 95).

Feminist groups worked with representatives of trade unions and of cen-
tre-left political parties in the early 1970s to bring pressure to bear on the
French parliament to reform the abortion law. Finally, after heated debate
in the French assembly, accompanied by a vigorous media-led public discussion, abortion during the first 12 weeks of pregnancy was legalised in
1975, initially for 5 years. In 1979, the reform was made permanent. In
addition, in 1975, an important series of laws were passed to forbid sex discrimination at work, to give equivalent rights to mothers as to fathers with
regard to running domestic affairs, and to give wives the same rights as
husbands in relation to the matrimonial home. At the same time the divorce
laws were reformed so that male and female adultery were defined in a
similar way, and subsequent legislation redefined rape and the penalties for
it.

Political parties were not slow to respond to the new mood of militancy
amongst French women. In December 1972, a statute was passed which
accepted that there should be equal pay for equal work. Two years later, a
State Secretariat for Women's Condition was established, and in 1978 this
became a delegated ministry. Moreover, in 1981, a Women's Ministry was
established under Yvette Roudy, which oversaw the enactment of a framework of laws to lay down a programme of equality in employment for
women. It has been claimed that during the 1970s, the French women's

movement changed "the universe of political discourse" (Randall, 1982: 246). Rejecting traditional norms, "feminists put forward a radical concept of gender relations in sexuality, emotional and economic independence, formal and real equality in marriage, the family and other existing relations of sexist domination" (Dahlerup, 1986: 99). It is undoubtedly the case that by the early 1980s some significant legislative changes had taken place and that French governments were placing greater emphasis on issues affecting women and were prepared to give them a higher priority than would have been the case a decade earlier.

The Italian feminist movement, as in France, emerged from the radical student movement of the late 1960s and quickly found itself in conflict with the Catholic Church and with the dominant Christian Democrat party over issues such as divorce reform, abortion and the removal of church influence from education. As in France, the movement was strongest in major urban and industrial centres such as Rome, Milan and Turin, where it could draw support from long-established political and cultural traditions of radicalism. In the early 1970s, feminist activists worked through hundreds of consciousness-raising autonomous women's groups such as Rivolta Femminile (Female Revolt), the Collettivo Femminista Romano (Roman Feminist Collective) and Lotta Femminista (Feminist Struggle). Such groups were keen to stress that they were part of an evolving movement that was not in any way connected to the existing political structure, that they excluded men, and were egalitarian and participative in approach rather than hierarchical (Dahlerup, 1986: 29). Inevitably, however, they were viewed suspiciously by local Communist and Socialist party organisations whose agendas were dominated by economic issues and not by social concerns, which could potentially weaken the unity of the working class. In the early 1970s, the Italian Communist Party castigated feminists as 'petty bourgeois' and 'individualistic' and argued that Italy was "not ready" to confront women's issues (Katzenstein and Mueller, 1987: 135).

However, the struggles to liberate Italian women attracted increasing support, and one important area of success was the establishment of medical centres to treat working class women, which helped to forge links between feminist activists and the local community in cities like Turin. Up to two million Italian women became involved in feminist campaigning (Lovenduski and Hills, 1981: 200), and many of the new recruits, especially amongst younger women, were keen to form alliances with existing political and professional organisations or to work within them. Despite such differences in approach, the Italian feminist movement as a whole was particularly successful in enlisting support for legislative change from trade unions and even, ultimately, from the largest opposition party, the Communist Party and has been described as "the largest, most vital and successful" women's movement in Europe (Quoted in Randall, 1982: 238).

In 1970, the Italian parliament approved a divorce law, which allowed for civil divorce after a five-year separation. The Catholic Church immediately began to campaign to overturn it, and looked to its traditional areas of support, including large numbers of women in rural and semi-rural areas, to back a referendum to reverse the legislation. However, when the referendum was held, in 1974, nearly 60 per cent of the population voted against any change to the new law, despite the fact that 68 per cent of women and 53 per cent of men had been against its introduction in 1970 (Dahlerup, 1986: 35). Though women's groups had supported the campaign to maintain the new law, they had viewed it as a fight in support of civil rights and democracy rather than for women's rights. Now the outcome of the referendum suggested that further reform favouring women's interests was a real possibility.

According to Italy's 1931 Penal Code, abortion was punishable by imprisonment. By the late 1960s, it was estimated that between one and three million Italian women per year were securing illegal abortions, despite the fact that the code was still operative (Dahlerup, 1986: 34). In response to feminist activity in the early 1970s, a campaign began to collect the half million signatures required to bring about a referendum to legalise abortion, and in 1973 a socialist deputy introduced a Bill into the chamber of deputies to achieve the same goal. As the Catholic Church and its allies tried increasingly desperately to hold back reform, feminist activists working with their allies in the trade unions and in the political parties of the left mobilised ever-bigger public demonstrations in favour of change. In 1975, two mass protests attracted first 10,000 and, later in the year, 30,000 supporters, and in the 1976 national elections, pressure from women's groups contributed to significant electoral gains by the parties of the left. As the chamber of deputies debated a measure that would allow abortion but with doctors, rather than women themselves, being given the power to take a final decision, 50,000 protesters took to the streets. Finally, in 1978, a new abortion law was passed which represented a compromise between feminist activists' demands for a woman's right to choose and the opposition to abortion of the Catholic Church. Women over 18 could in future obtain abortions up to 90 days after conception in public hospitals on medical, social or economic grounds. However, doctors and health staff were allowed to refuse to carry out abortions on grounds of conscience. This concession was immediately invoked by large numbers of medical staff and had a serious impact particularly in southern Italy, where it remained difficult for women to secure abortions, despite the new law. Whilst feminists felt that the reform fell far short of what they had demanded, pro-life groups were appalled at the new provision, and organised a referendum to overturn it. However, the percentage of those voting to maintain the abortion law was even higher than the level of support for divorce reform in 1974. 67.9 per cent of those who took part in the referendum, held in 1981, supported the legalisation of abortion. But attempts by Italian feminists to petition the Chamber of Deputies to pass a law prohibiting and redefining violence against women, an area of particular concern especially in southern Italy, were not successful in mobilising enough political support for the measure.

Nonetheless, another significant change had taken place in 1973, when the use and advertising of contraceptives was finally permitted. Two years later a new family law was approved which asserted the equality of marriage partners and of their responsibilities in relation to the education of their children. In addition, in 1977, in order to bring Italian law into line with European Community law, an Equal Pay Act and Equal Opportunities Act were introduced. Thus by the end of the 1970s, the pressure exerted by feminist campaigns had helped to bring about political and social change in a country in which women had not hitherto played a very active political role Women's groups had successfully challenged the power of the Catholic church and the preconceptions of the predominantly male Italian deputies and had placed women's issues firmly on the Italian political agenda.

In Spain, the strong position of the Catholic Church under the dictatorship of General Franco, which lasted until his death in 1975, greatly restricted women's social and economic freedoms. Divorce, contraception and abortion were all illegal and adultery was severely punished. Wives were expected to obey their husbands, to concern themselves with family and domestic chores and with religious observance, and not to work outside the home. However, the development of the Spanish economy and particularly of the tourist industry in the 1960s helped to create a more open society and to promote social and cultural liberalisation. The educational and employment opportunities available to women began to increase substantially by the late 1960s, and a number of women began to join in left-wing political activity aimed at the ending of dictatorship in Spain.

Nonetheless it was not until the mid-1970s that a feminist movement as such took shape.

As in other European countries, feminist activists divided into radical, socialist and equal rights groups and debated the merits of separatist organisation and activity as against working through established political organisations. However, they united in pressing for the legalisation of divorce, contraception and abortion and for the end of discrimination in education and employment. Franco's death in 1975, which coincided with the proclamation by the United Nations of 1975 as International Women's Year, gave a boost to the new women's movement, which was further encouraged by the emergence of democracy in Spain. A new constitution, established in 1978, prohibited discrimination on grounds of sex and proclaimed equal rights for men and women. In the same year, the ban on information about and sale of contraceptives was removed, and a network of health centres, to provide guidance on family problems, was established. Civil divorce became possible in 1982, and two years later abortions were legalised, although, as in Italy, health workers could refuse to carry them out on moral grounds. Because abortions could only take place if the mother's life was in danger, the foetus was malformed, or the woman was a rape victim, feminists objected that the measure was far too restrictive and furthermore was not to be provided free by the state. However, the measure represented a significant advance, which had been partly brought about by pressure from women's groups, though the growing strength of the Socialist party in the national assembly was probably a more important factor. By 1985, it is estimated that there were more than 600 women's groups in Spain, but many of them were very small, and only about a fifth were explicitly feminist (Dahlerup, 1986: 205). Nevertheless, many different strands of feminism were active in the ten years after Franco's death, both in the major cities and at regional level, and helped to contribute to the significant changes in the social and political climate, which took place.

Britain and West Germany

There are many similarities between the feminist movements that developed in the late 1960s and 1970s in Britain and West Germany. Both drew inspiration from developments in the United States in the 1960s and emerged from the student protest movements of the late 1960s. In both countries, the agenda was set by radical or socialist feminists rather than by liberal or reformist groups. Moreover, both movements had much greater success in stimulating local campaigns and promoting political change at local level than they did in influencing the national agenda.

In Britain, a broad range of radical and socialist women's groups were active in the 1970s, but they remained relatively small in membership and rarely co-ordinated their campaigns. They have been described as a "deliberately dispersed collection of groups, campaigns and political structures with no single ideology" (Dahlerup, 1986: 109). In 1983 it was estimated that about 10,000 women were active in some 300 groups, with a further 20,000 active on the periphery, but such numbers were very modest compared to the 3 million women in 1978 who met regularly in Britain to pursue a wide range of activities through such organisations as the Women's Institutes, Townswomen's Guilds, WRVS and the Mother's Union, but who did not for the most part regard themselves as feminists or see themselves as participating in a 'combative engagement' with male supremacy.

The four main demands of feminist activists in the 1970s were free contraception, equal pay, educational and job opportunities, the availability of 24-hour nurseries and abortion on demand. As far as abortion was concerned, the 1967 Abortion Act had legalised abortion on a number of specified grounds up to 28 weeks, and while feminists were unsuccessful in their campaigns to liberalise the legislation, they were able to mobilise mass support and draw on considerable trade union strength through the establishment in 1975 of the National Abortion Campaign which co-ordinated the efforts of some 400 separate groups and organisations. Thus in 1975 and again in 1979 they were able to prevent two attempts by backbench MPs to restrict the provisions of the 1967 Act[45] . While free contraception and adequate child care facilities were not achieved in the short term, the Labour administration, which came to power in 1974, introduced a Sex Discrimination Act in 1975, and followed by the Employment Protection Act. These pieces of legislation gave women a statutory right to paid maternity leave, protection from unfair dismissal during pregnancy, and the right to regain jobs up to 29 weeks after giving birth. The establishment of an Equal Opportunities Commission also held out some hope for women of a move towards equal pay and equal opportunities in future years.

---

45 In 1975, James White's Private Member's Bill to restrict the 1967 Abortion Act got as far as a second reading, and in 1979 John Corrie drew first place in the ballot for private members' bills, and tried again, unsuccessfully, to get a bill restricting abortion onto the statute book. Eighty thousand people joined in a march organised by the trade union movement, with input from women's groups, to express their opposition to the measure.

Feminist activists were most successful in initiating political and social change at a local level. Activists highlighted the extent and trauma of rape and of domestic violence suffered by women, and in 1972 Erin Pizzey established the women's aid movement. By the end of the 1970s, 99 women's aid groups and 200 Women's Refuges had been set up. One concrete result of this activity was the introduction of the Domestic Violence Act in 1976, whereby women could get a court injunction to restrain a violent husband or partner. By 1981, 16 Rape Crisis centres had also been established, partly because of pressure on local councils being successfully mobilised by individual women's groups (Lovenduski, 1986: 78). Another development in the late 1970s was the establishment of women's health centres, which offered a range of practical advice, help and counselling services.

Feminist activists tried hard to highlight women's continuing oppression at the hands of men, and the virtual absence of women from history textbooks. One result was the establishment of a number of publishing collectives, and the launching of the periodical Spare Rib in 1972, which helped to maintain the momentum of the feminist movement. Another was the establishment of women's studies workshops and the emergence of women's studies as an academic programme in a growing number of universities and polytechnics, which in the longer term helped to promote and to spread understanding of the feminist perspective. And significant for the longer term, in its strategy to work from within rather than to work through self-sufficient networks, was the establishment of the 300 Group, which aimed to increase to just under 50 per cent the number of women in the House of Commons, and which had recruited some 3000 female members by 1982.

In Germany, a strong women's movement emerged in West Berlin in the late 1960s and quickly spread to other major German cities. Radical feminist groups flourished in West German universities and focused on grass roots activism. Vigorous local campaigning helped to establish rape crisis centres, battered wives' shelters and publishing co-operatives, but feminists found it far more difficult to make an impact at national level. One of their earliest and most important aims was to bring into being a new abortion law, which would provide for abortion on demand. Though the Bundestag agreed a more liberal measure in 1975, it fell well short of feminist demands. Nevertheless, pressure from a broad coalition of women's groups and organisations had helped to bring about at least some change.

In 1973 the German Bundestag established a Women and Society Commission to look into the status of German women, and numerous measures were suggested by its subsequent report. However, concrete changes promoting equality were slow to be implemented, and a law providing for equality for women in the labour market was only introduced because of EEC initiatives. Between 1980 and 1990, hundreds of equality counsellors were introduced into regional and local councils and then in the civil service, political parties, universities and trade unions, though their powers to promote change were somewhat limited. As in Britain, while feminist activists were successful in promoting awareness of the range of problems faced by women in a local context, they found it difficult to bring pressure to bear on the government or on political parties to introduce major change into their national political agendas.

Conclusion

Thus by the early 1980s, feminist campaigning had not only challenged the political agenda within individual west European countries but had introduced new and imaginative approaches to political activism. They had asserted that while women felt oppressed by male-dominated political structures, and took little part in them, this did not signal a lack of interest in political issues as such but rather concealed a fundamental difference of view about what issues should be regarded as 'political'. Millions of women throughout Western Europe participated in campaigns to liberalise divorce and abortion laws, went on peace marches and became involved in environmental campaigns. As a result, they became increasingly involved in the political process while at the same time they developed new approaches to campaigning and effective ways of networking.

At the same time, the more flamboyant and explicitly feminist protests undoubtedly provoked a backlash. Female campaigning was met with derision and criticised as being too strident, reminiscent of the general reaction to the campaigns of suffragettes in the early twentieth century. Large demonstrations of women demanding the right to obtain divorce and abortion were seen by many older and conservative groups in society throughout Western Europe, particularly in rural areas, as threatening and deeply destabilising. Such activities provoked a spirited response, particularly from the Catholic Church, and pressure groups such as the Society for the Protection of the Unborn Child and Life were formed to lobby against abortion.

Yet, within a comparatively short period of time, where women's groups had a clear campaigning focus and the ability to construct broad networks with sympathetic groups on the left and centre of the political spectrum, they became a force to be reckoned with. The scale and impact of feminist campaigning varied from group to group and from country to country, as we have seen, but its cumulative effect was undoubtedly to transform the west European political landscape. Not only were 'women's issues', such as the availability of abortion and contraception, now firmly on the political agenda, but women themselves began to join in formal party political activity in greater numbers than ever before and to challenge the traditional structures they encountered with growing confidence.

References

Adams, C.T. and Winston, C.T. (1980) *Mothers at Work* (London: Longman).

Dahlerup, D. (ed.) (1986) *The New Women's Movement* (London: Sage).

Katzenstein, M.F. and Mueller, C. (eds) (1987) *The Women's Movements of the United States and Western Europe* (Philadelphia: Temple University Press).

Jenson, J. (1996) 'Representations of Difference: Varieties of French Feminism' in M. Threlfall (ed.) *Mapping the Women's Movement* (London: Verso), 73 108.

Kelber, M. (1994) *Women and Government: New Ways to Political Power* (New York: Praeger).

Lovenduski, J. (1986) *Women and European Politics: Contemporary Feminism and Public Policy* (Boston, Mass.: Massachusetts University Press).

Lovenduski, J. and Hills, J. (eds) (1981) *The Politics of the Second Electorate* (London: Routledge and Kegan Paul).

Randall, V. (1982) *Women and Politics: An International Perspective* (Basingstoke: Macmillan).

Threlfall, M. (ed.) (1996) *Mapping the Women's Movement* (London: Verso).

14. PEACE MOVEMENTS

Carlo Ruzza

Peace movements are amongst the most visible and widespread social movements. They have emerged in a wide variety of political contexts in response to different kinds of conflicts. Mobilisations have taken place against global geopolitical threats such as macro-regional re-armament programs, international crises leading to the threat of global wars, but also increasingly local wars and social conflicts rooted in ethnic tensions. Although they have tended to register peaks of activity and long phases of de-mobilisation and abeyance, they rarely completely cease to exist as they rely on a morally motivated activist base that keeps them alive even in the absence of viable political opportunities. Remaining active even in periods of generalised demobilisation through the work of small groups of dedicated pacifists allows a connection of cycles, a cross-fertilisation and a learning process in which concepts, protest tactics and resources can be re-deployed in different periods and different locations. In addition, the high media coverage of war and issues connected to war makes them – or at least some of them – internationally recognised and ideally connected through their public visibility. This provides a sense of geographical and temporal continuity which gives them social relevance and distinctive features, particularly in the West.

Peace movements' features are affected by the political context in which they emerge and the nature of the grievances they express. Their ideology of reference, protest tactics, supporting institutional allies and outcomes vary. For instance in the fifties they were often closely connected to a Marxist outlook, in the eighties they were often classed as New Social Movements and showed the characteristic lack of hierarchical structure and the theatrical repertoires of this kind of movements. In recent years they have developed in close association with the expansion of the third sector and the new no-global movements. Yet a common pacifist ideological core can be identified and traced across periods and contexts. In this chapter, I will begin by focussing on recent geopolitical events which in the last decade have substantially altered the prospects of these movements and their composition. I will then review the main ideological features and their recent transformations. I will analyse the main characteristics of recent European peace movements in terms of the mix of individuals and institu-

tions that have supported them and in terms of their grievances and outcomes. Finally I will examine the variables that affect their future
prospects.

A first distinction in peace movements should be drawn between movements emerging in democratic or relatively democratic political contexts
and movements emerging in differing or non-democratic contexts. The
presence or absence of democracy engenders distinctive features, which
differentiates peace movements and requires substantially different analyses. Variables such as the type and amount of repression and the movements' coverage in the media are different in democratic and
non-democratic contexts.

In non-democratic political contexts, movements might have to face
extremely strong state repression or conversely state attempts to utilise
them for propaganda reasons. This for instance was the case of peace
movements, which emerged in the eighties in the eastern bloc.

In western democracies, peace movements have often attempted to
maximise their visibility in the media arena – a strategy often difficult or
even impossible to achieve to non-western movements. There are for
instance local wars in Africa that have remained virtually unknown to the
rest of the world despite the effort of important local mobilisations. But in
the west the typical use of theatrical action forms have facilitated movements' salience in the media. Also their entrenchment in a diverse set of
institutions has enhanced their visibility. Peace movements have for
instance found a hospitable environment in Churches, local authorities,
some political parties, and professional associations such as associations of
scientists or doctors, and trade unions. Thus complex advocacy coalitions
have developed linking activists in institutional realms. In times of escalating conflict these coalitions form the basis for rapid mobilisation reaching
quickly mobilised networks such as schools, and citizens not affiliated to
institutions (Ruzza, 1997). These general features have taken somewhat
different characteristics in each of the most important movement cycles of
the period after WWII.

The History of Peace Movements

Peace movements rely on a body of concepts that can be connected to the
pacifism of early Christians. Peace movements' lengthy tradition has stimulated a large body of academic and activist research that dates back for
centuries (Martin, 1965; Mustro, 1986). It is a tradition that includes ana-

lytical works and historical analyses of specific geographical locations and geopolitical contexts and shows their historical and political relevance in a wide variety of contexts.

Recent History: The European and North American Geopolitical Situation

Several peace movements have re-emerged in recent times. Peace movements have taken off on a large scale in reaction to global threats and to civil wars. As for global mobilisations, in the fifties the first post war mobilisation emerged in protest against nuclear atmospheric tests and since then even if at smaller levels of mobilisation it remained a stable feature of Western and Eastern Europe.

Global Mobilisations

In the last twenty years three types of international peace mobilisation can be identified. Opposition to Pershing 2 and Cruise missiles marked a first cycle[46] that lasted from 1980 to 1985 (Kaltefleiter and Pfaltzgraff, 1985). Opposition to the Persian Gulf War constituted another cycle from December 1990 to March 1991. Opposition to a new conflict in Iraq also emerged at the end of 2002. These protest cycles were very wide. Protest embraced all European countries. In the U.S. a similar succession of protest events also occurred, the first being the Nuclear Freeze movement, the second the movement against intervention in the Persian Gulf, and the third another set of protest events against a new Persian Gulf war.

These three mobilisations share common features. They called into questions issues of imperialism and specifically the role of the US in matters of international security. But there were also substantial differences. The first mobilisation episode focused on the issue of nuclear weapons and was therefore directly connected to the anti-nuclear mobilisations of the fifties against atmospheric tests. Many organisational aspects had changed when a new wave of the peace movement took off in the early eighties, but the international situation of radical polarisation between two blocs was similar.

---

46 As Tarrow (1991) argues a cycle is characterised by a level of conflict which is higher than normal, by a simultaneous or near-simultaneous conflict within more than a social sector, by a diffusion of conflict within most of a state even if with different regional levels, by the utilisation of new action forms during the cycle which goes from one social sector to others and from some geographical locations to others.

In the eighties European peace movements developed against a background of a relatively stable geopolitical situation that underwent an increased polarisation and remained largely unchanged over the course of the movements' life, and roughly corresponded in the US to the movement for a nuclear freeze. The Reagan years were characterised by a situation of marked tensions between the superpowers. The division of Europe into conflicting Soviet and American spheres of influence was infused with a new ideological zeal. The rhetoric of the "Evil Empire" accompanied a massive escalation in defence expenditures and supported a conception of security that made nuclear war seem possible in the European theatre. This resulted in a general perception of threat that sustained and connected the European Peace Movements (Rochon, 1988). Furthermore, the fact that international conflict was polarised around two main actors, offered the movements a set of clearly defined and generally agreed-upon goals. Specifically, the refusal to accept the deployment of Cruise and Pershing missiles constituted the basis for an alliance among Peace Movements (Marullo, 1986).

Participation in the Peace Movement constituted one of the first occasions of significant interdependence between the social movement sectors of different European countries. Activists of different countries travelled extensively, not only within their own country, but wherever the front of the struggle was perceived to be. For instance, large numbers of German, Dutch and English activists went to Comiso in Sicily to engage in direct action with their Italian peers (Ruzza, 1990). Attempts were also made to include members of Eastern European peace movements, but there was a prevalent feeling that Communist manipulation in Eastern Europe was too strong to guarantee any significant independence in social movements.

The division of Europe into two blocs was such a long standing fact that it was taken for granted, and even created personal differences among activists too profound to be bridged. Among Western European activists, however, the common geopolitical situation was accompanied by a shared belief in the unacceptability of nuclear threat on which was based a common political platform of nuclear disarmament.

Despite massive mobilisations the missiles were deployed. However, soon after the international situation changed radically. Gorbachev started a program of reforms which over time led to substantial reduction of the nuclear arsenal of both superpowers.

Both the political and the cultural situation remained relatively constant throughout the lifecycle of the European peace movements of the eighties.

When Gorbachev began an internal and foreign policy inspired by new values of openness and a search for dialogue with the West, the impact on the Peace Movements was momentous. Perceptions of threat began to diminish and former activists became increasingly difficult to mobilise. Established goals of the movements became less relevant, or were actually achieved in the context of the East-West super-power summits, which to many symbolised and advertised the end of the Cold War.

However, the new climate was slow to emerge. While Reagan remained in office, the old ideological differences prevented a more trusting atmosphere from emerging in policy-making circles, and the media reflected a similar distrust. What completely changed the situation were the events of 1989. One by one, European Eastern states underwent radical political change that the Soviet Union did not hinder, and at least in the case of East Germany and Bulgaria, actively promoted. The 1989 events created a new social and political climate in Europe that significantly affected the social movement sector, as well as the cultural roots of its support.

In the span of a decade, dissolution of the Soviet bloc took place, effecting a further reduction of the sustained international tension that had characterised the cold war. Many peace activists point to the delayed effect of the movement in achieving these changes in the security arrangements. Other analysts mainly viewed the change as the consequence of an untenable economic situation in the eastern bloc. In any event, after the collapse of the eastern bloc the prospect for the peace movement changed substantially. The following international crisis developed in a radically different environment – a world in which there is only one superpower and in which wars increasingly come to be presented as guided by moral motives.

On August 2, 1990 the relevance of the European peace movement increased radically with Iraq's invasion of Kuwait. Washington reacted by immediately blocking Iraq's assets and obtaining international approval for an arms embargo. Soon after a multinational military contingent primary composed of American, French, British, Egyptian and Syrian troops was assembled.

Western European movements soon began to grow and mobilise (Brittain, 1991). A few days after the Congressional elections on November 6, President George Bush ordered a doubling of the 150,000 troops already present in the Gulf. On November 29 the U.N. voted to authorise member states to "use all necessary means" to implement Resolution 660 if Iraq did not withdraw from Kuwait by January 15, 1991. As the deadline approached peace movement activities steadily increased in intensity and reached the high mobilisation level of the early eighties. Well-attended demonstrations took place in all major European capitals.

Seven hours after the deadline the coalition launched an aerial offensive, within days flying thousands of missions. The rhythm of the demonstrations and other protest events further intensified. Soon many European high schools and colleges were mobilised. A February 23 deadline for a ground offensive passed, and a last minute Soviet proposal for a negotiated solution of the conflict was not accepted by the coalition. A "100 hours" war crushed the Iraqi military and inflicted heavy Iraqi casualties, forcing its withdrawal from Kuwait. Soon after the war ended the movement quickly demobilised, returning to a lower level of mobilisation supported by professional peace activists.

In 2002 a situation of tension re-emerged in the same geopolitical area. The background that led to a renewed attention to the Middle East was the terrorist attack that took place on September 11, 2001 when the New York twin towers and the Pentagon were attacked by hijacked airplanes flown by Al Quaeda terrorists. This brought a renewed focus on Islamic fundamentalism. The US administration declared a "war on terrorism." The first intervention took place in October 2001 in Afghanistan with the objective of dismantling the Taliban regime and its Al Quaeda supporters. Subsequently attention turned to Iraq – seen by the US administration as in some way associated to the Al Quaeda network. The US thus sought to mobilise a coalition to disarm it.

The situation reached a turning point after the November 2002 UN resolution (1441) which re-instated UN inspections in order to verify the destruction of weapons of mass destruction. However, activists could claim some success in pressurising the Bush administration into seeking a UN mandate for its campaign against Iraq. According to the resolution should 'material breach' of the disarmament process take place, military intervention would ensue. However, a majority of the peace movement continued to oppose intervention whether or not a UN mandate was secured. The movement coalition against the war continued to grow rapidly. Notable early manifestations included protest marches in London in September 2002. This new movement became even more visible in Europe at the European Social Forum held in Florence in November 2002 and then more massively in February 2003 on the eve of a possible military intervention in the region. On February 15, millions turned out in more than 600 cities around the world. Participation was particularly strong in Europe, with participation reaching one million in London and Rome. Participation in Asia and the US was more muted with about 20,000 joining a rally in New York. The movement embraced a wide variety of age groups and people of different ideological background. Participants included long-time activists as well as college and high school students and religious people from a variety of religious backgrounds. The protests were not successful in preventing the war from beginning on the 20 March, which resulted in a military victory for the U.S. led forces and the toppling of Saddam Hussein's dictatorship within a month. Protests continued during the war, though with reduced numbers in some countries such as the UK. Even after the defeat of the Iraqi regime, lower level protests continued though with the focus shifting to a perceived U.S. policy of rolling confrontation against what it defined as 'rogue' states threatening international security. The protests were interpreted by some commentators as crystallising a new international and, in particular, European identity formed in juxtaposition to the new U.S. policy. This possibly reflected a developing popular unease about a new unipolar world order, and in some cases growing anti-Americanism. This was a phenomenon recognised by some European leaders who utilised it in order to garner domestic electoral support, demonstrating the wider political uses and effects of this social movement.

Civil Wars

Besides these large international mobilisations, peace movements have also been active on more localised conflicts. Transitions from large international crises to local conflicts are often difficult for movements as the critical mass of allies and supporting institutions evaporates after a major crisis. However, often peace movements retain many of the resources accumulated during periods of escalating mobilisation, including funds, available meeting places, and pools of activists, and can use these resources even after demobilisation. For instance such a situation emerged in several movements after the cruise missile crisis. Remaining activists often channel these resources to oppose conventional wars.

The most relevant local wars have been those that have occurred in the Ex-Yugoslavia in association with the civil war that affected the entire region in the nineties. A prominent campaign – although on a different scale from the global peace movements previously described – emerged in the early nineties and declined after the interruption of the conflict, which took place after NATO bombing of the Serb army around Sarajevo in 1994. Later another relevant mobilisation took place in the late nineties in connection to the war in Kosovo in 1999. These mobilisations were aimed both against the actions of local military and paramilitary forces in the region and later against NATO intervention. As mentioned, a mobilisation also occurred in reaction to the Afghan conflict in 2001. European peace movements have also been involved for several years in humanitarian activities in the long Israeli-Palestinian conflict. To a lesser extent they have also been active in African conflicts, such as the Ugandan conflict and recently in the Sudan.

Other peace-movement related concerns tend to survive demobilisation such as opposition to the arms trade, peace education, opposition to the draft, fiscal protest against military expenditures, municipal initiatives, boycotts of multinationals, assistance to and exchanges with symbolic or war-ridden territories, and increasingly north-south interventions of humanitarian nature. In recent years boycotts have focussed on multinationals like McDonalds and Nestlé for promoting environmental practices, trade policies and dietary habits detrimental to the developing world and Shell for its dealings with a ruthless dictatorship in Nigeria. These boycotts show the connections between environmental and development concerns typical of the green movement and the north-south concerns of peace movements.

These are issues that precede and accompany large mobilisations but are often subordinated during international campaigns. These initiatives are more dispersed and different organisations privilege different campaigns. In recent years, in Europe, a relative convergence among de-mobilised national peace movements has emerged in relation to specific local wars.

Organisational Structures

Peace movements as with other movements are networks of individuals and political organisations. However, more than other movements they include a wide set of institutional allies, constituting in effect broad advocacy coalitions in each area in which they achieve saliency. The composition and commitment of these institutional allies have characterised peace movement structures over time.

In the fifties peace movements were often strongly associated with the left and were utilised in the ideological struggle that characterised the period. However, even in the midst of the cold war important non-leftist components characterised these movements. One can cite the fundamental contribution of the Catholic tradition for example. In the eighties the constituency of peace movements expanded to include large parts of the student movement in several countries and incorporated activists and structures of other movements, notably parts of the women's movement and of the environmental movement. This period is also characterised by the appearance of less hierarchical and intentionally less durable organisational structures in the social movement sector. These new largely informal structures responded to the values of anti-authoritarianism, which characterised new generations of activists and were identified and analysed by an emerging literature on New Social Movements. In these movements strong moral imperatives coexisted with an attempt to identify less personally constraining organisational structures where activists could find avenues for personal expression and self-actualisation. These aims also included the adoption of a broader repertoire of protest tactics that include symbolic and theatrical forms of protest (Scott, 1990)

At the turn of the century peace movements have undergone fundamental changes. They remain de-centralised non-hierarchical and theatrical in their protest repertoires. However, many individual participants and organisations have substantially strengthened the connection between their political activities and their intervention in civil society in support of humanitarian causes. Peace activity has for more activists than before come to mean work in support of refugees, trips to locations of conflict to witness their dissent and put pressure on state authorities, collections of food, medicines and other resources to send to areas of conflict, etc.

These activities are by no means new but they have expanded to the point that they constitute a fundamental change. It is a change that addresses a now dominant ethos of hollowed out states, which are increasingly unwilling, and incapable of coping with social problems – states farm out important areas of their social policies to the private sector. They relate to social needs by forming mixed public-private structures in charge of addressing welfare issues or by contracting out to organisations of civil society the task of intervening in what used to be a state remit. This has produced a larger often more responsible and often more resourced voluntary sector which has in many countries connected to the social movement sector in an organic way. Organisations have added to their political role as advocates one of providing concrete support for causes of traditional social movements concern, such as women, minorities and refugees. In this perspective peace movements have expanded their role and re-defined themselves as broad advocacy coalitions. This transformation has also been engendered by the perception of powerlessness and moral uncertainty that peace activists have often reported in reaction to civil wars – particularly the wars in Ex-Yugoslavia. Incapable of identifying clear lines of political interventions activists have then turned to providing support for victims of war.

After demobilisation following the end of the cruise missile crisis, peace movements had to make a difficult transition away from the clear international context on which they had concentrated. They chose a set of concerns that included local wars but came also to embrace related issues such as racism and xenophobia. In other words, the political approach to peace came to be more strictly integrated with a religious conception of peace that included personal relations among individuals in society. This expanded but also dispersed the remit of peace movements. Initiatives in peace education, initiatives against prejudice and other initiatives aimed at changing public opinion were adopted.

Another important change that has marked peace movements in recent years is the appearance of the no-global movement and the institutionalisation of the new movements of the eighties. The no-global movement has re-awakened attention to north-south issues and provided a large and rather undifferentiated pool of activism for peace movements.

The institutionalisation of the new movements of the eighties has resulted in a substantial increase of political credibility for social movements – in many cases, these movements are the natural allies of several peace movements. In certain policy areas such as environmental policy citizens trust these movements more than governments. This has granted powerful institutional allies to these movements and they have become embedded in certain political parties and local authorities. In so doing they have acquired resources that can be to an extent diverted to peace movements in times of necessity.

Finally, one important political development has been the growing importance of activist networks operating in relation to international and supranational structures of governance (see Keck and Sikkink, 1998). Social movements have concentrated their attention on the UN and the EU where they can exert influence that trickles down to the level of member states. These institutions are also often important sources of funding. For instance the European Union funds many projects that peace movement organisations conduct in the areas of support to refugees and migrants and in the area of assistance to development. Peace organisations are pressing for the entrenchment of human rights concerns at the international level. To the extent that this is happening and states come to define themselves at least partially as moral actors in the international arena, non-state actors have a political opportunity to constrain some of their actions. This therefore constitutes an opportunity for peace organisation advocacy (Risse and Ropp, 1999; O'Brien and Goetz et al., 2000).

Institutions and Public Opinion

As emerges from the previous discussion, Western peace movements are dependent for resources, political legitimacy and to an extent for activists from public opinion and from organised civil society. In many contexts they have relied on the voluntary sector, on churches, on some political parties and other institutionalised (and non institutionalised) movements. It is therefore necessary to identify the variables that spur these institutions to support peace movements and consider the impact of public opinion.

First one needs to differentiate periods in which a conflict appears imminent from periods in which this is not the case. Peace movements constitute political identities that are activated quickly when conflict resolution appears important but often only as weak identities as few individuals chose peace movements as their dominant concern in other periods. Those who do – often radical pacifists – constitute a committed minority which whilst important in linking different waves of mobilisation is generally unable to expand their support. Thus, one needs to separate support for specific peace campaigns from generalised support for peace movements. The World Value Survey examined direct identification with the peace movements at the end of 1999 in a period of absence of mass mobilisation, which was already somewhat removed from the conflict in Kosovo, and in 32 European countries percentages of respondents who stated that they 'belong(ed) to the peace movement' or 'perform(ed) unpaid activity for the peace movement' was generally very low – on average less than 1 percent (.98 percent belong, .77 per cent unpaid work). Higher percentages were registered in countries affected by societal or international conflicts (Greece 2.9 percent 'belong' and Northern Ireland '2.3 belong') and in countries with an old tradition of peace movement activities like the Netherlands (3.4 percent 'belong') and Belgium (2.3 percent 'belong'). A very different situation developed in 2003 where as mentioned support for the peace movement was generally high.

A fundamental reason for support for peace mobilisations is that the concept of peace is institutionalised as a positive political value in the discourse of a broad range of institutions and states but remains sufficiently undetermined to justify a variety of strategies and discursive frames in the pursuit of peace. In peace campaigns different frames often coexist allowing for the formation of differentiated coalitions. This was evident in the mobilisation against intervention in Iraq in 2003 when a majority of Western populations opposed intervention. Whilst pacifism – as a radical doctrine that unconditionally refuses any involvement in conflicts is a minority view, other approaches to promoting peace are shared by sizeable sectors of the population. Sectors of the population may identify with the strategies promoted by institutions closer to their political views and therefore contribute to broad fragmented coalitions without necessarily defining their political identity as mainly connected to peace movements at other times.

The reason why involvement in peace work is generally evaluated positively and expands significantly in periods when it is politically relevant is related to the so-called crisis of politics. One source of institutional attention common to the peace movements and to all social movements is the fact that they can provide legitimacy in a situation of perceived global crisis of political institutions. Politics is in many contexts associated with declining citizens' interest, declining voters' participation, and perceptions of ineffectiveness of Parliaments that are seen as unable to cope with the complexity of modern decision making requirements and with an increasing dominance of executives. Even the party system appears in crisis. Parties have become much institutionalised and strictly connected to the state in many countries. These features have led observers to posit a crisis of politics – a crisis to which movements appear able to provide a response by means of their perceived stronger connection to civil society.

This is often the case of peace movements whose connection to civil society and to local communities is possibly stronger, benefiting from the very fragmentation of these movements. In fact, if peace movements find it difficult to articulate a comprehensive political programme because of their dispersion in a host of supporting institutions, it is precisely their entrenchment in civil society that provides political legitimacy.

Ideological Features

When examining general attitudes towards the peace movements it is also necessary to consider the cultural images that form the cultural background in which media and movements interact. Regardless of a movement's organisational ability, which after the eighties was intentionally low for all

European peace movements, to be successful, protest must find an echo in relevant sectors of the population. The more society is alerted to a politically relevant variation of the concept of peace the more easily mobilisation will succeed. One can distinguish between images applicable to all peace movements and images that are relevant only to certain specific mobilisations.

Reviewing images connected to peace mobilisation, Melucci (1985) and Rochon (1988) compiled lists of prevalent images of peace with reference to the anti-cruise missile movement. However, these lists have also proved useful for the subsequent waves of the peace movement.

Melucci (1985) stresses a reaction to changes in military policies, which is expressed by both political actors within traditional political channels, and by atomised behaviours of fear of an irreversible catastrophe. He also points to a moral utopianism, which although always present and often embodied in sects, finds in the peace movement a new channel for expression. Thomas Rochon (1988) lists as factors underlying the emergence of the peace movement in four Western European countries a feeling of romantic anti-modernism and Christian pacifism, Anti-Americanism and Western European nationalism (Rochon, 1988). In the following mass mobilisation – in conjunction with the Persian Gulf War of 1991 – in addition to these images one needs to emphasise a new awareness of north-south issues and a focus on the neglect of international law perpetrated by the pro-war coalition. As in the previous cycle a synthesis of participating organisations' worldviews and their strategies to influence public opinion emerged (Coy and Woehrle, 1996). As in the previous wave the religious component was crucial and saw the active involvement of the peace churches and of sectors of the Catholic Church.

Anti-Nuclear Mobilisation and its Images

With reference to specific mobilisations, the most salient feature of recent decades has been the reaction against nuclear weapons. In Europe and the US, there are a series of images concerning peace that explain the differential success of different peace mobilisations (Weart, 1988). In explaining the success of the anti-cruise missile movement of the eighties one need to address the image of nuclear power. Both Melucci (1985) and Rochon (1988) point to a reaction to the nuclear threat of people with post-materialist values. These weapons came to be seen as the embodiment of a society run by big and distant governments that utilise nuclear technologies to intimidate citizens. Melucci argues that peace activists see the nuclear situation as a metaphor for the societal power to control information. On a symbolic level, the peace movement would then be an expression of a generalised reaction to the "artificial," "built" characteristics of social life. More generally, negative images of nuclear power predate the nuclear weapon issue. They provided the frame that the media used for discussing the peace movement when international tensions made the subject salient, and sharpened these images in the public's mind. International tensions made nuclear fear more pronounced. In the early eighties, the number of people concerned about international tensions grew constantly, as did the number of people who feared, and thought probable, a nuclear confrontation in the future. Without these elements, mobilisation efforts would have failed or more probably, would not have been instituted. The newly emphasised fears resonated with an older and deeply rooted distrust of nuclear power in its various aspects.

In this context one notes that in the eighties the peace issue surfaced in a moment of political vacuum for European leftist social movements, and offered a chance to revitalise protest politics by channelling the feelings of anxiety aroused by a tenser international climate, and by re-emphasising anti-imperialist sentiments. Peace movement participation was "encouraged" by existing leftist organisations, especially in Italy and France where the leftist tradition was stronger and the Ecologist movement was still in its infancy. The role of public opinion in creating availability for mobilisation was also crucial. Without public concern about nuclear weapons, it is hard to imagine that these organisations would have succeeded in mobilising millions.

In the eighties an anti-technological outlook was often manifest in large sectors of leftist and non-leftist public opinion and in the nineties and after it is a central concern of parts of the no global movement. Specifically, nuclear issues have always had a central place in popular imagery. Nuclear weapons are strictly associated with a fear of radioactivity, which in turn is connected to the theme of man as a creator of technological monsters who eventually punish him for his audacity. It is a restatement of the theme of Frankenstein, which decades of movies have made universally known. Dr. Frankenstein's transgression was to challenge natural and divine laws, and even more, to betray the ties he had with his creature and generally with humankind. In a similar manner, the fault of technological society was to have dared too much and given birth to a monster: nuclear energy.

Furthermore, the scientists' tie to their dangerous creation was thought to have suffered from their abdication of responsibility, the gift of their creature to the military establishment. The punishment was a future of annihilation and a present of disease. In particular, the disease theme has re-emerged in recent conventional wars in association with the use of spent uranium in shells.

Activists' condemnation was extensive – nuclear weapons leak radioactivity, their control is approximate; a nuclear confrontation could be triggered by a simple accident. The evil genie can escape the bottle at any moment. Even peaceful use of nuclear energy is generally not often accepted. For many nuclear energy should be banned altogether. A connection between the ecologist and the peace movement has traditionally been sought by peace movements and has been somewhat successfully accomplished, particularly in countries like Germany and England. Other activists accept technology in principle, but are aware of the dangers of most nuclear applications and advocate substitutes to nuclear technologies.

It is notable particularly in Germany that many former members of the peace movement now find themselves in government as part of the red-green coalition. This led initially to a decision to phase out nuclear power stations and later in 2003 to the German government making clear its opposition to a war in Iraq and leading to strains in relations with the USA.

The previously mentioned element of reaction to social control has particular connotations with reference to the nuclear issue, as some activists feel that it is implicit in the nuclear threat. Nuclear weapons are considered part of an Orwellian design of regimentation and administration of the world. They argue that the constant impending threat of annihilation secures the power of big nations over small nations, and within each nation, secures the domination of the superpowers' conservative allies over popular will. In a metaphorical sense, it also represents the power of "organised" society over the individual.

This theme is strictly connected with Anti-Americanism – clearly expressed by the frequent display of caricatured effigies of American presidents, and the repetition of Anti-American slogans. Another less frequent aspect of the reaction to social control was the desire for a "small and beautiful" society, free from big powers and their symbol, the atomic bomb. In the eighties this theme was often associated with ecologist motives expressed in opposition to nuclear power plants. In recent years, following the disappearance of a superpower and the scaling down of the nuclear arsenal, environmental and health concerns have taken precedence in terms of the fears raised by atomic energy.

Finally there is an element of moral utopianism. Religious activists are most sensitive to the "unjust" character of nuclear war. Catholicism has a long-standing concern with the morality of war (Musto, 1986). After the collapse of the Eastern bloc and of Communism as an ideological referent for the social movements sector, religious activism has grown in relevance, particularly as the main reference of long-term committed peace activists.

Conclusions

Peace movements have changed with the changing international geopolitical situation, with the increased importance of voluntary work connected to themes such as anti-racism and the impact of international and supranational institutions in supporting initiatives (Musto, 1986). However, they have retained their relevance and impact. An impact that consists in engaging arm experts in the context of security policy, in attempting to influence public opinion and sometimes succeeding, in mobilising other movements' constituencies on issues of principle (Meyer, 1995). In doing so they serve an important role in improving and deepening social thinking on the crucial theme of war and peace and in bringing the influence of civil society to bear over security policy – one of the most insulated and specialised policy areas.

References

Coy, P.G. and Woehrle, L.M. (1996) 'Constructing Identity and Oppositional Knowledge: The Framing Practices of Peace Movement Organisations During the Persian Gulf War, *Sociological Spectrum*, vol. 16:3; 287-327.

Brittain, V. (1991) *The Gulf Between Us: The Gulf War and Beyond* (London: Virago Press).

Diani, M. (1992) 'The Concept of Social Movement', *Sociological Review*, vol. 40: 1-25.

Downton, J. and Wehr, P. (1998) 'Persistent Pacifism: How Activist Commitment is Developed and Sustained', *Journal of Peace Research*, vol. 35:5; 531-50.

Kaltefleiter, W. and Pfaltzgraff, R.L. (1985) *The Peace Movements in Europe and the United States* (New York: St Martin's Press).

Keck, M.E. and Sikkink, K. (1998) *Activism Beyond Borders*. (Ithaca, NY.: Cornell University Press).

Lofland, J. (1993) *Polite Protesters – the American Peace Movement of the 1980s*, (Syracuse, NEW York: Syracuse University Press).

Martin, D. (1965) *Pacifism; an Historical and Sociological Study* (London: Routledge and Kegan Paul)

Marullo, S.L.J. (1986) *Peace Action in the Eighties* (New Brunswick: Rutgers).

Meyer, D.S. (1995a) 'Framing National Security – Elite Public Discourse on Nuclear Weapons During the Cold War', *Political Communication*, vol. 12:2; 173-92.

Meyer, D.S. (1995b) 'Polite Protesters – the American Peace Movement of the 1980s – Lofland, J.', Contemporary Sociology – *A Journal of Reviews*, vol. 24:1; 50-51.

Musto, R.G. (1986) *The Catholic Peace Tradition* (Maryknoll, NY.: Orbis Books).

Musto, R.G. (1987) *The Peace Tradition in the Catholic Church : An Annotated Bibliography*. (New York: Garland).

O'Brian, R., Goetz, A. et al. (2000) *Contesting Global Governance* (Cambridge: Cambridge University Press).

Risse, T., Ropp, S. et al. (eds) (1999). *The Power of Human Rights* (Cambridge: Cambridge University Press).

Rochon, T.R. (1988) *Mobilising for Peace* (Princeton, NJ.: Princeton University Press).

Ruzza, C. (1990). 'Strategies in the Italian Peace Movement', *Research in Social Movements, Conflict and Change*.

Ruzza, C. (1997) 'Institutionalisation in the Italian Peace Movement', *Theory and Society,* vol. 26; 1-41.

Ruzza, C. (2000). 'Anti-racism and EU institutions', *Journal of European Integration*, vol. 22:1. 145-171.

Scott, A.l. (1990) *Ideology and the New Social Movements* (London: Unwin Hyman).

Silverman, A. (1991). 'Where Have All the Peace Activists Gone?', Research in Social Movements, *Conflict and Change*, vol. 13; 153-70.

Tarrow, S. (1991). *Struggle, Politics and Reform: Collective Action, Social Movements and Cycles of Protest*. Occasional Paper 21, Centre for International Studies, Cornell University.

15. FROM PROTEST TO PARTNERSHIP?
Voluntary and Community Organisations in the Democratic Process

Tessa Parkes, Marilyn Taylor and Mick Wilkinson

Civil society, understood as the realm of private voluntary association, from neighbourhood committees to interest groups to philanthropic enterprises of all sorts, has come to be seen as an essential ingredient in both democratisation and the health of established democracies (Foley and Edwards 1996: 38).

Introduction

Voluntary and community organisations (VCOs) are seen by many as important routes through which citizens contribute to the development and implementation of public policy and to the democratic process. The work of Robert Putnam (1993; 2000) has linked engagement in voluntary and community organisations, or civil society associations, with the development of social capital and hence to the development of the civic norms and trust that, he argues, form the basis of effective local governance. Some scholars have gone so far as to suggest new forms of democracy based on associations. Thus, Hirst (1994) promotes a form of associational democracy, based on his belief that voluntary and community organisations can provide a counterweight to the power of both state bureaucracies and private enterprise. He sees 'voluntary organisations not as secondary associations but as the primary means of both democratic governance and organising social life' (Hirst, 1994: 26).

However, a number of scholars dispute this view. Salamon (1993) has argued that, while these organisations may contribute to democracy, they may also be an impediment or even an irrelevance. A growing number of scholars have been critical of Putnam's assumption that there is a link between voluntary and community association membership, social capital and democracy (see, for example, Foley and Edwards 1996, 1999; Union Institute 1999). Commentators on the related civil society discourse criticise normative assumptions, which ignore the conflicts of interest within it, the uneven distribution of power and resources, and the exclusive aspects of trust and association.

This chapter is based on findings from a two-year study[47] of the role of voluntary and community sector organisations in the democratic process in the UK. The research took place between April 2000 and April 2002 and included approximately 150 interviews. It had three phases: an initial set of 'scoping' interviews with intermediary bodies within the voluntary and community sector (VCS) and government; a series of interviews with voluntary and community organisations in four localities and at national level, and also with respondents from national and local government; and three case studies in particular policy areas. The policy areas covered were the environment, regeneration and policies relating to older people.

The study explored the contribution the sector makes to democracy from the perspective of both VCOs and the organisations they target. It also addressed how VCOs understand and pursue issues of effectiveness and legitimacy, and the way in which the political opportunity structure is changing. The focus for this chapter will be the nature of the contribution to democracy of the VCS; how our respondents understood democracy, how far they felt they contributed to it and where they thought they might be an impediment or perhaps be irrelevant to democracy. The chapter concludes by considering how this is affected by the changing political opportunity structure in the UK, which is highlighting partnership, governance and a more integrated approach to policy making.

What is Democracy?

In order to understand the contribution that voluntary and community organisations make to democracy, it is first necessary to define democracy. This is a major undertaking but we will confine ourselves to drawing two simple distinctions: between representative and participatory (or direct) democracy, and between instrumental and substantive views of democracy. By representative democracy, or what some authors call liberal democracy (Hewlett, 2000), we mean a system whereby representatives are elected by popular vote at regular intervals and take decisions on behalf of those who elect them in the interim. In this view of democracy, most citizens play a largely passive role. Control is exercised by the fact that citizens can elect different representatives at the next election if they are dissatisfied.

---

47 The study was funded by the ESRC, project number L215252049. The other members of the research team, on whose work we have drawn, were Gary Craig, Diane Warburton and Surya Monro.

Participatory or direct democracy, on the other hand, offers opportunities for citizens to come together and inform the policy process in a variety of ways and at different stages of the process – from agenda setting, policy formulation and revision, through to implementation, ongoing review, feedback and subsequent amendment.

Distinctions of this kind featured strongly in the responses of our respondents to the question about how they contributed to democracy. A number argued that the substance of their contribution would depend on how democracy was defined. Thus, VCOs probably did not contribute a great deal to representative democracy as defined above. However, many of our respondents saw democracy as more than this:

> A broader pluralist democracy ... is about ways in which ordinary people feel that they can influence things and have an effect on things (National VCO respondent).

For some, 'government by the people' – and some respondents referred to the Greek origins of the term – meant 'the people making decisions'. This meant, for the majority of our respondents, that democracy should be pluralist and participatory rather than majoritarian or representative. This also meant that people should have a wide variety of mechanisms through which to participate. Participatory democracy should allow people to influence what was going on around them and should mean that 'ordinary people' should feel that they can have a say. Some respondents went further, defining democracy as being about 'challenging, discussion and debate', on the one hand, or about decisions being taken locally when they are about local issues, on the other.

Where Representative Democracy Falls Short

Given the above, it was perhaps not surprising to find that many respondents, including respondents from the statutory sector, were critical of representative democracy – or at least drew attention to its limitations. Many respondents commented on the disillusionment with the political process that is felt by many people in Britain (and elsewhere) today:

> ... there is such a degree of cynicism about politics, both local and national, that I think some people engage in this work instead of the democratic process because they see the democratic process as being a waste of time (National VCO respondent).

Their criticisms can be summarised under five main headings: the limitations of the ballot box; the centralisation of government in the UK; the centralisation of power even at local level; the failure of local government to represent the interests of its constituency; and the advance of globalisation, which reduces the scope for influence even at national level.

Firstly, the ballot was seen as a very crude form of accountability – the most 'barren' part of the democratic system:

> The politicians drop the mandate of the people once they get in. If people allow this, democracy is a sham (National VCO respondent).

Voting figures in the UK, as elsewhere, are falling and respondents felt that there was a particularly marked democratic deficit in poorer areas where voting turnout was low and there was anecdotal evidence of mistrust.

Secondly, respondents were critical of the increasing power exercised by central government in the British system. The UK has a particularly centralised form of government compared with many other countries and central government was seen to maintain rigid control over agendas at all levels. VCOs felt that this limited the scope for influence at local level. It also put local government on the defensive:

> One of the interesting things in terms of democracy is that all these changes that are coming up are not the local authority any more. So, what is the role and function of the local authority? (Local government respondent).

Thirdly, the scope for influence had also been diminished, some felt, by the most recent reforms of political structures at local level. The introduction of a cabinet system in many authorities, as part of central government's modernisation agenda[48], had resulted in fewer, more powerful councillors engaged in policy development. In the view of a number of our respondents, cabinet members had less time to spend talking to groups and constituents, whilst those councillors outside the cabinet were seen as less able to exert real influence.

---

48 Recent reforms are encouraging cabinet government at local level, which focuses power in a small number of representatives. Other elected representatives are encouraged to play a scrutiny role.

Fourthly, there was much criticism of the operation of local government and the party system. Respondents commented on the poor quality of many local councillors, the exercise of patronage, and the unwillingness of elected politicians to share power, let alone to accept criticism. Some were also critical of what they saw as the adversarial nature of party politics in the UK and the 'dog eats dog' culture of politics at local and national level.

A final concern about the democratic system was the globalisation of power, which, some argued, was taking power away from all the institutions of representative government at national as well as local level. Business and multinationals were held to have 'unfair' and 'excessive' influence over civil servants and politicians. This was in part due to an imbalance of resources, in part because some politicians were held to be in the pocket of business interests, and in part due to the all-pervading culture of private enterprise. De facto, this again reduced the power that VCOs felt they could have over policy.

What do VCOs Contribute to Democracy?

So, what exactly do VCOs contribute to democracy? Some respondents argued that without the VCS, democracy would be moribund:

> Imagine what it would be like if there weren't any voluntary organisations and all we had defining the role of older people in our society was central and local government: it would be utterly dire (National VCO respondent).

Most respondents from government at local and national level agreed that the sector had a significant contribution to make, although with reservations that will be discussed later:

> Voluntary groups are essential to the democratic process – community groups bring incredible richness to this and they're able to identify where the state has forgotten people. Social change comes through small community and voluntary groups (Local VCO respondent).

They referred to a number of characteristics of the sector which allow it to make a contribution: some cited their face-to-face contact with people; many cited their diversity and their ability to bring a range of voices into the democratic process; others thought the fact that they were democratically organised themselves was a contribution. However, some took issue with this positive view, arguing that most VCOs were only concerned with service provision, or that contributing to the democratic process was not at the forefront of what many local organisations were trying to do:

> Some groups come together because they are sick of having no play spaces for their kids – they want resources and they want somewhere for their kids to play – it is an issue that people will fight for but they don't necessarily do it because they want to change the world or they want to change policy (Local government respondent).

One VCO commented that they had their work cut out with survival, another that they were usually concerned with *'sorting themselves out'* and not with what they saw as the 'wider issues'. Borrowing from social movement theory and Najam's classification of citizen organisations as policy entrepreneurs (1999), we have classified the contributions reported to us under two broad headings: mobilising citizens/capacity building and framing and influencing policy processes.

Mobilising Citizens / Capacity Building

It was suggested to us that engaging in VCS activity, even at the simplest level, could give people the skills, confidence and knowledge to engage in public life. Commentators like Robert Putnam would argue that the contribution to the democratic process does not have to be explicit. In his view, effective democracy is underpinned by the 'social capital' that engagement with voluntary associations provides. This is not an issue that our research was designed to test, but some of our respondents did suggest that involvement in social activities could lead to more political engagement:

> I've seen groups grow from being concerned about, for example, their pond, to a wider remit which includes the whole village (Local VCO respondent).

VCOs also took on a more explicit educational role. One national VCO, for example, saw its role as not only reflecting the views of older people, but also working with older people's groups to develop and support their ability to speak for themselves. For many organisations, this 'capacity building' is not about teaching people new skills as much as making them aware of their rights and responsibilities as citizens. Some engage in an explicit consciousness-raising process which is not about responding to outside agendas, but supporting people in learning through collective action and experience to define their own power, drawing for example on the work of Paulo Freire (1972):

> ... voluntary and community organisations have a role in the education of the individual or person in a broad setting because ideas are best formed when you are meeting with and talking to other people (Local VCO respondent).

Providing Opportunities to Participate

Many of our respondents argued that it was through VCOs that many people contributed to public life:

> People are so disenfranchised, except through the informal and formal groups that they belong to. That's the nearest they get to participating in a democracy (National VCO respondent).

What was particularly important about the sector for many of our respondents was that it engaged people through collective action, rather than as individuals:

> There are plans to try to involve individuals more closely but that will never replace the need or value of having voluntary organisations around to put an alternative view or express collective points of view (National government respondent).

Collective action allows individuals both to do more and to learn more:

> ... if you can carry other people with you then that should carry more weight – that is democracy, and to make democracy effective you have got to get people together in groups working for what they want (Local VCO respondent).

This can give people more power over their own lives, reducing dependency and involving people in transforming their own communities. A few respondents were more explicit about the political nature of their work and spoke about their role in mobilising individuals to be effective and active citizens through campaign work. Adopting a consciously political agenda was particularly important for excluded groups like black and minority ethnic groups:

> Black and minority ethnic groups will have to become a lot more powerful than they are at the moment if they are to be taken seriously. The council are beginning to realise that there are votes there. They could become more powerful by the leaders encouraging and educating their communities to become more involved – it is a huge political education exercise (Local VCO respondent).

This can extend to mobilising the vote, although the foundation for this is much broader:

> An important part of our work is encouraging people to vote. We have a role in ensuring that democracy works better (Local VCO respondent).

We found a small number of examples where voluntary organisations had worked with local government to increase the formal vote. In one locality, two Development Trusts held elections for their own trustees at the same time as the local authority elections, with booths in the same place. This increased the local turnout in those wards. Occasionally, respondents argued that the VCS could be a route for individuals to become local authority councillors, and there are of course a number of members of Parliament with a strong background in the VCS.

Plural Voices

VCOs can be seen as a channel for the views of those they represent and provide services to, or as a means of giving people voice directly. Respondents from both the VCS and the statutory sectors identified two characteristics which allowed them to offer this channel: the fact that they were often closer to the ground, and the fact that they could represent many diverse voices. In the first case, they were often able to access people who would not want to contact official agencies and to act as a channel for views that would not be expressed directly to power holders:

We meet the grassroots on a day-to-day basis in their own environments rather than cold, draughty school halls once every two or three months. I think councillors generally are just responding to letters, we are much more face-to-face with people and have a better understanding of issues on the ground (Local VCO respondent).

Many local councillors agreed with this. The VCS, one said, allowed them *'to take the pulse of what the community thinks'*.

However, of equal importance was the fact that the VCS could express a variety of voices. One respondent from a small national VCO asserted that it was *'good to have all types of discussion going on'*, and many organisations emphasised a commitment to 'the values of tolerance and diversity'. The important point here is not that individual VCOs are necessarily tolerant and diverse, but that the VCS as a whole allows for the expression of diversity and provides different ways of working, different values and philosophies. This is especially important if the views of the most excluded groups are to be heard. People spoke about the need for VCOs to help to *'level the playing field'* by giving structural support to minority groups.

The contribution of the VCS to pluralism not only has the potential to support social inclusion and social justice, important though these are. It also enriches the pool of knowledge and talent on which democracy can draw. For example, the sector allows a variety of avenues into public life and thereby accesses the skills and knowledge of people who are not attracted to mainstream politics, allowing people *'to find niches for what they want to do and how much time they are prepared to put in'* (Local VCO respondent). When it comes to single issues, VCOs often seem to be the only way to act.

Framing and Influencing Policy Processes

VCOs carry out research that informs or challenges policy decisions. They also communicate information up and down the system. They keep issues in the public eye and stimulate debate, and can sometimes change the way in which people think about issues. The move in government circles towards an emphasis on evidence-based policy makes this a particularly important role. Some government respondents found the VCS invaluable for providing feedback into the system. They are, said one local councillor, *'our eyes and ears'*.

VCOs generate information which can shape the policy process agenda. This again is a function recognised by both VCO respondents and those from the statutory sector:

> ... a lot of policies have probably originated from what voluntary organisations have been doing (Local government respondent).

In doing this, of course, VCOs seek to influence not only the statutory sector but all sources of power. A number of organisations from both the statutory sector and the VCS gave examples of how VCOs had brought issues onto the national agenda, for example on issues such as homelessness, carers and AIDS:

> ... at any one time there are a pool of things floating around that the Council could or should be doing, and the voluntary sector can flag up and push things up the agenda (Local government respondent).

They also bring new ideas and new solutions into the policy field by trying new things, being willing to take risks, and by supporting innovation.

Holding the System Accountable

Of course, the VCS input to the policy process is not always consensual and benign. They also challenge policy and the New Labour government has, in principle at least, welcomed this role. There was a strong sense, especially in some national organisations, of being 'watchdogs', holding government to account and challenging its agendas. Some VCOs also challenge the way the democratic process itself works. Black and minority ethnic groups, for example, have been particularly active in challenging the inadequate representation of minority groups in the formal party political system, while many groups have challenged the poor quality of much consultation. This kind of challenge forces politicians to remember 'the people out there', and reminds them of the concerns that such people have. It also reinforces the right of everyone to speak out. It is clear, however, that some government respondents find this difficult to accept, questioning the representativeness of critical VCOs. Whilst the UK national government has publicly accepted the right of the VCS to challenge and criticise policy[49], even when funded by government, there are examples nationally and locally where government-funded organisations, perceived to be critical, have found their funding cut.

Where VCOs Fall Short

In asking how far VCOs contribute to democracy, we focused on two questions. Firstly, we explored the extent to which they could be said to operate in a way that allows citizens and especially those who are under-represented, to participate more fully in public life and in the policy process (the 'mobilising' role). In doing so, we explored in particular the extent to which they were accountable to those they claimed to represent. Secondly, we explored how they negotiated the balance between gaining access to the policy process and the need to maintain their autonomy and distinctiveness, especially in an environment where opportunities to engage in the policy process were becoming more commonplace.

Accountability and Representativeness

Many VCS respondents, especially at local level, claimed that their contribution came from the fact that they were more 'democratically' organised than other bodies and that this both engaged people and gave the sector credibility:

> ... the voluntary sector as a whole is democratic and we make every effort to be very democratic in how things are done ... if any sector understands the concept of democracy it is the voluntary sector (Local VCO respondent).

However, others, from both the VCS and the state, questioned this claim. They argued that VCOs were often not representative, that they were not accountable, and they were too particularistic. While the sector as a whole may inject pluralism into democracy, these respondents argued that individual organisations within it were not necessarily 'democratic' in their operations:

---

49 This commitment has been made in the national 'compact' agreed between government and the third sector in 1998. This compact is a statement of the principles that should govern relationships between the sectors and has been followed by more detailed codes of practice (Home Office, 1998).

To what extent they can be generalised as representing the population as a whole I wouldn't like to say because in any organisation it's self selecting: the most active, the most confident, it is those who most passionately want to say something or do something who turn up in voluntary organisations (National VCO respondent).

In fact, it was suggested that VCOs could be patronising and exclude other voices. For this reason, some local and national government respondents felt it necessary to get beyond VCS intermediaries to the 'wider community': the 'real people'. Others acknowledged that there were some very 'suspect' voluntary or community groups and that some were a 'closed shop'. Against this, a number argued that it was not representativeness that was the issue – representativeness was in fact an impossible goal. What was more important in their view was accountability:

... you do not need a democratic mandate to protest – you need transparency (National VCO respondent).

It's open to abuse, but isn't every form of democracy? The important thing is to have safeguards against abuse – accountability is the biggest safeguard. If people have to report back; if the press have copies of papers; if there are frequent, regular elections so that if you end up with an organisation which is unrepresentative, you can get rid of them (National VCO respondent).

What also concerned many people, especially the smaller groups, was the fact that there was not a 'level playing field', and that some parts of the sector were able to have more influence than others:

... there is a key role for voluntary organisations in strengthening democracy, but it is important to be very clear about the limits. The arguments are accountability and legitimacy and whether or not people are having undue influence – undue in relation to their public effect – compared to others who may have reasonable cases that they are not communicating (National VCO respondent).

In this, there was support for Schattschneider's (1960: 35) famous contention that:

The heavenly choir of pluralism sings with an upper class accent.

There was thought to be a certain amount of collusion between local authorities and 'favoured' organisations. One council respondent argued that some principles were needed to stop this 'nobbling' from happening and recommended the 'compact' as a way forward. Other research we have done (Craig et al., 2002) has indeed suggested that local compacts have been used to make the relationship between elected local councillors and VCOs more transparent.

Another dynamic was the tendency for community groups to claim to be on the side of the angels, while accusing larger voluntary organisations of being undemocratic. There was a strong view amongst smaller organisations that neither the state nor the mainstream voluntary sector had their ear to the ground or had the democratic ethos that these smaller organisations themselves had. However, others felt this was far too simplistic and took the view not only that community organisations could be unrepresentative, but that professionals could be supportive of democracy; for example professional intervention could be an important means of mobilising grassroots action. In some cases, larger organisations could act as intermediaries for those with fewer resources, providing 'docking points' into the system that allowed smaller organisations to 'punch above their weight'. Some saw it as an important part of their role to support smaller organisations and service users in claiming their voice.

Insider or Outsider?

A number of respondents questioned how far VCOs could be said to contribute to democracy if they were delivering services as 'agents of the state'. They believed that VCS values were being eroded by their increasing role as contractors for state services. The implication was that, to the extent that state funders were dictating their agendas, the contribution that VCOs could make as alternative voices was increasingly compromised. This might be because of coercion on the part of state funders but it was just as likely to be the result of self-censorship, or the fact that those organisations that are in the business of providing services on contract to government simply did not have the time to engage in advocacy activities.

While other research in which one of us has been engaged suggests that advocacy did not suffer from the 'contract' culture in the early years of its introduction (Taylor, 1997), others argue that contracting is creating a division within the sector between those who act as government agents and those who can maintain an independent voice (see, for example, Dahrendorf, 2001). Thus, some community organisations were keen to distance themselves from larger VCOs who were seen as key players in the contract culture. However, a number of larger organisations we interviewed, some of whom did provide services on contract, also clearly played a campaigning role as well as providing development support for user-based organisations, so that service users could have their own voice.

The tensions between autonomy and co-option have been intensified by the partnership agenda. The decline in voter turnout and the clear disenchantment with politics at all levels has been one of the driving forces behind a central government programme which seeks to open up government and, particularly, to modernise local government. This has changed the policy environment both centrally and locally with important implications for the VCS. Most of our respondents felt that these initiatives were providing new opportunities for the VCS to engage with the policy process.

Government had embraced a more participatory approach and this, together with the increasing emphasis on evidence-based policy, had provided a framework for taking into account a range of interests; senior officials were more accessible than they had been in the past, and there was a greater freedom for them to talk freely and be creative.

This new policy environment is characterised by more communication across boundaries at all levels of government, more face-to-face contact, and more career moves, including secondments, across the boundaries. Viewing the state and the VCS as alternatives, as adversaries or even as totally independent, becomes increasingly illusory. At the local level respondents acknowledged the moves being made to revive democracy. The lead given by central government, they felt, had forced local public bodies to go through at least the motions of change.

However, doubts were expressed about the extent to which this new openness of the policy process actually translated into real influence at either national or local level. VCOs felt that they were getting their feet under the table but that there was some way to go before engagement would be meaningful; it was easier to voice concerns than to influence policies directly. Although gains had been made these were often viewed as small or peripheral. When there was general agreement on a particular policy initiative, there could be very fruitful discussions about details of implementation, but where that basic agreement did not exist, it was described as difficult even to get to the table. In addition, there were significant concerns about instrumentalism – of having to follow national government agendas and funding streams to the detriment of an organisation's own core objectives. Short-termism and the manipulation of consensus politics were endemic and a barrier to influence.

Despite the central government rhetoric of partnership, many local authorities were described as reluctant partners with an endemic resistance to sharing power. One respondent commented:

> Local government does resent community groups, particularly if they are independent. There is a de facto love-hate relationship (Local VCO respondent).

Some saw this as a defensive strategy, in the face of the erosion of the local authority role by central government. But others felt that local authorities were well able to defend themselves, turning the rhetoric to their own advantage by claiming to be *'the voice of the local community'* and trying to take the teeth out of VCS involvement by turning it into the *'sort of non-threatening consensual involvement that they want'*. The local government response varied between our case study sites. In some, there was indeed a strong resistance from councillors and officers who displayed a siege mentality, feeling that they were being squeezed from above and below: by moves to strengthen regional government, by neighbourhood management initiatives that sought to devolve budgets and decision making on services, by the various local partnerships and quangos that were being set up, and by the contracting out of public services to the private sector. In this environment, the VCS was seen as just one more wolf at the door.

It seems, therefore, that while many VCOs welcome the new drive for partnership and the prospects that it offers for a new institutional environment at local level, they feel that there is some way to go before public sector partners will really share power. Meanwhile they run the danger of being co-opted into public sector agendas under the guise of 'partnership', and of losing their independent voice. At the same time, however, there is a prospect that, with the advance of partnership, local government will itself lose its distinctive voice.

Martin Rein argued in 1989 that 'the future of the welfare state is the invention of institutions that are not public nor private' (1989: 70). One radical scenario is that the partnership agenda is opening up a new space between the public and the private, which could be seen as transforming the local democratic process. One of our respondents raised questions about the way in which new inter-sectoral partnership organisations were being set up and legally incorporated. As organisations that were neither public nor private, neither their provenance nor their accountability was at all clear. She argued that there was a brain drain from local government to these new partnership organisations, leaving behind a serious gap in expertise that could affect the capacity of local government to play the enabling role that many see as its future. Some commentators in the UK are even advancing the view that there is no future for local government (Stoker, 2001). Does this matter?

If the VCS contribution is about pluralism, then it could be argued that the state has a role in providing a level playing field (in relation to resources, access to power, etc.) and mechanisms to mediate between different interests. Some argued that part of that role should be to financially support the empowerment of organisations that might well be the state's critics – a phenomenon that has been a feature of the relationship between the state and the VCS, in some parts of the UK at least, for a long time.

In a parallel debate, Keane (1988: 7) criticises the neo-Conservative view that seeks to privilege civil society over the state and to popularise a distorted interpretation of the virtues appropriate to civil society. What civil society offers is the opportunity to bring a wide diversity of voices into the democratic process. Nevertheless, it is not possible to extrapolate from this to argue that the majority of organisations within it are democratic, or that the sector as a whole allows citizens an equal voice. To the contrary, Keane argues, civil society and the state are the condition of each other's democratisation. He sees the state as a device for enacting legislation, promulgating new policies, containing inevitable conflicts between particular interests within well-defined legal limits, and preventing civil society from falling victim to new forms of inequality and tyranny (1988: 15). Conversely, civil society should become a permanent thorn in the side of political power. Arguments about whether the VCS or the state is more important to democracy seem, then, to be fruitless. The views we heard from a predominantly VCS sample suggest that each has a role to play and that if either was missing, democracy would suffer.

Summary and Discussion

Respondents in our study generally believed that VCOs have a significant contribution to make to democracy. However, they did not contribute to representative democracy as commonly understood. Representative democracy was understood by many to be flawed. Instead, they considered that they contributed to participatory democracy in a variety of ways. They contributed to the development of the social capital that is said, by some, to provide the foundation for effective democracy. They provided people with the experience, confidence and education to act as citizens, both formally and informally. They ensured that democracy was informed by a plurality of interests. They provided opportunities for people to engage in the democratic process at a variety of levels and in a variety of ways, from the social to the political. In addition, a particular contribution was their ability to reach people who feel alienated from the political process.

If one aspect of the sector's role was to engage and mobilise people as citizens, a second aspect was to inform and frame political debate. VCOs provide feedback, transfer information up to decision-makers and down to citizens, and carry out research. They stimulate debate and put issues onto the public and political agenda. They hold government accountable and challenge its decisions, sometimes, if only rarely, even changing them. They act as a channel for the citizen's voice, especially the voices of those who normally go unheard – sometimes as conduits, but increasingly by supporting people to speak for themselves.

However, as we have described, there are limits to the contribution that voluntary organisations can make. Their contribution will depend on how effective they are in influencing policy – and some respondents questioned how far this was the case. Their contribution will also depend on how far they allow 'the people' access to the democratic process; for example, how democratic they are themselves.

What these misgivings illustrate is that the health of democracy is not determined solely by either state or VCS contributions. What is significant is the balance that is needed between the state and the VCS, if democracy is to work. The growing interest in local governance, as a new third space, which would be the major arena for policy generation at local level, offers one way forward. Those who criticise the resistance of local government to change may see this as a positive outcome. However, the shift from government to governance raises major questions about institutional form and democratic accountability, creates new sets of insiders and outsiders in the policy process, and requires new definitions of the democratic process, at least at local level. More thought needs to be given to the distinctive roles and legitimacy of different partners, and how representative and participatory democracy relate to each other, so that the strengths of each can be fully realised.

One national VCS respondent argued that the relationship between the sectors should not be about mutually exclusive circles (market, civil society, state), but that it did have to be robust and mature so that the different elements could work together on some things but also disagree. Another argued for a 'creative tension' between government and the VCS. It is clear that the VCS, taken as a whole, can bring a variety of voices into the political process and open up debate. However, as individual organisations, they will inevitably offer particular and conflicting voices, however 'democratically' organised they might be. Some respondents argued that it was the role of the state to arbitrate and balance the different interests, taking a strategic view. Whether these different roles are being combined to best advantage seems to vary from policy field to policy field and locality-to-locality. Our research suggests that, while this creative tension exists in some pockets, it is not yet a central feature of the relationship and there are still places where VCOs are still merely expected to do as they are told. However, it is perhaps towards this creative tension that emerging new forms of governance should be aspiring.

References

Craig, G., Taylor, M., Wilkinson, M., Bloor, K., Monro, S. and Syed, A. (2002) *Contract or Trust: The Role of Compacts in Local Governance* (Bristol: The Policy Press).

Dahrendorf, R. (2001) *The Arnold Goodman Lecture* (Tonbridge: Charities Aid Foundation).

Foley, M. and Edwards, R. (1996) 'The Paradox of Civil Society', *Journal of Democracy,* vol. 7:3; 38-52.

Foley, M. and Edwards, R. (1999) 'Is it Time to Disinvest in Social Capital?', *Journal of Public Policy*, vol. 19:2; 141-72.

Freire, P. (1972) *Pedagogy of the Oppressed* (Harmondsworth: Penguin).

Hewlett, N. (2000) 'Democracy: Liberal and Direct' in G. Browning, A. Hacli and F. Webster (eds) *Understanding Contemporary Society: Theories of the Present* (London: Sage). pp. 165-177.

Hirst, P. (1994) *Associative Democracy: New Forms of Economic and Social Governance* (London: Polity Press).

Home Office (1998) *Getting it Right Together: Compact on Relations Between Government and the Voluntary and Community Sector in England* (London: The Stationary Office, Cm 4100).

Keane, J. (1988) *Democracy and Civil Society* (London: Verso).

Najam, A. (1999) 'Citizen Organisations as Policy Entrepreneurs' in D. Lewis (ed.). *International Perspectives on Voluntary Action: Reshaping the Third Sector* (London: Earthscan Publications). pp. 142-181.

Putnam, R. (1993) *Making Democracy Work: Civic Traditions in Modern Italy* (Princeton, NJ.: Princeton University Press).

Putnam, R. (2000) *Bowling Alone: The Collapse and Revival of American Community* (New York: Simon and Schuster).

Rein, M. (1989) 'The Social Structure of Institutions: Neither Public Nor Private' in S.B. Kamerman and A.J. Kahn (eds) *Privatisation and the Welfare State* (Princeton, NJ.: Princeton University Press). pp. 49-71.

Salamon, L.M. (1993) 'The Non-profit Sector and Democracy: Prerequisite, Impediment or Irrelevance?' Presentation to the Aspen Institute Non-profit Sector Research Fund Symposium: *Democracy and the Non-profit Sector*, 14 December 1993.

Schattschneider, E.E. (1960) *The Semi-sovereign People* (New York: Holt, Rinehart and Winston).

Social Exclusion Unit (2001) *A New Commitment to Neighbourhood Regeneration: The Action Plan* (London: The Stationery Office).

Stoker, G. (2001). *Local Government You are the Weakest Link:* Goodbye. ESRC Seminar Series: Local Government and Local Governance in the UK (Aston University: September 2001).

Taylor, M. (1997) *The Best of Both Worlds* (York: Joseph Rowntree Foundation).

Union Institute (1999) *The Non-profit Sector and Democracy: Essays Exploring the Mission of the Non-profit Sector and its Relationship to Civil Society and Democratic Life in the United States* (Washington, DC.: The Union Institute).

16. PARTICIPATION AND PROTEST:
Mental Health Service Users/Survivors

Peter Beresford and Peter Campbell

The focus of this discussion is the modern development of participation and protest by mental health service users/survivors. This has taken place at both individual and collective levels. It relates to and raises issues about both the developing identity of mental health service users/survivors and the nature of their collective activities and movement. These can be seen as both related and distinct. In this discussion we shall try to explore both – mental health service users'/survivors' identity and their movement; the implications the two may have for each other and their implications for mental health service users' aspirations for participation and change in the future. Our primary focus is the UK, but this needs to be understood in the context of broader international developments, which reflect both similarities and differences to the British experience.

The Mental Patient Predicament

In the last twenty years, the mental health system, not just mental health services but the attitudes and practices of society towards those who use mental health services, has been under concerted attack. Among those acting on criticisms of the established system, the presence of one group of participants has been notable: people with a mental illness diagnosis. The contribution of this group is now evident in areas of the mental health arena where, until recently, their influence was impossible to detect. Nowadays people with a mental illness diagnosis are likely to be active in the planning, managing and monitoring of mental health services, in training, education and research, in public awareness campaigns, in debates about legislation. Although the extent of their influence can be questioned, there is little doubt that they have become stakeholders in the system (Campbell, 1999).

Action by people with a mental illness diagnosis has been very diverse and by no means entirely addressed towards the state of mental health services. Nevertheless much work has been dedicated to changing services and it is this aspect of action that primarily interests the government and the mental health professions. Partly as a result of this bias, it has become common for people with a mental illness diagnosis to be described as service users or simply users – certainly in the mental health field. But, in reality, the identity and naming of these people is much more problematic, both to themselves and to others in society. The proliferation of descriptions and self-descriptions in current use, for example – consumer, sufferer, service user, survivor, recipient, mad – is testimony to the uncertainties involved.

Most of the above terms, while familiar to mental health professionals, would not find easy recognition among non-professionals. On United Kingdom's streets currently, terms like 'mentally ill' and 'mental patient' would be more common and more easily understood. The description mad, repossessed and re-valued by some activists would be widely understood as a negative term seen by many as bordering on political incorrectness. But mental patient and ex-mental patient, characterisations from which many activists are seeking to escape, are likely to be viewed as realistic and acceptable by the majority of society.

The problem for most individuals whose distress is defined as 'mental illness' is that at one and the same time they are uncertain about who they have become and convinced that they are not who society thinks they are. Past centuries are studded with accounts of people whom society found mad protesting that they were misunderstood (Porter, 1987). In the last half-century such protests may have become more concerted but they are fundamentally the same. Today's mental patients (if we may characterise them as such) like their mad predecessors are struggling through confusion and uncertainty to achieve a positive evaluation for experiences that the majority in society (or at least, powerful individuals and institutions) are determined to confine within negative frameworks.

Becoming a mental patient is not an inevitable result of experiencing distress. Nor is it an instantaneous event. Rather it is the product of a process in which the interior and exterior reality of the individual is substantially and sometimes permanently changed. The way they think of themselves and the way others think of them is transformed negatively. They become someone different from whom they were before. At the same time they become different from most of society. A mental illness diagnosis and use of mental health services, although sometimes helpful in easing confusion and distress, effectively mark out the individual as a citizen of lesser value. This is confirmed by their arrival at the bottom of the pile – isolated, distrusted, largely unemployed and dependent on the welfare system.

Mental patients frequently find themselves on the margins of society and on the margins of non-personhood. Their alien-ness, their distance from ordinary people, is confirmed by widespread perceptions that they are irrational, incomprehensible, unpredictable, lacking in insight.

Their doubtful position on the human hierarchy is frequently revealed by penal and animalistic imagery in the popular press. They are 'discharged', 'released into the community'. They are 'detained' and 'caged'. In a fundamental sense they are seen as failed or failing human beings, a burden and a threat to others, violent, victims, incompetent, unpredictable, both wrong and in the wrong, second-class citizens if citizens at all, a nuisance, incapable, without credibility. Whatever their individual stories or potential futures they are bounded by society's deep and persistent prejudices about madness.

Faced with such an array of socially sanctioned and negative attributes, mental patients face a long, difficult journey to create and assert a more positive identity. While they may reject negative characterisations, these beliefs are so powerful and pervasive that it is difficult not to absorb them. They form a destructive accompaniment to all efforts at self-discovery, dictating mental patients' image of themselves and discouraging creative action towards change. If all people derive self-esteem through a positive orientation towards the good, as the philosopher Charles Taylor claims, mental patients, on the margins of personhood, are more disoriented than most (Taylor, 1989).

Possibilities for Change

Although traditional mental patient identities have a strong hold, recent developments within the mental health system carry promise of allowing mental patients more positive new identities. Closure of the large mental hospitals/asylums has de-stabilised mental health services and called into question some of the psychiatric certainties. In the first place, the mental patient has become at the least a community mental patient, living alongside other citizens rather than segregated behind the walls of inscrutable institutions. Perhaps from this unaccustomed vantage point individuals will be better able to pursue new roles and identities. Moreover, the hegemony of the medical model as a framework for understanding the mental patient experience has come under challenge from other professional groups within mental health services: psychologists, therapists, occupational therapists. The situation, both within and outside services, has become more fluid. There is argument within professional circles. The general public is less convinced that they have fully mastered who community mental patients really are and where they must fit into society. As Peter Barham and Robert Haywood have suggested, service users are moving away from mental patient-hood towards personhood and a more equal citizenship (Barham and Haywood, 1995). Society no longer sees them as entirely other, while still believing that they are essentially different. In times of uncertainty, it may become possible to construct new identities.

At the same time, post-war the United Kingdom has seen action by numerous disadvantaged groups to challenge their traditional role in society. Women, black and ethnic groups, gays, bisexuals and lesbians have all sought a revaluation of their social roles and worked to develop more positive identities. Alongside them, disabled people have taken collective action to challenge stereotyping and prejudice, resulting ultimately in the passing of anti-discrimination legislation (Campbell and Oliver, 1996). Such activity has not been lost on people with a mental illness diagnosis. Since the mid-1980s, action by this group has grown, mirroring to some extent the action of other oppressed groups. New perspectives, new activities, new understandings have begun to emerge. The mental patient can no longer be seen as merely a burden on society. The possibility of a contributory role must now be acknowledged.

The Status of the Mental Health Service User/Survivor Movement

If the status of mental health service users' identity has been complex, changing and ambiguous, there seem to be similar problems with understanding the nature of the mental health service users/survivors movement.

Even the question of whether there actually is a 'survivor movement' remains unclear. For example, in a major and well-received book published in 2000, focusing on 'overcoming discrimination and social exclusion', Liz Sayce, a major non-service user commentator on 'mental health' issues, referred to user – run projects, user and self-help groups, user-led services and user activism among mental health service users/survivors. Her book developed the idea of a 'disability inclusion' model as a way forward and made frequent reference to the disabled people's movement. There was also frequent mention of the 'mental health community'. But there was minimal reference to a survivor's movement. It is only in the last chapter that there was direct mention of it, with talk of the 'growing power of the user/survivor movement (Sayce, 2000: 245). The emphasis was much more on the disparate activities of mental health service users, their interactions with 'allies', the mental health system and other initiatives identified as progressive.

In contrast to this, in their critique of mental health policy and practice, Vicki Coppick and John Hopton made a clear and strong assertion. They argued that:

It has been the growing collective activities of mental health service users since the 1970s and 1980s which has been of crucial signifi- cance in recent times. The mental health users' movement, as with other civil rights movements developed out of a quest for self-deter- mination, coupled with a fundamental sense of injustice at the way in which medical psychiatry renders mental distress meaningless. It is informed by the principle that everyone has the right to be taken seriously and have their experiences recognised as meaningful. (Coppick and Hopton, 2000: 50-51)

When Coppick and Hopton asserted that:

Crucially (this principle of the users' movement) includes the right to own and define one's own distress and to have a decisive influ- ence in finding solutions to that distress. (2000: 51)

We come on to even more uncertain ground. Not everyone would agree with such certainty that there is a 'service users' movement; that it is a civil rights movement or what its principles are. It is unlikely that active mental health service users would be agreed about this, let alone outside commen- tators. Marian Barnes and Polly Shardlow, for example, comparing mental health service users' and disabled people's organisations and groups, dis- tinguished between the strategies of the former, which they saw as based on a consumerist approach and of the latter based on 'citizenship'. (Barnes and Shardlow, 1996).

A project has been undertaken focused on the mental health service user/survivor movement, but significantly it has been based in a large men- tal health charity, The Sainsbury Centre, rather than a service user/survivor controlled organisation. The formal information we have about 'the move- ment' is limited and it is difficult to generalise from it. We would argue that there is a mental health service user/survivor movement, but it is difficult to be dogmatic about it. There seems to be reluctance among mental health service users/survivors to impose or sign up to a rigid or single set of views or beliefs. We understand this view. It may be related to their long- term experience of being subjected involuntarily to just such rigid belief systems, imposed on them in the psychiatric system. So it is difficult to set out a series of clear values and principles as agreed and adopted by the movement. But there do seem to be a set of core values at the heart of it, which do seem to be held, either explicitly or implicitly, by most if not all service users/survivors who are actively involved. There seem to be some recurring stated and unstated principles and beliefs among mental health service users/survivors involved in their own organisations. These revolve around:

- People having the right to speak and act for themselves
- The idea that mental health service users are not inherently inferior or pathological
- The view that service users have a right to a say in what happens to them

It may be helpful to put this consideration of the mental health service users/survivors movement in the broader context of discussions about 'movements'. A number of social theorists identified the emergence in the late twentieth century of a wide range of groups, including those of environmentalists, minority groups and welfare recipients, which they conceived of as 'new social movements' (Touraine, 1981; Oliver, 1996). Characteristics associated by theorists with a new social movement include that:

- They remain on the margin of the political system
- They offer a critical evaluation of society
- They imply a society with different forms of valuation and distribution
- The issues which they raise transcend national boundaries.
  (Oliver, 1996: 157)

Some disabled commentators have described the disabled people's movement as such a new social movement (Oliver and Zarb, 1989; Davies, 1993). Others have seen the disabled people's movement as a liberatory movement. Tom Shakespeare, for example, has distinguished between post-materialist and liberation movements and argued that the disability movement belongs to the latter category (Oliver, 1996: 158). He has said that:

> Most of the struggles mentioned ... are about resource allocation; women, black people and disabled people are crucially concerned with their economic exploitation and poverty. (Shakespeare, 1993: 258)

Such a discussion has not yet taken place in relation to the mental health service users/survivors movement, although it could be argued that it features characteristics of both models of a movement.

What Progress has Been Made?

Incompetence is a commonly presumed characteristic of people with a mental illness diagnosis. Alongside violence it forms the most important basis of misunderstandings about this group. For most of the last two centuries it has been assumed that people with a mental illness, mental patients, the mad, were not only incapable of living in society and contributing but were also, in a permanent and fundamental way, unable to discern their best interests and act in pursuit of them. This perception helps explain why consent to treatment has only been a relatively recent issue of concern and points towards the most important reason why compulsory treatment for mental disorders has been justified (Fennell, 1996). Although it is actually possible to detain and treat people with a mental illness diagnosis without their consent even when they have decision-making capacity, the popular justification for the use of compulsion is that 'mental patients don't know what's good for them anyway.' Attributions of incompetence and the accompanying loss of credibility are damaging assaults on identity.

Service user/survivor action has done a good deal to establish the competence of people with mental distress. Hundreds of independent local action groups now exist, run entirely by activists, not only involved in consultations about the design and monitoring of services, but also often running services themselves. Service users/survivors are also involved in the education and training of mental health professionals and in research. For a minority, but a growing minority, there is the possibility of taking an active role in relation to the mental health system. For service users/survivors as a whole, there are now more positive models of who they could become.

Nevertheless, people with a mental illness diagnosis remain compromised by the fact that they have less freedom, less control over their physical integrity than the majority in society. They are likely to feel differently about themselves because designated agents of society can intervene in their lives in such major ways. Their legal status marks them out as second-class citizens. Moreover, there is every indication that government will, in the near future, be extending their liability to compulsion into community settings (DOH, 2002). In this regard, service user/survivor action has not proved successful.

If legal discrimination of this kind has negative impacts, so too does the dismissal of major aspects of the experience of mental distress. This is particularly true of whole areas of what in traditional models would be called the psychotic experience.

Mental health workers, led by psychiatrists, will very often think of psychotic behaviour and perceptions as primarily symptoms of illness. They will dismiss the content of psychosis as meaningless or of only negative value. Such a response has a damaging effect on identity, particularly as many, although finding such experiences problematic, have a desire to understand them and integrate them into their lives.

Debate about the true nature and value of psychosis has become an important aspect of service user/survivor action. The Hearing Voices Network has been particularly important in questioning psychiatric understandings of key phenomena like hallucinations and delusions and in proposing coping mechanisms that do not rely predominantly on anti-psychotic medication (James, 2001). At the same time, the National Self Harm Network has worked with some success for the re-valuation and more sensitive understanding of self-injury (Dace et al., 1998). These initiatives are examples of the general desire of people with a mental illness diagnosis to decide for themselves what their lives are about and to resist professional understandings and interventions that seem insensitive to the integrity of the person. They are part of a broader challenge to the capture of the experience of mental distress within negative frameworks.

The Diversity of the Service User/Survivor Movement

Action by current and former mental patients is extensive and diverse, ranging from service provision through research to artistic activities. The widespread description of such actions as the work of the "service user/survivor" movement itself reveals a disparity at the heart of action. Although they are often used simultaneously and are not always intended to have profound and contrasting meanings, service user and survivor are not the same term. At the very least, the term service user is neutral about the mental patient experience whereas the term survivor is taking a definite and critical position. Some commentators, building on this difference, have claimed that self-described service users are reformist while survivors are radical, even seeking the overthrow of a mental health service dominated by psychiatry. Whatever the truth of such a conclusion, it is evident that service user/survivor activists may have different priorities.

Although action in the 1970s had a strong separatist bias, activity within the service user/survivor movement since the mid-1980s has been predominantly collaborative. At the time when significant numbers of independent action groups were beginning to be formed, mental health services were overtaken by a consumerist ideology, intended to place the consumer or service user at the centre of change. Mental health professionals, particularly managers, wanted to talk to, and, in favourable circumstances, to listen to the people using services. Independent action groups were one source of such people. The invitations to professionally defined forums went out, service users went in and to a great extent have stayed in ever since. As a result service user/survivor activists have often found it difficult to set and stay in control of their own agendas.

Partnership or Independence?

As we have already indicated, there are many strands of difference within the mental health service user/survivor movement. But this strand along lines of separatism and collaboration is one which seems particularly important and which it is likely to be particularly helpful to consider more carefully. It can be expressed and be seen to manifest itself in a range of ways; for example in distinctions between activities based on:

- Independent action and partnership approaches
- Reactive and proactive strategies
- Managerialist/consumerist and democratic/liberatory approaches to involvement

All these are interrelated. They raise fundamental questions for service users/survivors (and for us here) about:

- Whose agenda?
- Whose initiatives?
- Whose approaches to participation service users/survivors are getting drawn into?

There has been a considerable emphasis on partnership approaches to involvement in the context of mental health policy and practice. This has related to mental health agencies in both the health and social care fields. Most of the funding available to service users/survivors and their organisations has been to support such service related involvement, rather than for service users to get together to establish their own independent initiatives and activities. As a result, there has been a strong tendency for agendas to be set by the service system/participation providers, with service users/survivors and their organisations having to struggle to push these in the direction of their own values, priorities, strategies and goals. Such an approach to participation has also been associated with a particular focus on work relating to the psychiatric service system, rather than addressing broader issues facing service users, for example, relating to employment, income, welfare benefits, education, recreation, relationships and so on.

The model of participation, which has predominantly underpinned developments in the field of mental health, has been a managerialist/consumerist one. This originates with the state and service system, is focused on the needs and interests of the service system and is primarily concerned with gathering 'user views' and data to inform (and legitimate) the activities and decision-making of existing power holders. Thus the reality is not as Barnes and Shardlow have suggested that service users/survivors have necessarily internalised a consumerist model of involvement, but rather that that is mostly what is on offer.

This has extended beyond receiving and responding to requests to 'get involved' from the service system. These have greatly increased in recent years as New Labour governments have emphasised partnership, participation and empowerment in public policy, particularly in health and social care. It relates significantly also to where key service user/survivor developmental activities are located and who controls them. Many of the major activities associated with the service user/survivor movement are located in non-user controlled organisations. Thus projects concerned with collecting the historical testimony of survivors, with user controlled services, the history of the service user/survivor movement and discrimination against mental health service users have all been based in non-user/survivor controlled organisations. The same has been true of research and knowledge production and development. The biggest and best funded user-led and user controlled research projects have all been based in non-user/survivor controlled organisations. This includes organisations primarily based on a medical model of madness and distress like the Sainsbury Centre for Mental Health, the Institute of Psychiatry and the Mental Health Foundation. This is not to say that there have not sometimes been 'user controlled initiatives' within such traditional organisations. However predictably this can lead to tensions and problems about where decision-making authority actually lies, when problems or conflicts of interests develop, as they can be expected to.

This is in sharp contrast to developments in the disabled people's movement, where comparable activities and research have all been initiated and controlled by disabled people and their own organisations. The emphasis in the disabled people's movement has been on 'doing their own things'. Similarly the disabled people's movement has maintained a much stronger focus on developments outside the narrow disability service system – innovating and initiating rather than responding. This was reflected in its early prioritising of broader issues affecting the lives of disabled people. This has been embodied in its campaigning for anti-discrimination legislation to secure disabled people's human and civil rights, for freedom of information legislation and to secure independent funding for disabled people's organisations. Instead of focusing its activities on the existing service system, it instead pioneered and developed alternative approaches based on the idea of independent living. Here the most conspicuous development has been 'direct payments', which are now widely available by law to disabled people and enable them to select and control their own self-run personal support schemes and arrangements (Campbell and Oliver, 1996; Oliver, 1996; Charlton, 2000).

This tendency for mental health service users/survivors to do things 'in partnership' and in non-user controlled organisations raises a basic question. Does it actually matter? There are likely to be different views about this, but the question does at least demand discussion. In our view there are likely to be problems at a range of levels for a movement if key activities are located in organisations and settings outside its control. There are the obvious ones we have already outlined relating to how far it is able to decide what is done and set its own agenda. But there is also the issue of this approach perpetuating the symbolic, if not actual dependence of service users/survivors as a collectivity, which they experience individually. What does it say of us as service users/survivors that we have to rely on others and their organisations? Will this dependence help or hinder us in efforts to escape the medical segregation which is frequently imposed on service users/survivors and the restricted focus on 'mental health' when other much broader issues also impact powerfully on our lives? We should also not forget the pressures that such an approach imposes on individual service users/survivors who are involved. Working with traditional (often medically based) organisations is often personally stressful, difficult and disempowering.

At the same time, it is possible to see why it might be that service users/survivors have been pressured into this way of working. Since conventional understanding of them is based on assumptions about pathologies, deficiencies and unreliability in their intellects, minds and brains (as opposed to physical limitations), it is not surprising if they have had more difficulty getting support to do things 'on their own' as they undoubtedly have done. It has been much easier for service users to get jobs, grants and other funding in association with traditional non-user controlled organisations than 'on their own'. This has been a real if as yet inadequately discussed and researched constraint operating upon service user/survivor activists.

Issues of Philosophy

There is one other important difference between the disabled people's and mental health service users/survivors movement that may have particular relevance here. One of the early acts of disability activists who went on to found the disabled people's movement in the UK was to develop their own clear philosophical and theoretical position. This was based on a social approach to or model of disability (Campbell and Oliver, 1996). Previous medicalised individual models of disability were rejected as part of the structures of oppression and discrimination experienced by disabled people. What characterises the social model is that it distinguishes between impairment; the perceived lack of or loss of function of a limb or sense and disability; the discriminatory and oppressive societal response to impairment. The UK disabled people's movement effectively started with the social model of disability and based their strategy and objectives on it. In contrast, the service users/survivors movement has never developed or agreed its own philosophy or model of madness and distress. There has been no unifying model or philosophy underpinning it. This may reflect, as we have already suggested, a reluctance to sign up to any kind of orthodoxy. But it has also tended to mean that traditional medicalised individual models of madness and distress, based on a 'mental illness' model are still internalised and accepted by many members of the movement, often disguised by the use of terms like 'mental health' and 'mental health problems' and that the movement cannot necessarily be said to have a coherent philosophical base. In our view this has the potential to create difficulties when trying to determine and agree effectively the values, aims and objectives of the movement.

Partnership or Independence: a Case Study

The issue of the extension of compulsory 'treatment' beyond the hospital provides a helpful case study for considering the situation of the service users/survivors movement and the implications of approaches based on partnership and independence. The 2002 Mental Health Act White Paper, which included far-reaching provisions for compulsion, (including 'compulsory treatment orders' and pre-emptive custody for people identified as having 'severe personality disorder') resulted in an unprecedented alliance of organisations, including service users, advocacy, charitable, trade union, church and professional organisations, united in opposition to the extension of compulsory powers. The Royal College of Psychiatrists was in common opposition with radical local survivor's organisations. There has however been a sense for some time among some service users/survivors, that this Alliance has only been able to unite on the basis of the lowest common denominator of what could be agreed rather than on the basis of proposals consistent with the rights and interests of mental health service users/survivors. Mental Health Alliance, for example, is only committed to 'a reduction in the use of compulsory powers', not their withdrawal (Mental Health Alliance, 2002). In September 2002, the Alliance cancelled a march against the Draft Mental Health Bill because of concerns about negative public reaction following the high profile murder of two young girls in Soham. There was an angry response to this from many survivor activists and they reorganised a march as the No Force Campaign. Several hundred people took part and there was no negative response (GLAD, 2002).

Mad Pride, the radical grouping of survivors that has adopted a much more independent and sometimes separatist position, has highlighted the weaknesses of such an alliance. Pete Shaughnessy, one of its founders, who sadly died in December 2002, wrote:

> We think that (mental health charities) are too soft and trying to pander to the Government and middle England ... to show a united front we have limited our public attacks on Sane, and saying Mind are a mixed bunch. (Shaughnessy, 2002)

An obituary for Pete spelled out the position that he and Mad Pride adopted:

> Pete saw mental health ... as both the great civil rights issue of the twenty first century and the new rock 'n' roll. Mad, he argued, should not mean bad. People with mental health problems should be treated with dignity and respect and free from draconian laws. (Hart and Olden, 2002)

For many activist service users/survivors, the fear is that a revised Mental Health Bill will ultimately go to parliament with modified (but for them still unacceptable) proposals for compulsion, which will be accepted by the broader alliance, leaving service users/survivors politically isolated and unsupported.

Links with Disability: New Possibilities

In recent years, particularly the last two or three years, there has been a growing interest among mental health service users/survivors in the activities of disabled people and the disabled people's movement (Beresford, 2000; Beresford, Harrison and Wilson, 2002). This interest has been reciprocated and traditional barriers, mostly related to each group's concerns about being stigmatised by the identity associated with the other, have begun to be broken down. As a result contacts between mental health service users/survivors and disabled people and their different organisations have increased; there has been greater recognition of overlaps and similarities (as well as differences) between them and common concerns have increasingly been identified. There has also been a growing consciousness of the relevance of developments relating to disabled people for service users/survivors. This includes interest in the social model of disability and also the creation of the Disability Rights Commission, the extension of the Disability Discrimination Act, eligibility to 'passport' disability benefits and to 'direct payments'. The latter are beginning to offer service users/survivors the prospect of developing individual (and collective) support arrangements based on a social rather than a medical model, breaking out of traditional psychiatric services and thinking. The opportunities that this increased awareness of the broader disability movement and disability policy offers are likely to be of increasing significance to a growing number of mental health service users/survivors, challenging traditional professional, service and identity boundaries.

Prospects for the Future

There are grounds for some optimism about both the prospects of the service users/survivors movement and the capacity that service users/survivors have to transform their identity. It can be argued that much current action by mental health service users/survivors is not overtly aimed at achieving positive changes in identity but that all action tends towards this effect. While activists may ostensibly be discussing the details of improvements to mental health services, their very presence in the committee rooms challenges old prejudices and puts forward new roles. Mental health workers are forced to reconsider long-established ideas about mental patients' incompetence and lack of credibility. Through working together in relationships not entirely bounded by clinical or therapeutic considerations, there is a chance that the expertise of service user/survivor activists and, by extension, of mental patients as a whole will be recognised. Each appearance by an activist in a consultative process can be said to erode the negative frameworks within which service users/survivors usually operate and puts forward new role models. Such, at any rate, must be the hope.

However, in the wider society outside mental health services, it must be more doubtful whether the mere presence of service user/survivor activists in unaccustomed roles has a great effect. Whereas mental health professionals have frequent and often close contacts with activists, most people have little or no (conscious) contact with people who are using mental health services and remain almost completely ignorant of new actions that are being taken. They have no opportunity to see the more positive roles activists are starting to adopt and have little to set against the overwhelmingly negative characterisations implicit in mental patient status. This situation is largely confirmed by the mass media, which clings tenaciously to traditional scripts about madness, emphasising the essential strangeness of the experience of mental illness and the threat mental patients pose to the population in general. In such circumstances, the increasing appearance of personal testimony in coverage of mental health issues may not be sufficient to challenge long-nurtured stereotypes.

Service user/survivor action calls into question, directly or implicitly, common approaches to difference. Activists are aiming at a proper and positive approach to difference that does not deny its existence but ascribes it value (Craine, 1998). People who experience mental distress are a diverse grouping before their problems are categorised as mental illness. This diversity should be recognised to survive both diagnosis and service use. At the same time, while activists assert that in many ways people with a mental illness diagnosis are very similar to people without one (except as relates to the experience following from diagnosis), they are also increasingly confident in putting forward the proposition that this group has particular positive qualities as a result of, rather than despite, their problematic experience. The unenviable predicament of the community mental patient lies not in difference but in society's response to difference and imposition of divisions in response to its identification of it. Here may lay the fundamental challenge over identity for the future.

References

Barham, P. and Hayward, R. (1995) *Relocating Madness: From the Mental Patient to the Person* (London: Free Association Books).

Barnes, M., Harrison, S., Mort, M. and Shardlow, P. (1999) *Unequal Partners: User Groups and Community Care* (Bristol: The Policy Press).

Barnes, M. and Shardlow, P. (1996) 'Effective Consumers and Active Citizens: Strategies for Users' Influence on Service and Beyond', *Research, Policy and Planning*, vol. 14:1; 3–38.

Beresford, P., Harrison, C. and Wilson, A. (2002) 'Mental Health Service Users and Disability: Implications for Future Strategies, *Policy and Politics*, vol. 30:3; 387–6.

Beresford, P. (2000) 'What have Madness and Psychiatric System Survivors got to do with Disability and Disability Studies? Current Issues', *Disability and Society*, vol. 15:1; 167–72.

Campbell, J. and Oliver, M. (1996) *Disability Politics: Understanding Our Past, Changing Our Future* (Basingstoke: Macmillan).

Campbell, P. (1999) *The Service User/Survivor Movement, This is Madness: A Critical Look at Psychiatry and the Future of Mental Health Services* (Ross-on-Wye: PCCS Books).

Charlton, J.I. (2000) *Nothing About Us Without Us: Disability, Oppression and Empowerment* (Berkeley: University of California Press).

Coppick, V. and Hopton, J. (2000) *Critical Perspectives on Mental Health* (London: Routledge).

Craine, S. (1998) *Shrink Resistant: The Survivor Movement and the Survivor Perspective* (US Network Working Papers: Exchange and Change).

Dace, E., Faulkner, A., Frost, M., Parker, K., Pembroke, L. and Smith, A. (1998) *The 'Hurt Yourself Less' Workbook* (London: National Self-Harm Network).

Fennell, P. (1996) *Treatment Without Consent: Law, Psychiatry and the Treatment of Mentally Disordered People since 1885* (London: Routledge).

Department of Health (2002) *Mental Health Bill* (London: The Stationery Office).

GLAD (2002) *Common Agenda Newsletter* (London: Greater London Action on Disability, October).

Hart, S. and Olden, M. (2003) 'Radical Mad Pride Pioneer Mourned, Obituary for Pete Shaughnessy, *Big Issue*, No. 521; 5. 6–12 January 2003.

James, A. (2001) *Raising Our Voices: An Account of the Hearing Voices Movement* (Gloucester: Handsell Publications).

Mental Health Alliance, (2002) *Rights Not Compulsion, Mental Health Alliance Lobby of Parliament 23 October*, leaflet (London: Mental Health Alliance).

Oliver, M. (1996) *Understanding Disability: From Theory to Practice* (Basingstoke: Macmillan).

Porter, R. (1987) *A Social History of Madness* (London: Weidenfeld and Nicolson).

Sayce, L. (2000) *From Psychiatric Patient to Citizen: Overcoming Discrimination and Social Exclusion* (Basingstoke: Macmillan).

Pithouse, A. and Williamson, H. (eds) (1997) *Engaging the User in Welfare Services* (Birmingham: Venture Press).

Shaughnessy, P. (2002) 'On Community Treatment Orders (CTOs) and Injustice', quoted in *S.U.N. Newsletter,* December, Manchester, Survivors' United Network; 2.

Taylor, C. (1989) *Sources of the Self* (Cambridge: Cambridge University Press).

INDEX

Twenty feet, fifteen. We barked at each other, and I thought I should shoot, because it was getting too close, and then I thought about what would happen if I did: a "shooting team" would respond and investigate as if I was a perp; Internal Affairs would interrogate me, PK, and the rest of the team for hours. The bosses would look at PK and say, *Escaped prisoners, injured perp, and now a shooting, is this guy in control out there?* I waited and shouted again: *"Get your fucking dog off this fucking roof!"*

The dog stopped, and then a man called it from the darkness inside the stairwell. It growled, then turned around and went inside. I sat down and rested for a minute before leaving. As I passed the dealers' apartment on the second floor, the dog began to bark again.

I was glad I hadn't shot, but I was troubled by how the white noise of politics had impinged on my thoughts for the four or five seconds of the confrontation. When you make a decision about self-defense, the only thing that should concern you is self-defense—tactics and cover, the possibilities and necessities of threat and response. The dog could well have knocked me over, off the roof. I was not eager to shoot, but if I was obliged to—with intended consequences or unintended ones—there would be a lot of people asking questions, but only my partners and PK would ask, "Are you okay?"

I shook it off, and we set up another OP a few blocks away. Nothing had happened, after all, and I put it aside and went back to work. The threats we faced were real—PK had been shot by a perp. That moment remained with me, and it would weigh in some manner in the decisions I made each day—as it did for John, and PK, and Tony, Stix, Orville, Sammy, and Alicia—not just to shoot or not shoot, but how hard to push. Time would tell the virtue of our choices, and at least we still had time.

So we believed, as a week passed, and another, until we drove up to the Four-Six one afternoon to set up. We were cruising through the blocks—University, Tremont, Popham, Andrews—when we received the summons over the air to return to the precinct, forthwith. DI Cavanagh had retired, and we had a new captain. PK met with him in his office, for fifteen or twenty minutes. We stood in the driveway at the back of the precinct, apart by ourselves, wondering what nonsense was afoot. We were curious, I remember, but not especially concerned. Were we arguing about something? Maybe I don't remember what we were talking about, or how we felt, but I won't forget the sight of PK as he came out of the precinct. His face had fallen, he was pale and stunned. He took us aside.

"I'm out of the unit," he said, and he went on to explain, haltingly, that the new captain told him that relatives of John's perp, who was a homeless junkie, had hired a lawyer. Though the perp didn't remember being arrested, and had in fact fractured his skull in a car accident, some time before, he remained in the hospital. The lawyer called the *Daily News,* announcing that he was representing the victim in the "latest police-brutality case in the Bronx." The *News* called Headquarters for comment, and the comment was "What are you talking about?" The Job does not like to be surprised; Chief Anemone, the Chief of the Department, was said to be furious. An Interim Order had been issued the year before, after the Louima case, which said that if a perp is "seriously injured" during an arrest, the duty captain has to be notified. If necessary, a crime scene will be set up and the matter investigated immediately, to protect the Job from subsequent litigation. We didn't know that, and PK didn't—I believe the order had been issued around the time he was burying his son Paulie, and Interim Orders fell by the wayside.

I don't remember exactly what we said—*"Bullshit!" "No, it can't be!" "That's crazy!" "That's wrong! . . ."* I think I began to protest and scheme—I'd call Mullen, or—better yet—Chief Anemone, I'd go right into his office to tell him what was going on. PK shook his head, stricken, knowing it was done. I thought I'd never seen a sadder face, until I looked over at John. Oh, laddo . . . He said nothing, and then he walked away. I didn't see him for days, and he wouldn't answer the phone. After the futility of it all began to sink in for the rest of us, we all shook hands, and then we went home, too.

EIGHT

For the NYPD, the era that followed the Knapp Commission was as the Civil War was for the United States, bloody but necessary, proudly defining but remembered without joy. The Knapp Commission may have achieved relatively little, on its own terms, and there are not only institutions but individuals who can claim to have done more concrete good. But the Commission took place in an age of extraordinary change, and during its tenure it was the dominant fact with which all the other forces reckoned. Though cops have certainly done wrong since, singly and in groups, even the most bitter critics of the NYPD would concede that the transformation has been radical and enduring. I have seen well over a thousand people arrested, and have witnessed only one offer of a bribe. It may be too much to wish that such reforms could have come more cheaply than they did, with less sacrifice of what was good as well as what was not. The NYPD was denounced not merely for what crooked cops did, or what other cops knew, but what still other cops should have known, and it tore through them all like an accusation of child abuse, too terrible to believe and too important to ignore. Whether innocent or guilty, everyone that it touched was stained.

One of the more bitter paradoxes of the Knapp Commission was that afterward, the NYPD began to truly deserve the respect that was lost to it, it seemed, forever. The epidemic of gambling graft that had bedeviled the police since the beginning ended with Knapp. While the facts of the *Times* story were appalling but not altogether unfamiliar, the theory—that the scandal was in the coverup more than the crime—propelled a great scoop into a new paradigm of investigative journalism. The adversarial posture became a reflex: for the *Times,* the word "police" became primarily an adjective used to modify the noun "corruption" or, later, "brutality"; they got their story thirty years ago, and they've stuck with it ever since. No longer would cops get the benefit of the doubt.

The Knapp Commission might have died on the vine, but for a variety of political alignments and odd chances that were plotted so perfectly as to strain credulity. Mayor Lindsay, who, in the columnist Jack Newfield's phrase, "gave good intentions a bad name," kept a degree of racial peace in the city by sheer bribery. Whoever shouted loudest got a meeting, and often a check; millions of dollars were funneled to self-proclaimed "community activists" whose community ties were most evident in their criminal records; a city job was provided to a man recently released from prison for plotting to blow up the Statue of Liberty. Lindsay had run as a Republican for his first term as mayor and as an independent for his second, and he was gearing up for a presidential run, in 1972, as a Democrat. President Nixon had liked him less in each incarnation: long hostile to the liberal, Eastern wing of the Republican Party, Nixon saw Lindsay shift from an internal rival to an outright opponent. If the Knapp Commission was going to produce evidence that New York City under the Lindsay Administration was a cesspool, it deserved firm federal support.

For six months, the Knapp investigators had virtually nothing—what Durk knew was old, and rarely firsthand, while Serpico was a pariah—until one winter night when they stumbled on eight uniformed cops stealing meat from a warehouse. Whether it was burglary or a theft staged for insurance fraud, the wide-open indifference of the cops was startling to the investigators. The warehouse was owned by none other than James Reardon, ex-cop and ex-con, and likely an acquaintance of my great-grandfather. Reardon was the one-time partner of Harry Gross, the bookie who had brought down the mayoralty of William O'Dwyer. Reardon also wrote an engagingly novelized memoir, *The Sweet Life of Jimmy Riley,* which presents an unusual defense of the life of a cop on the take: *Don't knock it till you've tried it.*

It got worse: a few months later, the law of unintended consequences was bent, if not broken, when the author of *The French Connection* supplied the

Knapp Commission with its star witness. As his next literary endeavor, Robin Moore had chosen the story of Xaviera Hollander, a Dutch prostitute working in midtown, which would be entitled *The Happy Hooker*. Hollander had a problem with getting arrested; it seemed to happen all the time, no matter who she paid, and at least one of the men who took money from her turned out not to be a police officer at all. She decided to remedy the situation in a two-pronged strategy: first, on the advice of a lawyer, she contacted a reliably dirty cop named William Phillips to settle things on a more permanent basis. Second, she had her apartment wired by one Teddy Ratnoff, an otherwise dubious character who was a "genius at electronic listening devices," whom she met through Moore. Hollander claimed that Moore urged her to bug the place to pick up conversations for purposes of "authenticity," while Moore, at least as plausibly, said she hoped to blackmail influential johns into protecting her. Ratnoff was also trying to convince the Knapp Commission to use his equipment, and when he caught Phillips in a shakedown, he had a deal. Soon, Phillips did, too. "You can't make this stuff up," as they say, though plainly, some people did.

Whenever a bad cop is collared, there is a duel of clichés: is he the rotten apple, or the tip of the iceberg? The rottenest apples always work hard on the iceberg story, that they are random samples rather than standouts. When Phillips was taken in by the investigators, he flipped immediately—there was no conscience to wrestle with. As far as bad cops go, Phillips was the real thing—he called his uniform "the money suit," and he even tried to bribe the Knapp investigators. He was dirty early on, with his whole heart and both hands. His own term for his type—which he said was common usage, and later became so—was that he was a "meat-eater," a cop who aggressively pursued a score, rather than a "grass-eater," who took what came his way. In many ways, his profile was iceberg-ish: his father, whom he hated, was also a crooked cop, and his career, which had taken him from patrol to the Squad and back to patrol, was an encyclopedia of corruption. But he was also apple-ish, in that he was a solitary operator who didn't even socialize with other cops, and he had already been flopped from the Squad back to patrol on the slimmest of pretexts, which suggested that he was marked as a problem long before he was caught outright.

When the Knapp Commission televised its hearings, Phillips was the star witness. He told about what he did on patrol, shaking down tow-truck companies for car accidents, funeral homes for DOAs, bars to quash brawls, construction sites for code violations, drivers for everything. As a detective, he'd hit up complainants for their property and perps for their freedom. He made a profound impression, not least on a detective who thought he resembled the face in a sketch for a double homicide, also in a brothel, not far from Hollander's. Phillips was tried and convicted of both murders and sent to prison for life. The prosecution of Phillips was the source of great conflict between the Manhattan DA, Frank Hogan, and Knapp, and whether it proved or impeached the entire thesis of what was rotten in the NYPD, as a last-act twist, it was hard to beat.

Honest cops felt that the Knapp Commission was a hatchet job, long on sound bites and short on substance. They had a point, in that the Commission took credit for the indictment of a mere fourteen cops, not counting Phillips, of course. Citywide, there were sixty-two cops indicted in 1971, which was certainly a result of the scandals, though in 1968—ages, it seemed, before Serpico, Knapp, and the rest—there were twenty-nine. For old-timers like Frank Hogan, an icon in the criminal justice system who had succeeded the legendary racket-buster Thomas Dewey thirty years before, this kind of separate and temporary commission was regarded as a publicity stunt; for newcomers like Commissioner Patrick Murphy, who was largely kept out of the loop, it was a minefield. Knapp himself later said that he expected Murphy would—and should—ask them to disband, though the request never came. But for Murphy, who in his own words "based his program on yesterday's headlines," the additional media pressure helped steer his course.

For New York City in 1970, Patrick Murphy was the perfect commissioner, a "law-and-order liberal." He was from a cop family—one of eight children, where the boys became cops, the girls nuns—and he was the father of eight children himself. He had risen through the ranks of the NYPD, and then taken jobs in Syracuse, Washington, and Detroit. In Washington, after the King assassination, he ordered cops not to shoot looters, and there was little bloodshed. In Detroit, he instituted a firearms-discharge review policy, in which every shot fired by a cop had to be examined by every rank through the Commissioner; police shootings dropped precipitously. According to Robert Daley, his Deputy Commissioner of Public Information, he had no friends, no interests, and no ability to make small talk. In his first career with the NYPD, Murphy had spent two years on patrol before assignments in ESU, Headquarters, and the Academy. As a street cop, he was a rookie, but in time, Daley came to believe, Murphy didn't even care much about cops or crime, but rather management and public relations.

Under Murphy, there was an emphasis on local command, an early version of crime analysis, with a "Precinct Planning Sergeant" working on pin maps; there was computerization, and other technological advances; there were Anti-Crime Units in each precinct, and later a citywide Street Crime Unit, in which plainclothes cops and undercovers were deployed against mugging and violent crime, for the first time, rather than just against gambling and narcotics. These cops, who were about 5 percent of the Department, made almost a third of its arrests. As for internal reform, there was a purge at One Police Plaza: the chiefs were summoned to a conference, in which they found charts with their ages and longevity of service, and they were obliged to fill out a financial questionnaire. Responsibility for anti-corruption efforts was delegated to field commanders: if a scandal broke in their precinct or division, they fell on the sword. Instead of evaluating cops for their arrest records, Murphy looked at their conviction rates, and he flopped hundreds of plainclothesmen from Vice and Narcotics back to the bag. Ultimately, he stopped gambling enforcement almost altogether.

Despite these improvements, Murphy was not a friend to most cops, good, bad, or indifferent. Cops who knew there were grave problems in the Department but were nonetheless proud of what they did were a little stunned to hear him refer to the Job as "this monster . . . with all its pockets of power, its traditions, its mythology, its cynicism." Earnest discussions were conducted in Headquarters as to whether precinct Christmas parties should be banned entirely, or allowed with special permission as long as all receipts were submitted. (The Headquarters party went on as planned, of course.) In public statements, denunciations of corruption had been traditionally accompanied by some expression of support for the rest of the troops, a rote reminder that most cops worked hard and deserved respect; such words were often left unsaid by Murphy. The Job was getting harder: in 1970, major crimes rose more than 12 percent, and cops would make over a quarter of a million arrests that year. They were getting kicked more, bit more, and shot more—forty-five cops were shot and seven were killed in 1970, and another ten would die before the end of Murphy's first year in office. In the street, rich white kids and poor black kids shouted "Pig!" in cops' faces; the headlines proclaimed that they were thieves; and the boss didn't seem to disagree.

All the usual kinds of murders were up—bar fights, robberies, drug deals—but there was a new kind of homicide taking place, more and more often, in Harlem and elsewhere, that had cops terrified not only because they were the victims, but also because a lot of people refused to admit it was happening at all. A splinter group of the Black Panther Party called the Black Liberation Army was taking out cops. In April of 1971, the Panthers themselves had wounded two cops in a shootout in Harlem, as an epic conspiracy case against thirteen of their group was winding down into farce. It had been the longest and most expensive trial in state history, and the outcome depended chiefly on the testimony of two black undercover cops. The jury took minutes to acquit the defendants of plotting to blow things up all over town. The prosecution must have been on to something, though: during the trial, the judge's house was firebombed, and almost a week after the verdict, in May, two cops assigned to stand guard at District Attorney Frank Hogan's apartment house on Riverside Drive were cut down by machine-gun fire.

Two nights later, two cops responded to an Aided case in the Polo Grounds projects in Harlem. One cop, Joseph Piagentini, was white, and his partner, Waverly Jones, was black, and as they were returning to their car, they were followed by two young men. Jones was shot three times in the back and once in the back of the head, and died instantly. After Piagentini went down, the perps flipped both cops over, took their guns, and fired at Piagentini over and over as he tried to swat away the bullets. He was hit thirteen times and died on the way to the hospital. For the next cop killing, there was no political motive—it was in Brownsville, when a lunatic stepped out of an alley and nearly decapitated a cop with a butcher knife—and so too for the one after that, when a cop ran into three armed junkies holding up a candy store. No one knows what happened with the next one, a detective sergeant found in his car by the side of the Belt Parkway in Brooklyn, shot on either side of his head.

As it happened, the BLA hit men had moved west for the summer. In San Francisco, Waverly Jones's pistol was recovered after two men were arrested for shooting at a cop with a machine gun, which fortunately jammed. The next day, three men walked into a precinct and shot the desk officer dead and wounded a clerk. It was learned that these events were the second and third installments of a four-day assault on San Francisco cops—the first, a bazooka attack on a precinct, was a failure because the missile didn't work, while the last, another double assassination of black and white cop partners, was called off for unknown reasons. In the winter, however, the group returned its attentions to New York.

In January, a cop who stopped a car for running a red light was shot clean through with automatic-weapons fire; a day later, a cop was stabbed in the chest as he sat in his squad car. Three days after that, another pair of partners, black and white, named Greg Foster and Rocco Laurie, were walking up-town on Avenue B, near 11th Street, when they passed three men headed in the opposite direction. The three men turned, and one shouted "Shoot them in the balls!" and then opened fire. Laurie was shot six times, three times in the back, twice in the groin, once through his penis. Foster was shot three times in the back and once in the back of the head; then they shot his eyes out with three more rounds. They took the dead cops' guns, and two of them ran away immediately, while the third did a dance in the street. Murphy was in-clined against making any statement about the BLA, though the group sent a letter to a wire service claiming credit.

Within the upper echelons of the Police Department, there was deep skep-ticism of the idea of a conspiracy, and outright opposition to making such a belief public; regardless of its reputation for being crustily reactionary, Head-quarters is acutely sensitive to the political winds, which at this point were blowing hopefully toward the White House. Lindsay's proudest claim was that during his administration, there had been no riots in New York, though through his work on the Kerner Commission, he had defined "riot" as any disturbance larger than those that had happened under his watch. It was in this climate of mistrust and expediency that Daley made public the facts of the case as they were known. The Mayor's Office was furious—for them, in Daley's view, "two dead cops was preferable to Harlem in flames." Two days later, the *Times* received an anonymous call that a cop would be killed at eight the next morning. It proved true, almost: a cop driving alone in his radio car was hailed by a man who called him over to the curb and stabbed him. A week later, two more cops in St. Louis were shot with Laurie's gun.

One spring morning in 1972, in the Two-Five precinct in Harlem, cops called a "10-13," for an officer in need of assistance. The legitimate 10-13 had followed a false one, phoned in to 911 by a man claiming to be a "Detective Thomas," on the second floor of 102 West 116th Street. When Patrolmen Phillip Cardillo and Vito Navarra arrived, they saw that it was a mosque of the Nation of Islam, which was led by Louis Farrakhan. Although there had been a spate of false 10-13 calls by the BLA to draw cops into ambush, they went inside, where they heard scuffling upstairs on the second floor. Navarra ran up first, where he was met by at least fifteen men, but his retreat was cut off by more men downstairs, who were fighting Cardillo and shut the door. Cardillo was shot. Very quickly, there were more than a thousand people on the block; bottles and bricks rained from the rooftops; a police car was turned over and set on fire; and white reporters were doused with lighter fluid and ignited. Two members of the Nation of Islam were taken into custody, and there was some preliminary collection of evidence before the police acceded to Farrakhan's demand that all white cops be removed from the scene. At the hospital, where the Mayor and the Commissioner had gone to see the mortally wounded cop, Daley remarked that the disturbance was "close to a riot." It was the wrong word for Lindsay: "Riot? What do you mean, riot? There can't be any riot. There won't be any riot. It never came close to being a riot. How can you say such a thing?"

Though Cardillo was not expected to live, he lingered on for a week. On the advice of Deputy Commissioner Ben Ward, the police made no statement whatsoever throughout that time, a silence which seemed to support Farrakhan's claims that it was a reckless, racist, and premeditated assault on a house of worship. Ward was the highest-ranking black member of the Department—he later became Police Commissioner under Mayor Ed Koch—and as such he was acutely sensitive to a crisis in Harlem. He had also spent years in the trial room, dealing with cops accused of corruption and brutality, which may have affected his views. But he was also a lawyer, which made his insistence that it was illegal for the cops to enter the mosque simply bizarre. When Cardillo died, Murphy didn't go to the hospital, claiming he wasn't feeling well; then he flew to Europe for a conference the next morning. A brief statement was released, saying that Cardillo had died from a gunshot wound after responding in uniform to a call for assistance which later proved unfounded. The Mayor missed the funeral as well, campaigning in Florida. Officially, the Department refused to say that Cardillo had done nothing wrong, or even that it had been wrong to kill him. Ben Ward announced that the police had made mistakes, and apologized to Farrakhan. The commanding officer of the Harlem precinct, DI Jack Haugh, demanded an apology to Cardillo's family, and when it was not forthcoming, he resigned.

At one point, there was a single cop officially assigned to the investigation. The police were not allowed back into the mosque, which left them without much evidence or even a sense of the crime scene. Through his Hollywood contacts, Sonny Grosso was able to have a model of the crime scene built from the few photos taken. Sonny was in Harlem on another BLA murder on the day of the riot; he was at the mosque and worked the Cardillo case, often on his own time. After almost five years and two trials, a Black Muslim named Louis 17X Dupree was acquitted of the Cardillo murder. The judge called the political interference a "disgrace." No movie was ever made of that story, but Louis 17X Dupree found work in Hollywood, playing a police captain in a movie called *Supercops*. Sonny left the Department and took a job on *Kojak*. He also wrote a book called *Murder at the Harlem Mosque*. He told me that when he endorses his pension check, he writes "under protest" on the back.

. . .

"MOONLIGHTING" IS ONE OF THE FEW BITS OF COP SLANG that has worked its way into regular speech. Unlike "collar" or "perp," in which the cop context is plain, "moonlighting" has traveled so widely and well in the language that its police origins have been lost. It comes from the early days of the city, when men were drafted for the night watch. If someone had the inclination to pay a substitute, they were permitted to do so. You could see it as an aspect of decline in democratic ideals, or a pragmatic adjustment of the market to meet a civic need, but it marked an early separation of the police function from the public as a whole. Then, to moonlight was to work as a cop; now, at least for us, to moonlight is to work as anything else. To be a cop anywhere, you have to be a jack of all trades, but to be a cop in New York, most of us have to be a jack of at least two.

My own moonlighting was about to move on to the next phase, as I'd been encouraged to start thinking about writing a book. I had my doubts: any book would make it harder to remain anonymous, and a good book ought to make it impossible. I was still new—a rookie by some standards—though I was coming up on four years as a cop. But the pieces I'd written had begun to coalesce in my mind into something larger, much as the Job had become both ordinary and nearly all-encompassing for me. The skin on my hip was rough from the gun, and if I went on vacation, it took a couple of days to feel natural without it. I would reach down to pat it, not out of need but for fear that I had lost it, and the weight never left me, like the pain of a phantom limb. With the recent events at SNEU, I'd begun to understand that there was a quality to a cop's life that reminded me—maybe not by coincidence—of Senator Moynihan's observation after the death of JFK, that to be Irish is to know that, in the end, the world will break your heart. Ya gotta have a story, as they said, and I began to believe that I had one.

At first, we were determined to follow PK out of SNEU, to walk out en masse: his removal was so unexpected, so unsound and unkind. The cases of the escaped perps and the injured perp were run-of-the-mill mishaps that had occurred without malice or even real negligence, and they were re-dressed without deception. Wasn't it just a month before that they were fight-ing dirty to keep us? The justice of our cause was so compelling that it seemed that no one of decency would oppose it: PK was a great man and we were a good team. I just had to make them understand that. We went for a sit-down with the new captain.

Despite our crusaders' zeal, we'd all begun to wonder what kind of favor we'd done PK with our high spirits. Why did I think it was such a fine thing to hunt for junkies in the woods, so that we could knock down the doors of felons? Was this what a therapist would recommend for him? I remembered the look on his face when he caught up to me in Manhattan, with the perp over the hood of the car and the big dog in the back seat, or seeing Stix and John speed by on bikes, clutching the bumper of a city bus, or all the crazy chases in my car, with the black snow floating around inside and the red light bouncing off the dash as we vaulted the sidewalks. And yet when he went home with the news of the transfer, PK said, his wife cried for three days.

The Captain had come from another PSA, where the rumors of him were good: the word was that if you worked hard for him, he took care of you. A new commanding officer looks at the numbers and listens to the rumors. Our numbers would have been better than our rumors. The "Manson family" gibe wouldn't have warmed the heart of any manager, and one of the pre-cepts of the new, modern-management NYPD was to create a system where any part was replaceable—and to remind each part of that precept whenever necessary. On the other hand, in a police department where morale seemed to vary between bad and worse, a leader who created a team of cops who looked forward to work each day shouldn't be dismissed lightly. We had a chance, I thought, if we sat down and reasoned together. And if we couldn't, we had all resolved to leave SNEU.

I didn't expect we would settle our differences like rival dons, exchanging flowery tributes and veiled threats over espresso, but the minimum require-ment for a sit-down is a sufficient number of seats. The Captain genially re-ceived us from behind his desk, but the office was too small for our group, and those without chairs withdrew awkwardly back into corners. The Cap-tain didn't look like a cop or talk like one. His lowercase moustache, comb-over, and rumpled-short-sleeved-shirt-and-tie combination gave him the look of a back-office supervisor, familiar with the sales figures for each line of production. It heartened me to think we were both a big seller and a premium brand. If Compstat inspired terror in the upper ranks for its inquisitorial accounting—*You went up three homicides last month, but your felony drug collars are off ten percent?*—it inversely gave hardworking cops a sense of worth. You could think, I may be a number, but the business is numbers now, and all I have to do is add up.

The Captain said that Chief Anemone himself had flopped PK from SNEU, and so there was nothing he could do, even if he wanted to. The finality made all of our protests irrelevant, as if we'd barged into the governor's mansion to beg for a stay of execution, only to be greeted with the news that the electrocution had been yesterday and the governor lived next door. *Alrighty, then!* We could ah-tic-ya-late all we wanted, they'd already flipped the switch. When we said we all wanted to leave SNEU, he told us we couldn't all leave at once, right away. He praised us and soothed us, telling us that he knew how hard we worked; he also told us that it made sense for us to give the new sergeant a chance—we should meet him, at least; it was only fair. He also added that he thought the chief was right: what a boss did was keep you out of trouble, on the street and on paper, and our recent past showed that PK didn't have what it took to run a team. I asked about the last search warrant I'd gotten with Charlie, which would expire in a couple of days.

"I think we're going to have to let that slide. We're going to be looked at closely for a while, so it's a bad time for anything to go wrong. You can always go get another one."

We left the office. I didn't like how it had gone; I felt that we hadn't been persuaded as much as we'd simply been had. The speed of our acquiescence troubled me, and for all that he'd said that was sensible or flattering, other remarks made it clear that he didn't understand things as we did, or he didn't care, or it didn't matter. The Captain had dismissed the search warrant so casually that it seemed he didn't know how much work went into them, and his remarks about PK were insulting and gratuitous. I don't know if we would have been a better team to stay or go, and I wondered how much self-interest figured in our decision, and whether there was anything wrong with that: *Now I can take my kids to school in the morning—what am I going to do if they put me on day tours or midnights? Will I see much of my wife if I lose my steady days off? How will it feel to be back in the bag, to have to think about how many parking tickets I wrote this month instead of plotting clandestine meetings with informants and to work out the signals for the drop? What about our goatees? First they take away PK, now they're coming after our goatees!*

But PK was against our quitting. "You guys have each other," he said, "and I don't think I have much to teach you. To tell you the truth, I never thought I did—I more or less let you run, and it was great. But you shouldn't give up what you have together." He also told us that it sometimes happened on the Job that you had to take a fall, and if you accepted it with good grace, it could be quietly arranged after the passage of time to restore you to a fit position. What he had been offered or promised along those lines, he didn't reveal, but it was plain that he had been given some encouragement that all could be made right in due course. And though the transfer had been a sharp blow, he'd landed softly—the Captain had made him the "Gang Coordinator," a new title that permitted him to make his own schedule. He supervised one cop, Tom Frankenberry, a computer whiz who would compile photographs and other intelligence for a database. For Frankenberry, it wasn't especially heavy lifting, and for PK, it was less. He needed that, and we did: John wanted to leave most, to just disappear, but since the rest of us would be stuck in the unit for a while, he refused to "benefit" by our new situation: *I'm the one who wrecked the team, so I can't be the only one who gets out when it goes bad.* One departure is easy enough to manage, but when an entire unit has to be remade, there's more administrative work—though when Sgt. Clark and the Crime team quit, the summer of the Rape Detail, they were permitted to leave all at once, and without recrimination. That, too, would not be the case in the new regime.

For weeks, we floated, filling in for sector cars or footposts, not knowing what we'd do each day. Sometimes we worked together, sometimes we didn't. "Patrol is the backbone of the Department," the expression went, though cops usually revised the anatomical correspondent to "backside." The midnight platoon commander, a veteran lieutenant, was flopped to day tours as a result of our shake-up—technically, it had been his responsibility to notify higher-ups about the injured perp—which resulted in the loss of "night differential" on his paycheck. When we did our day weeks, he was not inclined to accommodate us. I thought about approaching Chief Anemone, an old-time cop with a fearsome reputation, hard-charging and flinty. Opinion among my teammates was mixed only in that some thought he would show me to the door, while others thought he would throw me out the window.

We wondered who our new boss would be, knowing that each name on our wish list was wished for in vain—O'Hagan would stay with Bike, certainly, and Fackler on midnights, and Clark would not pick up SNEU after leaving Crime. When the SNEU sergeant was finally assigned, it made all our speculation idle: he was new to the rank, and new to the command. He was younger than I was, I thought, and though he had a couple more years on the Job, they had been interrupted by long stretches in the military. There was no presumption or pretense to him, and when it was time for our sit-down, there were enough seats. He told us, "I know you guys have had a rough time lately, and how you feel about PK. I know you've done great work, and you know what you're doing. I don't want to change anything, and I don't plan to. All I'm asking is that you give me a chance." The dewy sincerity of the request—*the request!*—took us by surprise. We'd been punted around and shunted aside, and here was a boss asking for our permission to work with us. Tony laughed, and feigned brushing away a tear: "He's like a puppy!" We'd give it another shot.

To my amazement, two cops from Bike wanted to join us, George "Chicky" Mendez and Scott "Smacky" Mackay. Bike had lost some momentum when Tommy "Stretch" Dolan had left the Job for a better-paying small-town police department upstate, and Chicky and Smacky were motivated cops, eager to go out and make collars. Our setbacks didn't deter them, apparently, and they remained determined to work with us.

Within the team, the debate was brief:

"All right, it might work—there's one of you people, and one white guy."

"Can't we get another Italian?"

"I said, 'white guy.'"

"Fuck you, we don't want another Irishman."

"Smacky's not Irish, he's Scottish. You can tell because his name is 'Scott.'"

"It's as if Tony's parents named him 'Puerto Rican.'"

"Chicky's Puerto Rican."

"He's not Puerto Rican, he's Short-a-Rican, like Sammy."

"Then maybe we should get two of them, they're small."

"That's the thing about you people, you always have to push."

Chicky was the opposite of Sammy: outgoing and emotional, and a shameless comedian. He was the senior man on the team by several years, and he'd been in SNEU before, under Messer. Smacky was from upstate, far enough that his accent was almost Midwestern. In an OP, he gave out a scrip of a man in a "Payne Stewart cap," which left the catch cars wondering exactly what a "paint store cap" might be. If we were a unit in a World War II movie, he'd have been the farm boy, a big white guy, earnest and idealistic, whose small-town decencies were surprisingly disarming. I'd tagged along behind him on my first days on patrol, when my remark about how Melrose-

Jackson was a little on the slow side—during the heyday of Satan and Loochi, in fact—made him laugh. His eye was almost as good as Orville's.

It seemed that SNEU had bottomed out, and now morale began to creep back up again. There was a corner of the PSA basement that seemed ripe for conquest as an office: there were a few boxes of files and a few drums of mysterious chemicals, leaking on the floor. For a week or so, we cleaned it out and fixed it up, sweeping, mopping, scraping, and painting, singing SNEU spirituals as we worked. Frankenberry, who was good with sheetrock, walled off our corner from the rest of the basement, despite constant assaults from the Bike guys, who took the separation personally. PK and Frankenberry would share the office with us. The Sergeant requisitioned a few desks and cabinets from the quartermaster, and we pitched in with whatever else we needed: I brought in a carpet and a television, and a coffeepot and water cooler followed. A phone line was installed. A couch was discussed but it was disapproved, on the grounds that it might make the place too lounge-like and we would find it too irresistible to leave.

That kind of petty restriction had become increasingly common, and increasingly hard to take. The real purpose of the room was not so much to work as to wait: most arrest paperwork had to be done in proximity to the perp, and someone had to stay by the cells at all times when we had prisoners. But on our ten-to-six weeks, we had an hour or two in the morning while we waited for the van, and it was better to be out of sight when we had a cup of coffee and read the papers, or even, in fact, did work. And on four-to-twelve weeks, when you collared you often finished at three or four in the morning, and went back on the clock at eight, at which point you sat for hours until the DA called to write up the complaint. Even in the busiest precincts working at optimal efficiency, there is at least as much waiting as not-waiting in police work, and the arbitrary way they made that harder for us was deeply frustrating.

Elsewhere in the precinct, you could try to sleep in the lunchroom, but the television was on or people were there eating, and in the dorm—a tiny room with three sets of bunks with bare mattresses—cops on the late tours would come in to sleep for their meal hours. The midnight cops amazed me, on the few tours I stayed over, in their ability to fall asleep in an instant, as if a hypnotist had snapped his fingers. The cops would come in serial pairs for the three o'clock, four o'clock, and five o'clock meals, and collapse on a mattress, sometimes without even taking off their gun belts or vests. All of them snored like chain saws, and I swear there was one time when Koesterer began to snore even as he was walking in from the locker room. John brought a beat-up chaise longue into the SNEU room, but when I slept I usually just went facedown on the floor, glad that I'd brought in the rug.

Such were the workaday gripes of every cop, and they filled the conversational spaces when there was little else to talk about. For hairbags and burnouts, there rarely was anything else, and each new indignity was greeted with a measure of satisfaction for proving their resentment to be right. When any new cop first takes in this ambient sound of cynicism, it can be jarring and dispiriting. You think about how you threw your white gloves in the air at graduation, as the Mayor led thousands in cheering for you, or how you tried not to smile the first time you looked at yourself in the mirror in uniform, or how proud you felt the first time someone said, "Thank you, Officer," and the blast of bitterness breaks through like the voice of Tokyo Rose over the airwaves to the fighting men in the Pacific: *Why you fight for, GI Joe? General MacArthur, he no care about you! Your wife, she no wait for you! GI Joe, you be smart, go home!* At first, I tuned it out, but in time, I found myself nodding in agreement, or adding my bit. As long as it was a matter of healthy ventilation, I thought it was fine, and I could complain with the best of them. I had to be careful, though, remembering the comment from the first days on patrol—*The way you're going, you're gonna be burnt out in five years. . . .* Our complaint, however, was that we wanted to work but they wouldn't let us, and it sprung from a still-abundant reservoir of enthusiasm for the Job. We were becoming seasoned, not soured, and it looked like we were going to get back into things. I asked the Sergeant if I could take Charlie back in for another warrant, and he told me to go ahead.

Charlie had decided that he was finally ready to go to rehab, but he couldn't find a treatment slot. Though the DA's Office ran a program for addicted defendants, I made the case that we ought to do at least as much for people who are working for us as we did for those working against us, and they agreed. A representative for an eighteen-month, residential treatment program would be in next week to interview him. I went back to the woods to find Charlie and tell him. He seemed grateful but guarded, and I asked him: "You've been to rehab before?"

"Yeah, couple of times, but not for a while."

"What's the longest you were clean?"

"Nine years."

"When you slipped up, how long was it before you were back in the street?"

"Two weeks."

Charlie had barely been indoors for the last several years; for the past two winters, he'd slept outside, fearful of the shelters. What was it about cocaine and heroin that he loved so much? Did they love him back? For the near-decade that he was sober, it was as if he were hiking across an icy ridge, where any false step could let loose an avalanche, or give way to an abyss. He'd have a few more days to decide if life at the peaks or the valleys was more perilous. I'd take another trip to the woods, to see if there was some enchantment that I'd overlooked—through the hole in the fence with the snake strung through it, over the headless white chicken on the hardening ground, and then scrambling across the slope to the befouled camp beneath the bridge, where they lived like the trolls in the nursery story. Nope, I didn't see it.

When I took him in for the warrant, it went quickly. We'd been in front of this judge before, and she didn't ask Charlie anything. She did ask me, "Weren't you here with this earlier? Didn't I issue this warrant sometime last month?"

"Yes, your Honor."

"Why wasn't it executed?"

"Administrative reasons on our part, your honor. Our sergeant was—"

"All right, then."

"Thank you."

We left the judge's chambers, saying nothing until we were almost outside the building. Charlie would be going into rehab from there. "Listen," he said, "I appreciate all you did for me."

"That's all right, Charlie, you helped me out, too."

"I hope it was worth it for you."

"If it wasn't, I wouldn't have done it."

"And I'm really gonna try to do this right, this time—to clean up and stay clean, and go home."

"You can do it, I believe you."

We stepped from the side exit of the courthouse, out into the public daylight, for the first time without concern for who might be watching. He had his freedom. I shook his hand.

"Good luck to you, Charlie. Don't take this the wrong way, but I hope I never see you again."

That caught him for a moment, until he worked out the meaning, and he smiled. "I gotcha. But you know, if it doesn't work out, you know where to find me. Just come looking for me, under the bridge. . . ."

"Don't even say that, Charlie. Take care now."

I held the door for him and let him walk on.

• • •

THE FIRST BOOK BY A MEMBER OF THE NYPD WAS WRITTEN by the first Chief of Police, George W. Matsell, in 1859, and it was called *Vocabulum; or, The Secret Language of Crime.* While most true-crime writing offers lurid gore in the often thin guise of moral condemnation, Matsell's book is an amazing miscellany of slang, some criminal, some not. The book claims to be both a decryption of a universal underworld code—"The rogue fraternity have a language peculiarly their own . . . no matter what their dialect, or the nation where they were reared. . . . The language of the rogue in New York is the language of the rogue the world over"—as well as a list of funny or foreign words that poor New Yorkers use, which "are being interwoven with our language and many are becoming recognized Anglicisms." He fudges the difference between the secret languages of gypsy racketeers or the thieves' guilds of *The Threepenny Opera,* and the pidgin English of the streets, some of which has become proper, some of which has disappeared, and some of which has become more or less O.K. (from "oll korrect"). Sometimes you get the sense that he believes these words have invaded the language and have to be repelled, and other times he thinks it's pretty neat that we all get to use them now. The mix of censure and allure is further confused by the appendix, which includes glossaries for the terms used by "Gamblers, Billiard Players, Stock Brokers and Pugilists."

Words with which Matsell presumed his audience was unfamiliar included "booze," "bordello," "negligee," and "pimp," which seem to fit as ordinary words for impolite things. In the same vein, he cites "swag" for stolen goods and "scrape" for trouble, not to mention "bilk" and "bluff," which aren't even slang anymore. There is nothing criminal or even off-color in "duds" and "togs" for clothes, unless slang itself is seen as irreverent instead of merely irregular. "Birthday suit" for "naked" we still say, but "wooden coat" and "eternity box" for "coffin" we don't—it's hard to believe this kind of jokey euphemism has much to do with crime. It shows the same kind of wit to refer to pride as "starch," watered-down liquor as "baptized," or a black-clad widow as the "ace of spades." So too to call the tongue the "red rag," although the example is the real prize: "Shut your potato-trap and give the red rag a holiday."

Many words have gone, but some have come again: a "crib" was a house for the Bowery B'hoys of the mid–nineteenth century as it is for the rappers in the late twentieth. (Incidentally, a "rapper," according to Matsell, is a perjurer.) A lot of the technical, criminal terms are obsolete, such as those that describe MOs for thefts with female decoys, or that pertain to using inside men to make wax impressions of keys. I don't know of any recent arrests for "sweating" or "snagling," the first defined as "reducing the weight of gold coin by putting it in a bag and shaking it violently for some time, and then collecting the gold dust which is then worn off." "Snagling," of course, is "stealing poultry by putting a worm on a fish-hook, thereby catching the fowl." To "pork," in those days, was to "inform the coroner of the whereabouts of a corpse." On the other hand, to commit a robbery, then as now, was to "do a job," and to kill someone was to "hush," "stifle," or "silence" him, or to "make him easy"—all of which are clear in meaning, even when they're not current. To inform was to "peach," "snitch," or "squeal," and a bit of such information was a "tip." Except for "pigs," all of the words for cops are now out of date—"Philistines," "Moabites," "prigger-nappers" (literally, "thief-catchers"), "shadows," "trappers," "traps," and "stops"—but all of the slang terms for arrests are still in use: you could book 'em, collar 'em, pinch 'em, nab 'em, or run 'em in, ideally when you had 'em "dead to rights." Maybe you could infer that who we are has changed, but what we do has not.

The *Vocabulum* is more tourism than counterterrorism, but it makes the characteristic claim of cop books and crime books, before and since, that what is contained within is dangerous to know. It is forbidden knowledge, and a lot of people—*powerful people, you follow me?*—don't want you to know about this thing of ours, whatever it might be. When I talked to various editors about what kind of book I might write, I got a lot of questions that picked up on the whistle-blower theme—"What would you change about . . ." and "How would improve . . ."—which told of a presumption that any bright young cop would find himself locked in battle against the system, à la Durk and Serpico. And there was a moment of mutual epiphany when one asked, "So then, you're . . . *not* a reformer?"

And I said, "No, I guess not."

When the story of the book deal made the news, I took a couple of days off. Though I was able to remain anonymous in the stories, at least at first, since the whistle-blower theme had been sounded, I knew I had to take my team aside and tell them what was happening. They were all surprised, but they seemed to think it was fine and kind of funny. Tony said, "So that's why you type like a bitch!" Not long after, Stix gave out a scrip from an OP, and when I stopped the perp, I recognized him as a junkie we'd talked to about working as a CI. I put him against a wall, not gently, but I wasn't going to take him in. "Hey, it's good to see you again," he said nervously. "I hear they're writing a book about you." The remark captured perfectly his limitations as an informant, and we didn't use him afterward.

There was graffiti on my locker, the first and only time anyone ever wrote on it. Some guys had silly things written on theirs—"Papi Chulo!" and "Lover-boy," and Orville had "Orville Redenbacher," after the popcorn company—and others had graffiti with an edge to it, accusing them of being rats or suck-ups to the bosses. When one guy failed to qualify on the firing range, someone made an elaborate target out of black tape, with Magic-Markered bullet holes all over the outside, going up to the ceiling, and a little advice: "Try a knife." When I looked at my locker, there was a simple scrawl that said, "Self-Made Millionaire," which was not the worst thing I'd ever been called. A lot of people joked about it, and a lot of people slapped me on the back, and a lot of people said they wanted free copies, and a few said they didn't want to be mentioned in it. Some of them asked me how to write a book, and I told them I'd let them know when I wrote mine. I never heard a cross word from cops, and I began to wonder if the years of caution were a little paranoid. I trusted the cops I worked with, and they trusted me.

Not for the first time, not for the last, I had it all backward. I thought cops would give me a hard time, but the bosses would like it, if only for the enjoyment of having a Harvard guy to order around. I'd passed on earlier offers from Inspector Mullen to work at Headquarters, at the Office of Management and Planning—"the NYPD think tank," as Mullen called it—because it wasn't the kind of police work that interested me. But the fact that my chief concern was that the upper echelons would find me irresistible showed how wildly misguided I was—to the extent that cops cared, they seemed to think it was fine, but word came early and often that I made the Captain uncomfortable. A dozen cops approached me to pass on his comments: "I don't get that guy. . . ."

"I don't trust that guy. . . ."

"I'd watch my step around that guy. . . ."

"What's he think he is, some kind of Serpico?"

The Serpico remark was especially perplexing, because my idea of a scandal at PSA-7 had to do with the couch ban in the SNEU room, and if there were any deep, dark secrets at the precinct, they were secrets to me as well. Moreover, if I was Serpico, what did that make him? I went into his office and asked him if he had a problem with me or my side job, and if there was anything I could do about it. He amiably denied that there was anything wrong.

The search warrant was due to expire in a few days, and I'd set up a date and time with the Sergeant to execute it, arranging with EMS, ESU, and all the rest. The Sergeant was pleased with the work, and how our continuing efforts showed we'd accepted him as our boss. He'd neglected to tell the Captain about the warrant, however, and when the Captain heard, he called us into the office and asked me why he hadn't been told about it. The Sergeant sat there like a wooden Indian as I apologized for the lack of communication and fielded his questions about the CI and the apartment, which varied between the astute and the simply bewildering:

How can you trust this CI? Aren't they all addicts and liars?

If he's established as a CI, why hasn't he been turned over to Narcotics?

Why are you paying him out of pocket? He can turn around and make all kinds of allegations against you. . . .

I explained that it was a vacant apartment, used only for sales, so that there was no risk of running into kids or old people; that we wouldn't need a warrant if we spoke to the landlord, but we'd heard the super was in with the gang; that Charlie was reliable, and Narcotics didn't want him, and he was finished as a CI now, hopefully for good. The money issue wasn't addressed—as PK said later, if you don't understand that you have to throw these people a couple of bucks now and then, you don't understand anything. But the Captain's opposition seemed to stem mainly from not being told about it, and in fairness, if his cops were going to smash a door down, he ought to know. And since he didn't, we wouldn't. Another warrant went down the drain: a dealer would keep his money, addicts would get their drugs, and all would be free to do as they pleased.

The Sergeant didn't seem to know much about SNEU operations in general, and he knew nothing about warrants in particular. That didn't matter much, I thought, because we did. We didn't need guidance in the street from him, we needed cover in the precinct, but the loss of another warrant suggested that that might not be his strength, either. We began to have Team Meetings—or "group hugs" as Tony called them—in which our shortcomings would be somberly addressed and our successes generously praised. The praise had a kindergarten quality, as if he were handing out gold stars for us to stick in our coloring books, and the reprimands were also jarring, in part because we were unused to them, but also because the rebukes persisted long after the infractions had passed. Each meeting had to have an upside topic and a downside, and if there was no occasion for the latter, the reprimand from the week before was recycled. There was some motivational formula at work there, a military or management-seminar prescription for How to Maximize Employee Performance, but we'd been marching to our own music for a long time by then, and his speeches came to sound like a broken record from a radio station that never quite came in.

In December, I went to a funeral out on Long Island, calling in to say that I'd be a couple of hours late, and then calling again to say I'd be a couple of hours later. I should have just taken the day, but we'd taken off a lot since PK was gone, and we were all short on time. Though I got back to the precinct in the afternoon, that single day's lateness continued as a subject at Team Meetings through the next summer. One day around that time, I called in from Headquarters at the start of the tour, where I'd gone to pick up Uncle Eddie's personnel records. I got the Sergeant on the phone and said I'd be an hour late, but if he put me down as present for duty at HQ, I could stay to get the rap sheets for a new informant. He said it was fine, and he'd see me later, but for the next four or five Team Meetings he'd say, "And another thing—Ed, this concerns you—from now on, we start our tours here."

The nagging unease—literally, now that I think of it—that our little family was becoming a corporate subdivision didn't go away, but we were getting back to work, which took our minds off everything else for hours at a time. And though the Captain had canceled the last two warrants, he asked me to see what I could do with a would-be informant who had approached another cop in the command. The informant, whom we named Christmas in the seasonal spirit, was a frumpy, middle-aged crack addict who wanted a respite from her frequent arrests for trespass and possession. She was an easy number for a team of cops who worked where she lived, as they watched her dawdle from crack spot to dope spot the way another woman might browse from the bakery to the greengrocer. She knew most dealers, and no one paid much attention to her, which made her nearly ideal as an informant. She'd also run errands for other addicts, picking up drugs for them because the dealers didn't know them, or because they were afraid of being arrested themselves. I talked to the sergeant who ran that team, and he said they'd lay off her; I told Christmas that if she went somewhere or bought something for us, she'd be fine, but she didn't have a license to buy drugs, let alone sell them. Essentially, the law against trespass had been suspended for her.

What Christmas had to offer was a new crack spot opened up by an old dealer, one of the Jefferson brothers, who had been major players in that project for years. Both of the brothers had long rap sheets, and each had been identified by first and last name several times in kites, or drug complaints about the building. Because the spot had just opened, we wouldn't have a problem with the DECS, but there also wouldn't be any kites on that apartment. Steve Carroll, another cop from the command, told me he thought an old woman lived there, but that she hadn't been around in a while; she also had a middle-aged son with diabetes or some other health problem. It was an unexceptional situation, with certain small advantages—known perps— offset by small handicaps, such as an untested informant.

With Christmas, some of the usual problems presented themselves— instructed not to tell anyone that she was working for us, she promptly told her husband, and she changed her mind about coming to court on the day I'd arranged to get the warrant. I changed her mind back again, and John and I took her in to see Sam Ramer, an ADA who worked for Ed Friedenthal, a chief in the Bronx DA's Investigations Division. Eddie Ramirez, a cop from the Four-O, had a CI in as well, a yappy little character who was giving up his friends to save some time. Eddie told him I was writing a book.

"Yo! You won't believe it! Me, too! I'm gonna call it, *Papi, What I Been Through!*"

"There goes another good title, out the window."

After Eddie was finished, Sam wrote up our warrant and took us in to see the judge. Christmas was a bit scatterbrained but performed reasonably well, and we got the warrant. Since the Captain had asked for it, no political difficulties were expected back at the precinct. I was out of the building, a day or two later, when the inspector from the Housing Borough called in John, the Sergeant, and the Captain to explain what we had. I returned to the precinct sometime afterward and saw their faces, and wondered whether I should have been sorry to have missed it. The warrant had been canceled.

By each of their accounts, the meeting was nearly surreal. In the past, when PK had told the Inspector what we had in a warrant, he'd ask him any number of questions, but he liked PK, and PK had all the answers. Though the Captain, the Sergeant, and John knew the Inspector and the warrant less well than PK would have, the meeting was less of an inquisition than an outright repudiation: What nonsense it was, the Inspector said, he couldn't believe it! The DA must be a rookie, to write this up! The judge must be a rookie, too, to sign it! There were no kites in the building, and only a few collars—it was one of the safest, cleanest buildings around, a senior-citizens complex in such-and-such houses! John thought it futile to protest that it wasn't a senior citizens' building, and it wasn't in that project, and you wouldn't expect the accumulation of kites and collars since it was a new spot. The Inspector announced with vivid finality: "This baby's going right back up the vagina!"

The three of them thought the Inspector had lost his mind. I wondered, too, but since I'd heard a rumor that Narcotics had set up an intensive, long-term undercover operation there, I held out the hope that the Inspector might have been told to keep our people away for a while. I could even understand putting on a show like that to discourage us, and I took no offense at being kept out of his confidence—I'd had some recent experience with trying to get a large number of people to keep a secret. In the end, my guess that he might not be crazy was no better than their guess that he was—my warrant was gone, regardless, and the Captain would be extremely reluctant to attempt another one.

I still saw our street collars as the paycheck work, the daily basics, and if we could make something more of it, it was all for the good. It was as if we were oystermen, and the man who threw out his catch every day because he didn't find a pearl wouldn't be long for the business. But we were being told to throw away the pearls, too, and even to drop everything that shined a little when you opened it. Two days before Christmas, I got a call from a friend in the FBI, Jeff Drubner, to ask if I could get a couple of cops to ride with his people, to see where a suspect would take an undercover agent for a drug meeting with a Nigerian. I'd met Jeff a year or two before, at a party after the St. Patrick's Day Parade. I was in my dress uniform, and we were introduced fairly quickly, as we were the only armed people in the room. For a few minutes, we fell into the absurd, movie-cliché cop-versus-Fed standoff, sussing each other out, but we hit it off and stayed in touch. Jeff had once been assigned to investigate a threatening letter sent by a Nigerian national to the head of the New York office. The letter, which turned out to be more of a curse than a threat, had the effect of associating Jeff with Nigeria, where there is a significant heroin-trafficking network, and those barest qualifications made him the New York Bureau's Man for Africans.

Jeff needed a couple of bodies to ride in surveillance cars for the morning of December 24. Their man was to meet the dealer and travel to another place to talk; it was hoped that it was his house, so he could be identified. It would not be difficult, dangerous, or even interesting work, but because of the date, they didn't have the manpower available. It would be a pure favor, since we were working a double shift to leave early on Christmas Eve, starting at four in the afternoon and finishing at eight in the morning. The FBI might need us through noon. John, Stix, Tony, and a couple of others were willing to go, and I was referred up the newly tightened chain of command to ask the Captain if it'd be all right. He didn't seem pleased.

"What if somebody gets shot? How do they know who this guy is? What if it turns out Narcotics has a case going on him already?"

I said I'd have Jeff call him, and I left the office. An hour later, Jeff called me: "You know, if your captain just told me, 'I don't get anything out of this, so I won't let my guys go,' I'd have a lot more respect for him. But this is bullshit—what do you mean, 'What if somebody gets shot?' Well, it would suck, wouldn't it? Would it suck more than it would the day after, or yesterday? I told him, no one's even getting out of their cars. And how does he think we ID the guy, except by talking to him and following him? And not for nothing, who cares if Narcotics has a case—if it's good enough, they'd try to take it federal anyway. I'm sorry, but your boss doesn't know what he's talking about."

And so we slept in on Christmas Eve, and SNEU got to spend the holiday at home. Though it was hard to tell afterward, I think that the Captain grew more firm in the opinion that I was more of a problem than an asset, and even my zeal for police work was compromised by a dubious private agenda. Four recent efforts—three search warrants and what might have been styled a "Joint Operation with the FBI"—that I'd brought into his office as bouquets somehow turned into stink bombs. The Sergeant forgot to tell him about one warrant, the Inspector might not have told him everything about another, and even if I turned out to be closer to Sgt. Bilko than Frank Serpico, he didn't understand it all, and so he didn't want to try anymore. I asked the Sergeant if he still wanted me to get warrants, and he said he did, and then I asked if he thought the Captain still wanted me to get them, and he assured me it was the case. I didn't quite believe him, but I decided to act as if I did—if I proved to be a fool, they would be proven liars, which was a verdict I could live with. And in the meantime, I could go on working as a cop, which was all I wanted to do anyway.

. . .

THE NEW YEAR OF 1999 BEGAN WELL—ON NEW YEAR'S EVE, we were assigned to Times Square in plainclothes, and then sent back to the Bronx with loose instructions to "make periodic checks on major landmarks," which I interpreted to mean relatives and friends. PK and Frankenberry were in the SNEU room with us, and so when we were inside the precinct, it seemed like he was our boss again. Early in the month, we had some good collar days, and later in the month, we had some better ones—the Sergeant was away for a week, and PK took us out. While we did want the numbers to jump that week—*Let's make PK look good!*—there was no corresponding effort to diminish the new boss. The fact was, for every sergeant who had us, from Carroll, Carrano, Kelly through the new guy, as well as O'Hagan and everyone else who filled in to cover us, when we hit the street, we thought about the street.

Whether you were watching or catching, you concentrated on the perp: where his hands were, where he could run to, what he had done in the past. It was wearying but also exhilarating, as if you'd run for miles, and then decided to run more, and you were uplifted simply by the will to undertake the farther distance. Chicky and Smacky fit into the team as if they'd always been there, and in fact they'd been doing what we did longer than we had. Chicky would break us up, taking on character roles to slip into the OP, the most disturbing being a kind of spastic, hobbling and twitching his way across playgrounds into projects, arousing pity but not suspicion. One day, he dressed as a mailman, and so many people handed him letters that he truly transformed into a disgruntled postal worker. When Smacky was in the OP, he called out the action in the hushed tones and stop-and-pause rhythms of an announcer at a golf tournament: "The pitcher is a male Hispanic, with blue jeans, white Air Jordans, no belt . . . and he is, he is smoking a cigarette, left hand, no, wait, he's lighting it to give to a girl, looks like, stand by . . . yeah, it looks like a Newport, and he has a shirt that is blue, white, green, and red, the design is . . ."

"Smacky, you on?"

". . . the design is triangular, with a border of . . ."

"Smacky, you on?"

". . . circles and squares, the circles are blue . . ."

"Smacky, you on?"

"Somebody trying to raise me?"

"Yeah, I got a question for you."

"Go ahead."

"Do you get paid by the word?"

One day, Smacky had us take a player who was stepping off—we'd missed a couple of buyers, but he wanted us to take him with whatever he had, which turned out to be sixty-six slabs. He was wanted on a bench warrant, and he had another open Narcotics case. Smacky talked him into turning, and he gave up two apartments with guns and another with drugs; he was a player in the revived Melrose-Jackson gang wars, whose most recent casualty had been a kid who was blasted in the face with a shotgun the day before. Smacky worked through the night, but there were logistical problems from the outset and legal ones soon after; the ADA told him that the perp had a right to an attorney because of the open case, which is simply not true. Though they refused to move in the day after the arrest, I still thought we could make a deal a week later in the Grand Jury: he had felony weight six times over, he was wanted on a warrant, and he had another open case. But the next week, the ADA in the Grand Jury told Smacky that without buyers, they weren't going to indict, anyway—the offer would be for a misdemeanor plea, with a couple of months in jail. Smacky called me at home to tell me. I thought there might just be a communication problem, and I told him to explain that we already had cooperation, and that all we were asking was to hold back on the offer while we went after the guns, one of which might have been used to shoot that kid in the face. In any county in the state, the perp would have faced years in jail. Smacky told me to wait, they would bring it up to the supervisor. A couple of minutes later, he came back. "They said no. They're making the offer, today."

"Let me talk to her," I said. I started to get steamed.

"I don't think I should," he said. I didn't argue with him. Smacky had a better idea of when to quit than I did.

One of the nights out with PK, we did a double, working through midnight and hitting the crack spots at Mitchell Houses hard. OV and I were in the van, and we rolled back and forth down 138th Street, up and down Alexander, Willis, and Brook, picking up bodies. A scrip came over: *male Hispanic, twenties, black leather jacket with fringes on the sleeves, riding a little-kid bike, east on One-Three-Eight* . . . When we rolled up and grabbed him, he was wild-eyed and damp with sweat. We fired off questions and he fired back lies:

"What were you doing in the building?"

"I didn't go in the building!"

"We saw you in the building."

"I went in the building but no one was there!"

"We saw you talk to the pitcher."

"I went in the building and I saw the pitcher but I changed my mind—"

"Stop it."

"My brother's a cop."

"He must be very proud of you. Listen, tell you what, just give it up, gimme what you got, and I'll get you a Desk Appearance Ticket, you'll be out in a couple of hours."

"I don't got nothin'! My brother's a cop! Don't you have anything better to do?"

"Turn around and give me your hands."

I cuffed him up and threw him in the van: "Tell me the truth now or I'll put you through the system!"

And then he broke down, crying and shouting from the back of the van for another hour as we worked: "I'm a good person! I work across the street! I can help you out! Where's my money? I had money in my pocket! You stole my money! Let me go, my brother's a cop!"

At the precinct, he continued the double-edged harangue of pleas for mercy and threats of litigation. When Sammy put him in a cell, the perp told him that we'd stolen thirty dollars from him, and he was going to make a complaint. At that point, I was still inclined to write a summons for trespass if he came up clean on the search, a Desk Appearance Ticket (DAT) if he didn't, on his brother's account. His brother was supposed to be down the street, and his father had been called to get him, but he never showed up. When he repeated the Internal Affairs threat, I joined in with the "Fuck him!" crowd—which was everyone else—and decided to put him through, regardless. In the cells, he became the shop steward for the angry perps, loudly denouncing cops for being stupid and crooked and mean, then demanding candy, cigarettes, and phone calls. When we searched him, we found a half-smoked joint, with the acrid smell of angel dust. That explained a lot: angel dust is an animal tranquilizer that induces psychosis in humans, and a lot of cops have stories of how it took six large men to subdue a hundred-and-fifteen-pound dusthead. It wasn't as if crack was getting great press in the South Bronx in 1999, but it took a particular kind of idiot to wake up one day and say, "Angel dust is a product I've heard nothing but good about, and it's about time I was involved."

When I pulled him out for debriefing, I told him he was going to jail no matter what I wanted to do with him, or what his brother could do for him, because he had a warrant for an old summons, and he was also on probation. I said that there was no point in lying or crying, because it was just us in the room, and at least one of us didn't feel sorry for him at all. But if he wanted to help me out, I could keep him from being violated on his probation and thrown back in jail. He thought for a moment, and then he told me about dope spots, crack spots, dust spots, and the people he knew who carried guns. What was of unique value was that he worked in a video store, where a number of dealers had memberships, and he could pull out their cards for names and addresses. I told him to come back and talk to me again in a few days, when his head cleared.

The Sergeant congratulated us on our accomplishments while he was away, and he seemed to expend his energy in administration and requisitions for the room—file cabinets from the quartermaster, laminated precinct maps for the walls. Each of us was assigned a precinct map to color in the public housing with blue marker. I told him about the new CI, his possibilities and pitfalls, and he said to go ahead with it. Once, I asked him to sit in on an interview with the CI—in part, because I wanted a witness for each conversation—but he sat there listlessly, saying nothing and looking ill at ease, so afterward I asked PK. I hadn't written the Sergeant off yet, but the past week had rekindled hope that PK might return. When we were in the office together, PK remained the conversational center of gravity, attracting all the jokes and tactical questions. There was no disrespect—the Sergeant's official position was always acknowledged—but there was also no doubt about who we loved. Maybe the new guy would win our affection and trust, and maybe he would not, but we had had a father once, and the stepfather had yet to prove himself.

When the CI came into the precinct, I took him into the muster room with Chicky to start the registration paperwork. He couldn't sit still, couldn't shut up, couldn't concentrate or respond. He didn't want to sign the forms, didn't want his picture taken, and told Chicky, "Stop looking at me like that, you're scaring me!" Now and then, he'd catch himself, realizing that he came off as an eight-cylinder psychotic, and attempt some poor feint at normalcy, like when he looked over at Chicky's Yankee hat and piped up, "So, you like the Yanks? I love the Yanks! Yeah, baseball!" He was like a surrendering German soldier leaping from a trench, hands up and shouting, "Babe Ruth! Bugs Bunny! Betty Grable!"

When I finally got him to sign the forms, he signed in all the wrong places—where I sign, where the captain does—and insisted on "J-5" as a code name, which was a little James Bondish, and prematurely self-congratulatory. He'd done nothing yet but raise my blood pressure, and I didn't want him to get wrapped up in secret-agent fantasies. When he screwed up another set of forms and began to complain again about having his picture taken, I bellowed at him:

"How fucking dare you come into my house fucking high, bugging out, all fucked up, and try to play me like this! You fucking insult me like this, coming here, and expect me to do you favors with probation? Get the fuck out of here!"

And then he started to bawl, Yes, okay, so maybe he'd had a drink—

"YOU ARE LYING! YOU DID NOT HAVE A DRINK!"

Boo, hoo, hoo, it was all the stress, he was afraid to come, he'd been in jail all weekend. His face streamed with snot and tears, and I told him to clean himself up and go home. We'd try again in a couple of days. When we left the room, there was a little crowd by the door. It had been loud, and Chicky said he'd wondered how long I'd let it go before cutting off the interview or punching him in the head.

A few days later, he was back, a little on edge but otherwise of sound enough mind, and he gave excellent, detailed information about three spots where they held or sold dope. When it came time to pick a code name, I decided to make it a kind of Rorschach test, and lead him out into wider fields of self-image. I said I couldn't just let him pick it, because it might reveal specific information about himself—Charlie's code name had been the town he was from, which said too much, so we just called him "Chuckles." I asked him what his favorite animal was, and he said, "I don't know, all of them, dogs." Pushed for a specific, he said, "the little ones, like the kind they have in the Taco Bell commercial." I was deeply satisfied by his choice. "From now on," I solemnly intoned, "you have a new identity, and you will be known to us only as 'Chihuahua.'" He nodded. For days, "*Yo quiero* angel dust!" was the office catchphrase.

Chihuahua was still a loudmouth and an aggravation, but the information was good: there were kites on two apartments out of the three he gave up, and the names he provided, "Tony" and "Jamie M—" were both specified in the kites. Jamie was on parole for drug sales. Chihuahua said the third apartment was where most of the stash was, hidden behind loose bricks in the wall beneath the sink. An old man lived there, but Chihuahua hadn't been inside in a while.

"Can you get in?"

"Yeah, the old man's a little gayish. He'd let me in."

"Well, do what you have to do. If you have to take one for the team, you're authorized. Excellent work, Chihuahua. You may go now."

I walked through the buildings, and all was as described: the odd turns of the stairway, the tile pattern on the floor, the stickers and marks on the doors. There were glassines for the brand of heroin—China White—all over both lobbies. We had Tony identified with a drug arrest; we had Jamie's mug shot, parole record. The old man was still unidentified, but we were at least able to corroborate the door markings, which way the windows faced, what they looked out on; I stopped an old woman going into the building to ask for a young girl in that apartment, and she told me I must be wrong, because an old man lived there who didn't like girls. We didn't expect too much from Tony's place—it was a sale spot, so only a couple of bundles and weed would be on hand, but there should be a good amount at the old man's. And Jamie had volume and a gun, too. I kept on Chihuahua to get into each apartment several times within a ten-day period, and set up a date for him to come into court. I let the Sergeant know where we stood for each apartment, and that I would try for warrants for all three, but that I wouldn't be surprised if a judge held back for the old man's place. He said to go ahead and get the warrants.

Though Chihuahua had become far more manageable—and credible, at least about where he got drugs—I hadn't learned to like him any better. Smacky went with me, the sole volunteer. In the morning, Chihuahua was late, and he hadn't been in one of the spots over the weekend, as I'd told him to do.

"Did you go into Jamie's?"

"I can get in there any time."

"Did you go over the weekend, like we said?"

"Nah, but I can get in, any time."

"I thought I explained to you that we don't get a warrant because you *can* get inside. We get a warrant because you *were* inside, recently, and saw shit there."

"It's no problem."

"Yes, Chihuahua, it is. We were on our way to court. Can you get in now?"

"No problem."

On the way, he blathered, in his usual nails-on-the-blackboard manner, complaining that I never called him enough—though my calls were never returned—and about how he'd like to get involved in the Internet. "Listen, I could find out things for you guys, too. Hey, I got an idea! You know what would be good? If you guys got me a computer! If you all chipped in, it wouldn't be so bad for you. You know, I could find out a lot of things, and I'm really into computers."

I took another breath, and refused to look at Smacky because we would have broken each other up. "We'll see," I said. We drove to a place a few blocks from Jamie's and let him out, crossing our fingers that he'd come back. He did, no worse for wear.

At the CI room, Bea Moore and another cop from Narcotics arrived with their own informant to get a warrant for the old man's house. I don't know who made the mistake in issuing them a DECS number for our apartment— had we gone to court a day later, there might have been a serious problem. As it was, I felt badly for the Narco cop, Ocasio, who'd worked needlessly through the night with his own skell to set up the warrant, but he did provide the corroboration for the third apartment. I was there first, on paper and in fact, so there was no dispute of ownership, and Ocasio told me about another floor trap, with two guns and more dope. A couple of hours later, we returned jubilantly to the precinct, free of Chihuahua and with three warrants.

While a lot of cops go for their entire careers without getting a search warrant, and others might get one a month, it had been almost two years at PSA-7 since anyone had a search warrant before SNEU started up again with PK. They tend to go in runs, when a cop gets hold of a quality informant, and I was proud that I'd gotten three in one day from an informant who was so difficult to manage. I pushed for them because of the other corroborative evidence—I wouldn't have knocked a door down on his say-so alone—and the fact that I disliked him so strongly was a positive; I wasn't spending time with him because I enjoyed the company. I thought nothing of him as a person, and whatever he had to say about anything aside from drugs was of no interest to me. I had an appreciation for the fact that it could appear as if I chose to believe what suited me, but I had evidence to support his statements on the only aspect of his life that mattered to me. He was not a whole person to me, but a key to a door. And he fit.

And then I threw out my back. I'd done it once or twice before, since I'd become a cop, for no apparent reason. The first time, I was leaving for work, and as I locked up my apartment I felt an electric shock through my spine and fell to my knees. I managed to get to my car and I drove to the precinct, where I asked for the day off, and the next, which brought me to my weekend. When I'd been at the command for two months, an older cop had told me, "I wouldn't go sick for at least a year. Your sick record is one of the big things they look at for transfers and so on, and if you go sick more than a couple of times, they bust your balls." At the time, my peculiar reasoning on the subject was that if it turned out to be a serious injury, I wanted to keep it off the record so I could keep working. When my back went out the first time, it took about a week for me to get better, during which I made gradual improvements toward upright posture, like a schoolroom poster of evolution, from all fours to Homo erectus. This time, after I took the day, John came home to tell me that the warrant was off again. Though I was barely in knuckle-scraping Neanderthal phase, I went back for the next tour, where I spent most of it on the floor of the SNEU room. Again, I was glad I'd brought in the rug.

John told me that the Sergeant had called a Team Meeting, during which he announced all the problems the Captain had with me—that I had a tendency to run off and do things on my own, that there was something suspect in how I could call up DAs and ask for favors. John told me the team gave it back to him, and there were fierce arguments, but in another meeting with the Captain, they were grilled on the details on the warrants and didn't have all the answers. It would be a better thing in future, he said, if the whole team knew the warrant inside out.

When I went back in, the Sergeant told me that the Captain was concerned about Chihuahua's brother, the cop. We had an obligation to find out who he was, and to let him know what we were doing. I told him that the cop-brother issue had only come up the night he was arrested, as leverage for release, and that I didn't see it as significant. (I had brought it up with Chihuahua after the arrest, and he almost cried, telling me that he didn't want his brother involved.) Whether the brother gave his blessing—if there was a brother, and if he was a cop—we were past the point of approval: we had the warrants, and the only question was whether we would reap any benefit from them. Few people, cops or otherwise, would be delighted to learn that relatives are working as informants: they don't want to deal with what led to the opportunity, and they don't want to think about the risk. I'd talked to another cop who had a brother with his own legal troubles, and he told me, "I said to him, 'If my job doesn't mean enough to you to keep from fucking up, don't start throwing my name around when you get caught.'" I didn't expect enthusiastic approval from the brother, but it was also troubling to imagine it—what if he wanted to be involved, to have a say in what we did or how we handled Chihuahua? We knew something about the informant; we knew nothing, nothing, nothing about the brother. Moreover, we don't let *anyone* know that someone is working for us.

At the end of the tour, the Sergeant told me we were not going ahead with the warrants without the brother's name. There wouldn't be a problem, he said, the Captain just wanted the name and where he worked; the Captain didn't have to talk to him, but it was a small detail that needed to be cleared up. Even at the time, I thought the conversation had the same quality as my earlier talk with Chihuahua, when he asked me to buy him a computer—*"We'll see . . ."*—in its unreality and inequality, in the attempt to keep a straight face. I called Chihuahua and told him he was giving up the name. He began to whimper and I cut him off. He gave me the name and the precinct. I gave them to the Sergeant and went home.

The next morning, we waited uneasily in the SNEU room, as the Sergeant chose his moment to make his announcement: the warrants were off, this time for good. He had a confidence about him, an assured and superior manner with which he delivered the news that the Captain had talked to Chihuahua's brother the cop, and that he was a cop but not his brother, just a friend of the family. He pronounced it as if it were an investigative coup, that the Captain—the old fox!—had cut through to the truth of the matter, while we were chasing our tails. The warrants would be given to Narcotics to execute. "You guys are going to have to get things a little tighter next time, it wasn't quite there," he went on blithely. "We'll go for the training, search-warrant training, and we'll know what we're doing next time."

Where to begin? To ask why he'd lied to me about talking to the cop brother? To ask why, if he'd thought it was an important issue, they hadn't forced it beforehand? To ask how many warrants he had gotten? Or the Captain? Or merely to ask if the *Pop!* was audible when he pulled his head out of his ass? Instead, I asked him whose decision it was to cancel the warrant.

"It was mine," he said. When I began to challenge his reasons, he backed off, saying he canceled it only because he knew the Captain was going to. And the Captain canceled it only because the Inspector would have. I said I'd talk to either of them, but he forbade it. Chain of command, you know. He said, "I don't know what you guys think about me—think what you want, but I fought for this, and I fought for you, tooth and nail!"

"You canceled the warrant. Is that fighting for it?"

He conceded I had a point, but insisted he had fought, then returned to the circular diversion of chain of command. I don't remember exactly the order of things: Orville left the room yelling that he was quitting the unit; Stix jumped in on the "fighting tooth and nail" remark; Smacky said that he now knew how difficult it could be to get a warrant, and how much work goes into it, and that it was just plain wrong to have this happen. The Sergeant said that any of us could leave SNEU when we wanted, and the unit would go on without them.

I wanted to return to the cross-examination: "Everything about this warrant I told you about as soon as I knew it, and every next step I did was cleared by you. So why is it that the Captain thinks I'm running around and doing things on my own?"

"I don't know . . . he just thinks so. . . ."

"But you straightened him out, right, told him you knew everything and approved everything?"

"Oh, yeah, of course."

"But he just thinks that anyway, despite what you tell him, you don't know why."

"Uh-huh."

That afternoon, I called Bea Moore in Narcotics to say that we had warrants for them, and to ask when we could meet and go over them. There were only a few days left in their ten-day life, and the last one I tried to give them, with Christmas, had come to them too late. The Sergeant was in the office with me, and he began to scream as soon as I hung up the phone: "That's exactly your fucking problem! You're always running off and doing things on your own! This is not your fucking warrant! It's my fucking warrant! I will decide who gets it and who doesn't get it!"

I was floored. We went back and forth some more, but I stayed lock-jawed and lawyerly to keep my temper. Later that day, my back was still killing me, and I said I wanted to leave early. Permission was denied. He made us get in uniform and go out on patrol.

The aftermath was bitter and blurry. Stix asked Sgt. O'Hagan about going to Bike, where there were openings. O'Hagan brought it up with the Captain, who told him that no one was moving from SNEU. I took days off whenever I could. On one of them, John told me that Chief Dunne, the CO of the Housing Bureau, had come in to address the troops. He told everyone about how when he was the CO of a Brooklyn precinct, the SNEU team got warrant after warrant, their investigations were far-reaching, and it was a tremendous success. John said the Captain stood beside him, nodding in agreement. During another Team Meeting, the Sergeant announced that no SNEU business was to be discussed with any supervisor outside the immediate chain of command. The rule meant specifically that we were not to talk to PK.

We ignored the Sergeant and talked to PK all the time. PK could only shake his head. "What a shame," he said. "What a waste." Not long after, Frankenberry was driving him when they hit a truck. John and I were in my car when we heard it over the air, the weakened voice calling for help, the slow recognition that it was PK. We would have preferred to have been hit ourselves, and almost were as we flew to the scene, as John bellowed directions in my ear as we cut through traffic. The front end of their car was mashed in, and they'd broken the windshield with their heads. PK was pale and dazed in his seat, and he didn't move. I turned away for a moment because I could picture him dead. I put my hand on his shoulder and asked him how he was doing. He smiled and said, "Not so good. . . ."

Other cops came, the rest of the SNEU team and sectors from Housing and the Four-O. PK and Frankenberry had been driving down a street that was two-way for most of its length, but one-way for a single block, which was where they were rammed by a beer truck. It was an easy mistake, but they were at fault. The scene had a feel of thwarted force—*What can we do, dammit?*—and messages were sent back and forth over the air: *Ascertain the status . . . advise which hospital . . . close down the streets. . . .* Central asked if the ambulance had left yet, and the Sergeant said, "Not yet, Central—they're still bagging him up." Whoever was listening whipped around to glare at him, then ignored him again. John took PK's shield and put it around his neck, and we divvied up the gun, belt, and the rest of the equipment to safeguard as if they were relics. We followed him into the ambulance and closed the doors. "Don't worry, laddo," I said. "I found a bundle of dope in the back seat, but I threw it out." He almost laughed.

As we were about to leave, the Captain opened the doors to ask two questions, "Is he all right?" and "Who was driving?" It seemed to me that the real concern was in the second. I said PK was fine, and Frankenberry had been driving, and we left.

It is almost a wonderful thing to be hurt as a cop, or rather, there is something majestic in the spectacle of the Job taking care of its own. Highway entrances are shut down all along the hospital route; flashing lights and sirens guard the road as you pass, and escort you to your destination. The world is told that a cop is hurt, and that is all that matters. PK and Frankenberry had concussions and bruises, and they were treated and released in a couple of hours. We drove them home and they had a couple of days off.

Soon after PK returned, the Captain told him he was no longer the Gang Coordinator. He would be issued a Command Discipline for his "failure to supervise" his driver, and be reassigned to patrol on the four-to-twelves. The flexibility to take care of things at home was already strained—PK always used his vacation days early, and rarely had time on the books—and now he'd have none. He went to the Inspector and asked to be transferred to PSA-8, in the north Bronx. "I'm not a fuck-up," he said. "And I'm not going to be treated as one." The Inspector ran the Borough, which covered all of Housing in the Bronx and Queens, and PK was accommodated. The Captain seemed to regard it as a slap in the face, and I was happy to think so. But it was also clear that we were going nowhere ourselves.

NINE

There is so much to the City, so many little worlds on the wax and wane, pulling you in and pushing you out. You might be met by a wary eyeball through the peephole, or with wide-armed welcome, if you have a pretty face, a pocketful of cash, the name of a friend. The dress code could be black tie, or you might have to leave all your clothes at the door, or a simple weapons check would do. There are cafes and clubs where you can speak Amharic, Bulgarian, or Catalan, and next door to each there are others where you can leave the mother tongue and mother country behind. People come here to be dancers, bankers, witches, chefs; to take jobs that have been just invented or long forgotten, union jobs and city jobs. New York maintains civil-service positions for ostlers—they take care of the municipal horses—and may be the only city to do so since the Kaiser left Berlin. If you require other Bulgarian ostlers so as not to feel lonely, you might have a problem, but we have both Bulgarians and ostlers. And there may well be an enclave of Bulgarian ostlers—in Queens, most likely—that I just haven't come across, because I haven't looked. You can never get lost in New York, as long as you keep on moving, but you can get stuck sometimes. It depends on your stamina more than your sense of direction.

After college, I'd sometimes run into people who'd complain about the narrow sameness of New York, which for them meant a Wall Street job, an Upper East Side apartment, and a social life in which they took cabs to restaurants, clubs, and dinner parties where they met other young men and women who had not only gone to the same schools, but studied the same majors. Hasidim mix it up more, I thought. But later, I thought that I was doing the same thing. In the Academy, when Sgt. Solosky warned us against getting lost in the Job, it sounded a little laughable: *Make sure you keep your old, civilian friends. . . .* What was irresistible about this world—the gray polyester uniforms, the hours spent mastering the dogshit-disposal regulations, or the months of obedience-school drills to sit, stay, fetch? *Good boy, gimme a paw. . . .* Though most of my old friends had shamefully low arrest activity, I didn't shun them altogether. But absent the last step of dating another police officer, I was in as deep as you could get.

I kept much the same company, on duty and off. I'd become good friends with two cops who'd left PSA-7, McTigue and Killian—I would be in both of their wedding parties—and we'd catch bands at bars, Shanachie at Rocky Sullivan's, Pat McGuire at Marty O'Brien's. Both bars were dark and smoky, narrow and long, and you could look at pictures of JFK, RFK, Shane McGowan, and Brendan Behan from behind your pint. Chris Byrne played with Shanachie and owned Rocky Sullivan's, and he had been a cop for ten years before quitting to play full-time with his other band, Black 47. Brian McCabe had been his partner in Midtown North, before he became a detective sergeant with Manhattan South Homicide. McCabe's nephew was Pat McGuire, of course, and he played for George Kornienko, owner of Marty's, who had worked for Chris with the band and at his bar before striking out on his own. Both bars were cop-heavy, and the density of off-duty Irishness was Uncle Eddie-ish, but there was a generational irony, as well: "Rocky Sullivan" was the James Cagney character in *Public Enemy*; "Marty O'Brien" was the stage name Frank Sinatra's father had used for his boxing career. Still, you could hear "Danny Boy" on the jukebox, and the pipes, the pipes were calling, for us as they had for Pat Brown.

John broadened the circle still further. He was a joiner and an organizer, a natural coach—he ran the precinct gym and played on our softball and basketball teams. He'd see someone who'd fallen off his weightlifting regimen and snap, "Look at him, the fat fuck. He's swollen up like a blood tick." The cult of fitness was new to me, the calorie- and carb-counting obsessions, the supplements, shakes, and nutrition bars: "I was good today, egg whites and turkey, with pepper and ketchup. All protein, no fat."

"And it gives you a shiny black nose and a fine, glossy coat."

With the gym cops from PSA-7 that John was tight with—Eddie Tibbatts, Andy Bielawski, John Chase, Chris Esposito, Reynaldo "Ray-Ray" Reyes—we'd step out to the nightclubs now and then, tinning the doorman—flashing your badge—to cut the line. *Right this way, guys, how many are you? Where do you work? The South Bronx!* You'd keep an eye on some of the guys, wondering if you'd collared them, and keep an eye out on the girls, too, just to be fair. Sometimes, we'd hit the Copa, but I think I was the only one looking to make a case there. I knew we were going out when I could smell John's cologne from around the corner. Inside the apartment, I'd see him trying on various shirts and expressions in front of the mirror: *What about the blue short-sleeve, and a brooding scowl?* He'd examine his reflection with an air of sober detachment before concluding, "The mirror doesn't lie. I get better-looking every day."

"It's cold out, John, put on more jewelry."

"Ah, shut up, you prick of misery."

"That's a nice expression. Where's that come from?"

"My grandmother says it, about my grandfather."

Even Mickstat and Wopstat continued after hours: John became a member, and then a delegate, and then a trustee of the Columbia Association, the NYPD Italian fraternal organization. "You finally got your button," I said. "Who'd you have to kill?" He raised his hands, as if it would be wrong for him to say more: "I'm a good earner . . . and you should have tried the *szviadell'*!" Though we both marched on St. Patrick's Day, he took no small pleasure casually tossing me an Emerald Society card, saying, "Here you go. I got plenty. If you need anything else from them, let me know. The Irish owe us, big time."

My counterpunch was directed straight to the gut, where he was most vulnerable. A good night out for me would be at a restaurant—a legacy from high school, at the Commuters—and we did eat well, and most often Italian. At my regular places, the waiters took such good care of us that John took to calling me a "closet guinea." "Listen," I told him. "I've been to Italy and I've been to Ireland. What I don't get is why you people left." I said that there were Fitzgeralds in my family, and the Fitzgeralds were once the Gheraldini, who had left Florence before Dante did. Moreover, as I pointed out, one look at him could show that his family had offered a warm welcome to travelers from the North; with his blond hair and blue eyes, a Viking or two had clearly developed a taste for Sicilian cooking. I'd say I could out-guinea him, anytime, as my knowledge of Italian covered most of the menu, whereas the only words he knew were for insults and pastries. Several times, we breached the walls of the fastest redoubt of guineadom, a restaurant in East Harlem called Rao's, which is over a hundred years old and fits eight tables inside. Over the years, its clientele graduated by degrees from gangsters to Sinatra types, who were happy to see gangsters, to people who were happy to see the Sinatra types. Politicians and sports figures often went there, and more often were turned away. *Is Frankie in? Nah? How 'bout Frankie Junior?* Sonny Grosso had a regular table on Monday nights, and he gave it to me once. I went with John, Killian, and McTigue, and as Nicky the Vest took our orders from behind the bar, he said, "You guys like sports?" After three answers in the affirmative, he offered the curt instruction, "Turn around." We did, to witness Hank Aaron. Sonny was the Joe DiMaggio of our business, and I was more than a little proud to know him. He remembered my father and Uncle Eddie from years ago. A few times he invited John and me out, and as the roast peppers with *pignoli* and raisins arrived, he might wave a hand for a friend to come over, and wave again for the waiter to turn off the jukebox, and the friend would shiver the windows with arias from *Pagliacci*.

"Still unsigned, can you believe it?" Sonny said. "I'm taking him to Vegas, to meet people. . . ."

At times like those, I wished that the phrase "Prince of the City" had been unspoiled by irony. We were used to being cops by then, settled in our skins. In all the Irish bars, Italian restaurants, and many other places we went, to be a New York City cop was to be met with gratitude and respect. People knew that if there was trouble we would help, and if there wasn't, we could tell them a funny story they could repeat to all their friends. Because of us, they could walk around at night, and if they thought about leaving town, it was because New York was becoming too expensive, and not because they were afraid they'd be killed if they stayed. I liked the feel of a shield on my chest, and it began to make sense that you wore it over your heart. So Sgt. Solosky was right, after all, or maybe he should have warned us against being caught up in the Job when it had nothing to do with good guys and bad guys, at least not in the expected way. But probably not, because it wouldn't have made sense at the time to have reached a point in my career where everything was great about work except work.

. . .

I HAD BEGUN TO FEAR THAT WHAT HAD MADE ME MAD AND miserable over those months on the Job was more than a run of bad luck or bad treatment, but signs of a larger and darker disorder. From PK's departure from the team to his escape from the precinct, the Job had been dental-visit dismal, with hours of discomfort broken by jolts of pain, but at the dentist's, at least, you knew that the visit would end. The Captain's talk of Serpico began to take on an ironic resonance, because I certainly began to feel like a lonely crusader in a hostile system, no matter if my cause was nothing greater than to stop my work from being screwed up all the time by a couple of jackasses. Until then, there were bosses I didn't care for, but the general and final alignment had been that I worked for people who were in some way older, wiser, or better than I was, and bore good will to good work. My predicament was vertical: we had the odious Sergeant, and above him, a Lieutenant who avoided us like a train wreck, and then the wretched Captain, and then the enigmatic Inspector, and beyond that, who knew? It began to prompt the belief that I was the part that didn't belong, at least not there. Cops would say, "The Job is not your friend," and I suspected the expression was an old one.

After Knapp, the old heroes were regarded as suspect, at best. Their very success under the old regime was held against them—how could they thrive amid the corruption and compromise, untainted themselves? But the new heroes were treated little better, at least on the Job: Durk had to complain about the Narcotics Division on a talk show—not the preferred format for an interoffice memo—to start an investigation that led to the breakup of a major Mafia heroin operation, with the arrest of more than sixty traffickers, though he was left out of the case. When he shot a mugger off-duty, the *Times* ran a front-page story about it; when he was frustrated with a particular assignment, they ran an editorial about how the NYPD ought to find a position for him that was commensurate with his talents. He continued to work with the DOI, sometimes on interesting cases, sometimes not. With the passing of each administration, he hoped to be brought back for a significant position, and Mayor Koch did bring him back, but that didn't last too long, either. He was hard to place: friends would get him job interviews, and he'd ask his prospective employers what they'd do if he caught them doing wrong. When he retired, six years of his city service were cut out of his pension, in a dispute over whether they counted as NYPD time. As of this writing, it is still being litigated. The Job was not his friend.

Sonny Grosso and Eddie Egan were split up in 1967 and sent to precinct detective squads in Harlem and Brooklyn, respectively. They were celebrities then, and when the movie came out, they were stars. Aside from the predictable jealousies that fame and presumed wealth provoked, the hard-charging, rule-breaking, smack-'em-around-and-figure-it-out-later Popeye Doyle was the exact opposite of the image Commissioner Murphy wanted to project for the NYPD. Egan was as good a street cop as the NYPD ever produced, and Sonny told me, "He was the first through the door and the first to the bar. Perps in the cells used to brag about getting locked up by him."

Eddie and Sonny both began to moonlight in the movie business, one as an actor, the other as a consultant and later a successful producer. On the Job, their paths diverged less sharply, but all the same Sonny moved ahead steadily, while Eddie occasionally stumbled. He still made cases and collars, but the glory days were behind him; moreover, there was far more paperwork in the Detective Bureau than in Narcotics, and Eddie could barely spell. Most aggressive cops find themselves the subject of allegations of wrongdoing, and more than a few such claims surfaced about Egan. None of them was ever substantiated, but when he put in for retirement, he was hit with a slew of paper violations to stall his departure, while Internal Affairs continued to investigate. Chris Borgen, a Narcotics cop who worked with Egan and later became a TV reporter, said of him, "He's crazy, he's a fanatic, but honest he is. He just has no use for the dumb regulations, and no time for them. He nearly broke up Grosso's family because he kept on calling up at three o'clock in the morning saying, 'Sonny, we got to meet an informant,' and Grosso would go with him. He's a completely gung-ho cop. He loves being a cop. All he cares about is the Police Department."

Egan had been made a first-grade detective with less than four years on the Job, a record-breaking achievement. On the day before his Department hearing, he was summarily flopped to patrolman. He appeared in the trial room in his ill-fitting uniform, backed by supporters who included Roy Scheider, who played Sonny in the movie, and William Friedkin, who directed it. Egan was found guilty of various procedural infractions, as was expected, even though Murphy himself had since abolished some of them as onerous and wasteful. The judge gave him the maximum penalty—twenty days for each of the two sets of charges—and the matter was forwarded to the Commissioner. Murphy tried to fire him. After all, there had to be something, didn't there? Wasn't a cop like him who wasn't caught taking money simply too smart to be nabbed? And with all the Hollywood money, how would they be able to tell the clean cash from the dirty? Wasn't it safe to assume he's a bad guy and cut him loose? As it happened, Egan had made a total of $3,900 for all his work on the book and the movie. Though he was eventually reinstated, when he left the Job he owed back rent, owned a seven-year-old car, and had a bank balance of $89.79. Egan found some work as an actor, usually playing a cop, like an old gunslinger who retired to perform in Wild West shows. He ran a detective agency that failed, and a bar in Florida called The Lauderdale Connection. Egan died in 1995, at the end of my first year on the Job. Though he had his pension, he was broke at the end, and pretty much always in between. When he died, his latest wife was going to cremate him, but Sonny brought him back up from Florida and paid for his funeral, and arranged for a Marine Corps color guard to send him off. The Job was not his friend, either.

It was a radical moment for me, the awakening instinct that where I'd arrived was not a detour or a derailment but the intended destination all along. Should I ever have expected to fit in? I was unusual in my education and my side job but typical in my background, and common enough in the enjoyment and drive with which I worked. Only part of my problems had to do with my extracurriculars, and when I look back at the legends of the 1970s, most of them left the Job with the taste of ashes in their mouths. Maybe Sonny came to believe that it was a tragedy how the world had changed, because New York had reached a point in history where cop killers were treated better than cops, and maybe Serpico came to believe that the tragedy was that the world would never change, because the real culprits were not held to account. But both viewpoints as I imagine them sprung from a deep conviction that justice in New York City depended on the political courage of the NYPD, and these men feared that it was lacking.

In February of 1999, that sense of urgency began to awaken again in the city, with a degree of divided passions that had not been seen in decades. I came into work one morning and Angelo Ricci, our union delegate, began to pass the word: "There was a shooting in the Four-Three. Street Crime killed a guy, no gun on him. It doesn't look good." Four cops from the Street Crime Unit, who had been deployed there to search for the same rapist we'd hunted the last summer, had approached a man who was standing by a dark lobby. Many victims had been taken from lobbies, and more assaults had occurred in that neighborhood than in any other area. When the cops told the man to put his hands up, he withdrew into the lobby and reached to his waistband, and one of the cops thought he saw a gun and called out, and another of them tripped and fell as the gunfire began, leading the others to believe he'd been shot. In all, the cops fired forty-one times, and the man they killed, a West African immigrant named Amadou Diallo, was unarmed. He had apparently been reaching for his wallet. The encounter had taken place over a matter of seconds. When the cops realized what they'd done, one of them crouched down by the body and wept.

In the days afterward, the street static was heavy: the punks and the drunks were loudest, as always, but there was a palpable anger among legitimate people as well. The facts as they emerged didn't seem to favor the cops: Diallo had lied about political persecution on his immigration form, but he'd otherwise led a blameless and harmless life, earning a meager living as a street peddler downtown, though his family in his native Guinea were prominent and moneyed. The forty-one shots became a public fixation, cited as proof of the extravagant violence of the NYPD, and the Street Crime Unit in particular. Its motto—"We Own the Night"—was seen as a vigilante boast, though the logo in its entirety centered around a decidedly unmacho picture of an elderly woman walking in safety. (The old woman was an undercover cop, a reference to the decoy work of the unit's early days.) Though cops debated the tactics and the training of the four officers among themselves, there was little doubt that they had acted without malice, in the belief of a hideous necessity, the defense of their own and their partners' lives. Anyone who has had to challenge strangers on the rooftops and in the alleys of this city, who has confronted the furtive or forthright menace of sudden movement by half-seen hands, knows that instant of decision when gunshots can echo through a lifetime—whether that lifetime will last for a moment or decades. And few who had been there rushed to judgment.

Mayor Giuliani cautioned against a quick decision in the matter, which contrasted with his generally established manner. He had never enjoyed significant black support, having lost and then won in two bitter campaigns against David Dinkins, New York's first black mayor. The issues to which his administration was dedicated—crime and public order, welfare reform and cutting taxes—pitted him squarely against the left-liberal political establishment, which encompassed most of the city and almost all of its minority leadership. His style was combative and personal, and he gained enemies even as his support grew, winning a second term decisively as the city enjoyed such peace and prosperity as could barely have been imagined in my lifetime. Though the prosperity was concentrated in white Manhattan, the lion's share of the peace dividend went to nonwhite neighborhoods like the ones where I worked. The homicide rate had peaked at more than two thousand a year during Dinkins's term, and in the year of Diallo it would continue its dive, to about seven hundred.

In the public mind, Giuliani was not just the commander-in-chief of the NYPD, but a kind of incarnation of it—cops were seen as virtual mini-Giulianis. For six years, our successes were such that our association won both parties the reputation as the gold standard in their professions: he was the Big City Mayor, we were the Big City Cops. After Diallo, the next national news story from New York became the expected contest for Senate between the Mayor and First Lady Hillary Rodham Clinton, and Democratic leaders spoke openly of the need to transform his chief political asset into a liability. The theme that the price was too high, that Giuliani had "unleashed" the police, and "condoned" brutality for the sake of order, had been picked up by the opposition, which came to include most Democrats and much of the media, The New York Times included. The allegations flew in the face of all evidence: civilian complaints were down, and Commissioner Howard Safir, who succeeded Bratton, had fired more cops than his two predecessors combined. New York City cops shot people less often than in any other big city, and they shot people far less often than they had during the Dinkins Administration, and in the overwhelming majority of cases where they did shoot, there were unambiguous findings of justification. These facts were ignored and belittled, and Giuliani's reliance on them was even held up as evidence of his heartless and penny-wise indifference to the feelings of people of color. The Mayor and the cops never denied that Diallo's death was a tragedy, or that it mattered greatly, in human terms, but what it would come to mean in political ones would astonish everyone in the city.

You might have thought a lot of things by reading the papers then. You might have thought that the Dinkins Administration was a golden age of police-community relations, instead of the culmination of the crack wars and race riots such as those in Crown Heights. You might have thought that demagogues like Reverend Al Sharpton had become thoughtful and credible, when, as recently as 1995, he had made a vitriolic speech outside a Jewish-owned department store in Harlem, in which he used the words "the Jew" and "the enemy" interchangeably, and one man in his audience firebombed the building, killing seven people. And you might have thought that Giuliani's robust embrace of the NYPD would have made cops his most loyal supporters.

Before Diallo, the major police scandal of the Giuliani Administration had been the rape of Abner Louima by PO Justin Volpe, on the midnights in the Seven-O, in Brooklyn. Volpe thought Louima had punched him in the face, following a brawl outside a nightclub. After Louima was arrested, Volpe shoved a stick up his rectum in the precinct bathroom, causing major internal damage. The outcry in the incident's aftermath was fierce but relatively brief: an atrocity was alleged, and decisive action was taken. The assault was an aberration in every sense of the word, as even the harshest critics of the police would likely concede. Cops rightly took issue with certain aspects of the case—from the lies of the victim (his teeth were not knocked out by cops) to the ruthless zeal of the prosecutors, who dragged both the fiancée and father of one of the defendants before the Grand Jury—but on the Job, you heard little protest beyond a weak and wishful hope that it just wasn't so, it wasn't one of us. And cops knew that all was not what it appeared to be when it was claimed that one of Louima's alleged assailants had bragged, "It's Giuliani time!" Such a boast was as likely to come from a crack dealer in Bed-Stuy as a New York City police officer.

For years, the same moment of low comedy was repeated thousands of times in station houses, when a perp spat out his hatred for the Mayor to the cop who'd brought him in, expecting the provocation to be on the order of an insult to motherhood. The perp always had a look of beautiful confusion on his face when the cop shrugged and said, "That much I agree with you—I don't like him either."

The great achievement of the Giuliani Administration was the cut in the crime rate, and its instrument was the NYPD. Public safety laid the foundation for public prosperity, and cops could also be proud of their contribution to the city's recent and abundant wealth. And yet the NYPD didn't share in the reward: they were paid less than their counterparts in almost every large city in the country, though the cost of living was higher here than almost anywhere else. Cops in suburban counties like Nassau and Suffolk made nearly twice what we did, but cops in inarguably poorer jurisdictions, like Newark, New Jersey, also had salaries that were nearly 30 percent higher. We were partly to blame, in that the best that could be said of our union, the PBA, was that it was blind to the appearance of impropriety. One of our lawyers was caught gambling with union money, but when he was disbarred, he returned to work for us as a consultant, at still higher fees. None of the indifference and incompetence of the old union would have mattered much, had they secured for their members a decent raise, but after two years without a contract, the final settlement was a five-year package with small raises for three years, and no raise for two. There was an insurrection among the rank and file, and a new leader named Pat Lynch took over the union, but the damage had already been done. Giuliani had supported the police in every way but one, and for that, cops felt not just disappointed but betrayed. If there was any constituency in New York more alienated from the Administration than blacks, it was cops.

If Giuliani won the Senate race, he would be gone from Gracie Mansion the next year; if he didn't, he would go the year after that. The cops would remain to suffer the consequences of the Diallo furor for years to come. Most viewed the protests as highly dubious, mixing the well-intentioned with the plainly hostile and the occasionally surreal. Many commentators denounced the cops at these demonstrations for being deployed in "riot gear," which meant nightsticks and helmets. But cops always carry nightsticks, and the sole purpose of a helmet is defensive; I still can't figure out why the desire to avoid a head injury is such a grossly provocative act. Sometimes there would be five stories on the news about Diallo before there was mention of our sort-of-war against Serbia. We were daily witnesses to a search for truth led by Reverend Sharpton, whose first stop on his "national tour against police brutality" was at the headquarters of the Nation of Islam, which holds that white people were accidentally created in a laboratory by a pumpkin-headed demon. Diallo's mother joined him on his crusade, which was broadened in theme to denounce the police throughout the United States. Though Mrs. Diallo's loss was profound and her intentions were doubtless sincere, her own nation was a human-rights disaster—Amnesty International reported that an opposition leader was jailed because a police official had a dream that he would try to overthrow the state. Mrs. Diallo's grief was understandable, and Reverend Sharpton's stunts were predictable, but what was new in recent memory was how established figures and organizations were roused as much as the rabble. Politicians and union leaders, celebrities and clergy joined with racial radicals, ex-cons, and gang members for marches and photo-op arrests, as pundits intoned solemnly that the NYPD represented the most profound threat to peace in the city. The most astonishing assertions went unchallenged and unchecked, such as when Mayor David Dinkins blithely announced on a television news interview that the police would have opened fire on the young daughter of Bronx Borough President Fernando Ferrer, had she failed to obey their orders to stop her car. Was this where the healing would begin?

As the Diallo protest movement gathered force, it could still be argued that talk of a "crisis" in race relations in the city was overblown or premature, though the protesters labored long and hard to create one. There certainly was a crisis in the Police Department, in the soft science of morale but also in the hard figures of recruitment and retention. The coming years would see the retirement of one-quarter of the NYPD as the big hires of the early 1980s reached the twenty-year mark; other cops retired earlier, to take jobs in other jurisdictions, or to get out of the business altogether. There was great difficulty in filling the new classes in the Academy, and the valedictorian of one class quit the day after graduation, to take a job in Suffolk. Recently raised standards would be lowered again, and though the quality of recruits was defended by City Hall, one cop at Applicant Investigations told me that they were taking "just about everyone without a felony conviction." The Diallo protesters also blasted the NYPD for its lack of diversity, in that it was roughly two-thirds white in a city that was less than half white. But despite the failure of a ten-million-dollar advertising campaign targeted at non-whites, there was no crisis as such in "minority" hiring, either—Hispanic cops were roughly proportional to the Hispanic population, and I'd guess that officers named Gonzalez will become the kind of cultural cliché in the next century that patrolmen named Murphy were for the last two. The recruiting crisis faced by the NYPD was specifically in hiring black males, who made up less than 10 percent of the Department. But when Mayor Dinkins narrated a TV commercial showing a small black boy living in terror of the police, it was hard to envision how that made a practical contribution to solving the problem.

It may be overreaching to say that this feverish attention to scandal caused physical harm to cops—even when cops were gunned down by the dozens in the early 1970s, there were other forces at work—but it might not be, either. Who knows how many extra cinder blocks flew from rooftops at that time, or how many people watched from their windows as a cop struggled with a perp, and decided not to call 911 for help? When the rhetoric of scandal—rogue cops, racist cops, and so on—becomes the received idea, when we are so engrossed by exceptions that they seem like rules, we still send cops out, in ones and twos, into angry crowds, fighting families, and darkened alleys, though stripped of a measure of defense.

I wondered if Amadou Diallo died because the NYPD thought too little of the South Bronx, or too much. Whenever I heard about the forty-one shots, I thought about the fifty-one women raped. At the time of Diallo, there were just under two murders a day in New York City. Seven years before, there had been more than six. Four killings a day, mostly of men of color—some as blameless as Diallo, some not—were no longer facts of life here. The police tactics that saved these lives, from the "quality of life" crackdown and "stop and frisk" policies to cameras in housing projects to the very existence of the Street Crime Unit, which took in almost a thousand guns the year before— guns that were in play, in waistbands and in cars—had been opposed with shrill vigor by most of the protest leaders. The homicides that occurred around me rarely made the news, and of the hundred-odd murders that took place in the South Bronx that year, I doubt if ten victims were mentioned by name in the papers. In editorials, the debate was framed as a rift between the people who cared about the body count and the people who simply cared.

It is a relief, after all, that you can't care every time someone dies. But it can be chilling to see how people choose between the symbol and the statistic, passing over one death as an incident while elevating another to an issue. The Bronx DA personally arraigned the four cops who shot Diallo on murder charges, stating that his presence was necessary to send a message in the case—his second such act in his ten-year term of office, the first being for the Happy Land social-club killer, whose act of arson led to eighty-seven deaths. But police officers have also been killed in the line of duty in his jurisdiction during his term, and his absence at their killers' arraignments now takes on a symbolic weight.

A month after Diallo, we went to the funeral for Matthew Dziergowski, a cop in Staten Island who was killed when he drove into the path of a vehicle that was speeding toward his partners, who were at the site of a jackknifed truck. When you go to a police funeral, your job is to stand there for hours, at ease and then at attention, then at ease, then at attention again. That day was cold and rainy, which heightened the gloom of the occasion. The thick blue wool of our reefer jackets soaked up the cold water, and our feet went numb in our black patent-leather shoes. And I doubt I was alone in feeling sorry for myself, at times, and then feeling a little ashamed, for dwelling on my small and passing discomforts at such a tragic scene. When the hearse approached us, in our formed ranks, we raised white-gloved hands in salute. As the rest of the cortege filed past, I noticed that in the first cars, the limousines with family and close friends, no one looked out at us. Behind the rain-beaded windows, the faces looked down, or straight ahead, and several held their heads in their hands. Amid the hundreds who had come for the funeral, they remained alone in their loss. But as more and more cars went by, the focus of the passengers' attention seemed to shift outward, and the faces inside gazed at the ranks of blue. Their distance from the death—a matter of a few emotional degrees—let them take in the larger spectacle of mourning and tribute, which can have a power, in time, to comfort and to heal. Perspective is a blessing, and it can be had with a glance through the window.

I don't know much about the family of Matthew Dziergowski, but I'd guess that they cared as much about the color of the man who killed him as the color of his car. There are times it seems to matter, and times it doesn't. Two of the three cops who died in the line of duty the year before were black, Gerard Carter and Sean Carrington. Both were killed by black men, and in Carter's case, his killer was a teenager who had killed two men prior to that, both also black. The Urban League had published a report on cities that stated that one out of every three black men in their twenties was in prison, on parole, or on probation. It is a devastating number, and a national disgrace, and I haven't got the least idea about what to do about it, except for my job—which some would charge is part of the problem. Because the issues of crime and race—when they belong together, and when they do not—draw such awful and vociferous attention, too many people keep a kind of silence on these matters that is not entirely honorable, either.

There is an exercise I have seen a number of times in department training, which the instructor sets up by calling up a number of cops, black and white, from the audience. First, the instructor takes a black cop and makes him put his hands up on a wall, while two white cops flank him. "What do we have here?" the instructor asks. Several in the audience call out, "a collar" or "a stop." The instructor then puts a white cop on the wall, with two black cops holding him there. Laughter breaks out from the crowd, because no one wants to say "a mugging." The first lesson, of course, is of the power and danger of these stereotypes, which is of paramount concern to minority cops who work in plainclothes. But in watching the audience, I also noticed that the reactions tended to be the same across the color line, that black, white, and Hispanic cops tended to have the same reactions, of matter-of-fact nods for the first scenario and chastened laughter for the second. Over time and in the main, cops tend to think like other cops. One of the largely overlooked findings of the Kerner Commission, which studied urban unrest and decay in the late 1960s, was that black people said that black cops treated them no better than white ones did; they supported minority hiring strictly as an employment opportunity, without expectations of improved police-community relations.

We are responsible for our actions, to be sure, but our perceptions are formed in a long and often passive process. In street encounters, you have to remind yourself: *You never know.* But this wariness about exception suggests that there are, if not rules, terribly regular events that you learn to recognize, ever more quickly in time: *You know what you know.*

One day that spring, when we were bossless again, that lesson was repeated for me. The team was split up to fill in with sectors and conditions cars, and I worked with a team of seven other cops—all nonwhite, as it happens. We swept a lobby that was a steady crack spot, without success. As we filed out through the back door, a crackhead approached, a skinny white guy who was almost theatrically dirty, like a chimney sweep in a musical. He froze as he saw us, his relief at avoiding arrest spoiled by the realization that his pipe would remain empty, at least for a while. "The spot's shut down," I said. "If you want crack, come back in an hour, or try a block over." He about-faced and left, joining up with two other white guys, who hovered in the middle of the project grounds. They were not street people: they were younger, cleaner, and bigger, and they could not have stood out more if they were wearing tuxedos or cowboy hats. Because of their race, they could only be cops or criminals—and shabby amateurs, regardless—but they couldn't be just *people.* The three drifted off together. Several of us asked at once, "Are they cops?" I was instantly impressed by the idea of the crackhead as undercover, marveling at his mastery of disguise. I knew that white undercovers were rarely used in this area, but this was an operative of such surpassing skill that he could pick where he worked. The other two spoiled the scenario, however—even if a white undercover was in play, he would never have white "ghosts," deployed to discreetly follow him. But then one of the other cops said that he saw a radio in a back pocket, he was sure they were police. And then I wondered if they were with some other agency, and I shuddered to think of what state or federal group worked with the subtlety of the Bulgarian secret service. We stayed to watch them, more out of curiosity than the expectation of a collar. The two coppish guys began a series of lethargic migrations, back and forth across the grounds, from building to building. When they finally walked off, we rolled up on them, and all visual ambiguity disappeared at around twenty-five yards—and a strong olfactory read became available at ten. They drooled, they stank, their eyes rolled like dice, but in the distance and the dark, most of us had taken them for colleagues.

The history of race, the idea of race, is largely one of irrationality and cruelty, and there is no reason to expect that suddenly to change. When I hear black people complain about historic prejudice that endures in many and often not subtle ways, I tend to agree; and when I hear white people complain about set-asides and preferences intended not so much to keep them out but to bring others in, but having the same effect, I tend to nod along with them as well. I can be one hell of an agreeable guy, so much so that when a black cop said that I was one of the few white people she'd let in her house, I may have been more flattered than I should have been. I have been to see a judge, in plainclothes, with Orville, when he was told by a court officer that informants had to wait outside. And I remember reading about a black cop who was hired in spite of a robbery conviction, during a rushed drive to hire minorities. There is a troubled middle ground that most people occupy, myself included, where you shrug things off in order to be able to sleep at night, even if it means you're signing up for more tomorrow. You pick your battles, take small steps. As a cop, you have to take things day by day, case by case: if you collar a wife-beater or a dope dealer, you think about the household or the corner that is a little safer, for now, without dwelling on whether you've made some lasting contribution to the crusades against drugs or domestic violence—let alone whether these crusades are envisioned and equipped as they should be. And I thank God, or whatever party is responsible, that big-picture policy making on hot-button issues is outside the job description of a New York City police officer. It's easy to forget sometimes.

. . .

IT MAKES ME LAUGH—A LITTLE BIT, FROM A DISTANCE— that as that miserable winter turned to miserable springtime, the only harmony we had on the SNEU team was racial harmony. If nothing else, it was a reminder that things can always get worse. After my last warrant, I didn't fight anymore. I noted the periodic explosions with scientific detachment, observing that the screaming matches between the Sergeant and one or more of us seemed to happen every six weeks, at first, and then every four. All the little things that bothered us before—the sudden changes of schedule, the increasing demands for collars, the diminishing support—became less bear-able because there was nothing more to fight for. We'd begun to process our collars at the PSA again, but with our recent difficulties, we realized we were treated better as guests in other precincts than we were in our own house.

We went out to collar, or we didn't. One day, we had to wait so long for the van that finally we didn't leave the office. The Sergeant later told us that we were almost evicted from the room we'd built, but he'd managed to save us. None of us quite believed him. The remark also reminded us that our little corner of the precinct, which we'd built with our own hands—and our own money—could be taken away on a whim. When our numbers were down, the Sergeant told us that he might be thrown off the team himself, which didn't exactly spur us into fits of activity. We volunteered for dull errands that would have been insults before, like radio repair, making a day of it. The radio repair shop was in Jamaica, Queens, and if we went, Stix would call his wife, who would call her grandmother, who would walk to the corner poul-try market and have a chicken killed. She was a tiny woman who spoke only Italian, and she made everything herself—cheeses, roast peppers—and in the basement of her house, homemade sausage hung from the ceiling and the shelves were stacked with bottles of homemade wine. If something had to go to Headquarters or the Academy, we'd volunteer, driving slowly.

Still, we worked out of self-respect, and we worked because we liked it, not least because it provided a few head-clearing hours in which our oppo-nents were plain and the fight was almost fair. The fact that good work would reflect well on the Sergeant became a bewildering disincentive—it was the only poor power we had.

The Captain told the Sergeant to "do something with the kites"—the complaints of drug sales called in, that patrol could not respond to—since so many were in public housing. The most that might have been accomplished was that had we randomly arrested an individual who happened to live in a kite location, the Narcotics cop assigned—if we knew who he or she was—could have arguably closed that case. I pointed out that the vast majority of the kites were for apartments, which the *Street* Narcotics Enforcement Unit was not even permitted to address. Orders were orders, however, and for a couple of weeks, we were obliged to generate still more pointless paperwork for investigations that we were unable to conduct ourselves. Eventually, we stopped bothering. The wall maps were a source of pride for the new Ser-geant, so I took to coloring in lots more public housing—random blocks, at first, but eventually Yankee Stadium, the Bronx Zoo, and even islands in the East River became housing projects, by the stroke of my pen. Maybe it was a way for the world to become ours again.

The dreary Team Meetings continued: "The old man loves the walls. . . ."

"The old man loves the kites. . . ."

"From now on, we start our tour here, okay, Ed?"

"What happened yesterday can never happen again. . . ."

"Our days off are being changed—this is straight from upstairs, my hands are tied. . . ."

"We were this close to losing the room—I fought for you guys, tooth and nail. I can take an ass-chewing with the best of 'em. . . ."

When we did make it out, many of the unexpected moments of amazement or hilarity now took on grim and cautionary tones. Maybe it was because we cared less and let our guard down, or maybe it was that when we did care more, our trust in our judgment was more instinctive and complete. One day, John, Alicia, and I grabbed a crackhead, bent and scrawny but full of manic energy, who pushed away from us, hiding something in his hand. We knew it was probably drugs, but it could have been a razor, and he continued to resist, screaming that he'd just had back surgery even as he demonstrated surprising strength and agility. I held myself in check even when I knocked him down; after Alicia maced him, I cuffed him somewhat loosely, as he shuddered and howled about his ruptured discs. In the van, he began to rub his face against the seat, and I told him to sit still. He shrieked at me, "You shouldn't worry about how I'm sitting! You should worry about what's important! You should worry I got out of my cuffs! You're lucky I'm not a bad guy, I took my pills today, I'm not so crazy!"

And then he showed how he had freed his hands.

"You're right, that is important," I said. He had tiny wrists, bent thumbs, and his arm had been twisted around. This time, he got less slack, and within twenty minutes—one perp later—he began to scream again about his back, slamming his head against the window with his whole weight behind him. I thought the window would break, so we called it a day and took them in. Later, he told Tony that he didn't even have back problems; he just didn't want to ride around in the van for the next couple of hours.

There was one small consolation. When John took each perp's name for the paperwork, he turned away and said, "Oh! No!"

Alicia looked over and smiled brightly: "Another two numbers for Wopstat!"

Another night, we worked in light snow and gale-force winds. I always thought bad-weather work was better, since the perps were sloppy, anxious to unload their stash and head home. John and Chicky took rooftop OPs for the crack strip on Park Avenue, One-Five-Six to One-Five-Eight, the tall red projects of Jackson Houses, the taller concrete ones of Morrisania Air Rights, which were known as "Vietnam." The Sergeant got in my car without asking, which I took as an unwanted peace offering. The small talk we made was small indeed that day, but the set was busy: the first guy I took was on a bike, and the wind almost knocked us both down. When I rode his bike to drop it off at his apartment, two blocks away, I almost sailed there. The seller was in a car, and he hit off another buyer in a car, who drove up to One-Five-Eight before cutting left to Morris, where he was stuck at a light. We came up behind him, out of the line of sight of the seller, and we jumped out of my car, leaving it running. I took the driver out at gunpoint as the Sergeant approached from the passenger side, when the OP called out:

"The seller's moving, he's coming up your way!"

We didn't want the seller to see the stop, but the storm made the visibility poor and we had already committed to the act; beyond that, when the seller leaves, the set's done. The Sergeant yelled out, "We gotta move or the set is blown!" He ordered the driver back in the car and jumped in beside him. My car was still running, twenty feet behind. I wasn't going to get in a car with a crackhead who hadn't been checked for weapons and drive off into the snow. I also didn't want to leave my car. As their car began to move around the corner, I edged forward, keeping a midpoint distance between the two vehicles, watching both. Four facts occurred to me, in such bald clarity that they almost seemed numbered on a list:

1. I like my car.
2. I don't like my sergeant.
3. If I lose my sergeant, the Job will give me another one.
4. If I lose my car, the Job won't. . . .

And as I stayed put, I also thought, "What are you gonna say if the Sergeant is hurt? When they ask, 'Why weren't you in the car with him?'" That, too, came easily, and I answered myself as I would have answered them: "Because I'm not an idiot, that's why."

Buyer and seller were both taken without incident, however, and we went back in. The Sergeant went to the SNEU room to study for the lieutenant's test as we got to work. When John asked me where the drugs were, I told him to ask the boss, who held on to the evidence more often than not. John went downstairs and was told, "Ask Eddie." After John said that I didn't have them, the Sergeant began to yell for everyone to report immediately for a Team Meeting, on the subject of lost narcotics. They weren't lost, of course—Alicia had them, but John hadn't asked her yet—we never had and never did lose any product, but the Sergeant made us stop everything to listen to a ten-minute tantrum before he stomped out and went home.

In its way, his leaving was a kindness. Other bosses were forced to consider that SNEU's problems might be with management instead of labor. The desk officer had been barking at us to hurry up and get the perps out, but now he had to sign all our paperwork; two other sergeants were divided as to whether I should voucher the seller's car as evidence used in the commission of a crime or under asset forfeiture. We also had the buyer's car, and I'd locked the keys inside. He was a social worker at a hospital, and his ex-wife, with whom he still lived, was there to pick it up. She brought their four-year-old child along, and she explained that the back seat was loaded with groceries. John sat with her, feeding her lines to catcall to me: "We're waiting, Ed, you could be a little better organized. You didn't lose the keys, did you? Well? Where are they?"

I finally recovered them, and made a mental note to have a laugh at John's expense the next time the shit began to land on him. I didn't have to wait long, but I took no pleasure when it came: I worked through the night and into the next day, writing up the collar and taking the seller's car to the pound on the docks of Brooklyn. As the team came in for the four-to-twelve, I was leaving the precinct. The Sergeant ordered everyone into uniform and out on footposts, in punishment for our misbehavior the night before.

Though nothing bothered me as much as the vicious circus in the precinct, the cracked-out streets were not always a balm for the nerves. One day, when the Sergeant was out, Sgt. Rhoden covered us. We always worked harder then, hoping that someone might notice that we did better without our own boss. Tony and I caught a woman who ate her slabs of crack when we stopped her. Though we would have let her go, she decided to make a scene in the street, drawing a crowd, screaming that we planted drugs on her, that we raped people with broom handles—thanks again, Volpe—that we were racist white crackheads—Tony, too, apparently—and that she'd never been arrested. She finished by bellowing that she was pregnant and that she was going to sue us. That did it for me: I put my life in the hands of God every day, but I would never put a nickel on the table against a pregnant lady before a Bronx jury. As I put the cuffs on her, she screamed at the crowd that I'd stolen her food stamps. When I took her in, it began another twenty-four-hour odyssey that I dubbed Operation Lying Whore.

We filled the van, and took in bodies till we ran out of handcuffs—reasoning that seven would be a respectable number, eight would be a matter of principle, and ten would be a slap in the face. My collar was only the second, so poor Sammy and Orville had to listen to her rant for the next two hours till we came in. The perps were a loopy bunch—I told one to raise his hands while we searched him, and he began to pirouette, spinning around until the crack popped out of his pocket. Another tried to eat it as we approached, and I flattened him.

"Is it a hit?"

"Yeah, it's a hit."

My perp maintained her rage, hitting her high notes of Justin Volpe and stolen food stamps and miscarriage and lawsuits. The name of Volpe made us cringe. "He wasn't a cop," John said. She threatened to piss in the cell and demanded to go to the hospital. She looked me straight in the eye and said, "I never had any drugs. I would never do anything to hurt my baby." If I'd never met her, I'd have believed her.

When she returned from the hospital, hours later, I read the doctor's report: "Patient warned of potentially fatal danger of ingesting cocaine; patient denies ingestion. Patient complains of wrist pain from handcuffs and is given Tylenol. Patient claims to be three months pregnant but states that she plans termination."

I went home in the morning to shower and change before coming back in. As expected, most of the charges were dropped, but the ADA gave me a sympathetic ear on Trespass and False Personation, a relatively new misdemeanor which forbids giving a false name and address when in police custody. My prospects brightened considerably when I saw her rap sheet, which listed twenty-seven priors for prostitution and resisting arrest, with multiple variations on the names Tracy Johnson and Lisa Smith, neither of which was the name she gave me. Still, I reckoned that a Bronx jury might have at least as many whore buffs as cop buffs. And unless I had some kind of conviction for this arrest, I would most assuredly lose in civil court—when the DA declines prosecution, it has the effect of sending a telegram to a civil jury that the cop was flat-out wrong. The DA told me I needed proof that she was trespassing, in the form of an affidavit from the landlord, or I needed to prove who the woman who claimed to be both Lisa Johnson and Tracy Smith really was. At the Four-O, the affidavits were locked in an office, and no one had the key. There was a loose pile of out-of-date affidavits, in no particular order, that could cover a square mile of tenements. A cop who helped me at the Four-O shook his head before giving up, muttering, "If I saw how this place works when I was young, I would have turned to a life of crime, no question."

The search for the Lying Whore's true identity was equally exhausting, though a birth certificate she had used to apply for an apartment was finally obtained. I was relieved but also disgusted, as I might have found Jimmy Hoffa with all the effort it took. That spring, there were cops who made collars for guns and homicides, who took out savage gangs and sophisticated international conspiracies, but I have a feeling that years from now, when I sit down to tell war stories with other old veterans, I can say, "Those cases were all interesting and good in their way, fellas, but let me tell you about Operation Lying Whore. Very few people knew about it at the time, of course. . . ."

I'd had a trial for a minor but aggravating case, in which a drunk was having an argument with his wife, and she called the cops, but he wouldn't let us in. When we finally forced our way in, he fought us and gave one cop a lump on the head. The perp had screamed nonstop for six hours after his arrest: every white cop was a racist, every Hispanic cop was really white, and every black cop was a faggot. He spat at us in the cell and banged his head against the wall, yelling, "I want bruises!" He filed a complaint with the Civilian Complaint Review Board prior to his criminal trial, and after it, a civil lawsuit would doubtless follow, again in front of a Bronx jury. We had acted properly and the perp was on parole for armed robbery; nonetheless, everyone seemed confident of defeat.

The DA had already reduced the charges to Attempted Assault 3, the lowest level of misdemeanor, punishable by up to thirty days in jail. My ADA explained that even though the charges were less, at this level the defendant was not entitled to a jury trial, and they had greater hope for a fair hearing from a judge. In the Bronx, the conviction rate had dipped below 50 percent, and for misdemeanors it was even worse, as juries often didn't take the accusations seriously. I asked the ADA, "Do you ever prosecute jurors for perjury? Because it seems that every day, people swear under oath that they will listen to the evidence, and then they set out to sabotage these cases that can take years to put together."

"Well," she said, "we did prosecute the forewoman of one jury, not long ago. She was in the middle of a trial, and she asked the judge for a day off, because she said she had a doctor's appointment. A court officer noticed her in the building—she was a defendant in another case, and her trial started that day."

"That's a good one," I said.

During voir dire, the interviews for jury selection, each person is asked under oath about their experience with the criminal justice system, as defendant or victim, but usually not even the most elementary effort is made to corroborate those claims. One ADA told me about inheriting a murder case, after the first jury deadlocked. He checked the raps for the jurors and found that four had criminal records. None of those jurors were prosecuted. Nor was it policy to prosecute defense witnesses who were demonstrably lying— by providing false alibis, for example—because, as another ADA told me, if they win the case, they don't bother, and if they lose, "it looks like sour grapes." A cop told me about a brawl at court one day, when he saw court officers tackle a man who tried to escape from the Grand Jury. An undercover was testifying about a buy when the juror recognized him as someone he had sold to. Another cop told me about locking up a woman for buying crack, who begged for a Desk Appearance Ticket, because she had to get back to court, for jury duty—she was the forewoman on a Narcotics case, of course. The worst part about these stories is that when I told them to various ADAs, none were at all surprised; most of those I'd worked with I respected, but the institutionalized expectations were abysmal. They were too used to losing, and it showed in how they played the game.

At the trial of the drunken cop-puncher, however, the ADA surprised me on the stand by asking me where I went to college. As it would have been perjury to answer "Howard," I told the truth, and the perp took a plea. I'd have to tell my mother that my Harvard diploma had not been earned in vain, but in fact had proved essential to winning a conviction for Disorderly Conduct in the Bronx.

The lunacy reached such levels that you had no choice but to enjoy it sometimes, and maybe to add your bit now and then. When you went sick, you had two choices. You could go Regular Sick, which meant you had to see the District Surgeon on the next tour, who would determine when you had to come back, either for limited assignment or full duty. If you'd broken a leg, you'd get a couple of weeks off and a couple of weeks limited, working behind the desk or handing out radios. You could go Administrative Sick, for one or two days, without asking anyone, more or less, if you hadn't gone sick more than four times in a year. You called the precinct to notify a sergeant, and then you called the Sick Desk for a log number. But for some reason, when you called the Sick Desk, you couldn't say "I have a cold." The first time I called in with a cold, I was corrected: "You can't have a cold."

"But I have a cold. Why can't I have one?"

"We're not allowed to put that down. You have to say you have 'flu-like symptoms.'"

"Fine, I'll take it, put me down for a set of flu-like symptoms."

I didn't know what other diseases you were allowed to have, so for my next non-colds I tried out a variety of exotic ailments. The first one was Space Dementia, which Steve Buscemi had when his spaceship circled the comet in *Armageddon*. I think I identified with his inability to feel especially useful in saving the world from destruction. That got a laugh from a cop named Tommy Casey at the precinct, but it was recorded without irony at the Sick Desk. Maybe there was more of it going around than I thought. The next time, I went with Dutch elm disease, which, together with the gypsy moth, has wiped out many magnificent trees across the country. At the time, Dutch elm disease seemed a reasonable diagnosis because I certainly didn't feel like moving much. That one got by at the precinct, but I met unexpected resistance at the Sick Desk.

"I can't put it down that you have Dutch elm disease."

"Why can't you say I have Dutch elm disease?"

"You can't go Admin Sick with Dutch elm disease. You have to go Regular Sick."

"Right, I forgot. I guess I'll have 'flu-like symptoms.'"

"Okay, you got it. Hope you feel better."

And when my friend McTigue put in his papers to quit the NYPD to move to California, I advised him on his final illness. We'd had a few beers, and a death with dignity for him was not my highest concern, so I suggested that he call in with autoerotic asphyxia, a condition that results when self-pleasure and self-strangulation are combined, in the belief that oxygen debt heightens the climax. He called it in and got the days off, and he must have had a very bad case, because he never went back to work here again. Still, I talk to him often and he claims to feel fine.

· · ·

OUR PERSONAL LIVES BEGAN TO TAKE CENTER PLACE AGAIN, as maybe they always should have. Stix was getting married, Orville's and

Chicky's wives were having kids, Tony's mom was sick. I broke up with the girl I'd dated since the summer, when the Rape Detail had seemed an intolerable burden. Smacky left for Narcotics, finally, with the group that we all might have been a part of, when we were with PK. Alicia was thrown out of SNEU, after another Team Meeting was devoted to our shortcomings. She blew up at the Sergeant, yelling, "I do my job but I don't give a damn! I got my kids and my family! But these guys work too hard to be treated this way!" She had to be held back by us, and I don't doubt who would have won the fight. We began to talk about getting out.

Our career ambitions came to appear as not just a means of advancement, but a way of escape. But the sergeant's exam was given only every other year or so, and it might be another year or more before promotion; a transfer to a detective assignment, in the Squad or Narcotics, required them to need people and to want you, circumstances that often took years to coincide. John, Smacky, and Orville were determined to take the test; Tony, Stix, and I were determined not to, aspiring only for the detective's shield. I was determined not to step back: SNEU was our unit, not his, and he should go, not us. Sometimes, that seemed to be the likelihood, and that's why we stuck it out. Other times, I resolved that I would only accept being pushed up-and-out, but not back to patrol. I liked walking better than driving, but to walk again in the Village held no allure. And though the Village remained the biggest and busiest footpost, it had slowed down somewhat of late, which was good for everyone there, but not for me: I'd be running between domestic disputes and "stuck-occupied" elevator jobs, with fewer guns and robberies to make it worthwhile. We'd missed the boat for Narcotics, and no other specialized unit was picking up cops, with one exception.

I decided to go to Street Crime. Tony and Orville had gone for two weeks, earlier in the fall, and they made a gun collar on their second or third night. Tony especially liked the gun hunt, the nocturnal and freestyle prowl, but he felt that he could not in conscience join full-time. His reasons were the same for his refusal to become an undercover—the work could be exhilarating, but the risks were too high for a man with a wife and child. Kevin Gillespie, a cop from Street Crime, had been killed during a carjacking in the Four-Six two years before; Chicky had been one of the first cops at the scene, and he didn't sleep well afterward. Tony knew Sean Carrington, another former Housing cop who'd gone to Narcotics, who had also been killed in the Four-Six. Tony was inclined against Street Crime before Diallo, and afterward it seemed ridiculous. John, too, had been drawn to the unit—his brother-in-law, Rob

Reed, was assigned there, and he loved it. But he still blamed himself for PK's transfer from SNEU—and maybe he always would—and he was reluctant to expose himself to more risk. The four cops from Street Crime would go on trial for the murder of Diallo, and the unit was under investigation by Internal Affairs, the New York State Attorney General, and the Department of Justice, while politicians still clamored that they were "not being held accountable."

Even so, John agonized for a month over whether to apply with me, tilting one way and then the other before asking for more time, and then more, before finally declining. I began to have a deepening sympathy for his poor girlfriend, Julie, whom he'd dated for five years. John's reasons for not going were better than mine for going—he had a modest appreciation for how a split-second decision on the street can change things—but Street Crime worked for me in a number of ways: you had steady days off, and you worked from six at night to two in the morning. In my career so far, I'd worked a couple of years on a beat, a couple of years in SNEU, and so a couple of years on the gun hunt seemed to fit. As long as I had good partners, it offered far more fun and games than SNEU, with even bigger prizes: you wouldn't sit on a roof, looking for slabs and bundles, but instead drive all night, chasing guns. Search warrants would not be thrown away. Street Crime was not classified as an investigative assignment, and there would be no gold shield at the end of eighteen months. Whether or not that was well-planned or even fair, the result was that it drew cops for whom the work was its own reward. It was a guts-and-glory unit, and within the Job, some cops muttered the same complaints about them that police critics at large leveled against the NYPD. I thought it would suit me fine.

When I asked the Captain to sign my recommendation for transfer, he reacted as my mother might have if I told her I was joining the Foreign Legion. Now, it seemed, he wanted me to stay at PSA-7. But as usual, he packed his argument with as much stupidity as sense, claiming at one moment that the unit would be disbanded, and the next that I'd be stuck there for ten years with nothing to show for it—"And then you'll be sent back here." Throughout the speech, I'd interrupt, "But will you sign it?" He fumfered and told me to think about it over the weekend. When I pursued him again the next week, he signed the recommendation with a terse smile, but he omitted the section for the evaluation. When I dropped off the application at Street Crime, on Randall's Island, they sent me back to the Captain, who referred me to the Admin lieutenant for a few lines of modest praise.

That day, I also got my first Command Discipline, for having "unauthorized off-duty employment." Though the magazine pieces had been approved by a Commissioner, I hadn't filled out forms at the command level. My punishment was the lightest possible—"warn and admonish"—but I was also perturbed at the thought that this could be considered a fortunate resolution. I'd told people how much I loved the NYPD, of its wonders and dangers, and I got off with a slap on the wrist.

You have to talk to people about these things. I had Tony, Orville, Stix, Sammy, Chicky, and John to talk to at work, and John even afterward. Aside from Inspector Mullen, my chief consigliere on the Job was Mike Shea, a friend and neighbor who was then a newly appointed captain. Mike was a distinctive figure, military in bearing, with a crew cut and wire-rimmed glasses, and even off duty, he wore a coat and tie. He had an MBA and a law degree, and had turned down a free year of graduate school at Harvard to study for the captain's test. In the event that working at, living with, and writing about the NYPD somehow wasn't enough, I'd have dinner with Mike for a little cop talk. Mike thought that Street Crime was an excellent idea—that I'd like the unit, and that I'd work well there. He also knew the CO and would make a call for me.

Cops explain a lot of things by saying, "He had a phone call," and the "hook" is a long-standing feature of Department lore. The comment was most often made when it looked like a cop was about to get in a lot of trouble but didn't, or got a prize assignment without working very long or hard for it. But being called a "son of a chief" wasn't the same as being called a "son of a bitch," and it was rarely held against a cop who was liked or respected. There was so much unfairness on the Job, so much undeserved aggravation, that an unearned break was accepted by most fair-minded cops, if only because they would accept such breaks themselves. I had a more nuanced view of the value of a real phone call—not a casual "Let me know if I can do anything for you," from a captain at a racket, or a "My uncle's old partner was best friends with the Commissioner's nephew"—but a true "contract," a deal. I thought of them as resembling Internet stocks more than blue chips, in that their worth varied wildly from one moment to the next and depended on circumstances which were largely out of your control.

My father was a master of the phone call. He met every Police Commissioner from the fifties through the eighties, but an entire generation had come and gone since he'd retired himself—the rookies of his last days had already packed for Florida. My uncle Joe would often mention how he just went to

Ireland or Atlantic City with this Chief of Detectives or that Chief of Patrol, since retired, always ending the story with the line, "And he knew your father very well." My father was liked and respected, and he was around for a long time. Various friends had risen high: one friend, Andy Maloney, had become U.S. Attorney at the Eastern District, and he put John Gotti away for life; two others, John Sprizzo and Kevin Duffy, had become federal judges. And because my father had little ambition—at least of the conventional kind, preferring to remain a field agent for the entirety of his three-decade career—his influence was thus increased because he was not in competition with anyone at the FBI, and certainly not in the NYPD. He could take people to dinner at the Commuters and arrange for summer jobs for cops' kids at Con Edison, where he would work himself after retirement. But my father knew clearly the difference between influence and power, and understood the limitations of each. He'd tell me the story of a chief who had a favorite seat at a steak house, and when he'd arrive, the maitre d' would evict whoever sat there, and though my father never mentioned it, I assume that the chief didn't pay the full freight when the check came. "Only a couple of days after the chief retired," my father went on, "he went back to the steak house, and instead of going straight to the table, the waiter says, 'It's great to see you again, I'll let you know as soon as something opens up.'" The chief could have had a heart attack right there. But when you play that game, you're in it or you're out, and when you're gone, you're gone. People don't care who you used to be.'"

I wasn't anyone, really, and the fear of what I might become was a part of my problem at the precinct. The Serpico stuff was ludicrous—there would be no Conlon Commission to succeed Knapp. I would not testify in the halls of the Congress, answering questions before the cameras, as lawyers whispered in my ears and aides scribbled notes.

"Officer Conlon, is it your statement, under oath, that the Captain is a weasel?"

"Yes, Senator, a very big weasel."

"And the Sergeant as well?"

Whisper, whisper . . .

"More of a rodent, I'd say, Senator."

"Very well, then. Let's now address the matter of the couch in the SNEU room. . . ."

"With all due respect, Senator, there is no couch in the SNEU room."

Resounding laughter and applause . . .

At Street Crime, there was a push for minority recruitment, since one of the many criticisms of the unit was that it was mostly white. A new black executive officer—or XO, meaning second in command—had been brought in, DI Wheeler, who had been the XO at PSA-7. Wheeler had not been at the PSA long, but he was highly regarded, seen as someone who would remain a street cop at heart, regardless of how high in the Department he rose. When he stopped by the precinct, he saw Tony and Orville and made a beeline to them, asking if they were interested in coming over. They knew Wheeler and I didn't, and I hung back at the side like a homely girl at a dance. Tony had decided against it, but Orville seemed tempted, and I think if he'd demanded a chauffeur and a three-day week, Wheeler might have said, "Let me see what I can do." As it was, when Wheeler asked, "So, do you want to come?" Orville just laughed and said, "Where, from the frying pan to the fire?"

Not long into my Street Crime interview, it became clear that I'd remain in the frying pan for a while longer. I showed up in a new suit on my day off, and I was a little surprised to see that there were only black guys there. I knew a couple of them, including one friend, Crosby, from my Academy company, and we gathered in a little huddle, wondering about what questions they'd ask. Whenever a cop came out from his interview, he told us what they wanted to know, and we pored over the words like schoolboys with half the answers to a test. When I was sent for, a white cop approached me on the sly and whispered that he was glad to see a guy like me there. A passing sergeant looked at me and observed, "You must be Conlon, the white guy." The interview was conducted by a captain, a lieutenant, and two sergeants, who asked questions as they looked over my application, in which I'd written where I went to college in the same scribble that two out of three of my Academy teachers took, happily, for Howard. Other questions such as off-duty employment were finessed with understated generalities ("self-employed"). At first, I enjoyed the interview, breezing through the law questions and debating the tactical ones, asking as many questions back as were answered. Then the sergeant asked, "Where did you go to school?" I told him, and there was a pause, and the captain asked, "Did you write a book?"

"No, but I'm writing one."

There was another pause, and then he said, "I know who you are."

The subject went no further. That was my mistake. It would have been faster if the lieutenant had just pushed the button for my ejector seat, but instead he thought a moment and asked, "What if you were with a team that just worked out for half the tour, and spent the other half hanging out in a diner? What would you do?"

"I'd have to get off that team. I'm here to work, and besides, I'd be new here—if I didn't produce, I'd be gone."

The next question was ratcheted up a notch: "What if they worked out and hung out for six hours a day, but managed to make their collars in the remaining two?"

"I wouldn't want to work like that. But if they're good enough to grab gun collars in two hours, who am I to tell them how things are going to be different?"

It was an honest answer and a fair one, although utterly naive to the direction we were going. I got some sourpuss looks, and then it was on to the next level. "What if you found out that when they went out," said the captain, "they were taking money from stores?"

"That would be completely different."

"How is stealing money different from stealing time from the City?"

"One is a crime, one isn't."

From that, it should have been clear that I was finished. A few hours later, I was told that the board had given me the lowest possible rating. I'd failed on my responses to the "integrity questions." There were echoes of Orwell in the interview, from the suggestion that laziness was a crime against the state to the way that my failure to tell them the lies they wanted to hear reflected a lack of integrity. I was informed that I could appeal, or request another interview, but I decided I'd let it go for now.

Later on, John's brother-in-law, Rob Reed, said he was there when I was discussed at a supervisors' meeting, and the prospect of bringing a reporter into the unit, so to speak, at that point in history was a nonstarter. I could hardly hold it against them, but I wish they hadn't wasted my day off. The Captain approached John and remarked with an amused air that he heard about how my integrity sank me in the interview. It made me wonder who the Captain had spoken to, and when. I had a hard time believing he'd be any happier about me staying than I was, but he threw up roadblocks every time I tried to leave.

Our old CIs didn't seem to prosper any more than we did. Stix saw Chihuahua on the street holding a live earthworm in his hand, with which he was engaged in earnest conversation. A few months after I'd last seen Charlie, I ran his name and saw that he'd been collared again in Washington

Heights, for drugs, and in the spring, John and I went back to look for him under the bridge. With Charlie and Tommy, the little camp looked like a dump hit by a hurricane. Now, it was clean and orderly, enclosed by a wind-break of trash bags wrapped around broom handles. A mattress had blankets folded on it, and the collection of books and clothes in a shopping cart was piled up more or less evenly. New tenants, I thought—the idea that Charlie and Tommy had become house-proud made me laugh. There was movement behind the enclosure: another white junkie, with long hair and tattoos. We couldn't ask about Charlie directly, but as we drew him out, he said that he used to have a friend who stayed there, and for a while there was an old man, who wasn't a junkie but a recent widower who couldn't bear to sleep at home. I gave him a cigarette, and he relaxed. "Can you believe it?" he asked. "I've only been on junk for two years. I was a machinist. . . .

"We help out the cops here, look around if somebody's robbing or beating people or whatever. We don't steal. I help out, you know, but I won't inform. You guys did a great job here with dope, I mean, I gotta go to Jerome Avenue to score. It's a hike. But crack's still all over the place on University. I stay away from crack, though. Crack killed my sister."

Though we were not in the market for informants, sometimes they turned up regardless, like postcards sent to the wrong address. And since it's not against the law to read someone else's postcard, we tended to take a peek. John signed up a CI who named himself Gallo, which is Spanish for "rooster," when he stopped by the precinct to say he wanted to work. When we talked to him, all he had to offer was a stash spot in a tenement mailbox for the crack dealers down the street. I thanked him and sent him on his way. A couple of days later, when I was stricken with Dutch elm disease, he came back and found John, telling him about how he knew a guy who had seven guns to sell. John and I talked a dozen times on the phone, going over new facts and old omissions in the story, and again when he got home, but for that day and the next, John had to pull the whole load alone. I think I felt more sick from being out of the game than from Dutch elm, but we also decided that it would be better for John to run with it by himself. Gallo was his CI, and he had to to learn how to handle an informant and an investigation on his own. And we didn't need to dwell on it, but the fact that my mere presence might shitcan whatever developed was a risk to be avoided as well.

I wouldn't have wished Gallo as a "starter CI" on anyone. When he first came in with news of the man with seven guns, he only had a first name and no address for the perp. When told to find out more about him, he returned the next day, brimming with excitement about another guy he'd met, again with no address and not even a first name, who had a quarter kilo and a .38. A few days later, he was back with a story about a third guy in the Heights, with half a kilo and two guns; the first two perps were forgotten. Each day was entirely new, and in subsequent appearances, he told of a local guy who had a .38 for sale, and of the twice-weekly drug pick-up, in which four guys, all with guns, made the trip from One-Five-Three and Melrose to 175 Alexander and back. I thought there was something to each of his stories, but for all they were worth in terms of evidentiary or even investigative value, he might as well have told us to quit our jobs because he knew there was gold in California.

Gallo himself was a strange bird who cooperated for the double thrill of playing cop and criminal at once. He was awful about staying in touch, rarely calling when he said he would, with excuses that were sometimes plausible—"One of the dealers was with me by the phone!"—and sometimes just aggravating—"It turned out to be a great party!" Despite constant instructions, he would stroll right in the front door of the precinct, when the perps he was giving up were two blocks away. John was the good guy ("When you don't call, I'm afraid you got killed") and I was the bad ("If you do that again, don't bother coming back"). I took a stronger dislike to him when I found out he was a rich kid, the son of two doctors who owned a laboratory in Puerto Rico. He had gone to college in Arizona on a baseball scholarship, where he majored in business. Afterward, he came to New York and looked for a job.

"What kind of job did you find?"

"Counting money at a dope spot."

Though he was sentenced to probation when his dope spot was raided, Gallo got tired of the city and went back to the Puerto, where his fun-loving ways continued. He worked for the police, and he claimed that they almost let him make arrests himself. He wore a wire that helped catch a bank robber, and he testified at the trial. He asked us for a vest, and made it clear that if we wanted to give him a gun, he wouldn't complain. After a brief, bad marriage, his wife had him arrested for assault and burglary, but he nonetheless won custody of his kid, whom he handed off to his parents. He hadn't seen the kid in years. After bouncing around the island for a while, he decided to return to New York. He was looking for work, and he could use a little money.

At first, John had casino eyes: he wanted the seven guns and the two guns and the one and the four, plus the drugs—why not?—while we were at it. Shortly after, he calmed down a little, and even though we didn't expect to

go all the way through with a warrant, we began to look at it, to begin to verify the information just to ascertain his credibility. Gallo had gone back to the
spot in the Heights, and we schooled him on the importance of addresses
and apartment numbers. He gave us a building on the southeast corner of
Audubon and 180th Street, apartment #6C, and a perp named Tony who
worked for the phone company. We went there late one night: the building
had five stories, and there were no six-story buildings in the area. Sorry,
sorry, the next day, he corrected himself: it was Amsterdam and 180th. Later
that night, we found a six-story apartment building where the apartments
were numbered 61, 62, 63, and so on, rather than 6A, 6B, 6C. It was after midnight, but I told John to call him. Gallo said it was too late to talk, but he
would take us there tomorrow. He hung up the phone. "This guy isn't splitting atoms on his day off," said John.

"Give me the number," I said.

When he answered, he was surly: "Do you know what time it is?"

"Yeah, I know exactly what time it is, because I just wasted the last two
hours chasing your bullshit information. I told you how this is gonna work.
You don't get three fucking tries to get a fucking address right."

"I'm sorry, I'll take you there tomorrow."

"That's not good enough," I said, and I hung up on him.

We let him alone for a few weeks, and then John called him up again.
Gallo apologized, and explained that his aunt, with whom he was staying,
had a habit of listening in on his calls from the other extension. That was not
a bad excuse, in fact, but his credibility—at least in terms of elementary accuracy of detail—was so poor that I would not bring him before a judge, let
alone take a door on his say-so. But we always saw him on the corner with
the dealers, and bit by bit, he gave up plausible information about the weekly
trip to Alexander Avenue. We watched it informally for a while, and we identified the two regular travelers; Gallo sometimes went as one of the two extra
men. If a warrant was out, a car stop was definitely possible.

The problem was how to set it up for maximum effect—perps, guns, and
drugs—without getting anyone hurt or exposing Gallo as an informant. We
thought about telling Gallo to just run away, without the gun, but Orville
pointed out that you just shouldn't program that kind of chaos into an already volatile situation. We talked to a number of DAs and detectives for
ideas, though nothing seemed to fit, until John and I went to talk it over with
Sam Ramer. Sam happened to be having lunch with his boss, Ed Friedenthal,
the bureau chief, as well as two other DAs I'd written warrants with, Frank

Randazzo and Tina Petrillo. We had a little brainstorming session, everyone arguing upsides and down, legal and tactical, and it was a thrill to be with people who knew what they were talking about and were determined to make it work. If we took the two in the building, we'd lose the two in the car; if we took the car before the visit, we'd lose the drugs, and we still needed a pretext for the stop. I thought of it: when the car parked outside of 175 Alex, we would wait for the two to go in and out of the building, and just as they were about to get back in their car, we would grab them. We would take them for trespass, and their proximity to the other two men and the car would give us grounds to toss them, too. Gallo told us that he and the fourth man always waited outside the car, and Gallo would leave his gun on the car floor, in plain view. We would get four guns, all the drugs, and four bodies, but with a terminally weak case against Gallo and the other, less culpable perp. And two cases dying a natural death would halve the suspicion on Gallo.

We tacced it like a warrant, with diagrams of both locations, and all the assignments for OPs and tails, roadblocks and hospital cars. We must have had eighteen cops involved; it was to be the D-day of car stops. John presented it to the pack of bosses, and he defended it with far more diplomacy than I would have when the predictable objections were raised.

The Captain said he wanted everyone taken in the car: "I don't care if he's killed, I don't care if he has to go through the system, I don't want any cops hurt." John pointed out that Gallo was a volunteer, and that while he was willing to spend a night in jail for the case, and even to risk his life, we were in no position to tell him he faced real jail time by helping us. When that made no impression, John said that the plan was Bureau Chief Friedenthal's, and he was adamant that we adhere to it. It was precisely the right pitch. There was more give and take—

"We don't want a gun battle in a moving car."

"We don't want a gun battle in a foot pursuit, either."

"What if he doesn't show up?"

"What if there are more guys?"

What if the building collapses or the cars explode? Finally, the plan was approved, and we waited for Gallo to tell us when they'd be going. A few days later, he called: it would take place tonight, no earlier than ten, no later than ten-thirty. We took our places half an hour before and waited. Ten passed, and ten-thirty, and at ten-forty, orders were given to quit. After eleven, Gallo called to say it had been postponed. On another night, we planned it again, but Gallo again failed to appear. We would not get another chance, with the full manpower it required, and we debated uneasily among ourselves whether we should run with it alone, if we suddenly got word. It was a damn good plan, I thought.

Gallo continued to blithely drop by the precinct. He would ask random cops at the desk to borrow money, or for a ride somewhere. Once, he was stopped on his way downstairs to the SNEU office. His long-lost kid came to visit him at his aunt's, and he brought her to the precinct, too. I was disinclined to have anything more to do with him, but he told John that he'd run into the local kid with the .38, who was anxious to sell it to him. He could set it up whenever we wanted. John was against shutting him down completely—he couldn't give up the guns—and he decided to play it by ear.

I heard how it went at home, when he called me. Orville and I had done a day tour for court, and the rest of the team was out, too, leaving John and Sammy alone on the four-to-twelve. Gallo called and said the kid was meeting him in an hour; John picked the place, around the corner from the precinct, and sat in an unmarked van with Sammy to watch. He told Gallo to scratch his head like he had lice to signal when the kid was there with the gun. Gallo showed, the kid showed, the head was scratched, and John and Sammy moved in and took him. "It turned out perfect," he said.

Again, I felt like the ugly girl at the dance, but John was right when he said that there are times when you have to move at the moment or forget it forever. I was disappointed that I hadn't been there, though I understood why it had happened. But in a later, fuller account from both John and Sammy, I was even more frustrated, because "perfect" might have described the ending, but nothing else before it. From the start, Gallo called to say that the meeting was set, again ignoring instructions that we were to choose the time. And when the seller showed up, he wasn't alone, but with his brother, who also had a gun. John and Sammy watched them talk from the van, and then the brothers stepped off for a moment. Gallo then took the opportunity to stroll over to the van to let them know the play-by-play. When I heard that, I was horrified: had the brothers returned a moment too soon, it would have told them to prepare for an ambush. Gallo had put everyone's lives at risk because he couldn't wait to tell John how well he was doing. A minute after he returned to his place, the brothers came back. He scratched his head, and John and Sammy rolled in; the kid dropped one gun, and they took him; the brother ran and got away.

Gallo had another gun in the works, from a guy who lived in the Village, in one of my old buildings. John said, "This collar's yours, if you want it." I didn't want to lose the gun, but I wasn't going to let Gallo run rampant. I talked to Smacky in Narcotics, who was working for Sgt. Poplaski from the PSA, and both of them now worked for Lt. Zerbo. I figured that if anyone could lay down the law to Gallo, Zerbo could. It was the classic dilemma: whenever you asked for help, you risked losing control. I told John to decide whether we should keep him. His decision was that it was my decision. I thought about what I could live with and what I could not, about the collar and the possibility of casualties. Some of my partners had children and the rest of us would like to. I called Smacky and said, "He's all yours. Be careful." Gallo made one dope buy for them and then he disappeared.

. . .

THE WARM WEATHER CAME BACK AGAIN. WE HUNG IN AND hung out, worked and waited. Sometimes weeks would pass between blowups with the Sergeant, and after a few peaceful weeks, the chill silences would give way to jokes and casual conversation between one of us and him. Stix invited him to his wedding, which annoyed me. But he explained that since everyone else was invited, and we joked about it—how the sheriff would have to be notified that minorities were coming to town, or that Orville would park the cars and Sammy would do the dishes—it would be disrespectful not to invite him.

"But you don't respect him."

"I know I don't respect him, but he's the boss—and it's a slap in the face if I don't invite him. It'd be too awkward, too weird."

I didn't have to say that things were plenty awkward and weird as they were. The Sergeant sometimes rode in his own car in the field, which did minimize the fights over who would get stuck driving him. On occasion, it emerged that his separation from us was more than physical. He didn't really know the precinct, and once, when we charged a lobby to hit a set, he ran into a building half a block away. Another time, we looked at 550 East 147th Street for an hour before concluding that nothing much was happening and moving on. The Sergeant stopped at the precinct as we set up for another spot, and a few minutes later, he called us all back.

"I have a new spot, it's working, it's hot," he said, with excitement.

"Where is it?"

"Five fifty East One-Four-Seven."

"Um, Sarge, that's where we just were."

As our respect eroded still further, his assertions of authority became more frequent and desperate. Since the drug game was clearly not his forte, he lunged into any other kind of police activity that came over the air. All cops raced to 10-13s—"Officer in need of assistance"—wherever they were, but for robberies and gun runs, only cops in the immediate area should respond. The Sergeant would have us fly two precincts away for those jobs, driving at breakneck speed, and he'd bark orders at the scene even if lieutenants and captains who actually belonged there were present. The team took to calling him "Captain Chaos," and Orville resolved, "I am not going to drive with him again until my child is born."

Another time, he sent us out in the field, saying he'd catch up with us later. That day, John and I fought a guy I almost shot—hand in pocket, pointed at me, repeated refusal to remove it—and when the Sergeant arrived, he announced it on the air like a conquering hero: "Hey guys, I'm back! And I got the van!" John said, "I gotta say something to this dope," and picked up the radio: "Who gives a fuck where you are? Do us a favor and stay home!" I yelled, "Holy shit! No!" and tried to grab the radio from him. John laughed his head off—he hadn't keyed the mike—"You were afraid! You really were afraid!"

The Sergeant would complain about the numbers, and then he'd announce that we'd spend one day a week cleaning the office: "We'll call it Clean Day." He went away for a week, after telling us that he'd arranged for Sgt. Rhoden to cover us. On the first day, we told the four-to-twelve lieutenant—a new transfer—about the situation, and he smiled and said, "You're not going anywhere. I have other plans for you." He sent us back to get into uniform, and then he pulled cops who had regular sectors into conditions cars, and we filled in the sectors. Sgt. Rhoden asked, "What does he have against you guys?"

"I have no clue. The guy just got here, he hasn't even had a chance to hate us yet."

So it went for the week, and when the Sergeant returned, we told him what had happened.

"Maybe he needed to cover patrol," he said.

I said that wasn't the case.

"Yeah, he told me he was fucking with you," he admitted.

What was there to say? I remembered the line that went, "Hollywood is high school with money," and wondered, "Is the Police Department high school with guns?" I thought of my father trying to make me the messenger to Mike Kelly, saying that he had no idea what awaited him on the Job. That June was my father's eighth anniversary. My family went to eight o'clock mass in the morning, and then we all went to work. The family got together again for dinner later on, and my sister Marianne asked me how my day was. I said, "I grabbed a guy by the neck until he spat out his heroin." She covered her ears, and I don't think she's asked me how my day went since.

Still, there were little things at work that made us laugh. The way we talked, the way perps talked, the way the Penal Law and the *Patrol Guide* failed to describe the realities we knew. One cop was yelled at by his wife when she found a note in his pocket that said "ADA Smith" and a phone number: "Who is this Ada Smith, and what does she want with you?" One night when we were watching *Jeopardy!* on TV, a couple of the guys challenged me to call out the answers. I got them right, and Sammy nodded in approval as he remarked, "You're a regular Rogue Scholar." Sammy had a few other deft slips, my favorite of which was when he referred to the "Verbal Judo" course the NYPD was big on that year as "Gerbil Voodoo." I found a great OP for One-Five-Three and Melrose, from an apartment roof just down the block. John and I went up, and we gave out four bodies in five minutes, crouched down by the low parapet, which reached just above the knees.

"I wish I had a bucket to sit on," John said. Just then we both looked across the roof, at a clean plastic bucket of the perfect height, which we'd failed to notice earlier.

"You idiot!" I said. "What a waste of a wish! You could have had Cindy Crawford, a million dollars—and all you got was an old bucket on a South Bronx tenement rooftop. I'm ashamed to even know you."

"Still," John said, looking down. "It's a good bucket."

Other moments of fun made us think that in the end, we might have the last laugh. There was the bribery collar, which came about one day when Chicky, Tony, John, and I drove up University, in the Four-Six. Since we hadn't been back much since PK left, and we later took to processing collars at the PSA, our disappearance seemed to have taken on sinister overtones. I saw a Four-Six cop at Central Booking, who said, "I heard you guys killed a perp and got disbanded." I just shook my head. It was a novelty to be back, and when we stopped at a light, John had another surprise, as he looked over at the scrawny white guy in the Camaro next to us, shooting up. Some junkie intuition kicked in on Camaro's part, too, and he peeled out up the street, breaking right on One-Eight-One, down a one-way, against traffic. We didn't chase him, as such, because the streets were narrow and crowded, and our van had only a little dash-top light—there was no siren, and the horn was still busted. But Camaro forced other cars off the road, and he left so many pissed-off people in his wake that the whole neighborhood joined in to help us, standing at the corners to point out where he'd turned, until we found where he'd abandoned his car to flee on foot. Chicky and I jumped out to chase him down an alley while John and Tony rounded the block in the van. At the end of the alley was a six-foot wall with a chain-link fence on top, which the so-called Short-a-Rican vaulted like an Olympian, and then there was another alley, wall, and fence, and by the time we got through the block, we saw Camaro lying on the sidewalk, hyperventilating, twitching, and bleeding from the hands. Chicky and I were spent, too, and we just sat down next to him. Camaro was lucky we caught him—he wasn't even cuffed for fifteen minutes, because we let him breathe into a beer-soaked bag, and the street justice would have been unforgiving. As it was, when we went back to his car, the radio and his jacket were stolen. The neighborhood treated us like conquering heroes, like we were firemen instead of cops. Camaro looked like he might go DOA, and I asked the guys if anyone wanted the collar:

"Nope!"

"Nope!"

"Are you kidding me?"

I wanted to put this guy away for a while; he could have killed kids. At the moment, we had a hundred witnesses, but tomorrow we might have none. If Camaro went into cardiac arrest after his junkie triathlon of shoot, drive, and run, a few months down the line we would face a wrongful-death suit with nothing to show but four Bronx cops saying, "You shoulda been there!" I told John to spread the word that we didn't care about the radio, we just wanted to check the jacket for drugs, and he disappeared in the crowd. Moments later, the jacket was produced, but it was clean of dope and works. Chicky and I drove back in the Camaro, an immaculately restored 1982 model, tricked out with flame decals. One tire was flat from its jump over the sidewalk, but we took off the top and enjoyed the ride, screeching around corners in second gear.

When we got back to the base, John said the perp had cried the whole time. He was going into rehab the next morning, and his fiancée would kill him if she knew that he went back to the Bronx for a last shot. We didn't understand, he *couldn't* go to jail, it would wreck everything. His fiancée would leave him, and he worked for her family—he'd had chances before and he'd blown them. Handcuffed in the back seat, he couldn't help but notice how much Chicky and I seemed to enjoy the car. If we let him go tonight, he said, it was ours. Such was John's summary when we met back at the precinct.

"What do you want to do with it?"

"Let's run with it. Fuck him, for all we know, this is the only charge that'll stick."

Inspections was notified, and a detective, sergeant, and lieutenant arrived to give me a tape recorder and drill us on the niceties of entrapment—we could say, "Remember what we talked about?" but not, "Remember that offer?" I had the recorder in my shirt pocket behind a pack of cigarettes as I went into the cells to get Camaro. As I walked past the desk, a great veteran lieutenant named Brophy followed me and leaned directly over the mike for a confidential whisper: "Careful! IAB's in the house! Make sure that none of the perps dropped anything in the cells!" I tried to kick him and point to my pocket, but we were already inside, and what was said would be there for posterity. We brought Camaro out and talked to him for twenty minutes, but he seemed to have forgotten his offer. Over and over, I tried to look greedy while remarking, "That's some nice car," and finally he got it, offering that car and others, as well as to come over on weekends and paint our houses. I thanked him and we left. The Inspections sergeant took time out from our case to yell at a cop for walking in with his shirt unbuttoned, and the Lieutenant then grilled John on why we had engaged in a "pursuit" in an unmarked vehicle and why we didn't transmit it over the radio. John was disgusted—bribery was supposed to be for major players who manipulated and corrupted the system with real money, not this addled little sap who could barely remember his own name. "This is garbage," he said. "I will never do this again, ever."

I didn't agree. I told him that as I saw it, this might be the only way we could hold him accountable, since the drugs were gone. "Besides," I added, "it's another number for Wopstat."

Within a couple of days, our new lieutenant, Andy Johnson, let us know that the arrest was of some significance. A bribery collar was a big deal in the NYPD, as a hangover from the Knapp Commission days, and it won you a medal, and an entire career point, and an interview with the Integrity Review Board, which could arrange for a transfer to your assignment of choice. To put that in perspective, I'd begun to scramble to put together my "career path" application, for which an excellent annual evaluation could get you two or three points. A medal for a stupendous collar, like a bank robbery,

might get you half a point. A college degree would get you two. A year without going sick would get you one. You needed fifteen for a transfer.

I was short of points, since for the first two years on patrol, my sergeant
seemed to change monthly; I rarely saw him, her, or whoever it was, and my
evaluations were rated a quick "satisfactory," which awarded me a total of
zero points. I never thought or cared about those evaluations until I realized
that I'd worked my first two years for free. But it appeared that to make a
bribery collar—which was, in effect, simply to refuse to commit a crime—
would be worth more than two years of work and a couple of bank robberies
combined. The only thing that could have made me a more valuable police
officer would have been to avoid flu-like symptoms for several years running. It didn't seem very fair—it didn't seem sane, in fact—but a break
seemed to be rolling my way, and I wasn't about to dodge it.

A few days later, Orville, Frankenberry, and I grabbed the perps from an
armed robbery, I think. It was just before ten in the morning, when the 10-30
came over from a clothing store a couple of blocks away. We'd just finished
getting dressed when Chicky came in, saying, "It looks like Columbine High
School over there!" ESU and Hostage Negotiations were called in, surrounding the store with armor and guns; civilians fled the block, and neighboring
stores lowered their steel gates. The three of us rolled up on the scene as a
woman called over to us, in lowered tones: "It's those two guys walking
away right now, down the block! They changed their shirts inside!" We
jumped from the car and chased them, throwing them against a fence. The
cops who caught the job came around the corner, and we handed off the
perps. An hour later, they called the precinct for our names for the medal
write-up, and Orville said that it was he and I who had done it. I felt bad that
he forgot Frankenberry, but he wound up taking a better cop job upstate, and
Orville and I were left out of the story, regardless.

So it went that our hopes rose and fell. The months took their toll on us,
and the resentments built, and the separate concerns of impending marriages
and children, sick relatives and side jobs, made the daily indignities no easier to bear. We didn't always spare each other our frustrations. A lot of our
old street antics, the spirited improvisations and crazy chases, seemed needlessly risky for a game that was hardly worth winning. One night, when we
dropped off perps at Central Booking, I said that I didn't like how the perps
were cuffed—one hand apiece, on a chain, instead of individually rear-
cuffed. When you had a lot of bodies, you often ran out of cuffs, and it is difficult to herd ten single perps from the precinct to CB, and often again to

another precinct to lodge them, if CB was full. Partners should talk tactics all the time, going over each collar and confrontation like a football team studies videotape of last week's game, win or lose. If the criticism was offered in the right spirit, you were grateful to learn; if not, it could be construed as an insult on the deepest level. Because tactics became paramount in times of crisis, the talk of tactics was talk of much more: a good tactical cop is a good cop, saving lives, and a bad tactical cop is a bad cop, cowardly or dumb or otherwise lacking control. At a moment of crisis, where was your head, and where was your heart? What might begin as a discussion of training could quickly end as a verdict on character.

At the end of one Team Meeting, Tony told the boss: "Um, I don't think what you did the other day—when you went by yourself, and walked ahead of the perp back to the van—I don't think you should do that anymore."

"You're right, okay, that was old school," he admitted, as if the act was one of Shaft-style hyperconfidence. It wasn't old school, it was Special Education—nobody walks alone ahead of a perp, who hadn't been searched and wasn't cuffed—and it amounted to an open invitation to assault or escape. The tactics, and the temperament behind them, summed up the Sergeant for us: all who were supposed to follow him—us no less than that perp—were provided ample occasion to wonder why.

When I told John my thoughts on perp-cuffing, he agreed, and he went on to bring up something that had long been on his mind: "As long as we're talking tactics, Tactics Boy, how about how you ran after each of the three perps yourself earlier today—the first one, even after he was cuffed up, I made run across the street with me after you jumped the fence. And then the other two . . ."

I laughed.

"You don't care, do you?"

John was in his twenties, two hundred pounds of maintained muscle, a star of his high school wrestling team, and he always shot perfect scores at the range. I was none of those things. Seeing a partner hurt or worse was high atop the list of the many bad things any cop could imagine, and when John watched me go after someone bigger than myself, or after a couple of people, the thought of my excellent education going to waste didn't just cross his mind, it made him crazy. There might be things on the Job worth dying for, but three slabs of crack was not one of them.

But I'd stopped perps alone for a long time, made arrests alone for a long time—even in SNEU, it was often more practical. In some sets, the dealer would wait until he could unload a bundle at a time, and he might have the buyers wait, for five minutes or forty-five, and then ten people would walk off in ten directions at once. You split the difference—and not in a tough-guy way—between Academy tactics and street needs. If I did stop three at a time, I wouldn't move in to search them, but I'd hold them at gunpoint till backup came. These were not SWAT-team extractions by any stretch of the imagination—we didn't have black helicopters, we had my 1980 Oldsmobile—but to my mind, the risks were not reckless ones. Or they were no more reckless than anything else in the statistic-driven but slapdash enterprise of SNEU, and if we were going to do it at all, we were going to do it with guts. That was part of another give-and-take between John and me that had gone on for months: What do we give to this? Is it worthwhile? Do we quit the team, or quit without leaving, and force the Captain to keep us or him? When John was more despairing, earlier on, I said, "You ought to keep at it, keep collaring and taking things wherever they go. If you do go—when you go—you'll go out on top of your game. When some new sergeant or captain looks at your arrest record, deciding whether to take you in, he sees felonies every month instead of hearing stories about Captain Chaos, which he won't believe anyway." When I'd thrown in the towel, after the sixth warrant was canceled, John gave me the same speech. It was like the movies where escaped convicts are shackled together by the ankles: when one steps forward, the other follows.

John had been in SNEU for a year by then. The first half was beautiful, the second was hardly bearable. Even in the good times, with PK, John would sometimes confide his doubts in what he brought to the team: "It's like everybody has a gift, a skill, whether it's OV doing OPs, or you running with CIs and warrants. But me, I think that PK has me around because I'm a lot of laughs." He thought for a moment. "Plus, I'm good-looking and can lift heavy things." In the daily decisions of where we should work, who should watch and who should catch, there was a phase of noise in which our collective and single inclinations shifted one way and the next before settling. I told him, "If you want to be in the OP, don't ask, just get up in the OP. And if you want to get better, get better—don't wait to be helped." He did, and he developed his own eye in an OP, and in streets where even slightly dodgy-looking white people, like Stix or me, couldn't get into a building without getting made, he'd put on coveralls or a Con Ed helmet, or pick up a mop or a toolbox, and march in whistling.

Before he came to SNEU, John had driven bosses for months at a time, and he had worked in a Target Team at Mott-Pat, as well as on a solo footpost in Highbridge in the Four-Four. He had three or four gun collars, and had tackled a bank robber who had been featured on *America's Most Wanted,* checking the right building when a vast NYPD–FBI Task Force was fanned out in the area. But for the first years on the Job, he'd been living at home, sixty miles away, and finishing college at St. John's: collars and street action were not foremost in his mind. A chaotic schedule didn't suit him in other ways: he liked to eat, healthy and often, and to get at least an hour in at the gym every day. John was the most natural and least natural athlete I knew. He was great at games—softball, football, basketball—and when he went to the projects by our apartment for pick-up games, "Watch the white boy! Cover Whiteboy!" was the courtside chorus. But without almost constant attention to diet and exercise, he would have turned from Schwarzenegger to the Pillsbury Doughboy in months. John could gain three pounds by taking a long nap. He didn't like the negotiations over where the team would eat, which could take hours and result in a plate of grease and beans instead of grilled chicken and steamed vegetables from the Chinese takeout where they knew how to cook for him. At first, SNEU was worth it for the fun and the experience, and later he felt locked in like the rest of us, only more so, blaming himself for PK. But when the bonds between team members began to tense and fray, even for a short time, the sacrifices that he made to stay in SNEU began to seem pointless.

Because John and I were so close, I didn't want to be seen as his automatic partisan whenever there was some disagreement on the team. Whether we should do a double on the last one, for a longer weekend, or whether we came in early or late on the first one back, was routine debate that usually set the single guys who always wanted as long a weekend as possible against the family men who had other responsibilities and events on the schedule. As it happened, the three white guys were single, and the Puerto Rican, the Short-a-Ricans, and the Jamaican were married with kids. We'd always been able to work things out among ourselves, and when we were in higher favor in the command, we were usually accommodated for shift changes and days off. Patience and goodwill were no longer in such strong supply, however. As I saw it, if we fell out with one another for any reason, it would be a tragedy, but if we fell out with one another amid rancor and racial division, it would be a disgrace. There were no signs that our frustrations with one another and everything else were anything but color-blind, but I knew things could go very bad, very quickly.

At the end of a long night, one of the guys blew up at me for trying to get him to switch collars with John. John wanted a day tour the next day, to get out of the precinct early, but no one listened when he asked. The guy had a seller with unapprehended buyers, which he was going to write up as misdemeanor possession, since it would be dropped anyway and he didn't want to come in early the next day. The switch made sense to me, of course, but it could also be reasonably seen as none of my goddamned business. It was a brief explosion, and we both knew a day later that there was nothing more to it than tiredness and tender nerves. At the beginning of another tour, four of us were in the van, when John brought up my tactics again, in the hope of getting the other guys to urge me to be more careful. One of the other guys disagreed with him on a point. Within moments, the debate on tactics became a personal argument, and then a fusillade of shouted curses—"Fuck you!" "Fuck me? You're the fuck-up!" The other noncombatant and I sat in shocked and horrified silence. For me, a fight between my partners was like a fight between my parents—if they ever fought—and anything I could add would only make it worse. It was awful. The other two guys left the van for an OP, and John and I stayed in the van. We didn't talk much. All the perps were runners or fighters that night, and John was stuck in the van with prisoners while I rolled around in the street with one perp, who was over six-two and 220. It didn't improve his mood. The next week he went sick for a couple of days.

A week or so after he came back, the Sergeant gave us our evaluations. When I looked at mine, I saw that it praised my activity and integrity (the bribery collar gave me my integrity back) but stated that I "needed improvement following instructions and team cohesion." He might have been on to something with the cohesion issue. When John was brought in—his evaluation had the identical praise and reprimands as mine—the Sergeant told him that he'd better talk to me, because I "was on my last legs on this team."

"You can talk to him," John said. "I'm leaving. I'm going back to my old post."

The Sergeant was quiet, and then he asked, "Is it because of me?"

John shook his head and walked out. I didn't know what to think. Minutes later, I couldn't: a cop called over the radio that there was a barricaded perp with a gun, One-Six-Six and Brook. The precinct emptied, as everyone grabbed keys and jumped into cars. The Sergeant took the wheel of the last unmarked car, and Chicky, Tony, and I reluctantly hopped into the back. Racing to the scene, Tony yelled at the Sergeant the whole time: "Follow the marked car! No, the other one! Turn, no! Turn! Keep the siren on 'Yelp!'" Chicky tried to jump out of the car every time it slowed down. It was a spectacle: ESU and K9, scores of cops, taking positions around the garage door, a captain from the Four-Two trying to find a Spanish-speaking cop to talk to the complainant. The adrenaline began to dwindle when the complainant was asked, "Did you actually see the gun?" and the reply was shaky. Maybe it was a knife, and maybe the perp wasn't barricaded in the garage but had walked through it, and maybe he wasn't a perp, really. Maybe it wasn't even a knife. It all arose from a dispute over a parking spot. Maybe it was a really great spot.

A sergeant appeared on the rooftop of the garage, striding across to make sure there was no one hiding there. He looked commanding, despite the loss of urgency for our being there. Our sergeant must have thought so, too, because a few minutes later, another cop told me, "Your boss is hurt—you better go check it out." I saw the Sergeant limp across the street. John and I stood there. "Yeah, I guess." I went over to him, on the side of the building where he sat, wrapping a towel around his bloody calf. "You all right?" He said he was, and he explained that he had stepped through a windshield of a parked car, as he tried to vault onto the roof.

"Another sergeant was with me, he went through the windshield, too. He didn't get hurt, though, I don't know how. I don't know where he went, either."

"Huh."

I walked away to tell the guys—"C'mere! C'mere! You gotta listen to what this guy did now!"—and for the first time in a week, John broke into a smile. Tony and Chicky went on an extended riff on the theme of Captain Chaos.

When the Sergeant got into an ambulance, each of us asked him how he felt, and then walked a hundred yards away to make more jokes, out of earshot. The Sergeant limped over to say that he had to go to the hospital for stitches, and it wouldn't take more than an hour. As he turned, he must have felt the debate, even if he didn't hear it: "*Somebody's* gotta go with him!"

"I'm not!"

"Not me!"

"Fuck that!"

"Fuck him!"

Tony finally volunteered to go, calling out "Boss, hold up!" when he was almost back to the ambulance. I thought about how when PK was hurt, we were stricken, surrounding him like widows at a wake. When we drove back to the precinct, however, the desk told us to get into uniform: there were power outages in the neighborhood, and we were on alert. The news seemed to awaken some charitable instinct in us: "We can't! Our sergeant is hurt, we have to go to hospital. We have to be with him, what if he needs blood?"

It was good to laugh again. It had been a while. I heard that Warrants was picking people up, and I went to the Captain, to ask if he would consider putting my name in. He was with the captain from Vice, which had their office on the second floor of our building. The Vice captain asked if I needed to talk alone. No, I said—fortunately, it seemed—and I stated my business.

"You don't want that," the Captain informed me. He went on, "You're going to stay on the Job? What do you want to do with your career?"

"I want my shield, to be in the Detective Bureau."

He shook his head. "No, what you really want is to be a boss. Do you have enough time on to take the test? Did you file?"

I didn't want to be a boss, I said; I did have the time, I had not filed. The Captain said, "Warrants is a mess, the people there are miserable, they hate it there. You don't know what's going to be happening there." That was news to me, and it would have been news to them, too. Slowly, I said that I knew people who loved it there, and that it would get me my shield, and he interrupted, "You think a Squad is going to pick you up from Warrants?"

"They're not going to pick me up from SNEU."

There was no answer for that, and so he suggested that I go to Narcotics. I said that I'd go in a second, but there was no movement there, according to Inspector Mullen.

"Go as an undercover, you could work at Columbia," he said.

The Vice captain remarked, "If Mullen said there's no movement, I'd take his word for it." The Captain then suggested that I go to Auto Crime, which is like saying a good way to visit England would be to get a Rhodes scholarship. I said I'd talk to more people about Warrants and get back to him. I left it at that.

A day or two later, I ran into the Vice captain in the parking lot, and he said that I could come work for him if I wanted. "We only take cops as temps, you know. You'll be back here in six months, but you're that much closer to your shield. Besides, you'll wind up back here, and the Captain likes you."

The last part baffled me, but I ran to get John, and we went back to the Vice captain, to see if we could go together. He told us to fill out the applications right there. Vice, or Public Morals, as it had been known, was a far smaller unit than it had been in its inglorious past, and the work—underage and after-hours drinking, gambling, and prostitution—didn't seem so compelling, the success of Operation Lying Whore notwithstanding. But I did like the thought that I'd be taking up in 1999 what Pat Brown had begun in 1915, and that it would move me closer to the gold shield. On many days, had I been offered the chance to dredge the Gowanus Canal with a toothbrush, it would have been more appealing than PSA-7.

So it seemed that as each door closed, another one opened. John went to the Admin lieutenant to ask to go back to his old post, and he was told it would take some time. Weeks passed and nothing happened, and then he was told that he'd have to work with a rookie in a conditions car for a couple of months before it would be arranged. The Captain told him, "The way I see it, I'm doing you a favor, letting you keep your days off." John didn't see it that way, but that didn't matter. When he suggested that he and I go to a conditions car together, in the Four-Four, the Captain said, "Eddie Conlon is not leaving SNEU." It wasn't clear whether it was his decree or his bet that I'd stay, and it didn't matter. For my part, when I went to the Integrity Review Board, I was doubly hopeful that I'd finally get to leave the PSA, and that I could talk them into helping John as well. Though only the arresting officer was to supposed to benefit with the career point and the transfer, John had seen the perp shooting up, and he had been the initial recipient of the bribe offer. I filled out a set of forms for each of us, including the tantalizing section which asked for your dream assignments. At the interview, I gave a quick rendition of the collar to the sergeant who ran the Board, and she said that the arrest met their qualifications. When I began to argue that John's part was at least as important as mine, she thought for a moment before saying, "You're right. You don't belong here, he does. Have him call me to set up an interview."

I hadn't expected to be quite so persuasive. I felt like saying, *Are you kidding? I bet Timpanaro would have taken the car! Look at me, I'm an Irishman, you think I'd drive a Camaro with flame decals? That car is right up his alley!* I went back to the PSA and told him. Maybe I should have said that for each door that opened, another one closed.

. . .

OTHER DOORS SEEMED TO REVOLVE, IN THE MOST SURPRIS-ing ways. I talked to PK often, and he was doing well at PSA-8, where he was the SNEU sergeant. For a while, he talked about trying to import the lot of us, but I doubted that they would permit the wholesale loss of manpower at PSA-7. Later on, we talked about a few of us coming over—John and me, maybe—but we were uncomfortable with the idea of splitting up the team.

At PSA-8, PK had taken over their SNEU team, replacing another Sgt. Kelly, of course, who'd had his own problems with the CO there. The trouble prompted the other Sgt. Kelly's transfer to PSA-7, where he filled in to cover us while our sergeant was away, and then he stayed, as he was due for promotion to lieutenant in a few weeks. We had half a boss most of the time, and now we had two. The rumor was that our captain was angry at theirs for treating PK well, and so he returned the favor. Was it a Bedouin saying that the enemy of my enemy is my friend? The local translation was, "If you make my enemy Sgt. Kelly your SNEU sergeant, I will of course make your enemy Sgt. Kelly my SNEU sergeant." And so we remained a little people, wandering the desert, with our tents and our feuds.

One feud happened soon after the new Sgt. Kelly arrived, during a Team Meeting. For most of the month, we were on patrol, and our activity was low. That was no excuse, we were told: our day-tour weeks would henceforth be changed to one-to-nines, and no leave would be approved for the rest of the month. Chicky said he couldn't do one-to-nines, because he had to take care of his kid. If we changed, he'd have to leave the team. And then he got heated, telling the Sergeant how he was punishing us for circumstances that were out of our control, and to have one slow month and get this bullshit was in fact bullshit. "These are the best cops in the command, and every day we come in to collar, and every day we get a smack in the face. Nobody wants to do anything anymore, and we still collar!"

"You guys think you can do whatever you want, come in when you want, and it's gonna stop—and if anybody wants to leave, they can!"

"You go ahead and replace us, you're losing the best cops in the precinct!"

Chicky walked out of the room, shaking with anger. The Sergeant said we should have written summonses, even when we were getting punished, and so last month's low numbers were our own fault. He said that Sgt. Rhoden's team always had their own van, exclusively for their use, because their numbers were always good, regardless of quality. I said when our numbers were great, we still had to fight for a car every day and usually lost. Orville then told the Sergeant that it was because he didn't fight for us.

"You can't say that I don't fight for you, nobody fights for you like I do—"

"I did say it."

"What the fuck did you say, you—?"

"That's my opinion."

As the Sergeant began to scream and curse, Orville walked toward him and said, "I am thirty years old and I have two children. I am not your child. I didn't curse at you and you will not curse at me."

They both got up and approached each other, the Sergeant cursing and Orville dressing him down with pulpit fervor. Tony got up between them, then pushed Orville out of the room so he wouldn't smack him and get fired. Later on, Chicky said that when he went home, his wife wanted to call an ambulance, because he was so mad, she thought he'd have a heart attack.

The other Sgt. Kelly had been amazed by the ferocity of the ill will. He offered to talk to our Sergeant and Captain for us, but he said that we'd need to get some numbers for him, so he'd be in a position to negotiate. Most of the time, when we could work, we did, but there were other occasions when it seemed necessary to make a statement, even if it wasn't completely understood. One day, John took to giving out "phantom" scrips, sending the boss scrambling all over the streets to catch nonexistent buyers. John pushed it a little—"Okay, we got three female whites, in business suits . . . you can't miss 'em!"

"No luck? Huh. Nevermind, now we got a Japanese guy in a convertible. . . ."

"My God, are you blind? Forget it, forget it, this one—please, if you don't get these two, I don't know. This one's a couple, male and female, on a bicycle built for two. . . ."

The Sergeant still asked me to talk to perps, whenever any cop in the command brought in a prisoner who offered information. I wondered why we bothered, but I never said no.

I debriefed one perp, asking, "Would you buy guns?"

"No," he said, "I'd buy clothes."

I liked to think that my interview skills had grown acute with time and experience, and maybe that was the case. When Orville took a guy for a couple of vials, I asked him if he would be willing to work for us. He said, "Okay."

I asked him if he'd ever worked for the police before.

"Yeah, sure," he'd said, and he gave me the cop's name, Jerry Gonzalez, with the Brooklyn DA's Squad. He'd been caught for a sale and a gun, and he'd worked it off: a Jamaican drug ring had been wanted for a number of murders, and though the case was never made against them for the homicides, the CI had put them away for life, arranging buys for half a kilo of coke and twenty pounds of weed. Detective Gonzalez said the CI was energetic and reliable and a bit of a cop buff. The CI took on the code name "Paiton," which was close to the Spanish for "python," and though I never got what he meant by it, he could have called himself anything he wanted.

Paiton was thin and hungry-looking, with the immigrant's mix of deference and drive, anxious to please and determined to succeed. He picked up jobs working with Sheetrock and tile, and his hands always had homemade bandages coming off his cuts. He was struggling with cocaine addiction, buying it a couple of times a week, but he hadn't lapsed on heroin for over a year. Every day, after the methadone clinic, he had two- and three-hour commutes, before dawn and by subway, bus, and train, to his work sites on Long Island and in New Jersey. He'd been arrested a decade earlier for attempted murder, but he hadn't done time for it—"It was a family thing," he said, scowling. He was one of seven children, six of whom had become heroin addicts. He'd been partial to speedballs himself, combined shots of heroin and cocaine. When he inherited his grandfather's sugarcane plantation, one hundred thousand dollars' worth of drugs went into his veins in one year.

Paiton could be hard to find, sometimes. He had a wife and young children in the Four-Six, and elderly parents in the projects by our precinct. He also sometimes stayed out by his work site for a couple of days at a time. The first set he told me about, he gave us the wrong block, and John and I spent several nights walking through apartment buildings and over rooftops, trying to match what we saw with what he'd described, without success. But when we spoke again—whether I'd misheard him, or he'd misspoken, in his heavy accent—he said the coke spot was in his own building. Once we'd locked that in, he became extremely conscientious about calling me, providing all the detail I requested on such aspects of the layout as the door markings, the type and number of locks, and which way the windows faced.

The spot would be the most promising and challenging we'd ever gone after: it was on the top floor—the seventh—of a corner building, and they sold cocaine by the ounce. A customer would ring the bell, which turned on a light inside the apartment; a "doorman" would check the peephole, gun in hand, to see if he knew the face on the other side. If he did, he'd let the buyer in and walk him to the kitchen, where another dealer cut cocaine from the pile, weighed it on a digital scale, and packed it in tinfoil. The dealer also had a gun, on the table or under his leg, on his chair. In addition, one or two men patrolled the sidewalks in front of the building, carrying transmitters like those used for electronic car-door openers; if the cops showed up for a search warrant, an alarm would be set off before they reached the lobby. There was also a "panic button" behind the gum machines, outside the bodega on the corner, but Paiton thought it had been disconnected. It would be tough to crack.

Narcotics had done a search warrant on a sixth-floor apartment in the building earlier in the spring. They had made three arrests, seizing two ounces of cocaine and a .38. Paiton told me they were the same people, who had set up shop again on the seventh floor after the raid. I went to Narcotics and talked to a detective named Danny King, who'd done the earlier warrant. He was about to be transferred to the Intelligence Division, and he handed his case folder over to me, despite being yelled at by his sergeant, "Why don't you check with me before you give away the store—we got a CI who told us they started back up in the building, it was gonna be our case!" Because I'd DECSed the apartment, it was mine, but had Narco claimed that it was part of some investigation, I probably would have been forced to give it up. King gave me the old apartment layout, and he warned that the door had been so heavily fortified that they made it in only by chance—a customer was coming out as they were about to go in. "These are serious, professional people," he said. "The whole door frame was reinforced steel, with a steel bar across it. We would have had better luck knocking through the wall." He said that the building super was on their payroll, which Paiton had also told us. Paiton said that the seventh-floor apartment hadn't been fortified yet, but everything else looked daunting.

Sgt. Kelly had been encouraging, saying that his good relations with the Captain would allow us to move forward with the warrant. I wasn't so sure. The Captain had reacted to the news of the Vice offer with displeasure, telling John, apropos of one of their conversations about his move to a foot-post: "Neither of you is going to Vice, I put a stop to it. Vice does nothing for Housing." Weeks had passed, and the Vice captain had told us, "Don't worry about it, we just have to process the paperwork, do background checks, and so on. It won't happen overnight, but it will happen." I wasn't going to argue with him in any case, and the prospect of a new warrant discouraged me from bringing up the issue. At each phase of the investigation, the Captain had allowed me to go forward, and when I had enough for a warrant, he let me apply for one. There was no reasonable objection to what we had—the credibility of the informant had been vouched for by the Brooklyn DA's Squad, the perps were identified as known drug dealers, and the apartment was vacant—but in my police career, at least, the Age of Reason had long since passed, and nothing would be as simple as it should be.

When Tony and Sammy went to the Captain to get their applications for Narcotics signed, he hemmed and hawed, telling them it was awful and dangerous. Was the shield really worth it? How did they feel as minorities, knowing that the Job was "using" them for that kind of work? And though he did sign their recommendations, however reluctantly, he left them with the thought: How did they sleep at night, working with me? How could they trust me? What did they think about me, knowing that I was writing about them? Tony called me at home, over the weekend, to tell me: "That guy has a hard-on for you!" I didn't feel any better a couple of days later, when I was walking past the desk, and a sergeant called out, "Hey, I hear Timpanaro's going upstairs."

"Yeah?"

"Yeah, he got transferred to Vice. He must have some kind of hook, to go from Housing to Vice. Does he?"

"Not that I know. Can I see the orders in writing?"

There it was in the Telephone Message Log: PO Timpanaro is transferred for a ninety-day temporary assignment to Bronx Vice, effective 0001 hrs, 8/30/99.

When I went upstairs to ask the Vice captain what had happened, he said that because I wrote on my application that I'd been to Narcotics only for a month, someone downtown wondered if it meant that I'd been thrown out. Because he was on vacation at the time, he couldn't be reached to explain the situation. I asked if he knew when I might be coming, and he said that he didn't, but he expected it would be soon. When he first asked me to work there, it was with a cheery enthusiasm, but when I'd check in to ask about the status of the transfer, with John at first, and then without, the reception was increasingly cool. John asked me what I thought was going on.

"Well, as I see it, there's two options," I said. "One, it's what he says—it's just one of those things, a little clerical screwup. Or it's part of the ongoing, worldwide plot to drive me out of my mind."

Since the warrant was moving forward, there was less time to speculate. As far as I knew, I'd be joining John soon enough. The next visits I had with the Captain, however, showed that he'd given the matter some thought. As I sat in his office, answering his questions and listening to his suggestions about the warrant, he'd interrupt to remark, "What happened with Timpanaro? How did it happen? He must know somebody. Who does he know?"

I said I didn't know anything, which must have seemed disingenuous. I could lie when I had to, like I could speak Spanish, in a workable pidgin, though I sometimes thought that after years of being a cop in the South Bronx, I'd be better at both. You gotta have a story: *No, sir, you're not in trouble, but why don't you come down to the precinct to tell me your side. . . . Sure, lady, I'm sure your husband will turn up in no time, with a good explanation. . . . No, Lieutenant, I wasn't sleeping, I missed Mass this morning and I was saying a prayer. . . .* What I told the Captain was true, but it felt like a lie, even to me. I did know people—if I thought about it, I knew people who knew people who knew the President, and ditto the Pope, and yet here I was. I didn't trust the Captain, but for all I knew, he was oblivious to what had happened with SNEU, and had he had an inkling of its near-year of travesties, the Sergeant would have been sent to direct traffic on Staten Island. The Sergeant had cut communication between us, and this warrant, along with the accidental reincarnation of Sgt. Kelly, provided a brief resumption of face-to-face talk. But as it was, when we did talk, it reminded me of the movie scenes where two people drink tea, with one poisoned cup switched each time the other's back is turned:

"Is that your money you dropped, over there?"

Switch, switch.

"My mistake, I thought it was money."

"Quite all right—my goodness, I've never seen such a beautiful woman, so naked, right behind you!"

Switch, switch . . .

When the Captain ran into John after his transfer, he said with a smile, "Don't come back." He said a lot of people were mad at John for leaving us, for leaving his team. But he laughed when he said it, so John knew he was joking, there were no hard feelings, none.

The other guys on the team didn't have much to do with the warrant. We were all burnt out, and they were unbeguiled by the dubious possibilities of the moment. It would take time for the new Sgt. Kelly to earn their trust, and he was nothing if not temporary. For a warrant, there is too much work for one person to do, but there really wasn't enough for three people; even after John went to Vice, he worked with me almost full-time—his new team neither expected him nor expected much from him, as a temp. Paiton also proved useful to John, when the three of us went out to lunch one day. We went to a good restaurant near the apartment, since I didn't want to take the chance that Paiton would run into anyone he knew. The other customers looked at him oddly, especially when a foul smell began to rise from the table. He remarked vaguely on what methadone does to your body, and we ignored the stink the best we could. When we dropped him off later that afternoon, however, John admitted that he'd been responsible for the gas attack, but when Paiton confessed, he kept his mouth shut. John had taken Vice, he'd taken the Integrity Review Board, and now he'd taken my informant as his blame hound. Some partner he'd turned out to be.

We worked on a tac plan: we had to take out lookouts, before they could transmit a signal, and we had to freeze an entire block, so that if there were additional alarms, we could prevent them from being sent. We needed hallway people, lobby people, roof people, OPs from across the street. Paiton told me that they had an apartment on the third floor, with an even larger stash; if the players ran, they'd probably head there, and we could get a bigger hit if we let them run, as long as we kept them in constant view. One of the players lived on the second floor, which could be a second target of flight and opportunity, and another worker lived on the fourth floor. I put together a booklet for the project, a twenty-page handout of assignments, subject photos, lists of hazards and responses, and maps and diagrams of the apartment, building, block, and hospital route.

The Captain wanted Narcotics to be involved. He called Capt. Hoch, who was in charge of the Four-Six modules, and a sergeant named Tommy Mc-Partland was assigned to work with us. Capt. Hoch had been a lieutenant at PSA-7, working midnights when I had my beat in the Village. As soon as I was sent to Narcotics, the complications arose. Paiton told me the big delivery was on Friday evenings, for the weekend customers, and I set up the execution for Friday night, with Narcotics, ESU, EMS, and the dozen or more cops from the PSA. When I told the Captain, he said, "Friday's no good for me. Put it off." After it had been set up again, the Captain announced, "The Inspector wants undercovers to go and make a buy there. I think it's a good idea, too." Again, I was sent back to explain the change of plan. It was a bad idea—if a CI has an established pattern of buys, you don't make sudden changes before you hit the door. In a shop this professional, they wouldn't fall for it, and if they did, they'd figure it out later and kill Paiton.

I told Sgt. McPartland, who was incredulous, who told his lieutenant, Tom Casey, who was amazed, who told Capt. Hoch, who was dumbfounded. Hoch looked at Casey and said, "Tell me again why it is we're working with these people?" I didn't want to suggest that we say we tried and failed—how could I say to one captain, Why don't you jerk my captain around?

Fortunately, Sgt. McPartland had the same idea and no compunctions. He sent me away, saying, "Call me and let me know what time you want us to say we tried."

The next day, I told the Captain, and he said that we at least had to make a "controlled buy" with Paiton, so that even if nothing turned up in the apartment, we could find the dealers and arrest them for sale. Where the first suggestion was unwise, the second was impossible: we don't make arrests for sales to informants, because they would have to testify in open court. I nodded and walked out of the office.

Even Paiton started to call me, angry that we hadn't hadn't taken the place out, "They sell coke to ten-year-olds, twelve-year-olds, you can't believe it!" I did like his indignation—it was why I worked, too—but his expectations were not a factor in the schedule. And then he disappeared on a job for a couple of days. The Captain didn't like that. I didn't either, but I said, "This is not a guy with a secretary—you can't always get him when you want." Another day passed, as the clock ticked on the warrant, and the Captain told me to go to Paiton's house and drag him back here. I didn't. He lived in the same building as the dealers. The Captain demanded that I find him. I did. The Captain said that he and the Inspector would be content if we had Paiton make a pre-warrant buy on Thursday, and we would hit the door on Tuesday, the last day of the warrant.

SNEU had Friday and Saturday off; Sgt. McPartland had Sunday and Monday. I'd already finished work on Thursday when I found Paiton, and I'd been home for hours when I found McPartland. Later that night, we did the controlled buy, and it was quick and easy. It was also of no value. A pre-warrant buy can be made just before a search warrant is executed, to make sure the product is there—it's a kind of embarrassment insurance—but to do it four days ahead was just an embarrassment. So was going back to McPartland and Hoch, sometimes twice a day, to tell them the new demands and the changes of plans. When the Captain told Tony to drive him to the apartment to see it, he was in uniform, and he refused to go in a car with tinted windows. Tony said, "He had me circle the building six times—and when I tried to drive past at regular speed, he had me slow down again."

I delayed telling the Captain about the pre-warrant buy for a couple of days, because I didn't want to give him time for another brainstorm. Not every idea of his was a bad idea, but the fact that they arose as last-minute, make-or-break contingencies made me wonder if the real motive was to help. It seemed as if he didn't want to deal with it or me, and wished we would all go away. Paiton told me that the weekend drop was the heaviest, but each day, there was another drop, late in the afternoon. I set up the execution for seven, locking in Narco, SNEU, EMS, and ESU. We would tac at five-thirty. On Tuesday at around noon, the Captain told me, "Seven's no good for me. Let's make it around three." I didn't feel like trying anymore.

Back I went to Narcotics, where I promised that they would never, ever see me again. I was able to put it back together, a little later than the Captain wanted, not as late as I did. At our base, I ran the tac meeting for thirty cops, handing out copies of my handsomely produced booklet. As we were about to roll out, the Captain said he'd called the desk at the Four-Six, and they said to hold off for a while, they were doing gun buys in the area. Okay. We waited a while—I was happy to, in the pouring rain, which would make the lookouts dull—and then finally moved out. A few blocks away, we formed up and waited. Chicky and Stix had been in an OP an hour before, and Mc-Partland's guys would be sent in to the floor, then Sammy would go in and hold the elevator. Sgt. Rhoden and his team would take out the lookouts, from scrips provided by the OP. John and I would go in first with ESU, Orville and Tony would cover the roof, another sergeant and his team would watch the windows and the fire escape. More cops would hold the lobby and the other floors. The signal was given: the Narco guys went in, then Sammy, then Rhoden. And then we rolled up, and raced to the door, and we all couldn't fit in the elevator, so half the entry team took the stairs, beating us there. In the elevator, one ESU cop said, "I'm more nervous than a Polack on *Jeopardy!*"

We ran from the elevator and I pointed out the door, with its *"Somos Católicos"* sticker. A buzzer was going off inside the apartment: there was an alarm we hadn't gotten. ESU took the door in seconds—no fortifications, as Paiton said—then tossed in a percussion grenade, which shook the windows. They went in and cleared the apartment, and I followed. When the smoke dissipated, I saw the scale, a bag of cocaine, and foil on the kitchen table. There was no one there. Lt. Johnson got on the air: "Window security, is anyone on the fire escape?"

Pause.

"Window security, on the air?"

Pause.

"Window security, is there anyone on the fire escape or the roof?"

A message came back: "There's someone on the fire escape, but he's on the sixth floor."

Well, then. We were on the seventh floor, so a man on the sixth-floor fire escape was probably just there to water his plants. ESU pulled him back in, with machine guns trained on him. He was an older man, and I recognized him from his picture. "He's under," I said, and I cuffed him.

John and Lt. Johnson went out to check the fire escape, and looking down, John saw a silver semiautomatic on the sixth floor: "Gun!"

When he went down to get it, he looked through the window of the apartment where the man had tried to escape, wondering if there was someone else inside. Lt. Johnson called him to come back up, and we began to tear the place apart. We emptied the refrigerator and the pots from the stove; we ripped up loose planking and kicked in patches of new sheetrock to check for traps. There was a Santería shrine, of candles and dishes of liquid, in a closet. No one touched it. Inside the vacuum cleaner, behind the disposable bag, Sammy found a nice brick of cocaine. There were accounting books in the kitchen, four hundred dollars in cash, a strainer and a pestle, a bowl of rice to keep the drugs dry. The Captain was delighted, and he shook my hand several times. Of the sergeant who was supposed to watch the windows, he said, "That's not your fault—there's only so much you can do. It worked out." We continued to search, soaked in sweat. The bosses left. John and I high-fived each other and took polaroids of the catch.

At the precinct, I debriefed the perp. He didn't speak English, and so Tony translated.

"Ask him why he was there."

He answered, and Tony told me that he just wanted to go there.

"He just likes empty apartments? Ask him why he had the key on his ring."

He offered such a nonsensical explanation that Tony didn't bother translating.

"Tell him he insults me with his lies. . . ."

"Tell him he is charged with an A-1 felony, he can go to jail for twenty-five years. . . ."

"Tell him he insults me with his lies. . . ."

I brought in a picture of his boss, the owner of the spot. I told him he worked for him, we knew, we wanted him, tell us. He said he didn't know him, then he knew him from the neighborhood, but that was all, and that he thought he was back in the Dominican Republic.

He clammed up again, so I pulled back. I asked him if he had ever had a real job, where he lived, when he came here, if he was married, had kids. He came here in the eighties, his kids were still in the DR, he had been a super. I asked where he lived and with whom. He said he lived with his sister, across the street. He said he was illegal but his sister was in the process of getting her citizenship.

"Tell him that he just blew his sister's citizenship."

Tony did, and he said that his sister was legal, and she hadn't done anything.

"Ask him to guess what Immigration will think about a woman who's harboring an illegal-alien cocaine dealer."

An ugly bluff, but it half-worked: he took responsibility for everything that damned him, and lied about everything that might have helped diminish his culpability. The drugs were his, he said, but he worked alone, for no one, and he bought the drugs from a guy he met on Fordham Road, who he just met in passing, he didn't know his name but he thought he might live in Jersey. He took the gun with him from the kitchen because he didn't want to be blamed for it if both were found in the apartment, and the cocaine in the vacuum was all he had left. I told him that the next time he found himself fleeing cops with machine guns, it would be wiser to leave the gun behind. I told him to write down what he'd just said, but Tony told me he didn't know how to write, not even how to sign his name. I borrowed a tape recorder from Vice, and we had him go through it all again on tape. What a jerk, I thought. He did a year or so and was deported.

That arrest represented six weeks of work. I was mostly glad and mostly proud, and I tried not to think about all the pointless errands that were required, and how much better we might have done—more perps, more drugs, more guns—had we timed the execution as we should have. There was another panic button inside the bodega downstairs, which is why alarms were going off when ESU took the door. When I talked to Paiton, he asked, "What went wrong?"

"What do you mean, what went wrong?"

Paiton told me that he talked to the other perp in the apartment, the next day. The "doorman" escaped out the window into another, vacant apartment, where the super let him hide. It was on the sixth floor. He had a gun. I was furious—the sergeant who was supposed to watch the windows from the street had cost me a gun. When I told John, he pointed out that it might have cost him a great deal more—he was on the sixth-floor fire escape, trying to peek in the window. The gunman was there, waiting. What would he have done if John had gone in? With that warrant, I'd hoped to go out on the top of my game, to leave for Vice or anywhere else with a taste of victory, to wash away some of the bitterness of the recent past. It wasn't a failure, but I would come to see it as emblematic of many things, good and bad, including my reasons for leaving.

During one of my periodic visits to Inspector Mullen, he told me that Narcotics was picking up investigators again. He didn't have to ask me twice. I didn't look forward to the conversation with the Captain, and I waited until the day before I was leaving for vacation to have him sign my recommendation. I waited too long; he was out that day. The XO was there, however, and he was new. I got the signature and ran like a rabbit. When I went in for the interview, I had to come in on my own time again, and I was in the same suit, but the experience could not have been more different from the Street Crime fiasco. Inspector Mullen made a phone call for me, and so did Capt. Hoch; the Admin lieutenant at Bronx Narcotics, Brian Nicholson, was my second cousin, I think, but he could easily be promoted to first. At my interview, I went in to talk to a captain, a lieutenant, and a sergeant. We plowed through the routine stuff: I wasn't married, I had no kids, I could—and happily would, yes!—work late tours on Staten Island. The lieutenant was looking through my papers as we went on, remarking favorably on my arrests, then stopped cold: "Where did you go to college?"

I answered, and she asked, "Did you graduate?" I said I had.

The other two looked at me strangely: "What the hell are you doing here?"

"What did you study?"

I said English, and then the sergeant said, "You should write a book, I bet you will!"

And I said I planned to. The captain said, "Well, that's about it—you're in. But we have to sit here for another ten minutes or so, or it won't look right." We bullshitted with each other, as if we were old friends at a bar.

As Inspector Mullen told me, I'd be one of the first cops in the door when it opened, but he didn't know when that would happen. It could be weeks, but it might be months; he'd heard it would probably happen before Christmas—the interview was in October—but it was also probable that the rumor would prove false. I went back to SNEU. The other Sgt. Kelly was promoted to lieutenant and left the command. John was upstairs in Vice. The fights went on, and the work went on. One day when I was on vacation, Tony was walking a perp out of a project when someone threw a bottle of some noxious liquid—he later thought it might have been vinegar—from an upper floor, which smashed on the perp. For a moment, both Tony and the perp were blinded. Orville grabbed Tony and threw him in the van, racing to the hospital. Someone watching from a window called Internal Affairs, claiming that they beat up the perp, and all were called down for a GO-15, an official department hearing. I read in the papers about a cop killing himself at his precinct, in the locker room, before the day tour. He was from my Academy class. Someone said that his girlfriend had left him, and I didn't doubt there was some personal crisis, but I wondered why he came in to work to eat his gun. The Bronx motto is *Ne cede malis:* Do not give way to evil.

I hadn't been to the dentist in years, and when I finally went back, he didn't have good news. My dental chart came back with more red pencil marks than a dopey kid's homework. I would need root-canal and other work done, requiring a dozen visits over the course of the fall.

I told John that the thought of quitting the Job had begun to flash through my mind lately. It was not a decision that I weighed consciously, and I had no plans to quit. But the idea would pop up in my head, unbidden, like a fantasy, and it was a strangely soothing daydream, like thoughts of suicide are said to be for people in deep depression. In the mornings, I would sometimes think, "What would happen if I just didn't go in?" I told John about it, and he said, "Stop it. Don't even talk like that."

The next morning, when I woke up for the ten-to-six, I lay in bed for a while, dreading the impending tour. But as the sleep left my mind and I began to take stock of what lay ahead, I broke into a smile: "I don't have to go in for the ten-to-six, I have a dentist's appointment! I have root canal!" As I got dressed, I realized what had happened, and right then I decided I would quit SNEU, that day. If the Job made having my teeth drilled look like pleasure, it was time to make a career adjustment. At the precinct, I went directly to the Admin lieutenant, and prepared to stay in his office until I was transferred. John had waited almost two months for his footpost, and when he left for Vice, he was still in SNEU. I'd have none of that.

The Admin lieutenant was at his desk when I walked in. Before I even opened my mouth, he said, "Time to move on, hmm? Well, it's all for the best, probably. What do you want? We have spots open on the midnights . . ." And we went over the squad roster, looking at the possibilities. Eddie Wynne needed a partner, and I'd have been glad to work with him, but the midnights would be a big change. He said to think about it, and I said I'd get back to him by the end of the day. I called Eddie at home and left a message, and then I went down to the SNEU office to let everyone know.

My news was not the first of the day, nor the worst. The Sergeant had thrown Stix off the team for "insubordination," a suspendable offense. Stix hadn't even been around for most of the summer—after his wedding, he'd gone on his honeymoon, and then he'd broken his toe. He'd been back only a few weeks. Stix was stunned, and then he was enraged. The Sergeant had been a guest at his wedding. Stix had asked him a simple question that the Sergeant took as a challenge to his authority, and now even his career was at risk. He said he was going to the Captain, to fight it. I said that he should clear things up with the Captain at some point, but he should be careful what he asked for—did he really want to stay here? Besides, in all likelihood, the Captain already knew and approved. It occurred to me why the Admin lieutenant had expected a visit from one of the SNEU guys that morning, and why he was so accommodating—he thought I was Stix.

Later that day, when I passed the Admin lieutenant and the Sergeant standing by the Desk, I said casually, "I'm leaving too, Sarge."

"Okay," he said, and I kept on walking.

TEN

When I went to work midnights, it was discovered that I didn't have a nickname. You need one, for patrol, to talk casually over the radio: "Stix, you getting coffee?" "Chicky, did you check the roof?" "OV, T, GQ, can you swing by?" Nicknames never stuck to me, for some reason, and I always thought that nicknaming yourself was like talking to yourself, something that made you look foolish if you were overheard. So the Hat, Hawkeye, Hollywood, Gee-Whiz, Big E, the Count, Rollercoaster, and the rest pitched a few:

"Hemingway—nah, they'd know it was you."

"Ernest is better."

"Or Clancy—he'd be a good one to have."

"What about Edgar?"

"What from?"

"Edgar Allan Poe."

"What about Poe?"

Poe it was. As I thought about it, the fit was neat: Poe had worked midnights, too, weak and weary, upon a midnight dreary, in his most famous poem. He moved to New York City in 1844, the same year the legislation that created the New York City Police Department was signed. He wrote the first mystery story ever, called "The Murders in the Rue Morgue." I don't mean to spoil the ending for anyone, but the killer turns out to be a demented orangutan with a straight razor. There is a brilliant detective, an earnest sidekick, a mood of languor and gloom—all the hallmarks of a genre that has endured for a century and a half. No one else has done much with the crazy ape. Poe spent his last years in the Bronx, living and working in a cottage that is midway between where I lived and where I worked. I was a police officer in the Bronx, where some kids called the cops "po-po." Was it all coming together? Give me a minute.

Midnights for Poe seemed less a time than a territory, a place of woefully distant vistas, as if he were stargazing from the bottom of a well. A lot of that has to do with needing sleep, I think. Everyone lacked sleep on the midnights, and it may have been this state of worn-out wakefulness while the rest of the world was dreaming that lent itself to thoughts that meandered roundabout and far. Each precinct has a list of "cooping-prone locations"—out-of-the-way places, under bridges and by rail yards and the like, where bosses are supposed to check to make sure patrol cars haven't stopped in for a nap. The list is posted, and when you look at it when you're tired, it seems like a recommendation, a Zagat's guide for secret sleep, as if it might say: St. Mary's Park, with its rolling hills and abundant trees, offers superb concealment in a pastoral setting—we give it four pillows! On the midnights, we talked about sleep the way frat boys talked about sex. Did you get any last night? How was it? Nah, nah, but this weekend, believe me, I'm gonna go all night long! Though I asked practically everyone on the tour how long it took for your body to adjust to an upside-down life, only three people gave precise answers:

"Two weeks."

"Four months."

"Never."

Nevermore . . . Uncle Eddie finished his thirty-three years as a cop working midnights in the Bronx, and he would have told me, I know, that he liked it because they leave you alone. That's why I went. I would wait until Narcotics called, or Vice, away from the storms of SNEU. Stix would wait with me, until the Captain understood what had happened, or the Sergeant was thrown out, or enough time passed for no one to care anymore. We would have time to think and breathe. I didn't look forward to coming in to work, but I didn't hate it—root canal no longer rated as a relative pleasure. Stix said that his wife, Anna, thought that he seemed better, too.

We would be partners in Squad A, and Sgt. Yolanda Gonzalez was our boss. Sgt. G would be retiring in the spring, and the precious closeness of her departure, coupled with twenty years on the Job, gave her steadiness and perspective. Sgt. G was pretty and proper, sweet-natured as a schoolmarm, and the cops looked up to her and looked out for her, as if they were reform-school boys who'd found a sudden inspiration for homework. Since she was a veteran of the military and also of undercover work, the protective sense that she inspired in her cops might not have been entirely necessary, but it was certainly good to see. Of the handful of cops in the command who were closer to the end of their careers than the beginning, most of them—Linda McLean, Timmy Anderson, Mike Moxom, Harry Thompson—worked the midnights. They looked at us with sympathy and something akin to bemusement—what we'd been through might have been bad, but no one had been indicted or killed, and so tragedy-wise, we were still a little light. Years before, I'd been surprised to see Timmy Anderson, in the daylight and wearing a suit. He was heading to court. "Someone had the bad taste to die while they were wearing my handcuffs," he said wearily, cutting to the nub of a longer story he told me later, of a perp whose cocaine psychosis led to cardiac arrest, and who would haunt Timmy as a litigious ghost for long after. Did we have problems? *Lemme tell ya about problems. . . .* If nothing else, our SNEU saga made us part of the hard-luck fraternity of the NYPD, and the midnight cops welcomed Stix and Poe as the newest old-timers.

Still, it was a difficult adjustment, for Stix especially. He was so fastidious that when he ate a sandwich, he held it in a paper towel. Once, when he was getting dressed, he dropped his uniform shirt on the floor of the locker room, and promptly threw it back into his locker to take it home to wash.

"The floor is covered with toejam," Stix said.

"Your partner, he's a real perfectionist," observed another cop, dressing by his locker.

"That's one word for it."

Stix found it hard to get used to eating and sleeping on our new schedule, and he was often nearly delirious with exhaustion. In the first week, I think he asked me a dozen times: "Do you wake up at night and have breakfast? And do you go home in the morning for dinner? How can you have eggs at night, or pasta when your wife is having eggs?" For me, a perversely ordered life was somewhat better than the old chaos, but it was still hard. Though the schedule was not kind on either of our digestions, I grew weary of his reaction whenever we encountered any foul odor—he would wrinkle his brow, glare, and ask, "Did you fart?" Quite often, I had not.

On our first night, Stix and I guarded an empty apartment. A woman had made a complaint about her ex-boyfriend, and he had come back and fired a couple of shots at her. For an indefinite period, two cops would be stationed outside her apartment, twenty-four hours a day. Though she had been staying with relatives for some time, Stix and I didn't object to the assignment, and we devoted the tour to reading and the discussion of breakfast philosophies. We were assigned there another night, and then another. The silences grew longer and more leaden.

"Did you say something?"

"I didn't even *think* anything."

A cop from the four-to-twelves who was also on the Captain's shitlist had spent a lot of time there, until he got into even more trouble by bringing in a chaise longue. It made sense to me. A lieutenant from the Inspections Unit made periodic checks on us, I suppose to make sure we were doing nothing. On other nights, we were detailed to guard hospitalized prisoners, or to work inside, handing out radios or working the "T/S," the telephone switchboard, behind the desk.

I had never worked inside, and I didn't think much of the cops who chose to—who would want such a dull and easy assignment? I didn't change my mind about the "dull" part, but "easy" was revised after my first tour on the T/S, when I developed my first case of writer's cramp since college. It was well after four when I was able to look up from the "daily summons recap," which consisted of indexing and cross-referencing the five-digit control number for each day's master sheet with each summons. On the master sheet, I'd write the cop's name and six-digit tax number, the date of issue, and then the ten-digit summons number, and then the plate number if it was a parking summons, or the person's name, address, and date of birth, if it was a criminal-court summons, or the plate number, name, address, and date of birth, if it was a moving summons. Seventy-three summonses had been issued in the past twenty-four hours at PSA-7, and I learned each of them intimately. Then I had to count them again and break them down: back copy for us, front for court, each in its own envelope, with separate envelopes for the two summonses that were turned in a day late. When I finished, Sgt. G politely explained that I'd written the control number on the wrong part of the summons, on the tear-off strip on top that would be thrown away. "Forget it, don't worry about it," she said consolingly. "I don't know who looks at this stuff anyway."

One night, when Stix had a hospitalized prisoner—a seventeen-year-old asthmatic crack dealer—he got the perp to give up three spots, one with a gun, which he'd been inside within the last twenty-four hours. When he came in for meal, we ran the checks and IDed all three players—each with felony narco raps, one on parole. Stix talked to Timmy Anderson about it, and Timmy suggested that we take it up with the Lieutenant, who was usually gung-ho for this sort of thing. But when Stix approached the Lieutenant to say that we wanted to look into something, the Lieutenant laughed and shook his head. "It's a waste of time," he said. "They're never gonna let you guys do a warrant. Tell you what—instead of trying for the warrant, why don't you just run into that wall as fast as you can. Maybe that'll get it out of your system."

After a couple of weeks, Harry Thompson, who was the PBA delegate on the late tour, took us aside. "You guys might have noticed you've been getting shitty assignments."

Yes, we had.

"What happened was that your old boss reached out to fuck you guys. But if you guys write some summonses, get some collars, whatever, Sgt. G is gonna be in a better position to tell them that she won't."

"How are we supposed to get collars on a fixed post or T/S?"

"That's the thing."

It was the thing. Sgt. Gonzalez later had a word with us, as well. "Here and now," she said. "This is a clean start. Whatever happened in SNEU is past—I won't hold it against you."

"What did you hear that happened?" I asked. If I had to write a complaint for the "suspicious DOA" of the SNEU team, Stix and I would have been listed as the complainants instead of the perps. It was disquieting to hear that the common understanding might be otherwise.

"I don't know what happened," she said. "I heard it was something about a warrant. . . . I don't know, and it doesn't matter to me."

Stix said, "It wasn't like that, Sarge."

She nodded. "Like I said, this is a fresh start."

I would have liked to think so. Rumors in the precinct buzzed around like microwave signals, in high volume and low quality—various cops had told me, with utter confidence, that the Captain was beloved by the bosses downtown and had a limitless future; that he was hated and was on his way out; that he hated the Job and would leave the instant he was eligible; that he never wanted to leave and was desperate for promotion to deputy inspector; that the promotion was due any minute now; and that it was a flat-out impossibility, because—and this is on the highest authority, so don't tell anyone—no one in Housing would be promoted. Sgt. G's reference to the warrant had an understated accuracy in my case, but it had nothing to do with Stix. It was little wonder that the rumor mill did less to clarify than to confuse.

The degree of confusion became apparent when a cop informed me matter-of-factly that it wasn't the Sergeant who'd thrown Stix out, but the new lieutenant—who had gleefully sent us on patrol when the Sergeant was out, and who now was the precinct Integrity Control officer—on the grounds of "chronic lateness." Stix had been officially late once, when there was a hurricane. The new lieutenant put him in the Minor Violations Log, and the Sergeant wrote "counseled for tardiness" on his evaluation. It was the only recorded infraction in his career, since the Sergeant's later charges of insubordination were bluntly dismissed by Lt. Johnson. But other cops picked up the theme of the story, passing along remarks to the effect that no one liked the new ICO, and that he was bound to cause trouble. Finally, cops from SNEU told us that the Sergeant now claimed that he didn't throw Stix out, to anyone who wasn't in the room when it happened—"I fought to keep him, there was nothing I could do . . ."—which was a rather grand lie. Since Stix and I had eight hours and thirty-five minutes a night to think about it, I came to speculate that the Sergeant and the ICO spun the story together, since it suited one to look like a nicer guy than he was, and the other to look tougher. It deepened our mistrust of the bosses, and made gestures of support from other cops all the more touching.

When Angelo Ricci, one of our PBA delegates, heard that we were both out of SNEU, he marched in to the Captain to confront him. The Captain said that Stix and the Sergeant "had been butting heads for a while," and that I was trying to transfer just about anywhere, but it wasn't happening because "nobody trusts him." Angelo said, "What are you talking about? Everybody loves him—he's a great cop and a great guy, one of the best cops in the command."

"Well, maybe it's the supervisors who don't trust him."

Angelo left the office, saying, "You just flushed two great cops down the toilet."

As part of my escape plan, I wrote up the bribery collar and the last warrant for department recognition, to get the points for the transfer. I was given bars for Meritorious Police Duty and Excellent Police Duty, respectively. An EPD is the most basic police commendation, and an MPD, which was a step above, was the conventional award for a bribery collar. The bribery collar took a couple of hours, and it sidelined a junkie for a couple of months; the warrant took six weeks, and it disabled the operation of serious criminals, even if the effects were more partial and temporary than they should have been. It didn't make sense, but I made nothing of it. And then Sgt. Clark, who headed the precinct awards committee, told me, "I put you in for a Commendation"—one level above an MPD—"but the Captain said you didn't deserve anything. He said it didn't happen the way you wrote it up, and Narcotics did all the work. He didn't want to give you anything—I had to fight with him to get you the EPD."

Though we were free of the Sergeant completely, and I'd rarely see the Captain, their enduring reach rankled nonetheless. It was not right that such small people had such a large influence in our lives, and similar revelations spurred many cops into devoted study for the sergeant's exam and beyond. Things were bad-marriage bad between us, with the kind of intensity that depends on an element of mutuality. Time and distance might provide a better perspective. The Sergeant was eagerly friendly to me again when we saw each other, as he had been on the first days on the team. I was not friendly in return, but I did wonder whether, if he'd been a cop with us, instead of our ostensible leader, his shortcomings would have been so pronounced. He was a bad fit for us, but not a bad man, at least at first; most people have a breaking point, and we were his. He reminded me of certain clients from my defense days, who were decent enough people as long as life treated them decently, but whom three bad weeks in a row would send into coke binges and liquor-store stick-ups. For the Captain, it was harder to guess—if the Inspector hadn't canceled one warrant, or he hadn't canceled three, or my book news had stayed hidden for another week, or he'd been at the command longer . . . Then again, I thought, the hell with both of them. In one year, I'd made more collars than either had made in his career. For the past eleven months, I had done backflips for them; the next jump would be out. Stix and I resolved that if one of us were hurt, the other would keep them both out of the hospital; if it went worse for us, they were to be banned from the church.

The Sergeant and the Captain cost us faith, time, and needless aggravation, but the worst you could say of them—arguably, at the farthest reach—was that certain criminals owed them their freedom, since they had kept us from working as we should. To encounter people who were genuinely evil, we would have to leave the precinct. We didn't have to go far away. When we finally got out on patrol, we were out for an hour before we were called in for another fixed post, at a crime scene. There had been a rape at one of my old buildings on Washington Avenue, on a stairwell in Morris Houses. The scene encompassed three flights of stairs and the elevator that the perp had taken to escape. The victim's clothes had been thrown all over the stairs: a scruffy brown leather jacket and an orange sweater on one landing, tan pants and a pair of aqua-and-blue-striped gym shorts on another. Her shoes were there, too—gray leather ankle-high boots, each still laced up and tied. There was a condom wrapper on my floor and a condom two flights up. I had the bottom of the stairs, Vinnie Commisso had the top, and Stix had the elevator. I asked about what had happened, and a sergeant casually threw out a couple of details. My job was to stand guard over a pair of shorts, and it didn't really matter what I knew. I overheard that there were inconsistencies to the woman's story: she said she was going to the store, but she didn't have any money and never left the building. One detective on the canvass muttered that she must have been hustling on the stairwell: "We're gonna lock this guy up for Theft of Service." I told Stix, "You're gonna wait here for an hour, and then Crime Scene's gonna show up and say, 'We're not gonna get a print off an elevator button,' and walk away." That happened, only it took longer.

I stood next to a door covered with gang graffiti—"031" and "Tre 9 Bloods"—the babel of proclamations of who was a lover, who was a fighter, and who just was. I was careful not to lean on the wall because of the roaches, and then I wondered idly why there were so many flies in the hall, especially near the clothing. Two detectives from the Crime Scene Unit came and asked what we had, and I told them what I knew. Per their request, I called upstairs, "Hey, Vinnie, is the condom full?" They shone UV light on the clothes, which illuminates body fluids, but there was no evidence of semen. They bagged some of the clothes, and then one of them went to pick up the condom wrapper.

"Uggh, there's shit on it. Check the shorts," he said.

"You check 'em," said the other.

He did, and found they were full of excrement. Did it matter if she was a whore? Maybe it had started as a conversation about a deal, and maybe it hadn't. However it had started, he tried to move her to the roof, and she didn't want to go. They were in a public area in the middle of a sixteen-story building with eight apartments per floor. She had been stripped naked, and even forced to take off her shoes. Whether she lost control of her bowels out of pure terror, or in a desperate gesture to repel her attacker, she was raped as she sat in her own shit, and she ran home dirty and naked.

Moments like those cleared your mind of office politics, at least for a while. Not every job on the midnights was as heavy as that, but the jobs tended to be substantiated: "shots fired" on the four-to-twelves often meant someone wanted to clear out the kids in the lobby; "shots fired" on the midnights usually meant shots had been fired. At least half of our homicides were on the midnights, but a higher percentage of those were the "misdemeanor murders," the perp-on-perp hits. When Stix and I went to one, in the lobby of 180 Brook, the body had already been removed, but there were blood and brains all over. White feathers were also strewn about, and they began to drift away in the breeze, except for where they were stuck in the red pools and gray piles.

"What happened here, a pillow fight?"

"Nah, he had a down jacket, EMS had to cut it open to work on him. . . ."

In the lobby of a project on Webster Avenue, a member of the Bloods was ambushed by Crips and shot five times: in each hand, the chin, the belly, and the balls. An elaborate shrine had been set up for him, of candles, beer and brandy bottles, wilting flowers, and scribbled notes and pictures. The notes were from adults and teenagers, but the writing—penmanship, spelling, and everything else—were like kids' letters to Santa. One of them said more than the others:

2 guns up
Shawny AKA
Shady AKA
Waterbug
Let me drop some knowledge on you
I'm sure (God) will make sure that they 'pay' 'how' nobody knows he may send
them to 'jail to life' or he may choose to deliver them to his dogs, dogettes,
b-brothers and sisters
Much love Dutchman RIP
13 murders finest

Was God a Blood or a Crip? I wondered. Did they think of Him as the Original Gangsta? Too often in the projects, the knowledge was promised but never dropped. Two buildings away, a night or two later, we had another gun run—"Male black, dark clothes . . ."—in a lobby where there were eight or so guys hanging out. I knew at least two of them as dealers. We approached with holsters cracked, our voices reasonable at first—"Guys, lemme see your hands"—and several complied, and then the voice harsher—"Up, I said. Hands up!"—and the rest followed, except for one. He sat listlessly and stared at me, and Stix covered the rest as I closed the gap between us. He didn't move—*Get your fucking hands up!*—and I grabbed him, flipped him around and pushed him against the fence, twisting an arm behind his back. The guys on the wall began to shout: "Hey! Take it easy on him!"

"Go easy!"

"That's my cousin, he's retarded!"

"Hey, he's retarded, yo!"

I shifted tone, reassuring him that I just had to check, I was sorry, it would be okay. I patted him on the back as I continued to check for the gun. I felt bad for him, but if they knew what they were doing, the gun wouldn't be on the big guy, or even the shooter. It would be in any of the places the cops don't want or think to look: under the colostomy bag of the guy in the wheelchair, or in the baby carriage, or in the young girl's knapsack. You want to know why I roughed up the retarded kid? *Let me drop some knowledge on you. . . .*

At the daylit end of one tour, a woman hailed us to point out white smoke billowing from the top window of an old three-story house with a mansard roof on Courtlandt Avenue. We rang the bells and banged on the door, and then we kicked and kicked and kicked. It was a steel door but we were almost through when a man sleepily stuck his head out from the second floor.

"You all right?" we asked.

"Yeah, don't worry about it—it's just the radiator. This is a city building, nobody's here but me and I don't know how to shut it off. The Fire Department knocked the door down last week to get in, that's why there's a nice new strong one. Thanks anyways, guys."

Both Stix and I were downcast. "I was thinking of the Commissioner," Stix said. "Him saying, 'You saved their lives, where do you want to go?'"

"I was thinking the same thing."

Such were our thoughts, and we didn't lack time to think them. There were fewer jobs than during the day tours, and far less than on the four-to-twelves. Even on the weekends, they tended to taper off after two or three in the morning. You had more time on your own than on any other tour. It felt odd to be back in the bag, back on patrol, at this hour and at this time in my career. When I thought about my past and the past of this place, as we drove and the late hours drifted on, I wondered where I was going. It often brought on a terminal feel, which I would sometimes try to cure by looking at the cause.

One night, Stix and I drove to the corner of 132nd Street and Lincoln Avenue—a cooping-prone location, in fact, though it wasn't the intention for the visit—a dead end at the very bottom of the Bronx, with a warehouse on one side and a parking lot on the other. Across the black shimmer of the river, you could see Harlem and the salt piles along the highway. When I was young, my father told me that kids from Harlem had died playing in the piles, and each time I'd see them I'd think of the little black boys drowning in the white salt. The Bronx began here, physically, and it began here in history, too, when Jonas Bronck built his farmhouse. Not much is known about him: he was a Swedish sea captain who was induced to settle the area by the Dutch West India Company. A peace treaty was signed at Bronck's house between the Dutch and the Weckquasgeeks, who lived in what would become the Bronx and upper Manhattan, ending years of sporadic but bloody skirmishes. Bronck didn't have much to do with it, but his house was the only one around.

"When did he move?" Stix asked.

"I don't know, probably when they built the projects."

It was a funny question, anyway, because it made me think that the Bronx is a place people come from, and not where they go to and stay, if luck is on their side. It was also a place of slow beginnings: Bronck came here in 1639 to homestead, and at the beginning of the twentieth century there was still farmland in the South Bronx; it only became citified as they built the subway. A person alive today could have witnessed its entire metropolitan career: two generations as a vibrant, blue-collar boomtown, and one as a slum so ravaged and riotous that when people from outside struggled to describe it, they compared it to Berlin and Hiroshima at war's end, a place so defeated that its enemies felt pity. They also compared it to the moon.

Stix and I cruised up to 142nd Street between Willis and Brook avenues, a block with a row of little houses on one side and a school on the other. We had chased a lot of junkies down that street, when they bought heroin with the brand name "President," among others, from the projects on the corner. One hundred years ago, stonecutters from Pisa named the Piccirilli brothers had a studio there, where they carved the Lincoln Memorial, but I don't suppose the dope was named in any commemorative spirit. Four blocks up and two over, Mother Teresa's order had a mission. The work they did was holy and noble, but there was also something a little embarrassing about it, to have nuns reassigned from leper duty in Calcutta to lend us a hand here. There was a picture in the *Daily News* a few years back of Mother Teresa and Princess Diana, visiting together, and Smacky was there, standing guard, just out of the frame. A little farther out of the frame is the building where Rayvon Evans died. He was a little boy whose parents kept his corpse in the closet until it seeped through to the floor below and the neighbors complained. John had driven the Lieutenant there when the job first came over, and they looked at both apartments, but the family had already thrown Rayvon's body out the window. The parents were never charged with murder because there wasn't enough of Rayvon left to tell how he died. When it was on the news, I saw Sammy and other cops from the PSA in the footage, in the hallway of the apartment and on the street, but I was glad that wasn't my job. There is a garden dedicated to the little boy, but there is no sign of the stonecutters, the princess, or the rest. Memory is short here, but the past is transparent, and you can look back as far as you want, until the present compels you to see what's happening now. It can take time for your eyes to adjust.

Midnights magnify things, sets them in sharp relief against the empty night, like gems on black velvet cloth. You answer jobs for lonely people who seem more lonely at midnight, more solitary and sorrowful, like the chubby little woman who reclined in her armchair like a pasha after attempting suicide by taking three Tylenol PMs. Or the woman whose close-cropped, dyedrowned blond hair was going green, who denied trying to hurt herself, but whose boyfriend confided that she had tried, by slapping herself, hard. Domestic disputes are all the more squalid and small-hearted when they take place at five in the morning: two middle-aged brothers at each other's throats, hours before their mother's funeral. The place stank and the walls seethed with roaches. One brother had a weary and beaten dignity, and he sat on the couch with his overcoat and an attaché case, like a salesman who had just lost a commission. The other brother shouted drunkenly, jerking and flailing like a dervish because of some unknown neurological misfires. They had argued because he had started drinking again, with a friend, who had called to report the sober one for his lack of sympathy. I took the jerky one aside, to let him ventilate a little. In his room, which was littered with cans of malt liquor, certificates from the Army and alcohol rehab were on proud display, taped to the wall. As he punched his honorable discharge to emphasize that his had been a life of accomplishment, a sunburst of roaches shot out from beneath it. I wanted to punch his rehab diploma, to show that he still had some work to do, but I thought better of it. We knew that we would be back if we left them there, and we dreaded the idea of having to lock someone up before the funeral, so we asked the sober one if he would mind leaving for a while. He agreed that it was the best thing to do; we agreed it was deeply unfair. He used to work as a security guard and he had a business card, which he offered to several cops—on the midnights, cops back each other up more often—and I took it without looking at it. "If there's anything I can do for you gentlemen . . ." he said, and then he went out to walk until daybreak.

If some people call because they want someone, anyone, to talk to, there are others for whom we are the last thing they want to see. For them, we arrive the way the Bible says judgment will: like a thief in the night. It felt like that when we took a woman's children away. With Stix, Sgt. G, and her steady driver, Louie Malagon, I escorted two caseworkers from the Administration for Children's Services who had a court order to remove the one-, two-, and three-year-old kids of a crackhead named Pamela into their care. The midnight visit was a sneak attack, as she had dodged the caseworkers during the daylight hours. Our part was to be—not to put too fine a point on it—hired muscle. These jobs are always awful, even when they run smoothly, and this one did not begin well: when we knocked, a woman answered—"Who?"—and then delayed ten minutes, muttering excuses—"Hold on," and, "Let me get something on," and then, "Who is it, again?"—before surrendering to threats to kick the door down. She was just a friend, she said, helping to clean up—probably in anticipation of such a visit. Pamela was out, she said, and there were kids in the back, but they were Pamela's sister's kids, and the sister was out, too. As we went to see the children, another woman came out from a back bedroom. Three kids were there, sleeping, who looked as if they might have been one, two, and three. But the second woman was coolly adamant: "Those are my kids, and I'm not Pamela, I'm her sister, Lorraine! I can show you, you're making a mistake!" I thought, what are the odds, two sisters, each having three kids the same ages? Somewhat high, and then the sexes—girl, girl, boy—and the odds were a little more comforting—a long shot multiplied by eight, to be precise—but I was still glad it was ACS's call, not mine. We grilled both women but they never broke from their story, and we could find no baby pictures or prescription bottles or anything else that would tie these children to the case—there lingered a twinge of doubt. And so when Lorraine said she could prove it, if we'd let her call her mother to get their ID, we agreed, as it would clearly demonstrate whether we were professional public servants doing a difficult job well, or dim-witted repo men hauling off the wrong crackbabies. But Lorraine didn't call for ID, she called for reinforcements, and the apartment was soon flooded with angry women. Lorraine wouldn't give up her kids, clutching the oldest two, while we had the baby boy, and then another neighbor took a girl, and then Lorraine tried to get out with one kid, walking down the hall. More cops came, and one told her to stop, but a neighbor woman blocked him when he went to follow, then blocked him again when he tried to step around. She howled: "Call the cops! Call the cops and have him arrested! He ain't leaving till the cops come and arrest him!" It looked like it was about to boil over, when even more cops came, two of them running up twelve flights of stairs, and one had to lie down when he got there, and the other was rushed to the hospital with chest pains just after. The press of angry bodies made the apartment hot, and some women yelled for everyone to calm down, and some women yelled the opposite, and as we tried to dress the crying kids, some women tried to help, in earnest, finding their jackets and socks, while others were plainly angling to shoplift them. Lorraine had her last child taken, and she took a swing at a cop but one wrist was grabbed, then the other when it followed, and her friends took her aside, and after a few more eruptions of screaming, we got the kids out. One woman yelled, "This is why people hate the cops!" And though I thought very little of her and the rest of them, the Mothers United for Narcotics and Neglect, she had a point, because no one likes people who steal babies in the middle of the night. Although I was confident that we had done right, it felt wretched, and I didn't want to dwell on it. We had just started our tour.

. . .

THE MIDNIGHT TOUR IS ALSO CALLED THE FIRST PLATOON, the second and third being day tours and four-to-twelves. You begin at 2315 hours and end at 0750. There are three squads for each platoon, working five days on, two days off, five days on, three days off, so that there are two squads on patrol every tour. The five days are the "set," the two or three the "swing." If you have Tuesday and Wednesday off one week, say, you have Tuesday, Wednesday, and Thursday the next, and then Wednesday and Thursday the week after that. It takes some getting used to, because if you're working a Friday, you don't come in Friday, you come in Thursday night. Another depressing thing about midnights is that when you finish work, at ten minutes to eight in the morning, you don't say, "See you tomorrow," which would seem soon enough; you say, "See you tonight." Tonight began yesterday and tomorrow begins tonight, and the days become one rolling night.

You lose track of time on this schedule, much more than on any other. I started out on steady four-to-twelves, Sunday to Thursday. You could lead a more normally regimented life. For my first two years at the Morris Houses, I was busier than on the midnights, when I might cover an entire precinct. The crime rate hadn't fallen as far as it later would, and the hours weren't as late. I knew less local history then, and the landmarks I navigated by were of recent relevance: the pawnshop to check after a chain-snatch; the crackhouse where the baby had overdosed; the rooftop where they fought pit bulls, sometimes throwing the loser to the street below. Sometimes Stix and I covered that area on the midnights, but even with a better grasp of the place and more time to think about it, I still wondered why things had turned out as they had.

Morris Houses were named after Gouverneur Morris, a Revolutionary War hero and coauthor of the Constitution who served with Washington at Valley Forge, and who later established the decimal system of U.S. currency, inventing the word "cent." His half-brother, Lewis, was a signer of the Declaration of Independence, and he tried to get the Founding Fathers to establish the Capitol on the family estate, though the idea was more or less a nonstarter. The Morrises owned most of the South Bronx from 1670, and their name is everywhere: the neighborhood called Morrisania, in the Four-Two, where my beat was, and Morris High School, which graduated the industrialist Armand Hammer and Secretary of State Colin Powell, not to mention dance-school impresario Arthur Murray. The neighborhoods of Morris Heights and Port Morris are named for the family, as is Morris Avenue, although Morris Park, which was built over the racetrack where they once held the Belmont Stakes, is named after someone else. Yet I couldn't say they mean much to anyone here; Morris Houses was the place where the kids Bernhard Goetz shot came from—four thugs who approached the wrong lunatic on a subway, in 1986. One remained confined to a wheelchair, and I'd sometimes see him around. I locked up another one's sister for robbery, after a nasty girl-gang fight, and I can't imagine their mother said, upon each of her children's return from jail, "Gouverneur Morris and his half-brother Lewis must be rolling in their graves!" The Morrises made this place and helped make this nation, but they might as well have knocked up some local girls after a one-night stand, leaving nothing but their name.

It's hard to think of how things could have gone worse, though they certainly could have. On a map of what might have been, I could point out the spot where someone planned to shoot Franklin Delano Roosevelt during a campaign visit. It isn't far from where the ransom was paid for the Lindbergh baby, though the child had been dead a month by then. I could show you the spot on Bryant Avenue where Popeye and Sonny recovered eighty-eight pounds of French Connection heroin, though I wish I could drive by and say, "This is where we won the war on drugs." There are other local monuments to lost opportunity that are not all cause for regret, however. A few blocks away, at 1522 Vyse Avenue, Leon Trotsky lived for a year before returning to Russia for the role that fate had assigned him. When the story broke, the headline of *The Bronx Home News* read, "Bronx Man Leads Russian Revolution." Imagine if he had stayed here. John F. Kennedy lived in the Bronx for a year as a child. I wonder what he would have sounded like, if he'd stayed: *Ax not what yiz can do for ya country . . .* Lee Harvey Oswald lived in the Bronx as a young teenager, in Highbridge and Belmont. But JFK returned to Boston, and Oswald was sent to the Youth House, for psychiatric evaluation, and they would not meet for years, and not here, and they would not know that they had the Bronx in common.

When the time dragged, these scraps of fact that jammed my head like a junkshop's clutter tended to pop up more often. The Russian theme reemerged one night, when it was so slow that three patrol cars showed up for a dispute between two crackheads over a lost shopping cart. To pass the time, we conducted a thorough investigation, asking pointed questions: *What color was the cart? Do you have a receipt?* It was cold, and after a while, one of the cops said we should leave. But I was bored enough to want to talk to the crackheads, who relished the attention. I said to the cop, "They have issues, we can help them work through them, the relationship can come out even stronger than it was before." He looked at me and said, "Hey, I'm no Dr. Zhivago, let's get out of here."

On the midnights, there is a risk of drifting within yourself, trailing off on your own weird trains of thought, so that when the even weirder world intrudes, it is hard work not to laugh. In short, you get a little punchy sometimes. I felt bad after one job, for a few reasons. It was a sad case and they seemed like good people, an old man and his sick wife. He had an upright, military bearing, and she was a stick figure, with plum-colored bruises all over, gasping through her nebulizer, *"Ayúdame, ayúdame, ayúdame. . . ."* We made small talk, in broken English and Spanish, while waiting for EMS.

There was a picture of a young man in a police uniform, and the old man said he was his son, a cop in San Juan who had died at the age of thirty-four, from cancer. The entire apartment was a Santería shrine: cigars laid across the tops of glasses of clear liquid; open scissors on dishes of blue liquid; dried black bananas hanging over the threshold; tarot cards, change, and dice before a dozen statues of saints, including a massive Virgin Mary with a triple-headed angel beneath. They struck me as objects of pity and power at once. I wondered if it was the woman or the man who was trying to stack the supernatural deck in their favor, if disaster, past or impending, could be re-negotiated with the spirits and saints. And then I thought, *They keep the place up, but it's more House Voodiful than House Beautiful.* The line wouldn't leave my head, and I started to break up. I had to pretend to cough and walk outside, while Stix gave me a funny look.

You get in the habit of reading these scenes for signs, forensic or sacra-mental, as they both make the same point about sin and struggle in the fallen world. In Santería, shrines of candles and other offerings are often placed in the corner of a room, near the entrance; and in just that spot, in one apart-ment, there was a black-handled butcher knife, and blood that had not just pooled but piled, it lay so thick on the floor. There were dark sedimentary layers, and a clear overlay like varnish, which I was told came from the lungs. The woman whose handiwork it was explained what brought her to this sacrifice at the household altar: "Two years ago, my brother broke my leg in five places. I came in tonight, he sold my couch. He killed my mother. Well, she died from him and all his nonsense." She stopped talking for a mo-ment, and tried to shift her hands in her cuffs, as EMS took him out in a wheelchair, pale and still. "I didn't stab him," she went on. "He stabbed him-self by accident, in the back, in the tussle." Some objects tell simple stories of fierce violence, like the two-by-four, so bloody it looked like it was dipped in the stuff, used to collect a fifty-dollar debt one woman owed another. Others are more subtle and tentative, like the open Bible in the apartment of a woman whose brother, just home from prison, suffered some sort of psy-chotic break. "He sat there reading the Bible for a while, and then he just looked up and said he was going to kill me," she said. The Bible was opened to the first page of Proverbs, which says, in Chapter 1, Verse 18: "These men lie in wait for their own blood, they set a trap for their own lives." Maybe he only read the first part of the sentence. The woman's husband had just died, and beside the Bible was a sympathy card from someone named Vendetta.

As a cop, you look for patterns, for context and connections that tell a fuller truth than a complainant may be willing to tell. But sometimes the patterns themselves are deceptive; there are parts that belong to no whole. So it was with a matched pair of attempted robberies, twenty minutes and four blocks apart. Each perp was a male Hispanic, tall, slim, and young, in dark clothes (all brown in the first case, all black in the other), with a razor blade. In the second robbery, the perp wore a bandanna over his face and a wig, and the victim was cut in the hand with a razor. We packed up the complainants and canvassed the park that lay between the crime scenes, and we stopped a tall, slim, male Hispanic in his twenties, in all-black clothes, and when I searched him, I found a wig, a bandanna, and a razor in his pocket. If there was some doubt that the perps were the same, there was little that I'd found the guy responsible for one of them. Both complainants were sure, however, that he wasn't the perp, and we let him go. Since the weapon was a razor, maybe I should have remembered Poe and gone to look for the orangutan.

That was one kind of mystery, the puzzle of whodunit, which has a solution that is out of sight but within reach, like the winning card in three-card monte. There are other mysteries that raise questions that are far older and more open, and if there is a hint of a game in what unfolds, you feel more like a piece than a player. One night we went to a routine Aided case, an old woman with a history of heart trouble, whose breath was rapid and shallow. She moaned, *"Mami!"* as she sat on a red velvet couch, flanked by her young teenage granddaughters, and as she left with EMS, Stix told me that the old lady took care of the girls. We drove around for a while, and then we had another Aided case, a "heavy bleeder." When we went inside, a woman said, "She's in bed," and, "It's in the tub," and we checked on the teenage girl in the bedroom, who said she was fine, and then looked in the bathtub, where a fetus the size and color of a sprained thumb nestled in the drain. The head was turned upward and the eyes were open and dark. When the EMTs came—they were the same guys as at the last job—they asked for some plastic wrap or tinfoil, and they were provided with a sandwich bag to pick it up. As we helped them put the teenage girl in the ambulance, the EMT told me that the old lady had gone into cardiac arrest and wouldn't make it. Nothing else happened that night, and as we drove I thought about the two jobs, what they asked and answered, and what went through my mind was that for every one that dies, another one never is born. It was late but not late enough, not yet time to go home.

. . .

OCTOBER PASSED, AND THEN NOVEMBER, AND CHRISTMAS approached. In the beginning, especially, it didn't seem that John and I worked at the same job: I was a security guard, and he might spend a night drinking, going to bars where an underage police cadet would attempt to be served, or to see if he could buy a drink after four a.m. He was getting paid to drink beer. Technically, he was an undercover, but the assignments were not 007 stuff: he'd go to bodegas and try to buy loose cigarettes, or to Yankee games to scalp tickets. They locked up old men in social clubs for having a case of beer in the back room, or old ladies in bodegas for having policy slips or a joker poker machine. At first, I was jealous of the ease of his life, but later on, when I was back in the street, he was jealous of the stories of real police work. When people asked us where we worked, I noticed that he began to say he was in the Organized Crime Control Bureau instead of Vice.

Nonetheless, the time counted for his shield, and there were other perks. John was trained in the use of the "asp," the new, telescoping nightstick, which you'd extend with a flick of the wrist, and perps would run at the sound of it. He was sent to a day-long course on eavesdropping technology, where they gave out tote bags that were emblazoned SECRET SERVICE NYPD ELECTRONIC CRIME SEMINAR. He came home beaming, holding it up.

"How do you like it?"

"The logo's cool. It's just a shame they decided to put in on a purse. You're probably tough enough to get away with carrying it around, but you could also give it to your sister."

As Vice grew less attractive to me, it was becoming clear that the distaste was mutual. John asked the Vice captain about me a couple of times, and then he stopped, as the answer of "Soon, I think" grew testy and cool. More temps came into the office, and I came to suspect that this constant flow of new people was someone's idea of an integrity tactic, so that the cops wouldn't trust one another enough to steal. John worked often with another temp named Chris Verdejo, and we went out for dinner one night. Chris had just made a case that was featured on the front page of the *Times* sports section, when he took down a major counterfeiter of pro sports tickets. Chris had worked a Yankee game for scalpers, and he picked up a perp who had counterfeit tickets. Even the "legit" scalpers, who after all sold a real ticket, hated the counterfeiters. Chris developed his perp as an informant, and it led to a print shop where tickets for hockey, baseball, and basketball teams all across the country were produced. George Steinbrenner had assisted the police in the investigation, and it got great press. "I'm the flavor of the month!" Chris laughed. The Vice captain told him he could stay permanently, if he wanted, but later on said he couldn't manage it. Some inspector's nephew would be getting the spot. It reminded me to call Inspector Mullen, and offer myself up for adoption. At Central Booking one night, I noticed a cop from the Four-Seven eyeballing me, after which he asked if I knew Mullen. I said I did, but when he scrutinized my name tag, he shook his head and said, "I thought you were his son." If only that cop worked in the personnel office.

And then John received another unexpected notification. He was called up for the Fire Department, from a test he had taken five years before. The rumor was that the old list was resurrected because the son of one of the big bosses was on it. My cousin Brian had also been called. Both of them were the sons of firemen—my cousin Gerald, Brian's brother, was also on FD—and John's father had worked until he had a heart attack in the firehouse, refusing to go to the hospital until he was carried out. Mr. Timpanaro loved his job, as most firefighters did, while John's love of police work was a rarer and more complex commodity. A lot of cops went over to FD, like my friend Tommy Killian, but you never heard of firefighters who switched over to become cops, except for one or two who traveled from PD to FD and back, and were considered oddballs by both departments. Firefighters could arrange their schedules so that they worked two or three days a week; the camaraderie was legendary and the politics were minimal, next to our job; the public loved them. They died more often than we did, but they killed themselves less. For most people, there was no hesitation to transfer; for John, there was. John was not afraid of many things, and to date I was aware of two of them: he dreaded roaches, and he lived in fear that I might use his toothbrush and not tell him. I was *gabbados* and a *stunad*, thickheaded, but more important I was a *gavone*, a slob; he was a *skeevats*, who saw messy things as positively menacing. His skeeve-levels were nearly as high as Stix's, in the avoidance of doorknobs and of handshakes from bums, and once when I told him I was returning a pair of his underwear—washed, of course—he looked at me with unabashed horror and said, "Keep them." But the third thing he was afraid of was fire, I learned.

"If I see a guy with a gun, I chase him. I know the risks but I'm not afraid—I know I'm smarter, stronger, and faster than him, and that I'm a better shot.

I've been trained in tactics, and he hasn't. In my gut, I know I'm gonna win. But with a fire, none of that matters—a fire cares about me less than even the worst perp, and all I have to go against it doesn't matter. As a cop, I work in the worst part of the city, and the part I love best is the gun collars. If I went to FD, I'd go to the quietest corner of Staten Island, where I can work out all day and help cook and get a cat out of a tree once a year. I don't like fire."

And yet he decided he would accept the job. He went through another interview and medical, and was told he'd get a call on a particular Friday or Monday. The days passed, but then he was told the date had been postponed. When the next date passed without a call, he knew that the job wasn't there for him. My cousin Brian became a fireman, and John stayed a cop. I think he was relieved as much he was disappointed, but I was angry that the NYPD was such that even people who loved it would leave for work they hated, because there were so few real or rational reasons to stay.

Stix and I had begun to find our stride on the midnights, becoming a familiar team like Moxom and Parisi, Otero and Garcia, Flower and Thompson. We collared, and learned how to work an odd little cat-and-mouse OP for 175 Alex, handicapped as we were by uniforms and a marked car, available for jobs at any moment. The building had a back door, so we'd have to wait for someone to walk out in order to make a sneak attack on the dealers in the lobby. One night we had an inspiration to send in someone to open it up for us. We drove a few blocks away, to the prostitution strip on Jackson Avenue, and made the acquaintance of two ladies named Melissa and Snake. Snake explained that her boyfriend lived in the building and that she couldn't go there, but Melissa figured that opening a door for five bucks would be the easiest money she made that night. But we waited in vain—Melissa went to the wrong building, and Snake marched straight to 175 Alex to warn the dealers.

"What's the world coming to, when you can't trust a whore named Snake?"

We sometimes slipped in to work with Eddie Fackler and his conditions team—Eddie Wynne, Dennis Koesterer, Scott Griszcewicz, Chris Barry, and Danny Campagna, who set up like SNEU each night to collar. Eddie Fackler could "smell a gun," and his team brought them in routinely. I doubted that either of us would be able to join conditions, but to jump in with them to hit a set or chase a gun was exciting and nostalgic at once. We'd forgotten that the Job could be fun. If the midnights were never quite normal, they began to feel a little more familiar—we were in the streets, at least, and that was good.

As the holidays drew near, Sgt. G organized a Christmas party, where each cop had to bring in a dish from where their family came from, and that night we answered jobs from the precinct, like firemen, around tables of pasta, empanadas, and fried chicken.

Two days before Christmas, Stix was out, and I worked with a new guy named Tommy Rendo. We had a job for a smoke condition, from a fire that had been put out on the four-to-twelve, when someone lit up a couch in a project basement. A few people were gathered outside, unable to return to their homes because the building was still choked with smoke, and we sent a couple with a baby to the hospital for smoke inhalation. Though the Fire Department had come and gone, the building still seemed unsettled and unsafe. We propped the front doors open and waded through the ankle-deep sludgy water of the basement to open more doors, and then we walked up ten stories to open the roof doors—the elevators had been shut down—so the building could ventilate. On the walk up, the smoke was so thick we could barely see in front of us, and we had to wait on the roof for a while to catch our breath, dizzy and coughing. On the way back down, we checked each apartment, but we had to go back to the roof a few more times for air. I was ambivalent about leaving, though the firefighters knew what they were doing and we didn't. After talking to the people outside to find out which elderly tenants might be at risk, we knocked on a few more doors and then we left.

We had to do a "vertical patrol" at a particular building, and we drove there, a little dazed and short of breath, stinking of smoke. The door was locked, and we sat in the car for a while, waiting for someone to come out. There was a recent decision to make verticals "activity," as a formal and quantifiable unit of work, like a summons or an arrest, and now every cop had to perform several each night, in designated buildings, and to notify the dispatcher at the start and finish of each. I suppose it made some cops walk when they would have preferred to sit, but it struck me as still more pointless and wrong-headed bureaucracy—would beat cops have to fill out reports for how many times they said hello to people, and whether they got a pleasant response? Why didn't they just put pedometers on our feet, and count how many steps we took at the end of the month? At roll calls, a lieutenant said, "Listen, the most important thing is to just put them over the air, so we get credit for them," with the plain message that seeming to do them was more important than anything else.

Finally, a woman walked out of the building and said hello to us—for a point maybe, on the new scale—but we didn't feel like moving just then.

Tommy and I had a cigarette, to get the old smoke out of our lungs, and then we waited awhile longer. Finally, I said, "The hell with this," and we drove off. A few minutes later, the ICO raised us for a scratch, and twenty minutes later, we were called back to the command—he had been watching us, with binoculars, and had seen that and we hadn't gone into the building. He called me into his office, and gave me a speech about how shocked and disappointed he was: "I can't believe this! People say good things about you here! How could you do it, when you've got a rookie with you, who doesn't know any better? If Inspections caught you instead of me, this would have been a serious hit! What if there was a homicide in that building, and you put over the air that it was OK? I'm thinking about just writing the CD and getting it over with!"

As he spoke, he huffed up his sense of indignation, until he almost believed it himself. I knew it didn't matter, and I knew that neither of us really cared. I was on midnights in the South Bronx, on punishment posts more often than not, and there was little else that could be done to me. I also knew that he had me, dead to rights. I'd radioed that we'd gone into a building, and we hadn't.

I said, "What can I say? It won't happen again." Tommy and I went back out on patrol and checked the building, which of course was empty. Though I wasn't much concerned about the ICO, I told Tommy about a recent experience Stix and I had with him, when we were called in for a GO-15—an official department hearing, with union representatives—over a dent in the car. When we were assigned the car, Stix inspected it—checking the back seat for contraband, looking at the fluid levels, and so on—and he noticed a crimp on the passenger side, where the door hinge met the front panel. Every time you opened the door, the crimp got bigger, and after trying a few times, the two-inch gap became a three-inch gap. Cars pick up all kinds of nicks and scratches, and sometimes if cops dent the car more seriously, they'll pay a body shop to pound it out, rather than going through the fuss of the paperwork, or losing the car for weeks to the police mechanics. Once the accident is reported, the last cops to use the car are responsible for the damage; in this case, Comparetto and Clifford might catch a little grief, since someone gave it a kick on their watch. We were reluctant to report it, but we'd had enough trouble for ourselves, and the senior cops we talked to said we had no choice. The lieutenant at the desk said he'd have a look at it, as the ICO was walking by.

Had you seen the ICO look at the car door, you might have thought that he'd found a murder weapon; had you heard him, you might have thought that the homicide was of his twin brother. "I bet they were in a hit-and-run!" he said, as Stix and I stood by, unable to share in his mounting excitement. "There was a pursuit in the Four-O on the four-to-twelve, I bet they were in it and hit somebody! Let me see if they put it over the air that they were there!" and he raced back to pull up the printout of the job, certain that he was closing in on the culprits. Comparetto and Clifford, who each lived more than an hour away from the precinct, were summoned back at two in the morning. If they weren't so tired and enraged, they might have felt sorry for the ICO. As it was, they were informed of their rights to union and legal representation. The Accident and Investigation Section of the Highway Unit was called in, to photograph the dent and dust it for prints; the District Attorney's Office was notified of the possibility of criminal prosecution; a team from Inspections arrived to conduct the formal interrogation.

Lt. Mahoney, who had the desk that night, said, "Leave it to the Police Department to turn a hundred-dollar dent into a ten-thousand-dollar investigation."

And so it was with a mix of false confidence and real indifference that I put my thoughts of the ICO aside, when we went back in for meal at five. When we left, an hour later, Tommy told me that the ICO had decided to write us up for Command Disciplines. I said, "Turn around, I'm gonna talk to him, we'll say we didn't go in on my account." Tommy began to protest that whatever we did, we did together, but I said forget about it, let's just settle this, and we headed back. As soon as I walked into the ICO's office, he said, "Where were you? You stink!"

If anything, we smelled better than the first time around, and I told him about the fire. I said that we could have gone to the hospital and gone sick for the next couple of days, but we were the only Housing car covering the Four-Two, and that wasn't the kind of cops we were. My diplomacy was not what it might have been, but he'd left me with the clear impression the reprimand would be man-to-man. He hemmed and hawed, saying that he had to write me up because he'd talked about it in front of another cop, whom he *really* wanted to get—and eventually would, for taking days off while claiming to be in the military. Finally, he told me, "Don't worry, you're one of the Captain's best guys, you won't lose any time."

"I don't think it's right," I said, and I walked out. It was the morning before Christmas Eve, and I'd have the holiday off for the swing. When I went back in, the day after Christmas, our PBA delegate Harry Thompson told me that the Captain wanted to take three days, and it was non-negotiable. The

CD, for "improper patrol," would remain on my permanent record. My great-grandchildren would be able to look at the citation, much as I had been able to look at Pat Brown's. At the roll call, the lieutenant bellowed about what a fuck-up I was, and he sent Stix and me on another fixed post, for another threatened witness who wasn't home. It was more than a mile away, near Hunts Point, and the rest of the cops were ordered explicitly not to drive us there—we would take the bus. As we waited at the bus stop, for fifteen minutes, twenty, half an hour, the other guys kept driving up to us and saying, "C'mon, get in." "Forget about it," we said. "If they want us to take an hour to get there, it'll take us an hour to get there. If somebody gets killed, we'll be glad to explain why."

That would be my post for the next two weeks, sometimes with Stix, and sometimes with Parisi, who also had run afoul of one of the bosses. I sat there and read. One night, Eddie Fackler, Eddie Wynne, Chris Barry, and Dennis Koesterer got a gun, from a pistol-whip cab robbery. The perp hid in the bushes, reaching down to his ankle as they saw him. At the precinct, Koesterer yelled at him: "What the hell is wrong with you! I could have killed you!" "I had to straighten my sock," said the perp. Louie Malagon and Sgt. G got a gun, from a robbery at 169 and Cypress. Alex Otero and Louie Garcia got a gun, and Chicky got a gun with Sgt. Toth. Chicky had also come to midnights, a month after we did. He was tired of the fighting, too.

I called Inspector Mullen, and he said that Narcotics should come soon, not long after the New Year; I shouldn't worry about the CD, he said, but I had to have it adjudicated before the transfer. Harry Thompson was able to negotiate down so that it would be removed from my record if I stayed out of trouble for six months; my dark secrets would remain hidden from my descendants. I took the three days and signed the CD. The Lieutenant apologized for blowing up at me, and said that it was the Captain's orders. Once the two weeks were up, I could go back to work with Stix again on regular patrol.

On New Year's Eve, I was assigned to guard the PSA parking lot, and it was there that I greeted the new millennium. After five years of hard work in the NYPD, I was sent to stand there, freezing amid the empty cars, as the fireworks erupted somewhere out of sight, and the gunshots rang out, a little closer. I was with a new guy named Ullman—since he'd seen combat in the Israeli Army, "rookie" seemed patronizing—and we bullshitted away the hours. I tried to say what I liked about the Job, but it was hard to come up with anything. I didn't want to come off as a hairbag, though it wasn't far from what I felt. The Captain and the ICO both paid me visits, to make sure I was at my post. I think I said "Happy New Year" to them, but I don't really recall.

. . .

WHEN MY FATHER'S FBI FILES FINALLY ARRIVED FROM WASH-ington, eighteen months after I'd requested them, there were a lot of little surprises and one larger shock. For the NYPD, Uncle Eddie's career was contained in some fifty pages of paper, and Pat Brown's was summed up on an index card. The stack of documents on my father was more than three inches thick, and it comprised his initial application and the exhaustive research into his medical, military, family, educational, vocational, and personal history. His annual evaluations were also comprehensive, and included a medical exam. Once, when he was twenty pounds overweight, a pay raise was withheld for several months until he slimmed down, under a doctor's supervision. There were congratulatory notes from J. Edgar Hoover on his tenth and twentieth anniversaries with the Bureau, as well as for his marriage and on the births of each of his children. For his casework, there were many congratulatory letters from supervisors and outside agencies, but they were distinctly unilluminating: the names of his fellow agents were blacked out, and so were the names of the defendants. Since my father had the originals, I could see which gangsters and agents were involved, but none of the names had any special meaning for me. One did stand out: Robert Morgenthau, who wrote Hoover to thank him for my father's work on a case of the theft of nearly half a million dollars in American Express traveler's checks, in 1967, when he served as U.S. Attorney for the Southern District. In the letter, Morgenthau noted that the perps were in the Mafia, and he was especially pleased with how my father had been able to secure the testimony of one mobster even after his first cooperating witness was murdered in an unrelated matter.

Morgenthau had been the District Attorney in Manhattan since the early 1970s, and he was without peer in the country in terms of stature and longevity; in all of American history, only his predecessor, Frank Hogan, had a comparable record of innovation and integrity. I gave him a call and we talked for half an hour. "Sure, I remember your father," he said. "He was a terrific agent, one of the smartest if not the smartest around, an extremely bright guy. Did he go to St. John's Law?"

Fordham, I said. I asked him how he had jurisdiction in the case, since the airports were in the Eastern District, which was the junior partner and occasional rival of the Southern.

"Damned if I know. If they were looking at Manhattan, we had jurisdiction."

Morgenthau reflected on the changes in the U.S. Attorney's Office, which now had seven times as many assistants and produced half as many indictments, and how it was controlled more by Washington—from whom you needed approval for a wiretap application, for example. As a federal and then as a local prosecutor, he had worked with FBI and the NYPD for decades. "We had an extremely close relationship with the agents, to our mutual benefit, I think. With the Police Department, it was very uneven; it depended on the Commissioner and the Chief of Detectives, and it took time to build up confidence. You knew someone trusted you when they didn't ask who an informant was.

"Most of the time, we did very well with the Bureau, except for the time when [X] was there in New York. He was a real turkey. What did the agents call him, Cement Head?"

I did recall references to Cement Head as my father talked to my mother over dinner. Morgenthau went on to ask me what I was doing, and I said I worked midnights now, but I expected to go into Narcotics soon. "Well, if you want to work in Manhattan, let me know, and once you get your shield . . ."

When I hung up the phone, I was a little giddy. I was proud of my father, and proud to be able to talk to the District Attorney. I wasn't especially proud of my professional life in recent months. It wasn't fair to compare my career at that point to either of theirs, I knew, but I was willing to hazard a guess that they never had to put their verticals over the air. I was glad to have learned the Job from the ground up, but at the moment there was an abundance of ground, and up was not in sight. The law-enforcement world of Morgenthau and my father brought serious people to work on important cases; their efforts and methods reflected dignity and thought, and there was a gravity and grandeur to their cause. The return of stolen traveler's checks might not sound so lofty, but the perpetrators were part of a powerful and murderous criminal conspiracy in the most important commercial center in the world. By comparison, I was getting yelled at over parking tickets by bosses who weren't fit to shine Cement Head's shoes.

As I looked over my father's FBI files, I was taken with the differences between the Bureau and the NYPD. There were almost 40,000 cops in the city, which was roughly four times the number of agents in the entire country. Our

evaluations were one double-sided page, mostly of five-point numerical rat-
ings for dozens of qualities, some of which were purely nonsensical—"Spatial
orientation" and "Visualization"—and others which were well-meaning but
essentially moot. For "Integrity," should everyone get the highest score until
proven guilty, or should anyone who doesn't get a 5 be fired? The Bureau's
evaluations were far more detailed and substantive, and they looked at what
each agent brought to the institution, beyond their immediate workload—one
criterion was for how many new FBI employees the agent had recruited. Great
emphasis was placed on how agents secured and developed informants. My
favorite part was a section that praised my father's dictation skills—he was
called a "great dictator," in fact—which in my adolescent years, especially, I
understood.

Each note of congratulation represented a case: weeks and months of stake-
outs, wiretaps and raids, tips and the interrogations, moments of broad comedy and dull fear, and finally—it would seem by the fact of the letter—a
measure of satisfaction. There were no letters for cases that fell apart, of course,
for the non-arrests, the tentative informants who disappeared or clammed up,
the wiretaps where the conversants stuck carefully to talk of girlfriends and the
Yankees and what they ate for lunch. Failure spoke for itself, or rather it didn't:
the absence of reprimand in my father's files—weight-loss notwithstanding—
suggested that even when a case didn't work out, either nothing in particular
had been done wrong, or no one had held it against him.

That seems to have been the case with the great revelation of the files. I remember asking my father when I was young, "Hey Dad, didja ever kill anybody?" I suppose every cop's kid asks that, and since my father was in World
War II and then in law enforcement for thirty years, it was not an altogether
unreasonable question. But his face darkened at my idle enthusiasm, and as
far as I can recall, his response was more of a dismissal than a denial. It was
a rude question, as I know from having been asked it myself, many times,
and children who don't know better need to be taught. So when I came across
documents relating to an incident in the summer of 1961, when my father did
kill someone, the fact of it was as surprising as the form. It was in a traffic accident in the neighborhood, on Broadway at 256th Street. An elderly couple
walked across from east to west. My father was driving northbound on
Broadway. The woman lagged behind, having reached the middle of the
street while her husband was already at the curb; a car sped southbound, and
the woman hesitated, then turned suddenly back into my father's lane,
where he struck and killed her. There were a number of witnesses who of-

fered consistent testimony about the second car, which fled and was never found, and the woman's husband did not pursue a case against my father. Since he was not at fault, I almost wonder why he never told me about it. I think if I'd had a driver's license—I got mine only a week before I went into the Academy—the story might have found its way into a cautionary tale. I asked my mother about it recently, and she paused a moment before she told me, "We were married only a few months then. He came home, and he said— he had a hard time telling me about it—he said it was the kind of thing that was so awful and unreal that he wanted to run away. He couldn't believe it was happening."

What did I know about my father? When he'd come home from work, he'd take off his hat and say, "Traffic was bumpita-bumpa," and for years I thought the phrase must be Italian. He drank Sanka and put Brylcreem in his hair. Every night, he said his prayers on his knees, beside the bed, but when he wanted to sneak into the Fordham gym to go swimming, he would drive past the security guard and bark, "Father Maloney!" Often, he was as direct as a billboard, but there were times when he was a literal sphinx. Once, a college roommate of mine who was visiting asked him three questions in quick succession: *How did Napoleon's army retreat from Russia? How does the Israeli mafia work? How long does it take to become a federal judge?* Though they were odd questions, they matched my father's interests in history, crime, and politics, and he traced the route of retreat, described a typical electronics-store bust-out scheme, and in response to the judicial question, he returned to reading his newpaper and said, "How long is a piece of string?"

I was twenty-six when he died, but we had lived under the same roof for most of those years, and even when I left, it was for his old home. He was a good storyteller and I was a good listener, which acquainted me with much of his biography, the facts and his feelings about them. We were each one of five children who remained close to their siblings, geographically and otherwise, providing an ample if sometimes contradictory pool of recollections. We were in the same line of work, which we seemed to regard with the same complex intensity. Further understanding would come as I grew older, when I would have children of my own to annoy me.

There were no other real surprises in my research, only bits and pieces that were pleasant to read or funny to think about, as when I found letters from his Marine Corps buddy, Nathan Perlmutter, who went on to head B'nai B'rith. I knew he was friends with Perlmutter; I didn't know that Perlmutter called him "Jocko." While it was uplifting to hear from Morgenthau, "Sure I knew him," I wonder what I would have said if I ran into a man who could say, "John Conlon, of course. He killed my wife."

I didn't know what to make of that, or how much. Mostly, I would have liked to know what he made of it—whether he ever forgave himself, or whether he felt he needed forgiving. For me, it pointed up one of the ironies of police work, of how people take dangerous jobs for the security they provide. While my father was at war, his mother died in bed; after almost ten years as a G-man, he killed a woman who was crossing the street. Work isn't as dangerous as life; you could get hurt or killed on the Job, but off-duty, everybody has to die sometime. Maybe work helps to put that in perspective. If it doesn't lend meaning to your death, it should lend purpose to your life. The NYPD had done that for me, for four years, and then it hadn't, for one. As a percentage, that was adequate; at present, it was not. I wanted to look forward to going to work again. The night was getting old.

. . .

FROM THE SIXTIES THROUGH THE EIGHTIES, THE LANDSCAPE of the Bronx was a record of public failure, high and low, from the powerful, such as Robert Moses, who moved through the Bronx like Sherman through Georgia, evicting thousands to build highways, to the scavengers and predators among ordinary people, who made ordinary life impossible. Since then, the landscape has changed for the better, and the record has been rewritten, often quickly and well. And it was easy to forget how most of the great landmarks of the Bronx remained throughout the burning years. The Yankees continued to play at the House That Ruth Built, no matter the distractions. Crowds still went to the Bronx Zoo, where the American buffalo was saved, a hundred years ago, from a small breeding herd. At Woodlawn Cemetery, people still paid respects to Herman Melville, Duke Ellington, and their own remembered dead. Miles Davis is buried there, too, now, beneath a shiny black headstone that calls him "Sir Miles Davis," with the *i*'s dotted with musical notes. Across the north Bronx, thousands of acres of parkland—from Wave Hill and Van Cortlandt Park, by the Hudson River, to the Botanical Garden, to Pelham Bay Park and Orchard Beach on the Long Island Sound—were enjoyed, though sensibly only in the daylight. Near Hunts Point, there is a cloistered convent where nuns pray in silence behind high stone walls. They lit candles as the neighborhood burned, confident that their fire would endure. The synagogue that was open through the 1990s on

Intervale Avenue was now the Thessalonia Baptist Church for All People. A menorah and two Stars of David are still visible on the cornice, carved in the worn stone. What had they prayed for, when the temple was their own? Maybe the prayer was, *Get out, schmuck, get out!* and their prayers were answered, too.

James Lyons, the borough president in the 1930s who chose the corpse flower for us, hoped that "Borough of Universities" would become the nickname for the Bronx, as Borough of Homes and Borough of Churches were for Queens and Brooklyn. It never stuck. NYU abandoned its Bronx campus, but Fordham stayed. Poe became friendly with the Jesuits there when he lived nearby, and he spent some time in their library and grounds. It was called St. John's then. He wrote his poem "The Bells" about the bell in the University Chapel, because it irritated him. Poe died from politics, it could be argued, or maybe even from democracy. Four years after he moved here, in 1849, he was on a lecture tour to raise money for a magazine when he paid a visit to Baltimore during an election. His health was poor and he had long struggled with alcohol. Somehow, he fell in with a political gang who enlisted him to become a repeat voter, paying him with liquor after each trip to the ballot box. He was found, incoherent, in another man's clothes, and died four days later from the binge-voting and drinking. Poe Cottage remains, just below Fordham Road, though it was moved twice from its original location, a few hundred feet away. There isn't much to it. It is a small and cheerful place, with low ceilings and wide-planked floors. The portraits of Poe show an intense look and a top-heavy head, with a vast brow, as if made for fever, and the small mouth, "which was his only defect, showing weakness," in the view of a family friend.

Poe was buried in Baltimore, and his wife, who had died two years before, was moved from the Bronx and interred with him. If he haunts anyplace, it would more likely be Baltimore. I wonder what he would have thought of the South Bronx, at its worst; what his ghost would have made of our ghost town. He wrote about loves lost to death at an early age, and he set his tales in ancestral houses gone to ruin. He might have easily adapted his castles and crypts to the abandoned factories and the tenements whose graffitied walls fell down, leaving them open like cabinets. He might have said, *Don't change a thing!* Then again, such a landscape might have left little room for the imagination, or offered too much. Poe was a dark romantic, who worked to make something lastingly beautiful out of what went wrong with his life— if he were a convict, he would have been the type who spent his sentence decorating his cell instead of plotting an escape. A great city can't think that way, and here, we have done the opposite, bulldozing over our mistakes, building on top of them and hiding them from view, and we almost expect that in another generation, we'll tear it all down and start again. And so there is another, more dramatic difference: when something came back from the dead in Poe's world, no good came of it: *It is the beating of his hideous heart!* . . . When the Bronx came back, more people wondered how than why, but no one supposed it was purely for revenge. The phrase "with a vengeance" does come to mind, when I look at Charlotte Street—or the next street over, called Suburban Place—the center of several blocks of well-tended ranch houses, reminiscent of Levittown and other postwar developments. There is something a little surreal about the neighborhood, with its fences and lawns, given both its past and its surroundings, which are still plenty rough. You could look at it as a plot twist in a mystery story as unexpected as anything in Poe. *Ne cede malis.* Do not give way to evil. You had to wait for it, and be accepting of surprise.

· · ·

THE FIRST THREE MONTHS OF THE YEAR 2000 WOULD PASS before Narcotics finally called. I went on vacation for almost a month of it, and I went on strike for the rest. I worked as I always had, but I gave my arrests away and I wouldn't write any more tickets. I would do my job, but without benefit to the Captain. The little act of mutiny was liberating, and when I was not preoccupied with rumors that Narcotics would call this Friday, or the next, I enjoyed patrol as I hadn't in a while. As theater, there is no match for it, and even the way you engage the spectacle is like something a kid would invent—you knock on a door and someone has to tell you a story.

We had a domestic dispute, where the female complainant barely spoke English. I asked what her husband had done, and she cried, "He killed me!" Another lady, who ostensibly did speak English, had a fight with her neighbors, because "I don't socialate with Puerto Ricans."

"Why don't you try a little socialating, ma'am? They're not bad people when you get to know them."

We locked up a guy for choking his girlfriend, and as I was filling out his paperwork, I asked what I thought was an employment-related question— "What did you do in Jersey?"

"Six years."

"You shoot somebody?"

"I shot up a place."

"A place?"

"Mostly I shot the stereo."

After another attempted drive-by murder, the miraculously unwounded complainant gave us a strangely unemotional recounting of events, until he noticed that the windows of his own car were shot out: "This is the second time they shot at me tonight. . . . Holy shit! Look at my car!" Half an hour before the end of tour, another job came up: *10-34, assault with a weapon, the weapon is a frying pan.* . . . "Jeez, do you think this one could be domestic?" In the hall outside the apartment, a closetful of men's clothes had been strewn on the ground and splashed with bleach. A large woman met us at the door in a nightgown, shuddering with rage: "I want to make a citizen's arrest! It's my husband! For what? Adultery, that's what! No? Of course not—adultery is not a crime, 'cause the men write the laws! I want female cops the next time!"

We asked to talk to the gentleman in question, and she retreated to the back of the apartment. When he emerged from the kitchen, it was clear that he'd been out the whole night, and the fun he'd had might have been worth the trouble. "Look at this!" he said, pointing to the clothes. From the back of the apartment, there must have been half a dozen kids, all young, peeping out of rooms and creeping down to investigate. He brushed them back with the reflexive indifference of a horsetail swatting at flies.

"You see this?" he asked, holding up his eyeglasses, which had been twisted into a scribble of wire.

"Yep," I said. "I see your kids, too."

He shook his head. "I swear, Officer, I did not touch another woman, I was sniffin' coke with my bloods all night, I'm still flying!"

He agreed that it might be a good idea to leave for a while, but he was concerned about what she would do to his aquarium. "I'm like a father to these fish," he said, pointing to the large and well-equipped tank, where three huge black-and-orange oscars gulped in the water with malignant looks. "You know how rough these fish are? Look, they love me!" He dipped his hand in the tank and the fish nibbled his fingers. A few of the children tiptoed down the hall again, and again he waved them away.

On Sunday mornings, as the dawn burned into day, swarms of gulls descended on the uncollected trash, hovering and dropping in the cold clear light. On rainy nights, we might drive for hours, looking for drug dealers who were standing close to puddles. One night, Stix spied an enormous rat nosing around a sewer cap in the middle of the street. He sped up to it and then stopped short. The fat rat scuttled away in safety.

"I couldn't do it," he said.

"Professional courtesy?"

Half an hour later, he turned to me and said, "You're an asshole." I smiled and nodded.

A lot of times, Stix brought in food for me from Anna's deli. His own diet was the subject of intense curiosity on the midnights, and Sgt. G and Louie Malagon always asked him what he was having when they raised us for the scratch. "Just some plain pasta and a little *fanook*," he'd explain, holding up a plastic bag of what we finally decided was, in English, raw fennel. Tentatively, they tried some, and for a brief period Stix initiated a mini-craze for *fanook*, and some cops took it up with the airy nonchalance of sophomores with clove cigarettes. I wasn't converted to *fanook*, and neither did I take to the tofu heroes that Stix was also partial to. Then again, he didn't sell them very well: "If you don't like it you don't have to eat it—you don't have to be polite. I mean, I gave Chicky one and he threw up—it's not for everyone."

Stix had struck a bargain with the Admin lieutenant—if his numbers were good for a couple of months, he could go back to a beat on the day tours. It was a fresh-out-of-the-Academy assignment, but it would give him his life back. They wanted fifteen tickets a month from him, and thirty tickets could reasonably be seen as the price of his freedom. But as we sighted a car with an expired inspection, Stix went into agonies of indecision over whether to write another ticket, since he had written the same car for the same infraction a week before.

"Should I do it?"

"I don't know."

"Do you think it's cheesy?"

"Do what you want."

So went the first of eight verses. Finally, he seemed to decide against it, and he ran the plate in the hope that he would find further discouragement— "Maybe it's an old lady, an old man . . ."—it proved to be registered to a thirty-four-year old woman who lived half a mile away.

"She's probably living in sin," I said. "Why don't you write her for indecency?"

Still, he wasn't sure. "This has been a real emotional roller coaster for you," I said as we drove away. At the end of the block, he turned around and came back again.

"Would you like me to pray on it with you?"

"Fuck it, somebody else is gonna."

He wrote the ticket.

On the night after the Diallo verdict, we had two encounters with French-speaking, West African Muslims. We recovered a stolen car that belonged to a woman from the Ivory Coast, and we tracked her down at her apartment in Harlem from a phone bill in the back seat. She was grateful for our efforts, despite the hour. And shortly afterward, we stopped a livery cab that blocked traffic to pick up a fare. The cabbie was all manic hands and explanations, and he couldn't come up with any paperwork at all—no hack license, not even a driver's license. I told the fare to get another cab and went back to our car to run the plate as Stix continued to talk with him. Stix returned, and to my surprise he had all the paperwork, which was entirely correct and up to date—the man was just nervous when we stopped him, whether he was afraid he was getting a ticket or the fear ran deeper. Stix said, "When he gave me this stuff, he kind of flashed a twenty with it."

We talked over the rules of engagement for a bribery collar, and what it might mean—though the Integrity Review Board had done nothing for John, after nine months and counting, the possibility of an escape for Stix, not just from the midnights but from the precinct, appeared like a map of buried treasure. We thought for a moment, and then Stix said, "Nah—forget it. It's not like this guy's a drug dealer."

"Yeah, you're right. This guy comes from a country where the cops might beat him up, lock him up, if he doesn't offer money. He's scared, he doesn't know."

We returned his paperwork to him, and I told him that the next time he picked up a fare, he had to pull over to the side of the street. He thanked us and drove off. When we returned to our car, however, neither of us felt that the encounter had gone quite like it should have. We followed him and pulled him over again, and again he was nervous.

"Listen, relax," I said. "You're not in trouble, you're not getting a ticket, you're getting a talking-to. You had money in your hand when you talked to my partner, and we both know what you meant by it. I want to let you know now that we don't do that here—you could have just turned a traffic ticket into a serious crime. I know you're a good guy out trying to make a living, so I just want you to know that—don't do that again, okay?" We shook hands and he drove off again.

When you have time, you have everything, and on the midnights, it can seem you have nothing else. When it's busy, the busyness is strange, the hectic activity out of place for the night, and when it's quiet it's strange, because it strikes me as going against the sleepless nature of the City. It is a contradiction, I know. One night, we raced to the scene of "shots fired" from a subway platform, which EMS had put over when they were driving past. A number of passersby confirmed it, but the shooter was long gone. Four hours later, with little to do in the intermission except for driving around in the dark, we received another job of shots fired, from an apartment right next to the train. Inside, a lovely old couple pointed out the hole in the window, the neat chute the bullet cut through the hanging basket of African violets, littering stems and leaves on the floor. "I love my plants, they're my babies," the woman said, more concerned for what had happened than what might have. She was a kind of grandmother to the neighborhood, and had been for generations. There was a picture on the wall of her with Mayor Lindsay, who had given her a house for a dollar a year to take care of local children. "Give your plants a big drink of water," I said. "And I'll play them some nice soothing music, too," she added. We found where the bullet hit the back wall—not far from Mayor Lindsay—but we had to hunt for the slug for a while, before we found it under the refrigerator. The heat and speed and impact had transformed the sleekly lethal missile into an oddly shaped glob, like a scoop of mashed potato, harmless and pointless. It was a big slug, probably from a .45, and it would have taken her head off had she been watering her plants. It frightened her, to be sure, but she had slept through its arrival and she would sleep again, now that it was gone.

The bullet took less than a second to travel from the barrel into their home, but in my mind—from when it was heard to when it was found—it was a four-hour journey, and I could picture it in slow motion, floating over like a soap bubble on a windless night. Both perspectives were true, the explosive instant and the glacial glide, and I was glad to be able to see each of them, in the luxury of time. The old couple, I'm sure, were glad of it as well. That night passed, as did the long night of the South Bronx. And those who survived that nightmare, even now can sleep through the worst, sure of the morning.

ELEVEN

On the night I found out I was transferred, I drove home singing in
my car. For the next two weeks of Organized Crime Control Bureau training in Brooklyn, I sang on the drive there in the morning
and I sang on the way home, and I would have sung in the classroom if it
wouldn't have aroused suspicions about why I'd gone to Narcotics in the
first place. Stix had gone to work for Sgt. O'Hagan a week or two before I left,
and he'd become used to daylight again. John had come back from Vice, and
had finally been reassigned to his old footpost in the Four-Four. One afternoon, I did a tour change and we worked together, idly checking out our old
spots in between jobs. The next day, he collared and signed up a perp as a CI.
I was at dinner downtown with my new girlfriend, who got to hear me talk
on the cell phone about crack and kites and DECS from the appetizers
through coffee. Ultimately, he decided to hand the package over to Smacky
and Pops in Narcotics, and when he informed the Captain afterward, he
was offered semi-grudging congratulations for his work and complaints
about having given it away. Stix and John had gotten what they wanted,
and it was good enough, for now. "Partners come and go," Mike Moxom,
a veteran midnight cop, told me. He also said, "You can put this in your

book: What comes around, goes around." I sang it in my car, along with everything else.

For a while, it looked like I was the last happy cop in the NYPD, at least for the moment. It was a strange time to be singing: two weeks before I left for Narcotics, a cop from PSA-8 SNEU killed a man named Malcolm Ferguson in a struggle for the cop's gun during an arrest for drug sales. Ferguson had an extensive criminal record, and he had half a dozen glassines of heroin in his pocket when he died; his death was controversial primarily because it took place in the Four-Three, where Diallo was killed. Nonetheless, the cop received death threats from the Latin Kings, and on my last midnights, I was assigned to guard his house, sitting outside in a marked patrol car. John was assigned there, too, on the four-to-twelves, and he'd go up and visit the cop, partly because it was a better hour and partly because it was in his nature to reach out. In the event of the second-worst-possible outcome from a SNEU op, we knew, a patrol car could have been parked outside our apartment door: we had all been there, struggling alone with perps in project halls, wondering if we could reach the radio before he reached the gun. PK had been that cop's boss, too, though he wasn't working at the time of the shooting. PK told John that the man was an excellent cop, who felt he had no choice: "He said, 'It was him or me. . . .'"

The day after my transfer, an undercover in midtown asked a man named Patrick Dorismond for drugs. Dorismond took offense at the question and began to rough him up. As they struggled, his "ghost"—the cop assigned to tail him from a distance—interceded, and Dorismond was shot fatally by the ghost. Dorismond had several arrests, for a gun, robbery, and marijuana sales, and he had been most recently accused of hitting his girlfriend as she held their child, but he had no convictions for serious offenses. The altercation was difficult to understand, to say the least, in that it ostensibly began with his refusal to commit a crime. Dorismond was also Haitian, as Louima was, and that stirred anger, as did the Mayor's release of his arrest record. Several years before, Giuliani's release of juvenile arrest records had quelled the controversy in the killing of a machete-wielding felon named Kevin Cedeno in Washington Heights, which some politicians had previously styled the execution of an innocent. The cops in the Ferguson and Dorismond cases were nonwhite, which blunted the accusations of racism only somewhat—they expressed institutional rather than individual racism, apparently—and both were cleared. But the reaction against the police from so many quarters had become so vehement and reflexive that morale plunged still further. The

Narcotics team in the Dorismond case was led by a Sgt. Richard Romano, whose brother was the star of the hit sitcom *Everybody Loves Raymond,* and both brothers were featured in a recruiting ad for the NYPD, in which Ray Romano praises his brother for being the real success in the family. The ad had just begun to run when the Dorismond killing occurred, and as the protests began to mount again, Sgt. Romano announced that he'd had it, and quit. The recruitment campaign was not a success.

Still, I was delighted to be there, and I reported to work with an immigrant's zeal: *Your American floors, it is a privilege to scrub them.* The two weeks of training took place in trailers on a fenced-off quarter of the Brooklyn Army Terminal. They trained investigators, undercovers, and supervisors for OCCB, and they also trained dogs. Periodically, an instructor would quit her explanation of buy reports or case management as the sound of canine assault rose from the lot. "I'm not going to kid myself about how interesting I am, next to this," she said. "Take five." We would all rush over to the windows to watch a German shepherd attack a cop, biting at his padded limbs to yank him to the ground.

As with any police training course, it took twice as long as it should have, though the instructors tended to be veteran detectives from Narcotics who knew how to tell a story. One told about the elaborate sting operation designed to catch a wanna-be mafioso named Henry Vega, who had killed an off-duty cop named George Scheu in 1987 when Scheu tried to stop him from stealing a car stereo. A social club was built and populated entirely with undercovers posing as made men. Vega was desperate to be accepted, and he was allowed to insinuate himself, bit by bit, into their midst. When he begged to be allowed to join, he was asked if he could be trusted to carry out a hit. Vega then bragged about killing Scheu, and his statements were recorded.

The lecturers from other specialized units—Asset Forfeiture, Major Case, TARU (Technical Assistance and Response Unit, which did everything from installing wiretaps to installing hidden cameras)—varied more widely. The hours might crawl during a discussion of radio frequencies and UHF signals for the "kels," or transmitters, that undercovers wore, or of "traps," the custom-engineered concealed compartments for carrying drugs or guns in cars: "In a 1989 Ford Taurus, we found a trap in the center console by clicking the headlights twice, turning the radio to AM, and turning on the windshield wipers. In a 1995 Lincoln Continental, the trap was in the trunk, and to activate it you had to turn the engine on, off, and on again, put the car in neutral, and turn the defogger to maximum. For this Ford Explorer . . ."

We field-tested drugs, gathering around a long table in which little heaps of white and beige powder were spread across a dozen sheets of paper. You took a blue plastic scoop like a flattened toothpick to drop a dab of powder in a clear plastic packet with glass ampules inside. For cocaine, there were three ampules of reagent, and you broke them left to right: if the fluid encountered cocaine hydrochloride, it turned pink, and then the next ampule turned it blue, and the final ampule turned it pink and blue, with the blue layer rising thinly to the top. For heroin, there were two ampules, for which the first remained clear and the second flushed green, sometimes with a dramatic suddenness. Some piles tested negative for both, and one tested positive for both, and we dipped in the piles and shook our packets with the earnest studiousness and easy jokes—*Hey, this is good shit!*—of high school biology students dissecting frogs. We did the same for marijuana, which flushed gray, then purple, then purple and gray.

During the breaks, we would step outside and gather in little groups to talk or smoke cigarettes. There were almost forty of us: investigators, undercovers, a few sergeants, one lieutenant. The cops clumped together by borough, either because they knew each other before, or were likely to afterward, as the group would be sent to Brooklyn and Manhattan North. I clumped sometimes with a cop from the Five-Two named Ricky Duggan, and a sergeant named Jimmy Gildea, who had been in Narcotics as a cop and had survived a shooting. Sometimes we went out to lunch together, but more often I disappeared to read the papers in a restaurant by myself, or to meet with my Ryan cousins, Mary and Catherine, who lived in the neighborhood. There was a time-killing aspect to the two weeks, but I didn't object.

On the second-to-last day, Lt. Russo, who ran the program, announced, "Unless you were at dinner last night and had the opportunity to say, 'Howard, pass the salt,' you are going to Brooklyn North and Manhattan North. That's where they need people, and that's where you're going." "Howard" referred to Commissioner Safir, and when they read the list of assignments the next afternoon—

"Alvarez . . . Brooklyn North . . .

"Baker . . . Brooklyn North . . .

"Buono . . . Manhattan North . . .

"Calderon . . . Brooklyn North . . .

"Conlon . . . South Bronx Initiative . . ."

—more than a few people turned around to look. *Howard, pass the salt.* I was a little surprised myself. I'd talked to Inspector Mullen, who'd been transferred to Queens, days before I went to Narcotics, and Lt. Nicholson—my cousin—and Pops, and they said they would try to get me to the Four-O. The idea of Manhattan North wasn't unattractive by any means—I could work uptown, amid the violence and depravity that make cop life worthwhile, and then go to court downtown a couple of times a week, where my girlfriend lived. But the Bronx would remain home and work for awhile longer. I still sang on the last drive back from Brooklyn.

. . .

WHEN I GOT TO THE SOUTH BRONX INITIATIVE, AT THE PRE-cinct which had housed the old Fort Apache, Chief Tiffany called me into his office to welcome me to the command. He told me that he liked one of my pieces, how it reminded him of a Fellini movie. I blinked and thanked him: this was a change. Later on, he told me about a federal agent who had asked him about corruption, and his testy response. "I said to him, 'You recall in the *Inferno,* when Virgil and Dante are about to enter the seventh circle of Hell?'" He looked at me, and I nodded, in vague assent. "The stench was so awful, they had to step aside, to acclimate before going in. But down they went, as we do. Too many of the feds keep bankers' hours, they don't get too dirty or go too deep. That's why corruption happens, I think, and it's part of the risks of the Job." What the chief said about corruption didn't bother me, but what he said about Dante did; would there be a test, or did they ask about it in Compstat? *The Commissioner wants to know why damnations are down for hypocrites and usurers. . . .* Narcotics could be a tricky business, I knew, but I hadn't expected this.

Lt. Nicholson was similarly welcoming, as were Pops and Sgt. Billy Clune, who were the sergeants for the module, and Capt. Mahony, who was in charge of the Four-O teams. When Lt. Zerbo saw me, he said, "Ah, fuck, not you again."

I grinned like an idiot. One of the guys told me, "Don't worry about Zerbo, he just talks like that. He'll never hurt you."

I said, "If Lieutenant Zerbo kicked me in the balls every time I walked in the office, I'd still be happy to be here."

When I worked there two years before, there were ten teams that covered the Four-O; now, there were four. Pops and Billy Clune each had a team, and they reported to Zerbo, but there were other familiar faces: Smacky and Billy Clark had arrived the previous year, joining Hector Nolasco in the PSA-7 contingent, and John Reilly, Rob Richardson, Adam Leibowitz, Abe Garcia, Dexter Powers, and a few others. I was assigned to Billy Clune, but both teams worked together so often and in such combinations that I never quite figured out who was assigned to which.

Billy Clune's father had been a cop, and his brother was a cop, a lieutenant in Midtown South. His was the attitude of the veteran: *Don't go crazy and don't get hurt. Let's take care of business, make our overtime, and go home.* He called everyone "Atlas" or "Slim," even his infant son: "Atlas Junior was up sick all night, poor fella." Clune was even-keeled and easygoing, except for when cops complained about assignments. "Try getting stuck in Internal Affairs for two years, Atlas," he said. "Then you can bitch about having to stand on a corner for a couple of hours. Arright, Slim?"

Most cops found the Internal Affairs Bureau distasteful to some degree, and the unit had first choice of supervisors who put in for OCCB or the Detective Bureau, which made many of them hesitate to leave patrol. At IAB, a routine operation might involve calling in a job of drug sales, where the caller specified that the stash was under the mailbox. An IAB surveillance van would watch the cop respond: if the dealer wasn't around, would the cop mark the job "90-X" and move on, without checking under the mailbox, or if he checked, would he just kick the drugs down a sewer? The appropriate response would be to search for the drugs and find them, and then to raise a boss over the air to apprise him of "found narcotics," and then to return to the precinct to write up a report and voucher them. The result was the same as if the cop had kicked them down the sewer, though the correct procedure might take the cop off the street for two hours. Doubtless there was division and mistrust even within IAB over how to address such situations, where the actions were technically improper but essentially right. The unit had the responsibility of arresting cops whenever it was necessary, and for cops in bad relationships, the vindictive 911 call from a significant other was a conventional weapon. It was no great pleasure to respond to incidents where cops were guilty of domestic violence, either.

Pops had also been stuck in IAB, and while he wasn't glad to be there, he was more forthright in his acknowledgment of its necessity: "We had an uncle try to get done in this place in Harlem, it was both a crackhouse and whorehouse. They had a 'security guy' at the door, who told them not to do the uncle, he could be a cop. Anyway, a couple of days later, the uncle goes to court, and he sees the 'security guy' is a cop, on modified assignment at the courthouse. Turns out he's been on modified for years, he molested his ten-year-old niece or stepdaughter or something, but she wouldn't press charges. The Job wouldn't let him have a gun, but they couldn't fire him, either. Our case against him is in the Trial Room now."

Pops was driven, determined to make collars and cases, to make things happen. His heart was in the Job, and when we did B&B, his mood lightened after each successful set. Pops was close to PK at PSA-7, not least because they had both lost young sons to illness—a heart ailment in Frankie Poplaski's case. But where PK had a sense of kindly quiet about him, with Pops you felt the urgency of his resolve, that he would not let time go to waste. Pops worked federal cases and he worked closely with the Four-O Detective Squad, especially Bobby Addolorado, who was assigned exclusively to homicides. Bobby had a number of superb informants, and he shared them with Pops for Narcotics work. Though the primary responsibility of a Four-O Narcotics module was, not surprisingly, narcotics in the Four-O, Pops would scramble to make cases happen, no matter where they led. As John Reilly, the senior man on his team, liked to point out, "The shield doesn't say, 'Only for use against drugs in the South Bronx,' it says, 'Detective, City of New York. . . .'"

With Lt. Zerbo, we had a man whose experience began in the late 1960s, before Durk, Serpico, and the Knapp Commission, and had continued through the blackout, the financial crisis, and Son of Sam killings of the mid-seventies; when crack and AIDS first appeared in the early eighties, he was barely midway through his career. In the spring of 2000, he was as physically active as anyone on the team, and mentally, he was on his own level. There was a letter on his wall from a bank president in Yonkers, thanking him for catching a bank robber. Lt. Zerbo had been on line to make a deposit, and he'd chased the perp on foot for blocks through a snowstorm. As I drove him one afternoon when we were doing B&B, he glanced at a man getting into a car, a white Honda with New Jersey plates.

"Pull over," he said, and I did. After a moment of conversation with the would-be driver—he had no license—he told me to check the trunk. I found a bulletproof vest. Lt. Zerbo had recalled that the car was involved in a case they took down six months before.

Lt. Zerbo never failed to surprise you, whether by walking past your desk and taking a handful of your lunch—even if you were eating it, and even if it was pasta—or by passing an offhand remark that began, "That reminds me of when I was in the seminary. . . ." The seminary? There might have been a Father Zerbo, a Monsignor Zerbo, a Bishop Zerbo? *This is a reading from effin' Ephesians, so shut your damn mouths. . . .* But Zerbo also looked out for his cops, and if there was a problem at home or with the Job, he was a trusted advisor and a formidable ally.

Zerbo was hilarious with perps, having heard thirty years of the most dire threats and inventive lies. One perp, who was shouting about how he'd sue us because he knew we were going to beat him, was shut up by the nonchalance of Lt. Zerbo's remark: "Well, we used to beat people up all the time in the old days. Now, we're not allowed to anymore."

Another time when I drove him, he took me down Weiher Court, a block-long street in the Four-Two. Weiher Court is a classic landscape of the old South Bronx, where a little fortlike house stands out like the Alamo over a junk-strewn field of weeds. "They chased Twymon Myers all the way from the subway down to here," he said, pointing to a spot in the field. Twymon Myers was a Black Liberation Army hit man who had taken part in the murders of several police officers; Sonny Grosso had been hunting for him in Harlem when he was called to the Cardillo killing at the Nation of Islam mosque. Zerbo went on, "And he hid under a mattress, with his gun, ready to blast whoever lifted it up. But they never checked underneath it. When they finally did get him, at One-Five-Two and Tinton, there were all these cops with machine guns, shotguns, all this heavy artillery—but what killed him was one regular cop who took him out with his .38. There's still a bullet hole in the streetlight there, I'll have to show you some time. . . ." I did look for it later on. Chief Tiffany had told me, too, and I found it one afternoon: a kidney-shaped hole, some three inches by one inch, where two large rounds had grouped together. It was hard to tell how much wider it had become in time, and it didn't even look like a bullet hole anymore. It was another place where a killer was killed, in a place that had seen a thousand killings since.

Chief Tiffany and Lt. Zerbo both had an appreciation for local history, though each seemed to draw different conclusions from it. I'd given the chief two books that I admired greatly, by an author named Jill Jonnes, *We're Still Here,* a history of the South Bronx, and *Hep-Cats, Narcs, and Pipe Dreams,* which told of drugs and drug enforcement in this country over the last century. The subject matter might be of interest to the Chief of Bronx Narcotics, I figured, and I was correct, as I haven't seen either book since. If he saw me outside having a cigarette, he'd stop and talk about the books.

"This block was tenements, this block burned," he said. "If you've been around this neighborhood as long as I have, the change is nothing short of miraculous. That's because of us—a lot of it is, anyway. What I love best about it is how when the kids play baseball or stickball here on the sidewalk, they play right in front of the precinct, and our stoop—or the front door, or the doorknob sometimes—that's third base for them."

A few weeks later, as we were loading up the equipment for a warrant— the hand-held ballistic bunkers, crowbars and hydraulic door-openers, fire extinguishers and flashlights—the stickball game didn't stop for us, and the ball bounced near Lt. Zerbo's head as he stepped out. As the ball was thrown back near him, he snatched it out of the air and brandished it in front of the eight-year-olds. "I told you kids a thousand times, this is a police station, and you can't get in the way when we're working! Well, the game's over now, because I have the ball!"

. . .

NARCOTICS HAD WHOLESALE AND RETAIL SIDES TO IT: THERE was Buy and Bust, and there were cases, which developed if an uncle got a phone number for a dealer, or a CI made an introduction, and we would buy into the crew, from grams to ounces to kilos, until you were ready to take them down. Cases were labor-intensive and paper-intensive, and months of work could lead to the purchase of a half-kilo of soap flakes, but they were the only way you could rip out a drug crew by the roots. Some teams— bosses and cops alike—lived for cases, the reach and the depth of the game, while others preferred the simple and semi-predictable exercise of Buy and Bust. B&B was Basic Bullshit, and Boring Bullshit, and Bread & Butter, and we did it two or three times a week. The work was half-familiar from SNEU, and half-familiar again from having done it for a month two years earlier, and the procedure was learned in short order. Before we went out, the ar-resting officer would get eighty dollars or so in "buy money"—known as "bim," for short—to photocopy, laying out the tens and twenties on the ma-chine so that each serial number was recorded, and then give it to the uncles. Sometimes you'd mark the bills with an X or a stroke of red pen, so you could recognize the bim in the street. The sergeant would write up a tac plan, list-ing each cop's role for the day—arresting officer, or "A/O," catch cars, the prisoner van, known as the P-van, uncles, and ghosts—the radio and car assigned, and the list of spots to hit. Most spots were steady ones—One-Five-Six and Courtlandt, One-Four-Eight and Willis—though particular addresses would be added if there had been a recent shooting or homicide, or if it was a kite location, an apartment or lobby for which someone had called in a complaint about drugs sales. We would gather up our equipment and head to the cars. The A/O would drive the boss, strapping the receiver in the back seat and sticking the antenna on the roof by its magnetic base.

Outside, the Sergeant would test the radios and the kels:

"Four-O Leader to uncle car, on the air? Okay, Uncle Abe, you're on C Channel? Uncle Dex, you're on B? Abe, gimme a kel check."

"Kel, kel, kel, kel, kel—you read me, Leader?"

"Coming in five-by-five. Uncle Dex, gimme a kel check. . . ."

The kel was a one-way transmitter, which only the sergeant and his driver could hear, but the ghost wore a regular radio, with extensions that allowed him to transmit and receive without being seen.

"All right, Bobby Rich, can I have a ghost check?"

If the equipment worked, we headed out for the first set, deploying the cars in a rough perimeter for each direction the perp might run, ready to move in case the uncle was steered elsewhere.

When everyone was in position, the sergeant would put it over the air: "Four-O Leader to uncle car, you on? You ready?"

"We're ready, Leader."

"Okay, uncle car, you got the green light, you got the green. Field team, be advised, the uncles are out of the car. Repeat: the uncles have stepped . . ."

In the sergeant's car, you heard the uncles strike up a conversation over the crackle and static of the kel:

"Yo, you working?"

"Wassup, anybody out?"

"Anybody got work?"

They were pick-up lines, of a kind, and each uncle had a style: Dex and Teddy had a suave reserve, while George and Abe tended to be up-tempo and avid, and Curtis and Damian were somewhere in between. As a female, Janet found that sellers often wanted to sell themselves to her. Abe's hustle always sounded like he was in a nightclub: quick and eager, loud enough to be heard above the music, definitely interested but never desperate: "Yo, baby! C'mon! You *know* me! You saw me *last week!* Are you kidding me? *I ain't no cop!* C'mon now, don't be like that. You and me, you and me, let's get them krills and we'll fire 'em up together, we'll go right up to the project roof and *beam up!* No? Arright, if that's the way you wanna be, I'll just go up the block . . . No? Arright then, let's do it. Gimme two . . ."

They had to connect, and their hunger for connection sometimes reminded me of guys on the make for women, and sometimes it reminded me of actors at an audition, hungry for a break. While their styles varied, I wondered whether there was a need to convince, or a drive to perform. For some, that inner thrill was plain to see, though for others it was simply how the job was done, and if they had to sing for their supper or scream for it, that's what they did, though not for any special love for song or screaming.

As the uncle talks to a seller or steerer, the ghost watches and reports: "Uncle Curtis is in conversation, female Hispanic, One-Four-Eight and Brook, blue hoodie, black pants, Yankee cap . . . looks like we have a positive buy. . . ."

The kel failed constantly, for a couple of seconds at a time or for longer. The uncle never knew, of course, because it was only a transmitter. The uncle would have a visual sign for "positive buy"—pulling up his hood, lighting a cigarette—for the ghost to read and tell the field team, but the ghost often had to pull back, or step inside a store, or look away for a moment, if his scrutiny of the uncle appeared too purposeful.

"Stand by, Leader, I gotta step off a minute, they're getting raised on me, I gotta step off the block and I'm dropping my ears. . . ."

"Catch up to him, ghost, and give him the cut-off sign, give him the cut-off, we're gonna wrap it. . . ."

The kel would cut in and out as the signal bounced through the landscape of twenty-story projects: "Positive buy, Leader, we have—*sssssshhhhhhh*—male, that's repeat—*sssshhhhhhhh*—wearing—*sshhhhhhhhhhshhhhhhhhhhshhhh*—right on the corner of—*ssssshhhhhhsshhshh.* Okay, Leader, you copy?"

If the conversation was in Spanish, the static might be scarcely less intelligible, though the sergeant could read the tone, and pick out *yayo, bomba, sí, no.* The field team would wait in their cars, in dull boredom if the uncle found no one who would talk to him, or in heightening apprehension if we lost contact. Sometimes, we'd have to charge into a building or fan out through project grounds if we lost the uncle for too long; fortunately, none of our uncles was ever in trouble then, and when we'd find them—talking on a bench or in a stairwell—you could run past, as if you were looking for someone else, or you could put them both on the wall, hoping that the uncle hadn't been made. Usually, the uncles worked in pairs, so that if a buy was made, the ghost could remain on the set to watch the seller while the uncles returned to the car. The uncle would fill in over the radio whatever was missed on the kel transmissions. Sellers were "subjects" and buyers were "Ps":

"Okay, Leader, the set has three pieces, the female black who steered me, and the two male Hispanics. The hand-to-hand is the tall one in the red jacket, it says 'Chicago Bulls.' Also, there's three or four Ps, who came all at once, and are heading south on Brook . . ."

"All right, forget the Ps for now—what's the product and how much did you spend?"

"Twenty, and it's D, the brand is 'HBO.'"

"All right, Field Team, let's move in. . . ."

And we'd go, all at once if it was a one-piece set, or a car for each subject at their last known position. There were runners and fighters, as there had been in SNEU, when I worked the same sets, but they ran less and fought less, it seemed. We had better equipment, more cars, more people, and more experience, which together would tend to reduce misadventure, but sometimes I thought that it was just a matter of the perps getting older, too. When we moved in and took the subjects, the uncle car would drive by for a confirmatory identification.

"That's them, Leader, you got 'em both. . . ."

"Ten-four, that's a wrap, everybody—Field Team to the Four-O, uncles, you can take it back to the barn. . . ."

When the undercovers returned to our base, they had to field test and voucher the drugs they'd bought, and write up buy reports: *At T/P/O I UC#123 approached JD Braids (M/B/20, 5'8" 150, blue shirt, blue jeans, short braids) in front of 550 E 147 St. and asked him if he had dope. JD Braids asked "How much do you want?" and I responded "Give me two." I then handed JD Braids $20 USC/PRBM and he approached JD Newport (M/H/40's, 5'5" 130, Newport T-shirt, green shorts) and handed over the USC/PRBM for small objects taken from the rear of his pants. JD Braids then handed me two glassines of heroin stamped E-Z Money. I then left the scene and notified the field team of what transpired.*

Visibility: Clear

Weather: Sunny

USC/PRBM stood for "United States Currency/Pre-Recorded Buy Money." "JD" meant "John Doe," and the uncle could have called JD Braids and JD Newport "JD Blue" and "JD Green," or whatever he saw as a distinguishing characteristic. JD Gap Tooth, JD Bald, JD Stutter would all be fine, JD Heavy would be preferable to JD Fat, but JD Stupid, JD Ripe Shorts, JD Face-

Only-a-Mother-Could-Love—no matter their accuracy—might later suggest to a jury that the undercover was not taking his work entirely seriously.

In the early 1970s, when Narcotics did B&B, they did B& . . . B, as the field team picked up subjects days and even weeks after the uncle had made a buy. The delay protected the undercover from exposure, as the seller might have to guess the cop from hundreds of buyers, but it also weakened the case, and it's hard to imagine a modern Bronx jury voting to convict. It amazed me how some of our uncles could buy drugs in the same precinct two or three times a week for years—Dex and Abe would do that, and so would Janet and George, though at least their street work would be broken up to monitor Spanish-language wiretaps for months at a time. There were at least thirty steady sets, from individual apartments to the wide-open pill and methadone market of One-Four-Eight and Willis, where the junkies sold "spitback" from little plastic juice bottles. (Methadone must be consumed on site at the clinic, and spitback is just what it sounds like.) There was enough turnover at the steady sets and enough new spots to allow them to work—carefully, and on the move—but all the uncles had stories of being run off a set by perps who recognized them from the last time around. Few of the undercover cops who have been killed died because the perps thought they were cops, but rather because they thought they were attractive victims or fellow criminals—when we were in SNEU, the uncle who killed the perps on 160 was being set up for a robbery, and Sean Carrington's killer thought Carrington was coming to rob him of his stash. Sean Carrington was Rob Richardson's cousin. Rob spoke at Sean's funeral, parts of which were televised, and so his own undercover career ended. After that, Rob only ghosted.

A new uncle was expected to make eight buys a month, give or take; if they couldn't buy, they might be transferred to a different area, but continued failure meant a return to patrol. Uncles who were established were given more slack; they might only work major cases, or in time they, too, might be moved, voluntarily or otherwise. After three years, undercovers "flipped" to investigators. Because Narcotics depended so heavily on undercovers, there were star performers who emerged, and were courted like seven-foot-tall high school juniors by college basketball coaches, with whatever poor perks the sergeants and lieutenants had to offer:

"Listen, if you work for me, we'll do anything you want—we'll go to Manhattan, we'll go federal—anything! And believe me, I'm tight with the chief, if we run with something good—sky's the limit, overtime-wise. . . ."

Some investigators claimed that this encouraged a prima donna attitude among certain undercovers, and you did sometimes wonder when an operation with a dozen cops, planned for weeks or more, was suddenly called off when the uncle said, "I ain't feelin' it, boss." And some of them doubtless scammed on occasion, but I also heard the flip side from other uncle friends, who said that bosses especially, but also cops, tended to change their attitudes about them. In time, they came to be treated more like informants than colleagues—they weren't worked with as much as they were dealt with. I didn't see that in our office—maybe because I was an investigator—but I heard a lot one night from an undercover who worked in Queens, who told me that the change was profound: "I was a cop for five years before, and so it wasn't as if I was used to being talked to like a human being—but this really surprised me. You have to get into it a little, whoever you want to be as an uncle—white-trash guy hitting the city, biker guys, local dealer who's not afraid to mix with the ghetto. And you dress up, or grow a beard, or buy different clothes or whatever, and you have to forget about being a cop, how you deal with people as a cop. But what shocked the shit out of me wasn't how I bought into it, but how other cops did. Other cops asked the boss for a day off, it was 'Yes,' or 'No,' but me, I thought every time I asked him for something he looked at me and *wondered*. . . ."

On B&B, you always had to be alert for the runners and fighters, not to mention the shooters, but it became fairly routine for undercovers and investigators alike. Not so the search warrants, though we did several each month: the moments before entry were always heavy with adrenaline, and the people on the street always stopped, jaws agape, as the convoy of cars pulled up in front of a building, and the cops in raid jackets ran out with rams and shields. My first warrant there was through John's CI, just after I got back from training. I rode with John and John Reilly to the tac point, and as we waited for the signal, Reilly turned to me and said, "This is the best part of the job." I nodded. You never knew what waited for you on the other side, whether it was more than you expected or less, or something entirely different. I remember waiting in the car with Rob Richardson, who would ram the door for an apartment where there were supposed to be several submachine guns, as he shook his head. "I got kids," he said. "I ain't feelin' this."

The bigger guys—Reilly, Leibowitz, Smacky, Clark, and Richardson—usually handled the ram, and the number of hits it took to knock in the door was always noted wryly afterward:

"What did that take you, four? Five? Hector says six. Maybe it's time to hit the gym. . . ."

Or, "Yeah, so it went down in one shot, my daughter has a tougher door on her Barbie town house. You could have sneezed on it and got in, so get over yourself. . . ."

Once you were in, another set of worries took over. We took a door one morning for a dope dealer, a man in his mid-thirties, who had a record of armed robberies. When we got in, we found only an old woman, who began to hyperventilate and clutch her chest, chattering rapidly in Spanish about her heart. She lived alone, she said, and she thought she might die. We all felt uneasy, as I had years before, during Operation Hindenburg. The apartment was small but cluttered, as they all seemed to be, and it would take some time to go through it. I was glad to notice several men's coats hanging on a rack outside the closet, and more men's clothing in a back room: it meant that her son stayed there, often enough, if not every night. Her little lie gave me my first hope, and as I went through the coat pockets, I came up with a couple of bags of heroin. The dope made us happier than it would have any junkie—the little glassines were our passports out of lawsuit country—and I handed them to Pops, smiling. The search always played out with the heady, heartless drama of a hand of blackjack, card by card—

Hit me!

Yes!

Hit me!

Yes!

Hit me!

Oh, I shoulda stuck. . . .

Your instinct is like an overeager hunting dog, pulling you in the right direction but sometimes on a trail that has long gone cold: you think to check the watch box for the stash, but it's full of empty glassines; you feel a metal weight in a sock, but it turns out to be a wrench. *Of course, I always keep my wrench in a sock.* You wonder: Does he want his stash close by and convenient, so he can grab it for a quick sale? Or does he keep the weight or the gun hidden in a box under loose floorboards, where no one will find them in a robbery or raid? What looks new, and what looks different? How much can I break?

The dope put us in the game, and when Pops showed it to the old woman, she seemed to recover her composure, and she toned down the silent-movie theatrics to daytime-TV level. After I went through the coats, I checked the closets and found one with more men's clothing. On the top shelf, there were black plastic grocery bags, and I tore them open to find stacks of old phone bills, twenty-year-old report cards, letters to friends in prison. One bag had a box shaped like a stick of butter, only larger, in red and green Christmas wrapping paper. I opened it up and found a brick of heroin, some fifty bundles, neatly double-stacked. "Hey, Pops! Have a look!"

Pops had called for an ambulance for the old woman, as a precaution, but she seemed to feel much better now, after being assured that she would not be arrested. I went back to my closet, through the pockets of coats, pants, and shirts hung up on the rail, and then down below, to the boxes of shoes. There were lighter boxes for dress shoes, and heavier ones for boots, which made me a little excited when I lifted up the first one, thinking that the weight was metal. And then I got to a box that was too heavy for boots, and it felt just right. I opened it to find a new Smith & Wesson nine-millimeter, and boxes of rounds. *Hey, Pops* . . .

And Pops was even happier when our subject returned. He'd been out in the neighborhood, but when he spotted the ambulance in front of his building, he rushed home in concern. At the apartment, he hurried to the EMTs, as Pops stepped in beside them.

"What happened? Is she all right?"

"Who are you? Do you live here?" Pops asked.

"I'm her son, I live here, what's going on?"

"Your mother's fine, but you're under arrest. Turn around and face the wall. . . ."

. . .

OUR TEAM TOOK IN HUNDREDS OF PEOPLE EVERY YEAR, AND Narcotics took in thousands, even tens of thousands. You could picture a chow line leading to the massive wooden precinct door, with its green copper lanterns and worn stone steps, a line of young hustlers and old dope fiends, aging players and new fools, reaching down the block and even past the horizon. The size and sameness of the problem could be daunting, or dull, depending on your mood. I was past my disenchantment with work, but not yet truly re-enchanted by it, and maybe the Job for me was like drugs were for Charlie, a cycle of detox and retox, rehab and dehab, a trip through happy hell and back. I needed to find Charlie again, or another Charlie; to find a face in the crowd that was more than a number—five hours of over-time, to be precise—a face with eyes and ears, and a big mouth. Anyone in the chow line could prove to be my underworld guide, or at least have a piece of a map—they knew where the crack was cooked for Brook and One-Three-Eight, or they'd witnessed a murder on a Saturday night in the sum-mer of '95. Everyone knew something, or something that could lead to it, provided you could reach them, and provided you both made the time.

You hoped to make a case, something sustained and substantive. You tried to talk to everyone. Sellers tended to know more than buyers, but that rule was riddled with exceptions: a seller might only know the person he worked for, at one place, whom he met in the lobby when his stash ran out, while a buyer of long experience might know all the major dealers in the neighbor-hood, at every level of the organization. You could often spot perps who you felt might be receptive. You might have a word as you fingerprinted them, planting a seed of speculation before you put them back in the cell, returning in half an hour to ask, "Didn't you say you had to go to the bathroom? C'mon, I'll take you." Others resisted, and you found yourself in a position of peculiar reversal, as if you were on a Parole Board, and had to beg a con-tented prisoner to consider life beyond the cell block. *"Naah, on the outside, I hear you have to pay for the gym, I think I'll stay. . . ."* And some you succeeded in persuading proved that their first instincts were right, that it was better for them to remain. Still, you keep on talking.

When I signed up the first informant, no harm came of it, but no good did, either. We had taken three young guys for selling marijuana, and one of them was a marked Blood, with three cigarette burns on his shoulder in a triangle pattern. At the precinct, he surprised me by his extreme discomfort at taking off his clothes when I searched him in the bathroom. Most perps in Narcotics have been arrested many times, and many have spent years in prison, and that kind of self-consciousness falls away soon enough, if it was ever there to begin with. The other two dealers seemed to look up to him, and the combi-nation of gang seniority and criminal-justice novelty marked him as a person of interest. Since we both knew that he faced no more than a night in jail, I couldn't bargain seriously with a reduction in sentence, but it gave me an idea of what I could work with on him. I took him out on the fire escape and gave him a cigarette.

"So what's up? You never been locked up before?"

"Nah, never. . . ."

"Yeah? That means never-never, or you only count convictions?"

"Nah, never—I got a ticket here and there, but I never got taken into the precinct."

"Well, that's 'never,' then. How do you like it?"

He shook his head.

"You're not supposed to. You work?"

"Nah . . ."

"Go to school?"

"Nah . . ."

"What do you do for money, if you don't mind my asking—remember, we're just talking here, I never read you your rights, so nothing goes beyond us. You make enough money selling weed?"

"Nah, that was just—that was just tonight. I got a settlement, my father was killed, run over by a car. My Grams keeps thirty thousand in the bank for me, for when I turn twenty-one. Also, I get Social Security."

Oh. So he'd be out tomorrow, and he had plenty of money. What did I have to offer? I thought a moment, and went on, "Well, that's nice. You turn twenty-one next year, right? You got a girl, you got kids?"

"Yeah, I got a girl, we gotta a little boy."

"Okay, then. Well, listen, Joe—can I call you Joe? My name's Ed—I'll get to the point. I can help you, and you can help me. For now, you're set up pretty good, and I won't lie to you by saying getting locked up for weed in the Bronx is the end of the world. But it is on your record, and some people are very narrow-minded about hiring drug *dealers,* I mean, everybody has their fun when they're young, but this is *dealing,* and a lot of employers, they're still a little funny on the subject. Your check stops after your next birthday, and even though thirty Gs sounds like a lot, you and your girl can live for a week like rich people or live for a year like poor people—believe me, it's not all that much. Cops make thirty a year to start, and everybody knows cops make shit. So you gotta be serious about your future, because you won't have it easy, even if you don't get in trouble again, and you get to take showers with your girl every night instead of thirty other guys. Big guys, and they're winking at you. And you can say no to me, or you can say yes—it's all the same to me, but for your sake, and your kid's sake, you should see if we could work something out. You wanna talk to me?"

"Yeah, arright."

"The only thing I ask is you gotta be honest. If you lie, it's over, and you got an enemy. If you don't know something, say, 'I don't know.' Don't tell me what you think I want to hear. And if you can't say something, say, 'I can't say,' or 'I won't say'—don't try to play me, 'cause that's a lie, too. Let's start basic. You're Blood, right?"

He shifted uncomfortably, and fingered his red beads.

"Come on! You got the burns, you got the beads, you and me both know that if you wasn't Blood, real gangstas would beat your balls off."

He paused a moment, and then he said, "Yeah, I'm a Blood. They everything to me, they family. Blood up!" He talked about them with the misty-eyed nostalgia of a veteran of Omaha Beach. "I couldn't give up anything on my Bloods."

"Okay," I said. "How about the Crips?"

"I could do that."

After telling me about certain Harlem Crips he knew who carried guns, he gave me his home and cell-phone numbers. He chose "Damu" as his code name, which he told me was Swahili for "blood." I said he wasn't free to commit crimes, and if he saw other Bloods hurt someone, he had to tell me.

"Yeah, but my Bloods, they—"

"Listen, I'm close to cops, they're my friends, they have my back, they mean everything to me. But right is right—if a cop crossed the line, if he was robbing or beating people or hurting girls or whatever, that's on him. And I ain't going to jail for nobody, and neither should you. You understand?"

Slowly, he nodded, and agreed. We shook hands. It was classic jerkology: in ten minutes of conversation, I'd talked him into breaking his most sacred oath, and I was pleased with both of us and with the thought of what we might do together. But I never saw him again—he was wanted for armed robbery and had skipped out on his bail. It hadn't been his first arrest, by a long shot. He had lied to me about his past, of course, but we spoke little of his past and at length of his future, and in his hope for a long and untroubled life, he was as sincere as anyone. I think he believed that his past might not catch up to him, or that he might have an ally on the police before it did, and had the fingerprint system not been computerized, he could have been right. Blood in, blood out. So much for Damu, who resumed his place on the chow line, and sent me back to mine.

My next informant took less persuasion, but more patience. He came over as a buyer, with a perfect scrip for a crowded city street—*Male Hispanic, blue tank top and shorts, with a hat with a big purple-and-yellow umbrella on it, holding a bag of dope*—and he was amenable to work from the beginning. He called himself "Lesty," which was his broken-English version of "Lefty," and I worked with him for months. Lesty wasn't bright, but I was never sure how much was lost in the translation and how much was lost in the heroin. I would ask him how many spots he knew, and he'd think hard and come up with one or two, but whenever I told him of a new spot to try—usually for a kite—he often knew it anyway. Things tended to occur to him quite a bit later, as when I asked him if he knew anyone who had or sold guns.

"Gonz?"

"Yeah, gonz, you know—*pistoles.*"

"Nah, I don't know nobody with gonz."

But he did, he remembered a week later—two brothers were always pestering him about buying guns from a connection they had in the Heights. But they would deal only with him, Lesty said, and he couldn't bring anyone else. Our office wouldn't pay for the guns with an untested informant, even after I'd IDed the subjects—Flaco and Gordo, or "Skinny" and "Fats"—who had several priors, including an arrest for attempted murder. Had Lesty been able to bring someone, he could have brought another CI or an undercover—without being told which it was—and still another introduction could have been made later on, providing another layer of insulation for Lesty. As it was, we would be paying street prices for a gun, without a case against the seller, because we couldn't have Lesty testify in open court. John Reilly suggested I call ATF, and after the call was transferred through a series of indifferent secretaries and desk agents, I met with an agent who sounded so excited he almost dropped the phone:

"When can we meet?"

But when I told my bosses, they told me to go slowly, because one of our chiefs was at odds with one of theirs. The political squabble had imperiled the future of the NYPD-ATF Task Force—it was later disbanded—and the agents I spoke with weren't even part of that. Still, I set up a meeting, and the two agents met with Lesty. Others in the office cautioned me about working with feds, much as cops in SNEU were wary of Narcotics: if the little dog invites a bigger dog into the pack, they might bring down larger game but find that there was less food to go around. As I saw it, the worst that could happen would be for them to cut me out altogether, and though I wouldn't be happy about that, at least they'd be using Lesty properly.

When we met, one of the ATF agents spoke Spanish, and again there were revelations: Lesty had no problem bringing someone else along. I asked the agent to ask Lesty if he didn't understand me the first time, or circumstances had changed, and Lesty smiled and nodded. The agents asked him all the questions I'd asked—make, model, color—as well as one I didn't think to: Did the guns look brand-new or old? They were new, "still in the box," which made them less interesting: new guns would be from a store in Georgia or Virginia, and the case would probably be fairly uncomplicated, as the gun moved north through two or three sets of hands. But if they were older guns, guns with histories, they might have bodies on them, and ballistics could link them to shootings in Brooklyn and murders in Jersey that might otherwise have gone unsolved. The agents were eager to meet again and set up the buy, and they were so friendly that I was a little concerned, as cops or New York-ers are rarely so cordial. But I handed over my material on Flaco and Gordo, and let them sign up Lesty. And they never screwed me, because I screwed them first, or rather, screws were turned on both of us, from higher levels.

Lt. Zerbo broke the news to me that the politics had doomed this effort, and that we would not be allowed to work together. I called the first agent to apologize, and we both bemoaned the stupidity. A few days later, as I was figuring out how Lesty could make the buy with one of our uncles, I got a call from a lieutenant from one of the other modules:

"Detective Conlon?"

I liked the sound of that, but the warmth of his tone made me suspicious.

"Still a PO, Lou. What's up?"

"You have this address DECSed on One-Three-Nine Street?"

"Yes, I do."

"Well, we're here, we want to get an emergency search warrant. Flaco sold weed to one of our undercovers and ran on us, inside his house."

"I take it you know about the gun under the bed."

"Uh, yeah. But I know it's your spot, and I wanted to make sure it's okay with you."

"If you're there, you're there, Lou, but I should talk to Lieutenant Zerbo first."

"I spoke with him already. It's okay."

"I guess it's okay with me, then, too."

My case fell apart, for the second time. So it went: sometimes the wheels turned and the cogs caught and broke, and sometimes they caught and meshed, sending other wheels turning in the machine. Lesty caught for the guns, and then he spun out, and then the guns caught on another one of our wheels, but then Lesty spun out and caught onto something else, making buys into Bloody Rich's crew. That, too, was a federal case, part of a far more collegial collaboration of the NYPD with the U.S. Attorney's Office.

Bloody Rich was the subject of "Operation Hellbound, Phase Two"—I wondered if Chief Tiffany had come up with the Dantesque name—which would be prosecuted under federal conspiracy statutes. John Reilly would be responsible for the narcotics aspect of the investigation, while Bobby Addolorado of the Four-O Squad took charge of the shootings and homicides. Reilly and Addolorado had handled the first Operation Hellbound, which was directed against another violent drug gang called the "Thief David" crew, which ran crack in and around Millbrook Houses. Thief David had been at war with Bloody Rich, and fortunately a truce had been reached just as the case was taken down, which meant that Thief David's people were in business with Bloody Rich before they were locked up. The prospect of twenty- and thirty-year sentences inspired thoughts of cooperation against their new allies, whose present freedom could be exchanged for their own.

Phase Two was off to a rocky start. Bloody Rich had beaten an attempted murder rap, a year before, for shooting it out with the cops after a Buy and Bust. Bloody Rich's people had begun a shooting war with another crew, and one night one of his lieutenants was shot on a streetcorner in a drive-by. When it happened, John Timpanaro and John Parisi, with whom I'd worked midnights, had filled in a patrol sector, and they headed to the scene. They saw the shooters' car, and gave chase: the perps abandoned the car and fled on foot, and one of them knocked over a kid on a bike and rode away, abandoning the bike when he fled into a project. Timpanaro ran him down and collared him, as both of them gasped for breath in a stairwell. Though the gun wasn't recovered, the perp was charged with the shooting and the robbery of the bicycle. But the bike owner was content to have his bike back and declined to press charges; the shooting victim was uncooperative as well, reasoning that his people would take care of things in their own way.

At that point, the wholesale and retail aspects of police work came into conflict; there were competing demands for immediate results, and for lasting ones. That year, 2000, homicides would rise 50 percent in the Bronx, and though all crimes, murder included, were still a fraction of what they were seven years before, the trend was sharp and ominous. Though Compstat had brought about a greater integration between the separate fiefdoms of the NYPD—in this case, the Four-O Precinct for the Patrol Bureau, the Four-O Squad for the Detective Bureau, the Narcotics modules assigned to Capt. Mahony in the Organized Crime Control Bureau, and of course, the Housing Bureau of PSA-7—the harmony was not quite pitch-perfect. As Bloody Rich's feuds heated up, the CO of the Four-O would be grilled at Compstat for the escalating rate of shootings and homicides, and the bosses downtown demanded arrests. Often, the Squad knew who the perps were but there was no basis for an arrest, or the case would fall apart, as John's shooting-robbery had. Once, Capt. Mahony came back from Compstat fuming that the CO of the Four-O had announced that all of his recent problems were due to Narcotics and Housing, which left him and my old captain holding the bag. Capt. Mahony looked at me tentatively and said, "I know you had your differences, but your old CO doesn't seem to be such a bad guy. . . ."

I laughed. "I'm just happy to be here, Cap."

I was happy enough. Now, I was on the team that played through, one of the big dogs that the little dogs asked for help.

As charges of ignorance and arrogance were traded back and forth, the precinct SNEU and Anti-Crime teams would be sent to the hot spots for quick results, which sometimes conflicted with our investigations. Timpanaro had returned to the PSA from Vice and had moved again from his old footpost to Anti-Crime. Though he still planned to take the sergeant's test, he hoped to get picked up by a detective squad in the meantime. The Captain ordered John to collar a guy who was wanted by the Four-O Squad, despite the fact that a "wanted card" had been issued, which meant that he had been identified in a case, and was unequivocally Squad property. The Squad Commander, Jimmy Ruane, chewed out John for taking the collar. Ruane was a friend of Pops's, and he had been a sergeant with the Four-Four Squad, where John hoped to go. Pops told me to pass along a message to John, and I relayed it: "If you get picked up by the Detective Bureau, let Pops know. His buddy Jimmy Ruane might be able to help you out to get to the Four-Four."

"Uh, yeah—I just met Ruane the other night. . . ."

I had no quarrels with anyone. I kept mostly to myself, eyes open and mouth shut, as I had during my first days as a cop. I didn't miss the fights, but there was a detachment, which I recalled from when I first came to Narcotics, a degree of remove that was a result of the division of labor between undercovers and investigators. If you didn't have an active CI, or it wasn't your turn to "get on" as the arresting officer for B&B, weeks might pass when you didn't even talk to a criminal. There was a disconnection, though I wasn't sure how much it mattered or what it meant. When you were in the field, a team had to work cohesively, to know their positions and their subjects, when to move out and when to move in. At the same time, there was little need to know much about any given case, and I found that perplexing and somewhat uncomfortable. You could float through Narcotics, and I didn't like floating.

Our office had two major cases that year, Operation Hellbound and Smacky's wiretap case. I knew Hellbound fairly well, as Lesty had made buys for it, but Smacky's case was largely mysterious to me: by the time the wire went up, Smacky had several binders of DD5s, or "fives"—the standard detective memo—as thick as phone books, and it would be almost a year from the first buy until the case takedown. It began as a routine CI buy, and then an introduction was made for an uncle; phone numbers were exchanged as we bought in greater and greater weight. Dex and Teddy were the uncles in that case, and in one of the first major buys, they met one subject in the Bronx and traveled to Manhattan to meet another at a diner to conclude a sale. The second subject had not been identified, and so we didn't know his past or his propensity for violence; the level of transaction had moved up into the range of ounces and thousands of dollars; and traveling always brought an additional degree of risk, whether the subjects spotted the tail or we lost the uncles. When the uncles met the subject in a "flash car"—a Mitsubishi Gallant from the small fleet of rental cars at our disposal, which was not so flashy but deemed a better mid-level dealer vehicle than our stodgy old Mercedes four-door sedan—there was tension in Pops's voice as he called the tail like a horse race:

"Arright, they're off . . . south on Third, east on One-Four-Three . . . north on Morris . . . okay, I'm off—you on 'em, 402? They're probably going across to Manhattan on One-Six-One. . . ."

"On him, Leader, this is 402, he's north on Morris. . . ."

"Everybody, everybody, he's north on Morris, keep on parallelin', keep on parallelin' . . ."

"Okay, Leader, they took the left on One-Six-One, I'm out—368's coming across on One-Six-One, copy?"

"Copy—I can't hear you 368, you on him?"

"On him."

"You gotta tell me, you gotta tell me—everybody still parallelin'?"

"Parallelin'—Pops, we're north on Courtlandt, coming up on Six-One. . . ."

"That you, Eddie? Ten-four. . . ."

I rode with Fran Nugent, one of the senior men on the team, and peppered him with questions about the case.

"Who are the uncles?"

"Dex and Teddy, I think."

"Where are we going?"

"Somewhere in Harlem or the Heights."

"What are we buying? How much?"

"How am I supposed to know?"

"And what about—"

I didn't bother finishing, because Fran began to laugh.

"So basically, when we go out on a case, most of us don't really know what's going on?"

"Pretty much."

"Oh."

What I didn't know didn't matter to the case, but the headiness of that hour was heightened by the uncertainty: the uncles met the subject at a restaurant in Hamilton Heights, and we took positions around the perimeter. You didn't want to double-park with the engine running, because you looked more like cops, but then again you might, so you could move quickly if you had to. The kel faded in and out, and one of the subjects left the restaurant and headed toward me and Fran. Fran's hair was red as a siren, and I wasn't too close to passing as a local, either. Too late to move, Fran cut the engine and we dropped our seats back, so the car looked empty. He passed by, oblivious to us. The uncles made the buy, safely, and went back to the Bronx. We followed soon after, and I didn't think about the case again until the next buy.

· · ·

THE SHIFTING AND PROVISIONAL NATURE OF THE WORK WAS inevitable, to a large degree, but other interruptions and adjustments of routine were easily avoidable. That year, apparently as a kind of morale-lowering experiment, our days off rotated three times, from Friday and Saturday in the spring, to Tuesday and Wednesday through the summer, to Sunday and Monday in the fall. Our daily schedules also changed, well, daily—and the next day's tour might be posted and adjusted several times over. With some modules, the tours were changed to fit the schedules of the bosses, and the whole team might come in late one day so the sergeant could see his kid's Little League game, or come in early so the lieutenant could have a night on the town; other modules kept fairly steady tours. For us, Lt. Zerbo changed the tours purely for reasons of professional gain—to do a late buy or an early warrant—and while you had to respect his decision, I never figured out how the cops with families could manage that flexibility. Even without a family, it was a strain, and it was the chief objection that John cited whenever I relayed offers from Pops or Chief Tiffany for him to come over to Narcotics.

In addition, there were the details, a uniformed assignment to a protest, parade, or some other special event. In the spring and early summer, we might have one or two a month, but as the summer turned, they began to pick up to twice a week. From Labor Day through Thanksgiving, New York City would host the playoffs, the World Series, and the U.S. Open. We had the United Nations anniversary, in which hundreds of heads of state were gathered in midtown for a week. That fall saw Hillary Clinton's run for the Senate and Al Gore's run for the Presidency, and the Clintons and Gores were in town constantly, together or apart, to campaign and raise money. We lined the motorcade route for hours beforehand, and froze the blocks before the cars passed, shutting down sections of the city. The Narcotics Division had four thousand cops, a pool that was tapped without hesitation for any of these events. The office joke was that OCCB didn't stand for the Organized Crime Control Bureau but "Other Commands Can Borrow." You might have several days' notice for them, but you might not, and when you came into work you were told to get in uniform and head out. The detail notices said NO DEPARTMENT VEHICLES and NO OVERTIME, but you always took a department car, and you usually did overtime. Your plans for the day—a CI buy, catching up on paperwork, or whatever else—were done. Though I was on vacation for the major disaster that year—the Puerto Rican Day Parade, in which numerous women were sexually assaulted—even the most peaceful details had moments of confusion and ill will, as cops were assigned for the day to a place many had never been before, without radios, and with little information. When I had to work Shea Stadium for a Mets–Braves game—Atlanta pitcher John Rocker had recently given an interview in which he denounced New Yorkers of all colors and preferences—I was assigned to a parking lot, where numerous drivers asked me for directions to various highways. When my first answer—"I have no idea"—seemed to invite denunciation and debate, I revised it to "Take the first left." For all I know, those people are still lost in Queens.

You had to be there hours before: at the precinct an hour and fifteen minutes before the muster, and at the muster hours before the event. On the Fourth of July, we had to be at the precinct at a quarter to four in the morning for a muster in front of the *Intrepid* at five, whereas the events would not begin until after ten. We were a slow-moving, slow-thinking herd, lowing in the dark for coffee, until someone found a bagel store on Forty-fourth Street and we ambled over en masse. The pre-dawn river chill gave way quickly, and the sun was hot and strong. The crowds gathered to watch the great wooden ships of forty nations sail up the river.

The spectacle was majestic, but after I'd stood there for ten hours, twelve, fourteen, in the blazing sun, my appreciation wore thin. We had booklets with the listings of berths for each ship, and schedules for when they sailed, but everything had been changed after the printing, and we had no answers to the questions from Argentine and Japanese and German tourists about the *Esmerelda* or the *Zenob Gramme*. A tidal condition had forced the flotilla to turn back down the river, and the crowds who had gathered above 72nd Street saw the ships only in the distance, and then in retreat. As they moved downtown, the street crossings were closed, and people were shunted to Fifty-seventh Street to cross, and then down to Fiftieth, and then to Forty-eighth, by cops who told them that the next crossing was open, or the past one had been. We had to keep the sidewalks moving, and if your attention lapsed for seconds, the crowds filled in and blocked traffic. No one was supposed to cross the West Side Highway where I stood, but if a man came up to me and said his elderly mother couldn't walk anymore, or his kids were worn out, I'd quietly let them through. And if it seemed safe, I'd let more across, until some captain would shout that the lines had to remain intact, and I'd hold them for a while. And then someone would come up in a wheelchair, and I'd let him through, and then the rest of the crowd would shout, "Why can't we go, too! What's wrong with you!" One woman shouted in my face, "My feet hurt, and you wrecked my day!"

At the Harlem Day Parade, the daylit hours were crowded with families watching the majorettes and marching bands, the Masonic lodges with dapper gents in Sinatra-era suits with gold-embroidered fezzes, calypso bands, and stilt-walkers, strutting and bouncing a dozen feet off the ground. After the sun set, however, there was an edge in the air, and it seemed that the families didn't leave as much as fled. The afternoon had been bright and balmy, and we wore short-sleeved shirts; now, we shivered in the chill and waited for dismissal. Bloods began to move down the streets in packs, in red jerseys and bandannas, and the children who remained alone after dark looked like they were accustomed to running the streets at night. A fat girl of about ten danced in the street to the rap:

Shake your ass
Watch yourself
Shake your ass
Show me what you got
Shake your ass . . .

She did a side-split on the pavement and ground to the beat, and a bony little boy of seven or eight hopped up onto her thigh and danced on it.

The parade went on an hour after schedule, and then two, and a last sound truck appeared in the distance, surrounded by a dancing crowd, determined to finish the route. A captain decided to close off the street, and we lifted the wooden barriers to block the passage. When the crowd saw that the street was closing, they raced ahead to the barriers before they shut, and some leaped over them. As the gap closed and the mass of the crowd drew near, they surged and started to stampede. Kids were mashed against the barriers, and the cops were pushed back, and the captain called out, "Stand fast! Hold the line!" The crowd poured through one corner, and I saw a cop stumble; I began to push through toward her, furious at the captain for forcing a confrontation, when he gave the order to pull back the barriers and let the crowd through. "Let 'em stop 'em at 125th Street," he muttered in disgust. The cop was all right, and I stepped back to the side, and I began to wonder why I was more angry at the captain—who had made a stupid decision, certainly—than the crowd, who risked crushing children so they could dance in the street for three more blocks.

The Palestinian "Day of Rage" didn't promise to be such a pleasant afternoon either. I remember watching Lt. Zerbo make up the detail roster in the office, pencil in his mouth, as he said, "Hmmm . . . I don't think I'll send Leibowitz to this one." The protest was to take place outside the Israeli Embassy, and a few cops noted that it fell on Friday the thirteenth. "It's much worse than that," I added helpfully. "The date's 10-13"—the radio code for "Officer needs assistance." As it happened, the protest was peaceful and uneventful, with one moment of near-catastrophe. I was with Clune, and his brother the lieutenant was there, too, and we amiably passed the time on our side of the barricades. I stood in the sunlight on a corner, my gaze drifting from the crowds in head scarves who carried signs on one side of the barricades, to the crowds in business suits who carried briefcases on the other, when my attention was caught by a middle-aged man who wore an Israeli flag around his shoulders like Superman's cape. He marched with great determination toward the thick of the protest, followed by an entourage that included half a dozen teenage boys.

"Hey! Hold on a second, there!"

Beautiful, I thought, it's the Palestinian Day of Rage and I'm going to collar a rabbi. The Clune brothers and a few other cops rushed over with me to intercept them. I recognized the man as a controversial rabbi who had last been in the news for denouncing a convent on the grounds of Auschwitz as "an abomination." The rabbi said he was exercising his First Amendment rights, and the boys behind him nodded with wild looks in their eyes, ready to meet their fates on the corner of Forty-second Street and Masada. Another, younger rabbi pressed us with questions, as if trying to trap us into an admission of guilt.

"Can't the rabbi walk up Second Avenue? Isn't this America? Are you saying to me that the rabbi *can't* walk up Second Avenue? Are you *ordering* the rabbi not to walk up Second Avenue?"

"Yes, I am telling you—ordering you—saying to you, asking you, if you want. But the rabbi can't walk up Second Avenue."

Third Avenue, yes. First Avenue, yes. Second Avenue, no. By the way, did you get these boys' parents to sign permission slips for suicide? In the end, Super-Rabbi and his crew were content to march in a little circle on the far corner, well attended by police, and no harm came to anyone. The Day of Rage had become a Day of Mild Annoyance, as so many of them did that fall.

The West Indian Day Parade, over Labor Day weekend, was always dreaded by cops: it would be a twenty-hour day with huge crowds and flatbed trucks piled twenty feet high with speakers that turned out reggae, calypso, and soca at tooth-loosening volume. In the past, drinking had been permitted and cops had turned a blind eye to marijuana, and there had inevitably been violence after sundown. This year, the Mayor banned beer sales, and there was concern that the reaction might be stronger than if people had been allowed to drink. Just about everyone in the office would work, and I expected to, but the day before it happened I couldn't get out of bed.

My back had gone out again, a little worse than before. I knew what to expect, and I knew I wouldn't be moving the next day, still less standing for twenty hours. I was more concerned with what Lt. Zerbo would say, and how he'd react to the "sudden illness" that kept me from the longest day of the year. It was three or four more days before I returned to work, and as I walked into the office, Lt. Zerbo shook his head, an expression on his face that would curdle cheese.

"Don't even talk to me, I don't even want to hear it."

"But Lou, I—"

"But what—what happened?"

"My back went out."

"Oh. Okay. You all right?"

"I'm better, I think."

I was better, and a few days afterward I hardly felt it at all. And then it came back again, and never really left. For a while, changing posture from sitting to standing hurt, and I had to ease into each, and choose which might be more useful for the next few hours. I tried to be sneaky about it, the way an alcoholic slips into the bathroom and comes out with a mouthful of peppermints. If I couldn't stand up right away, I'd pretend to have an itch or tie my shoe until I could try again. The pain would go away for a few hours, and I was hopeful that it would stay away, as it often had. I just wanted to get better, or at least to get sick and get better, on a clearly defined timetable. What was not possible was to be on restricted duty indefinitely, not quite good enough to be in the field, but not quite bad enough to be allowed to stay home. There just wasn't enough to do in the office—even when my own casework was backed up at its worst, it could be dispatched in a few hours. If restricted-duty status continued for more than a month or so, I would be reassigned, and though working at the front desk at Narcotics would be far better than Central Booking, I didn't want to do either.

The pain drifted down from my lower back to the left kidney, and then to the left hip and leg. The condition is called sciatica, and it comes from the vertebrae compressing a nerve. I tried acupuncture, which felt fine at first, but walking back to my car I thought my leg was being yanked out of its socket. I staggered into a pizza parlor and sat at a table, tearfully ordering a slice. I went back a week later and told the Chinese woman what had happened. "You okay," she said. "Health take time, like beauty."

The way I moved was neither healthy nor beautiful. After a search warrant, Leibowitz told me, "You run like Walter Matthau in *Grumpy Old Men*." One afternoon in early September, I worked in the surveillance van with John Reilly to shoot video of one of Bloody Rich's spots. Reilly had a severe toothache, and I was half doubled over with my back. It was nearly ninety degrees outside, and we had to keep the windows shut, which drove up the interior temperature to well over a hundred. We also had to keep our movements to a minimum, so the van wouldn't rock. We ate handfuls of Advil and drank quarts of water, sweating it out as fast as we consumed it. As each junkie doddered up to the stoop where a dealer named Omar manned the stash, we zoomed in and out on the faces, dripping sweat on the camera, keeping our groans low. I would have liked to have that afternoon listed as a count on the indictment against Bloody Rich—Aggravated Backache, in the First Degree—but less imaginative legal minds prevailed.

We kept at it, as the cases closed and opened, the CIs came and went. Lesty had disappeared. He was going to be evicted, he told me, and he asked me for two thousand dollars to cover his back rent. I said that wouldn't be a problem, if he got me twenty guns or a couple of kilos. He didn't leave a forwarding address. Another informant took his place, sent to Pops by Bobby Addolorado. Sol was scrawny, pocked, and patchy-skinned, and she often seemed near physical extinction from her various drug-related illnesses—hepatitis, shingles—but she made it painfully clear that whatever its condition, her body was available for Ricky Duggan to ravish. I'd gone through OCCB training with Ricky, and he'd come over to the Bronx from Manhattan North that summer. His manner was cheerful and otherwise unflappable, except with regard to Sol. When we took her out for CI buys, she'd return to the car with crack or heroin, and we'd ask her what the seller looked like or where he kept the stash. Sol would gaze dreamily at Ricky and respond, "Ricky, alls I wanna do is lick your ears."

Often, she brought her boyfriend Mike along, who either went with her on the buys or waited with us in the car. It was, I suppose, what you could call an open relationship, because Mike would gleefully tell of having sex with Sol's young niece in the shower the day before, or how he shot a video of Sol with several friends in bed together. "I directed it, I produced it, I even wroted it," he said brightly. "Well, I co-wroted it."

"Aren't you a lucky fella," I said. "So you have no problems with Sol and Ricky being an item?"

"Hell, no. Ricky's the best!"

"You couldn't ask for better, Mike."

We paid them money and took their drugs, and then we dropped them off on a desolate block to return to their own diversions.

"What nice people," I said. "I'd like to see a lot more of them."

We took them out one night, as Ricky and I sat in the front seat, sending Sol off on her little errands. She continued to profess her love for Ricky, which he laughed at, until just before we dropped her off.

"Oh my God," he said, shuddering.

Sol called out cheerfully as she left, "Bye now, Ricky, I think I'm pregnant, and I hope it's yours!"

"What happened?" I asked.

"She hiked her skirt up for me to see," he said.

"Like Sharon Stone, in *Basic Instinct*?"

"She did what Sharon Stone did in *Basic Instinct*, but I couldn't really say it was like *Basic Instinct*. I think I'm going to have to tell Jennifer the engagement's off, indefinitely."

"In *Basic Instinct*, Sharon Stone didn't show her colostomy bag, did she?"

"No, I don't think she did."

"There's no shame in seeking counseling these days, Ricky, the Department has a number of fine services, and confidentiality is assured."

"I might have to take advantage of that."

When we took Sol to court for warrants, she was usually somewhat restrained, at first, in surroundings which had not always been so hospitable or so profitable for her. She was polite to the ADAs, and she often waited until they had elicited some legal information from her before she asked, "Do you like jokes?"

Sometimes they said they did, and sometimes they said they didn't, and neither answer mattered to Sol, who had one performance piece of which she was very proud: "Okay, so there's this guy? So he gets out of jail, and he's so horny he goes to Coney Island and picks up the first hooker he sees. She goes, 'How much money you got, yo?' And he says, 'Five bucks.' And the ho' goes, 'Fuck that!' And he goes, 'C'mon! I just got out, you gotta fuck me, five bucks is all I got!' So she takes the five bucks, and fucks him under the boardwalk. And the next day he's itchin' and scratchin', and the next day and the next, and the doctor says, 'Yo, you got crabs, mothafucka!' So he goes back to the boardwalk to look for the ho', and he says, 'Yo, bitch! What's up with you! You give me crabs!' And she says, 'Whaddaya expect for five bucks— Red Lobster?'"

I always laughed when she came to the part about the doctor. It reminded me of Crazy Larry's notes to his ex-girlfriend, on hospital stationery—*You got the AIDS, Bitch!*—or maybe there was a South Bronx doctor with that exact bedside manner. A few ADAs laughed, but more than one felt it necessary to caution her, "That's a good joke, but you have to promise you won't tell it to the judge."

I don't think Sol would have sold out her own child, but there was no price for him, yet. In one case, she looked through a "set book," which contained photographs of subjects, and as she flipped the pages, she said, "That's my father . . . that's my real father . . . that's my uncle . . . that's my godson. . . ." Once, she gave up her cousin who was wanted for a stabbing when she met him at a family party, calling the Four-O Squad to say, "Hello, can I have a cab at 180 Brook . . . ," as a prearranged signal to the detective who had the case.

A lot of the cops wouldn't deal with Sol, because she operated at several skeeve-levels above their threshold. For some reason, Leibowitz usually chose the moment when I was eating to tell me about her latest endearment:

"And she got out of the car, and she squatted down right there—"

"I'm trying to eat here. . . ."

"And she takes a squirt right there in the street, and—"

"Hey! Adam! Save it!"

"Hey, sorry . . . you gonna finish that sandwich?"

Sol was an unusual young lady, to be sure. She would mention offhandedly how much crack her mother used to sell, or how she used to rob dealers herself, sticking them up at gunpoint and making them strip naked. Though she weighed about eighty-five pounds, she reminisced about how she tipped the scales at over two hundred when she spent a year in Rikers. "Yo, I *really* liked the food there. I'll show you a picture if you promise not to laugh. . . ." But Sol made sense to me, because she was in it for the money, and that single motivation made her more manageable than many less objectionable informants.

In dealing with informants, my pitch had always been rational, to show perps that they had a choice, and why working with us offered better prospects than fighting a charge. I hustled them in the sense that there was a technique to the persuasions, but I never lied or even exaggerated. I could offer money or freedom, on a sliding scale. If the deal was for freedom, I avoided explicit terms to the effect that three buys and a warrant gets you from two-to-six to probation, because I didn't have the authority to adjust a sentence, though I could make my case with most ADAs. If it was a money deal, I told them exactly what they could make—on each set, fifteen dollars a try, thirty dollars a buy, and a hundred for a warrant if it was a hit—and if the office didn't have the money at the moment, I covered it myself. The approach was effective, as far as it went, but it encouraged a tendency to expect perps, or anyone else, to calculate advantage and risk in side-by-side columns. It's what I would do, I supposed, and that was the mistake: we were not the same. And not because I was a cop and they were criminals—though that was a real distinction, in that I didn't wake up wondering where to get my dope, let alone whom I would rob or rape—but because everyone has a percentage of themselves that makes no sense, and there is a percentage of people who never make any sense at all. I had to remind myself that the lines of human thought were neither straight nor clear, but it was a better lesson when the perps took it upon themselves to remind me.

We set up to watch Smacky's wiretap subjects—the still-unidentified JD Red and another man—come from the Heights to meet a Bronx dealer named Mike. JD Red carried a VCR in a cardboard box. They waited outside a pizza place, and we waited in cars around the perimeter of Mott-Pat, with uncles and ghosts floating through the project grounds. They waited and then they walked, and then they waited again, and then Mike met them, and all three walked again, into a building. We waited, tensely, wondering whether to move. We didn't want to take them yet, but the thought of what we might miss lingered like an itch—what if this was the big drop? We wanted to take in JD Red, just to identify him, but we didn't want to let him know that he was being watched, let alone overheard. As they stepped out of the project lobby, JD Red no longer had the VCR box, and we moved in and took them for trespass. We took them to PSA-7, hoping they'd believe they'd been picked up by Housing cops instead of Narcotics, and checked the name that JD Red had given us. If JD Red had a gun or a kilo on him, we would have been glad, but as it was, we had what we needed and hadn't been made. As we walked him out, however—Smacky, Billy Clark, and I, who were all from the PSA—a cop called out jovially, "Hey, what are you guys doing here? You're not in Housing anymore, you're in Narcotics!"

JD Red turned to Smacky and gave him a strange look. Smacky said nothing, and I shuddered. Would he have to write another binder full of fives to explain how the case was destroyed? No, I thought, one page would do. None of us mentioned it to Pops or Zerbo. I was anxious to look at the transcripts from the tap over the next few days, to see what they had taken away from the encounter. I found out when another dealer named Angel called JD Red, and while I was relieved to see that we hadn't been made, I was amazed to see his take on it. JD Red didn't think in circles but circuits, repeating figures of grievance and ego, and could pull facts like taffy. It was classic perp logic:

> "What's up, bro, I heard about what happened to you!"
>
> "Yeah—nah, but I was out quick. They got me only for bullshit trespassing, yo."
>
> "What, coming out of the house?"
>
> "Nah, I was inside the building and shit, in the fucking projects, and I was waiting, you know, for my man . . . in the lobby and shit."
>
> "Yeah, you serious? And they took you?"
>
> "Yeah, man, they took me for the little bullshit, yo. I was telling them, 'Yo man, you know you wasting your time and my time.' And he said, 'Well, I'm not really wasting my time, 'cause I'm getting overtime.' And I said, 'Ain't that a bitch. . . .'"

That part was true—Billy Clark said it. Angel had some questions about Article 140, Section 10 of the Penal Law, which Red explained fairly well:

> "I don't understand, you waiting for a friend, how they have that right just to take you, bro?"
>
> "If you don't live in the project, okay, you not supposed to hang out in the building. I told them, 'Listen man, be honest, it's cold out there. You know it's cold out there. You know, we ain't commit no crime, you know, we just standing here, staying warm. I had told them I went upstairs to my friend's house but there was nobody there.'"
>
> "Right."
>
> "You know what I'm saying? And we're just waiting for a cab to come."
>
> "Right."
>
> "You know? And then he said, 'All right, well what apartment your friend lives in?' And shit, you know, and I couldn't really remember the apartment, you know, so I had told them it's the twelfth floor, the first door to the left, this and that. So he says, 'All right guys, just don't hang out inside the building, y'all could stand outside.' So we stood outside waiting for my man."
>
> "Right."
>
> "And them motherfuckers went and knocked and shit, it was some black lady that opened up the door. And she said, 'Nah, I don't know . . . you-know, you-know, because I had to give them my name, and shit, she said, 'No, I don't know no Eric, this and that.' And ahh, nigger radioed in, yo. The next thing

you know, like four DTs and shit, two vans and two fucking cars, bum-rushed us, man, it was like, 'What the fuck is going on, yo?' And he was saying—you know the cop came, and shit, he said, 'You know, I don't like no fucking liars.'

That part was true, too—Smacky said it, and it was a good line, because it made it seem that we brought him in because one cop was angry about what he said, instead of many who were interested in what he did.

"And I told him, you know, just because we're standing in the fucking building, c'mon man, I could see if we selling drugs . . ."
"You a grown man. . . ."
". . . or robbing people or something, you know. . . ."
"You ain't no kid. . . ."
"I told him, he said, 'But you know, it's the law, you cannot trespass.' I told him, 'Listen, okay, that's the law—it's true, you right about that. But you know that's a bullshit law, yo!'"
"Yeah, no doubt."
"I could see if I'm some young thug and shit, hanging out around the building to mug somebody, or sell drugs, you know. I told him, 'Yo, I'm an older man, you know what I'm saying?'"
"Right!"
"I told him, 'That's not right, man.' I told him, 'Listen, if I bet you anything, if I was an old lady or a man with a cane, y'all guys would never arrest us. But being that we look like we're from the street or whatever, that's the reason why y'all took us in.' You know?"

I was happy to hear that. It meant that even Red thought—his own case aside—that cops enforced the law selectively but sensibly. Angel took a different perspective:

"They were white, right?"
"Yeah, two white cops, and shit. You know . . ."
"Prejudice."
"I told him, 'Yo, I'm too old for that bullshit!' I told him, 'What you think? I'm gonna be an idiot and stand right there selling drugs? You gotta be kidding me!' I told him, 'If I was selling drugs, I woulda been the fuck out of there. . . . I'm forty-one years old, you think I'm an idiot, yo?'"
"I hate white people. . . ."

JD Red was no darker than Dan Quayle, with red-brown hair that gave him his JD name.

But clearly, when he looked in the mirror, he didn't see the same things that we did. There was no realization that we were on to him, but there was also no recognition that we had any right or reason to be. *It's not as if he were selling drugs!* His indignation was sublime, in its way, as he was a drug dealer who was talking to another drug dealer, about having just delivered a quarter-pound of cocaine:

> *"Oh yeah, I knew, I knew I was gonna be out quick, but you know, thank God, man, because, uh . . . Just before that happened and shit, I had a hundred of them things. You know what I'm saying? And I took it to my man."*
>
> *"Thank God, man."*
>
> *"In that building, you know what I'm saying?"*
>
> *"Yeah, yeah."*
>
> *"So I was waiting for my man to come down and shit, 'cause you know, he had to—uh, you know—he had to kick up the cash and shit."*

Red had dropped off a hundred grams of cocaine—almost four ounces—and Mike was going to cook up ten grams into crack, for Red's sister to sell. Angel said that his mother and stepfather also sold drugs, and then went on to say that he had been at Mike's that morning to buy crack but the quality was bad—*"I disapprove, you know—I'm-a get rid of it . . . but it's gonna take me long, niggas ain't feelin' it. I hope he ain't get it from you."*

The two went on to talk about their pride in their families and their business, which appeared to frequently intersect:

> *"And let me tell you, I won't give you no garbage—you know what I'm sayin'?—because to me, what's important is that you make your money, 'cause if you don't make your money, then I can't make no money."*
>
> *"Your word is good. You know what I mean? And my family tells me that."*
>
> *"Uh-huh."*
>
> *"I'm proud of you, and I take that very serious."*
>
> *"I know what's good and what's not good. I've been in this shit like twenty-five years, you know what I'm saying?"*
>
> *"You could teach me, bro. . . ."*
>
> *"Yeah, you know—hey, we all teach each other, you know?"*
>
> *"Yeah."*

"That's how I've learned, and I've taught other people, too . . . whenever I put my foot in the bucket, I make sure I get myself out of it, you know what I'm saying?"

"No doubt."

"'Cause I mean, it's too many years experience in this fucking world, you know what I'm saying? Not that I know it all—'cause I don't—and it's always good to reach out, you know what I'm saying? But whatever I get myself into . . . thank God, knock on wood, you know?"

What struck me was how Red cast himself as an injured party, how his sense of order had been violated, if not, technically, his rights. He sounded like a stockbroker furious at a traffic cop who had ticketed him for speeding, making him late for the 0650 express train. He sounded exactly like the stockbroker, in fact, who might have been expecting agents of the Securities and Exchange Commission, but was positively offended by the lowly flatfoot. And Angel understood completely. Angel's parents were dealers, and maybe his children would be, too; Red's own quarter-century in the trade itself spanned generations. It had been bred into them. Maybe my great-grand-children would arrest theirs.

I thought about how his sense of the normal was as remote from my own as that of a Berber tribesman or Prussian colonel. But then I considered that I was not an entirely logical creature myself: I was thirty-five years old, with a good education and a bad back, and I spent my days grabbing crack dealers in the South Bronx. What had been bred into me? I had occasion to think about that, a week or two later, when we had a Christmas party at Louie's on East Tremont Avenue, where part of *The Godfather* was filmed. It is a pivotal scene: the Corleones are at war with Sollozzo, Tartaglia, and Barzini; Don Corleone has been shot, and he is threatened further in the hospital; in his first encounter with the law, Michael's jaw is broken by the corrupt police captain, McCluskey, who is on Sollozzo's payroll. At home, Sonny and Tommy Hagen, the consigliere, debate their options, when Michael proposes that they agree to a sit-down with McCluskey and Sollozzo, where he will kill them both.

Sonny laughs at him, impressed at his ambition but dismissive of his ability: "Hey, what are you gonna do? Nice college boy, who didn't want to get mixed up in the family business . . . now you want to gun down a police captain? Why, because he slapped you in the face a little bit? . . ."

"It's not personal, Sonny, it's strictly business."

As I watched the scene again, I wondered which was true: was it for his family's sake, or his own?

McCluskey is old, oafish, crooked, and brutal, and no matter how perfect the character, the role is one that stretches historical reality—a captain might be in the mob's pocket, but he wouldn't be a personal bodyguard for a gangster. His risk of exposure would be too high, and the gangster could certainly do better than a cranky geriatric. But McCluskey's first line as they sit down at Louie's is one of my favorites in the movie: "How's the *Italian* food in this restaurant?"

The emphasis brims with disdain, barely conscious and barely concealed. There is something in the way that line is spoken that reminded me of my older relatives at Italian restaurants, fumbling with a menu before ordering lasagna because it was the only dish with a name they could pronounce.

"Good. Try the veal, it's the best in the city," says Sollozzo.

Wine is brought, but the only glasses are for Michael and Sollozzo—it is their little revenge for his being Irish. They speak Italian, but it is not hard to follow: *Padre . . . rispetto . . . molto difficile . . .*

As he's rehearsed with Clemenza, Michael asks permission to go to the bathroom—"You gotta go, you gotta go"—and returns with a .38.

He sits down and listens, barely—*"Tuo padre . . ."*—and then he shoots Sollozzo in the forehead, as McCluskey sits, open-mouthed, a forkful of the best veal in the city suspended in the air. Michael shoots him, too, and drops the gun, as he's been told, and though he was told not to run, he starts to, just as he reaches the door.

When we sat down to dinner at the Christmas party, I said, "How's the *Italian* food in this restaurant?" but I don't recall getting too many laughs. I didn't try the veal. If I was the only one who appreciated a joke, I was happy to laugh alone. It may have made a few people raise their eyebrows, but I didn't much care.

You never really know what your own reputation is, or how your view of yourself conforms with those around you. I was liked, I thought, and I got along with everyone in the office. The occasional jokes about going to Harvard or writing a book were infrequent and good-natured, and when someone was genuinely interested in one or the other, they'd approach me quietly to ask about them. As far as my eccentricities, they were not extreme: I dressed like a bum but I drove an old Cadillac and drank martinis; I could wreck a desk with paperwork; I read all the time—books, newspapers, magazines. Ricky Duggan said I looked like a panicked junkie if didn't have anything to read, tearing around the office for last week's *Post*.

I was quiet in the office and kept a low profile. I didn't have a desk, or even a drawer in one, and so no one was used to looking for me in any particular place. I used my own car again, for the freedom and convenience it brought, and if I had business to take care of that didn't need another cop, I took care of it alone. Early on, before I built up a caseload, I had some free time, and later on, when I didn't, I had a lot of errands like picking up rap sheets at Headquarters, or meetings with ADAs or CIs. I became a PBA delegate, and I got a day off each month for union meetings. Our office went out on most days, for B&B, CI buys, or case buys, but if we weren't doing anything, I'd take off—I did have another job to do. Billy Clark took to calling me "The Phantom."

The tag reminded me of something, and when I looked through my father's scrapbook, I found a poem that his colleagues had written on the occasion of his twentieth anniversary in the FBI:

John Matthew Conlon, the Phantom, Will-of-the-Wisp, each day
Reporting to work every morning, folding his tent and fading away.
Oh, Gray Fox, we wonder how you disappear in a Flash.
You can make the elevator in the record time of a hundred-yard dash.

However, we know you are working, because it's easy to see
How happy you are when you arrest someone and deprive him of Liberty.
Of all the Agents on 26, there probably is no other.
We bet you would be happy even if you arrested your brother.

On the opposite page of the scrapbook, there was another poem, and I wondered if it was composed by the same Agent-Poet, or if—God forbid—there were two in the office.

He joined the ranks in '51
And sat down to take a rest.
While waiting for his interview
He swallowed the Reader's Digest.

The magazines piled high and high,
His wife was pressed for space.
John took the kids from the bunk beds,
The books will take their place. . . .

And as we sign him in today,
Never fear and be not reticent,
For John will always change his name
To protect the pure and innocent.

My teammates might not have been entirely unfamiliar with the figure of a book-loving cop who drove an odd car—a Volkswagen Beetle, in my father's case—but when I thought about the similarities it was almost embarrassing: a casual attitude toward punctuality, and a penchant for aliases . . . Sometimes I wondered whether I was coming into my own, or merely repeating what had been my father's. In either case, there were worse ways to be.

By the end of the year, I was confident in my new assignment, and comfortable with my bosses and partners. It was not as it was with SNEU, with its intensities of camaraderie and cause, and if I wasn't singing in my car anymore, neither was I looking forward to a root canal. The next year, I would be made a detective, as I'd determined when I first put on a uniform and threw my gloves in the air. But there was no sense of culmination on the horizon, and that troubled me somewhat, as I looked ahead. I didn't want to just collect the gold shield like a paycheck, but there was no particular reason to leave, and no particular place to go. There was little I could do about it, except to keep working and hope for a case that would engage me, that would lead to some kind of Door. I had no expectation of a French Connection, but I needed a renewed sense of purpose and place. And after being shamed by Chief Tiffany into brushing up on Dante, I began to think that the problem might be that work didn't stink enough—I didn't have to pause before descending to the next level of Hell. As you go on in the Job, your career should follow a double arc, down and up at the same time: as you get better, the work should get worse, to graver tasks and tests. For Dante to find his Door, he had to head where it hurt to go: Are you feelin' this? *I ain't feelin' this.* Good, this must be the way.

Only one thing did hurt for me, more and more, and that was my back. I had trouble standing up, or moving very fast or far. My posture was like a question mark, and on B&B, I took to standing outside the car as we waited on a set, so I would be able to run if we moved in. In January, they kept me in the office for a week or two, and then I would go on vacation, and then I would have surgery. I wouldn't work again until May, but on New Year's Eve of 2000—for the true millennium—I worked the Times Square detail for the first time in my life. The crowd swelled up to our post at Fifty-ninth and Seventh, filling up the pens in the center of the street. The New York Athletic Club opened a room for us with a coffee urn and donuts, and we slipped out of the cold now and then. Snow was banked hard and high on the sidewalks, and I helped a little girl clamber up to see over the crowd. Japanese tourists asked me where they could go to the bathroom, and I laughed. All the crowd fell silent as the count wound down, and we had a clear view of the ball as it descended through the neon canyon of Times Square, the first of all the lights, the last of the year.

TWELVE

For five months, I lay down and thought. Often, I felt old. In some ways, I was old: had I gone on the Job when I was twenty, I'd have been a few short years from retirement. It might have been the painkillers, but when I looked back over the six years I'd been a cop and the hundred and fifty that the NYPD had somehow managed without me, there was no clean line between them. I had begun a year after Giuliani and Bratton had been sworn in, but I'd lived in the city and worked in the courts when Koch and Dinkins were in office. As a cop, I would talk to Inspector Mullen, Chief Tiffany, or Sonny Grosso about the major events of the 1960s and 1970s, of Phillips, Serpico, and Leuci, and sometimes I thought that they talked to me no differently than they had with their partners at the time. So, too, it was with my father's friends on the Job, who began work in the 1950s, and even in the 1930s, in Jim Falihee's case. Falihee had been a chemistry major in college and planned to become a doctor, but the Depression intervened, and he spent most of his career in the Bomb Squad and the Police Laboratory. He could reminisce about the World's Fair bombings of 1941, and hunting for Nazi saboteurs. Falihee's time began as Pat Brown's was ending, and in Pat's rookie years, the old-timers doubtless groused about how Teddy Roosevelt had damn near ruined the Job. *The beer pail is empty! And the spittoon is full!*

Mother of God, if my father ever lived to see the day when they let Eye-talians into the New York City Police Department . . .

If these generations ever came together, I could tell them about how computers had changed things, how we didn't take fingerprints with ink or photographs with film, and Uncle Eddie and Sonny Grosso could recall when television was invented, and if Pat Brown was still talking to us, he could reminisce about when the automobile made its debut. But all of us could talk about walking footposts on winter nights, and how the sergeant would touch your shield to check if it was cold. All of us, from each end of the century, knew the green lights of the precinct, which hearkened back to centuries before. We could talk about shoe-flies and rackets, roll calls and rounds; we would even know some of the same paperwork—the UF 61s and DD5s. We might even agree that the time of the Irish had passed, but maybe it had always been passing, and always would. And Sonny would likely complain about that less than the rest. We would see eye to eye about many things.

No matter how natural it felt to be a cop, and no matter the pointed weight of heredity and history, it was by no means inevitable that I had gone on the Job. When I was younger, I had never read mysteries, and I had no pronounced interest in crime, true or otherwise, until I happened into a job in criminal defense. Sometimes I wondered what had happened to my old clients from CCJA. I remembered poor Cecil, who cut off his stepson's crack-crazed head, and how he'd look down and mutter, "I would not be able to say," no matter what I asked him. Not long after we'd banished him to Montserrat, I read about the hurricane that wiped out much of the island. I caught another name in the papers a few years later, just after I'd gone on the Job, I think. A one-paragraph item in the *Daily News* told of an off-duty cop who stopped at a gas station as it was being robbed at gunpoint, and he shot the perp in the chest. The perp was Dondre, who had last played with guns with his best friend Kataun. The gas station was in Greenpoint, not far from where his grandmother lived, reading her John le Carré novels. Dondre was twenty-one, and he must have just been released, if he maxed out as a juvenile. He would max back in again; so much for second chances.

For a while, I stayed in touch with Jack, my first client, and his mother, Maria. I wrote to Jack in prison, after Maria told me that he was getting in trouble again with gangs there. He had joined the Five Percenters, which was affiliated with the Nation of Islam. I was concerned for Jack, and angry, not to mention a little confused: Jack was Puerto Rican, and not even dark-skinned, and he had no brighter a future with black supremacists than he would have with the Klan. His fights and gang activities cost him his first chance at parole, and he spent three years in prison. When he came home, I went over to his house for dinner, and the time showed on him. At eighteen, he was bigger and stronger, but he had a nervous quickness to him, as if someone had just turned on the lights. We had fried chicken and rice and beans, and we made polite small talk. Jack handled his knife and fork clumsily; he was unused to metal utensils. When the bell went off on the microwave, he jumped. "I thought it was the panic button," he explained. "You know, for when they do lockdown."

When Jack talked about "up north," it was as if he'd been at college or in the Army. I was uneasy with his nonchalant tone, and how it suggested that further confinement would be less of an adjustment than freedom would be. Nor did I trust the parroted references to "keeping it positive" and "not being a follower." After dinner, when he walked me back to the subway, I had even further misgivings. I watched him watch the street, rapid and roving, combat-ready. In the prison corridors upstate, the high-alert attitude might have been defensive, but on streets of Brooklyn, he looked predatory, on the make. At the subway, we shook hands and assured each other we'd stay in touch.

"You be careful out here, Mr. Conlon."

"I told you, you don't have to call me 'Mister.'"

"All right, but you be careful—there's a lot of knuckleheads out here."

"I always keep an eye out for knuckleheads, Jack. You take care, now."

Ten years passed before I thought to call again. It took some time to remember the name of the Catholic social-services agency where Maria worked. I wondered for a moment if she was still alive, or if Jack was. I talked to a nun at the agency and persuaded her to give me Maria's home number. After the first ring, I almost hoped to get an answering machine, so I could hang up and call again after thinking about what message to leave. But Maria answered, and though I was certain she would remember me, I wasn't prepared for her reaction:

"God has sent you! God has sent you! Oh, thank God, my goodness—it's so good to hear from you. . . ."

Nor did I expect to hear news that would make me as elated as her greeting. Jack had gone to college in Maryland, and he stayed there after graduation. Now, he was married and had two children, and he worked as a counselor for troubled kids. He had a master's degree, and he had nearly completed his Ph.D. I'd been afraid that he'd find his way back to the knuckleheads, but I never expected that it would be on these terms. We talked some more—about her health, which had been uneven—and my own career adjustments, which she was happy to hear about. She gave me Jack's number in Maryland, and I called him.

"Oh, my *Gaaawd*—Mr. Conlon!"

And we talked for a while, about his kids and his wife and his job and his Ph.D. He was as casual about his striving and his hard-won substance as he had been about panic buttons and lockdowns the last time we'd spoken. Was there anything so strange about that, going from life to life? No, I thought, but so few people manage it so well. I thought about his intermediate-school teachers and the people at St. Barbara's who saw such great things for Jack, and how even after he became a criminal, and then a prisoner, and then an ex-con—it had been a short period, but it had not been a long life—they remained undaunted in their hope. For a moment, I felt like an absentee father, and I laughed at myself for the vanity. But I told him, "Jack, I'm proud of you," and I think he was glad to hear it. Anyone can learn from their mistakes, but it takes a savvy or a sanctity beyond ordinary measure—St. Augustine comes to mind—to make those mistakes mean so much, to whomever is willing to listen.

As they told us in high school, the word "vocation" meant a calling: you knew when you heard it, and you went. To prepare for our freshman year, the Jesuits gave us a book about the history of the order, telling of St. Ignatius Loyola, the founding soldier-saint who devised a form of meditation, and of other missionaries, martyrs, and scholars. The last chapter had been torn out, which we found highly intriguing; what secrets were being withheld from us? In fact, the chapter had been removed because it discussed preparation for the priesthood, and the school feared that it might scare off parents who were hopeful for grandchildren. Three of my classmates entered the priesthood, though all three eventually left. Would there have been more if the last chapter had not been torn out? Would they have stayed? Maybe the voice that called had fallen silent, or other voices called louder.

I had two vocations, cop and writer, which called not only to me but to each other. Much of police work is storytelling, from the journalism of an investigation, to the post-arrest sales pitch to the ADA. I always felt a little superior when a sergeant or an ADA looked at my paperwork and said, "This is very well written, you know." I felt the opposite after my first evaluation for Narcotics, where the marks varied from average to above, until Clune explained that Lt. Zerbo did that for everyone, so that later evaluations would reflect progress. "I'm not sure what to say about this," I said. "But maybe that's because my 'Judgment' is only average, three out of five. I could go one way or another."

"Don't be insulted. He was going to give you a three in 'Communication,' too, but I thought you'd take that a lot more personal."

I thought for a moment. "You're right, I would have." In any case, I was less unhappy than the teammate who wondered whether the purported tribute of being a "well-rounded detective" was a jibe about his weight.

On duty and off, cops are storytellers, but when a group of cops tells stories, there is usually a degree of self-consciousness if a non-cop is around. Sometimes it's because you have to break up the story to explain a bit of slang or procedure, but more often it's out of a wariness that things won't sound right, that the cop will look as rough and rude as the work can be. Even when the purpose of police work is to disclose a secret, to reveal a true mystery—who stole what from where, who killed whom—there is a shifting balance between the unsaid and the said. A patrolman is entitled to use his discretion, and on some days, the D is heavier than others. More is left out because it's too dull to explain rather than because it's dangerous to share, and many omissions really aren't either—in one verse of my father's FBI anniversary poem, there is mention of an extremely valuable and delicate old painting he recovered, which he tossed in the back seat of his Volkswagen, amid the coffee cups and peanut shells. Until he retired—and maybe after— my father would have said of the painting story, "Let's keep that one to ourselves, why don't we?" It is easier to talk your way into trouble than to talk your way out: cases are often solved because criminals talk—bragging to their friends, yapping on a tapped phone—and convictions are more likely after a confession. *How does a fish get caught? He opens his mouth.*

But ya *still* gotta have a story. For cops, despite the Blue Wall of Silence and the Fifth Amendment, the well-founded fear of the media and an adversarial legal system, sooner or later, we are all called to testify. It saddened me to hear a story about a rookie who chased a perp to a rooftop, where the perp fell to his death trying to escape. Though there was the expected street-corner chorus crying *Murder!* the Squad had moved in quickly, finding several witnesses who corroborated the account of an accidental death. Before the rookie could give his statement to Internal Affairs, however, he was taken aside by an old hairbag, who said, *Listen, kid, listen to me, ya hafta say you weren't there, ya hafta say you never made it into the building, ya can't trust anybody, trust me on this. . . .* The rookie had done nothing wrong until the interview, after which he was fired. No doubt the old-timer is generous with his advice still, enjoying his pension in Florida. *Poor dumb kid, he didn't listen. . . .* Nobody ever says *nothing,* not even a monk. Our silences are as articulate as our stories, are part of them, and they too can be held against us. In *A Man for All Seasons,* Thomas More correctly insisted that under the common law, silence indicates consent. More had refused to take the oath of allegiance to Henry VIII as head of the Church, and hoped to keep his head in spite of it. He did not beat the system, and though Sir Thomas became St. Thomas, he would have preferred survival to either title. If you don't have a story of your own, one may be supplied, and you may be surprised, not happily, by how well it fits.

. . .

FOR PAT BROWN, I HAVE A COPY OF WHAT IS CALLED A "TEN card," which lists his disciplinary record as well as the barest administrative data: assignments, addresses, and shield numbers. His first six years were spent in the 172nd and 148th precincts, neither of which exists today, and then in June 1914, he was transferred to the 15th Inspection District for a series of ten-day temporary assignments that extended for four years. In 1918 he moved to "BBH," Brooklyn Borough Hall, and then to "HD," Headquarters Division, for two years, with a note that says "200 Ex Com." In 1920, there is a severe-looking note that says "Ex Com Revoked," marking a return to patrol in Brooklyn, with another temporary posting to the Brooklyn DA's Squad before promotion to sergeant in 1926. He had been a cop for twenty-one years, and he spent his remaining twelve between the First Precinct, "the old First," on Old Slip, near the Fulton Street Fish Market, and in the 78th, in Park Slope, in Brooklyn again, from which he retired.

For most people, these notes would be hieroglyphic; for me, the risk is not failing to understand what they say—though I don't understand them completely—but rather reading too much into them. In the spring of 1914, when he was first transferred, the city was consumed with the Becker–Rosenthal scandal, in which a police lieutenant was sent to the electric chair for the murder of a gambler. Such events, then as now, invariably provoke a frenzy of administrative housecleaning. Moreover, it was just after the inauguration of Mayor John Purroy Mitchel, the reform candidate who beat Tammany in the wake of the scandal. Whether Pat Brown was seen as a man who could be trusted not to take a penny, or someone who could keep his mouth shut, advancement presented itself in a time of political crisis. His move to Head-quarters similarly took place during a period of political transition, a month after John F. Hylan took office as Mayor, ousting the reformer after one term, as was the pattern. Hylan, a Brooklyn Democrat, was regarded as "honest but befuddled" and had an obsession with the subways—he had been a rail-road conductor until he was fired for nearly running over his boss. His police commissioner, Richard Enright, was the first former NYPD officer to occupy that position; he was best remembered for giving out solid-gold shields to wealthy supporters, known as "Enright's Millionaires." Whether there was a Brooklyn hook or a cop hook at the changing of the guard, it pulled Pat Brown to the center of things. The center, as the late Lt. Becker might have told him, is not always the best place to be.

1920: Ex Com Revoked. It sounds worse than an ordinary transfer, cer-tainly, though there is no mark against him on his disciplinary record. The 78th Precinct was near his home in Brooklyn, and had he seriously crossed his bosses he would have been sent to the Bronx. Nonetheless, for most cops, a purely lateral move from the capital to the provinces is rarely a step up. Re-gardless of whether 1920 was a year of great professional turmoil for Pat Brown or simply occasioned a routine administrative shift, it was then that the marriage broke apart. I can guess wildly if not well about what hap-pened: he was caught taking money, or caught not taking money, or he was taking money and never got caught, but he lost it when he left Headquarters, after he fought with his boss, or his boss lost a fight, or there was no fight, but two years was considered to be the proper term for a cop at HQ. Or his boss was promoted to Brooklyn, and he followed him there. Or he learned the trade of the shakedown in the city, so when he hit the boondocks, the rubes were ripe for the picking. The sudden loss of income pushed him into bitter-ness, or the sudden gain in income made him want to live like a playboy. I don't know what happened. I do know that most cops bring their work home with them, when it's going badly; that they carry the smell of the streets on them even when they change clothes. And even though, as a plainclothes-man, he walked better streets than he had on patrol, the smells were often worse. It might be worth noting that 1920 was also the year that Prohibition went into effect.

Pat Brown spent the next six years in Brooklyn, as the city came to realize that the good times didn't end with the Volstead Act. Tammany reached its heights under Governor Al Smith, who was the first Catholic candidate for President, and from whom his onetime and ungracious protégé Franklin

Delano Roosevelt lifted much of the New Deal. In 1925, Jimmy Walker convinced Smith that his rakish ways were behind him to secure the nomination for mayor, and for a time he had the city fooled, too. Walker was known as "the Night Mayor" and "Beau James," and he embodied the city far better than he administered it. When a Long Island casino he was visiting was raided, he slipped into the kitchen and put on an apron to watch the cops haul off the other patrons, his girlfriend included, as he ate beans with the dishwashers. He remarked that it wouldn't do for a man in his position to turn up in a "rural hoosegow." Walker was *the* man about town, all wisecracks and diamond stickpins, who co-wrote a hit song, "Will You Love Me in December As You Do in May?"—a question which, if considered political in nature, was answered with a resounding "No!"

Pat Brown was a boss himself by then, having been promoted in 1926. He worked in the 1st Precinct in lower Manhattan through the Walker years, remaining until a few weeks before Fiorello La Guardia appointed his great reformer, Lewis Valentine, as Police Commissioner. It is hard to read the transfer as a coincidence. The 1st was not the Tenderloin—it encompassed the financial district and some of the waterfront—and as such had a relatively tiny permanent population. It was never known as a red-light district, though its bankers and sailors must have had some nearby diversions, but waterfronts were famously useful to organized crime in general and bootleggers in particular. By the length of his stay and the timing of his departure, I would assume that the command had some value for Pat, as well as some risk. The 1st Precinct covered Headquarters and was uncomfortably close. Prohibition had been repealed, and Valentine was about to arrive when he returned to Brooklyn, to the Seven-Eight, in Park Slope, where he finished his career in the NYPD in 1940.

Pat Brown did not leave much of a paper trail I have his ten card and the menu from his retirement dinner; beyond that, there is a clip from *The Brooklyn Eagle* of Wednesday, June 14, 1916, which raises more questions than it answers:

TRIED TO "BUY" POLICEMAN?

Brown Says He Was Offered $10 to Drop Case

Charged with attempting to bribe Patrolman Patrick Brown of the Fifteenth Inspection District, who had arrested his friend, Joseph

Lopoma, 45 years old, of 52 Dooley Street, was held on $1000 bail for a hearing by Magistrate Geismar in the Coney Island Court yesterday afternoon. The officer states that in the corridor of the court yesterday Lopoma offered him $10 to discontinue the complaint of selling liquor without a license, made against Basile Peccelro, 23 years old, of 50 Dooley Street.

Peccelro was arrested by Patrolmen Brown and Daly, charged with distributing and selling to a construction gang boxes of bottled beer. He pleaded not guilty and was held on $500 bail for examination on June 16.

They were indeed different times. If Pat Brown was someone else's relation, what would stand out for me in the story would be the old New York ethnic casting, of Irish cop, German or Jewish judge, and Italian defendants with dubiously spelled names. The bail is extraordinarily high, somewhat understandable for a defendant charged with bribery, but appalling for a man accused of providing beer to laborers. As a Bronx cop, it's somewhat refreshing to see criminal cases treated with firm dispatch, but it is hard to be nostalgic for a system so petty and cruel. My guess is that the bribe was too little, or too late. I wish there was better to say, and more, without offense to ancestral spirits. When a relative came to my father for advice about a newspaper column that he felt was disrespectful to his late brother, my father pointed out that, as a matter of law, you cannot libel the dead. If Pat Brown could not sue, I figured, he was well within his rights to haunt me.

Whenever I find myself in an out-of-the-way part of the city, I like to walk around a bit, or to stop by with relatives or friends whom I haven't seen in a while. If I think about it, I'll know somebody just about anywhere in town. One day I gave John Timpanaro a lift to Kennedy Airport, which put me in the far reaches of Queens on a balmy spring afternoon, so I decided to pay a visit to my great-grandfather. It would be our first meeting. At St. John's Cemetery in Middle Village, I meandered amid groves of marble angels on high pedestals, moneyed and majestic and sentimental, and I could almost feel the cool of the moon-colored stone. I passed a bunkerlike mausoleum that bore the name Profaci, which with some injustice but better luck escaped becoming a brand name of a Mafia branch, now known as Colombo. The brand names are there, too: Colombo, Gambino, and Genovese, and other bosses, like Carmine Galante, who helped organize the French Connection; Salvatore Maranzano, the first "Boss of Bosses," who founded the Commission and the Five Families as Prohibition ended; and Charles "Lucky" Luciano, who became the next and last true Boss of Bosses after killing Maranzano. John Gotti would be buried there, too, in time.

So Paddy the Cop finally got his table at Rao's, I thought, or a spot at the bar at an eternal, underworld Copacabana. I would have gotten along with him, I think, despite myself. New York has always been full of heroes who are hard to like and villains who are hard to hate. My mother and her sisters never spoke with him, in any real sense, but Pat Brown did speak with his daughter-in-law, Marie, by telephone a few times, and she recalls him with some affection. Then again, Marie had a knack for getting along with some very difficult men. My great-aunt Marie Doherty Brown Marcus was a jazz pianist from Boston. While she was still in her teens, her mother brought her down to New York for her first job, at Keen's Chop House, and told her employer, "My daughter is a good Catholic girl, Mister, and if she has any problems here, you'll have me to answer to!"

"Yes, Mrs. Doherty, of course, Mrs. Doherty, she'll be fine here," was the response from Dutch Schultz, perhaps the most murderous gangster of his day. Schultz himself was gunned down not long afterward by his underworld colleagues, after announcing his intention to kill Special Prosecutor Thomas E. Dewey. Schultz was a fairly dour character, as Marie remembers him, though she was thrilled when he included her in his visits to the Cotton Club in Harlem, where she watched her idols Fats Waller—he had given her piano lessons when she was young—Cab Calloway, and other jazz legends play. From there, she went to work for Frank Costello at his Venetian Palace, where, on one early occasion, there was an apparent misunderstanding between them as to the nature of the entertainment she was to provide. He sent her to play at a private party of mobsters at a hotel room, and she was utterly stunned to see the singers remove their gowns before the first verse. When it appeared that one of the hoods expected her to follow suit, she fled the room and went back to the club, where she hunted down Costello and gave him an earful, much as her mother had done Schultz, and he apologized profusely, saying he had no idea it was that kind of party. Once Costello was straightened out, she told me, she had no more problems. She met Lucky Luciano there, and thought Bugsy Siegel a "very nice man," who called her "the Coca-Cola Kid," because that was all she drank. Her public was thick with Public Enemies.

Marie married Jack Brown, and for a time they had an act together in the clubs and hotels of Manhattan and Brooklyn. She played the piano and Jack sang, and when I asked what "their" song was, she laughed and said, "Melancholy Baby," as if it held some clue as to why their marriage was not to last. Few people now recognize that song except as a punch line, but it seems to have been the national anthem for the underworld in its tender moments. At the Venetian Palace, a gangster requested it, and when Marie told him she'd gladly comply, after playing a prior request, he put his cigarette out on her gown. In turn, she broke a chair on his head. Some capo resolved the matter by giving her a hundred dollars. ("The gown only cost five dollars to have made, plus the fabric!" she recalled, triumphantly.) When asked what Dutch Schultz's favorite song was, she told me, "Melancholy Baby." Asked if she ever met Meyer Lansky, she said, "Yes, I'd see him on the beach in Miami, he was a very nice man. Always wanted to hear 'Melancholy Baby.'"

Lost in the cemetery, I grew melancholy as well. A groundskeeper gave me directions to the office, and then gave me a look of pity when he saw me circle past again, a few minutes later. When I found the office, I waited for a woman behind the counter to stop taking calls, though the phone seemed to ring every ten seconds. She seemed like a new or nearly retired teacher, not quite in control of an unruly class. "No, I'm sorry, but no quotes, no hyphens, no nicknames," she said, as if handing back a homework assignment. "I think so, I'm pretty sure, but let me check," she said, putting the caller on hold to check another aspect of post-mortem etiquette. "The father's Catholic and he's in the grave. The mother isn't either—but she's ready to go. Can they go in the grave together?" The answer was yes, as she thought, and I thought it was an easy question. Even a nostalgic one, harking back to a more defined age, with sharper edges. When she had time for me, I told the woman I was looking for Patrick Brown, that he had lived in Brooklyn and died in January 1946. I didn't say why I was there, and she didn't ask, though there was a moment when we both seemed to expect an explanation. I did feel a little guilty, as I was there to work—though whether to dig up Pat Brown, or to bury him again, I wasn't yet sure. She gave me a map that looked like a place mat and traced a route from the office to the grave, filling out the coordinates for section, range, and plot, "8—G—22," in this case.

I found him easily enough, at a green edge of the cemetery, beneath a sycamore tree. Beyond the fence was Woodhaven Boulevard, and a generic commercial strip: gas station, motel, car wash, auto body. He had a modest gray granite stone, polished and clean, with a cross flanked by two camellias. On the lower left side was his name and dates, and on the lower right was space for another. Mom had told me that his second wife, Margaret Cramer

Brown Sullivan, was buried with him, and the absence, the pointed absence, said either that she was buried elsewhere—against her wishes, as my mother recalled them—or that no one had attended to the inscription. I sat down by the grave and intended to say a prayer, but instead found myself daydreaming about things. Was I the first to visit him in twenty years? Thirty? What would he think? I felt like I was there to serve a subpoena. After a while, I went back to my car, but found I had lost my keys; they must have fallen out of my pocket as I sat by the grave. As I walked back, a woman carrying two bouquets of flowers asked me, "Do you work here? Where can I find some water?" I said I didn't work there, and I didn't know. "But I need it for the flowers," she said, as if I might have been holding out on her. Back at the grave, I found my keys and remembered to say a prayer, a Hail Mary and an Our Father, before I took to daydreaming again, if you could call it that, because the day itself was like a dream, pointless and portentous at once: I got lost while looking for my great-grandfather's grave and found his wife missing, and then I forgot to say prayers and my keys were missing, and a woman asked me for water for her flowers because she thought I worked in a graveyard. I wondered if another piece would make the whole thing clear, and then as I reached the path again I met with another item that carries a certain charge of symbolism in my culture: a dead rat. It was not just dead but flattened and skeletonized, softly gray and almost transparent, like a pencil sketch of itself. It was as if a certain ancestor had slipped me a subtle and coded message, and when I did not rise to the challenge, the telegram would have to be sent. *We can do this the hard way or the easy way. . . .*

Back at the office, the woman was surprised to see me again. I explained that my step-great-grandmother was missing, and asked if it was simply a neglected inscription or whether she was with a party named Sullivan, whom I believed to have died in the mid-fifties. At a Catholic cemetery, there is never any shortage of Sullivans, and there was—I won't say digging— some work to do. Two Hispanic women came in, with their place-mat maps, about to ask for directions, and to spare the woman from distraction I took it upon myself to explain how to find the section they were looking for, and how to read the codes on the stones. "You should get a job here," one of them said, and the woman who worked there looked up from her lists of Sullivans to say, "It's yours for the asking." I was glad the woman with the flowers wasn't around. After a while, the deed to the Brown grave was found, and it showed that Margaret was not there; I called my mother to ask her date of death—she died in the eighties, it turned out, at the age of eighty-five—and we were eventually able to ascertain that she was in fact buried with her second husband, John Sullivan, as well as his first wife. I found them—some two hundred yards from Pat Brown—and saw the three names: wife, husband, wife, on a stone almost exactly like Brown's, with a cross and camellias, but twice the size, with a well-tended bed of begonias in front. I sat down there, too, and began to feel indignant, as if I'd found them out. And I also felt bad for Pat Brown, to have been left out altogether. My mother was certain Margaret had intended to be buried with him. On the back of the gravestone were several different names, probably also relatives, but the words had a sneaky look, like the answers to an exam written on the back of the hand. I thought, *This is how it turned out for you, poor Pat: forever with the knuckleheads, stood up by your date.*

. . .

SUCH WAS MY SICK LEAVE, FROM JANUARY THROUGH MAY IN the year 2001, when I became fit again for duty. I had been back at work for three weeks when it appeared that I was due for another change. A friend of a friend had dinner with Police Commissioner Bernard Kerik, and when I got home from work one night, there was a message on the machine. "I talked you up. Don't be surprised if you get a call from Kerik, sooner rather than later," he said. "And don't be worried if you do." I was glad for the warning, because the call from the PC's office to Bronx Narcotics came the next morning. Admin called me at home, and told me I had to report downtown "forthwith." I had a detail that day—a teachers'-union protest outside of City Hall—where my sister Marianne would be among the demonstrators, and I wanted to arrest her. "Go now," they told me. "Forget about showering and shaving, just get there as soon as possible." I did skip the shave, but I showered, as a favor to both of us.

I had never been to the fourteenth floor of One Police Plaza, which housed the offices of the Police Commissioner. I waited in the oak-paneled foyer and uncertainly told the cop at the Desk that I was Officer Conlon, of Narcotics, to see the Commissioner. We looked at each other for a moment. I wondered whether he thought his seat there was a punishment or a privilege. After ten minutes, I was shown inside, through an open work area of cubicles and computers, modern and dully functional as the building itself, and then into the Commissioner's office. The windows were wide and looked out over lower Manhattan, with its towers and lights, its power and money, and the Commissioner sat at the vast carved wooden desk that had belonged to Theodore Roosevelt. He was eating lunch—tuna on pita bread, Diet Coke, I noted—and I wondered whether I was supposed to salute. I wasn't in uniform, and the Commissioner doesn't wear one. I half-saluted, which seemed like a fair compromise.

He nodded and fired off questions:

"Where do you work?"

"Are you happy there?"

"What do you want to do on this Job?"

Narcotics, yes, to be a detective, I told him. He nodded.

"Do you like being a cop?"

"I love it when it doesn't suck, sir."

He nodded again.

"Loyalty is very important to me," he said. "And I trust you. I'd like you to come and work for me—speechwriting, research, whatever else." His chief of staff, John Picciano, walked me out, and said I could take the weekend to think about it. I would come back in on Monday to tell him what I decided. I thanked him, shook his hand, and fled.

I didn't know what to think. While I was honored to be asked, I had become a cop precisely to avoid work that entailed a suit, a commute, and a cubicle. At the same time, the speed of the offer showed that there was no real definition of my duties, and that offered room to maneuver. I had recently run into an acquaintance who told me he was working in an arson unit out of Headquarters. As far as I knew, only the fire marshals investigated suspicious fires, but it showed that there were all kinds of interesting things happening downtown of which I knew nothing. There were any number of small, specialized details that were created—the Art Squad, Hostage Negotiations, even a one-man team who investigated cases that involved Santería—because the right cop had the right idea, and the right boss listened. That was a possibility, I thought. It was also possible that my duties would primarily consist of licking stamps.

At the office the next day, Chief Tiffany drew me aside on the way in. "C'mere, Eddie," he said, with a puzzled look. When Admin had told me to report to the PC, I wanted to keep it quiet, and so I told them to say that I was called in for a random drug test. In retrospect, it was not a clever story, because it didn't so much cover the real reason as much as mingle with it, and the rumor thus circulated that the Police Commissioner personally wanted to test my urine. After I explained, the chief laughed and said, "I didn't think you were in any trouble. Let me know what you decide, but I don't think it would be good for you to say no."

On Monday morning, on the drive down to Police Headquarters, I happened to look down at my clothing. In my haste, it seemed that I had put on a black suit jacket and a pair of blue pants. On the fourteenth floor, there was the same wary exchange of glances with the cop at the desk—"What is this guy about?"—and I was sent in to see Chief Picciano. I must have had the look on my face of a kid who was sent to the principal, because he spent five minutes reassuring me that I wouldn't be in trouble if I declined the offer. Like a lot of outer-borough street cops, I believed in some inconvertibly primitive place in my heart that there was a catapult on the roof of One Police Plaza, and that if you crossed someone who was influential, they launched you through the air to Staten Island, where you landed on the pavement in a uniform that was too small, and you spent the remainder of your career on a corner, watching empty buses pass.

"Yes, sir," I said.

"You wouldn't actually be working for me or the Commissioner," he said. "You'd work for Deputy Inspector Rising. Let me take you to meet him."

"Yes, sir," I said.

Chief Picciano dropped me off at DI Rising's office, where I glanced around for the catapult as I thanked him.

"Listen, relax!" he said. "Don't worry about it—you're not in trouble!"

"Yes, sir."

But I was in trouble: too much good luck can be the same as bad luck, I knew. When I worked at CCJA, the office had a case of a guy who had his troubles with drugs, did his time, and then cleaned up and went home. For years, he worked as a truck driver, getting by, honestly but barely. One night on his way to work, he stopped at a bank machine and crossed his fingers. He knew that he had just over or just under twenty dollars in his account, and if it was $19.75 he'd be screwed, but if he had $20.25, he could take out the bill, buy some gas and food, and get through the day. He closed his eyes when he punched in the request for the twenty, and felt dizzy with relief when the cash slid out of the machine. When he checked his balance, he could barely stand: a bank error had put more than fifty thousand dollars in his account.

He didn't go to work that day, nor did he for many days afterward, and shortly he met a woman who convinced him that the habit he had abandoned almost a decade before was more than supportable for a man of his newfound means. So it was that through his extraordinary good fortune he became a client of Consultants for Criminal Justice Alternatives.

Deputy Inspector Rising was friendly and polite, but I'd been deposited in his office like an extra filing cabinet; in time, he'd find a place for me, but at the moment I was taking up space. I said that I'd always been a street cop, and that I had my reservations about working in an office. I said that I was due for my detective shield in a couple of months, and that I didn't want to derail my investigative time for this assignment, no matter what.

"As a matter of civil-service law," he explained kindly, "the PC can make you a detective tomorrow. It's purely discretionary.

"Another thing you should know is that the Commissioner doesn't really speak from prepared text. He happens to be a good speaker. At a funeral, he'll stick close to a written speech, but he's good off the cuff, and what I try to do for him is to set out five or six talking points he should make, and he takes it from there."

"Oh."

I had never heard the Commissioner speak. On the news, commissioners only seemed to say, "There will be a thorough investigation," which I'd never written before, but I supposed I was up to the task.

"So offhand, I thought of a couple of things you might do. You're in Narcotics, and the PC worked in Narcotics, and so whatever you might be able to bring to the table in terms of policy, we'd be happy to hear. In terms of more concrete things, one is that when a cop gets a Letter of Commendation, you could personalize it—make the cop know that we really understood and appreciated what they did, instead of just sending a thank-you card for stopping a bank robbery. The other is that you could write letters to the Parole Board, when cop killers are up for parole. That happens a lot more than you think, and it's an important thing that these cops who gave their lives are not forgotten or overlooked."

These were valid points, and important tasks, and my heart sank to hear them. I doubted that a real policy role would emerge, not least because I didn't have any big new ideas, which left letter-writing in the portfolio of tasks. But I liked DI Rising, and I thought that maybe there was space to improvise. I said, "I don't know if this work is going to take three hours a week, or sixty. But in my gut—and this is why I do this, why I am a cop—I have to have the opportunity to do some kind of enforcement work, so that if there's some down time—one day a week, four and a half days a week, however it works out—I get to go outside. It's an honor to work for the Commissioner, and I would never say no to him, but it just wouldn't work for anybody if I stopped being a cop."

DI Rising said that he had worked for Chief Tiffany, too, and he understood why I would be reluctant to leave. I trusted Rising, but I didn't want to work at Headquarters. It might be important, but it just didn't sound like police work.

And so I talked to my consiglieri: Inspector Mullen first, who told me, "Did you ever hear the expression, 'This is an offer you can't refuse?' This is that offer. Don't say no. Even though they say there won't be recriminations, there may be recriminations, just because someone else is pissed off that you had the PC's ear for ten seconds. More importantly, this is an opportunity— go have a look at Headquarters, at the largest and most important department in the world. Do it. Why not? If you're on the Job for life, this is an opportunity that might not come around again. Go ahead. And did I say that this is an offer that you can't refuse?"

Chief Tiffany agreed, and Capt. Mahony put it even more bluntly: "Listen, Timothy McVeigh is gonna have a longer shelf life than this guy. Go there, suck it up no matter what, and in six months, you work wherever you want to." As it happened, Kerik did survive McVeigh, but the point was taken. If you were a soldier, you were a soldier, and whether you were told to stand at attention for twenty hours or to write love letters for the PC, you did what you were told. Rising had left open the possibility that I could find some enforcement work, my other duties permitting. In my head, a jingle began to ring:

Commissioner Kerik is the mightiest of men,
If you do a push-up, he will do ten . . .

And I put it out of my mind. When I told Lt. Zerbo, he thought for a moment and said, "You're a douche bag."

I laughed. I hadn't quite expected to hear that, but time would tell if it was true.

"A douche bag. Look at you, and look at him. He should be working for you."

It was one of the more roundabout compliments I'd received, but I'd take it.

My first day of work would be the next Tuesday, after Memorial Day, when I would accompany Rising and the Commissioner to the Police Academy graduation to get a sense of Kerik's speaking style. Friday would be my last day of B&B, and on Thursday night, we all went out for a farewell dinner. Most of the people who had left the team did so without even a handshake—Leibowitz went to Queens, Nugent to midnights—but I liked my teammates and bosses, and I was determined to commemorate the occasion. I had been happy there, and I took my reluctance to leave as a sign that I was destined to, because if I'd been as desperate to go as I had been at the PSA, the departure would have been postponed for months.

It was not a late night, but B&B began the next morning at seven, and we all felt it a little. A foot pursuit into a project on One-Four-Six helped get the blood running, and I was almost feeling normal again when the base raised Clune on the radio, telling him that I had to call the Commissioner's office, forthwith. I was driving him, and he gave me a worried look as he relayed the message. When I called DI Rising, his tone was grim.

"You better get down here right away," he said.

"Uh, we're in the middle of B&B," I said. I wondered if it was the wrong thing to say; maybe at One Police Plaza, they considered the wishes of the Commissioner to have priority over the next three crack vials from Courtlandt Avenue.

"All right," he said. "Get down as soon as you finish up."

I didn't want to leave it at that, as the conspiracy theories ricocheted in my skull.

"Can you tell me what's going on?"

"I don't think this is going to work out."

I thought again: What had I done? I didn't have a dead hooker in the trunk of my car, did I? Maybe they reviewed the file footage of my second interview, and noticed the mismatched pants and jacket. What had happened in the two days since we'd last shaken hands?

"Is there anything I should know?"

There was a pause, and then he said, "No, it's nothing you did. But I don't think it's gonna work out. Just get down here."

Clune made a remark about a refund for my farewell dinner. We hit a couple more sets and I headed downtown.

DI Rising was mercifully blunt: "I hope you didn't go out and buy a bunch of suits, but this isn't going to happen. I'm sorry, I was looking forward to it, I hope you were too. Basically, down here we don't just have to think about what's right and what's real, but how things look. The PC signed a book deal last week, and for you to come here now makes it look like you're going to write it for him. We can't have it. Believe me, I'm sorry, I'm embarrassed and the Commissioner feels bad about it too. I hope you didn't make any big arrangements."

"Well, we did have my farewell dinner last night."

"The Commissioner wants to make it up to you. Do you want to go anywhere? I can't promise the Joint Terrorism Task Force, but . . ."

He left it hanging like that, and I said, "Can I think about it over the weekend?"

"Sure."

I shook his hand and left. I was ecstatic: I was getting alimony, and I never even had to kiss the guy. I called Clune to say we'd have to set up a welcome-back dinner, and then another farewell right afterward. I also called Timpanaro and told him to start thinking about what we should ask for—we'd talked about working together again, but the opportunity never seemed to arise. Now, it might: Rising had offered a big favor, but maybe I could make it two slightly smaller ones. Or two big ones.

My friend Brian McCabe was a sergeant at Manhattan South Homicide, and he had told me that after I got my shield, I should think about coming to work for him. Compared to the Bronx, Manhattan South had relatively few homicides, but whatever they had tended to be high-profile. You would catch glimpses of Brian on the news for the perp-walk in cases like the Carnegie Deli murders, where five people were shot, three fatally, during the robbery of a marijuana dealer. Manhattan South Homicide also worked like the old Confidential Squads for the Chief of Detectives, in that they filled in and helped out whenever some situation presented itself—the theft of an antique Torah, the escape of a dangerous prisoner—and the chief wanted special attention to be paid.

But I had to wonder: if I was murdered, would I want someone like me to catch the case? Maybe they could start me off with something easy, a practice murder, in which the victim wasn't quite dead, or the killer hadn't quite left. They could wean me on easy manslaughters until I cut my teeth. In answer to my question, I thought, Yes, if I was killed, I would be content to have someone like me assigned to the case, even now. But how much better would it be later? When I called Brian, he was a little cool to the idea, explaining that the rumor was that his Squad was going to be cut, and that for me to arrive—with a white shield, no less—while others were facing eviction could be complicated. Now was not the time. I thought again, and asked him what he thought about Manhattan Robbery. He said that it was a fine idea.

The Manhattan Robbery office was on 12th Street, but it covered the entire borough from the Battery to Inwood. Homicide was an "assist" squad, working in collaboration with the precinct detective who caught the case, whereas Robbery took over cases themselves, usually if a pattern was established where crimes crossed precinct lines. If a liquor store on East Eighty-sixth Street was held up, the case went to a 19th Precinct detective, but if the same perps hit a liquor store on West Eighty-sixth Street, in the 20th Precinct, and a bar on Thirty-eighth, in Midtown South, it was designated a pattern and assigned to Manhattan Robbery. "You'll get real bad guys, real good cases," said Brian. "And you'll get to be in Manhattan. How many years have you been in the South Bronx now? Maybe it's time for a change."

Though it seemed that John planned a different career every week—he had in mind the boss route, through the sergeant's exam, but also a detective's shield, and law school, but also maybe the Fire Department, or a better-paid cop job on Long Island—there was one thing of which he was certain: he was tired of PSA-7. Anti-Crime had made a number of gun collars through the winter, largely though his work, but they'd been dry for months. He cast about for some outlet for his competitive drive, and one day, he announced a victory in a field that I am sure no one had ever thought to view as a contest: the Adopt-A-Senior program, in which cops volunteered to help the elderly. "I kicked ass!" he crowed. "You shoulda seen these old ladies, there was a busload of 'em. Most of 'em, forget about it—they whined, or they smelled, or they just sat there, like nothing. But there was one great one, Mrs. B, and I snapped her right up. What a nice lady! And so clean! You shoulda seen the other guys, they were so mad!"

John wanted to go to a precinct Robbery Squad—a RAM, or Robbery Apprehension Module, which the busier squads maintained as a separate unit—specifically, in the Four-Four, which had always been among the busiest in the city. The Integrity Review Board continued to assure him that something was in the works, but two years had passed since that promise had been made. More important, the Police Commissioner had recently revived the "upstairs route" to the Squads, telling each precinct CO to select three cops for the Detective Bureau. It had been a traditional means of ascent for the hardest-working cops to move from patrol to a team like SNEU or Anti-Crime, and then upstairs to the Squad, where a shield was awarded after eighteen months. It was a sensible progression, in that the cop knew the terrain, and I never understood why it had been discontinued. For all my problems with the CO of PSA-7, I respected his choices for the Detective Bureau: Tony Marcano was the first, and he went to the Four-Two Squad in the fall. Timpanaro and Eddie Wynne were the next two names, though the rumors placed one first, then the next, but neither moved as winter turned to spring. Mike Shea—then a precinct commander on the Upper West Side—told me that all three of the cops he'd recommended were already gone. We didn't know whether it was because the Housing Bureau was given second-class status, or because PSA-7 was, or if there was some other complication, but after eight months, there had been no movement for either John or Eddie Wynne. John didn't take long to say that Manhattan Robbery sounded fine to him.

At the same time, I reminded him that we had been made offers before, and they hadn't come through. A year and a half before, just before John had gone to Vice, we went out to a party in Manhattan, where I saw a man at the edge of the crowd with a familiarly watchful manner. I whispered to John, "Look at him—I bet he's a cop."

John said, "Good eye you got there. He happens to be Joe Dunne, the Chief of the Department."

"Well, I was right, then, wasn't I?"

As it happened, John was friends with someone Dunne knew, and he went over to say hello. Ordinarily, I wouldn't have followed, but as this was my root-canal phase, I walked so closely behind him that he poked me in the eye when he pointed back to introduce me.

We wound up having a few drinks together, and Chief Dunne asked us where we worked, and we explained that we were partners, but there had been an administrative mishap with my transfer to Vice. He offered to take care of it, and wrote down my name. I felt lottery-ticket lucky, and wondered why I was wasting such a great favor on such a small matter. But when that night ended, I worked in SNEU for another month, and on midnights for six, and another five in Narcotics before I got a call from his office, asking me if everything was all right. "Now it is, yeah," I said. Chief Dunne was a highly respected thirty-year veteran, and since he was responsible for the safety of eight million people, my temporary transfer should have been on page 5000 of his "To do" list. Still, the offer was made, and I was disappointed.

A few weeks after the party, on a midnight, Stix and I guarded an empty apartment for eight hours again, watching the roaches on the walls and discussing the unnatural aspects of breakfast at night. When we finished talking about that, Stix decided we ought to talk some more, to pass the time. "It's all who you know," he ventured. "That's the lousiest thing about the politics on this job."

I spat on the wall at a cockroach. "If only that was true!"

And so with the new offer from the PC, I told John that it looked as good as these things got, but you never really knew until it happened. When I wrote to DI Rising to say that I wanted Manhattan Robbery for both of us, he wrote back to say that he hadn't expected it to be a "two-fer," but that he'd do what he could.

. . .

IN THE MEANTIME, WE WAITED, ME IN NARCOTICS AND John at the PSA. He had run into our old CI, Christmas, in the holding cells. He took her phone number and passed it along to me, and Pops spoke with Sgt. Rhoden about giving her a pass if his team only saw her trespassing. She was not much the worse for wear after the two years since I'd last seen her. She was housewifey, in an odd, rundown way, and it was easier to picture her in a bathrobe, rye and soda in hand, dusting the knickknack shelf as she wept at the soap opera, than it was to imagine her scoring crack in the projects. Nonetheless, Christmas began to work again with enthusiasm, making buys every week. The first warrant she gave us was for a 350-pound woman who sold heroin. "She's a big woman, in a dress like a tent."

"JD Tent she is, then."

When we hit the door, she lay sprawled in her bed, bare naked with her legs spread, and the team nearly turned around without searching the apartment. Other warrants followed: Christmas was working on crack spots, weed spots, and dope spots for me, and she could hardly keep track of them. Christmas was ditzily affectionate and absentminded, like an elderly aunt who kept looking for the handkerchief she kept in her hand. Her voice was nasal and Noo-Yawky, and her thoughts left her mouth as soon as they entered her head.

One Saturday afternoon, we sent her out on a few routine buys. Clune and I sat off in the middle of a quiet block of warehouses, in a car with tinted windows, waiting for her to return. As she emptied her bra of crack and heroin, a thought occurred to her.

"Oh, yeah! Ah, I meant to ask you guys but it slipped my mind. Are you interested in guns and shootings and stuff, or only drugs?"

Clune and I looked at each other.

"Sure, we cover guns and all kinds of things. Why do you ask?"

"Well, you remember how I told you about Shaka?"

"Yeah, he sells crack, green tops over on One-Five-Three."

"Right, so anyway, I went over to his place the other morning, and he was out of 'work,' but he said that he was having a fight with his mother over his girlfriend, because she was staying there and anyway, he says he can't keep his gun in the house anymore, and he wants *me* to keep it. So anyway, I say my husband, Louie, he's very old-fashioned, and he wouldn't want the gun in the house, especially because my mother-in-law is so nosy, you know? I mean, she's a very nice lady, but—"

"Christmas?"

"I mean, she is my mother-in-law, and Louie is very straitlaced, and—"

"Christmas?"

"You know, I hope she doesn't stay so long this time. I mean, the apartment's in her name, but still—"

"Christmas?"

"Yes, Eddie?"

"Where's the gun?"

"Oh, the gun, it's in the bedroom closet, but I can't keep it there. If Louie knew, oh my God, I bet he'd throw me out!"

"You're right, Christmas, you can't keep it there. You have to give us the gun."

"All right, I'll go get it."

"Hold on a second."

Clune and I thought for a moment, and asked, "What's Shaka gonna say when he comes back for the gun?"

"Oh, that's no problem, I'll just tell him Louie threw it out."

We thought again.

"That's not a good story, Christmas. Tell us a little more about Shaka, why don't you?"

"Oh, he's all right. I mean, I don't think I have to worry about him."

"Well, he does sell crack for a living, and we know at least that he used to carry a gun. What's to keep him from getting another one and using it on you?"

"I guess."

"Tell you what—the best way to do it is, you come out of the building and we stop you and pretend to lock you up. There'll be a crowd, they'll see everything, Shaka is gonna hear. That way, he owes you a favor, instead of you owing him a gun, you follow? You have to lie low for a day, maybe stay at your daughter's or somewhere, and then it's all over."

She pursed her lips and frowned.

"I don't think so, Eddie. You know, I don't *like* getting locked up."

"That's the thing, Christmas, I'm not sure you heard me. We wouldn't *actually* lock you up, we'd just take you away so it *looked* like you got locked up. I know it might be a pain in the ass to have to disappear for a day, but in the long term, it's a lot less aggravation."

She shook her head. "No, my mother-in-law, she would not want to hear about my getting locked up, and Louie—forget about it. I'm not gonna do that, I can't. I'll just tell Shaka I lost it."

For Christmas, an arrest was a routine occurrence. It had happened to her fifty times in her life, two or three times a year in the last twenty years, and it was a waiting-in-line kind of aggravation, like other people experience in holiday traffic. You don't like it but you deal with it, and if you can't, you should skip the beach trip on the Fourth of July, or the in-laws in Jersey on Christmas, or the crack dealer's every day. And though I saw that she was being childishly stubborn, petulant in her refusal to accept a small inconvenience to avoid a threat to her life, I didn't have it in me at the moment to push her hard. She looked like a little old lady, and I didn't want to make her cry.

"How about this, then. You tell Shaka that Louie found out, or he was about to, and you had to get the gun out of the house right away. You were taking it over to his place, and you saw cops in the building, so you had to ditch it."

"I'll say I threw it out the window."

"No, you won't say you threw it out the window. Do those projects have windows in the stairwells? You threw it down the trash-compactor chute, that way it's gone for good, and it's still on him, if you tell the story right— you did him a favor, and you almost got jammed up for it."

"Oh, okay!"

And then we let her out of the car to go home to collect the gun. She returned in fifteen minutes with a little black knapsack, slipping into the back seat of the van. She handed the pack forward and Clune took it, gingerly, and handed it to me. I opened it and there was a .45 pistol and a box of ammunition, each wrapped in a bandanna. We gave her money and sent her home. We had a crime but no case, and while getting the gun off the street was the primary task, I wasn't content to leave it at that.

Nor was Christmas, however, and she took it upon herself to open up new avenues of prosecution. The next week, she called me, hysterical:

"He's going to kill me!"

"Who?"

"Shaka!"

"What happened?"

"I was sitting in front of my building with my girlfriend, and he came up to me and said, 'Yo, I need that thing back.' And I said, 'All right, lets go upstairs and get it.'"

As far as I recalled, that was not what she had been instructed to say. I was interested in hearing her improvisation, and I didn't doubt that, as she walked Shaka through the graffiti-covered and trash-strewn lobby and rode the elevator upstairs, she might surprise herself. They entered the apartment and she led him to the bedroom, where she made a show of searching the closet.

"Oh my God! I can't believe it! It's gone!"

I bet she clapped both hands to her cheeks. "What did he say?" I asked.

"Oh, it was bad! He was cursing and he said he was gonna kill me! 'I got no problems taking out a woman,' he said, and he demanded to know what happened to the gun, I had to get it back. I said my brother was here over the weekend, he musta taken it."

"Do you have a brother?"

"Yeah."

"Does Shaka know where he lives?"

"No, that's no problem, he's straight, never in trouble, and he lives in Virginia. But Shaka told me I better come up with the gun, or I have to come up with six hundred dollars to pay him for it. Can you get me the money?"

"What I gotta do is think. What you gotta do is what I tell you. Remember last week, I told you we'd pretend to lock you up, and that would have solved the problem? And you wouldn't do it? And then we came up with another story, and you said you'd do that, and you didn't? And now we got a big fucking mess to deal with. You know what I'm saying?"

She agreed with me, weeping. What a dingbat, I thought. And she was my guide into the criminal underworld. If she'd been leading Dante, he'd be lucky to get into Hell, let alone out of it. I told my bosses, and the consensus was that we'd just have to move her: we weren't going to pay for a gun that we already owned.

I had a few ideas: What if we have Christmas call Shaka to say her brother gave her the gun back? We set up an exchange, she gives him the gun, empty, and we jump Shaka when he takes it?

What if he has ammunition?

"Okay, what if we take the gun to the range and disable it, take out the firing pin?"

What if we lose him during the takedown? And then, what if he gets the gun fixed?

"Okay, how about . . ."

Capt. Mahony said, "So this shemp wants his gun back? What do you suppose he wants it for? And with the six hundred, don't you suppose he's gonna pick up another piece? I haven't looked this rule up lately, but I don't think the Police Department is supposed to be in the business of buying guns for crack dealers. Nah, the only thing to do is to move her."

If a witness or an informant is threatened, we can put someone up in a motel for a few days or a few weeks, but more permanent accommodations are arranged through the DA. I thought Christmas's viability as an informant was coming to an end, and that we would have to eventually relocate her, but I didn't want to go through all that effort without a collar to show for it. I had an idea: Why didn't we supply her with the felonious brother she'd fabricated? There was an undercover who worked in another precinct, who could arguably pass for a relative of Christmas—though I wouldn't stress that aspect when I told him about the case—couldn't we send him in as her brother, wearing a wire?

Capt. Mahony was averse to that, too: it wasn't an ordinary gun buy, Shaka was coming in angry, feeling like he got ripped off, and the risk was too high. If he escaped, or if something went wrong, there would be too much to explain. The objections were all valid, and I couldn't override them. I did like the idea of fabricating a character to fit my addled informant's offhand lie, and I suppose it was a good thing she didn't claim the .45 was taken by the Gun Fairy.

And so I went to see Sam Ramer. He liked the case, and he said he'd run it by Ed Friedenthal to see if they'd take it. Ed Friedenthal said, "So you want us to pay for a gun we already own, huh? Well, why not?" He set up a meeting with the DA's investigators.

There were two DA's Squads, one of which comprised active NYPD officers assigned to the office, and another of investigators employed by the DA, many of whom were retired cops. We would work primarily with Frank Viggiano and Rocco Galasso, both of whom were retired NYPD. Rocco had worked as an undercover in the 1980s, and he volunteered to become Christmas's brother. I didn't know Rocco well enough to make any jokes about the family resemblance, but his colleagues were kind enough to pick up the slack.

We sat down with Inspector Nasta, who had just retired from Bronx Narcotics, Viggiano, Galasso, Ramer, and a few others, and went over the scenario. Shaka had priors for robbery and drug sales, and there had been a lot of shootings recently in the project where Shaka lived, and while he was not known as a major player, he sold crack in a competitive market, and he felt the need for a gun. A .45 had been used in a recent homicide there. It was proposed that Rocco try to buy crack from Shaka, as the gun sale was only a D felony, while drug sales were a B. I also said that I thought we had Grand Larceny, a C felony, as Shaka had threatened to kill her when he demanded money, which was the legal definition of extortion. It was decided that Rocco would call Shaka first, and we'd tape the conversation.

"So that's the setup," I said. "I don't know what you'd call it, exactly."

Several voices in the room said, "It's a reverse sting."

At least I wouldn't be in the pawn shop like my father, with my finger in my pocket, pretending to have a gun. But as soon as the plans were in place, Christmas began to make changes.

I brought her in to Sam's office, and we were going over the story when she corrected me on a detail: "No, Shaka didn't say he'd kill me, Eddie, he said he'd beat me up."

That was relevant, and at a certain level, I was glad to hear it. I pointed out, "You told me he'd kill you, when you called me the first time. You remember, 'I got no problems taking out a woman. . . .' What did you think he meant, dinner and a movie?"

"Did I say that? Well, you know, I was very upset. I think all he meant was he'd beat me up. Also, he'd tell Louie, which would be real, real bad—he'd throw me out, I know it, and—"

"Okay, we gotcha."

We looked up the statute. Threat of death was downgraded to threat of physical injury, a class C to a class D, no worse than the gun possession or sale. But for the final charges, we'd have to see what Shaka said on the tape, and what he did if he agreed to meet with Rocco.

And then the process of arranging a new life for Christmas began, setting up a new apartment, reapplying for welfare, and arranging for a treatment program, which didn't interest her at all. In fact, she didn't think there was much wrong with her old life, aside from the business with Shaka. It suited me, too, in its way. When I first signed her up, I told her that she didn't have permission to do anything with drugs, other than what she did for us—if she was caught for anything on her own time, it was her problem. Often, she'd run to pick up heroin or crack for a neighbor, sometimes as much as two or three hundred dollars' worth, for which she'd be given a couple of vials. She made no effort to conceal these activities, but I'd learn of them only as absentminded afterthoughts, and she broadly construed this kind of thing as field work, which of course it was. OCCB guidelines took an altogether narrower view, but if addicts quit just because I told them to, I could eliminate half the crime in this country without getting up from my couch. I didn't worry about Christmas hurting anyone but herself, but that was an abiding concern.

A few days later, she called me again, in tears. "I can't move, I don't want to, I don't care. . . ." The prospect of leaving husband and home now seemed unbearable. Her safety was my concern; her happiness was not, especially since it seemed to depend on the freedom to buy drugs in the neighborhood she knew best. She met Shaka on the street, she said, and he hadn't threatened her: "As a matter of fact, he was real friendly, real nice to me. Like before."

I asked her, "Why? What did you tell him?"

"I told him I'd give him the six hundred dollars on Friday."

"Do you have six hundred dollars to give him on Friday?"

"No."

"So what are you going to do on Friday?"

"I thought I'd go to my daughter's in Jersey for the weekend."

I didn't argue with her. Christmas was a quintessential crackhead: the next ten minutes were the only ones that counted. She had bought herself a weekend of peace, and she would deal with Monday when Monday came. And when it did, I knew that Shaka would persuade her to cooperate far more effectively than I could have.

On Monday night, she called me again, crying. Shaka had seen her when she returned from her daughter's house. They were no longer friends, it seemed. Christmas had told him that her brother from Virginia would be coming back, and they could work it out with each other. We were back in play.

We set up the phone call in a small room at the DA's Squad, with Christmas, Sam, and Rocco. Rocco had been an extraordinary undercover, and more than a few cops told me stories about times when dealers had held guns to Rocco's head. Not all of the dealers had survived, but Rocco clearly had. For Rocco, this caper was light exercise, and all the more fun because it had been a while since he'd had a chance to stretch. We all felt an exhilaration, reminded of how much like play our work could be, that even when it was life-threatening, it could have the goofy freedom of summer camp.

I turned on the recorder and headed the tape, "The time is fifteen hundred hours on July 12, 2001. This is Police Officer Conlon, shield number 9786, of Bronx Narcotics, along with Lieutenant Rocco Galasso of the Bronx DA's Squad, and a confidential informant, dialing number . . . for the purposes of a monitored conversation."

The number for the cellular customer you have called is no longer in service. . . .

"The time now is fifteen-oh-two hours, on July . . ."

I handed the phone to Christmas, but a little girl answered. "Nah, Shaka's not here now. Maaaa? Do you know when he's getting home?"

Another call, not long after: "The time now is fifteen thirty hours . . ."

When they spoke, Shaka wasn't happy. I listened on another extension, with the mouthpiece off, so he couldn't hear me breathe. Shaka took a tough stance:

"We got a problem, me and you, and bad things are gonna happen if you don't fix it. There's gonna be big problems, if you don't get me the gun, or the money. . . ."

It was a good beginning, but he hadn't talked himself into the charges yet: "my gun," or "the gun I gave you to hold," would determine possession more clearly, and while "bad things" was better than "big problems," the threats were vague. Christmas said that her brother was here, and that the two of them had to deal with each other now; Shaka refused, but he didn't hang up when Rocco got on the phone: "Hey, Shaka, what's up? What's going on with you and my sister?"

And so began a strange conversation. Shaka was a lot less tough. Rocco sounded as Virginian as Sonny Corleone. Rocco told Shaka that he had no business getting his sister involved with guns; Shaka said that no one had forced Christmas to do anything, and now someone owed him the gun or the money. Rocco said the price was too high—he was from Virginia, and guns were cheap there. Shaka asked why he took his gun, then, if he could get them so easily—good point, that—and Rocco said that a friend had sudden need of it. Shaka got scared: "What if he does something with it, and it gets back to me! What if he does something with my gun?"

That worked. Rocco turned it around: "Don't worry about it, I wiped it clean, nothing can get back to you. What about my friend, though—is anything you did with it gonna get back to him?"

Shaka said it wouldn't, which was disappointing but not conclusive. He said he wanted his money, now. Rocco said he couldn't do that, just yet. Shaka seemed to find a measure of courage as he thought about the money, and we wanted to get him stoked up, to make threats on tape, without putting Christmas in further danger.

Rocco went on. "Listen, Shaka, I'm gonna get you the money, but six hundred's too much. And besides, I got things to do for a couple of days, things to do with people, but I gotta know if my sister's gonna be okay—this is between you and me now, and we'll straighten things out—but I can't worry about her. Shaka, you gotta tell me if I got anything to worry about."

"We got problems. She owes me money. I ain't gonna say what's gonna happen if you don't set things straight."

"C'mon, Shaka, don't play games with me. Me and you gonna have problems, you threaten my sister, arright?"

There was a pause, and Shaka sounded like a sly and nasty ten-year-old brat. "I might have to tell Louie. . . ." Rocco and I made the same face: what a pussy, what a loser, what a piece of shit. That's the threat the crack dealer makes when you take away his .45: *I'm telling on your sister, she's gonna get in trouble. . . .*

And he even backed off that threat, as Rocco alluded to the people he had to see, the things he had to do, that would delay the payment for a few days.

"What people?"

"Shaka—*people,* you know?"

"What things?"

"You know—*things.* Things . . . *with friends . . .*"

It did sound ominous. We all were impressed. Shaka gradually warmed to Rocco—he was excited by him and afraid of him, and it looked like he was finally going to see some money. An hour before, he didn't even believe that this bizarre redneck-mafioso character even existed, and now they were in business together. They made an appointment to meet in two days, with four hundred dollars. Even Christmas was delighted with the show, and took to referring to Rocco as her brother so naturally that I felt compelled to ask, "You do realize, Christmas, that Rocco is not your brother?"

"Oh yeah, I know . . . but I want to get used to talking like he is."

"That's fine, I just have to make sure that we're on the same page."

We worked through lunch, and Sam ordered from a nearby diner for us, where the DA's Office had an account. He asked Christmas what she wanted to drink.

"That's okay, Sam, she brought a beer," I said. The bottle cap had set off the metal detector downstairs when I'd brought her in. Sam suggested that she save the beer for later.

I could have used one, too. No matter how it concluded, I would be stuck with Christmas afterward, and I still thought we'd have to move her. Even if Shaka didn't have her killed, there would be others happy to rid the neighborhood of an informant. And I knew that Christmas would feel the pull of home again, once Shaka was behind bars. We couldn't force her to go anywhere, or to stay away. I'm still not sure if it was for my benefit or Christmas's, but I worked out a twist for the last act.

We set up a tac plan, readying our radios, cars, kels, binoculars, and vests. We drove out to the projects and set up in position. There was apprehension as Rocco waited, and we listened to the OP narrate Shaka's approach.

"Okay, he's coming down the block, he sees Rock, he's up to him—it's okay."

"Okay? Does he look pissed?"

"Nah, he hugged him."

Viggiano reported the next conversation from over the kel: "He didn't bring him any crack, the lazy bastard! I could come up with ten vials in fifteen minutes in this neighborhood!"

Rocco handed him the money, and we swept in. Shaka looked stunned, and betrayed—*Holy shit! What the fuck!*—but as he was cuffed and thrown over the hood of the car, he saw that Rocco was in cuffs, too. And Rocco seemed to be getting worse treatment than he was—*It's over, now, scumbag! We gotcha!*—as they were whisked away, in separate cars.

Shaka was taken to a room at the DA's Squad, and left to imagine what great conspiracy he had stumbled into. When we confronted him, it was less of an interrogation than a kind of guided meditation on La Cracker Nostra:

"Do you have any idea who you've been dealing with?"

"This is big-time! Interstate! Federal! You're not in a precinct, are you?"

"This goes way beyond you! This goes deep!"

"We've been on to this guy for a long time, Shaka."

"The Virginia Mafia! Nobody fucks with them!"

"We got him in a room down the hall—this guy gave up his own sister! You're lucky you got out alive!"

Shaka didn't know what to believe, and held his head in his hands. We staged another, highly visible arrest of Christmas later that afternoon, so word would leak back to him in jail. I tried to imagine Shaka's conversation with his lawyer, as he tried to explain the garbled cabal. The lawyer must have considered an insanity defense; she had a highly puzzled expression when she approached Sam Ramer to ask what had happened. Sam rolled his eyes in a bored, heard-that-before dismissal and offered eighteen months. The lawyer went back to Shaka and gave him her advice. He took the plea, and Christmas went home to Louie.

. . .

THE WEEKS PASSED, AND I BEGAN TO WONDER ABOUT THE delay at Headquarters. Now and then, I'd check in with DI Rising, and he'd allude to the political complexities of the placement. The PC could put me anywhere, I knew, but I also knew there was more to it, and the last thing I wanted was to be dropped in a place where I wasn't wanted. I'd landed softly at Narcotics because people knew me there, from cops to the chief, and I hadn't forgotten the last miserable year at the PSA. It didn't take much to make things hard, and I could wait until things were right.

John's frustrations rose and fell, and we were soon reminded that a job change was not always for the better. My cousin Brian was a firefighter now, and that June, on Father's Day, his house in Queens lost three men fighting a conflagration at a hardware store, started by two kids who knocked over drums of gas in an alley. The scope of the loss seemed unimaginable—three men in one day, from one house—and firefighters from all over the country attended the funeral. John didn't talk much about his lost opportunity to go to FD, and eventually he wouldn't count it among his regrets. I had to laugh when he was passed over for a job in a Long Island police department, if only because his sister was offered a position. His sister Barbara is a wonderful person, the mother of three children, but prone to announcements such as, "I could never arrest an Italian, and besides, if I saw any criminal, I'd run the other way." Like most departments, the NYPD sets a minimal academic standard, after which they try to weed out the demonstrably unfit through a psychological exam and background checks. The Long Island department had instead hired consultants to develop a hodgepodge profile for their ideal candidate, who would be married instead of single and preferred math to reading; the New Haven police had adopted a similar strategy and made headlines for their refusal to hire a candidate on the grounds of excessive intelligence. I laughed a lot less when John told me that the Long Island job would have effectively doubled his salary. But in mid-July, as I was in the thick of my Christmas carol, John got his own present: he was picked for the RAM, and was assigned to the Four-Four. That could work out, we figured— he'd know what he was doing with a robbery case, and he could teach me when we got to Manhattan Robbery.

That was a hard summer at Narcotics. There were no public controversies, as there had been with Dorismond and Ferguson the year before, but two cops died in a private horror. A male undercover had dated a female undercover on his team, and when she broke it off, he went to her house and killed her before turning the gun on himself. We'd all known the male undercover from PSA-7, and liked him—he'd been a good cop, effective on the street, cool and low-key in person. Sammy had worked with him at Narcotics. Pop told me that IAB would be watching the funeral, and anyone who went to his wake on job time or in uniform would be written up—he wasn't a cop anymore, he was a cop killer, and no official tribute could be paid. But another cop from the PSA lost his father within days of the murder-suicide, and both wakes would be held at the same funeral home, at the same time, and it was customary to send a van of cops in uniform to pay respects. Would they make the cops change before going from one room to the other? I spread word to the PSA to watch themselves, but I'd miss the funerals, as I had to go to a wedding out of town. When I got home, I found I'd missed a third—Mike Shea's mother had died as well.

We had Sundays and Mondays off, but through July and August, we worked late every Saturday, sometimes until six or seven the next morning, and began again early on Tuesdays. The weekends felt like a brief overnight, and if I had a personal life—my girfriend and I had broken up, and I had another job—I might have resented it. For a time, it seemed as if it rained every B&B Saturday, and that we had a pursuit that led to a car crash, but even on cloudless days, the chases could go awry. Once, a seller disappeared into the middle of the projects, and we spread out along the perimeter as he was sighted again, and we closed in, walking slow, then walking fast. When he saw us, he broke into a run. I saw the perp cross the street as a civilian's car drove up, unable to stop, and he tried to vault the hood one-handed like a stunt man, but the moving car threw him. I watched him land on the street,

bouncing off his shoulder, stand unsteadily and run again; I watched the horrified woman in the car, who thought she'd hit an innocent pedestrian; seconds later, she saw him get up, and then the cops follow, and she broke out
laughing. As I ran past her, I gave her the thumbs-up, and she nodded and
drove on. The perp cut down the block, and though he'd slowed, he was still
running. I stepped into the street and stopped two Spanish guys in an old
Toyota, opened the door, and jumped in the back: "Turn around! Follow him!"

They screeched a U-turn and barreled down the street, delighted to be
deputized. I don't think they understood English, but they knew exactly
what was going on. Two cops on foot had already caught the perp and put
him against the fence, and all three were winded and gasping for air. I
stepped out and thanked my drivers, and they drove off, grinning. For all I
knew, they had three kilos and a machine gun under the seat, but we were all
happy with the spontaneous moment of cooperation.

On another day, an uncle went to an apartment to buy heroin. The dealer
said that she was out, but she could get some more. "Stay right here, and
would you keep an eye on my kids?" There were two of them, both under
five. The dealer was gone for fifteen minutes, half an hour, forty-five . . . the
field team grew apprehensive. "Anything on the kel, Leader?"

"Stand by, Field Team, the uncle is baby-sitting. . . ."

Maybe when the dealer later realized that she'd left her children with a
police officer instead of a random junkie, she'd feel a little better. Maybe one
day the kids would appreciate that, too.

Every other Saturday, we did a late tour for B&B, and on the off weeks, we
worked a case at a nightclub, where at long last I got to be an undercover. The
club put on "raves," all-night dances with techno music and designer drugs.
Alcohol wasn't sold, and the crowd was as young as thirteen and fourteen.
There had been overdoses and a report of an unconscious girl dumped in a
back alley by the bouncers. White teenagers would flock in from the subway,
and parents in station wagons would drop off the kids at the club, as the local felons cruised around the edges, almost disbelieving of their good fortune. There was a strong underground culture to the raves, which I couldn't
begin to describe without feeling old, or sounding like my father might.
Some of the drugs, such as Ecstasy, we knew about, while others were entirely strange—GHB, ketamine, and other chemical combinations that I forgot as soon as I heard them. What was with these kids? Was there anything
wrong with good old-fashioned heroin? At the briefings, we were like G-men

in the Eisenhower days, trying to pronounce "beatnik" and "hashish" after the manner of the in-house hipster:

"Gentlemen, repeat after me: 'Lay some of that mary jane on me, Daddy-O. . . .' Got it? Together, now! *Lay some of that mary jane . . .*"

I intended to ask Clune if I could file a line-of-duty report for the loss of dignity when I found out that infant pacifiers and glow-in-the-dark wands were mandatory costumes—the former reduced teeth-grinding and the latter supplied hours of fun, waving slowly in the dark, to the properly medicated. Ricky Duggan and I would go for our team, and Pops brought in two other white uncles who worked the north Bronx. They studied a video and said, "We'll need parachute pants." Parachute pants were funded. Everything was: bribe money to skip the line, admission, money for candy, non-alcoholic drinks, glow sticks and pacifiers, of course, and lots of drugs. I would have a video camera with a night-vision lens, and all of us would have "fireflies," pins to put on a hat or shirt that flashed an infrared strobe light, so I could find them with the night vision in the darkened club.

The subjects of the operation were the security guards, whom we had been told by an informant were selling the drugs. The club had a vast open dance space and smaller rooms, and a section like a bazaar, with a table where drug-free rave literature was handed out—I picked up leaflets, to figure out what to buy—and booths for candy, gum, water, and CDs. In the smaller rooms, groups of kids would huddle on the floor to hug each other, or just to collapse, panting and gasping like runners at the end of a race. We were told to keep an eye out for open sex acts, and we were indeed vigilant. Ricky and I spent some time at the piercing booth, watching the young girls line up for punctured eyebrows and bellybuttons. "Go for it, Ricky—surprise your fiancée, Jennifer, with a nice tongue stud," I said.

"I really want one, but I think it would be wrong to spend taxpayer dollars on it."

I nodded and we bought more glow sticks instead.

At first, we had a lot of laughs: the scene was novel and bizarre, and after all, we were getting paid to spend a Saturday night at a club. But after a few hours, we had headaches from the relentless and barely changing beat of the music. You'd see a beautiful girl, but when you got a closer look, you'd realize she might be fifteen years old. The night wore on, and fights broke out: I watched an enormous bouncer argue with a teenager, and then pick him up and shot-put him: he sailed ten feet through the air, smashed through a door, and landed on the sidewalk. As an undercover, I had no gun or shield, and the music was too loud to call for help; an arrest would have ended the investigation, and we had planned to develop the drug case into a larger tax case against the club. But if the teenager had a broken neck, I had no choice. I strolled over a few paces to get a look at him on the sidewalk. The kid popped up from the gutter and danced like a marionette, screaming that he had to get back inside.

One of the other uncles handed me a couple of bags of weed, which I pocketed. "They said they had something called 'Special K,' too, but I didn't know what it was, so I said forget about it." I checked my drug-free rave pamphlets and said, "Go back and buy the Special K."

At first, we bought from whoever offered, but then we concentrated on the bouncers. One of the freelance dealers confided that the bouncers sometimes took them into back rooms and stole their stashes. *Thank you, sir, I'll be sure to add that to the report.* We worked our way in to the bouncers, who were deft as dealers, well organized and well supplied. I shot footage of sales until one of them approached me and said that I couldn't film anymore. After witnessing the shot-putting incident, I thought his politeness suspect, but he didn't demand the tape. I would have been happy to add on a robbery charge to the eventual indictment, but I would have preferred to skip the assault. I called Pops on the cell phone and met him around the corner, to hand off the camera and the drugs. "You look sharp," he said. I took the pacifier out of my mouth and told him where he could go.

When we worked the raves, we'd stay till six or seven in the morning, arriving back at the base in sunlight, exhausted, to voucher the drugs. We bought liquids, powders, and pills from large men in security shirts and headsets, as the cars with out-of-state plates pulled on to the block to drop off their children. The nights seemed to go on as long as the midnights had, with the same strangeness, the daylight bedtimes and breakfast in the dark, and a different strangeness, as we worked while pretending to play. The case would continue as we IDed subjects and ran checks, copying down plates and investigating business records. But the party would go on without me.

In mid-August, I got an e-mail from DI Rising, telling me to call him right away. He said, "Here's what I can do for now—you and your partner can go to any Squad in the city, tomorrow, and by the end of the year we can look at Manhattan Robbery. Where do you want to go?"

I told him that John had been at the Four-Four Squad for a couple of weeks now, and that I'd like to run things by him first, but it sounded good to me. I would call him back tomorrow. In fact, I wanted to stall for time. I had a few cases that I wanted to clear, and I also had four free days off for the PBA convention, which would lead into Labor Day weekend. I could use the break. When I called him back, I asked if we could delay it through Labor Day, and he said, "I don't think you should. You never know what's gonna happen." He was right. There could be an incident or a scandal—if a Four-Four cop got in trouble, or someone from Narcotics did, it could be suddenly impolitic to make changes at either place. I thought of all the near-certain non-events of my career—the SNEU team going to Narcotics, Street Crime, Vice, Manhattan North Narcotics, Headquarters, even Manhattan Robbery, maybe—and how differently things had turned out despite all my effort, luck, hustle, and hooks. When the door opens, you go. I said, "Okay, then. Let's do it." I'd finally be going to the Detective Bureau, to the Four-Four Squad. Effective midnight, I was gone.

THIRTEEN

The word "investigate" comes from the Latin *vestigium,* for footprint, and came to mean "to follow a trail." I arrived at the Squad before the news of my arrival did, and when I introduced myself to the bosses, the truth of my announcement had to be checked downtown, as if I might be an impostor. After I said hello to whoever else was in the office, I went back to Narcotics to pack up my things. Though the drive was no more than fifteen minutes, my investigators had beaten me back on the return trip. When I saw Ricky Duggan, he said, "Geez, the phone's been ringing off the hook about you, they want to know what the deal is."

"What did you tell 'em?"

"Great guy, hard worker, all that."

"Good, throw them off the scent."

So too at Admin, when I went to say my good-byes up there—"We've had a bunch of calls from the Four-Four. . . ." It hadn't been an hour since I'd set foot in there, and my footprints had been tracked back to Narcotics, Housing, and beyond, to my off-duty work. I came clean with them right away. They were detectives, after all, and it was their job to find out.

When I started out on my beat in the Village, I'd take my collars to the Four-Two, where I was a guest twice over. I was a new cop amid older ones, a Housing cop in the NYPD. The PSA was less than two years old, an air-conditioned and freshly painted cinder-block box, while the Four-Two had been built just after the turn of the century, cobbled together from pieces of dungeon and saloon: a high oak promontory of a desk with a brass rail, behind which an old Irishman decided who was served and how; in the back was a dank row of iron-barred cells, foul-smelling, dark, and covered with graffiti that could have been scrawled by the Birdman of Alcatraz. When I went upstairs to the Squad to have my perps debriefed, I was a three-time outsider, and I sometimes hesitated before I crossed the threshold, half expecting that they'd release the perp I'd brought in for trespassing and charge me with trespass myself.

There was nothing distinctive about the Squad, built on the cheap and badly maintained, with scuffed floors that looked like they were mopped once a week with the same bucket of dirty water. Detectives doubled up on desks beneath fluorescent lights; wanted posters papered the walls over the layers of peeling, military-surplus paint; rows of file cabinets broke the rooms into alcoves. Sometimes there was nothing distinctive about the men there—they were all men—who seemed to have taken on the worn-out look of their surroundings. But they had a way of looking at you, especially if you walked in without knocking, that reminded you that first impressions can be deceiving: there was more to them, and more to this place. If you took the time, you began to notice why. Detectives were unencumbered by the vests, belts, and sticks of patrol cops, and their movements were lighter and looser; it also made them more individual, more themselves. Their shields were on their belts, exhibited with the casual undraping of the suit jacket, a brief movement of the left hand that showed a flash of gold. Some wore their ties unknotted, with the ends crossed over in the center of their shirts, secured with a tie tack; it had an aura of old custom, like a homburg or a monocle.

Cops were standardized and general-purpose, dressed alike and designed to react to everything—disputes, traffic, broken elevators, loose dogs. Patrol had the most immediate part of the Job, and the most important. But while this immediacy was a great thrill, it was also the limitation: even if you got the first look, you rarely heard the last word, or even the middle of the story. The arrival of detectives at a crime scene signaled the end of patrol's responsibilities beyond the preservation of evidence. If there was a body on an apartment floor, they would slip in to draw a weeping woman aside, offering condolences while aiming questions. On the street, they might fan out into the crowd that had gathered, drawing out people there, too, for a quiet word, or to conceal a card in a handshake to speak in private later on. Their purpose was to inspire confidences, and their manner reflected confidences won, and a self-confidence; they carried themselves with a Broadway swagger even on streets that had never seen bright lights.

For almost a century, the Detective Bureau was its own separate kingdom within the Department, beginning with Inspector Thomas Byrnes in the 1870s and ending a century later. Byrnes, an Irish immigrant and Civil War veteran, was made Chief of Detectives after solving a three-million-dollar robbery from Chase Manhattan Bank. He instituted a high degree of professionalism in the Bureau: the mug shot and line-up were his inventions, and the police began to be known as "the Finest" at this time. He created a "dead line" at Fulton Street, the northern border of the Financial District, below which known criminals were summarily arrested if they happened to venture. Byrnes himself was a master detective, with an encyclopedic knowledge of the MOs and territories of individual perpetrators. He collaborated on several books, including *Professional Criminals of 1886*. The state legislature made the Detective Bureau a separate division of the NYPD at his request. His unquestioned honesty led to promotions after Boss Tweed fell in the 1870s, and then to Byrnes's becoming Superintendent after the Reverend Charles Parkhurst's sensational denunciations of vice and police corruption in the early 1890s. In 1892, after Congress assigned federal marshals to the polls, a Tammany district leader issued orders for police to arrest them if they committed "breaches of the peace." Byrnes told each of his captains he would "take the buttons off him" if he did so, and none did. Reformers like Lincoln Steffens and Jacob Riis, who generally had little praise for the police, admired him personally. For Steffens, he was "simple, no complications at all—a man who would buy you or beat you, as you might choose, but get you he would." And Riis mourned his retirement, musing that "chained as he was in the meanness and smallness of it all, he was yet cast in a different mold. Compared with his successor, he was a giant in every way. Byrnes was a 'big policeman.' We shall not soon have another like him."

But many detectives followed who would become nearly as well regarded and well known, and for many decades, New York knew its good guys as well as its bad guys by name. Joseph Petrosino, the first Italian-American in the NYPD and the founder of the "Italian Squad," put more than five hundred mafiosi in prison, and he was killed in revenge while on assignment in Palermo in 1909. More than a quarter of a million people, mostly Italian immigrants, turned out for his funeral on the Lower East Side. Broadway

Johnny Broderick, also known as the "One-Man Riot Squad," once tossed Legs Diamond into a dumpster. Johnny Cordes was a two-time Medal of Honor winner who didn't carry a gun, and who found jobs for two perps who had shot him when they were later released from prison. The bank robber Willie Sutton provided an admiring blurb for a biography of Frank Phillips, the detective who captured him: "He's just about the best there is. You never felt safe if you knew Phillips was after you. If Mike Hammer ever read the record of Frank Phillips's accomplishments as a detective, he would undoubtedly pass a few snide remarks about Mickey Spillane's ability to create a super-sleuth." In the 1950s, the Detectives Endowment Association would have annual parties at the Waldorf and the Plaza, where the likes of Frank Sinatra and Dean Martin would perform. Though the independence of the Detective Bureau was curbed by Commissioner Patrick Murphy as part of his modernization of the NYPD—Murphy had strong ideas about preventing crimes, but little experience in solving them—it retained a measure of its old autonomy and character.

Then as now, cops with ambition became bosses or detectives, and the former was not an option for those without a talent for politics or test-taking. The Bureau also drew cops whose view of the Job was essentially romantic, an evergreen game of tag with the bad guys, profoundly boyish in its excitement but adult in its consequences. More than anything else, what a detective does is talk—to witnesses, victims, perps—and talk them into talking; you chose your own words as you chose your own clothes, and you rose or fell on your style. When I'd talk to friends like Brian McCabe, he'd say things like, "The Squad is the Job. Hurry up and come here."

The Four-Four was one of the busiest squads in the city, closely knit and conscious of tradition. The Three-Four in Washington Heights and the Seven-Five in East New York, Brooklyn, had traditionally dueled for first place in homicides during the crack wars, racking up eighty or a hundred bodies a year, but the Four-Four, which was a fraction of their size, was always close behind. And while the Three-Four and Seven-Five had seen reductions in crime as dramatic as any in the city in recent years, the Four-Four began the year 2001 with a homicide on each of the first four days of January. Within blocks of East 161st Street and the Grand Concourse, the Four-Four contained Yankee Stadium, the courts, the DA's and Borough President's offices, and the Bronx County Building, which had housed the Democratic machine that had put FDR and JFK into the White House. In *The Bonfire of the Vanities,* Tom Wolfe called this corridor of influence "Gibraltar":

All over Gibraltar, at this moment, from lowest to the highest, the represen-
tatives of the Power in the Bronx were holed up in their offices, shell-backed,
hunched over deli sandwiches, ordered in. . . . You could ascend to the very top
of the criminal justice system in the Bronx and eat deli sandwiches until the
day you retired or died.

And why? Because they, the Power, the Power that ran the Bronx, were ter-
rified! And they ran the place, the Bronx, a borough of 1.1 million souls! The
heart of the Bronx was now such a slum that there was nothing even resem-
bling a businessman's sit-down restaurant. But even if there were, what judge
or DA or assistant DA, what court officer, even packing a .38, would leave
Gibraltar at lunchtime to get to it? . . . You were an alien in the 44th Precinct,
and you knew at once, every time Fate led you into their *territory . . .*

After six years in the South Bronx, the Four-Four was a small adjustment, but the Squad would be a true change. I felt like I was holding my breath a little, not from a Seventh Circle stench—though Dante and Virgil began their transit to Lower Hell there, the realm of the violent, where I was headed, too—but so that I would not be heard as I crept in. Housing had had its own Squads, before the merge, but since leaving my beat, my contact with precinct detectives had been sporadic. I didn't know many of them, and I didn't know all that much about what they did or how they did it. It was as if I was peering over the edge, readying for the jump, and I was glad to have Timpanaro there with me. I felt like giving him a little poolside shove—*Let me know how the water is*—but he leaped in first, and he loved it.

When John arrived the month before, in July, he attended a seven-day De-tective Bureau orientation. For several of those nights, I was out for dinner with friends downtown, and John would join us on his break, beaming and dressed in new suits, telling us how various bosses had welcomed them, in-cluding the Chief of Detectives himself, and the tone seemed to be that of an awards ceremony or an initiation to a secret society. He carried himself with a sense of delight, of having arrived, and by the last day, I almost expected him to produce a key to the city. He told a joke from the orientation: "They set up a weekend down south, in Virginia, for the best investigators in the country. They have cookouts, lectures, softball games—all that—and everybody has a good time. In the end, on the last day, they say, 'We're gonna have a demon-stration, see what everybody's got.' They go out to the woods, with two guys from the CIA, two guys from the FBI, two guys from Bronx Homicide. They have a little white rabbit in a cage. They let it go, and it scampers off into the woods. The guy waits a little bit and says, 'Okay, first up is the CIA—go out and find that rabbit!' The two CIA guys run off and disappear, and in ten minutes they come back with the rabbit. Everybody claps—'Great work! Look at these guys!' And then they let another rabbit loose, and they wait, and the guy says, 'FBI—you're next! Go get 'em!' And the two FBI guys go off in the woods, and everybody waits, but in an hour, they come back with the rabbit. 'Good job, guys, good job!' Finally, Bronx Homicide is up. The rabbit goes, and they go out after it. An hour passes, and another hour, and another. It's starting to get dark, and everybody's getting worried—they're gonna have to send out a search party for the Bronx guys, forget about the rabbit. As the sun goes down, they get ready to head into the woods. Just then, Bronx Homicide comes out of the woods with a bear. One guy has it by the neck, and the other guy is kicking it in the balls, and the bear is saying, 'Okay! Okay! I'm a rabbit!'"

A month later, I heard the joke, too, at my orientation, and though the Chief of Detectives did welcome us, there appeared to be far less fanfare. We were on day tours instead of four-to-twelves, as an apparent hedge against us enjoying our dinner breaks too thoroughly: a cop in Brooklyn had worked a midnight, drank through the day at a strip joint, and returned for another midnight when he ran over a pregnant woman and two children, killing them all. It was a gross tragedy, and the Job reacted grossly in turn: any cop who had been near him that day was punished, it seemed, and a rookie who had gone to the strip joint was fired. It was the way the Job offers an apology, and the mood was sorrowful and sour. The move to the Detective Bureau was a lateral one for me, moving over rather than up, and though I was content that I'd made the right decision, I wasn't singing in my car.

In Narcotics, at its best, you are an entrepreneur, with the freedom to choose cases or even invent them, as I had with Christmas, and follow wherever they led. Just before I'd gone, in August, I had the beginnings of a case with great potential. That month, my sister Regina had married a man named Michael Pacicco, who ran a family jewelry store on 47th Street, in the Diamond District, who called to tell me that a vendor of his, a Russian, had been sold fifty thousand dollars' worth of fake gold. When I talked to the Russian, he said the sellers were connected both to his in-laws and to organized crime, but he said that he was fed up with their stalling, and he wanted the police to help. It was a bit of a tricky situation: for the crime of Grand Larceny to have been committed, it would have to be shown that he was knowingly sold false goods, and it would have required him to wear a wire. It took a dozen phone calls to shop the case around, and it was only after I heard that Morgenthau loved cases with the Diamond District and the Russian Mob that I was able to find a receptive audience with the Manhattan DA's Squad. As it happened, the Russian ruined the case—he told the perps he had gone to the police—but the two men were taken down a year later, as part of a multi-million-dollar stolen-property ring. Manhattan gold fraud didn't have much to do with Bronx Narcotics, but I thought that Pops would be able to smell the overtime all the way to Forty-seventh Street. As John Reilly would say, "The shield says City of New York. . . ." The open-ended nature of the work was the best part of Narcotics: you went out to see what the stories were.

In the Squad, you were a historian, and the stories came to you. You couldn't get just any bad guy, you had to get a particular one, who had done a specific thing to a distinct individual. It seemed narrow at first, and later it felt oppressive, not least because of the shift in the audience. In Narcotics, a collar brought some relief to a building, a block, a neighborhood; even with one less dealer or one less gun on the street, the benefit you provided was an environmental one, and as such it was to some degree abstract. For gun and drug cases, the complainant is the People of the State of New York, and they didn't call to tell you to hurry up while you worked a case, or to thank you when you finished. In the Squad, they did: you had victims, living or other-wise. It had been a while since I'd worked for real human beings, and the shift was refreshing at times, and at others it was a burden.

The Detective Bureau would be as novel and challenging as my first days on patrol, when the Academy, at least, had provided six months of theory be-fore the practice. You began the day with the 60 sheet—the list of complaints for the previous day, which someone from the Squad would skim each morn-ing, through reports of nuisances and crimes, lost property and missing per-sons, to see what would become a case. The 494 sheet determined who "caught" the case, from the catching order: there were three two-man Rob-bery teams, A, B, and C, each working from four in the afternoon through one in the morning for two days, from eight in the morning through four in the afternoon the next two, followed by two days off. The cops on each team alternated catching for the tours they worked, and the day-tour team caught from midnights as well. The case folders were assembled by hand, folding the cardboard, punching, stapling, and clipping the 61 and the fives on the right side, and all other documents—computer checks, vouchers, pictures—on the left. Most of the fives you typed were pink, but you typed blue ones for arrests. There were the case-closing classifications, amenable and non-amenable, from A-1, for an arrest by the Detective Squad; D-1, arrest by patrol; B-5, transfer to another office, like Transit for subway robberies or Bronx Robbery for patterns; B-7, inaccurate facts; C-2, when a witness can no longer identify a perp; C-3, uncooperative complainant; C-4, all leads exhausted. B-15 also meant that a complainant couldn't ID, or an arrest by patrol, but only sometimes. There were procedures for issuing wanted cards, conducting line-ups and showing photo arrays. Most of it was brand-new to me, and much of what I did know I hadn't done in years.

There was a feel of age to the place, a consciousness of legacy. Unlike most of the Job, there were men who were not bosses who had gray hair. When I looked at the old Homicide logs, leather-bound ledgers that were older than the building that housed them, I saw how we averaged about fifty murders a year in the early 1980s, crested to over eighty in the crack years, and had come down to the thirties more recently. The logs were yellowed and the pages were crisp, divided into columns that listed location, weapon, motive, and the name, age, and race of victim and perp. In the 1980 log, there were a fair number of elderly Irish and Jewish ladies in their seventies and eighties, strangled or bludgeoned at home during burglaries; the race of one victim was listed as "Y," which stumped me for a moment, until I saw the victim was Chinese, and the detective meant "Yellow." Other motives were set down simply as "Homosexual," and child-abuse cases were categorized as "Discipline." Some of the detectives in that log had come on the Job soon after World War II, and men they taught had retired just before my arrival. They were men who could have worked with my father, and to be there felt like I was closer to him than ever, in type and time.

The Squad was run by Lt. George Corbiere, with two sergeants, Larry Sheehan and Tom Rice, while the RAM was headed by Sgt. Scott Adler. From Corbiere, especially, I began to understand some of the intensity of pride that John had felt at the orientation. There were few precincts as dangerous and few Squads as dedicated and driven. Sgt. Adler talked about the "adulthood" of the Squad: he was here to help with anything I asked for, on duty or off, and he should know about any major developments in the former, but I was my own man. I liked that. I certainly liked it more than when he said that he valued neatness and he didn't want smoking in the office. As I tapped the pack of cigarettes in my pocket, I thought of how Capt. Mahony would sometimes stop by my desk just to stare at the alp of paperwork. I told Adler my preference for the B Team, of Danny Scanlon and John Timpanaro, and he said that it sounded fine.

I slowly began to understand the layout of the Squad, the roles and rotations: the separate five-day chart for the two-man Burglary team and the three detectives assigned to Domestic Violence. The RAM took robberies and grand larcenies from persons, which generally meant chain snatches or purse snatches. Ron Kress and Steve DeSalvo were the A Team, and Keith Clinton and Jimmy Reilly made up the C. Most cops in the Squad began in the RAM, as there was an average of upper-middle seriousness to the cases, from the kid-who-punched-the-other-kid-and-took-his-jacket stuff, to commercial robberies and stick-ups in which the victim was shot. The Squad took everything else, from homicides to cases of aggravated harassment, which required nothing more than a phone call to the threatening phone-caller, telling him to come to the office. The A, B, and C teams on the Squad worked on the same rolling chart as the RAM—two nights, two days, two off—and in the event of homicides, shootings, or other heavy cases, the entire office responded to the scene. The senior men were Mike Rodriguez, his brother Steve, and Eddie McDonald for the A team, Bobby Nardi and Bobby D'Amico for the B, and Bobby Colten, Al Rosario, and JR Carter for the C. On my first day there, I listened to JR talk casually about his recent trip to Florida to collect the hit man a woman had hired to kill her husband. There was no need to point out that I was the new guy, because I was well aware of it myself; I respected all of them a great deal and I showed it, I hoped, without servility. Billy Coakley introduced himself by asking jovially, "Are you a dump job or an IAB plant?" I thought before answering. "A little of both."

As I grappled with the new faces and forms, further investigations were conducted: I had worked with Jose Morales's sister, Janet, in Narcotics; Capt. Hoch knew Scott Adler, and Larry Sheehan knew my brother John—his daughter and my niece Elizabeth went to kindergarten together. When Corbiere asked how I'd gotten here, Larry Sheehan said, "Clearly, this is a transfer by osmosis." His nickname was Vocabu-Larry. That was easy to remember, but it was harder to tell Glynn from Flynn, and Flynn from Flood. John Flynn had worked with Uncle Eddie in the Four-Seven: "He was a barrel of fun. . . ." And John Flood must have had some Jesuit training, as was shown when a perp called to him from the cells, "Where's D'Amico at?"

"Listen, guy, I'm gonna tell you two things," he barked. "First, D'Amico's not in, and second, in this Squad we never, *ever* end a sentence with a preposition. You got me?"

For the first few days, there was little to do with me, and I listened and watched. One morning, a midnight cop named McNamee told Danny Scanlon about a collar he'd made the night before, of gang members at a prostitution area the cops called "Pickle Park." A group of Bloods had set upon a gay teenage boy working the area, but they were driven off by another teen prostitute, a transvestite with a bullwhip. Another morning, the Squad was crowded with chiefs; I slipped into my desk and pretended I had work to do. Someone knocked from the interview room, which was a few feet away, and when I opened it, an eight-year-old boy stood before me and said, "I have to go to the bathroom." He had killed a four-year-old boy, stabbing him in the neck with a pen. They lived in the same building, and the eight-year-old had bullied the smaller boy for a year. He stabbed him when the four-year-old was sent out to the garbage disposal in the hall to throw away a diaper. I led him out to the bathroom, and then I took him back, and locked the door again.

I stuck with John, picking up bits and pieces from him. While he had only been there a month, he'd worked in the precinct on and off for years. He wanted the Four-Four to work with Scanlon and Jose Morales—he had known them from his old footpost, when they were on Four-Four SNEU. Danny and Jose were the young turks of the precinct, aggressive cops who came to be known as Batman and Robin on the busier corners. Jose had come upstairs just before Danny, and he was on the B Team, on the Squad side. John and Danny were all hustle and heat, and they called each other on their days off to talk about how they could finagle the next gun collar. John had been on a hot streak from the moment he arrived: there were a couple of good collars after canvasses, and a gun collar after a foot pursuit in the park; he had also caught a few great cases, including a cab robbery where the perps shot up the car. On my first day back from orientation, I came in as John and Danny were setting up a gun rip for the next day, with a guy they'd stopped the night before for a traffic violation.

Danny was as hard-charging as Popeye Doyle. He'd worked for eight years in the Four-Four, and he couldn't drive down a block without an old complainant stopping the car to say hello on one side, and an old collar calling out, "Hey, Batman!" from the other. And Danny would stop and talk to each. Once he'd collared a perp, Danny treated him like an old schoolmate, joking about past times and planning to meet again: "Tell me for real—you got a gun at home? Who does? You know who's carrying? Let's help each other out. . . ."

If it felt like I lived in a police state sometimes, Danny made my world look relatively civilian. Though he was a first-generation cop—his mother was from Mayo, as my grandmother Delia was—one of his brothers, John, was a sergeant in Street Crime, and his other brother, Brian, was applying to the FBI. He met his wife, Lily Roque, when they were partners in SNEU, and she still worked at the Four-Four, in Community Policing. They had two children, Nina and Danny Jr., and while the little ones had not yet expressed any job preferences, there was an easy bet to be made on what they'd do. Danny had begun as a cop in the Four-Four and fully expected to end his career there, in the Squad, and to stay past his twenty years.

At first, Danny was welcoming but wary with me; John's endorsement counted for something, but you never knew how you'd work out as partners, balancing rhythms and personalities for fifty hours a week. Taking on a partner was more like an arranged marriage than a blind date, and in our business especially, you didn't just take someone's word for things. Compared to OCCB, detectives in the Bureau operated with tremendous independence: they came and went from the office without asking permission from a boss, and they decided the course of an investigation as they saw fit. Because no one thought for you, you and your partner had to think alike, or at least to disagree with respect. With Danny, I deferred to his experience in most matters, and with John, the combination of an old partner and a new assignment was the perfect balance of the familiar and the strange.

When the prospect of living and working together suddenly presented itself, John and I looked at each other and wondered if it was such a good idea. It had been two years since we were steady partners in SNEU, and at first, work was so much fun that we were happy to talk about it at home, and then it was so miserable that the bond formed a natural defense. We'd planned to partner up again, but as the time passed, the plan became almost a figure of speech—"Next year in Jerusalem!"—as John didn't want to go to Narcotics and it didn't look like I was going anywhere else. Over the summer, it seemed that things would work out: John would learn the robbery trade at the Four-Four, and then he could teach me at Manhattan Robbery, maybe at the end of the year. Maybe then, too, he would stun his longtime girlfriend, Julie, with a proposal. She was in the third year of her medical residency, and I advised him to do it at the hospital, where she could receive necessary treatment. From the time he'd moved in, he'd planned to propose to Julie the next Christmas, or the next Valentine's Day, and then on vacation in the spring, but the signs were never quite right. Three years of holidays and trips had passed, and it had even been a year since he'd asked me to be his best man. I was honored, and I asked him to be my pallbearer in return:

"Just you—not five other guys. I want you to carry the coffin yourself, on your back, and give me five squat-thrusts coming and going from the church."

"No problem. That gives me, what—a good three, maybe four years to get in shape."

"Four years, easy. Here's my rough draft of the best-man speech: 'Good riddance.' How's that sound?"

John thought for a moment. "You know, I've heard worse."

We decided to give it a try—John was on the Island on his days off, and with the detective's chart, it felt like you lived with your team: you went in late on the first day and left early on the last, and the middle two ran together for the "turnaround"—the night tour ended at one a.m. and the next day began at eight, and half the Squad slept over in the precinct. On work days, life was work.

One afternoon, I went with John to Lincoln Hospital to interview Alfonzo, his complainant for a stabbing-robbery from the night before. Alfonzo had been waiting to hail a cab for his girlfriend when two men approached from either side and cut him in the leg and chest. Other detectives had interviewed him that night, and he was hostile and uncooperative, and when we looked up his record—the "victimology," conducted in every case—we saw his prior arrest for robbery. Often, these victims feel a sense of professional courtesy toward their colleagues, and they prefer to shoot them instead of having them arrested. It was an unpromising beginning and an unprepossessing setting, but for me it was a pure thrill. Patients and doctors alike looked at us, and someone called out from the waiting room, "Ooh, FBI!" It was like on my first day of patrol, when the drunk in the blue styrofoam cowboy hat had called out, "There's a new sheriff in town!" And though no one had their facts quite right, then or now, I was flattered nonetheless. When you wear a suit in a room full of suits, you look, at best, like you belong there; when you wear a suit in a place full of sweatshirts, everyone else wonders if they do. When we stopped to announce our visit to the woman at the information desk, John dropped his voice half an octave to the finest Squad-guy tone, grave and confidential, but willing to share in the secret, just this once, for you: "Timpanaro and Conlon, Four-Four Squad," he said, as he pulled his jacket half-aside to show the shield. "We're here to see . . ."

The suave and serious mood was broken when we stepped into Alfonzo's room. He seemed to be playing with himself. I said, "Ahem . . . hey, Alfonzo, how are you feeling? My name is Conlon and this is my partner, Timpanaro, and—"

John gave me a little shove, and I looked at him, and followed his nod.

"We'll give you a minute, excuse us," I said, as we withdrew.

Outside, John said, "You couldn't see he's pissing in a bedpan?"

I shook my head sadly: "Sometimes you have to look past the obvious, to get to the truth. Frankly, I'm not sure if you have much of a future in this business, John."

Alfonzo had suffered a deep cut to the side, requiring fifty stitches to close; he was both heavily sedated and in pain. He didn't know why he had been attacked, he said, but he thought he knew one of his attackers, who didn't live too far from him. We asked what he looked like, and he gave a description so detailed he might have dressed him that morning: twenty-year-old male Hispanic, hair in three thick braids, a tattoo of a Chinese character on his neck, wearing a Cincinnati Reds cap over a black do-rag, a gold chain without any ornament; a black jacket with red piping down the sleeves, black Air Jordans with red laces. Most people couldn't provide such a description if they'd studied a photograph for ten minutes, and Alfonzo had a split second before the stabbing. John asked if the perp sold drugs, and Alfonzo said that he did, on One-Five-Seven and Gerard. When I asked what he sold, he responded without hesitation, "Red tops."

Alfonzo's portrait of his attacker was a self-portrait as well. Though he didn't have any drug collars on his sheet, his familiarity with the product and perp was not that of a spectator. It didn't mean that we didn't want the case or wouldn't work the case, but we had to establish whether Alfonzo wanted us to—he could be our complainant now, or the perp in next month's homicide, and while it wasn't quite all the same to us, there was only so much we could do to gain his cooperation. When I looked at the 61, I saw that today was Alfonzo's birthday, and I offered congratulations. He began to cry a little, saying that he never had any luck, how he tried and tried. . . . We let him go on for a moment, and then John said, "Do you want to work with us on this, Alfonzo? I mean, we want to get this guy for you, but do you want us to help? Some people don't want to deal with cops, for whatever reason, they've been in trouble before, whatever. You ever been in trouble before?"

Alfonzo's hiccuppy whimper opened up into a full-throated sob: "The only time I really got locked up was on my birthday, two years ago! I got drunk and took a TV . . . a birthday present . . . one birthday in jail, another in the hospital . . ."

Whether it was the kind words, the birthday coincidence, or the morphine, when we walked away, it felt like we'd rescued the case. The other detectives had been discouraging before we went in, and maybe we made an additional effort to draw Alfonzo out, just to defy expectations. It was a good feeling to be able to shift the circumstances, to make Alfonzo someone you were glad to help, and to take off running. It also felt good to work with John again, to tag-team an interview to draw out facts or feelings, and to talk it over afterward, noticing details, pointing out problems and possibilities.

It felt right, the rhythm of the place, the professionalism and the pride. There was far more paperwork than I expected, and more time spent in the office, where the phones could ring without rest. One afternoon, after a series of calls that asked, "Is this Crown Donut?" I picked up with the intention of taking their order, but it was the sergeant at the desk, downstairs.

"There's somebody here, wants to see one of you guys."

"Who? You got a name?"

"Nah, but from who they describe, I think they want that skinny new detective."

"Conlon?"

"Yeah, maybe."

"Send 'em up."

When the skinny new detective caught his first case, John, Danny, and I made another hospital visit, to talk to Ethan Prescott. Ethan had been walking home from a family party late one night, when a man followed him from the subway and asked for change. Ethan knew what was coming next, and so he walked faster, when the man stepped up to him and cracked him in the head with a pipe. Hours later, he came to, and someone helped him to his apartment, a few blocks away. For the next two days, he was in and out of consciousness, and it was not until a social worker came to visit him that help was sought. Ethan had AIDS, and his injuries would have been severe under any circumstances, but here they might have been lethal. His jaw was broken, and he had developed an infection. He would be happy to work with us, he said, but we had to understand that there were other things on his mind.

As a case, it was not altogether lost: Ethan thought he could recognize the man, but it was unknown when he'd be able to get in to view pictures, and by that time, his memory might have faded. He did remember getting a phone call when he lay delirious in his apartment: a credit-card company asked whether a particular charge was authorized, after someone had signed the slip "Evan Prescott," and the merchant had become suspicious. He had two credit cards, and he wasn't sure which company had called, but when he got home, he'd look at his bills and know which. There might be a problem finding the bill, however, as he was preparing to move, and his belongings were all in boxes. It was a slim chance, but someone at the store should remember him, and might have a videotape, and if we were extremely lucky, the perp might have been arrested at the scene. We went back to the office and I typed my first DD5 for my first case, on the long pink sheet. It felt strange to write my new command, "44 Robbery Apprehension Module," and I tried to remember how long it had felt strange to write "Narcotics," and wondered how it would feel to write "Detective Conlon" in a few months. But when I look at that five now, by far the strangest thing about it is the date, which presaged a change far greater than any from Housing to Narcotics to the Detective Bureau. The date was September 10, 2001.

. . .

IT WAS IMPOSSIBLE TO THINK THAT THE TWIN TOWERS WERE now a part of "old New York," lost like the Third Avenue El, Ebbets Field, or the Polo Grounds, of a piece with the age of pushcarts and cobblestone streets. Their stratospheric, clean-lined reach defined the modern skyline: they had an utter simplicity and a vague symbolism, like an equal sign or a number—two? eleven?—that didn't demand to be understood, and were at once truly awesome and a little dull. My sister Regina and her husband, Michael, returned from their honeymoon two days before, on a cruise ship that entered New York harbor at dawn. Regina took pictures of the Statue of Liberty. She didn't think she'd want a picture of the Twin Towers, any more than she'd take a picture of my mother's house. We'd been there so often there was no need.

We had gone to the World Trade Center since it had opened, to my uncles' restaurant at the underground level of the PATH trains to New Jersey. There were three uncles—Joe, Herman, and Victor—and three businesses, a bar called the Trade Inn, a coffee shop, and the Commuter's Cafe. My family had gone since the 1970s, and my friends had gone since the 1980s; the tradition ended in 1993, after the first bombing. Herman was at the coffee shop when the bomb went off in the underground garage, and there was chaos and near-disaster in his escape. Afterward, the restaurant and coffee shop didn't re-open, and in the years since, Victor and Joe had died. Only Herman and the bar were left by the year 2001, and I thought of them an hour after I arrived at work on the morning of September 11.

I'd caught a case the night before, and at 0848 hours I was looking at the report for a commercial robbery—gun, bodega, two males, one with a promi-nent gap in his teeth, I was glad to learn—when a shout went up from the lunchroom. It wasn't so loud or extreme, only slightly more than you might have heard at a tie-breaking touchdown. And like a football game, there was instant replay, over and over. I walked in and watched the plane hit. It looked small, like a private plane, for a hobbyist or a local charter. If I hadn't been new in the office, I might have expressed my opinion, which would have been that there was room for accident and coincidence, that we shouldn't jump to conclusions. I might have pointed out that a plane had struck the Empire State Building once, and there had been nothing sinister about it. Our TV flickered a little, but the image of orange flame and black smoke, silver skyscraper and blue sky came in unbroken in my mind. I watched it play over and over, and then I stepped out of the room again, and then there was a greater shout, and I went back in. Another plane, another tower, banking in from the south, and striking with such force that it left an exit wound.

"We're at war," said Sgt. Adler. "Let's suit up. Everybody in the bag."

I don't know if I was especially collected or a bit numb. I called my mother to tell her I was all right, and I called a few others, to spread the word. When-ever a cop is shot in the city, everyone who had a relative or friend on the Job feels a jolt of dread. I felt *too* safe, and I ran through my own potential casu-alty list: Herman probably wasn't in yet to open the bar, but his son, Steve, was a cop in the First Precinct, which covered the World Trade Center. He worked the midnights, which finished at 0750; had he left yet, and had he gone there? The Fire Department had gone down en masse, and I had two cousins, Brian and his brother Gerald, and Tommy Killian, and a list of other names, less close, that ran longer than I could count. I wasn't even sure where my brothers worked—one a lawyer, the other at a bank, somewhere downtown. Steve Rodriguez had talked to his wife, who worked in the south tower, after the first plane hit the north. "They're telling us not to evacuate," she told Steve. "Get the fuck out, now," he said. Steve grabbed a car with his brother Mike and two other guys from the Squad, Bobby Colten and Rocco

Farella, and they sped downtown. People in the towers began to leap to their deaths. Some of them were on fire.

My uniform was at home; I didn't have a locker yet and was sharing John's. Another plane struck the Pentagon, and another had been hijacked and was somewhere over Pennsylvania. Most cops were grim, but now and then someone made a forced, whistling-in-the-dark joke about Arabs or war. One cop was in a state of high agitation, nearly yelling, "My aunt works there! My aunt works right there! Fuck that! Man, fuck that!" I wanted to tell him to calm down, but I also wanted to smack him. One tower fell, trembling and blazing, and the black smoke shot up as if released from the core of the earth. A column of steel and glass became a column of ash, rising ever higher. As we watched, it was as if the air had been sucked out of us. The second tower fell, with the same haunting motion, the same stop-action descent, floor by floor, from something to nothing, like a magician's top hat, disappearing with a snap. I thought how everything was landing on my last uncle's last bar. I went home to get my uniform.

As I raced home on local streets, a flashing light on the dash, John called from Long Island. "Should I come in?" he asked. "I don't know how you'll be able to," I said. "Everything's shut—bridges, tunnels, trains." I said I'd call him back. Just after noon, we all mustered outside our new Headquarters on Simpson Street; Detective Borough Bronx had taken over the building from Narcotics over the summer. We awaited our assignments, and some wondered whether we would guard bridges or airports or the perimeter of the Trade Center, but others speculated that we would go to the morgues. Forty thousand people worked in the two towers, and though it was early in the morning, and many had left after the first plane hit, there were estimates of five and six thousand dead. We milled about in the street for hours. A city bus came to pick up detectives and went downtown; a captain sent out a few carloads to collect water and flashlight batteries from supermarkets. I struggled to think of something useful to do, and then I went to a diner and ordered dozens of sandwiches. They didn't take a dime off, not even for the coffee. It's a slippery slope, I suppose. Danny came in, and I called John again, who was already on his way; the bridges had been opened for emergency workers. When he got to Simpson Street, he said that he was the only one on the Throgs Neck Bridge coming into the city, and he stopped his car for a moment and stepped outside. The day was perfect, a balmy, windless moment of Indian summer, and he looked at the empty gray span and the empty blue sky and then downtown, at the geysers of smoke on the skyline. And then he thought, "Maybe this isn't the smartest place to be," and he sped off the bridge.

Someone said, "The whole first platoon at the First Precinct was wiped out." That didn't make sense: the first platoon is the midnights, but the plane had hit fifty-eight minutes after end of tour. Maybe they meant the second platoon. That meant that my cousin Steve would be all right, but a lot more cops would be dead—three times as many would be at work during the day. I calculated odds, as if it mattered. Someone said that there was a separate morgue being set up just for cops and firemen. A detective named O'Hagan from the Four-O Squad was called off the line; his brother was a fireman. I knew the family: I'd gone to high school with one brother, Joe, and another was a lieutenant in Narcotics. Ron Kress said that someone saw Steve Rodriguez on TV, running into the south tower just before it fell.

The hours passed, and the sun set, and we stood idle on Simpson Street. Sometimes we'd drift into the building to watch TV, to hear more rumors and wonder why we were kept on what seemed like the quietest street in the city. I don't think there were many robberies or assaults that day, but anyone who called 911 didn't get an answer. At ten o'clock at night, half of us were dismissed until four in the morning, the other half until four in the afternoon: we would be on seven-day, twelve-hour shifts until further notice. John, Danny, and I would be back at four in the morning. We went home and tried to make calls. My brother Steve had flown to England the night before, and we hadn't heard from him. I wasn't worried; he wasn't here. My firefighter cousins were alive, and so were the Tretters. We didn't sleep much before we went back in.

Another twelve hours passed, milling about in uniform on Simpson Street. I kept my wallet full of cash and brought back more food. More rumors circulated: carloads of uniformed city cops were being turned away from the site; one story, which was more than a rumor, told of twenty cops from the Four-Four who had gone down in uniform during their twelve hours off, only to be cursed at and sent home by some captain. Not everyone was desperate to play a part: the agitated cop who worried for his aunt later called in sick. His locker was broken into, and a yellow stripe was painted down the back of his uniform. I heard that he later resigned. When volunteers from Massachusetts and Pennsylvania were interviewed on TV at Ground Zero—though it wasn't called that yet—the mood became belligerent. They wore hard hats and were covered in ash, and said how they just got in their cars and came over to help. People shouted at the TV: "What the fuck's up with that?"

"We got dead brothers there, and they turn us away?"

"We got NYPD ID cards, uniforms, and shields, and it's get-the-fuck-out, but this guy shows up with a shovel and it's 'Welcome, brother!'"

I thought about how the President would arrive in a day or two, and I wondered how secure the perimeter might be. Would there be a Phase Two of attacks, or a Phase Three? New York had changed its driver's licenses not too long before, and the first time I saw one, I looked at the guy who handed it to me like he was trying to pull a fast one. How well would any other NYPD cop, or FBI agent, let alone a National Guardsman, recognize a legitimate license from Indiana or even from New Jersey? And yet Ground Zero was teeming with out-of-state cops, firefighters, volunteer firefighters, and paramedics, not to mention freelance volunteers who offered food, counseling, clean socks, water, Bibles, and everything else that could conceivably be of use. They came with truckloads of things, from rescue dogs to homemade lasagna. It was a scene of improvised nobility that may have been commensurate to the evil that provoked it, and yet in terms of security, it was a travesty, at least from my TV set. By the end of the day on Simpson Street, fewer cops were watching TV, and more were scheming how to get down there to work.

John had talked to a cop at PSA-7 named Bobby Tucker who had managed to get in at Ground Zero the day before. After a twelve-hour shift, we met him at four in the morning and drove down to the site. Bobby had brought hard hats, and we put on respirators, raid jackets, and dusty boots, and we marched past the National Guardsmen at the perimeter as if we'd just stepped out for a break. There was an uncanniness to it all: the sight of soldiers on Canal Street; the movement and noise in the predawn hours; the air acrid from smoke, with a sour, chemical tang. I passed restaurants where I'd eaten, offices where friends worked, the apartment of an old girlfriend. It was still dark, but there was a kind of anticipatory underglow, of light waiting in the wings, though we would not be glad for the sunrise. We turned a corner and saw what had been Seven World Trade Center, and stopped. What had been fifty stories was now five or six. It didn't look like it had fallen down. It looked shattered, broken apart by hammer blows. It stank like it was rotting and burning at once, as if the next of kin couldn't decide on burial or cremation. It was gone.

We passed on wordlessly to Ground Zero. There were hordes of cops, fire-men, construction workers, many collapsed along the sidelines, exhausted, or staring blankly at the piles. There were steel I-beams stuck like darts in the towers that surrounded the site, and on a row of old buildings, cloth and pa-per hung like confetti from the fire escapes, flattened back from the blast. Cranes lifted up sixty-foot girders made of four-inch-thick steel, twisted like shoelaces. There was a mountain of broken things, and pits that led to still more devastation below. It didn't look like war, or even a war movie. It looked like a monster movie, where some great beast had punched holes in buildings and battered down the city. You found yourself standing, staring, forgetting about time. The sun rose, and it was another beautiful day.

We made our way into the piles and fell in line on the bucket brigade. A hundred cops passed five-gallon drums full of rubble from the center of the pile to the perimeter, and passed back the buckets, empty. Teams from FEMA in blue jumpsuits followed their dogs to pick a spot to dig, and the line fell back from where the dogs thought there might be life, moving toward each false hope, a bucket at a time. A hundred feet before us, a six-story section of facade from the North Tower stood, undulating double columns of steel that meshed like a screen. It gleamed silver in the new daylight, regal as a tiara. Fires blazed behind it and black smoke plumed. We passed back buckets, and larger pieces of plank and rebar by hand, and now and then there was an ex-plosion, as air rushed into a new void and fed the fire. You would stop and stare, and then someone would tap you on the shoulder and pass back an-other bucket. The hours passed, and the hundred million tons of wreckage began to shift to the side, handful by handful.

There was a great blast, and the ground shook, and the facade trembled and nearly fell as the flames roared behind it. Some people broke from the line and ran back—John scrambled a few steps back—but I just stood there. It would have crushed us if it fell, but the facade shook and held. The line re-formed, but then the FEMA team told us to break for a while. We joined the others off to the side, to sit and stare at the pile. I saw Billy Clune's brother, the lieutenant, and he told me that a Corrections officer had stolen watches from a jewelry store. I saw another fireman I knew, who told me that Tommy Killian was all right. We waited and watched, wondering when the bucket brigade would form up again. The cranes and cherry pickers and earth movers rumbled on; it seemed like there would be fewer opportunities for the digging to go on by hand, and still less point to it. No one had been res-cued from the collapse, but some had been hurt in the recovery. We'd been at work nearly twenty-four hours. The bucket brigade fell into line again, but we went home.

At work, we stayed in the office, in uniform, awaiting the summons. As the hours passed, we pulled out cases and began to type up fives from our notes. If we couldn't work, we might as well work. It was fitful and half-hearted, but it had to be done. If you had a gun stuck in your face in August, it was going to wait a while, but not forever, and doing anything was better than nothing.

There were no casualties among my family or closest friends. Steve Rodriguez had made it: his wife had left the building, which had collapsed before he was able to get inside; he was knocked back by the collapse to wander blindly in the blizzard of ash. Mike Rodriguez had injured his knee, and he would be eventually forced to retire. Rocco Farella, who had gone with them, said that you could only recognize cops by the silhouette of gunbelt and nightstick. My brother Steve's best friend, Dave McGovern, had gone from the NYPD to the FDNY, as many cops had. As he struggled out of the rubble, a falling body killed the fireman next to him, a partner from his house. That's what we heard; Dave didn't talk about it.

People I'd known for twenty years had died, like Mike Armstrong. Mike had given me a job as a doorman the summer after my father died—his father was the super of a building on Fifth Avenue—and the Armstrongs had a St. Patrick's Day party every year. Mike worked at Cantor Fitzgerald, the company that had the largest number of casualties that day—their offices were just above where the first plane hit. There were guys from my high school, Matt Leonard, Greg Trocchi. And others I'd known less long but fairly well, like Dennis Mulligan. Mulligan was a cop who became a fire-fighter, and he'd gone out for years with McTigue's twin sister, Kerry. At his wake, my old Narcotics team had shown up—I hadn't known that Mulligan's brother was a sergeant in Narcotics as well. My sister Marianne called me in tears about Mulligan; she had dated a fireman in his house, and they were friends. There was Bronco and Tom Foley, firemen I'd met through Tommy Killian. Of the other three hundred forty-three firemen, I'd look at their faces in the thumbnail-sized newspaper ID photos and wonder how many I'd recognize instantly in life. I did recognize the O'Hagan brother; I'd met him. Among the cops, I knew their faces better—Driscoll and Coughlin and the other Bronx ESU cops, and Mike Curtin, a sergeant in ESU in Brook-lyn. My cousin Mark, an emergency-room doctor at Bellevue, had worked with Curtin as part of the FEMA Rescue and Recovery team in Oklahoma City, and he told me about how Curtin searched through the voids, making sure that all the bodies were removed with ceremony and dignity.

You heard the rumors: there might be six thousand dead, seven. Three Arabs in a van filled with explosives had been stopped by the NYPD on the West Side Highway, or on the New Jersey Turnpike by troopers, or just before they made the George Washington Bridge by the FBI. My friend Cahill's wife, Renee, called me, overjoyed, to say that she heard that cops trapped in a pocket had shot their guns to summon aid, and then she called me in tears to say that they had committed suicide. What had happened—if anything, I guessed—was that the rounds went off in the heat. Letters laced with anthrax began to arrive in offices, killing more, and you heard rumors about that, too.

You began to hear the stories about the near-misses and the hideous coincidences: one woman who was fired the Friday before, another who had quit, but had come in that day to clean out her desk. The man who had the week off because his wife had just had twins, but he needed to collect some papers to work from home. The other man who worked where the plane struck, but who was in the lobby when it hit, cursing at an obnoxious security guard who made him come down and sign for a delivery. Every casualty seemed to have a cruel twist: they had just gotten engaged or married, their wives had just gotten pregnant or given birth, they had finally gotten a promotion, or a dream job in a company on an upper floor.

The days were still beautiful and limpid, but the F-16s made the air shudder as they circled the city, and the smoke still rose from downtown. We waited and watched, and our part was not long in coming. We were to go to the Fresh Kills landfill in Staten Island, which had been the city dump until it was shut down two years before. "Kills" is from a Dutch word for "stream," but no one needed to point out the irony. It was a man-made mountain of trash, foul-smelling and besieged by thousands of gulls. The refuse would be trucked in from Ground Zero to the landfill, and we would pick through it for body parts, the black boxes, and other evidence. A city bus brought us from Simpson Street in the late afternoon, and as we went out over the George Washington Bridge, I gasped to see planes flying, commercial jets taking off from Newark. They were big and slow and close, and I hadn't seen one since before the eleventh, when I might not have noticed. I gasped again on the bridge, where a vast American flag was draped between spans. It was larger than the sails of the largest tall ship from the summer, and it moved weightily in the wind, and when it snapped it sounded like a cannon. As we drove south down the turnpike, whoever wasn't facing east got a soft elbow in the ribs, and a nod, a tilt of the head—no one said anything—to take in the sight of the new skyline, the city that had been remade. Manhattan itself is like a skyscraper, tall and narrow and ascending to a point. The Twin Towers seemed to pin down the toe of the island, to fasten it to the earth when it might lift off altogether, out of carelessness or pride. As we looked out the window, a pillar of smoke and fire had replaced them on the horizon, a terrible and temporary monument.

The bus driver was from the Bronx and didn't know the area, but one cop was from Staten Island and he directed us to the dump. We crossed back over the bridge to New York and left the highway on a gravel road that led up to the great plateau of trash, which loomed like a fortress in the declining afternoon light. The bus ground through the gravel and lumbered through the potholes, and at the entrance to the landfill, a gray-haired woman in a raincoat held up a sign that said GOD BLESS YOU. Our bus followed a dump truck up the hill and over the plateau, which had lots the size of football fields for the debris, and lights on stanchions, and, at the far end, a scattering of trailers and windblown olive drab tents. The wind was constant and the air was rank. We got out of the bus by the trailers, one an NYPD command post, the other for the FBI. To the left was the Statue of Liberty, unchanging in its pose of vigilance and welcome; ahead of us, across the harbor, was the Battery and the tragic aspect of lower Manhattan; above us was a sky that to the east was a deepening violet and in the west, orange as fire. A tattered flag that had been recovered from the rubble was strung between tents, lashing in the wind.

This was history, I knew, as much history as my home had seen since the Civil War. I had a disposable camera and I snapped a picture. A captain approached me and whispered not to do that again—"A chief saw a cop do that, and he almost fired him on the spot. This is a crime scene." I waited till he left and snapped another, though the light had gone. A group of FBI agents posed in front of the flag, and an official photographer took some shots of them. The gulls whirled and called raucously overhead. One tent was for recovered FDNY equipment, and it housed a loose array of helmets and boots, tools and bunker gear; in another were a few damp cardboard boxes, marked VALUABLES and IDENTIFIABLES, with a few wet twenties in one and a growing heap of credit cards and licenses in the other. There was a supply tent and a mess tent and a trailer for the Medical Examiner. Sometimes it looked like a military outpost and sometimes it looked like a mining camp.

We wore white Tyvek suits—a thin plasticized-paper coverall—along with hard hats, goggles, surgical masks, work gloves, and rubber boots. We looked otherworldly, like men from space, or men who were going there. Were there a hundred of us, or two hundred? It was hard to tell. Most of us were NYPD detectives, since the chief was correct, at least, in calling it a crime scene, and as such it was the responsibility of the Detective Bureau. There were also FBI and Customs agents, Port Authority police, and a variety of volunteers; some had their commands written on the back of their suits in magic marker. There were racks of picks, rakes, hoes, and shovels, and we grabbed our tools of choice and spread out over the piles.

At first, there appeared to be little order. The fields were long and broad, and there weren't enough lights. The well-lit areas were searched over and over, while the dark areas went unexamined. Dump trucks rolled in and unloaded more wreckage, and bulldozers scraped the fields clean, and the little people in white suits scampered out of the way of the monstrous machines, sometimes with seconds to spare. Goggles blocked our view, and the grinding roar of the engines was deafening; we could hardly see or hear anything coming, as we picked through the rubble like gulls. Sometimes you were picking away when you felt a slap on the shoulder, and a figure in white, masked and goggled and helmeted, shouted something you couldn't understand. And then more shouting, and a hand was pointed at an oncoming earth mover, thirty feet high, and you ran off to the side. You didn't know if they saw you; they didn't seem to slow down. Sometimes you were that figure, shouting, slapping, pointing, to someone else on their knees in the debris fields, and they ran off behind you. I stuck with John and Bobby Nardi, and there was a lot of that, watching your back as you picked through the rubble, as the convoys rolled in from the city, with what once had been the city on their backs. In a few hours, a loose sense of organization took hold, and instead of drifting across fields like migrant workers, teams of a dozen formed around each new load as it was spilled out on the ground. A bulldozer would spread it out, clearing the larger pieces of metal and concrete, and then we would clamber into the pile and pick through it by hand.

There was everything there, and nothing. The dirt wasn't even dirt; not earth, but a blend of ash and dust—concrete walls, wooden desks, the people who sat behind them—broken, burnt and hosed down. The largest pieces of structural steel were deposited off to the side, but twenty-foot sections of I-beams and concrete boulders the size of cars arrived on the trucks. There were little things that had survived and big things that hadn't, and there was a sense of the miraculous and the—what? the counter-miraculous? The steel head of a hammer seemed to be attached to a head of human hair, wavy, greasy, and gray, fanning out like an old-fashioned feather duster. What was this? I lifted it to show the mutant next to me, in the practiced pantomime of the deafening, silent piles: shoulder shrug—*What?*—pointing—*This?* It was a freakish crossbreed, half-hammer, half-wig. The goggle-man lifted his mask to yell, "Fiberglass handle! Heat on fiberglass handle!"

There were a lot of bones. There were yards and yards of fire hose. There was white metal from the hulls of the planes. There was a Toyota, mashed flat. A lot of single shoes. There were all kinds of documents, some in perfect condition, from Cantor Fitzgerald, Blue Cross Blue Shield, Aon. I found the personnel file for an Irish Williams, with a reprimand for being late in June 1992. I hoped Irish Williams was late on September 11. All the warranties and guarantees, limited liabilities, risk assessments—had they been voided? All the projections, conditions, and contracts, the paper that is to the corporation what coral is to the reef, just as monumental, just as fragile. For a while, I came across a lot of little yellow pebbles, and I'd always stop when I saw them, because they looked like teeth. We had white plastic five-gallon drums, and we filled them with bones. You got a feel for them, and after a while you could tell them from plastic molding or wooden sticks, but to be certain, you would break them. They had a certain give, unlike cable or a dowel. It felt sacrilegious at first, but it saved time.

When we broke for meal, we were starving, and we stripped off our muddied Tyveks. We were soaked to the skin with sweat. There was another tent full of T-shirts, sweatshirts, and socks, and I changed clothes several times that night. At first, the only supplies they had were hard candies, packets of butter cookies, and Salvation Army coffee, which required faith to drink. Firemen arrived, with vanloads of hot food—pizza, lasagna, sandwiches— and we looked at each other with gratitude and pity: they were sorry for us, because we had to dig, and we were sorry for them, because of what we dug out. The firemen laid out the food for us and left for the tent with their gear, tenderly cradling recovered boots and helmets as if they were infants. We went back into the fields.

At the end of the night, we filed back into the buses, exhausted. I looked out over the fields, with the pole lights and the convoys, the cranes and bulldozers shifting and spreading the remains of sixteen acres of city across the foul, muddy ground. I thought, this is where the world goes, after the world ends. We all fell asleep, and woke to find that the bus driver had gotten lost.

We slept again, and woke in the Bronx. At home, John and I spent half an hour trying to yank our rubber boots off, falling back like stooges. I boiled myself in the shower for half an hour, but I could still smell the dump.

. . .

THAT DAY BLENDED WITH MANY AFTER, ARRIVING JUST before sunrise or dawn, for brilliant twilight hours of purple and golden skies before they turned bright or dark. F-16s in pairs and trios patrolled from the air. The Statue of Liberty held a torch, and the city still burned. I stopped to watch a single silver hearse creep down the road, wondering why there was only one. Helicopters descended from the air, and the roar of the rotors as they set down outmatched the roar of the trucks. For one helicopter, we were called in to hear a speech. A captain spoke with a bullhorn that barked and squealed, but when he turned it off, most of us couldn't hear him. There were cynical grumbles from some people—*I don't need the "Attaboy," let me work or send me home*—but I wanted to hear what was said, and I pushed to the front. The Captain introduced Barry Mawn, head of the New York office of the FBI, and Mary Jo White, U.S. Attorney from the Southern District. Barry Mawn had a heavy Boston accent, and he looked a little like my father, silver-haired and solid. He said that the casualty count was now estimated to be seven thousand eight hundred people, and that he had worked airplane crashes before—it might have been Flight 007, but the bullhorn brayed again—yet this would be much harder, very different, and mostly ours. I couldn't catch much of what Mary Jo White said, but the theme seemed to be "Thank you." Others came to the site, in SUVs—this commissioner, that chief—sometimes to speak, and sometimes just to see it, and the reception was always polite but mixed; there was always something awkward about them. Sometimes we had to stop when they came, and sometimes we didn't, but they would drive away or fly, clean and warm, and we would return to the mud to dig for corpses. *Next time, bring a six-pack. . . .*

You might go to the landfill with one or two guys from the Squad, or you fell in with a group of eight or ten other detectives, to join a sergeant's detail roster. You looked around for people you knew. I worked one day with Mike Donnelly, whom I'd met when I was in SNEU and he was in HIDTA, an NYPD-Federal task force. He was in Bronx Homicide now. He'd known Uncle Eddie at the Four-Seven and was nearing retirement himself. He was with his sergeant, named Duggan, and I jumped on their roster. I asked Sgt. Duggan if he had a brother named Kevin who went to Regis High School. He said that he did. I'd seen Kevin last at a steak house, where I was out with friends, and Kevin had proposed to his wife.

"How's he doing now? Still working in construction?"

"No, he went on the Fire Department a couple of years ago."

I waited a second. "Is he okay?"

"Yeah, he's okay."

The Homicide guys talked about the smell, which was sour from the methane bubbling up from the ground, as well as from the carnage that had been trucked over from Manhattan.

"It's bad here, but not too bad," said one.

"Not as bad as it gets," another agreed.

Mike looked at me and said, "The really bad smell you get from a body, the real putrescence, is from the gas buildup, which makes the body swell. When it pops, it's real bad. But these bodies, well, most of 'em aren't going to be whole, so at least you won't get that. At least mostly, I think."

We watched as the gulls circled like vultures and dropped down on a spot on the ground, fiercely picking. One guy stepped forward, and another, and we broke into a run, waving our arms, to chase them away. The birds had descended on what could only be described as a hemisphere of meat, wet and gray. We stood over it and peered down, speculating. It wasn't a brain: it was smooth tissue, unpatterned, and it was too big, almost the size of half a volleyball.

"I think it's an ass cheek," I said.

"I think you're right."

Someone flipped it onto a piece of cardboard with a stick and carried it over to the Medical Examiner's trailer. When the gulls descended again in another spot, fifty yards away, we ran after them again, waving, but as they alit they tore apart a strip of cloth, and there was no body to be seen. We couldn't have them there, eating people, but they had their uses, too, like pointers on a hunt. A few days later, Danny Mullarkey, who was on the B Team, told me that a falcon had been brought to the landfill, perched in its hood on the falconer's gloved hand. The falconer walked out toward where the gulls whirled and dipped, and then he unleashed the leather hood from the bird and released it. It shot out in a long, low, and direct line of flight, scattering the flock like a shot. From there, it ascended in a widening arc and circled the sky above the landfill, like a guardian spirit. The gulls fled and didn't return, and we never saw them again in such numbers.

The night with Mike Donnelly, I found novelty dice, the kind of jokey knickknack that someone had kept on his desk. Each side bore a line—"Go out with friends," "Work out," "See a movie"—with advice to stop and enjoy life, to seize the day. I tapped Mike on the shoulder and showed it to him. He looked through his goggles and nodded. And then I rolled it on the ground, and the side that came up said, "Take the day off." Mike and I pulled off our masks and stepped aside, and we sat down on the generator for a cigarette. We looked at it again: *Take the day off.*

"Poor bastard," said Mike.

"Maybe he did take the day off."

Mike smiled and slapped me on the shoulder.

The cadaver dogs began to move through the piles, young German shepherds, light-footed over the scrap metal, almost dancing as they sniffed. One had a hit beneath a sheet of white metal that I realized was part of the hull of a plane. The dog lay flat and barked. I lifted it up, hesitating. Would I find a face there? One had just been found thirty yards over, hanging like a rind on half a skull. I didn't want to and yet I did, because it meant that part of someone would go home. I lifted the metal up and the dog sniffed below, and the handler pulled it back. I threw the metal away and got on my knees with a flashlight, sifting through the rubble. Rags, sticks, rocks, twisted little broken things, but no one, or nothing that had been part of anyone, that could be seen. We looked at the dog accusingly, as if she'd lied, and she whined. And then I realized that there might not be any body part to see, but that there were people everywhere, or a broad effluent of humanity that permeated the fields. A while later, another dog hit on me, pointing and barking. I waved it away: *Get out of here! I'm not dead yet, I only smell like it.*

As time went on, the landfill developed into a more permanent encampment, with long tents shaped like onion domes built over steel frames, and trailers and sheds for the mess tent and the decontamination station. The tents were covered inside with cards from schoolchildren, mostly decorated with hearts, stars, and flags, though some drew crying faces, or figures leaping from an inferno. In addition to the piles, there were details for the grapplers and the sifters. The grappler was a crane with a claw appendage, which would pick out large pieces of metal and strew them on a field, and then we would look through them. The grappler took almost an hour to lay out the pieces, and it took ten minutes to walk through them. I didn't like that; I was bored, and I froze standing there. I huddled by the light generator, and burned a hole in the ass of my Tyvek suit. The sifter was better: you stood along one of two belts that ran from a central funnel, which dumped debris through two grades of screen. Each belt carried out rubble, and we stood at the sides like an assembly line, snatching out items as they rolled past. It was hypnotic at first, and then it was dizzying.

The operation became more regimented and efficient, week by week, even as the first wave of emotion passed, and the unison of shock and rage and sorrow was tempered by cold and exhaustion. Though most of us worked with little rest and less complaint, pettiness inspired pettiness, in thought if not in act. You did notice that some people didn't seem to leave the mess tent for the entire tour, and there were rumors that some had snuck away early. We drove our own cars to the site at first, but after a few weeks we had to park in a lot down below, where we were taken up in Department of Corrections buses. The top of the site was a sea of rock and mud, and it was terrible for your car, but I'd also heard that the bosses were concerned that people were stealing rakes. Bobby Nardi said that one boss gave a speech before the tour, berating people for taking pictures, and suggesting that it wasn't cops who took rakes, but volunteers. Bobby was disgusted: "These people had come on their own time, from Ohio or Florida, to spend their vacations digging for the dead. What harm would come from a picture? Would the word get out that the towers came down?" For me, the no-car rule was exasperating—you didn't know whether you'd sweat in the piles or freeze at the grappler, and if I brought my car, I could change clothes, bring my own food, and read on the breaks. I wasn't going to ride like an inmate on the prison bus, and I just drove past the cops who guarded the entrance. Sometimes they yelled or hit the siren, but I just kept going; I figured they wouldn't chase me, and they didn't. I always felt elated when I went past, in my petty, private rebellion, a guilty thrill as if I'd robbed a bank. I found a teddy bear in the pile, wearing a red T-shirt from the International Organization of Operation Engineers, with the slogan *Labor Omnia Vincit*. Labor conquers all.

. . .

WHEN WE DIDN'T WORK, WE SLEPT, AND FOR WEEKS IT seemed we did not sleep. But the sleeplessness accounted for a small part of the bewildering loss of proportion, the confusion of purpose: Was our duty to the dead, or the living? Which victims would we tend to? Aside from the landfill, there were other details: traffic posts, Yankee games for the playoffs and then the World Series. Sometimes we had one day a week to work on our cases, and the cases kept coming in. It was not long before the perps tired of watching patriotic television and returned to the business of stick-ups and muggings. Within days of 9/11, we had a triple shooting, the classic warm-weather ghetto bullshit, which now seemed an affront to history, or a bitter resumption of it: *If we don't get back to thug life, the terrorists will have won!* The victims were no better than the perp, who had let off rounds over drugs, or a girl, or a look, and no one was talking. Relatives raced to the hospital to remove the victims' contraband before we arrived. One victim's mother had witnessed the shooting from a window, but during the interview, the only firm opinion she expressed was that she did not want us to look in his room. I wanted to collar them all for treason. Four days after the Towers fell, I caught my first commercial robbery.

John and Danny had gone to Queens on another case that Saturday afternoon, and I went to the scene with Matt Crowley. Fifteen minutes before, a man walked into a travel agency off the Grand Concourse, where a woman worked alone behind the counter. It was the kind of Dominican place that provided every service that could fit into a hundred square feet: they booked flights, sold cell phones, handled money orders and wire transfers—there was even a barber chair in the back. She didn't speak English, and the perp didn't speak Spanish, but he made himself clear, holding a gun in his waistband and stepping behind the counter. Though there was more than a thousand dollars in the cash box, he pulled the gun on her and said, "Is that all there is?" He seemed uncertain, confused; he stepped back from the counter to try to close the roll-down gate, trapping them both inside, and then he stood there for a moment, with an apologetic air, and left. Ordinarily, there would have been plenty of Spanish-speaking cops around, but we had to piece together phrases of two broken languages to try to put together a story—

"*Qué color?*"

"*Blanco.*"

"He was white?"

"No, *como,* like white."

"Light-skinned?"

"*Sí,* I think you say."

"Was he Spanish? Dominican? Boricua? *Habla él español o inglés?*"

"*No, blanco.*"

"He spoke white?"

"*Sí.*"

No one on the street had seen him leave, and we canvassed with her, without success. There were no cameras in the store, and the patrol sector would wait until Evidence Collection came, to see if there were fingerprints to lift. She couldn't come with us to view pictures, she said, but she would make an appointment later on. The woman was twenty years old, months in the country and weeks at the job, terrified by the robbery and frustrated by us— by the language barrier, and the dunning dullness of investigative procedure, the waiting, watching, testing, the same questions, over and over, five different ways, when all she wanted to do was go home and collapse. In Saudi Arabia, they cut off the hands of thieves, and at moments I felt the policy had merit.

There were times when the "old Job" and the new circumstances did touch upon each other, albeit obliquely. At John's cab shooting from August, a beeper was left at the scene. He tracked it down to a particular store, and we went to interview the owner, who was from Yemen. He looked nervous when we entered. We asked him if he'd had any problems with people since 9/11, and he said that he hadn't. We showed him the beeper and he looked it up on the computer. There could be a problem, he said. Ordinarily, when a customer buys a cell phone, they deal directly with the company, filling out an application with pedigree and credit information. But he bought beepers in bulk, and he took in monthly fees from customers who might only have a first name, and no phone number—the computer might show only whether the account was current. This beeper had belonged to an Arlene, with no last name, and it had been deactivated. But that beeper was one of eight bought for different women by a certain "Don Q." The store owner didn't even want to say the name, but rather pointed out all of Don Q's girls on the computer screen. "He's a pimp?" Looking around nervously, he told us all he remembered about Don Q—an approximate last name, his brother's name, and so on.

When we left, we wondered how we had benefitted from recent events in that interview. In uniform and out, I'd made a point of buying newspapers and cigarettes from Arab stores, and asked if they'd been given any trouble; all had said no. The owner had been exceptionally helpful, perhaps at some risk to himself—Don Q, we later found out, sold guns as well as girls—but there was also something suspect in how much he knew. When I last bought a beeper, the store owner might have guessed I was a cop, but he certainly didn't know my brothers' names. Regardless, we now had a solid lead for the shooting, and the Yemenite store owner, along with all of our Arab concerns, receded for a moment beside the new and eager hope for a collar.

For me, at least, one benefit of the endlessness of the days was that I soon felt as if I'd worked with my new partners for years. In the beginning, Eddie McDonald, John Swift, and Chris Perino had been unfailingly helpful, hovering over John and me to look over our paperwork and answer our countless questions. Steve Rodriguez would say, "Don't think like a cop, think like a defense lawyer." For shootings and homicides, the whole team went out, Norbie Tirado and Matt Crowley, who had come from Street Crime, Danny Mullarkey and Jose Morales, Bobby D'Amico and Bobby Nardi. Morales and Mullarkey were a study in contrast: Jose was coolly disciplined, a former Marine sniper and Gulf War veteran, whose heavy-lidded eyes and deep voice added to his sense of watchful reserve; Mullarkey was a firecracker and the office troublemaker. His caffeine intake was closely monitored, as was his spit cup for his chewing tobacco, which often looked dangerously full. When someone slept over in the dorm, Mullarkey liked to pose them with the teddy bear from Domestic Violence and snap a picture. Bobby D'Amico was so meticulous and professional that the joke was that when he closed a case, the perp's whole family pleaded guilty. D'Amico, who had spent his entire career in the Four-Four, served as almost another sergeant in the office. Bobby Nardi had just reached his twenty-year mark that fall, but he had no intention of retiring. He saw being a detective as a vocation. "I think being an astronaut would be a better job, maybe," he said. "But other than that, I can't think of anything. Is there a greater responsibility than catching a killer?" Sometimes, Bobby said he wouldn't retire until all of his homicides were closed. He talked about movies a lot, which many cops seem to, maybe because they have to picture things and figure out a story. He said to me, "Do you remember Al Pacino in *Heat,* when he says he dreams at night of a dinner party full of all his unsolved homicides, and they stare and him, eyes black from eight-ball hemorrhages? It's not like that, at least not for me, but you could tell he talked to homicide detectives. You do sleep better after a collar, and you sleep really well after a conviction. It's like, 'Rest in peace,' for both of you."

Everyone had a useful story, whose moral seemed to be to stick to it, and ask questions, and don't be surprised because you'll always be surprised. There were things you could do, and things you couldn't, and things you could try, where time would tell. Bobby Nardi had worked for Jack Maple, the architect of Compstat and much else, when they were in Transit; in tough spots, he said, he often asked himself, "What would Jack do?" Maple would bring a chaise longue to a perp's door, so he could wait him out; he also devised a chain-snatch trap for decoys, so the "sleeping drunk" cop had his chain attached by fishing line to a wig, and the cops could follow the chain-snatcher through the crowd, once they stopped laughing. Bobby D'Amico explained that you could lie during interrogations—"We have your fingerprints on the knife!"—but you couldn't lie with a prop; you couldn't type up a report that said, "Positive identification of fingerprints to Joe Perp." In a case that had been overturned on appeal, he said, detectives had invented a "lying machine," assembled from a salad bowl attached by wires to a photocopier, which had a piece of paper with the word "LIE" on it. When the suspect was brought in for interrogation, the salad bowl was placed on his head, for the machine to read his thoughts: "Okay, Joe, say your name is John."

"My name is John . . ."

A detective pressed the COPY button. *Click:* LIE.

"See? This machine never fails. Say your name is Jim."

"My name is—" *Click:* LIE.

"Okay. When I ask your name, tell the truth . . ."

After the response, the detective at the copier simply didn't press the button. Joe saw the futility of fighting the system, and confessed to the murder. But the higher courts felt that he was taken advantage of, and I see the wisdom of their decision. *Click:* LIE.

Early in his career, D'Amico caught a suicide, a young man who hanged himself, which appeared to be a routine tragedy until he received a call from the Four-Seven saying that the girlfriend was missing, too. There was a downpour, and as he and his partner waited in the car, reluctant to re-invade a house in mourning, a young man rode up on a bicycle and said that the suicide had said to him last week, "What if I told you I killed my girlfriend and buried her under my bedroom floor?" They returned to the house and the devastated family to check the bedroom. A rug covered a plywood floor, which had one section fastened with new screws. After calling a captain and ESU, they broke apart the plywood and the oak floor underneath, and then they dug down two feet through dirt. The captain was embarrassed, the family was horrified, and the room looked like a coal mine. "Are you sure you want to go on?" asked the captain. "Just a little further," Bobby said, and after another foot, they hit concrete. It was the body of the girl, entombed. The boy believed that she had given him AIDS, and as he had sex with her one last time, he strangled her. Then he buried her in his room. The next day, he took his own life.

Bobby Nardi caught a homicide when a young white drug addict from the suburbs named Guy was dumped at a hospital with a fatal stab wound. A hospital cop caught the license plate, and it was traced back to another white junkie, who said that they had come into the city to buy drugs. Though they didn't have any money, Guy knew a dealer named Snake who he thought would give them credit. At Snake's place, Guy patted him on the head to show his friend how cool he was with his ghetto dealer. "I ain't no fucking cat," said Snake, stating the obvious. Guy continued, and Snake stabbed him with a broken broomstick, and both junkies staggered out. Bobby and Danny Mullarkey made their way to Snake's house and asked him if he knew Guy. Snake said matter-of-factly that they'd recently had a fight, and agreed to accompany them to the precinct. As they left, Bobby noticed something odd about how Snake walked, and he asked politely, "Are you blind?" When Snake said yes, Bobby said, "You could hear the air leak out of Mullarkey's body. It was the only time I ever saw him speechless. Snake said it was self-defense, I wrote a statement for him and he signed it. I've never heard of a blind man charged with murder, let alone one who signed a confession. When he testified at the Grand Jury, the jurors' mouths dropped open the minute he walked in, and they stayed open as they sent him right back home."

D'Amico and Nardi had decades of experience; for Scanlon and Morales, the Four-Four was their backyard; and though Mullarkey had come from Street Crime only two years before, he knew it almost as well as they did, through sheer drive. The three of them knew every major case in the office, and they ping-ponged names and theories with headachy speed:

"Rocco's hommie, I hear it's T-Money, he's lucky the Jamaicans didn't find him."

"I heard Baby Blood was involved, he had some kind of grudge."

"Nah, Baby Blood's all about the West Side."

"Didn't he have a beef with Mike Murder?"

"Nah, not Mike Murder, just 'Murder,' a guy from the West Side."

"What about West Side? He's in or out?"

"He's in for a hommie, but in Pennsylvania . . ."

They knew the people, and they knew the job, and when a case broke, they fell to it with the avid and total, face-to-the-ground focus of a pack of bloodhounds. At times I felt like a happy mutt who had fallen in with them, believing we were chasing a Frisbee. I barked gamely and ran alongside, wondering when the "fetch" part would begin. But ignorance is not bliss for a detective, and there were cases in which I chased my tail so fiercely that had I caught it, I would have torn it out by the root.

In October, John and I responded to a robbery at a parking lot in a mall. A twenty-one-year-old gofer named Jasper had been sent to the bank with eleven thousand dollars in receipts and had been jumped. Or so he claimed. When I asked him what had happened, he blinked and moaned, as if he were unable to speak, unable even to understand the questions, and he retreated hastily to the hospital. Prior to his case of the vapors, his story was that as he walked through a hallway, an unseen assailant snuck up on him, punched him in the head, grabbed the money, and ran off. The hallway was twenty paces from the office, but instead of returning, he proceeded to the end of the hallway, up a long flight of stairs to the street-level lot, and then all the way to the back of the mall to report the theft to the security office. He acted like he'd gone ten rounds with Mike Tyson but looked as if he'd overslept on a hard pillow: he had the faintest swelling on the cheek, and a half-inch scratch on the jaw. Jasper had been arrested twice for robbery, and he'd recently finished parole. It was a plain lie and a bad story, but up to a point, it was the perfect crime.

And Jasper's story was only the first negative to disprove. The "robbery" had taken place in a hallway between two video cameras, but there was no tape. The guard who monitored the cameras was a woman named Keisha, who happened to be Jasper's close friend. She made a great show of pressing buttons and pulling tapes, first handing us a cassette of month-old footage, before trying to insist the recorder was broken, when it was working perfectly. Ray, the manager of the parking lot, was equivocal: after telling us that Jasper was lazy, dishonest, and about to be fired, he realized it looked bad for him to hand so much cash to a criminal, and became guarded in his statements. Another employee, Caroline, later whispered to me that Ray had told everyone not to talk to the cops, and that Jasper had talked about stealing the money for weeks. Caroline was a complainant in another case at the parking lot, in which a couple in a car had robbed her, she said, because she was too slow in changing a hundred-dollar bill. That video was of terrible quality, and the camera was pointed too high to catch the plate; several other employees even suggested that Caroline had concocted that story. We knew it was Jasper, but did he do it with Keisha? Or even Ray, or Caroline? Or with someone else? I could have asked them, I suppose. I did try.

I asked the management company not to fire Jasper or Ray, but they said they had to fire Jasper, not least because he'd lied about his criminal record.

The security company laid off Keisha, for unrelated reasons. When Jasper came into the precinct the next day, he couldn't even tell a straight story about where he'd slept the night before: he was at his house, but really at his girlfriend's, but not really at his girlfriend's, because he'd left before going to sleep . . . but I didn't get to ask him about much else, because I was sent out to man a vehicle checkpoint at Yankee Stadium twenty minutes later. And I never got another shot at him: a lawyer called to say he wouldn't answer any more questions. The first time I brought Keisha into the office, I had to take her right back to work, as a threatening letter closed down the precinct with an anthrax scare. The next time we talked, we spoke for hours, and against all expectations, I came away convinced of her innocence; she agreed to tape a phone call to Jasper, though he wasn't home. It occurred to me that Jasper might have set up the robbery between the cameras anticipating that his actions would be recorded, and the absence of videotape was an accidental benefit. The more we talked with Caroline, the more we doubted her sanity: on one occasion, she said that a woman had written down the plate number of the car in her earlier robbery, and that she had it on a scrap of paper at home. She'd had it for weeks, but she'd forgotten to tell us. When we drove her to Manhattan to get it, her daughter said, "Oh, *that* piece of paper, Mommy? I threw it out last night, when I cleaned the kitchen. . . ."

On the day I left Jasper's interview for a vehicle checkpoint, I thought about how to handle things. I wanted to throttle him for his mock-innocent pose and his pissy little fibs, and for the fact that as most of the city wept and helped and prayed, he was plotting a phony stick-up. But mostly I hated him because he was a second-rate hoodlum with a second-rate scam, and it looked in all likelihood as if he'd outsmart me. I wanted time to work this one, and time was the last thing I had. How long ago had it been, when I was brooding about the lack of intensity at work? Two months before, a collar might require ten words for charges to be brought: "At T/P/O defendant was in possession of a controlled substance." *The Squad is the Job, Eddie, hurry up and come here.* Thanks, McCabe. With all these details, we couldn't do cases; the perps didn't wait for us, the complainants didn't understand, and the Job didn't care.

· · ·

THE CASES KEPT COMING IN, SOMETIMES THREE AND FOUR a day. You read through the complaint, hoping that the facts offered immediate promise—a named or known perp, a distinctive description, a plate number or other viable evidence—or that they foreclosed on effort from the outset: an arrest had been made by patrol, or the complainant couldn't ID. Every robbery complaint, open or closed, became a case in the RAM. Some could be closed by simply reiterating the facts on the complaint, but the standards were constantly being raised before a case could be closed: reinterview the complainant to make sure he can't ID, recanvass the area to make sure there were no witnesses. The worst were the complainants who said they wanted to pursue the case but didn't; they made appointments to come in but never showed, and then they assured you they would come in the next time. When you called them, you found their phones had been disconnected, if they even had phones, and then you had to go to their homes to try to talk to them, repeatedly, before you could send a case-closing letter, C-3, uncooperative complainant. If they moved without telling you, you had to call the post office to try to get a forwarding address. You couldn't make the visits alone, and the B Team was fortunate to have the extra man, so that if one of us needed a few hours to type up paperwork, we could still go out in the field. I had to agree with the ex-boyfriend of one crackhead complainant who'd gone missing, when he told me with disdain, "This is a whole big bunch of unbelievable!"

"If it isn't on a five, it didn't happen," we were told. Everything had to be documented, and if you interviewed three different people at the scene of a robbery, you had to type three different fives, each headed by names, dates, and numbers. And I do mean type, on a long pink triplicate form, with carbon-paper backs. Errors were not correctable on the back two copies, one of which went into the case file, and few were not marred with typos. If you closed your eyes when you walked into the Squad, it sounded like a 1940s movie set in a newsroom—*tap-tap, tap-tap-tap . . . Get me the City Desk, Lepke Buchalter just broke out of Sing Sing!* We may have been the only police department north of Tijuana that still ran on carbon paper and typewriters. The air conditioning never worked, and on hot days, the fans sent unattended fives fluttering like autumn leaves. When we got days off again, I didn't have a day off that I didn't work on cases at home, because there was so little time for work at work.

The lousy cases swamped the good ones, and both were both swamped by details, and John and Danny might have theirs on different days from mine, and I might not have anyone to go out with, as the Squad was equally swamped. The volume of work was overwhelming—we would have more than a thousand robberies that year—and I was brand-new, and we were at war. Robberies were often harder to solve than homicides, the Squad guys told me, because most killers know their victims, whereas the large majority of robberies occur between utter strangers. The administrative epilepsy of the Job added to the chaos: Sgt. Adler was informed one day that he had been transferred to Special Victims, as Sex Crimes was now known; he was not particularly worried, as he had been transferred four times in the last year, and each time it had been rescinded, but this time it stuck. He was replaced by Sgt. Mike Guedas, who had been in the Four-O. Guedas was similarly surprised by the move, as he'd been transferred from Narcotics a few weeks before.

In spite of everything, I learned how a case broke: someone said something, someone left something, someone saw something. None of these occurred at the behest of the detective. Few perps were as accommodating as the man who choked and robbed a woman on the street and was trying to drag her into an alley when a Good Samaritan intervened, driving him off. The perp dropped some papers, which included a snapshot of himself, and a note with his address that said, "Directions to my house." It was Danny's case, and he was pleased with it.

"Get over yourself," I told him, "Scooby-Doo could have solved this one."

Information often did surface, over time, when another perp hoped to trade his way out of trouble, but you couldn't clear your desk and wait for it. You evaluated each scene for video, fingerprints, or DNA, in descending order of likelihood, and asked about traceable items taken, most often a cell phone or credit card. Though more and more stores have security cameras installed, perhaps one in five provided usable footage. Some of them never worked, and the merchants hoped the mere sight of them would deter thieves, like a "Beware of Dog" sign; others didn't have recorders and were used only to watch for shoplifters in the back aisles. Many reused the same tape every day for months, so that the faces were like the image on the Shroud of Turin, and were just as haunting, and just as unhelpful. For one bodega robbery, I had what appeared to be a tape of excellent quality, until one overexcited worker ran back for the video and mixed up the buttons on the recorder, leaving me with two seconds of robbery footage and a longer sequence of Danny, Matt Crowley, and me entering the store. Absent these possibilities—and they were absent, mostly—you showed the victim pictures. A photo hit was sufficient for arrest, but the ID had to be confirmed in a line-up. A positive identification was the most emotionally compelling evidence you could provide in a case, and if those two words—*That's him!*—were delivered with steadiness and passion, they trumped all the science in China.

We showed the victims photos on a computer, which contained pictures of all defendants arrested since 1997, when the system was introduced. Though the computer was a great improvement over the mug books, it was temperamental and glitch-ridden, but the viewers could be, too. You'd tell them to clear their mind and think back, and remind them to concentrate only on the faces, and not to focus on clothing, hairstyle, or facial hair, which could change. I had one complainant who said, "That looks like him, but no . . . the man who robbed me, he was wearing a hat." I patiently explained that when the perps were photographed in Central Booking, they had to remove their hats, and that in life, also, even the most devoted hat-wearers take them off sometimes.

"Look at the face and remember. If you want to, imagine him in a hat."

"Oh, that's him!"

If you had a specific perp in mind, you would print out a photo array, with the perp and five "fillers." If the perp had something distinctive about him—a scar on the cheek, say—you had to either find scarred fillers, or do a little cosmetology with white-out on each cheek, which might well obliterate the only thing about the perp that the victim remembered. But if you had only a general description, say, of a twenty-year-old male "white-Hispanic" who was five-eight and weighed a hundred and fifty pounds, complainants would have thousands of pictures to look through, and their eyes would grow so dull from watching that the perp could literally melt into the crowd of faces. The more you knew or could guess about a robbery, the better you could narrow it down. Wolf-pack street robberies tended to be semi-spontaneous and local, and you would run everyone of that description in the precinct, knowing that some of them had been arrested for drugs or assaults but not necessarily robberies; solo and commercial robbers were a different, more dedicated breed, and you might run everyone of the scrip who had been arrested for robbery in the borough. Transracial identifications through photos were often troublesome. If a Chinese delivery boy looked at a computer screen with six black faces, he might say, "That's them!"

If the complainant saw a resemblance to the perp in several pictures on the computer, you might print them out and have the complainant look again. One detective suggested I have the complainant rate each on a scale of one to ten. I felt terrible for one elderly woman who didn't seem to grasp the concept.

The perp had followed her to the door of her house, and as she looked for her keys, he punched her in the head and took her purse. Out of the dozens of photos I showed on the computer, she picked out ten possibles. I printed them and told her to rate them.

"Mmm . . . six."

"Okay, looks kinda like him. How about him?"

"Seven."

"A little better. This one, now."

"Nine."

"Really? You're almost definitely sure?"

She shrugged. At the next picture, she said, "Ten!"

"Ten! It's definitely him?"

"Oh, no, not at all."

"Are you more sure of the ten than the nine?"

"I wouldn't say that."

It was like she was calling out bingo; I stopped the rating system shortly thereafter.

For most robberies, a line-up had to be conducted, and it is a peculiar institution, beloved by cartoonists and screenwriters but by neither the police nor the defense. Line-ups often took hours of work, and some ADAs demanded them even when the victim couldn't ID, or the perp and victim knew each other well enough that it wasn't necessary. You got the feeling that if these ADAs were prosecutors at Nuremberg, they would have wanted six million line-ups conducted. The suspect sits with four or five fillers, who are safe from prosecution, though a detective named Brian Walsh told me that a complainant of his once picked out a filler as the perp from another mugging a week before. Line-ups were conducted at Bronx Homicide, on Simpson Street, and a man named Robert was the exclusive subcontractor for line-up filler in the borough. You would page him and say what you needed—male blacks, male Hispanics, dark-skinned or light, bearded or not—and then he'd call back in fifteen or twenty minutes with a little posse assembled, who were willing to sit for ten minutes to make ten bucks. While the arrangement was more convenient than scouring the streets, there was still a class-trip chaos in putting it together: you had only one car, and Robert and the fillers needed a ride, and the complainant usually did, and the perp always did. Robert often joined the line-up as filler—he was medium-everything, height, weight, skin—and could write a far longer book than this one about the murderers, robbers, and rapists he's sat beside, the miracle sextuplets of Simpson Street.

A detective from Bronx Homicide helped run the viewing, and Mike Donnelly, who was also on the B Team, was usually there when I went in. He led me through the procedure, which, like a lot of police paperwork, seemed tough as taxes the first time I did it, and like signing your name by the third or fourth try. Our line-ups were conducted with the subjects sitting down, with a sheet of black plastic pulled up to the chin, and wearing either baseball or ski caps, so that differences in clothing, height, and hairstyle were irrelevant. Mike told me to stand beside complainants at the glass, and to reassure them that they couldn't be seen. "It's obvious when they're afraid," Mike said. "They look from face to face, and when they see the perp, their eyes pop out of their head. You can't tell them which one to pick, obviously, but you can tell them to tell the truth, and that everything will be okay."

In the first line-ups I helped conduct, there were immediate identifications, there were thoughtful negatives, where the complainant scrutinized each face, one by one, and shook her head no, saying this one looked a little like him and that one looked a little more like him, but her perp was not there. False negatives, however, were profoundly frustrating to watch. At my first one, the complainant was so afraid that he could barely look at the photo arrays, as if the face in the picture would yell at him, *Your money or your life!* When I stood behind him for the viewing, as the blinds were raised over the mirrored window, I watched his head as he looked down the line. He paused for two or three seconds at filler one, filler two, filler three, and when he reached the suspect in position four, his head almost twisted off his neck.

"No, I don't see him."

"Take your time, look at everyone."

He glanced at one, then six before turning away again.

Other complainants were uncanny in their visual acuity. One victim, named Alec, picked out a perp in a photo array even though his identical twin brother was positioned, by chance, right next to him—they had been arrested together earlier in the summer on a drug charge. The sole difference between these genetic doubles was that one brother weighed fifteen pounds more than the other. Alec's eye was such that it properly trumped science, which could not have told the perp from his brother. In the line-up, Robert's fillers all had facial hair, while the perp was clean-shaven, and I had to cover them from the nose down. Alec could essentially see five pairs of eyes, but he chose without hesitation. There was something medieval in a line-up, like a witch-trial, but there were moments where guilt was as manifest as if the perp turned green and floated up into the air, praising Satan. "Okay, that's a positive ID."

I kept at my first case, Ethan Prescott, for weeks: he was in and out of the hospital, and I had trouble obtaining his new address from his social worker. When I finally visited him, he opened the door and looked at me without recognition.

"Ethan? How are you feeling? I'm Conlon, the cop who has your robbery case."

He thought for a moment, and said, "Sorry, I didn't . . . come in."

I wondered if he was losing his memory, and he might have been, but that didn't explain the hesitation at the door. As I followed him inside, he said, "I don't know if you knew, but I was blind in one eye before, and now, well, since I got hit, I lost eighty percent of the vision in the other eye. I have infections, I'm at the hospital all the time, I'm getting registered with the Guild for the Blind. I want to thank you for your help, but I haven't found the credit-card statement . . . you can see I'm not unpacked, and I might not be. I do appreciate you trying, but it's not the first thing on my mind right now, or the second. . . ."

When he did call me with a credit-card number, the company told me it was incomplete, thirteen digits out of the seventeen required; by the time I spoke with Ethan again, it was lost. In the meantime, the credit-card company was taken over by another, and the bank had merged as well, and I was bounced between dozens of account representatives, customer representatives, legal departments, and law-enforcement contacts. I had his name, date of birth, and Social Security number, and no one could find his account. It infuriated me because I suspected that if Ethan called asking for a hundred-dollar credit extension, every bit of information would be at hand in seconds. It was only after writing a true tearjerker of a letter to the latest company that I received an attentive response, but by that time, the account had been long canceled, and any information on where the card had last been used was gone. I checked every arrest for possession or use of a stolen credit card in New York City, but none had any relation to Ethan.

Pity and pique, they were what drove you in a case. I worked for Ethan out of compassion, and against Jasper out of pride, and a third case fell somewhere in between them, a double motive to help and to hunt. A young Dominican immigrant named Luis delivered two large pizzas (one plain, one pepperoni), a lasagna, and a large bottle of soda to an apartment where no one answered. The order had been called in by cell phone, which the pizzeria usually didn't accept, but it was a fairly large order, and it was sent out. After waiting at the apartment, Luis went back downstairs, where he was approached by five or six teenagers, one of whom had a knife. Luis remembered the biggest one, who had dark skin and cornrows and stood over six feet tall. They surrounded him and knocked him down, punching him and kicking him, and took the food. They also took his gold chain and bracelet and a walkie-talkie. When Luis returned to the pizzeria, bloody and bruised, the news of his robbery had already reached them—the perps had called on the walkie-talkie to tell them, laughing, and they called with more clever comments until closing time.

The pizzeria was the best in the neighborhood, and I'd eaten there for years. Whenever I stopped by, I asked for Luis, and we wound up talking often. He was a good guy, a hardworking immigrant who had never been in trouble, and I could see that he came to believe I would catch the people who had hurt and humiliated him. If the kids had just looked to scam a free meal, neither of us would have been especially put out, but they beat him, and took his jewelry, and called the pizzeria to cackle about it through the night. I had a decent complainant, gratuitously nasty perps, and a phone number, and I was confident I could make a collar.

I called Sam Ramer for a subpoena for the cell phone, and it came back to a Kevin Wilson, whose billing address was a small apartment building two blocks from the robbery. When I drove up with Danny, he said, "Oh God, not this building. I don't think there's anyone here who I haven't arrested. And the lady on the third floor, where we're going? The mother of all skells." I had run the building, and there were only three skells that I knew of, three brothers, Khaleed, collared for sodomizing a twelve-year-old boy and menacing a man with a shotgun; Saleem, aka Abdool, car thief and gunman; and Abdul, aka John, armed robbery. We went upstairs and knocked on the door, setting off a stampede of footsteps inside.

"You check the fire escape, I'll wait here," said Danny.

Whatever dignity a suit adds to your bearing when you enter a courtroom, it is subtracted several times over when you wear it dangling from a fire escape. But I scrambled up, ducking past the windows on the lower floors, whose residents might have been within their rights to take a shot at me. Peeking into the apartment, it was empty, as far as I could see. Eventually, a young woman answered, letting Danny in, and me after, through the window. Astonishingly, Kevin Wilson was in a back bedroom, sleeping, and his lack of flight provided some small testimony of innocence. Luis had told me that he remembered best the tall one, with dark skin and cornrows, and Kevin was that; he was also thirty-three years old, twice the estimated age of the perps. Still, it had been dark out, and Kevin looked younger than thirty-three, and no matter what, he was coming in to talk to us. We spoke sweetly and he agreed.

While Kevin might have been a first-class liar, I believed him when he professed ignorance of everything I discussed with him, including ownership of the cell phone. He was staying in the apartment as part of a large and shifting network of young men who knocked up the Mother-of-Skells' daughters, or young women who had been knocked up by her sons. Kevin hadn't even knocked up a skell-daughter himself, but he had begun to date one midway through her pregnancy. He wasn't dumb, but he was a little soft, and while he had done time for drugs, he had stayed out of trouble for more than eight years. He had stayed out of most things—jobs, permanent addresses—and the idea that he had a cell phone was flattering but unreal, as if I'd asked him where he'd parked his Porsche. As I continued to talk to him, Danny Scanlon began to call numbers from the phone records.

"Hello, this is Detective Mullarkey from the Forty-fourth Precinct," he'd say, "and we have a real situation here. We have a young man who's hurt, he's unconscious, and we need to identify him to tell his family. I'm calling numbers on his cell phone, hoping someone can tell me his name. Do you recognize this number?"

After a few tries, Danny got a fifteen-year-old girl named Jasmine, who recently got knocked up herself by the owner of the phone, whom she identified as "Sincere." And though neither Jasmine nor her mother thought highly of Sincere, who had recently dropped out of sight, they saw through the ruse and would not provide his real name. Danny did confirm that he lived at the address in question, and that he was about eighteen years old, and he seemed to get a reaction to the name Abdul. I took Kevin's picture and let him go.

When I put Kevin's picture in a photo array, Luis didn't pick him out, and I didn't expect him to. But he also didn't pick out Khaleed, Saleem aka Abdool, or Abdul aka John. Kevin was tall and dark-skinned, and Khaleed was tall and light-skinned, and the aka's were short and dark-skinned, like the other five perps that Luis said he couldn't identify. The aka's were there, I was sure, and though I could bring them in, I couldn't arrest them unless they confessed. Danny and I dropped in on Mother Skell, who claimed that her boys were traveling in various southern states. We told her we had to talk to Sincere about Jasmine, and if we could work it out, maybe her family wouldn't press charges. Mother Skell spluttered with indignation, "Why, every boy in the neighborhood was into her, dirty thing! My son had *nothin'* to do with that." She seemed relieved that we were only interested in a trifle like statutory rape, and as we left, she shook her head and said, "Some people just don't know how to raise kids. . . ."

Of the three cases, Jasper might well go down the drain, and Ethan definitely would—it was effectively over—and I was at a loss for what to do with Luis. Whether Sincere was Abdool or Abdul, I knew he was a part of it, and maybe both were, but the tall one with cornrows was the only one who stood a chance of conviction. But things turn up, unexpectedly. Some time later, I helped Ron Kress with a line-up for one of two perps who had robbed and beaten a retarded eleven-year-old, savagely, for a dollar. It took place in an apartment lobby with a video camera, and we all flinched when we watched the tape. Since I'd spent a day on the case, I knew it, and when a tip was called in saying that the other perp was in front of his building, right now, Danny and I ran out and scooped him up.

It was not a difficult interrogation. Before we could even mention the videotape, he said, "I'm sorry, I know I shouldna done it." He blamed his friend, though he was the one who had broken the kid's nose, pounding away as the kid staggered in the lobby. He was sixteen, and this would be his first adult arrest, though he admitted that he had spent three years in juvenile detention after he stabbed someone at the age of twelve. He didn't know the kid was retarded, and he became frightened, knowing that the crime was more serious than he thought.

"I'll be honest with you, this could go either way," I said. "It's your first real arrest, but the kid was beaten bad, and it's on videotape—we'll get into that later—and with a retarded kid, all bets are off. That's gonna make people mad. Maybe the judge had a retarded niece or son or brother. Maybe the judge is a retard himself! There's a lot of them!"

He nodded gravely, but the remark seemed to slip past Danny as well. The perp confided that he had a friend named Marquise who had several guns in the house. Danny had him call to say he had a job set up, the robbery of a crackhouse, and Marquise agreed without hesitation to meet with a pair of .9s. We got a scrip of Marquise: sixteen years old, six feet tall, dark skin, cornrows. Danny, Keith Clinton, and I staked out the location, but Marquise never showed up. I took the first perp in for a search warrant, and before dawn the next day, we took the door, but Marquise wasn't home, and neither were his guns. His room was a shrine of Bloods graffiti, and there were .38 rounds and a speed-loader in the hamper where he said the guns would be. I pressed the first perp, one last time: *C'mon, what else you got? What else did Marquise do?*

"Well, lemme see . . . there was this pizza guy, Marquise and a couple others called in an order and jumped him. . . ."

Here was my first true hunt as a bloodhound, a long pursuit over hard ground, and I'd found my man. But when I put a picture of Marquise in a photo array and took it to the pizzeria, I was told that Luis had moved back to the Dominican Republic. I should have stuck to chasing Frisbees.

Those were hard collars to lose. The easiest ones to make were the domestics, like the squirmy man whose children's mother put a razor to his neck and emptied his pockets, for "child support," she later explained, though her children had been taken away long before. Or cases that were essentially assaults, like the man whose neighbor led a crowd who stomped him and took his wallet. Both parties were Guyanese, and once I picked up the perp, I thought about letting him go—he said that the complainant had started the fight by smashing him in the face with a bottle, and he had two dozen stitches to back up the story. The complainant admitted to drinking five shots of vodka before the argument, the perp to fifteen of rum. But the complainant had five children and no arrests, while the perp had no children and several felonies. Finally, the perp lied about his arrest record to me and continued to insist that he and the complainant were great friends, regardless of the stitches, so I decided to go ahead with the arrest. But as the ADA took the complainant through the story again in minute detail, he mentioned that the mob that took his money was considerate enough to return the wallet to his pocket afterward, without his noticing. The ADA turned to me and asked, "Have you ever heard a story like that before, Officer? How long have you been on the Job?"

I shook my head. "Not long enough."

The easiest collar was one that was made for me, by Jose, Danny Mullarkey, and Bobby Nardi. A complainant named Michael Monroe had been brought into the station by patrol after he hailed down a car: he had been taking pictures by the Bronx Terminal Market, on the river, when a man approached him with a knife and demanded money. Michael had only twenty dollars, and the perp made him walk to a bank and withdraw another sixty. I was out with Danny Scanlon on another case, and so I arranged to have someone from the Squad show him pictures. That was all that there was to be done—a couple of rounds of pictures and canvasses—and I would pick up the security video from the bank later, to see if the perp appeared on camera. An hour later, we heard Danny Mullarkey on the radio, calling for another car where the robbery had taken place. We raced over to them, and they were cuffing up the perp.

When Bobby Nardi heard about the robbery, he took Michael out on another canvass. He'd caught a homicide in the area earlier that year, of a man stabbed as he walked over the bridge from Manhattan, an apparent robbery. There were no solid leads, but something was bound to break from the crew of whores and thieves who hung around the Market after dark. Michael thought he spotted the perp but said he wasn't sure. "Tell you what," Bobby said. "Why don't you get out of the car and call to him, 'Why'd you do that? Why'd you rob me?'" Michael gamely did as asked, and the response was, "I didn't rob you! You gave me the money!"

The answer was funny, but the story was a little funny, too. The walk to the bank was over twelve blocks, into a crowded and well-patrolled area. The perp waited outside the bank, and Michael could have stayed there, or notified the guard. And the perp didn't take the camera equipment, which was worth ten times as much as the cash he received. On the canvass, Mullarkey asked Michael, "Was there anything sexual happening there? If there was, it doesn't matter, but we should know about it going in."

Michael didn't react defensively to the suggestion, saying that he was there to take pictures, nothing else. In our car, the perp protested loudly on the ride back: "I didn't rob nobody! Motherfucker wanted to suck my dick, and he only had twenty bucks! He got more, I took the money and split!"

It was a good story, and on the face of it, it was a great deal simpler and more logical than Michael's. Michael had a slightly nebbishy quality, kindhearted and absentminded, like a bird-watcher stumbling into a battlefield, his binoculars trained on the hummingbird as the bullets whistled past. But his explanations had their own logic: the perp had taken his wallet before they left for the bank, and his license showed where he lived; if he gave the perp the money, he could get the wallet back, and it would be a fair price for peace of mind; if he didn't take any sudden action, no one would get hurt. Once the perp ran, Michael had called the cops immediately. He also asked to call his girlfriend, saying she'd want to wait with him for the next few hours.

I left him in the interview room and hashed over the story with Nardi and Mullarkey. The perp repeated his claims, with vehemence. We tilted one way, then the other.

"What about the cameras? Why didn't he take them?"

"He's a crackhead. Cash-and-carry, he gets money and he's out."

"Okay, let's look at the blowjob. First, this Michael guy doesn't blink when I bring it up. A guy who begs crackheads to let him blow 'em, who pays them for it, is probably not real proud of himself. He gets beat for a couple of bucks, he goes home, he doesn't make a big stink about it. This guy calls the cops, then his girlfriend."

"And not for nothing, but a hundred bucks for a crackhead blowjob seems a little . . . above market."

"Oh, yeah, what do you usually pay?"

"It's not what I pay, it's what I charge."

Maybe that wasn't such a smart comeback after all. I ran both of them, and that cinched it: while the perp had a long sheet, including half a dozen robberies, Michael had never even made a police report. At the complaint room, the ADA listened to the story and said, "That's exactly what happened to another ADA last week! He's walking through the park by the courthouse after lunch, and a guy comes up to him and says, 'Gimme ten bucks.' The ADA says get lost, and the guy says, 'Gimme ten bucks, or I'll call the cops and say you wanted to suck my dick!'" The ADA knew better and didn't care—no cop would take out his handcuffs, even if he believed the beggar—but there was probably a small but reliable percentage of men who would spend ten dollars to spare themselves the indignity of the accusation. You gotta have a story, and the perp stuck with his.

Within the Squad, that kind of collaboration was necessary and expected, but the responsibilities to other cases was a strain, when you had so little time for your own. Danny might have visits to make when John wanted to catch up on typing, and I might have to help with a line-up from the C Team if Reilly or Clinton had a collar. We also had to cover the home invasions and carjackings that would be assigned to Bronx Robbery, if they weren't available. There were only eight or ten detectives there, and they were stretched as thin as we were; we'd often have to respond, examining the scene and conducting interviews, writing up fives and other reports. The job might take the entire tour, and the case would be handed off at the end of it. If the case looked like a loser, it was a relief, but more often there was some promising, playable angle, and it was frustrating to let it go.

A successful debriefing could also take up an entire tour, though if it went that long, it tended to be productive. Two cops named Kevin Costello and Bobby Nugent made a great collar, taking three perps with two guns after the robbery of a laundromat. The first perp stuck by his ridiculous story: he didn't know his co-defendants, who lived around the corner from him in a distant part of the Bronx; he had found the gun in the street, moments before; he had stopped by the laundromat on a sudden urge to wash his coat and gloves. But the second perp gave it up without hesitation.

"It's a mistake, we all make them, God knows," said Danny.

"When you write down what happened," I said, "be sure to say how sorry you are about it. That's important for the judge to see."

When he finished writing, Danny said, "That's good. It's obvious you're a good guy, come from good people. Who do you live with, your Moms?"

His mother, his twin brother, a younger brother, and a cousin from Boston.

"That sounds good. There's another thing. With all the guns involved in this, we can get a search warrant for your house. We don't want that, and you don't want that."

"We come crashing through in the middle of the night, and everybody gets locked up. Everybody. Is there something there that shouldn't be, a gun? Where's the gun?"

"Arright, there is a gun, but you sure my Moms won't get in trouble?"

"Not your Moms, not your brothers, not even your cousin from Boston. What kind of gun, where is it?"

The sawed-off shotgun was exactly where it was said to be, over the closet in his room. We told him how well he had done, how he'd started to turn his life around, to make things right. But we knew he wasn't being completely honest: no one's first mistake is a three-man commercial robbery with two guns. We pushed harder, and he gave up two more commercial robberies, for a barber shop and a parking lot, and of numerous Mexican delivery boys. And Chinese delivery boys, there were more than he could begin to remember. *That's the problem with robbing Chinese delivery boys, you're hungry half an hour later.* With the second perp's confession, we were able to break the third, though the first stuck to his story.

Danny said that he felt he could talk anybody into talking, with enough time. He once broke a perp in eight words. A crackhead beat his girlfriend bloody and took her gold chain. He didn't remember most of it, he claimed. Danny asked, "When's the last time you saw her alive?" In general, both he and John had a buddy-buddy style of interrogation: *You got a girl? You got a picture? Lemme see. . . . Nice. She got a sister? I'm gonna tell the judge, no bail for you, I should pay her a visit and keep her company. Nah, I'm foolin'. . . . But serious, I wouldn't leave that piece of ass alone too long, you know what I mean? I can help you. . . .* John and Danny were better actors than I was, or at least different kinds of actors. They could muster up an instant intimacy, a brotherly bond, improvised on the quick. I was wary of the we-have-your-fingerprints kind of chicanery, if only because these gambits locked you into a factual stance, and if the perp didn't buy it, it was hard to recover a position of authenticity or authority. While I could conceal my disdain for a subject, I could never pretend affection. Maybe I was more of a method actor, who had to work from a place of conviction. I had to range around to find a point of connection, to spitball and think, and to make the silences weigh on the perp rather than me: *Do you have children? Do you love them? Do you want to see them? Do you believe in God? Do you believe in luck? How about yours, do you believe it's good, even today?* For one perp, I read his horoscope: "When's your birthday, wait . . . Look at this, 'Everyone will understand if you concentrate on your closest loved ones.' And in the other paper, 'Don't wait for others to come to you—approach them first and make things happen.' Is this a sign, or is this a sign?"

I needed a sign, too. Or rather the opposite, a case of substance, that I could use to show I could do this, not least to myself. Though John and even Danny did not have a great deal more time here than I did, they had both proven themselves, collaring on serious cases. Even when a case was closed with a big break—the mask came off during the home invasion, or the perp called home on the stolen cell phone—the very luck of the break seemed a token of justice, of fortune favoring the brave. Though we were trained to be skeptical of coincidence, over time, luck felt like talent, and it was.

Livery-cab robberies in the Bronx had been high-profile for two years, since a slew of cab robbery-homicides had raised the issue in the press. I caught a cab robbery—and a break—in which one perp put a gun to the driver's head, and the other grabbed his neck, and said, "Give him the money!" The driver, a Rwandan immigrant, could identify only the man with the gun. I could identify them both, however, almost immediately, from a digital security camera in the car. Though the robbery itself was not on film, a series of pictures showed them getting into the cab, after which one of them put on a mask. It was such a good picture that it ran in the *Daily News,* and two days later, a neighbor of one perp called, and we picked him up, and he gave up the other, whom we grabbed a week later. The first perp, the gunman, who went by the name K-Lo, had just finished parole after doing two years for the robbery of a ten-year-old boy; the other, Diba, had just come out of prison after doing nearly six years for several armed robberies. K-Lo was wearing the same coat he wore in the photo—a mustard-yellow snorkel jacket with a fur-trimmed hood—and he carried the newspaper clip with his picture in his pocket. K-Lo and Diba both made extensive statements in which they admitted to being there but professed innocence of wrongdoing, blaming each other for everything. Diba was the more persuasive, and the one without the gun, but his knowledge of the take—"It was about two hundred and seventy-three dollars"—was impressive for a bystander.

But in some cases, luck was not enough, nor was talent, let alone truth. I didn't know what else you could bring to bear, but I was still new. I was glad it was Danny's case, and I wasn't even in the office the night a man named Tareek robbed one Arab deli, then went down the block and robbed another one. For Danny, the second robbery was beautiful because they had a video in the store, which captured everything, including the counterman hitting him in the head with a hammer, and the first one was beautiful because patrol caught Tareek on the street, as he ran from the second one. The first victim identified him right there, but Tareek was already back at the precinct, bloody-headed, before the second report was made, and the law required that for that complainant, a line-up had to be conducted, at least a day later. Tareek was picked out in a photo array, but when Danny went to get the second merchant for the line-up, he was told that the man had returned to Yemen. Tareek was only charged with the first robbery, and he testified at the Grand Jury that the cops had always hated him, and framed him, and beat him terribly—*Look at what they did to my head!* All evidence of the second robbery was inadmissible, including the videotape of how the injuries were actually incurred. The ADA was also unable to question him about his twenty prior arrests. The first victim testified, as did the cops, but the Grand Jury believed Tareek. Danny was investigated by IAB, however, and though he seems to have been cleared as well, he was told that the videotape was "inconclusive."

But Danny was at least as happy as I was when the Latent Print Unit called to say that the prints lifted from the cash box in my first commercial robbery, at the all-purpose Dominican store, matched the left middle and index fingers of Tareek. I picked him up at court—he had a case for assaulting a Corrections officer after being jailed for domestic violence, though he was at liberty, again, for both cases—and did not try to interrogate him; he was too seasoned a perp to fall for anything I might have tried. When I brought him into the precinct, he said, "Who'd they say I robbed now?" I put it down on a five. While he matched the description—large, light-skinned, in his thirties—the victim couldn't remember his face anymore, and she did not pick him out. But on the way to Central Booking, I drove past the store, and he said, "I've never been inside there." I put that down on a five, too—it eliminated any alternative explanation for the prints.

In the Grand Jury, the victim testified about the robbery, of her terror and the gun, and the perp's strange behavior, trying to close the gate on them. She hadn't been able to pick him out of a line-up, but the description matched. She was young, pretty, and sincere, all you could ask for in a witness. Tareek was not young or pretty, but he seemed to have mustered some sincerity when he testified that the cops had always hated him and framed him, and though he didn't remember what he was doing on that day, he was never in the store. And he was a Muslim, and he loved his children, and he was probably taking care of them at the time. Or maybe he was partying, but he wasn't in the store. He had no idea how his fingerprints had gotten there, but I had a vendetta against him, after a confrontation we'd had when his uncle was shot in 1996. He presently had a lawsuit against me, he said. I had never set eyes on him before the arrest. And the Grand Jury again set him free. The ADA told me that a woman called out as he left, "Give your baby a big kiss good night tonight!"

The ADA called me to tell me, but I didn't call Danny, who had already left for the day. At least one of us should have a decent night's sleep. What did I lack here? Something was seen, something was left, something was said. I'd even been lucky. And I could not credit the loss to mere luck, because it was not the first time it had happened. K-Lo and Diba were also set free by the Grand Jury, by two different panels. K-Lo said the entire case was a conspiracy, that he had never been in the cab, and the picture had been fabricated by the police, probably on some kind of super-computer. The jacket had been planted on him, and the *Daily News* clip had been planted in the jacket, and he signed the confession only because I put a gun to his head. He made me sound like one of the elders of Zion. Diba said that the robbery had happened, all right, but he was simply a passenger: when K-Lo pulled the gun, he was as surprised as anyone. I didn't have the heart to tell the cab driver, who had come to America from Rwanda to escape unreason and hatred. When I told Sam Ramer, he offered condolences, as if I'd told him about a death in the family; he understood. He said that if it made me feel any better, he thought these runaway decisions represented a kind of addled optimism, that the jurors wanted desperately to believe that these perps were not as bad as we said. As a gesture of faith in human nature, however, it was not what I needed at the time.

FOURTEEN

One night before working at the landfill, I didn't sleep; I couldn't, moving from couch to bed, TV to book, looking at the clock to see if I could get five hours, three, two ... There was an old cop adage, said of perps in the cells: *Only the guilty sleep.* I was guilty of plenty of things; why couldn't I sleep? I packed a kit of aspirin, matches, and disinfectant, and I put on coffee. By the time I arrived in Staten Island, I was ready to pass out, maybe from the guilt of driving past the guards. I had the sifter that day, watching the channeled rubble roll by, steadily brown, with bits of glass that shone pale green, like new shoots in the spring loam. If I looked at the ground, it swam, not with the steady run of the sifter belt but with a seasick, heaving flow. I couldn't look at the ground, I had to watch the belt. There had been fewer bones the last few tours, but still plenty of plastic, credit cards, and the like. Today, there was the head of a putter, a full bottle of perfume, three twisted spoons. A city map rolled past, and I picked it up: the page was open to Staten Island and Fresh Kills. A bike seat, the air bag of a car, two purple bras, still with store security tags, thank God. On breaks, I stepped through the seething, creamy mud, and the wind was putrid and white with dust, the gusts skimming like pale riders over the fields. I dozed off in my car and Danny called. I went back to the sifter. A poster for Excalibur Extravaganza Limousine Service: a jumbo jet over lower Manhattan, the plane heading right for the Twin Towers. I was looking for bodies and finding only ironies, and as the belt moved the rubble, the ironies were gone, too.

For a while, there was no rubble, either, and the belt passed by, empty. We stood there, watching it. A baseball-sized steel sphere popped up from below, and a cop rolled it back against the direction of the belt. It rolled of its own momentum, but as it slowed, the belt kept it rolling forward, even as it came back to the cop who threw it, its force never fully spent. The ball was tossed again, spinning forward as it rolled back. We all watched, mesmerized, as the ball was thrown. What is the physics term? Inertia? Bodies in motion tend to stay in motion, bodies at rest tend to stay at rest. The phrase rolled through my head each time the ball rolled on the belt, forward and back, in motion and at rest. I don't remember much else.

Other duties and details required more than sleep to endure without despairing. The city had barely begun to recover from 9/11 when another plane crash brought more devastation. American Airlines Flight 587 was bound for the Dominican Republic when it went down in Rockaway shortly after takeoff, killing 265 people. There were no survivors. Most of the dead were Dominicans, and while the Dominicans in New York are concentrated in Washington Heights, there were significant numbers in the Four-Four. Detectives are obliged to make official death notifications, and I went with John Flood to tell a man that his son had died.

While it is no pleasure to surprise anyone with news of this kind, our redundancy made the task seem pathetic, even cruel. But what if the family was estranged, and we brought fresh sorrow instead of stale? What if they didn't care? We knocked on the door and the house was full: relatives milled about, and a heavyset man sat at a table, a bottle of rum in front of him. There were grief counselors from American Airlines. We both stood there for a moment, and John Flood began, "I'm sorry to have to tell you this, sir, but the body of your son Miguel has been found."

The heavy man wept and looked down, and several arms were thrown over his shoulders. And then he looked up, staring at us through his tears, and asked, "What about the other three?"

The other three? His wife, his daughter, and another son had gone down with the plane.

There was too much of this. This was far harder than it should be. New miseries seemed not only beyond bearing but beyond imagining, rolling up like rubble on the sifter. Keith Clinton told me that the body of a flight attendant was found, still hogtied. By the luck of the draw, I never had the Medical Examiner's detail, which was generally preferred to the landfill, since it was indoors. But when Danny had the ME, he told me that seven firefighters were brought in. The first time John had it, he said, it was so easy that when he got it again, he felt twice as lucky to be spared the elements in Staten Island, natural and otherwise. After, he didn't feel lucky at all:

"It was the worst, my worst day on this job. I start at 0400, get there half an hour early to get on a decent roster. There's one sergeant who looks like he knows everybody—'Hey Tony, hey Phil!'—like he was there every day. I decide to go to him, he'll have it good. Turns out, he wasn't there much at all, or maybe nobody likes him. He gets 'escort.' Next thing you know, you gotta get in all this gear—hospital scrubs, masks, booties, long gloves, short gloves, the whole nine, bundled up worse than a surgeon. Turns out, the job of an escort is for when a cop or a fireman comes in, or any part of a cop or a fireman comes in, they get a cop to walk them in. We get on line, ten a.m., we wait outside. I'm like, 'Hey, this detail's a bunt!' Then we all gotta go out, get to attention, an ambulance comes. We stop, dead silence. The ambulance has two or three cop cars in front of it, two or three behind. The lieutenant who runs the detail yells, 'Preee-sent *arms!*'

"We salute, and a body bag comes out, with a flag on it, and they put him on a regular rollaway stretcher. They take the flag off, they fold it up by triangles till it's a little package and put it under the stretcher. Then they put another little American flag on top of him, like what a kid would wave at a parade. So there's always a flag.

"They take it inside. It's a full body bag, a full one. 'Present arms,' again, and they open it up. It's bunker gear, a fireman's jacket, a boot—the rest if it, you couldn't make out. It stunk like all hell. A guy in front of me got that. The next one comes in—same thing, salute, walk it in from the ambulance, salute. It's a foot. I'm up next. It's like eleven-thirty when it comes in. This time, the body bag looks real full. There's five or six tables, this one goes to the main table. The medical examiners open it up, and it's a full body, full uniform, it's a cop. He's got Hi-Tec boots, cargo pants, uniform top, shield, nameplate, gun on the side in the belt. All the everyday cop things you see—extra magazines, belt keepers. The body's intact. He was burnt a little but he was mostly dirty. He was buried. That's why he came in as a whole body, but the firemen were smelly soup in bunker gear. They had air, they burnt.

"Stunk like all hell. The body was like the Crypt Keeper in *Tales from the Crypt,* shrunken. It was like the fat in the skin was sucked out, it was around the bone. The cheeks were sunken, the eyeballs were sunken. The face, the face was frozen, and it looked like it was screaming. The 'I'm gonna die!' look, preserved. Like he saw the I-beam hit him, and the face stopped there.

"The guys get to work, like it was nothing. This is what they do. One hand has a leather glove, they take that off. They cut the clothes off, the gun belt, he's naked. The stink is worse. One of them cuts off his pinkie toe for DNA, they sliced it off right there in front of me and put it in a tube. They take measurements, height and weight, head to toe. They put him back in the bag, back on the stretcher. I couldn't believe how they picked him up, no mask, no gloves.

"Next, they yell, 'Escort!' I'm there, I never left. They had two PBA delegates, union delegates, to take his stuff back at the end. Some people are looking, gawking a little, and for the MEs it's like nothing, but the whole thing's so respectful. You know?

"Okay, there's three different stations. First, there's fingerprints. There's an FBI guy there, two NYPD. One's a white shield, I think his family has a funeral home, he's a mortician. They lift up the hand, they feel it for the texture. They got incense burning, but it still stinks, when they open up the bag again, it's like a ton of bricks. The two of them are playing with the skin on the hand, it moves more than yours or mine. One says to me, 'Do me a favor, hold his hand up.' They got me holding up his dead arm. They play with the finger and they inject something in it, it swells up, and then they try to roll a print. It's no good. They try another finger, they inject that. Negative. Another guy grabs a scalpel, he cuts around the finger, all around the tip, he wiggles it so it gets real loose, and he starts pulling up the skin. It gets caught on the nail. I don't know if he took off the nail, I think he took it off over the nail. Then he takes the skin and he slips it over his own finger, rolls it in ink. He gets a perfect print. He cuts off maybe eight of the fingertips, the skins, and he rolls for prints. I was a little too involved. I'm moving body parts, holding hands. All in the stench, looking at the corpse.

"The whole thing takes forty-five minutes, and we zip him back up. Next stop is dental. Oral surgeons, dentists, whoever else. Four guys. They tell us to take a seat. Again, they unzip, and the smell hits you. . . . They gave us the option to wait outside, but I figure I'm the escort, I gotta stay with him, he's a cop. They hacked his face up. They cut his face open and cut his whole jaw out, they cut the fucking jaw right out of the face. They analyzed each tooth, all the molars, eye-one, eye-two, all of them. We were there an hour an a half. That was the worst one.

"The last stop, X-ray. Unzip, board underneath, the chest X-ray, torso. We had to stand outside for that. Finally, there's checkout. They hand over the property to the PBA guys, check off the list. ID card, shield and gun. They zip him up again right there, and the Lieutenant takes the little flag from the top of the body bag. 'This poor sap deserves better than this.' The big flag goes back on top. The Lieutenant yells out, everybody comes to attention, the meat wagon's out front. We snap a salute. I was overwhelmed by how respectful and courteous the Job was for this.

"I stood outside the rest of the day. I didn't want nothing to do with nothing after that. I smelled him and held the rail of his stretcher for two hours, I held his hand for almost an hour. I didn't want nothing to do with nothing after that. The face sucked in, like he was screaming. The look. That was the only full body that day. Noreen O'Shea was working with me. She got off easy, she got a little finger or something.

"I couldn't eat for a long time after. You have it in your system, that DOA smell, you feel it in your clothes, you feel it on your breath, even in the fresh air. That's fucked up. They got me holding up his dead arm. The shitty part was that I'd be standing beside him, and there was a poster on the wall with all the dead cops' pictures, and I'm looking at his live face on the wall, and his dead face in front of me."

As the weeks passed, I saw John's mood darken, his teeth clench more and more. He didn't see Julie because of the schedule, didn't eat right, didn't work out, couldn't study for the sergeant's test, which was a few weeks away. His streak of good collars and even good cases ended, and his desk piled up with fives on complainants who didn't show up or changed their stories, who couldn't ID but wouldn't admit it, of visits to empty houses. "I feel like a secretary," he said. "I haven't done police work in months." Scott Adler called to ask him if he wanted to work on a special task force for a pattern rapist who had assaulted a dozen women in the Bronx and Queens, ranging in age from eight to fifty-eight. He would have steady days off, and a flexible schedule, and he would be exempt from details. Instead of two dozen cases, most of them petty, at least in what was required of him, he would have one tremendously important one, and he would have the rest of his life back. I loved working with John, and he was welcome to live with me as long as he liked, but especially in the weeks after September 11, we were together twenty-four hours a day, seven days a week.

"Do you want to come?" John asked me. "There's more spots open. . . ."

It would be a temporary assignment, he said, for a few weeks or maybe months. But Eddie McDonald, from the A Team, had been on the task force for Isaac Jones and his fifty-one rapes—Eddie had obtained the confession, in fact, with Bobby Dellano from Homicide—and that temporary assignment had lasted two and a half years. At the Four-Four, I was exhausted, but I was exhilarated, too. I was finding my stride in robberies, in the Squad, and with Danny. We'd call each other on our days off to figure out cases, or talk shop over dinner. Maybe it would be three months or six before I felt comfortable and competent enough to think about going over to the Squad and catch homicides. I'd know it when the time came, when to make the move. I told John that I'd stay. I called DI Rising, too, to say that I was going take a pass on Manhattan Robbery. This was the place for me. I told John there were no hard feelings, and I taped a sign to his bedroom door that said "For Rent." He looked at it and shook his head, laughing. "*Gabbados.*"

"*Stunad.*"

"*Gavone!*"

"*Prick of misery!*"

"You hungry?"

"I could eat."

"Let's go out . . ."

We'd partner up again, in time—it was a twenty-year road, and we weren't half done. *Next year in Jerusalem . . .*

It was one of the smaller coincidences, I thought, that he left as we had started in SNEU, for a pattern rape detail. Of the old SNEU team, Tony was in the Squad, in the Four-Two, and Orville had never left, though he was now on the list for sergeant. Chicky and Stix had returned, from the midnights and from Sgt. O'Hagan's team. Eileen Brown had been the boss, and then Tommy Clark, and they said that things got better again, almost as good as they had been with PK. My old antagonists—the Captain, the ICO, and the Sergeant—were all gone. Alicia had gone to PSA-8, and Sammy was still in Narcotics. Smacky was a SNEU sergeant himself, in the Four-Seven. PK had left PSA-8 for the Medical Division, which gave him a car to take home, and flexible hours. His boys were getting bigger, and walking better. Though he was now and then tempted to return to "real" police work, the temptation passed; he had done his share, and he'd keep what he had. I talked to him every month or so, and his voice always brought me back: *Laddo!*

I'd run into other cops from PSA-7, sometimes at crime scenes, where I'd be the Squad guy in the suit, asking the questions: *Whaddaya got, kid?* Some

were impressed and some weren't; at one commercial robbery, Eddie Tibbatts interviewed me as I interviewed the victim:

"Eddie C! How ya doin'!"

"Eddie T! It's good, good. Hang on—so your hands were taped like this,
you said? Did he bring the tape or find it in the store?"

"That's a nice suit. Sharp! The dry cleaning must add up, though, huh?"

"Thanks, yeah, it does—sorry, you said the three guys had masks and
gloves. Did they take them off ever, did they touch anything?"

"Didja hear, John Chase is in FD now?"

"Yeah, I heard—and you said you have an alarm? Did you call the company?"

"Thursday night, the Copa, whaddaya say, me, you, and Johnny T, we
hit it!"

"Absolutely!"

Eddie T could always put things in perspective. A night out, a night in, a
breath, a break: any of them, all of them, were all I needed, and they came, in
time. We were all struggling, I knew, even the most veteran detectives, and I
wondered what perversity it was to take comfort in the idea that it would get
no easier with experience. And to think there were brand-new investigators,
like me, with their own cases and details, who couldn't even type. At Fresh
Kills, the wasted landscape was infernal, but we would leave it after twelve
hours, alive. The damned that Dante stuck in the mud were those who made
themselves miserable in life: "Once we were sullen in the sweet air . . . Now
we have this blackened mire to be sullen in." I was ready for my next run-in
with Chief Tiffany, but when we met again, the lesson was not from literature. He said, "What we're doing at the landfill is unique in human history, I
think. At a certain point, you would have expected us to give up. Was it the
Battle of Stalingrad, where they bulldozed over it and planted trees? There's
never been anything like this, looking through a hundred million tons of
wreckage by hand, looking for each individual person," he said. I kept my
complaints to myself, nodding. Maybe this war would end, as the Trojan War
did, when the bodies of the fallen came home.

In the supply tent, the pictures of people identified from the landfill began
to accumulate, firefighters and businessmen, IDed by fingerprints, bones,
DNA. The next time I had the detail, I saw Billy Clune and a few guys from
the team—Abe Garcia, Jimmy Donovan—and he told me, "They got a foot the
other day, and I think they got a pelvis in Area D." His department van was

parked next to my car. "How'd you get up here? Never mind, I don't want to know." For our meal, we stripped off our Tyveks, washed our boots, and entered the chow line, as Salvation Army volunteers from Kentucky and Texas ladled out bratwurst, potato casserole, and Salisbury steak, items that had disappeared from Manhattan restaurants before La Guardia left City Hall. In acknowledgment of the cultural divide, they put up a cardboard menu: FRIED POSSUM, BOILED POSSUM, AGED POSSUM, FRESH POSSUM. DESSERT: SQUIRREL PIE. Their kindness and cheer made it hard to complain; they didn't have to be there. As I ate in my car, I read *The Thin Man,* with Nick and Nora Charles, the elegant couple who solved elegant crimes amid wry dialogue and many cocktails. On a visit to Manhattan, the Charleses have become embroiled in the disappearance of a wealthy and eccentric inventor. Nick gives some shrewd interrogation advice to NYPD detectives on how to approach the inventor's venomous ex-wife:

> *"The chief thing," I advised them, "is not to let her tire you out. When you catch her in a lie, she admits it and gives you another lie to take its place and, when you catch her in that one, admits it and gives you still another, and so on. Most people—even women—get discouraged after you've caught them in the third or fourth straight lie and fall back on either the truth or silence, but not Mimi. She keeps trying and you've got to be careful or you'll find yourself believing her, not because she seems to be telling the truth, but simply because you're tired of disbelieving her."*

I made a note of that and returned to the sifter. The observation startled me with its acuity, given the book's breezy style. The value of an interrogation was not always that you arrived at a truthful statement, but that you drew out a story, a character, a line, and kept them coming, and wrote them down. You had testimony, and testimony has its own truth, if not about what witnesses did or know, then about who they are. If I could remember that, I might get along in this business. *The Thin Man* became a movie with many sequels: *After the Thin Man, Another Thin Man, Shadow of the Thin Man, The Thin Man Goes Home,* and *Song of the Thin Man.* Though the series declined in quality, the characters remain irresistible: they had fun and found things out. The "Thin Man" figures only in the first book—he's the missing inventor, not Nick Charles—but it worked, so they kept it, and few people seemed to notice and fewer seemed to mind. If I could remember that, too, maybe the skinny new detective had a place here, after all.

• • •

AT THE SQUAD, THERE WAS MUCH MOVEMENT: LT. GEORGE
Corbiere would retire and Lt. George Tagliaferri would replace him, followed
by Richie Vasquez, before Jimmy Ruane returned to the Four-Four; Larry
Sheehan would retire also; Mike Guedas would be reshuffled to the Four-One,
and then the Four-Three, and Timmy McCormack would fill his spot; Tommy
Rice would be sent to the Four-Two, and back, and then to the Four-Seven. In
the RAM, Ron Bolte would come and go, and Jimmy Mangan and Owen Clifford would come upstairs from patrol, and then Rachel Silva and Barry
Jones. They asked me how to do things; I wasn't the new guy anymore, or at
least not the newest. One of Owen's first collars was of an armless man, and
Owen had to ink his feet to take footprints for identification. I asked Owen
what he got him for, and he paused a moment before responding, "Forgery."

"Eddie, you wouldn't believe it," he went on. "He could do everything, he
could smoke a cigarette, he could write, he had better penmanship than you
or me. He could do everything but wipe his ass." Realizing the next question,
Owen added quickly, "I called his wife to come in."

It began to feel as if I'd worked with Danny, Jose, and the others for ages,
and it felt good. And detective work began to resume the balance of our attentions, bit by bit—and maybe not by chance, my cases seemed to get better,
even as I got better at them.

In the last century, the jails in New York were run by the Department
of Charities and Corrections, and these dual motives applied for us today.
Charities and Corrections, pity and pique: the victims looked to us for justice,
for a compassion that was larger and longer-lasting than the contempt with
which they had been treated. We rarely got their money back, and certainly
couldn't unspill their blood, but even when we didn't get the perp, we could
help them move on by showing our sympathy and perseverance. There was
the two-year-old boy who was picking a flower for his grandmother when a
crackhead knocked him down and snatched his chain. That case will never
close for me, though I may not get the crackhead, but the father and grandmother were heartened to see the neighborhood covered with bilingual
posters advertising a two-thousand-dollar reward. There was the case of
the fifteen-year-old whose face was set on fire in a Puerto Rican–Dominican
drug-gang war (last score: Puerto Ricans up, four shootings to two), in which
Mullarkey scammed the perp into surrender, telling his mother we'd heard

of threats to his life. If there was charity in the baby-robbery and face burning, my Dominican counter-abductions were pure correction: the first victim was taken from the street into a vacant apartment, duct-taped, and pistol-whipped. In a moment of Clouseau-like inspiration, he decided the acquaintance who unexpectedly called an hour before must have been responsible, and the next day, he and a friend took the acquaintance for a ride at gunpoint. They demanded the address of his family in the Dominican Republic and told him they would all be killed if he didn't supply the names of his accomplices. It was all drug-related, I was sure: I collared the first victim, and his friend fled the country. That case will always be closed for me. Another correction case was for the Bloods who stomped a little African kid for a few dollars. As I drove one perp to the line-up, he boasted, "You watch, I'm gonna be out for New Year's, see the ball drop in Times Square."

"The only balls that are gonna drop for you are your cell mate's on your chin," I replied.

Danny almost drove off the road.

The Squad is the Job, Eddie, hurry up and come here. . . .

If an investigation followed a trail to one person, or one place, offering the satisfaction of hard-won arrival, there were detours and diversions that were horrific, or hilarious, or haunting, or all of them at once. You felt like you stepped into a comedy sketch sometimes, or even a fairy tale. Jose caught a kidnapping, in which a teenage mother had met a friend from school at a laundromat; the other girl offered to take the baby for a while, and even to go out and get some Chinese food for them. An hour passed, and then two, and then eight before the mother finally called the police. The perp lived in the Heights, and Danny and I canvassed there in vain all night, checking in on the corners and at the hospitals. In the morning, the baby was returned, safely, but it was the interval that fascinated me, when Jose told me what had happened: the perp had taken the baby to the house of a boy she had slept with, a year before, knocking on the door at midnight.

"This is your daughter," she told him. "We had twins, but the boy died."

I wonder if she expected to be rebuffed or embraced, presenting her changeling, the true lost child with the imagined one, and I wonder if the embrace was what she wanted, because the boy woke his mother, and she summoned relatives, who brought presents and made food and admired the new baby until nearly sunrise, when she excused herself for a moment and left. She went home to sleep, abandoning the baby in a carriage on the sidewalk in front of her parents' house, where it was discovered by a news crew. The boy and his mother waited awhile, trying to take it all in, before they left for their own local precinct.

"My wife and child are missing!" he said.

I still feel for that boy, who lived a lifetime in those hours, and all of it a lie.

Another evening, I spent a few hours with Bobby Nardi in New Jersey on computer searches for a car involved with one of my cases; a friend named Jimmy Abrams was a cop at a small, prosperous, sleepy town in that state, and he was of great help. On the drive back, Bobby and I talked about how different our jobs were from his, though we were cops, a few miles apart.

"God bless these guys. They make nearly twice our salary, and what do they have to deal with?"

"Traffic, sometimes."

"Exactly. And us, here? What we gotta do . . ."

As we pulled into the precinct, a man staggered down the street and collapsed over the hood of a patrol car, spouting blood from three holes in his chest and one in his face.

"I've been shot!" he screamed.

But wait, it's even funnier: a woman had just pulled up to the cops to ask for directions to the highway; she had gotten lost on her way back from a Mets game.

"Is this a dangerous neighborhood?" she asked, as the near-corpse stumbled over, howling, as if on cue. The man lived, of course—as the cop adage goes, the perps survive machine guns, while we die from paper cuts. The victim had just been released from prison, and he was beating his girlfriend in his car when one of the drunks from the corner told him to lay off. The drunk wasn't a perfect gentleman—he'd been hitting on the girlfriend every time he saw her, drunk or sober—and the girlfriend ultimately chose the beater over the shooter. *Ah, love.*

I began to play a larger part in other cases in the office, to earn my keep in the Squad. Jose caught a homicide, when a man named Gio argued with his girlfriend's nephew over returning a videotape—*Bait,* starring Jamie Foxx— and shot him in the chest. Danny and I searched his apartment, and I came up with his grandmother's address on his parole discharge papers, beneath a couch cushion. We trapped a call to her phone, and an hour later, he leapt from his friends' closet into the waiting arms of Jose, Timmy McCormack, and Brendan Mallon from Homicide. The next day, Danny and I transported him to Central Booking, and we pushed him for the gun:

"Listen, Gio, I know you made a statement last night, and it's one of two stories—it was an accident, or it was self-defense. You can take a plea or take your chances with the jury, and they're gonna think it's your fault or the other guy's. But either way, the gun was there—you didn't throw the bullet at him. Now, if some kid finds that gun and plays with it, and something bad happens, that's all on you—that's your fault, because you played cute with us, now."

At first, Gio told Danny that he'd thrown the gun in the woods by Van Cortlandt Park, but now he told me that he'd put it in a tar bucket on the roof of his apartment. Often, the mood tipped back and forth between the adversarial and the almost amiable—Gio had come into the precinct fighting, and he left it making deals; the gun admission had won him a plate of steak and eggs. He and I began to get along.

"Man, I shoulda come out shooting the other day when you guys got me. . . ."

"C'mon Gio, would you rather be dead? Or full of holes, pissing in a bag the rest of your life, in prison? Now, who knows? Maybe you beat this, you're out in a year. . . ."

"Yeah, you're right."

"What you should have done is run. The apartment you were in? The roof of a church is right out the window. Me and another guy were waiting for you on the street, but who knows, maybe you could have beat us. . . ."

"Yeah? Shit! No kidding!"

He said he wanted to go to the hospital, because his arms hurt a little. At the hospital, rear-cuffed and in leg irons, Gio tried to pick up girls. When an aide walked past, he ran his game on her—"Mmmm, look at you, what a fine woman . . ."—and I laughed at him.

"C'mon, how does that work for you, on the outside?"

"I can't complain, Conlon."

"Well, I bet this lady's looking for somebody with gold chains, not steel ones."

The aide started laughing. "It's a little more my style!"

When a young blonde walked past, he nudged me and said, "That's all you, Conlon, that's all you!" The blonde was a medical student, who stood beside us with two or three others when the attending doctor examined Gio. Danny made sure they saw where the medical-treatment form said MURDER as well as "complaint of ache in wrists." Gio ignored the doctor as he extended his arms for the examination, staring at the blonde.

"Yo, what's your name?" he asked her, abruptly.

She was surprised, but didn't betray any nervousness: "My name is Laura."

He paused a moment, and then cocked his head back and forth for the introduction: "Laura, meet Conlon. Conlon, this is Laura."

He smiled and winked at me. Danny informed me later that I did in fact blush.

The doctor attempted to continue his examination with all seriousness. He asked about past illnesses and medications, if Gio used drugs, drank, or smoked. For the last, Gio stammered, "I smoke a cigarette or two, now and then, but do you mean . . . I mean, the last two days, it's like nonstop, two packs, three . . ."

I offered my assistance: "What I think the doctor means, Gio, is how much do you smoke when you don't shoot people."

"Aww, man, Conlon, you blew me up! And I just hooked you up!"

I was starting to feel hooked up. Or unhooked, in truth. As Sgt. Adler said on my first day, there was an "adulthood" to the Squad, which I didn't fully appreciate at the time. Though the supervisors ensured that certain things were done, or done on time, in a narrow sense, we did what the case required, not what the boss did. I wasn't sure if it was a trait of Irishmen or second sons, but the history of my relations with authority, at least on the Job, tended to split sharply between strong admiration and near-mutiny. Here, I was my own man, fatherless, as it were, and if I was free to succeed, I was also deprived of an explanation for failure. I hadn't expected to be unready for it. The word "perp" itself is a kind of misbegotten son, lost in the law: at the root of "perpetrate" is "father," in *pater,* which extended to a sense of mastery or accomplishment. At first, to perpetrate meant only to do or achieve, for neither good nor ill, but its early usage by lawyers led it to mean "to do wrong." There was a lesson there, somewhere.

It was an interesting thought, of the kind that I tried to keep to myself, though more must have escaped than I remembered. When Danny and I passed an apartment building on the Grand Concourse, Danny jabbed a thumb at it and said, "You know who that was named after? The guy who invented the nickel." I looked quizzically, at him and then it, before I saw the building was named The Lewis Morris. All right, it was his half-brother, Gouverneur, who came up with the word "cent," but close enough. Another time Danny and I were out with Bobby Nardi when I noticed we were passing 1455 Sheridan, and we pulled over. We went to look at the building, an old prewar apartment house. As I explained our purpose, Bobby was excited but Danny just shook his head.

"This is where Lee Harvey Oswald lived, when he was a teenager," I said. We fanned out into the lobby, a half-century late for the canvass.

"Across the street, it's Taft High School. Do you think he looked out and thought about presidents?"

"Where did he live? What apartment?" Bobby asked.

"A basement apartment is all I know."

"Maybe he carved his name in the wall."

There had to be something here that meant something, at least to us. I scanned the mailboxes; the names were almost all Spanish, but none, alas, was Castro. The walls were stucco, painted a mustard-yellow color, tediously free of graffiti. As we walked out, I noticed decals on the front door, and one stood out, rather dramatically, for a livery-cab company: KENNEDY RADIO DISPATCH.

"Sometimes, it all fits. . . ."

Danny was relentless, approaching each encounter, each interview, with the belief that someone always knew something: if you didn't have a gun, you knew someone who did, or knew someone who was wanted, or someone who should be. You never had nothing. On a day that I was out, patrol made a robbery arrest; Danny debriefed the perps, who admitted that their intended victim was a drug dealer. Danny took the dealer and eleven kilos of cocaine. But outside of the Four-Four, I was happy to tell him, he was clueless as a tourist. When we had to pick up a perp at his job, as a concessionaire at the Midtown theater where *Sweet Smell of Success* was playing, I had to urge him to slow down, to time our arrival. We got there just after the curtain opened, and the manager asked if we could wait until after intermission to make the arrest. "In the meantime, why don't you enjoy the show . . ." At last, we'd made it to Broadway . . .

But the real mark of a detective is the interrogation, which at its deepest level is a matter of convincing a perp to trust you more than he trusts himself, and then betraying that trust. *Trust me, trust me, it's my mother's maiden name. . . .* To go in, get it, and get out without looking back had not been the way I'd lived my life, and I was uncomfortable with the thought that I might become comfortable so doing. I wasn't sure I had it in me. As Sonny Corleone tells Michael, *You gotta get up close like this, and bada-bing! You blow their brains all over your nice Ivy League suit. . . .* And then I remembered a time when my father returned home from a garage sale with a tent. He was in an abstract and slightly melancholy mood. "It's a sad story, really," he said. "The lady who had the sale, her son was on a camping trip. They had a gas heater in the tent, and it leaked, and the kid died. His best friend, too. Tragic, absolutely tragic. That's why I tell you kids to be careful about gas. . . . Wonderful woman, the mother. Catholic. Anyway, the tent was brand-new—used once—and cost three hundred dollars. The woman wanted two."

"How much did you get it for, Dad?"

Without a beat or even a break in the mood, he said, "I walked away three or four times, got her down to twenty. Now, what's for dinner?"

Alas, I thought, I had it in me, and I might as well use it. I caught a case after two new cops named Calamari and Mattison made an outstanding collar of a vicious assault on a nurse. The perp had slipped into the hospital and happened upon his victim in a storeroom; when he tried to rob her, she started to scream, and he jammed his fist so far down her throat that he ruptured her tonsils. The cops were in the emergency room on an unrelated stabbing when the perp ran through, bloody-handed, yelling, "A lady back there needs a doctor!"

The crime had taken place at about six in the morning, and the perp was asleep in the cell—still cuffed, his hands in paper bags to preserve the evidence—when I came in at eight. I let him sleep a few more hours before taking him upstairs. Although a confession might not be essential in this case—he had been IDed at the scene by the nurse, and her DNA would be collected from his hands—we wanted the case to be Bronx jury–proof, and for him to go away for a long time. I brought him coffee, candy, water, and soda, and I read him his rights. He didn't give me much in return. His name was Jerry Mapes, he said, and he didn't remember anything. He said it was his birthday, and he'd been celebrating with an eighteen-hour angel-dust binge. He said he'd never been arrested, but he'd neither worked nor gone to school for ten years. He wanted to go back to sleep. Only the last statement was true. But one of the real difficulties of interrogation was not telling truth from lies, but rather telling the relevant lies from the reflexive ones. As former prosecutor Thomas Puccio said of Robert Leuci, the crooked cop hero of *Prince of the City,* "You'd have to completely replace his blood with sodium pentothal in the hopes of getting the truth."

I wondered if he was wanted for something else, something worse. Without a real name, we'd have to wait for his fingerprints to find his history. No one does nothing in the Bronx for a decade with neither a pay stub nor an arrest record to show for it, and certainly no one with a taste for angel dust fails to leave a mark. And though I knew he was lying, I knew that there could well be vast gaps in what he remembered.

"Is there anything you want to ask me, Jerry? I mean, you wake up on your birthday in a jail cell with blood on your hands, literally. Me, I'd want to know how the party went. You haven't asked. Sit up when I talk to you. Matter of fact, stand up."

Jimmy Mangan was watching through the window, and he told me later that he thought I was going to hit the perp. But I was doing what they told us to do in the Academy when we thought we'd fall asleep in class. We stood together for the lesson. I asked him how he got money, and he said his mother gave it to him. We talked about his mother for a while.

"So you tell me she's on her knees scrubbing floors six days a week, on her knees in church the seventh. Works for you, prays for you, gives you money, you spend it on angel dust. Does she say that when she gives you the money, does she say, 'Here, Jerry, go out and hurt somebody, anybody, especially yourself? There's always more floors I can scrub, Jerry, don't worry, the back, the knees are fine'? Does she say that to you? Does she say that, Jerry? Answer me!"

"No, she don't say that. . . ."

"Is your name really Jerry? Is that your goverment name? It don't matter what I call you, what you say, you know—I don't know if this is the first time you ever did something, or if you're on the run from killing nuns in Hawaii—we got these fingerprint computers now, they'll say who you are in an hour. . . ."

"Can I sit down?"

"Sure you can sit down, if you don't fall asleep. You can't sleep now, Jerry, this is the most important hour of your life. You made a mistake, there's no way around that. But now—only now—you get a chance to tell me what happened, what really happened, to show your side, to put a human face on it. So the judge don't say, 'This is an animal, he's gonna die in jail!' So the judge says, maybe, 'Look, this guy made a mistake, but he owns it, he takes responsibility, he's a man. Drugs fuck you up, he knows it now, let's get him in a program and move on. He's a man, let's move on.' You understand me?"

"Yeah, I understand."

"So what happened in the hospital?"

"I don't remember."

"C'mon, Jerry, I thought we were talking here."

"It's Antoine, Jeffrey Antoine. That's my name."

"Arright, that's good, Jeffrey. So what's going on here, why you hiding your name?"

"I just got out of prison, I did eight years for robbery."

There it was, the first opening, and if there was one, there would be more. It showed a low-grade con cool: his first instinct was to admit nothing, but he was beginning to realize that his instincts would not help. He was starting to give in to me; we were at the tipping point. At the same time, I realized with a chill that if Calamari and Mattison hadn't caught him at the hospital, we might not have caught him at all: his arrest photo predated the computer, and I would have shown the nurse hundreds of useless pictures. He'd gone to prison just before I'd come on the Job, and all that had happened since was new for him. Maybe he knew about DNA from television, but he knew nothing about digital fingerprints or much else. In terms of the modern criminal-justice system, he was like Rip Van Winkle, awake in a later world. I'd try to work that, as well as some old tricks. He'd probably fallen for them before.

We began inching closer to the crime scene, as he conceded memory after memory: he remembered the afternoon before, and then the night, and then the hospital, which door he had entered, how no one had stopped him. He remembered wandering around to look for the bathroom, and finding the linen room instead, where the nurse told him to leave. And then he didn't re-member anything else.

We had run his past arrests, and several of his robbery victims had been fe-male, which I felt was telling. A robbery is rarely just about money. As St. Au-gustine wrote, when he was a child, he used to steal pears from an orchard, and they were sweeter because they were stolen. Even when he wasn't hun-gry, he found himself back in the orchard. "I stole them simply that I might steal, for, having stolen them, I threw them away." Perps who repeatedly choose women in their twenties and thirties, as Jeffrey Antoine had done, had to be attracted by more than the paycheck. Although Jeffrey had no sex crimes in his history, there was a sexual element to his predatory patterns, and in the wanton excess of his assault on the nurse. I wondered if he realized it himself.

"Jeffrey, this is good, this is good so far, but it isn't enough. I know you've been away for a while, a lot of what we do now, how we do it, it's all changed. Did you ever hear of Megan's Law?"

"No."

"It's named after a little girl that was raped and murdered. It makes everybody register who does any sex crimes, it puts 'em on a list, and it tells the whole block. The neighbors know, everybody, that their wives, their mothers, their kids aren't safe. And people have got killed over it, even people who didn't deserve it, people who got mistaken for somebody on the list. You sure you haven't heard about it?"

"Nah . . ."

"Well, I can show it to you, you can look it up. Because what I'm saying is—and I'm not saying it, she is, the nurse is—that you tried to rape her. You tried to get in her pants. And her pants are ripped, we have 'em."

"Nah!"

We did have the pants, and they were ripped, but even the nurse had said that Jeffrey wanted only her wallet.

"Now I'm not gonna try to tell you what it's like upstate, you know better than me, I can't tell you anything about prison you don't know. But you know time goes by different for a straight-up robber than it does for a rapist. You know how it goes for them. A stick-up guy, he gets his respect. A rapist, forget about it."

Jeffrey shook his head. "I have never, ever laid my hand on a woman like that. Never. All I wanted was her wallet, and I covered her mouth to stop her screaming. . . ."

"That's right, Jeffrey, that's good. You were fucked up on dust, but all you wanted was to keep the party going. You didn't want to hurt nobody. You even tried to get help, running through the emergency room, calling out the lady needs a doctor, right? Why'd you say that?"

"I didn't want her to get hurt. I tried to get a doctor for her."

"That's right, Jeffrey, that's important to bring out. Now, the DA's here with a video camera, and when we talk to her, you gotta be sure to say how you tried to get her help. . . ."

Months later, I testified at a hearing on the admissibility of the confession. As we watched the video, I watched Jeffrey Antoine, and he covered his mouth with his hand the whole time. *How does a fish get caught?* Good instinct there, Jeffrey, you should have stuck with it.

Danny and I talked about going to the Squad often enough. Robbery had been good to us. Many cases took on an assembly-line sameness, and we made factory decisions for their disposal: kid with a new jacket, lady with a chain, Chinese delivery, bodega; IDable or not, evidence or not, pattern or not, even lying or not, for the repeat customers on the first of the month, "robbed" of the rent on the way to the landlord, wouldn't you know! Home invasion, carjacking: let me give you the number for Bronx Robbery.... You'd look across at the Squad, and see a room full of typists as they moped between homicides, tapping out fives for Aggravated Harassments and teen-age Missings. But then you'd catch a good case, something live and moving, with victims and perps each spurring you on, and it got you hot-blooded and hungry. "It's got meat on it," we'd say, and meat was made for eating.

I caught one case with so much meat on it I still haven't finished the meal. A simple bodega stick-up—man with gun, a thousand in cash, two packs of Newports ("I guess he's trying to cut down," Danny noted)—became a pattern the next day, when he hit the same place again, with a partner. In the week that followed, the case didn't break as much as it shattered. Even the bad leads paid off—a tip led us to knock at the wrong apartment door in Queens, where a terrified Moroccan threw two pounds of hashish out the window—but the leads were mostly good: a nickname surfaced from the streets, Igor, which turned out to be a real name. We tracked down his mother—*Did you really name him Igor?*—who said was staying in Connecticut; the Connecticut cops said that he was wanted for nine robberies there, and a shooting. He was on the run with a woman, Sharlene, who had taken her two-year-old son with her, and when I talked to her father—*You gotta help me, Detective, you gotta, I don't know if my grandson's alive, I don't know what to do, you gotta help, you gotta, I work so hard, I haven't slept*—he gave me the license plate of their car. On the day we got Sharlene's picture on TV—whether she was a hostage or helpmate, she'd brought a baby on a crime spree—the car was spotted at two more robberies in Manhattan. In one, Igor put a gun to the head of a six-year-old boy, threatening to kill him if he didn't get the money. The next day, I got a call from Sharlene's father—*God bless you, God bless you, you saved my grandson*—telling us that she had surrendered to the cops in Connecticut, and that she had agreed to return with us to help find Igor. When we picked her up she was the picture of flustered innocence and mild apology, as if she knew she shouldn't have taken a ride with a friend who'd been drinking. She asked permission to go to the bathroom before we drove back, and when she returned, she flashed a quick smile and said, "Sorry for the hold-up!"

"You'd oughta be," said Danny.

Though Igor had sworn bloody oaths to die before he'd go to jail, when we found him, he peeped out from under his blanket like a kid playing peeka-boo and meekly raised his hands. He was dope-sick, and I kept him going on a junkie's banquet of grape soda and Pop-Tarts, aspirin, antihistamines, and Newports. At the line-ups I had trouble finding male Hispanics without moustaches, and a cop from the Four-Four named Eddie Perez sat in as filler. He slumped in his chair with an absent look, but duly noted each of Igor's boasts about the crime spree. I put them down on a five. The Manhattan cops connected Igor to another bodega stick-up, and fingerprints put him at another, and Sharlene told us about a pizza place—again, he put a gun to a child's head—and when I thought we were finally done—we got his accomplice, too—I got a call from a cell mate of Igor's at Rikers Island, saying he'd told him about more robberies, three convenience stores in Massachusetts, a seventy-five-thousand-dollar payroll heist in Puerto Rico. . . . No, I thought, I'd stay at the Four-Four for a while. Maybe we'd have to make a trip to Puerto Rico, when the weather got colder, combing the beaches and bars with my case folder. Maybe a good case never ends, if you keep on investigating, as every trail leads to another trail, and the footprints meet other feet. The case can go as long as you can go, as long as you keep on walking, as long as the world is round. I'd recently run into George again, my old hit man and armed robber from my days on patrol, and he was back on the streets: Ray-Ray Reyes from PSA-7 had picked him up for a blunt collar. No, I'd stay at the Four-Four for a while.

And though I'd passed on the offer to go to Manhattan Robbery, I did take a trip downtown. If I didn't follow the Bronx motto myself—*Get out, schmuck, get out!*—I could at least send my cases to a friendlier venue. New York is, after all, the capital of second chances. Mike Rodriguez had been working on a triple homicide that would be prosecuted by the U.S. Attorney's Office, and I asked him to see if they might be interested in a few robberies. Mike told me that they were definitely interested, and after we hammered out the details— yes, the cab made trips to Newark Airport, which fell under the Hobbes Act, which regulates interstate trade—I testified in the federal Grand Jury and obtained an indictment. K-Lo and Diba, who had robbed the Rwandan cabbie, had a cute act that played in the Bronx, but I doubted it would make it on the main stage downtown.

"What are they looking at, in terms of sentence?" I asked one of the U.S. Attorneys.

"Let's see . . . offhand, I'd say at least twenty-five for this robbery, but maybe with their records, both of them could be looking at mandatory life."

I winced. For a moment, I felt bad for them, but it passed. I knew I would not have to arrest K-Lo, who was already back in jail. After he'd been emancipated by the Grand Jury, I was looking through old cases, and I found a carjacking that he might fit. I called the detective who had the case from Bronx Robbery, Maria Roman, and suggested she show her victim his picture. It was a hit. When I saw K-Lo in the cells, I walked over to him.

"You don't got nothin' on me," he sneered.

"You have no idea. You are done."

When I reached out to Diba's parole officer to tell him that I'd be lightening his caseload, he told me that I was too late; Diba had been locked up a week before, for the armed robbery of a convenience store on Staten Island. The offer there was fifteen years, but Diba could now add a zero to the figure.

I thought about sending Tareek a card, telling him to enjoy his freedom while he could. Instead, I called downtown again, and suggested that the robbery of a Dominican wire-transfer/travel agency was the definition of a crime against interstate trade.

"We're interested," the U.S. Attorney told me. "Let's get this going—can you fax me down his rap sheet?"

"No problem, but you better make sure there's enough paper in your machine."

You guys, you poor guys, I thought, you shouldn't have beaten me the first time. You gotta have a story, pals, and I got yours.

• • •

BECAUSE OF ADMINISTRATIVE MYSTERIES THAT I HAVE YET TO comprehend, my promotion date was on, then off, then scheduled with me, then without, and I wasn't sure of it or myself until the day before it happened. My dress uniform hadn't been dry-cleaned since St. Patrick's Day, but it seemed serviceable enough. I got a tie clip from Bobby Nardi, and swiped white gloves from John. My wallet was on the dog's choke chain that Uncle Eddie had always used; I reported to Police Headquarters in a Cadillac, as Pat Brown would have. I carried other tokens and tributes, and the day itself was a testament to my father, of advice heeded and ignored, all for the good. We had to arrive a few hours early to hear some speeches and fill out forms, for dental plans and next-of-kin. An hour before promotion, we practiced mounting the stage, stopping at the edge for a salute, and then stepping to the center to rehearse an odd cross-armed gesture, the point of which I didn't understand. As we took our seats, I scanned the back for faces: family and friends, old partners and new. There was John, and Mom, trying to get the camera to flash; there was Mike Kelly's father . . . there . . . Inspector Mullen; there—my high school buddy and old codefendant, Eddie. Why hadn't I thought to invite any informants?

It felt too good to be true, and so it was fitting that the promotion ceremony began with a movie, projected on three screens. A montage of cops in action—walking and running, helping people and holding them—it was a powerful and professional piece, beautifully shot and edited, narrated by James Earl Jones, who began by saying, "This is the NYPD . . ." in the sweet but cellar-deep baritone with which he once said, *Luke, I am your father.* If it went a little heavy on the daredeviltry—ESU rappeling from rooftops, helicopters rising over the skyline, boats charging through whitecaps of the harbor—no one complained. There was footage of 9/11, the Towers burning and falling, and ash-dusted cops at work at rescue and recovery. Then came the faces of the twenty-three cops killed. Everyone was glad that a break for speeches followed, so we wouldn't take the stage red-eyed and sniffling.

No one could not think about the dead, the three thousand gone. My sister Regina had just told me about my uncles' bar, the Trade Inn, and how the workers had recently dug down to that level. A camera crew had followed them, and Regina saw it on TV. Commuter's was set against the foundation wall, and it was untouched, intact, with the napkins folded on the bar beside bowls for peanuts and pretzels, the glasses hanging from the racks, undisturbed except for a film of ash. If anyone had been inside when the planes struck, they could have remained until the rescue workers arrived, lacking nothing but ice for their drinks. I could have told the customers that we didn't pay there, because of my father, because the owners were family, and they could put the drinks on me. My tab would still have been good.

And maybe you couldn't call it a miracle, because no one had been spared by its survival. But you could take it as a sign, even a sacrament—that's what they taught us in high school, that a sacrament was a sign—that showed there is always some refuge, even in the depths of the fire. I cleaned up my face with my white gloves, and I was glad when I remembered they were Timpanaro's. Moments from now, there would be another sign, not a sacrament but a little act of alchemy, when my tin shield would be turned to gold.

The Commissioner couldn't be there, and the First Deputy Commissioner, Joe Dunne, would preside. I'd met him three years before, when he was Chief of the Department and I was trying to hustle my way into Vice. Now, I was glad I hadn't gone, and he was giving me what I wanted most. Dunne would retire at the end of the year, and his speech was often halting and heavy with emotion. Oaths of office were administered for detectives, sergeants, and lieutenants. He had a few words about each position, but for detectives, he had the least: "The gold shield of the New York City detective is the most prestigious in the world." They began calling names, and we filed out, and I mounted the side of the stage and saluted, and when I reached Dunne at the center, I understood the cross-armed gesture—he shook your hand as he gave you a certificate. I felt as golden as my shield. Dunne laughed as I shook his hand.

"Good for you, Eddie, so far you're the only one who's come up smiling. . . ."

An odd thing had happened to my cop shield a few weeks before. My number was 9786, and the seven had fallen off, for no reason I could fathom. Was it because I'd been there seven years? When I handed in the shield, they looked at me oddly; I was handing in damaged police property, which should have been reported earlier. *What if a perp had found the seven, and built a new shield around it?* The cop shrugged and tossed it in the box. The Department would take my old shield and fix it, and maybe next year, a new cop would pin it to his uniform. After so many years of inheritance, it would be my first bequest: an old shield that was broken and remade, and that I'd carried for a time.

ACKNOWLEDGMENTS

Years of thanks to my agent, Owen Laster, at the William Morris Agency; to my editors at Riverhead, Chris Knutsen, who brought the book in, and Julie Grau, who brought it home; at *The New Yorker,* where the pieces began with Amanda Weil and David Kuhn, under Tina Brown and David Remnick, through Susan Morrison and Alice Truax, whom I still owe dinner. I walk upright today because of Dr. Michael Platzman, Dr. Frank Petito, Joan Durcan, Dr. Patrick O'Leary, who operated on my back, and especially Dr. Kevin Cahill, whose family has offered steadfast friendship. Much of the book was written while enjoying the hospitality of John, Duff, and the late Lambros Lambros. My teachers from high school and college, most notably John Connelly and the late William Alfred, have my abiding gratitude.

Among friends from the Job and around it, I thank here whoever isn't mentioned in the text, and apologize in advance for omissions. Good looking out: Peaches McGillicuddy, Scott Hungreder, George Stevens, George Shannon, Jimmy Sullivan, Lynn Awe, Tony Ingui, Bobby Gerardi, Dave Sin, Alroy Scott, Lisa Bartolomeo, Mike Burke, Tony Stendardo, Mike Lowery, Tommy Sileo, Tabitha Bronstein, Greg Bundza, Angelo Polite, Bobby "Cheech" Perez, Jimmy Cronin, Rob Knapp, Chris Lynch, and Chris Murphy from PSA-7; Nefti Gomez and Lt. Manente from Narcotics; Lt. Truta from the Academy; Lt. Brian Burke of DCPI; Brian Monahan, for his early encouragement; Carl Cespedes, Glenn Bresnan, Timmy Nichols, Kenny Sparks, Vic Cipullo, Paul and Kim Morrison, from the unions; Scott Nicholson and Conor McCourt at TARU; Chief Daniel

Mullin, Counselor Eddie Hayes, and Special Agent Elizabeth Gaine Callender, who helped plot my escape; Pete Tarsnane, Jimmy Conneely, Augie Paese, Nicky Ciuffi, Bobby Grant, Ray Byrne, Izzy Hernandez, John Schwartz, and Lt. O'Toole at Bronx Homicide; Scopac and Carson for transport; from the Four-Four Squad, PAA's Leland Chase and Jackie Green, Inspector James O'Neill, Mike O'Brien, John Hennessy, John McCarthy, Moe Acevedo, Lenny Crawley, Jimmy Hanvey, and Billy Polotaye; at the Bronx DA's Office, Meredith Holtzman, Tom O'Hanlon, Christiana Stover, Licet Tineo, Michelle Rodney, Dana Roth, Dan DeFillippi, Lisa Mattaway, Honey Cohen, and Odalys Alonso; at the U.S. Attorney's Office, Dan Gitner, Mike Scudder, and Bill Craco; Judge John Keenan and Commissioner Nicholas Scoppetta, for their time; for various acts of aiding and abetting: the Deiters; the Kusners; the McTigues; the Timpanaros; all Boas, Drakes, Duffies, Evers, Horans, Lawsons, Lillies, Mailers, Marshalls, Patons, Paynes, Rushes, and Stones; the Kellys of 35th Street; the McGraths of Bay Ridge; Lynn and the Flying Fishers; the Phillipses of Charleston; the McCabes of Woodhaven; the Castells, Princes of Havana; the Ryans of Point Breeze; the Driscolls of Beara and Boston; Adam Stern; Keith Kelly of the *Post*; Meg O'Rourke; Aida Turturro; Liz Phelps; Colin Callender; the late Mike McAlary; Mrs. James Draddy; Giovanni Porcelli; Tommy Shaw; Gus and Che; and everyone at Park Place, especially Helen. You are now all deputized. *Sláinte.*

ABOUT THE AUTHOR

Edward Conlon is a detective with the New York City
Police Department. A graduate of Regis High School
in New York City and of Harvard, he has published
articles in *The New Yorker* and has been included in
The Best American Essays 2001. He lives and works in
the Bronx.